Arise, England

Arise, England

Six Kings and the Making of the English State

CAROLINE BURT &
RICHARD PARTINGTON

faber

First published in 2024
by Faber & Faber Limited
The Bindery, 51 Hatton Garden
London EC1N 8HN

Typeset by Faber & Faber Limited
Printed and bound by CPI Group (UK) Ltd, Croydon, CR0 4YY

A CIP record for this book
is available from the British Library

ISBN 978-0-571-31198-9

Printed and bound in the UK on FSC® certified paper in line with our continuing
commitment to ethical business practices, sustainability and the environment.
For further information see faber.co.uk/environmental-policy

2 4 6 8 10 9 7 5 3 1

To our families

CONTENTS

PREFACE

Because this book has been a long time in the making, we have incurred many large debts of gratitude! Our thanks begin with Christine Carpenter, whose inspirational undergraduate supervision, clarity of vision, penetration, rigour and magisterial research sparked career-defining interest for us and many, many colleagues. Christine saw the polity in later medieval England fairly and dispassionately. To her, despite the individual self-interest of political actors, it was a means by which the common good could be and was maintained – rather than a cynical and dreary creator of disorder. In this way, building on earlier, ground-breaking work by the great K. B. McFarlane and her own doctoral supervisor Gerald Harriss, her research challenged an existing historiography that focused upon an alleged struggle for power between and among kings and nobles, each of whom supposedly pursued personal aggrandisement with scant regard to the needs of the country. We owe her more than we can say – intellectually and personally. Many of Christine's former students have similarly provided us with generous support and help: Benjamin Thompson, John Watts and Helen Castor have always willingly read our work and given critical advice and encouragement, and we are also enormously grateful to Mark King, Andrea Ruddick and Andrew Spencer, similarly generous with time and assistance. Dan Jones has always offered cheerful and welcome counsel, and John Bethell has been a great sounding board. This book could not have been written without these people, to whom we give heartfelt thanks.

We owe gratitude to many other medieval historians. It was an honour to benefit from the advice of the late Jim Holt and the support of the late George Holmes. Since then, David Carpenter, Peter Coss, Michael Prestwich and Magnus Ryan have always been willing to provide help and advice. This book's chapter on Henry III is deeply indebted to David Carpenter's wonderful work. The second volume of his biography of

Henry III came too late to influence us, but the first volume was pivotal to our understanding. Sandra Raban, Rosamond McKitterick, Ted Powell, Carl Watkins, Rowena Archer, Philip Morgan and Christopher Page have inspired us. Similarly, we have greatly enjoyed our interactions with European colleagues as we have discussed how politics developed in England, the British Isles and continental Europe. It is common themes that have come through most strongly, and we have been enriched – intellectually and otherwise – by our European connections.

Beyond the community of medieval historians, great encouragement – and the title of this book! – has come from the inspirational David Reynolds. The late Derek Beales, Tim Blanning, Tony Badger, James Mayall, Paul Cavill and Mark Goldie have given vital support. At school, Frances McGee, Alan Steenson and Jim Robertson were critical to our development as historians, for which we remain ever grateful. Frances has provided us both with friendship in our adult lives.

The many friends and non-historian colleagues who have surrounded us throughout our working lives may – through this book – now see what sort of history we actually research and write! Your warmth, generosity of spirit and humour have kept us going so many times. We hope you enjoy reading what we have written. We won't be setting a test!

It has been an enormous privilege to teach so many brilliant, dedicated and delightful students – and to learn from them. Their questions, original and telling perspectives and – in some cases – own research have inevitably influenced and informed us. As any researcher who teaches agrees, the pedagogical process – having to define, distil and reformulate as you explain – is central to developing one's own understanding. Cambridge undergraduates, postgraduates and visiting students – many from international backgrounds – have, over many years, moved, pushed and taught us. We are so grateful to them all.

Both of us received research council funding for doctoral research, without which we could not have entered academia. Our Cambridge colleges – Sidney Sussex, Churchill, Murray Edwards, Pembroke and St John's – have provided stimulating environments for our research and the settings for much of our teaching. We have many colleagues across a wide variety of subject areas to whom we are deeply thankful for the community of scholarship from which we have profited. Churchill and Pembroke have been very generous with the provision of the sabbatical leave that has made this book possible, while the Newton Trust provided vital funding for a year's sabbatical for Caroline to complete this work.

Our editors and copy editors at Faber have been wonderfully supportive. Emmie Francis has done the bulk of the work reading drafts and our book is incomparably better for her excellent counsel. Our thanks go also to Neil Belton, who originally signed us as authors, Fiona Crosby, who picked up the book in the final editorial stages, Robert Davies, whose copy-editing was terrific, and Ian Bahrami, who worked wonders under huge time pressure towards the end. Our agent Andrew Gordon deserves a very grateful mention for helping us to secure our contract, and subsequently putting up with more delays than we suspect he thought possible!

Finally, and most importantly, family. We are both first-generation university students from the north-west of England. Without the encouragement, inspiration, tireless work and refusal to accept second best of our parents, attending university would have been difficult and studying at Cambridge impossible. It is a matter of personal sadness that three of our parents have not lived to see this book published. We miss them every day, though we take great solace from our relationships with our brothers and our wider families. To young people from backgrounds like ours, recognise that, without you, places like Cambridge are weakened and dulled. Have confidence in your ability, worth and value; aim as high as you can; and believe that you belong in the places to which you aspire – because you do belong there, and those places need you.

It is commonplace in prefaces for the authors to take responsibility for any errors in their work. We do that *a fortiori*!

INTRODUCTION

In 1199 John 'Lackland', the youngest son of Henry II, seized the English throne following the death of his brother, Richard the Lionheart. The accession of the infamous 'bad king John' ushered in a dramatic, definitive reign, and with it two of the most tumultuous centuries in English history – centuries whose impact upon England and its neighbours, and more widely upon British and European history, is hard to overstate. Between them, the thirteenth and fourteenth centuries saw numerous political crises, including three civil wars and the depositions of two anointed kings. Social upheaval was almost as dramatic, with rapid and near-catastrophic population loss in the first outbreak of a new pandemic known as the 'Black Death', large-scale popular rebellion in the Peasants' Revolt and the emergence of a religious movement known as Lollardy.

Crisis, though, also brought momentous advances: Magna Carta, which placed the monarch under the law and thereby confirmed English and – in time – arguably the Western world's liberties; the extraordinary development of English royal government and the unique 'common law', its centrally organised and managed legal system; and the striking advance of English foreign policy, military organisation and feats of arms. All these contributed to the rise of Parliament, so central to our modern sense of Englishness (and even Britishness); the genesis of a system of national taxation; massive growth in the reach of the king's authority; the conquest of Wales and the attempted conquest of Scotland under Edward I; and, under Edward III, dominance of the European political stage as England's armies swept all before them on the field of battle.

The State in 1199: A Precocious Child

In 1199, many features of what we can identify as the state were already present in England: the realm was defined and the country had long recognised the sovereignty of a single king, responsible for its internal order and external defence. There was a substantially centralised and relatively sophisticated government bureaucracy: extensive royal financial accounts were kept in the Exchequer, and the Chancery, or king's writing office, was well established, issuing government instructions. A single legal system, the common law, accessible to all free men and women, had existed since the mid-twelfth century, and was unique to England. In no other European realm did a king's writ run so unfettered across his lands; and nowhere else had his people such ready access to royal justice. While it was not the only available source of redress, regulation or dispute resolution in the realm (manorial courts held by greater landholders provided immediate justice to tenants; church courts regulated moral behaviour; and arbitration could settle disputes), it was by far the most important means by which justice was done and order maintained. This was particularly the case in relation to criminality, and the vital social and economic building block of landed property.

From its inception, the common law enabled the king to fulfil, as never before, his central duty to protect life, limb and property throughout England. It did this by creating an infrastructure of royal courts acting locally, serviced by a cadre of justices and clerks. The common law served the king's needs, too, by providing him with a way to ensure that his royal rights were maintained and that the pecuniary profits that came with those rights kept flowing into the royal coffers. Even in the small number of areas where independent judicial liberties still existed, lordly justice increasingly aped the king's courts.

Things were somewhat different in respect of external defence. Henry II had re-established, for the first time since the demise of the Anglo-Saxon kingdom in 1066, a national scheme for defence, but without yet fully harnessing the power of the nation to its own protection. Henry's Assize of Arms of 1181 had created a hybrid system for raising defensive armies, in which the mounted knights and esquires of the royal household and the king's mercenaries – often crossbowmen – were backed by infantry recruited nationally for feudal service. As the king's lieges, able-bodied men were now obliged to equip themselves militarily and serve for up to forty days each year. But while this system provided large numbers of foot soldiers to back the cavalry and archers otherwise engaged by the king, the troops could be poor in quality and unreliable in service. Transportation to the Continent and maintaining military supplies by sea were an ongoing challenge, despite England's status as a leading maritime nation. Although no royal navy yet existed, Richard the Lionheart (who reigned from 1189) created 'king's ships' – vessels owned or co-owned by the monarch and usually moored at the Tower of London – and instituted regular shipping surveys to establish which merchant vessels were available to be requisitioned (under the king's feudal prerogative) for royal service.

The king had also to maintain, in the face of French royal aggression, his vast territories in France – the lands of the Angevin or Plantagenet kings. But these lands abroad were a personal matter for him as their lord; they did not concern his English subjects as a point of national interest. At the end of the twelfth century, while a failure of defence in England was certainly a matter for national consternation, questions of foreign policy and war were largely for the king and his greatest landed subjects to ponder. They were not yet the subject of national debate.

The Common Law: The State's Most Vigorous Limb

While the emergence of Parliament might be widely cited as the key state development of the thirteenth and fourteenth centuries, the state institution that arguably grew most fundamentally – with the greatest impact upon the people – was the common law. From its very inception, it was intended to be accessible to ordinary people across the country. Cases could be brought locally either by the purchase of a judicial writ, which cost sixpence – roughly a day's wages for a skilled labourer – or by persuading a panel of 'good and lawful' local men (a so-called 'presenting jury': a lineal ancestor of the grand jury that survives in the US judicial system today) that one was a victim of a crime and that a named person or persons could reasonably be suspected of having committed it. As it developed, the common law continued to be broadly accessible, but by 1399 the number of writs and other procedures available to the aggrieved had grown unrecognisably in response to the clamour of demand for 'the king's law'. The

3

effective operation of the law also allowed kings themselves greater capacity to rule – and potentially rule well. It became a vital manifestation of the burgeoning state for the monarch as well as his subjects.

With this expansion, the apparatus carrying the common law to the people also underwent dramatic change. Before 1199, the so-called 'general eyre', the great judicial mechanism by which the king's law was initially transported to the shires, had already seen its most useful functions separated into offshoot judicial commissions of 'assize' and 'gaol delivery'. These were able to deal with property disputes and felonies more quickly than the eyre, which at best visited each county only once every four years. During the late thirteenth and early fourteenth centuries, the general eyre fell into abeyance, to be replaced largely by those mechanisms that had originally been created only to supplement its work. The commissions of assize and gaol delivery were regularised and then combined, so that a single set of justices in each region both 'heard the assizes' and 'delivered the gaols'. In the mid-fourteenth century they were effectively merged with another local judicial tribunal, the so-called 'peace commission', creating the 'justices of the peace' (JPs). Through the 'quarter sessions', the JPs provided ready access to the common law, up to four times each year, a sixteen-fold increase in accessibility compared with the general eyre. (Today, the direct descendants of the JPs – the magistrates – remain fundamental to the operation of justice in England, Wales and Northern Ireland; a central instrument of the modern state was created almost seven hundred years ago.)

For a minority of litigants the common law was also accessed via the great courts at the political centre. Two major courts emerged, by a process that remains somewhat obscure, from the royal court or *Curia Regis* in the late twelfth and early thirteenth centuries. The, first, the court of Common Pleas, was fixed at Westminster by Magna Carta; the second, King's Bench, initially travelled with the king, but became largely established in the same location – within Westminster Hall – around a century later. The remit of Common Pleas gradually evolved mainly to comprise cases involving significant debts. King's Bench, as the senior court in the realm, initially sat only when the king was present; but as the common law grew, so did the business of the court, until it became impractical to have the monarch in situ. King's Bench dealt with cases in which the Crown had an interest, however indirect, but wealthier landowners, including the most prosperous peasants, could prosecute their enemies there too, usually for trespass within the context of a land dispute. The other legal development at the centre was the rise of non-common-law cases of 'equitable jurisdiction' or 'equity', in which the monarch's authority was exercised to provide 'natural justice' – via the king's Council, the Chamber or the Chancery – where common-law mechanisms could not (usually because the common law as it stood had not envisaged the precise circumstances pertaining in a particular case).

Pivotal developments also occurred in respect of 'extraordinary' disorder – serious local unrest and what we might term 'political' crime: rebellion, conspiracy, corruption and tax evasion. Starting in embryonic form in the 1230s, but expanding dramatically from the late thirteenth century, commissions both of inquiry and 'to hear and determine', or 'oyer and terminer', to use the contemporary parlance, were sent into the localities; the latter added 'determining', or the power to try cases, to the 'hearing' of a commission of inquiry. Inquiries and determining commissions could be issued both in response to an individual petition, and proactively by a king concerned about disorder. Great inquiries were repeatedly used by kings in the fourteenth century, and resulted in the imprisonment and fining of allegedly corrupt justices, officials, knights and nobles on a grand scale.

The State in Arms: Professionalising the Military

Under Edward I and especially Edward III, English arms were transformed. The national system of feudal military service established by Henry II was replaced by a professional army, led by nobles and embedded in local and regional social networks. Moreover, this army learned to fight differently – to devastating effect.

The array, or feudal summons, of common soldiers established by Henry II continued, though with a twist: increasingly, 'hobelars' (light cavalry) and longbowmen, rather than infantry, were arrayed because they were more useful in skirmishing warfare, as well as on the field of battle. A new form of recruitment was added in the late thirteenth century, however:

indentures or contracts for war. Nobles and senior knights were contracted to fight for specific periods of time, in specific theatres of war, and with specific numbers of troops (whom they recruited directly); all received wages from the king, agreed in advance. In the fourteenth century these military innovations were taken to their logical conclusion, and by the mid-1340s, English armies were typically raised and led by contracted noble lieutenants on a regional basis. Gone was the marginally fit, poorly equipped, slow-moving and cumbersome feudal infantry, accompanying the old-style heavy cavalry of the nobility and royal household. In place of both were more compact, fully integrated, highly professional divisions: uniformed, equipped with the most up-to-date arms and armour, expertly supplied and comprising – radically – equal numbers of men-at-arms and archers. Where previously a distinction had existed between elite mounted knights and common foot soldiers, now, as men-at-arms, the two rode together to battle and dismounted to fight on foot as a single unit, alongside massed longbowmen who were also transported by horse. The king's armies were highly mobile on the march and dominant on the field, and were transported overseas in naval operations conducted by professional admirals on an unprecedented scale.

Developing tactics were equally ground-breaking, enabled by the end of the old, socially embedded distinction between cavalry, infantry and archers. Although the English retained the capacity – where necessary – to mount cavalry charges, their favoured approach in battle was now to fight on the defensive, often dug in. The intense fire of the massed archers – whose arrows the king procured literally by the million – devastated the advancing soldiers and horses of the enemy before the archers' comrades, the men-at-arms, stepped forward to complete the grim work with sword, Dane axe, mace and war hammer. This new way of fighting was so successful that the English retook the lands lost to the French in the thirteenth century, and in the late 1350s John II of France, David II of Scotland and Charles, duke of Brittany were all captured in battle. Such was the importance of these military changes that historians have termed them a military revolution.

6

Footing the Bill: The Advent of Parliament

Over the course of the two centuries, Parliament was created, and expanded both its membership and its function, particularly from the reign of Edward I, when community representation was increased. In the fourteenth century the two parliamentary houses of Lords and Commons emerged. The former comprised the lords temporal and spiritual: respectively, the dukes, earls and other great lords summoned by name, and the archbishops, bishops and (occasionally) abbots of the great religious houses. The latter included representatives of the cities, boroughs and counties, usually two from each. While Parliament's main purpose from the outset was to consider royal requests for taxation, it quickly began to consider wider matters of public interest, including the state of the peace and, increasingly, foreign affairs and war. One of its most important functions was to act as a conduit for petitions for the redress of grievances, initially from individuals or local communities, but, from the early fourteenth century, also from the Commons collectively, often in relation to legal or administrative issues. It was in Parliament that laws came to be enacted. When this first took place it was solely at the behest of the king. But over time both the Lords and Commons took the initiative in law-making, until legislating became a crucial dimension of parliamentary activity.

The exact terms upon which Parliament would agree to grant money to the king were rapidly finessed. Kings promoted the idea that the protection and defence of their own interests was synonymous with the common good of the realm – in other words, their subjects' well-being – and requested what was in effect national taxation in the national interest. This was because it was only through taxation that they could hope to raise the sums of money necessary to wage warfare, particularly after Magna Carta. From the outset, in kings' minds this included provision for the protection of royal lands outside England as well as the more obvious defence of England's borders, but it seems that their subjects did not initially accept this broad conception. By the late fourteenth century, this had changed: royal lands in France were firmly believed to belong to the Crown of England and Parliament even proactively voiced its own concerns about threats to them. It was by this time a very active participant in, and at times driver of, the dialogue about defence and foreign policy. But despite this, the king could not simply demand taxation at will. Over the period covered by this book, Parliament put in place caveats to the king's freedom in this regard. First, it carved out for itself a role in determining the true necessity of the demands being made. Second, late in the thirteenth century Parliament forcefully expressed the view that, no matter how great the necessity, taxation should never have the effect of impoverishing the king's subjects: it should not, in and of itself, damage the common good. This set parameters around what the king could reasonably ask of his subjects.

Developments in taxation and the role of Parliament meant a fusion of the king's world with the public world of the realm – that is, the king and his subjects together. The community of the realm, through Parliament, took joint ownership – with the king – of the English Crown's rights. It was now a case of the nation engaging in a joint-stock enterprise, under the king's leadership, to do what was best for England and the Crown.

State Bureaucracy and a Civil Service

Given the huge expansion of the state across the years between 1199 and 1399, it is unsurprising that government bureaucracy also grew dramatically. Under King John a fundamental, though seemingly straightforward, change came when government began systematically to archive the commands it issued through the Chancery by a process of enrolment. The charter rolls recorded royal charters – establishing markets in towns, for example; the patent rolls recorded the king's publicly expressed appointments and instructions; and the close rolls recorded those that were private or personal. Under Henry III the fine rolls were added, recording financial deals between the king and various of his subjects. Before the end of 1399 the Chancery had fully matured and was complemented by offices for the privy seal and signet seal. It was with the great seal that Chancery writs or letters were ordinarily closed or validated. But increasingly the king's more personal privy and signet seals were used, which provides us with historical records and an indication of the king's direct involvement in the issuing of particular government instructions. By the late fourteenth century, the government was issuing some forty thousand letters each year under the various seals. A financial parallel was the emergence of the office of the royal wardrobe as a more nimble and mobile financial office, to complement the Exchequer. Its development initially came in time of war, but after war ended, its utility endured.

The growing state infrastructure had also to be staffed, both at the governmental centre and especially on the ground, in the localities. This was not straightforward: it is easy to forget that, before the economic revolution brought by global trade and industrialisation, people were much poorer than they are now, and no medieval state – England included – could afford a standing army or navy, or a police force permanently stationed in the localities. But, in the judicial sphere just as in the military sphere, English kings across this period were able to harness the resources of their subjects to the national interest and then increase the effectiveness of provision with professionalisation.

This phenomenon is most clearly visible in the emergence of legal education. With the growth of the common law, a legal profession – a cadre of lawyers, hierarchically arranged – was extant in London by the mid-thirteenth century. Surviving registers of legal writs and the so-called 'year books' of legal arguments evidence the proliferation of legal training shortly thereafter, which accompanied the learning on the job completed by trainee attorneys or sergeants-at-law (respectively the medieval equivalents of solicitors and barristers within the present-day English legal system). It was only in the late fourteenth century that the Inns of Court (where barristers still train today) first appeared, but there is no doubt that would-be lawyers were being educated in a similar fashion many years before this. They resided with other trainees – including in the Inns of Chancery, where government clerks also received their training – obtaining instruction and guidance together.

The careers of royal officials at the centre and in the localities witness the process. From the outset, the royal justices of the central courts included the most able lawyers in the land, drawn from the ranks of the sergeants-at-law in Westminster. Rubbing shoulders with such men in, say, the court of King's Bench would be an ever-growing plethora of trainee and practising attorneys, whose educational milieu was broadly similar; centred on the Inns of Chancery and in some cases (though by no means all) preceded by a period at university in Oxford or Cambridge. An attorney whose education included canon (as well as civil) law might opt to enter the civil service and become a royal clerk in one of the offices of state, receiving religious benefices from the king by way of reward. Another attorney might decamp to the localities to serve as the steward, or chief judicial and administrative officer, of a great lord, or to practise as a lawyer or commercial agent, or might use his legal knowledge principally to manage his own estates.

Across the country, these men deployed their knowledge in the service of the king, often working alongside men who had built up legal knowledge by observation and self-teaching. Moreover, their wider skills (often including languages – Latin and Norman French as well as English – and accounting) were broadly applicable to royal service, making them highly useful not only on legal commissions but also with other royal assignments: collecting taxes, making surveys and extents, and conducting the array, for instance. Some served regularly as Members of Parliament, representing the locality in which they lived and worked. Finally, those with the right background and inclination for military service were additionally valuable to the king – not just on the field of battle, but also in the organisation of logistics and the maintenance of supply-critical military matters. The most able and trusted among them might even be sent on royal diplomatic missions, alongside senior nobles, bishops and justices.

The latter, who were the king's chief lieutenants and principal advisers in internal and external rule, were national or even international figures, but also embedded in the localities, straddling national and local interest. While the great landholders of the realm were a warrior caste accustomed to serving the king in war, the rise of the state, and in particular the rapid and sustained flowering of the common law, brought them into royal rule in the counties as royal justices. This originally occurred in times of marked disorder and it remained the case that the Crown might respond to a local outbreak of crime or violence by commissioning great lords, as well as the most experienced lawyers, to investigate and punish it. Ideally the lords were attentive to royal concerns while remaining alive to local circumstances and needs. This made for nuanced, responsive and effective rule.

In such situations they were overtly providing muscle – the power to enforce – as well as local leadership. But such power – borrowed by the

Crown on the strength of its authority and in any case generally in the interests of local stability – was latently exercised in a magnate's 'country', or region, even when they personally held no royal judicial appointment. This is because they were typically connected with local royal officials, who, knowledgeable in the law, frequently acted as their stewards or attorneys, or witnessed their charters or grants. These connections must have made it harder for disputants or criminals to resist those officials. Without a permanent local police force or salaried bureaucracy in the shires, the monarch relied on the nobility and greater gentry for routine enforcement, and over the course of the fourteenth century that reliance became more systematised than ever before.

The next tier down in the hierarchy of royal commissioners comprised the senior lawyers and administrators among the local gentry, who were usually appointed as sheriffs (the king's senior administrator in each shire), or alongside the justices of the central courts as commissioners of the peace or of oyer and terminer. Local lawyers and administrators receiving less high-profile commissions (for example, to collect taxes, conduct the array or, after the Black Death, enforce the labouring legislation enacted to protect the economy) tended to be gentry of slightly lower status or lesser experience.

The extent of change in the English state over the two centuries to 1399 meant that the state apparatus in the king's hands by the end of the period would have been quite beyond the compass of the monarchs of the late twelfth century. It was so remarkable that it remains fundamental to the state today. By 1399 the king had at his disposal a highly sophisticated governmental and legal infrastructure both at the political centre and in the localities of his realm – even in the remotest areas. He presided at the apex of a political community with a deep sense of national identity and mission, which, if he led it effectively, worked in partnership with him in England's interests – not least through its representative body, Parliament. Among the critical functions of that body was approving taxation under an established system of national finance. This substantially funded the defence, via a professionalised military, of all the king's lands, in the British Isles and in France, which were regarded by the people as matters of national interest: their interest as well as that of the king. In short, in 1199 feudal kingship in England was starting to claim a more public, national authority.

By 1399 there existed national monarchy underpinned by a sophisticated infrastructure that is eminently recognisable as a nascent state.

A Note on Sources

What makes it possible to tell the story of these two centuries in England with such vividness and in such detail is the extraordinary variety and volume of the surviving source material. Chronicles (or contemporary histories), political songs and poems, letters and especially government records – instructional, financial and legal – provide exceptional insight into the past. One can write a history of England in the thirteenth and fourteenth centuries in a way that is essentially impossible for other European states.

Central to this are the government records, now located in the National Archives in Kew. From early in the reign of King John – probably thanks to Hubert Walter, the great Angevin administrator John had inherited from Richard the Lionheart – a wide range of formal documents was systematically catalogued by the king's officials. Royal commissions and other orders, charters and grants, diplomatic and other letters, and financial records were all carefully filed. Perhaps most importantly, legal cases brought before the king's courts at the centre were enrolled for the purposes of future reference; and later, when justices of assize, gaol delivery, oyer and terminer, and the peace were operating in great number in the shires, it became common practice for them to deposit the personal copies of cases they had heard in the central records when they returned to Westminster. Faced by millions of legal records, carefully written on parchment in the neatest Latin (and occasionally Norman French) script, the historian can only wonder at the tedium involved for the scribes – tedium evidently relieved by the enchanting doodles and sketches they occasionally made in the margins of documents. It is through such a sketch on a legal record that we know what a highwayman's murderous club-like weapon or 'trailbaston' (after which the 'trailbaston' judicial inquiries into roaming criminals of the early fourteenth century were named) looked like. In the face of this humanity, we feel, as we hold the record, as though we are stepping seven hundred years into the past. Likewise with the extant wax seals, pendant on contracts for military service: the historian's hand is now where William Bohun, earl of

Northampton's hand lay in the early 1340s, as he contemplated embarking for war in Brittany.

Although the vital and revealing legal records deposited by the itinerant justices survive inconsistently, they are sufficient in number and range for us to understand how the common law worked in the localities, who used it, and with what motivation and what consequence. The records of the central courts and offices of state survive almost completely intact. Only the hungry mice of past centuries, plus water and fire damage from mishaps in storage in the Tower of London, long ago, make the historian's work – occasionally – more challenging. The array of information and insight that can be gleaned from these records is astonishing. We know who was suspected of having stolen this person's brass cooking pots or that person's horses, in this county or that county, and on which days in which years. We know that, when a Lincolnshire man was killed on Christmas Eve in 1338, his brother was suspected of being the guilty party, and that, in the same county in the same year, Alice Lacy, countess of Lincoln accused the sheriff of Lincoln – who was retained by her former brother-in-law, Henry, earl of Lancaster – of having stolen a great leviathan of the sea (a whale) from the shores of her manor of Sutton. We know the names of the earl of Arundel's Welshmen who apprehended Lord Charlton in 1331. We know what King John had for Christmas dinner in 1211 and how much he paid his tailor; and we know that Edward I threw his daughter Princess Elizabeth's coronet into the fire in fury in Ipswich in 1297. The records tell us which ships carried early cannon (following the invention of gunpowder artillery), and that Edward III was heartbroken when his beloved daughter Princess Joan died of the Black Death at Bordeaux in 1348. They tell us that he entrusted his life to God and believed that God held it safely in his hands through many grave dangers. Indeed the government records, easily and understandably characterised as formulaic and dry, allow the hard-working and interventionist kings, who engaged and corresponded proactively with their officials, to step straight from the parchment as large as life, belying the commonplace among historians that we can only know such figures two-dimensionally.

The chronicles are far less voluminous and comprehensive, but they provide us with vibrant colour, personal detail, contemporary perspective and eyewitness insight. They also tell us things that the instructional, financial and legal government records do not, such as how battles were actually fought (as opposed to how much it cost to fight them) and, occasionally, what political actors said. We have to be cautious with them, because their authors were engaged in a literary art and may accordingly have taken artistic licence – inserting assumed speeches at pertinent moments, or echoing, consciously or otherwise, the classical and biblical texts that they knew so well. That said, we also know by cross-referencing their comments with governmental records that some chroniclers could be incredibly well, and accurately, informed, and that figures in government and politics, including kings, valued their information and acumen, consulted them and supplied them with appropriate source material.

Those in the early part of our period were mostly produced by monks outside London, who were principally creating archives for their abbeys or priories. The amount of evidence or commentary on national affairs therefore varies significantly, but plenty of chronicles extensively discuss what was going on beyond the abbey or priory gates. By the early fourteenth century the situation had begun to change, and secular clerks (clerics who were not based in monasteries), especially from London, came to eclipse the monastic chroniclers, writing most of the best works on the reigns of Edward II and Edward III. Given London's growing size and importance as England's governmental and economic centre, it is no surprise that so many of these writers should have heralded from the city. The fourteenth century also saw a handful of works by laymen writing from first-hand experience, such as Sir Thomas Gray's *Scalacronica* and the Chandos Herald's *Life of the Black Prince*.

Despite the change in the balance between monastic chronicles and those produced by secular clerics and laymen, the former tradition remained (just) alive during the first two reigns of the fourteenth century. The monastic chroniclers had much to contribute in relation to Edward III's military campaigns, and this remains valuable to the historian. During Richard II's reign, the monastic chronicle tradition rose again, probably as a result of high drama – in the form of the Peasants' Revolt of 1381 and Richard's deposition in 1399. The greatest work produced in these years was by the St Albans monk Thomas Walsingham, who, among many emergent and talented monastic chroniclers of Richard's reign, was unrivalled in his ability to create an engaging narrative.

The chronicles illuminate the period between 1199 and 1399 in very specific ways. Sometimes they are repositories of unique copies of government documents that have been lost, or they contain first-hand accounts of events or descriptions of people: Matthew Paris's *Chronica Majora*, written at the abbey of St Albans in the mid-thirteenth century, includes the only surviving copy of the so-called Paper Constitution written by baronial critics of the king in 1244. And the late thirteenth-century chronicle written at the abbey of Bury St Edmunds, a staging post for royal journeys to and from Scotland, contains information about the negotiations for Edward I's marriage to Blanche, the sister of Philip of France, found nowhere else. It is likely that this account came directly from Edward himself, when he was staying at the abbey. The secular clerks' chronicles were often equally well informed. Perhaps the most famous chronicle of Edward II's reign, the *Vita Edwardi Secundi* (or *Life of Edward II*) was written by a cleric based somewhere in the Severn Valley in the west of England. Its account of the circumstances of the earl of Gloucester's death at Bannockburn in 1314, where the English forces were routed, contains minute detail that is overwhelmingly likely to have come from an eyewitness with whom the writer was connected. The author of the *Vita* arguably understood the nature and importance of the hostile relationship between Edward II and Thomas, earl of Lancaster better than any historian writing since.

It would of course be a mistake to assume that chroniclers were always correct or accurate: Sir Thomas Gray's *Scalacronica* is a first-hand military account, written in the 1350s in prison in Edinburgh, following Gray's capture by the Scots. In it he reflected on Edward III's military campaigns of the previous two decades, in which he had participated. But Gray's depiction of events is at times misleading. He seems to have been something of an embittered contrarian, or perhaps factual reality was sacrificed to dramatic effect. In other cases, chroniclers were only as good as the information they received from others, which could itself be distorted by failures of memory or even due to propaganda. Perhaps the starkest example of this is the circulation to several monastic houses of the 'Record and Process' of the removal of Richard II from the throne in 1399 by

Henry IV, which many authors subsequently copied into their chronicles. (The document was also written into the parliamentary records.) Its purpose was to justify Henry's usurpation of the throne and it was littered with untruths. So, while they can provide us with important information, the chronicles and histories of the period must be used with care.

To varying degrees the chroniclers opined on circumstances or people as they documented events. This can be invaluable to historians – again with some caveats. Unsurprisingly, many communicated religiously influenced moral messages, and were quick to condemn: the author of the *Vita* makes repeated biblical references, regularly accusing the principal political actors of pride and avarice. Many chroniclers firmly believed that God's judgement decided the outcome of battles – as, to be fair, did most contemporary military commanders. (Too often, letters from the front comment on a victory or defeat solely as a judgement of God, whereas what the historian craves is an explanation of where exactly the archers were placed, and why.) The chroniclers were naturally also affected by their wider attitudes and those of society: xenophobia is a strong theme in Matthew Paris's chronicle, for instance, just as it was in political discourse during Henry III's reign. The personal circumstances of the chronicler could be equally influential: Peter Langtoft's and other northern chroniclers' opinions of kings in the late thirteenth and fourteenth centuries were inevitably influenced by the rulers' actions concerning Scotland. The same can be said of some of the French chroniclers who wrote about English affairs. Two chronicles of Richard II's reign were written by French authors who were in England at the time: one was accompanying Richard's new queen, the French princess Isabella, and staunchly supported close royal control; the other travelled with Richard on campaign in Ireland, and similarly defended the king's actions. Patrons, too, who commissioned chronicles, obviously influenced the opinions expressed by their writers, particularly as the fourteenth century progressed, and more chronicles were produced at the behest of individual nobles. (In Richard II's reign, several of those who wrote chronicles had noble patrons and took a strongly pro-noble line.)

Perhaps the best way to see the chroniclers is akin to modern-day political journalists, and to assess their writings accordingly. The chroniclers often convey useful eyewitness information, because of their high-level political connections – even with the king – or sometimes because they were themselves at the heart of the action. That might have been at the political epicentre in Westminster or London, or on the front line of Scottish attacks on northern England. And while they were rarely neutral in outlook, they did not pretend to be. It is for this very reason that the colour they provide is so interesting to historians. Their value to us lies precisely in their human perception of what was happening around them. They represent another way in which the remote past speaks to us.

No voice could cry more directly than the surviving political songs and poems. The *Song of Lewes* of 1264 celebrated Simon de Montfort's civil war victory over royalist forces that year, and the *Outlaw's Song of Trailbaston* lambasted the new trailbaston commissions of 1304–7. A similar rebel cry in the face of powerful and insistent royal justice was made by *The Tale of Gamelyn* in 1340. Later, in the north Midlands in the 1350s, *Wynnere and Wastoure* reflected inconclusively – in a post-Black Death, changing world – on the different perspectives of the 'winners', men such as merchants who made and kept money, and 'wasters', knights and others whose focus was on consumption and display. Such works provide insight into dissonant views that might otherwise be lost to us amid records and chronicles that substantially reflect an establishment outlook. The reign of Richard II is notable for its poetry. Geoffrey Chaucer was connected to the court and the political world, even though his writings were primarily humanistic, social, philosophical and universal. His friend John Gower claimed to know King Richard directly. His most famous work, the *Vox Clamantis*, spoke to the condition of society, but, interestingly, contained references to Richard's kingship that were revised to present the king more negatively during his reign. Almost certainly also composed under Richard's rule, in the north Midlands or north-west of England, was *Sir Gawain and the Green Knight*, an incredibly rich religious text that begins with a tour de force imagining of the court of King Arthur at Christmas, now thought to be descriptive of the court during celebrations in the reign of Edward III.

This rich and in certain respects unique source material permits us not only to tell the story of England in 1199–1399 in real detail, but also to understand and paint often intimate portraits of some of the leading political actors even beyond the strict realm of politics. It was these figures, real people, not pasteboard caricatures, who drove either deliberately or accidentally the developments that took place in our period. Their characters, motivations, actions and responses were complex and at times contradictory. They were not the good kings and bad kings of historical commonplace. This book will show how their stories, with all their drama, intrigue, personal triumph and tragedy, are inextricably intertwined with the grand narrative of the emergence of the English state.

KING JOHN, 1199–1216
'A Tyrant rather than a King'

Introduction: The Great Charter of Liberties

In 1215, at Runnymede on the Thames, a group of armed nobles presented a charter that quickly came to be known as the great charter of liberties, or *Magna Carta Libertatum*, to that 'tyrannous whelp' (to use the chronicler Gerald of Wales's epithet), King John. On 15 June, at their mercy, and therefore with no choice but to agree to their demands, John formally issued Magna Carta (as we now know it) to the realm. In so doing he ended the civil war that had raged in the preceding months, and the group of rebel nobles promptly renewed their allegiance to him as king in return. On the face of it, peace seemed to have been restored.

The Charter made a reality of many of the demands that same group of rebels had made in May and June, promising to bring to heel a king whose financial and other exactions had been greater than those of any of his predecessors, and who had reduced a number of his greatest nobles to humiliating penury. Magna Carta did this by formally placing the king under the same 'common law' that his subjects had to abide by, stipulating that he could not take the property of those subjects at will, imprison them without due process or deny them justice. Its confirmation in June 1215 meant that things would potentially never be the same again. It redefined the parameters of royal authority.

But this was not the end of the story: the fact that Magna Carta had to be forcibly imposed on King John indicates the extent of his resistance to it; he had no intention of honouring his pledge. He took the earliest opportunity to throw off its shackles and the civil war inevitably resumed. Instead of acting as a peace treaty that provided clear terms of engagement to both parties for the future, Magna Carta, whose legacy has loomed large over the eight succeeding centuries of English history, was therefore, in the first instance, a failure. But so important had its principles become that it could not simply be ignored, and the eventual price of peace in the civil war was its reconfirmation in 1217, made possible by the fact that John had been succeeded by the infant King Henry III.

As the name accorded it by contemporaries signified, Magna Carta really was, at its heart, a charter of liberties: an attempt to protect individual and collective rights against arbitrary government, even if those who drafted it had their own interests clearly at the forefront of their minds. The crisis in which it was produced came about as a reaction to the arbitrary power of the Angevin kings. But at the same time, it was also an acceptance of the benefits brought by that government and the nascent state in England, particularly subjects' access to a common legal system. In other words, the barons wanted continued recourse to the benefits Angevin government had brought, particularly independent justice and due process, but they wanted it to be implemented in a predictable way by a king who consulted with and listened to his subjects. The principles Magna Carta enshrined became embarkation points for the development of Parliament, national taxation and cultural identity, and its timeless principles of good government and subjects' rights have remained a core part of England's constitution ever since. The grant of Magna Carta by the king in what is likely to have been a muddy field (this being England) in Surrey in June 1215 is central to our understanding of the long-term development of the English state and nation.

The Angevin World in 1199

King John and his Angevin predecessors Henry II and Richard I were not simply kings of England. The realm represented only one element in a vast and sprawling Angevin empire, so called after Henry's title 'count of Anjou', which encompassed land in south-west, western and northern France too: Aquitaine, Poitou, Maine, Touraine, Anjou and Normandy. It was a huge territory to defend and control, larger even than that directly presided over by the main rival of the Angevin rulers, the king of France. French ambitions to control directly more of the territory over which they claimed overlordship – which included most of the Angevin lands – had increased over time, as had the monetary and other resources available to the French Crown. When John came to the throne in 1199, Henry II and

Richard I had already lost some ground to the resurgent Capetian dynasty of France, both financially and territorially. At the same time, the late twelfth and early thirteenth centuries saw the Angevins confronted by one of France's greatest kings, Philip II, the first to term himself 'king of France' rather than 'king of the Franks', who ruled France from 1180 to 1223. As his attitude to his title suggests, he aimed to bring all France under his control, and was given the title 'Philip Augustus' by one chronicler in tribute to how much of that ambition he achieved. Clouds were darkening on the horizon across the Channel already in 1199. It would take a strong and talented king to manage and retain this huge empire.

In England, the Angevins, and to some extent all of their post-Conquest predecessors, had worked hard to make a practical reality of their theoretical authority over their realm, but there were also sensitivities and fault lines. While some elements of Angevin government, such as Henry II's great common-law system, were welcomed by the king's subjects in England, others were resented and even resisted. In the north of England in particular, which was not used to the yoke of government in the same way as many other parts of the realm, intrusions were often resisted and independence strongly asserted. It was a situation that called for careful handling and the utmost diplomatic skill.

'Bad' King John

King John's personality was almost wholly unsuited to the challenges he faced; in fact, so bad were his faults deemed to be that he has been subject to some of the worst vilification of any leader in history. First, contemporaries argued, John was a coward. One chronicler, William the Breton, said that when the French king invaded Normandy in 1204, John had declared that he would 'stay in a safe place with my dog'; he had, it was said, 'a doll's heart'. In other words, he was cowardly. Another chronicler christened him 'softsword' because he was said to prefer peace to war. Even his own brother Richard is said by one chronicler to have mocked John's lack of courage: 'My brother John is not the man to subjugate a country if there is a person able to make the slightest resistance' (wrote Roger of Howden). When he was not shying away from fighting, he has been presented as sexually predatory and immoral: the chronicler Roger of Wendover argued that there were 'many nobles whose wives and daughters the king had violated to the indignation of their husbands and fathers'. Wendover also noted that when John received appeals to save Chateau Gaillard in Normandy, Richard I's great fortress taken humiliatingly by the French king in 1204, he was apparently 'enjoying all the pleasures of life with his queen'.

John's cruelty, pathological insecurity and ability to alienate potential friends were almost legendary. It was reported that he had a habit of sniggering at others and encouraging his friends to do the same, but it is for worse than this that he is notorious: he allegedly starved forty knights to death after a military victory at Mirebeau in 1202 and Wendover describes him as having men hanged by the thumbs, having salt and vinegar put in prisoners' eyes, and having them roasted on tripods and gridirons. Wendover's successor as the chronicler of St Albans, Matthew Paris, wrote that John was a man whose 'punishments were refinements of cruelty, the starvation of children, the crushing of old men under copes of lead'. But perhaps the worst of the crimes alleged against John was the murder of his own nephew and rival for the English throne, Arthur. Evidence for this is far from extensive, but what exists suggests that it is very likely that John at least ordered the murder, even if he did not commit it in person. It is perhaps no surprise that fears of assassination are said to have kept John unblinkingly awake throughout the night.

While there is no doubt that some of the stories in the chronicles about John are at the very least embellishments of reality, rarely has any king been so negatively depicted. The medieval world had no doubt, after his death, that he had joined the ranks of mortal sinners in Hell. Vilification has continued into much modern historiography, too.

The chroniclers were, in the end, engaged in a literary art, and this, plus their tendency to biblical or classical allusion (whether direct or indirect), left them prone to exaggeration. Beyond the chronicles there is limited evidence. But contemporary or near-contemporary criticism of John was so legion and varied that it is hard to imagine all the other condemnations of him were unjust. Other kings simply do not suffer this scale of disparagement. Furthermore, much of the John-centred 'gossip' recounted by the chroniclers fits so well with what we know of John's actions from elsewhere in the sources that the picture of his character that emerges is compelling – if more nuanced. Such a personality is hardly suited to any sort of leadership, let alone kingship, and that did not bode well for his reign.

John 'Lackland'

John's journey to becoming king of England was, given the number of heirs Henry II produced, a highly unlikely and improbable one. With four elder brothers, William, Henry, Richard and Geoffrey, John never expected to become king and was repeatedly taunted about this and mocked by at least one of his brothers; he was part of what can only be described as a profoundly dysfunctional family. Born on Christmas Eve in 1166, John was not only the youngest son, he was the youngest of all Henry II's eight *legitimate* children. William had died long before John was born, having succumbed to a seizure aged only two in 1156. But that still left Henry II with four legitimate sons for whom he needed to carve out individual inheritances. As the youngest, there was no likelihood, should the state of play remain as it was in 1156, that John would ever hold much in the way of significant lordships, let alone become a king, a duke or even a count.

In 1169, recognising the need to divide his vast territories between his offspring before they began to assert themselves independently, Henry II moved to give each of them a sense of their inheritance. The eldest, 'Young Henry', now aged fourteen, was to have his father's personal inheritance, consisting of England, the duchy of Normandy and the counties of Anjou, Maine and Touraine. Richard, aged eleven, would have the huge duchy of Aquitaine and its appurtenances (the counties of Auvergne, Limoges, Périgord and La Marche) and Poitou. And Geoffrey, who was ten, was to have Brittany; he was in fact already betrothed to the duke of Brittany's daughter, Constance. This settlement left nothing for the youngest son John, aged just two, who in consequence increasingly became known as *Jean Sans Terre*, or John 'Lackland'. Henry II, in no hurry given John's age, was content to wait for opportunities to arise before attempting to secure an inheritance for his youngest son. Since John was very young, his endowment was clearly not pressing. Nonetheless, this settlement – or lack thereof – was an inauspicious start for the young prince.

If Henry's actions in 1169 were designed to bring certainty and unity to the familial situation more generally, they failed abjectly. Although Young Henry was crowned king of England at Westminster in 1170 (undergoing a coronation in advance was designed to secure the succession and achieve recognition of his authority), and Richard was similarly enthroned as duke of Aquitaine, this was not to lead to any practical power for the two sons. Henry II continued to rule his territories in person. As they got older, his sons' relative impotence began to rankle with them, despite Young Henry showing no potential to be an assiduous and cerebral ruler – he much preferred parties and tournaments to business. Nonetheless, in due course, encouraged perhaps by their mother, Eleanor of Aquitaine, whose own relationship with Henry had become tested, he and his brothers decided that they wanted proper recognition.

Tensions became explicit in 1173 when Henry II sought to make provision for John's inheritance by agreeing his marriage to the daughter of the count of Maurienne, whose territory was in the Savoyard Alps. Needing to provide something on the Angevin side in the agreement with the count, Henry offered three castles in Anjou: Chinon, Loudun and Mirebeau. It was a good deal for John and Henry II. But it overlooked one critical thing: these castles had already been promised to Young Henry. This whittling away of his inheritance added insult to the injury of his having been denied any practical authority since 1169, and it proved too much for the eighteen-year-old. He swiftly allied in rebellion against his father with the French king, and with his brothers Richard and Geoffrey, and his mother Eleanor, each of whom had their own reasons for resenting Henry II.

The alliance of sons and wife, operating with the blessing of the French monarch, Henry's arch-enemy, indicates how embattled this family was. When we consider its leading members, explaining how relations between them went so badly wrong is easy. Henry II presided over a great empire with noted intellect and charisma, and great energy as well as a powerful personality; but he was given to violent fits of temper, and demanded total subjugation and obedience from his subjects: this was, after all, a man who – indirectly or otherwise – ordered the brutal murder of the archbishop of

Canterbury, Thomas Becket, and who insisted that no one at court should be able to sit down while he himself remained standing. He was, in other words, as authoritarian as he was capable. He could also be insincere and deceitful.

In his wife, though, he had met his match. Orphaned at thirteen, Eleanor had inherited the duchy of Aquitaine and been quickly married off to the heir to the French throne, Prince Louis. It was an important match because it promised to bring yet more of France under the French Crown's direct control. Shortly after the marriage Eleanor's new husband succeeded his father as King Louis VII. But this was not a happy marriage. Eleanor gradually made her displeasure at their continued union known to Louis and cited their consanguinity as the reason why their marriage should be annulled. Although he was initially resistant to this, when confronted with their repeated failure to produce a son and heir, the previously devoted Louis acquiesced, and accepted the verdict of the French bishops that the marriage should be annulled. In 1152 Eleanor left Louis and returned to Aquitaine, taking her duchy with her.

Within the space of just over two months, twenty-eight-year-old Eleanor had gone on to marry nineteen-year-old Henry, duke of Normandy and count of Anjou, who in 1154 was to inherit the English throne and become King Henry II – a move that seems to have been completely unsuspected by Louis. Exactly how and when the marriage was agreed is unknown, but it was fast work and both parties stood to gain from it – Henry by acquiring Aquitaine through Eleanor and Eleanor by acquiring a powerful protector, as well as (in due course) a second queenly diadem. The new partnership was not only something of an insult to Louis, but also threatened to undermine his position. In response he wasted no time, sweeping quickly with an army into Henry's duchy of Normandy. But it was futile – under two months later Henry had seen off Louis's forces, just as Eleanor had repelled his advances during the latter part of their marriage. The French king was humiliated.

Given their respective personalities, the alliance of Henry and Eleanor promised to be a fiery one. Together they could either be all-conquering or mutually destructive; they managed to be both in turns. Between 1153 and 1166 Eleanor gave birth to eight children, but by 1168 she was back in Aquitaine. The long-term rule of the duchy was in acute need of attention, following a revolt by members of the powerful Lusignan family, and Eleanor, with Henry's blessing, intended to provide it until Richard, her son, who was to succeed to the duchy, reached maturity.

Yet Eleanor lacked the power to assert herself in her homeland as completely as she wished, because Henry had given her control neither of revenues nor of military resources. Like her sons, she found that Henry II guarded power jealously; similarly, she was not prepared to countenance the lack of power. In 1173 she had to watch in silence as Henry granted Toulouse to Count Ramon of Toulouse, a man whose family had seized it from her family, in Eleanor's eyes illegitimately. In so doing, Henry secured the homage of Ramon, which was vital to Henry's overall strategy to strengthen his position in France at the expense of the French king. However, the grant involved giving away his wife's claim, and there can be little doubt of her unhappiness at this turn of events. It was under these circumstances that she joined Young Henry's rebellion that year. The rebels underestimated the strength of their enemy, though. Henry, quickly amassing a powerful force against them, destroyed their rebellion and captured Eleanor in the process. She was then imprisoned in England, an act that shows the lengths Henry was prepared to go to in order to avoid future revolt. But the defeat of the family rebellion did not bring to heel his sons, and his relationship with them was to continue to be a source of tension throughout his remaining years.

Given all of this, things did not look good for *Jean Sans Terre* in the early 1170s. Furthermore, the planned marriage alliance with the count of Maurienne had faltered, and so he remained without a continental inheritance – though his father had identified him as the future lord of Ireland in 1177. Fortune, or rather death, was to lend him a helping hand. In 1183, dysentery removed his eldest brother, Henry, the cavalier lover of games and hunting. In 1186, Geoffrey – described by the royal clerk and chaplain Gerald of Wales as 'a hypocrite, never to be trusted, and with a marvellous talent for feigning or counterfeiting all things' – received an arguably suitable comeuppance when he was trampled to death after falling from his horse in a tournament. This left only twenty-year-old John, and Richard, now aged twenty-four. The two were very different from each other. Richard had all the assets of a paradigmatic medieval ruler and constituted a far more formidable successor to Henry II than his elder brother would have been. A narrative of the Third Crusade written posthumously in the 1220s described him, somewhat prosaically, as 'tall, of elegant build; the colour of his hair was between red and gold; his limbs were supple and straight. He had long arms suited to wielding a sword. His long legs matched the rest of his body.' Richard was also intelligent and learned, once even correcting the Latin grammar of Archbishop Hubert Walter. John, too, was intelligent and well educated, but unlike Richard he was short, at about five feet and five inches, and stocky.

With the death of Young Henry in 1183, the impressive Richard had become Henry II's chief heir. But he was now expected to surrender Aquitaine to John (their middle brother, Geoffrey, having been amply catered for by receiving the dukedom of Brittany through his marriage), something he was not prepared to do. The old king, in another display of dysfunctional family relations, therefore encouraged John to take the duchy by force – without providing him with the soldiers to do so, although John obtained them from his brother Geoffrey. This again pushed Richard into the arms of the French king, now Philip Augustus, following Louis's death. The situation was only ultimately calmed by Henry's death in 1189 and Richard's swift accession to his full inheritance – including Aquitaine. By now, of course, Richard regarded John with suspicion and, perhaps in an attempt either to buy off his opposition or to bind him closer without granting him any major continental lordships, confirmed his brother as lord of Ireland and gave him a number of very substantial grants of land within England – but crucially did not recognise John as his heir. This was an honour reserved instead for Arthur of Brittany, the young son of his deceased brother Geoffrey.

Given their history of severely troubled family relations, it was highly likely that John would seek to undermine his brother. Soon he was offered an opportunity by Richard's departure on crusade in 1190. In 1187, Jerusalem, the jewel in the crown of the crusader states, had fallen to Saladin. It was a devastating and ignominious loss, and Henry II and Philip Augustus had quickly laid aside their differences in order to commit to a new crusade, together with the Holy Roman Emperor, Frederick

Barbarossa. Henry's death, though, left no alternative but for Richard I to fill his father's shoes. While he was away John plotted to boost his own position. Initially he attempted to alter the line of succession and make himself heir to the English throne, but he could not secure support. Later, when Richard was captured by Leopold, duke of Austria, on his way back from crusade, he tried again heading straight to the court of the French king, who was no ally of Richard's, to perform homage to him for Richard's continental lands. He then secured the assistance of an all-too-willing Philip in his bid to invade England to claim Richard's throne. The move was frustrated by the fact that Richard's councillors in England, under the authority of his mother Queen Eleanor, whom Richard had made regent, refused to recognise John's authority. John was thwarted again. But it had been a closer call than Richard would have liked.

When he was freed in 1194 following payment of a huge ransom, one of his first acts, unsurprisingly, was therefore to deprive his brother of his lands. (Philip Augustus wrote to John to warn him that Richard was free: 'The devil is loosed.') However, active enmity between the brothers did not last long. Given his disparaging comments about his brother's military ability, it is unlikely that Richard believed John would pose a real threat once he was back from the East. It may even have been that their mother intervened in the dispute between them. In any case, within a year, having abandoned Philip Augustus and prostrated himself before Richard at Lisieux in Normandy, John was restored to his English lands, but was allegedly told he had behaved like a child and had been led astray. The veiled threat in Richard's words was clear: if John wanted to have a chance of succeeding his brother, it was not in his interests to act against him again. It was one thing to try to claim the throne when Richard was a captive in Austria and Germany, possibly never to be released, quite another when he was a free man, with the legitimacy of his position and ample support to call on. For the next five years, John wisely remained a staunch supporter of Richard, helping him to regain lands in France from Philip Augustus and enjoying some personal military success. He played his new role so well that from 1197 Richard recognised him as his heir.

How should we read John's early actions? From his perspective, his elder brother had refused to deliver to him the duchy of Aquitaine, and the grants of lands in England in lieu, despite their financial worth, were scarcely compensation for the absence of coveted and more prestigious continental lordships. If John were to have a substantial inheritance, he cannot be blamed for concluding that it would have to be of his own making. Moreover, had he shown indecisiveness at this stage, it might have cost John what he saw in the long term as the biggest prize, and his due: the succession to the throne of England ahead of Arthur of Brittany. The decisive assertion of a claim to rule through a show of force had made all the difference on more than one occasion in the last hundred years, so to attach too much censure to what John did in 1194 might be unfair in the context of the time. He would make a bid for the throne again on Richard's death in 1199, but the difference this time was that he did so from a much stronger position, having finally displayed real political acumen by faithfully serving Richard for sufficiently long that the latter had been persuaded that he should make him his heir.

From 'Lackland' to King

On 6 April 1199 Richard I's death was a surprise: 'At a time when almost the whole world feared the king of England or praised him,' a contemporary lament said, 'he was snatched suddenly from this life.' Richard was engaged in peace negotiations with Philip Augustus at this point, the aim of which was to facilitate a new crusade to recapture Jerusalem proclaimed by Pope Innocent III. Philip was nonetheless still determined to take any available opportunity to undermine the English king in his duchy of Aquitaine. Richard was therefore busy at work on the eastern margins of Aquitaine dealing with the rebellious viscount of Limoges, who had been encouraged by the French king, when disaster struck: he went out one night, without armour, to observe how the siege was progressing and was struck in the shoulder by an arrow from a single crossbowman from the castle. He was badly attended to by surgeons and died less than a month later from a subsequent infection in the wound, in the arms of his beloved mother – a muted end to an illustrious career.

Although Richard had confirmed John as his heir on his deathbed, a widespread understanding that renewed tensions had emerged between the brothers just before Richard's death in 1199, together with the ambitions of their nephew Arthur of Brittany's associates and supporters, meant that John had little choice but to seize his inheritance immediately and with force. In the face of this task John had to contend with the fundamental structural problems that had also affected the rule of both his father and his elder brother: against a background in which the Crowns of England and France both sought to advance their positions at one another's expense, there were seemingly endless opportunities for dissatisfied, alienated, ambitious or cynical local lords to form alliances locally, regionally or nationally with a view to promoting their own interests at the expense of the king of England. This, combined with the Angevins' strong personal ambitions and sense of their individual rights, Philip Augustus' machinations and manoeuvrings, and the patchwork of different cultural and political norms that criss-crossed the Angevin empire, meant that politics took a shape that now seems extraordinarily internecine. John's personality was to exacerbate this problem in the coming months.

In practice, John had to secure four great blocks of territory if he were to emerge triumphant in 1199: England; Aquitaine and Poitou; Normandy; and Maine, Anjou and Touraine. Lack of support for Arthur in England meant that John's position there was relatively guaranteed; it was on the Continent that he had to take serious action to prevail over his nephew.

The threat from Arthur and his supporters was greatest in Anjou, Maine and Touraine, which bordered Arthur's home territory of Brittany. Were Arthur to be successful across the three great counties, he would dominate and effectively close off the main route between Normandy and Poitou–Aquitaine. It was to this area, then, and specifically to Angers and Tours, that both he and the French began to move soon after Richard's death. Realising the seriousness of the threat and the need to secure these lands, John himself moved quickly from Brittany (where he had been when Richard died) into the Loire Valley. He promptly took control of the key castles of Chinon and Loches, the former being the Angevin treasury, which gave him access to vital resources for sustaining military conflict. However, he was swiftly forced to withdraw by troops raised by Arthur's mother, Constance, who also secured Anjou's capital, Angers. Soon, rebel lords of Anjou, Maine and Touraine, at the forefront of whom was William des Roches, Anjou's most important lord, declared for Arthur. Des Roches's position is surprising as he had previously been a knight of Henry II and a loyal adherent of both Henry and Richard I. Like most of the lords of Anjou and Brittany, his support for Arthur may have resulted from their own customs of succession: Arthur had a strong claim as the son of John's older brother Geoffrey. On the other hand, des Roches's position may have been more cynically reached as a result of the provision of attractive incentives: Arthur had offered him the stewardship (governorship) or seneschalcy of Anjou in return for his support, and had intimated that he would play a key role in the new regime. John for his part seems not to have made any similar undertakings.

The likely loss of Anjou, Maine and Touraine, the Angevin heartlands, was a significant blow for John. Having tried and failed to take refuge from the rebel lords at Le Mans, the capital of Maine, which declared for Arthur, and with Philip Augustus fast approaching to offer Arthur support, John was forced to retreat hastily into Normandy, where he managed at least to secure from the Norman lords his acceptance as duke of Normandy in Rouen on 25 April. This was a significant coup and, with Normandy reasonably safe, he was soon able to move back to Le Mans, where he meted out punishment for its support of Arthur, destroying both the castle and the city walls. He then headed to England to be crowned on 27 May. There Arthur had almost no political platform, and John took control with relative ease, backed by William Marshal, earl of Pembroke, who had a long history of service to the Angevins, and who also raised timely (for John) questions about Arthur's 'evil' advisers. Following the succession, John immediately abolished Richard's 'evil customs' in June 1199 as a mark of gratitude to, and favour for, his new subjects. He could not afford to lose their support.

With England and Normandy secured, John could turn his attention to Aquitaine and Poitou, where the assertion of his claim was not straightforward: he was a relative stranger there, his last visit to the duchy of Aquitaine having taken place over a decade earlier. Yet what John did have – and Arthur and Philip Augustus did not – was the support of his mother Eleanor. Her practical assistance would be crucial in securing control for him, and although she was now in her seventies and had been looking forward to retirement, she did not hesitate to provide. In early May 1199, within a month of Richard's death, this formidable woman placed herself at the head of an army that inflicted punishment on Anjou for its support of Philip Augustus and Arthur. She then moved into Poitou and Aquitaine, visiting many major towns and cities and distributing patronage as she went in a bid to assert her authority, and by extension that of her son. John joined her on her perambulations. After this, in late summer, she did homage to Philip Augustus for Poitou on John's behalf. This provided John with an excellent formal foundation for securing Poitou in the long term, because by accepting the homage Philip had effectively acknowledged this part of John's inheritance.

Philip, meanwhile, had been focused on preventing John from making a definitive assault on Anjou, Maine and Touraine, which were still holding out for Arthur. Philip's strategy had hitherto been to attack the eastern marches of Normandy around Évreux (explaining why he had seized it so quickly after Richard's death) to draw John away from the Loire Valley, and he was back in the north by late summer to continue with his plan. Feeling reasonably secure in his hold on Normandy, however, John was content to take a modicum of risk there, and in September 1199 he proceeded south to try to secure Anjou, Maine and Touraine. It was a clever move because the impetus now shifted to John: Philip was forced to leave Normandy and follow.

John's earlier attempt to bring Anjou to heel by force, involving as it had retribution for the decision of so many of its lords and some of its key towns to support Arthur in the disputed succession, had unsurprisingly not secured submission. However, a critical misstep by Philip Augustus soon turned the tide in John's favour. This reversal of fortunes was the result of the actions in Anjou of William des Roches, the key lord who had initially supported Arthur. In May 1199 William and Philip jointly took the fortress of Ballon, just north of Le Mans, during the struggle against John. But Philip then refused to hand the fortress over to William himself or to Arthur, and consequently William and Philip quarrelled over what Philip saw as des Roches's high-handed behaviour. When in the following month John launched an impressive attack on Maine, significantly undermining the French king's authority in the region, supporters of Arthur were forced to make terms with John; and in the ensuing negotiations des Roches met the English king. He was persuaded that Philip Augustus' support for Arthur was simply a ruse to mask his own ambitions, a tale that fitted well with des Roches's own experience when dealing with Philip at Ballon. John also promised des Roches the seneschalcy of Anjou in the event of his success in securing the county, confirming the grant made to him by Arthur and Philip. This was one of John's few diplomatic triumphs: des Roches was brought back into the Angevin fold, and he went on to broker a settlement between John and Arthur's supporters at Le Mans in September 1199. Philip now had no real choice but to make peace, and so talks between the French king and John began in January 1200, concluding on 22 May with a treaty agreed at Le Goulet in southern Normandy, in which John was formally recognised as Richard's heir. 'Softsword' had prevailed.

Yet the achievement of the Treaty of Le Goulet is not simply the story of a victorious John and a defeated Philip. Even in victory the situation John found himself in was, territorially and practically, a degree worse than that experienced by his brother in 1189: the treaty emphatically laid out and acknowledged the territorial gains made by Philip since 1189, gains that had significantly reduced the size of the duchy of Normandy that John now held. The Treaty of Le Goulet also established Philip's claim to be John's overlord in the lands he held in France – excepting Aquitaine, whose rulers had never owed allegiance to the French Crown. This had always been theoretically the case, and Richard I had himself acknowledged it, but enshrining the relationship in a treaty raised the stakes: John now formally held many of his lands as a feudal tenant or vassal under Philip's suzerainty. He would have to do feudal homage to Philip for the lands in question, and, perhaps most importantly, John's own subjects in his French lands could, if they chose, appeal to the French king as John's overlord if they were unhappy with John's rule – in particular, his judicial judgements. In territories where recalcitrant or trouble-making local lords had always been difficult, this represented a huge prospective challenge, along with a mischief-making and aggressive French monarch. Furthermore, if Philip overrode one of John's judgements, and if, for reasons to do with local political control and the maintenance of order, John refused to accept the overturning of his judgement, Philip could declare him a contumacious vassal or rebel, and confiscate his lands in consequence. It is clear from the start that Philip meant fully to enforce those rights in a way that none of his predecessors had. Given the previously informal nature of the exercise of overlordship by French kings, John may have misunderstood this. On the surface, the Treaty of Le Goulet looked like a good settlement for John, but in reality it was a Trojan horse through which Philip Augustus might in due course penetrate the citadel of Angevin tenure in France.

The Empire under Threat

Despite the Treaty of Le Goulet, John knew that he could not take the chance of lowering his guard in the north and east of the duchy of Normandy in 1200. Nor were his lands further south safe. Philip was clearly bent on strengthening his territorial position within France and would take advantage of any opportunity. And so, following the peace established in 1200, John immediately began to counter Philip's influence wherever he could. In Poitou, he made a number of concessions of land to Poitevin lords, while his mother Eleanor managed to form a constructive relationship with Hugh le Brun ('the Brown') of Lusignan by granting him the territory of La Marche, directly to the east of Poitou, which he greatly coveted. The Lusignans were among the most important Poitevin families and any alliance might prove vital in the future.

What neither John nor Eleanor had anticipated, however, was the rapidity with which the sands of lordly relations would shift in the area – a sudden rapprochement between the Lusignans and the counts of Angoulême, by means of the betrothal of Isabella of Angoulême, the count's heir, to Hugh le Brun, inevitably came as a surprise. We have no details about how or exactly when this was achieved, but John and Eleanor must have been sure that if the marriage went ahead the resulting territorial settlement would bring together two great tranches of land in northern Aquitaine, changing the balance of power in the region dramatically by bringing another independent force, in the form of a Lusignan–Angoulême partnership, into the equation. This had the potential to undermine Angevin authority in the region as a whole by providing another significant focal point for their subjects to play off.

The situation created by the betrothal was challenging, but John had a solution. Having recently repudiated his own wife, Isabella of Gloucester, on the grounds of consanguinity – they were cousins, and the archbishop of Canterbury had from the first condemned their union – John was free to make another marriage. The real reason for John's abandonment of Isabella was not related to concerns about his spiritual position, though. Instead, he almost certainly felt he could do better, having first been betrothed to Isabella by his father when he had little inheritance to hope for. He must have concluded that as king of England he could aim for a higher-status wife, and he quickly managed to secure his own betrothal to Isabella of Angoulême in place of Hugh le Brun: for Isabella's family too, marriage to John, given his landed status, wealth and power, trumped marriage to Hugh of Lusignan.

The match promised to bring the house of Angoulême fully into the Angevin fold as partner, drawing the counts away from the French king. Of course, it also threatened to alienate Hugh le Brun, whom John at the same time made no effort to compensate for his loss of a wealthy and advantageous marriage. As a result, by the start of 1201 serious rumours of rebellion had begun to circulate in Poitou. Eleanor of Aquitaine, who by this time had had to retire in ill health to the abbey of Fontevraud, worked hard from her sickbed to turn disaster into triumph for her tactless and headstrong son. She had laid solid diplomatic foundations, but John, as would so often be the case, simply could not discern that this was a time for negotiation and compromise, for a degree of humility in victory. Instead he gave orders to his officials to confiscate La Marche from Hugh le Brun and to 'do . . . all the harm they could' to Hugh's brother Ralph, who held the county of Eu in Normandy.

Unsurprisingly, in June 1201 Hugh and Ralph appealed to the French king, technically John's and by extension their feudal overlord (and therefore previously not their ally), saying that John had attacked them and despoiled their lands without justification. Luckily for John, Philip had his own concerns, and was not ready to use this as a pretext to wage war on his Angevin adversary. Instead, he encouraged John to make peace with the Lusignan brothers and give them a fair trial in his ducal court, while urging the brothers to stop their sieges in Poitou. John had been thrown an unexpected lifeline. But here he made another damaging mistake, clearly failing to see the risks inherent in the combination of this situation and his new position as a vassal of the French king. Refusing to negotiate with the Lusignans or provide them with a trial in his court, and instead charging them with treason against both himself and Richard I, he challenged them to a duel with his own men to prove their innocence. In so doing, he effectively guaranteed that they would lodge a further appeal with Philip. Even then, John might have walked away from this potential fiasco relatively unscathed, because Philip again tried in late 1201 to induce him to provide the Lusignans with a fair trial. However, John's overconfidence led him to delay. When he finally offered a trial, he did not offer safe-conduct for the Lusignans, which meant they would be in fear of their lives if they made the journey. John was able to argue as a result that they had declined his offer of a trial, but it was a reckless path to tread and demonstrates his unwise machination.

Meanwhile, the French king continued with his diplomatic efforts in the face of John's actions, but when all else failed, and now occupying the moral high ground, Philip Augustus finally required John to come before the French court in Paris at Easter 1202. John refused, saying he was only obliged to go to the borders of the duchy of Normandy and not beyond. The French royal court at Paris inevitably and immediately rejected John's defence, and judgement was passed against him. But this was not just as count of Poitou: the French court deemed him to have forfeited all the lands he held from the French Crown because of his stubborn refusal to appear before his overlord. Philip was quick to declare Arthur as John's successor and to take his homage. This was a preface to a full-scale assault on Normandy by Philip, the legality of which was dubious given that the court judgement had not actually deprived John of the duchy. Doubtless Philip was looking for any excuse to seize John's lands. However, the failure of diplomacy and judgement on John's part was abject and staggering – he had made things very easy for Philip.

The Inheritance Lost

In late spring 1202, Philip began to make a series of outright assaults on Normandy. John needed friends but found himself short of allies.

Meanwhile, Arthur and his forces were causing problems in the southern part of John's French territories, starting with a progress along the Loire Valley; by late July they had moved south from there and were pursuing Eleanor of Aquitaine as she, in one of the final efforts of her life, headed for Poitiers to arrange its defence. She failed to make it all the way there, taking refuge in the keep of the castle at the small town of Mirebeau just north of the city, where Arthur's forces besieged her. At this time John was in Le Mans preparing to make an assault on Maine and Anjou, but now diverted quickly to relieve his mother. Covering over eighty miles in a southward march in the space of just forty-eight hours to get to Mirebeau would prove to be one of the few martial glories of John's reign. With William des Roches, his new ally, John stormed the castle at dawn, surprising those who besieged it before they had even had their breakfast. Eleanor was rescued and Arthur and his allies, including the Lusignan brothers, were captured.

This might have been a pivotal victory, enabling John to restore his position just as he had done in 1200. But he made further serious mistakes. First, he created yet more enemies and disregarded norms of chivalry by sending the besiegers to prison weighted with chains; many died in the process. Furthermore, having promised to take counsel from William des Roches, who had masterminded the relief of Mirebeau, John now instead decided to remove Arthur to prison in Falaise in lower Normandy. Humiliating an ally as vital as William des Roches – the very man who had denied Philip Augustus victory in 1199 when Philip had been similarly high-handed over the fortress of Ballon – was only going to end badly. Des Roches duly defected back to Philip Augustus, taking with him a significant number of other lords. John had compromised his own position throughout the Loire Valley, a critical linking point between his lands in Aquitaine and Normandy, and hugely valuable in its own right.

Only now did he realise the importance of his relationship with the Lusignans, and swiftly released them from the harsh regime of imprisonment that had been inflicted upon so many men captured at Mirebeau. In return for their release they promised loyalty, but in reality they had no intention of allowing John to subject them to his whims again. They went on to betray him as soon as was expedient. Beyond Normandy John was confronted with more and more rebels throughout 1202 – his reputation preceded him.

By early 1203 Philip's star was definitively in the ascendant. It is reported that John, panicking, had Arthur murdered at Rouen (where he had been moved from Falaise); some accounts even declare that John performed the act himself. According to the annals of the abbey of Margam in Glamorgan, when John 'was drunk and possessed by the devil, he slew him with his own hand, and tying a heavy stone to the body cast it into the Seine'. This chronicle account of John murdering Arthur was written in an abbey of which the Briouze family were patrons, and may well have been based on a first-hand account: William de Briouze had been a significant advocate of John's claim to the English throne in 1199 and was for several years thereafter a great favourite. He had also been the man who had captured Arthur at Mirebeau in 1202 and stayed with John in his service afterwards. Whatever the details, few doubt that it was at the very least on John's orders that Arthur was killed. The act brought Arthur's loyal Bretons out into a war of vengeance against John, and by autumn 1202 they quickly seized the city of Angers – just as they had done on John's accession in 1199.

Meanwhile, Philip was launching a further series of attacks on eastern Normandy. With the situation worsening, John realised that he needed significant reinforcements and began preparing for a major campaign, mustering men in central Normandy, from where they could easily travel in any direction in response to an emerging threat. Early in 1203 his position began to unravel further with the loss of the great castle and Angevin treasure at Chinon in Touraine, perhaps inevitable given the amount of support John had haemorrhaged. John decided to advance south, but he was quickly forced to turn back and abandon his position in Anjou, Maine and Touraine. Soon all his lands on and around the Loire had been lost, the core of his Angevin inheritance.

On the eastern flank of Normandy, Philip Augustus stepped up his assault, and the castles of Conches and Vaudreuil quickly fell, enabling the French king to move to lay siege to Richard I's great castle near Rouen, Chateau Gaillard, which was now isolated. The castle had been one of Richard's proudest achievements: he described it as his 'beautiful daughter' whose walls he could hold 'were they made of butter'. It was – and remains – an extraordinary tour de force in military architecture: commanding the cliffs above the Seine, it formed a defensive complex – easily linked by barge to the Angevin arsenal at Rouen and thereby to supply from the sea – that effectively blocked any ingress that Philip Augustus might seek to make into upper Normandy. Inspired by the latest concentric castle design, seen by Richard in the Holy Land and reimagined in Normandy in even more compelling form with no fewer than four tiers of formidable defences, it ought to have been as impregnable as any fortress in the known world, and to have sealed Normandy like a cork seals a bottle.

What happened to Chateau Gaillard over the next few months cemented the fate of Normandy. Like any castle, its garrison needed provisions. John tried to get supplies to it by attacking the besieging French forces. But the rowers moving up the river with relief supplies were slower because of the strength of the current and they missed the troops who were coming across land. The failure of the rendezvous meant that the French forces were able to intercept the relief supplies and defeat the land army. At this point, John moved west to try to distract Philip's attention by attacking the Breton forces, but Philip was resolute before the castle walls and the diversion tactic failed. With the continental inheritance for which he had fought so hard collapsing around him, John rushed from France to England in December 1203 to raise new resources to enable him to return to France in spring 1204. But he was too slow. Chateau Gaillard fell to Philip Augustus in March.

Despite John's failure to provide relief supplies to the garrison in 1203, however, the castle was not starved out; it was taken by a mix of force and politics. Chateau Gaillard's structure was key. Under normal siege circumstances, its defences should easily have held out, but what Richard I had never expected was that his opponents would have a period of many months to attack the castle; the failure of John's political position condemned Chateau Gaillard to months of exactly such grinding assault. When the castle fell on 6 March 1204, John's last hopes of any defence of Normandy fell with it, the rest of the duchy quickly coming into French hands.

Little had John known when he crossed to England at the end of 1203 that he had left France as de facto duke of Normandy for the last time.

By spring 1204, with Normandy lost, his problems on the Continent mounted. Eleanor died soon after the storming of Chateau Gaillard, and a number of towns and lords quickly realised that they must pledge allegiance to Philip Augustus if they were not to be punished as opponents by the dominant leader in the region. It was the end of a great empire. On one side of the Channel, Philip Augustus celebrated the achievement of his crowning glory; on the other, John could only rue his ignominious failure.

England's Full-Time King

In the years that followed, John would be away from England for only brief periods in 1206, 1210 and 1214, spending more time in the realm than either his father or brother. His personal presence alone would inevitably make this a very different reign from either of his predecessors', but John's preparations for a fresh assault on Philip Augustus on the Continent also required a greater accumulation of resources than ever before: there was now no Norman wealth to contribute to the effort, and any campaign would this time be one not of retention but reconquest of a vast swathe of lands. Furthermore, Philip Augustus' own ambitions did not stop at the shoreline of France – more than once after 1204 he actively made preparations to invade England, with the notion that his son Louis would become king. In fact, as early as 1205 the spectre of invasion loomed large: in his pomp, and having wasted no time, Philip was already attempting to assemble aggressive allies who might join him by virtue of their own landed claims through their wives: men like the count of Boulogne and the duke of Brabant. Concerned about the gravity of the threat, John took urgent action late in 1204 and early in 1205 to ensure that England's borders were defended. In January, he demanded a vow of fidelity from every adult male in the country 'against foreigners and against any other disturbers of the peace'. Constables were appointed in the localities to raise forces in the event of invasion. Meanwhile, naval defences were created, often from scratch, with frantic shipbuilding taking place, especially on the south coast.

Philip must have been hopeful of building a coalition and forming alliances with nobles within England: a number of those lords who held extensive lands in England were also landowners in Normandy, and were not straightforwardly aligned to either the English or French king. The earl of Pembroke, William Marshal – who had given important support to John in England in 1199 and who had led the unsuccessful attempt in 1203 to relieve the garrison at Chateau Gaillard – had felt the subsequent fall of Normandy as devastatingly as John; he lost a great deal of land. So it was understandable that, having been offered an opportunity in 1205 to make a deal with Philip Augustus for his lands in Normandy, he should have been willing to pay 500 marks for a guarantee that the French king would leave those lands alone for a year and a day, and to promise to do homage to him for them thereafter if they remained intact. He was clearly keen to ensure that his relationship with Philip Augustus was a positive one in the future. Marshal was not the only one to come to such an arrangement: Robert, earl of Leicester did so too, thereby saving his Norman lands.

Others in the same position decided, however, not to make such arrangements, perhaps because they were more fearful of the potential impact on their lands in England. Earl Ranulf of Chester, for example, decided against reaching an agreement with Philip, who went on to redistribute the earl's forfeited Norman lands among his followers. Another group left French lands in the hands of younger sons, and therefore retained at least a familial foothold on both sides of the Channel. There is no doubt that a number of English lords were willing to come to arrangements with Philip Augustus in relation to their Norman lands, but there is no evidence that he would have been able to bring large numbers to his side in support for an invasion of England, in part due to the nobility's interpretation of the likelihood of Philip prevailing over John in England. In March 1205, with Philip actively raising an expeditionary army, John met his nobles to ask for their support, and they wasted little time in agreeing to supply him with all their might in defending England; forces were ordered to muster in May.

But all was not well within England. In fact, despite their promise of loyalty to John in defending the realm itself, many lords were becoming increasingly disgruntled with his rule. This was expressed later in 1205, when John attempted to take the fight back across the Channel by mounting a campaign in Poitou. John's opportunity to launch a campaign arose from the fact that Philip's prospective allies among the princes of the Low Countries had proved reluctant to fight across the Channel, critically undermining the planned invasion. This meant that in 1205, as spring turned to summer, England was no longer under serious threat, and John immediately moved to the front foot and tried to take the fight back to Philip – but faced with demands for service overseas, the English nobles refused in large numbers to muster. English brakes had been applied to John's continental ambitions; he was not going to find the realm as amenable as he had presumed.

A steady accumulation of grievances at John's dealings with the lords had built up since 1199. The first problem was his personal relationship with the nobility as a group; he tended to eschew their services and surrounded himself with paid mercenaries, or men whom he had cultivated himself and who owed their position not to their inherited landed wealth or status as Conquest families, but to him. The nobility did not feel as though they were his natural counsellors, a role that, as his key military commanders and soldiers, they were traditionally expected to play, exactly as secretaries of state do now with prime ministers and presidents. Moreover, at the start of the reign John had agreed to the restitution of lost rights for his subjects in England but had failed to deliver on his promise. In 1201–2 he had toured the country selling privileges and confirmations of liberties which lords, among others, were obliged to pay fines to obtain, thereby raising large sums of money, while in 1203 he had implemented a novel tax on movable goods, which was paid, so far as we know, only by the lay nobility and bishops, and may have been punitive as a result of their alleged desertion of him. At the same time, in a precursor to later action, he had begun to threaten to confiscate land if a debtor was unable to pay what he owed to the Crown, a move that must have worried many.

Secondly, John's behaviour towards individual barons and earls was unpredictable. The fundamental problem arose from his application of the principle of carrot and stick to induce loyalty – he punished some in order to enforce what he considered their reluctant or dubious loyalty, while rewarding others in order to secure their support. It was an attitude that infantilised the nobility, and assumed fundamental antagonism towards the monarchy rather than support for it. While they were sensitive about what they saw as their own local rights and jurisdictions, it is clear from how nobles acted towards the king that they both wanted and needed their monarch: the king was the only one with the authority, God-given after all, to resolve disputes between them, and to lead them in battle, and by the early thirteenth century, they depended on the smooth operation of the all-encompassing common-law system over which the king presided. He therefore served a vital role and they were, quite simply, loyal unless provoked to be otherwise. He was equally willing to take all manner of financial or other offerings – both great and small – for judicial suits, the effect of which was to confuse justice with patronage. The former was supposed to be dispensed by the king as the fount of natural justice. But this should have been a matter of equity and impartiality, not of favour. And certainly justice was not supposed to be purchased.

The extent of the king's demands and the vagaries of his behaviour were particularly felt in the north of England, defined in the period as everywhere above the River Trent. John was in the north – often making long perambulations – in every year of his reign other than 1199, 1202, 1203 and 1214. By contrast, Henry II visited on only eleven occasions during his thirty-five-year reign, and Richard the Lionheart only twice. John's presence had a significant impact because when the king was physically present in a locality, the financial demands associated with royal government tended to be applied with greater force and alacrity. When he visited a locality, John also levied fines and amercements (financial penalties) on an unprecedented scale. Moreover, certain aspects of Angevin rule, for instance the Forest Law (that is, the law protecting hunting for the king in large areas of land adding up to about a third of England) and the collection of so-called Jewish debts (debts owed by the nobility and others that had reverted to the Crown on the deaths of Jewish moneylenders) burdened the north more heavily than they did the south. In the case of Jewish debts this was because the most prominent moneylenders, foremost among whom was Aaron the Jew of Lincoln (who had died in 1186), had been active in the north.

Although John was more absent from the north in the early years of his reign – his presence being demanded elsewhere by the need to secure the throne and then by threats to his continental lands – nonetheless the governmental records contain long lists of so-called financial offerings that people made to the king in the period (a better term than 'offerings' would be 'extractions' because they were certainly not voluntary). Some £6,000 was extracted from Yorkshire alone during an extensive royal tour in 1201. The individual offerings that added up to these major sums were varied in nature: in York, the citizens were even forced to give John £100 for his benevolence because they had not met him on his arrival; he had consequently taken hostages from among them, for whose release this £100 also paid. Roger of Howden, with all the drama we expect from contemporary writers, wrote that an earthquake took place in Yorkshire shortly before John's arrival, and that when the king did come, 'He perambulated the land and ransomed the men of the realm . . . asserting that they had wasted his forest.' John's reputation for greed is indicated by the fact that Roger also stated that, when John arrived in Hexham, 'He heard that there was buried treasure at Corbridge. He had men dig there, but nothing was found.' Roger of Wendover mentions that John had taken large amounts of money from the north during the 1201 tour.

The increased weight of government in the north under the Angevins greatly affected its most substantial nobles. By 1199, their jurisdiction was already being challenged by judicial eyres and forest eyres (both of which involved royal justices circulating through the counties hearing cases, the former hearing all manner of legal cases in the localities, particularly property disputes, and the latter cases relating to the royal forests), tallages (a form of arbitrary taxation levied on liberties and boroughs) and other money-raising measures, as well as by royal visitations. John was to take all this further, and, as was the case elsewhere, it was accompanied by unpredictability, perceived greed and needless cruelty on the part of the king.

Another aspect of John's intrusive and heavy-handed government was that, as elsewhere in his territories, he increasingly imported new personnel – favourites and outsiders, some from his lost French territories – into local office. The men who were appointed to these offices were, as well as often being from across the Channel, regularly from relatively humble backgrounds, and would receive extensive patronage from the king which cut across existing expectations. One, Robert de Vieuxpont, was even given the hereditary lordship of Westmorland.

The discontent caused by the imposition of so many financial burdens, the king's unpredictability and the promotion of so many new and unknown men, often foreigners, not only in the north but across the whole of England, had been clear as early as 1201. In that year quite a number of earls, especially northerners, had failed to respond to John's summons for a campaign in Normandy. Refusing to come to Portsmouth for the muster for the proposed crossing to the duchy, they instead met at Leicester and stated that they would not go on campaign 'unless [John] restored to each of them their rights'. In the face of this John acted swiftly, not by making concessions, but by taking hostages and effectively enforcing service, with the result that many nobles went on to accompany him on campaign overseas – but hardly under propitious circumstances.

Distrust continued, and when the king returned to England in 1203 he accused the nobility collectively of deserting him – a far from reasonable accusation since so many had campaigned with him. Towards the end of 1204 northern England was close to being in a state of war with the king. Unsurprisingly, in March 1205, when the nobility agreed to support John in defending England against Philip Augustus and the dauphin Prince Louis, they also made their king take an oath 'that he would by their counsel maintain the rights of the kingdom inviolate, to the utmost of his power'. John thought that in so doing he had secured their obedience, but by the summer his hopes were to be disappointed: the reality was that he had simply not given enough guarantees or engaged in enough acts of good faith to convince men to serve with him on the Continent.

Many of the burdens John imposed in the years to 1205 resulted from a mixture of his acute need for money both before and after the loss of Normandy, and his desire to make the governmental machinery more all-encompassing and imposing. In both these areas, John's personal oversight of, and the efficiency with which he deployed and expanded, the Angevin governmental machine were both significantly greater than under his father and brother. This was the case even before the loss of the continental lands brought him back to England on an almost full-time basis and generated greater burdens. This created tensions, particularly in the north of England, which was not used to this sort of royal rule. But the situation was also significantly complicated by John's paranoia and mistrust of his greatest subjects, and the way in which these were expressed; nobles cannot have known if they would be singled out for flattery or destruction, and the resulting situation must have been at best unsettling and at worst terrifying. By preferring the counsel of his own mercenaries and confidants, often from outside England, John had also begun to drive a further wedge between himself and his greatest nobles.

Thwarted Ambitions

The refusal of the nobility to serve with him on the Continent in 1205 came at the same time as a succession crisis – not that of the king. In July 1205 the archbishop of Canterbury, Hubert Walter, died. For John, needing to place his own administrators and supporters in the highest clerical ranks so that they might access benefices and therefore not burden the Crown financially, this presented an opportunity. It was also probably a matter of principle to John that he should have a key say in the appointment of the new archbishop. After Walter's death, he went straight to Canterbury in order to try to promote his own candidate. There, he found the monks of the priory of Christ Church Canterbury, who were attached to the cathedral, at odds with the bishops of the province of Canterbury over who should elect the archbishop. The monks argued that they had the right to appoint one of their own to the archbishopric without any other input, whereas the bishops claimed that they had a right to a voice in the election. John persuaded both groups to wait until the end of the year to go forward with an election. In the meantime, they appealed to the pope for a decision on who had the right to choose. But a faction among the monks decided not to wait and elected their prior, Reginald, on the condition that the pope subsequently approved that decision. They sent him to Rome with letters to that effect, perhaps not expecting Reginald to rewrite the script and announce himself to have been elected without mentioning that condition.

By autumn 1205, John was therefore struggling to assert his kingly authority in both the ecclesiastical and the lay spheres. In the first of these, a rogue prior was arguing to the pope that he was now the archbishop of Canterbury in the face of John's own wishes to the contrary, and in the latter his nobles were refusing to accompany him to campaign against the king of France. John must have been furious on both counts. He had proceeded with uncharacteristic diplomacy over the archbishopric and still failed. Meanwhile he had pursued his foreign ambitions with single-minded purpose, and just as it looked as though a window of opportunity had opened for him, he had been thwarted. The failure of the 1205 campaign might have been a salutary lesson for John about the fundamentals of his relationships in England, but he was determined to launch another campaign as soon as possible. As he would do when faced with a crisis again in 1212, he seems to have embarked not on amending his behaviour, but on a personal tour of the country, paying particular attention to the north, throughout the autumn and winter of 1205–6, which was patently aimed at bringing his recalcitrant lords into line.

John's chosen methods of persuasion took their usual form of a combination of threats and bribes: Earl Ranulf of Chester, for example, was given the lands of the honour of Richmond, but a number of other lords were made to surrender their lands. When the now elderly Angevin loyalist William Marshal pleaded in 1205 that he was unable to join John in an expedition to Poitou because of his homage to Philip Augustus, whose vassal he now was and whom therefore he could not fight, John angrily accused William of treason. Luckily for William, his fellow magnates refused to pass judgement on him. That John thought such a man could be treated in this way is telling. What Marshal is alleged to have said to his peers during this altercation with the king is remarkably prescient: 'Be on alert against the king: what he thinks to do with me, he will do to each and every one of you, or even more, if he gets the upper hand over you.' He could not have summarised the situation more astutely.

Where the archbishopric of Canterbury was concerned, John felt his own personal presence in Canterbury was needed if he were to hold sway given the recent turn of events, and so his tour in the winter of 1205–6 also involved some time there. When he arrived in December 1205, his first action was to demand to know why Reginald seemed to believe himself to be archbishop despite there having been no formal and proper election. Reassuring the outraged king that they had not made an election, the monks then held another vote in John's presence, unsurprisingly choosing the king's own candidate, John de Gray, bishop of Norwich. However, the drama turned into a farce when Pope Innocent III then refused to acknowledge the new election because it had been made while an appeal to him about who had the right to choose the archbishop was still in train. By March 1206 Innocent had summoned more monks from Christ Church Canterbury to Rome to take part in a third election, and by the autumn he had in addition informed the bishops that they were not entitled to participate. But the monks were divided between Prior Reginald and John de Gray, and so Innocent proposed an alternative candidate, Stephen Langton, who, despite being born in England, had spent most of his life in France and was therefore heavily associated in John's mind with his arch-enemies.

John was deeply unhappy and refused to give his assent to Langton's election. This did not deter Innocent, a man (like the Angevin kings) famous for his inflexible sense of his own prerogatives, and he went on to consecrate the new archbishop in May 1207. There almost inevitably followed a refusal by John to allow Langton into England, let alone Canterbury. In a move typical of John, he decided to drive the monks of Christ Church, who had caused him a good deal of trouble in all this, into exile. For good measure, he also took possession of all benefices of Italian clerics in England and banned the papal judges from the English church courts.

But the reality remained that John had failed to prevail in relation to the pope. Innocent III even ignored John's demands for guarantees that the election of Langton against his will would not set a precedent. There was consequently a complete impasse. Innocent drove up the pressure by responding to John's continued opposition to Langton's appointment with an interdict, banning all sacraments from being performed in England. In return John confiscated clerical property, making clerics pay fines to receive it back and turning a huge profit in the process. Despite several attempts to negotiate a truce in the next few years, the pope and the king remained irreconcilable, and in November 1209 John was excommunicated. This meant in theory that anyone deposing John had the pope's blessing. For now, however, that was certainly not on the cards. Ironically, John and his nobles mostly found themselves of one mind over this: the great lords agreed with the king that the pope had to recognise that the election of

Langton would not set a precedent if a settlement was to be brokered. The impasse prevailed.

John was more successful in his demands on the nobles than in his quarrel with the pope. His actions in the autumn and winter of 1205–6 enabled him to amass a sufficient force to launch a campaign in summer 1206. When he wanted, John could be extremely beguiling, and of course his threats to individual lords' landed security were potent as inducements to loyalty. The result was that, in early June 1206, his internal 'diplomacy' took him to La Rochelle with a significant following of nobles. He swiftly retook northern Poitou, forcing Philip Augustus to rush to the border between Anjou and Poitou in order to prevent further progress. With Poitou largely regained, he was content to agree a two-year truce with Philip in October 1206. Neither king was yet ready for a more extensive campaign.

The Campaign for Reconquest

The success in south-west France in 1206 was cause for optimism. When John set sail for England, therefore, his luck seemed to have turned, and from the moment of his return he started to make plans for one of the most ambitious campaigns of reconquest of Normandy across the Channel that had ever been attempted. But it was an all-or-nothing bid and would require financial underpinnings (and therefore impositions on his subjects) of such an order of magnitude that failure, and the consequences of failure, were unthinkable. So the royal government in England came to be even more oppressive, more exploitative and more aggressive in the financial sphere than before – this could not fail to increase resentment and produce a febrile atmosphere.

One of John's first actions on his return from the Continent was to call together a Great Council of the prelates and nobles of England to meet with him in January in Oxford, where he requested a tax of one-thirteenth on movable property from both groups. The clergy resisted, but he claimed to have gained consent from the lords for a lay tax, stating that it had been granted 'by common counsel and the assent of our Council'. It seems more likely from the evidence that no one in the meeting had dared to argue with him. In his statement about the tax, John also claimed that it had been agreed 'for the defence of our realm and the recovery of our rights'. Where previously kings might only have called on feudal service from their tenants-in-chief (usually nobles or senior members of the gentry) for the second of these, John was now claiming that his subjects had agreed that the Angevin inheritance was a matter for the realm as a whole. In essence it represented an attempt to normalise the granting of taxes by his subjects, and therefore recourse by the king to public funding, for continental campaigns. As a result all laymen had to pay to the king twelve pence in every mark (a mark amounted to roughly sixty-six pence) of their annual revenues and twelve pence in every mark on their 'movable' goods (mainly saleable corn and livestock). The resulting collection of over £60,000 provoked such opposition that John did not dare to attempt such a novel experiment with revenue-raising again, but his attempt to elide his private Angevin inheritance and the realm of England would in due course be echoed by his successor.

Other revenue-raising measures were also instituted. A new forest eyre began, raising huge sums of money for the Exchequer through fines; Jewish debts and Jewish moneylenders were exploited to the full, with the collection of debts in Crown hands vigorously pursued. At the same time, heavy taxes were imposed on living Jews: in 1210 alone the Jews of Bristol were taxed a staggering £45,000. Not only did this damage England's burgeoning credit economy, it also impoverished the king's Jewish subjects, and impacted heavily on some of the most indebted members of society, often nobles and lesser lords. Crown debtors generally were also subject to increased attention, and threatened with the confiscation of their property if they could not meet the terms. Simultaneously, John held on for extended periods to bishoprics and abbacies vacated as a result of the death of the incumbent, enabling him to claim the revenues that accrued in the interim. By early 1213 there were seven bishoprics and thirteen abbacies in the king's hands bringing in large sums of money.

The king could also fine subjects who committed infringements of the law or other misdemeanours, and he could accept payments for justice – to expedite cases, for example, or to permit a hearing in the first place. John did this energetically throughout the reign. In the period from 1207, however, payments for justice became more and more common, peaking in 1210–12 as the pressure for money for the alliance John was seeking to construct on the Continent mounted significantly. At the same time, the pipe rolls (the financial records of government) show increasing numbers of fines being paid for the king's benevolence and for release from the king's prisons.

The same dramatic increase in pressure can be seen in relation to feudal revenues, particularly the 'feudal incidents' – fees paid for permission to marry or inherit land, for example. The value of a feudal incident was not regulated and was, strictly, subject to the whim of the king. So, if John charged one person £15,000 to inherit his father's lands, a payment known as a 'relief', and another £500, he had done nothing that it was not within his power to do, even though there was broad agreement by the early thirteenth century that £100 was actually the most reasonable sum to charge. If the heir who had been forced to pledge £15,000 defaulted on his payment because he simply could not raise the funds the Exchequer demanded, the king could confiscate his land, or take his children as hostages, without any means of redress. Of course this was not new under John. What was new from 1207 was the sheer regularity and magnitude of the charges.

The scale of the demands made by John brought the fact that there were virtually no rules about what he could and could not do into stark relief. His subjects' vulnerability to the vagaries of his will was made all the more threatening not just by John's acute need for money; at the same time, his innate fears of treachery were mounting and he increasingly used reliefs and fines to place barons he did not trust in fetters of debt to the Crown, threatening dispossession to enforce obedience among those who were struggling to pay if he thought they might be likely to betray him.

Two men who particularly suffered as a result of John's suspicions were William Marshal and William de Briouze, who dominated South Wales, the southern Welsh borderlands (or March) and Ireland, and who had both been among the king's most trusted advisers in the early years of the reign. Tensions first erupted in Ireland in 1206 when the justiciar of Ireland, Meiler fitz Henry, seized one of Marshal's castles, Offaly in Leinster. The same happened to Briouze in Limerick. Marshal's and Briouze's tenants naturally fought for their lords and sent word to them across the Irish Sea about what had happened. The two lords protested to John about the behaviour of his justiciar and John conceded to allow the return of any of Briouze's men, together with booty that had been seized. But he did not propose to return the city of Limerick, which had been occupied. He also gave permission for Marshal to visit Ireland in 1207 to make a survey of his lands, but then decided to require custody of Marshal's second son and of the earl's English and Welsh castles as guarantees of his loyalty. In autumn 1207 he ordered Marshal to return to England and went on to give a number of lands to those Leinster lords who looked as though they might be willing to desert Marshal. (This suggests that the justiciar's first actions against Marshal and Briouze had in all likelihood been taken on John's orders, rather than independently.) John also confiscated the sheriffdom of Gloucestershire and the custody of Cardigan and the Forest of Dean from Marshal. When the earl returned to England, another lord, Meiler fitz Henry, launched a number of attacks on his possessions in Leinster, but these were repulsed by an able body of knights the earl had left behind as a precaution. John was consequently forced to compromise with Marshal, but still emerged with the upper hand: Marshal had to pay around £200 to receive Offaly back and was made to sign a new charter regarding his earldom of Leinster. This restricted his rights and extended those of the king. Thereafter Marshal sensibly kept a generally low profile until John pardoned him in 1212. His case is a good example of John's suspicion of treachery, even where, given Marshal's record of loyalty, it was extremely unlikely that he would launch any challenge to the king.

John arguably provoked treachery from Briouze by acting as he did. Briouze had helped John to gain the English throne in 1199 and was a natural ally. Yet despite giving him early favour, the king became increasingly suspicious of him, even demanding hostages in 1208. Briouze's wife Matilda refused, allegedly saying that she would not give her sons over to a man who had murdered his own nephew, referring to Arthur in 1203. Her husband tried to smooth things over, but John, probably even more fearful of treachery now, sent his officials to arrest the whole family. In the event, those officials arrived too late: Briouze, Matilda and their children, fearing the worst, had already fled to Ireland. Once there, Briouze had to evade capture. Initially he took refuge with Marshal, and later with Walter de Lacy, lord of Trim Castle in County Meath, Ireland and of Ludlow

Castle in Shropshire, who was married to Briouze's daughter. Rumours abounded that the Briouzes and the Lacys, who had both been instrumental in asserting royal authority in Ireland earlier in John's reign, were attempting to start a rebellion there. The situation was serious, and it was of John's own making.

Rebellion across the British Isles

John could not mete out the punishment he wanted to the rebels over in Ireland because rumours of a possible rebellion in the north of England in response to the impositions of recent years forced him to divert there in July 1209. John's policies in respect of Jewish debts, the tax of 1207, the royal forests and feudal incidents, while probably not intended to have a greater impact in the north than elsewhere, nonetheless had. At the same time, the scale of the appointment of officials who had served John loyally on the Continent and who were, following the loss of lands in 1204, in need of billets in England, was so extensive that by 1209 there had been massive changes in personnel. Many local notables had been displaced in the process. What made the situation even more threatening for John were rumours that had begun to circulate at the same time that the Scottish king, William I, had entered into an alliance of mutual support with both Philip Augustus and some of the English lords. At the start of John's reign, King William had demanded the cession to Scotland of both Northumberland and Cumberland, refusing to do homage to John for the lands he held in England. In entering into a new alliance with the French king, William had seen an opportunity to assert himself. With both the north on the verge of rebellion, and the arms of the Scottish and French kings for the northerners to run into, it would have been doubly risky for John to depart for Ireland. Instead he travelled to the north in July 1209, taking the feudal army with him. Once there he met the Scottish king, who, faced with John's forces, and devoid of a significant army himself, quickly made peace with demeaning terms, agreeing to pay the king £10,000 and to hand over two of his daughters as hostages to his good behaviour.

William the Lion's swift capitulation enabled John to resume his focus on raising money and enforcing baronial loyalty in England and Ireland.

In May 1210 he took the opportunity to sail across to Ireland to impose his authority. This move was successful: John humbled the great English nobles whom he suspected of fostering rebellion there, and although William de Briouze escaped back to Wales, he offered to make peace. This being John, the matter was not left to rest: the king was hell-bent on pursuing Matilda de Briouze – who had spoken out so dangerously about Arthur of Brittany's fate – and remained in Ireland to do so. Only after she had fled to Scotland and was captured by a Scottish lord was John willing to do business with her husband. Briouze agreed to raise the money for his wife's release but instead fled to France, fearing for his own life, in the process showing little thought for his wife and children. He cannot have anticipated what would happen next, a series of events that was ultimately distilled into one of the most famous stories in the history of the period: Matilda and her sons were allegedly starved to death in prison on John's orders, a story of staggering cruelty that is all too easy to believe, given what we know of John's personality.

When John returned to the mainland in August 1210, he decided to take pre-emptive action to prevent any further distractions from the business of his continental campaign. This meant bringing to heel another vassal about whom he was growing concerned in an increasingly febrile political atmosphere. Llywelyn ab Iorwerth, prince of Gwynedd and undisputed leader of the native Welsh, had extended his own territorial position within Wales so extensively that John judged him to be a clear threat to the position of the English king. The latter's authority in Wales derived not from his territorial presence, which was actually quite limited, but from the fact that Henry II had made a deal with Rhys ap Gruffudd of Deheubarth in 1171–2, which he had consolidated in 1175–7, that Rhys acknowledge Henry as his feudal overlord. Overlordship meant that the English king was entitled to hold estates when their holder died and the heir was too young to inherit, and that, as in England, lands fell to him if he confiscated them from their lords, as was the case with William de Briouze. Prior to Llywelyn ab Iorwerth, Rhys was the predominant native Welsh prince, so he could claim the authority to do this.

From his accession John had approached Wales in much the same way as he approached England, Ireland and Scotland. He wanted to make the practical reality of his authority more tangible, and so he visited the Welsh Marches frequently once he was back in England after 1204, though typically deployed inducements to build relationships with a number of native Welsh princes. In fact, while he was careful to articulate clearly how he defined the terms of the overlordship that had been agreed in the 1170s, he was initially able to create a good working relationship with Llywelyn ab Iorwerth, who had established his pre-eminence following Rhys ap Gruffudd's death in 1197 (Rhys's own family having been riven by disputes about succession). John's success with Llywelyn resulted from the fact that he was quick to recognise the enhanced status of the prince of Gwynedd in practical ways, arranging the marriage of his own illegitimate daughter to the prince, together with granting Llywelyn the manor of Ellesmere in Shropshire in 1205. Llywelyn had even accompanied John on his campaign to the Scottish border in 1209. It was unusually diplomatic.

Yet establishing an initial pre-eminence was not enough for Llywelyn, who was keen to ensure that his position *within* Wales was unchallengeable, and he set about annexing southern Powys and making inroads into Ceredigion. For King John, Llywelyn's power had to be diminished. He mounted two campaigns into Wales in 1211, the second of the two raiding into Gwynedd and forcing Llywelyn into an utterly ignominious truce in which he was forced to surrender the Four Cantrefs, a key region in North Wales. John's mercenary captains who held office in border counties, men like Engelard de Cigogné, sheriff of Gloucestershire and Herefordshire from 1210, and, in South Wales, Fawkes de Breauté, bailiff of Glamorgan since 1207, then proceeded to embark on a programme of castle-building as a way of cementing John's position.

Continental Disaster

By the end of 1211, John had halted, at least temporarily, both those whom he believed posed a threat to him in the British Isles and those who really did. The result was that he could give his full attention to the Continent, where the situation had begun to look favourable for a new campaign. John's continental strategy after 1206 had been to create an intricate web of alliances with other lords and princes in order to launch a combined attack on Philip Augustus. It was in principle a good plan, promising to split Philip's forces by requiring him to make war on at least two fronts when the time came, both to the north-east and to the south-west of Normandy. But progress in realising the strategy had been slow in the first few years: although in 1207 John had secured the support of Otto of Brunswick, claimant to the German throne (Brunswick's claim to the throne would prevail in 1208 and he was also to become Holy Roman Emperor in 1209), and thereafter had built alliances with princes in eastern Germany with Otto's help and with the aid of considerable financial incentives made possible by John's extractions from his English subjects, it was only in 1211 that further major figures were brought on side. In that year the count of Boulogne, upset by the local application, at his expense, of Philip Augustus' expansionist inclinations, began work to re-form the grand coalition in the Low Countries that had previously been so useful to Richard the Lionheart. It looked as though cracks were emerging in Philip Augustus' position, which until recently had appeared impregnable. This opened up opportunities for John by early 1212.

First, though, he had renewed problems in Wales to contend with, when Llywelyn ab Iorwerth of Gwynedd allied with other native Welsh princes in June 1212 to launch retaliatory attacks on English royal garrisons. The alliance had come about because the princes were, in light of the recent campaigns, collectively afraid of what John's recent masterful assertions of his authority in Wales meant for them, and the attacks unsurprisingly included some on the castles that John's mercenary captains had built during the course of 1211. In response, John initially focused on a mission to relieve the pressure on garrisons, but he then decided that a full-scale campaign stood the best chance of eliminating the threat from the native princes. This necessitated the diversion of the troops he had planned to take to Poitou, who were now ordered to muster at Chester in August. John planned for the army to build castles as they advanced into Welsh territory, firmly establishing Angevin dominance, and to that end he gave orders to the sheriffs across thirty English counties to raise more than two thousand men skilled in carpentry and other essential crafts and more than six thousand labourers to join the muster, a foreshadowing of Edward's actions several decades later. John meant business.

But even the Welsh campaign was not to be. Just before the army set off, John received rumours of a baronial plot that aimed either to murder him or to hand him over to the Welsh. As the Barnwell chronicler put it, the desired outcome was clear: it was 'to choose someone else as king in his place'. John had no choice but to cancel the muster immediately. He put his eldest son into safe custody and began to seize suspected nobles' castles and demand hostages. Knowing they had been found out, two participants in the plot, Robert Fitzwalter, lord of Dunmow in Essex and Baynard's Castle in London, and Eustace de Vescy, lord of Alnwick in Northumberland, fled the country. But what accounted for this sudden action on the part of Fitzwalter, Vescy and their confederates? There is no evidence that the plot was directly linked with earlier opposition. In fact, it seems to have been hastily put together sometime between July and August 1212, possibly prompted by a decision by John to order an inquiry into feudal landholding and service on 1 June 1212; this may have led to fears about what he intended to do with the returns, especially given his continental plans and ambitions. The opportunity to act was provided by the distraction of the Welsh rebellion.

Fitzwalter and Vescy were the only two lords who failed to cover their tracks effectively, but we know very little about their motivations. Both were vilified by chroniclers and even by some modern historians: one of King John's modern biographers, Wilfred Warren, memorably wrote that they were 'baronial roughnecks' who 'put out stories of John's lecherous designs upon their womenfolk' and who were 'simply out for John's blood'. But these are caricatures at best. In 1212, Fitzwalter had until very recently enjoyed a good relationship with John. His tenure of a large swathe of land in England made him one of England's greatest territorial magnates, and he had been the recipient of early favour from John, receiving the custody of Hertfordshire in 1202 and a pardon for all debts owed to Jewish moneylenders the same year. He was involved in the defence of Normandy in 1203, but under pressure from Philip Augustus surrendered Vaudreuil, one of two key castles in the east of the duchy, which fell just before Philip began his siege of Chateau Gaillard, and whose loss opened the door to the fateful attack on Richard the Lionheart's defensive *pièce de résistance*. The circumstances of the surrender of Vaudreuil were (and remain) shrouded in mystery, and this led some at the time to suspect Fitzwalter of treachery, though in fact there is little evidence of that; King John certainly does not seem to have thought this himself. That Fitzwalter was one of the lords who went with John willingly to Poitou in 1206 would seem to suggest he remained loyal; he was certainly in receipt of favour from the king in this period. As late as 1210 he had received a grant of land, and served with John in Ireland that year.

Both Fitzwalter and Vescy had until only very recently had a strong record of loyal military service. From this, it seems that their relations with John can only have deteriorated shortly before 1212. One contemporary theory as to why this took place is that John had supported the prior of St Albans in a dispute with Fitzwalter over Binham Priory; another is that John had made a bid to seduce Fitzwalter's daughter. None of the alternatives put before us to explain Fitzwalter's treachery in 1212 seems to offer a compelling argument when taken alone, and it may be that a combination of factors contributed to his actions.

What is much more likely, especially given that it is highly probable that they were not the only plotters in 1212, is that they and their confederates had grown very concerned about John's behaviour and intentions. Although we cannot trace individual links between the plot of 1212 and earlier problems, the trend is clear: in 1209, John had had to journey to the north of England following rumours of a rebellion; and in 1210 he had been forced to pursue his fallen favourite William de Briouze to Ireland, fearing he might lead an invasion. Opposition was building. The Irish campaign was about establishing John's authority firmly there, but Fitzwalter and Vescy, and others accompanying the king, were surely perturbed by the single-minded pursuit of William de Briouze, and of William's son-in-law Walter de Lacy, and Walter's younger brother Hugh, earl of Ulster – who had harboured both William and Matilda – and then by the gruesome murder of Matilda and her children. There may also have been a much wider backdrop to these concerns: John's impositions on the nobility in the years since 1206 had been of unprecedented magnitude. Fears about the inquest into feudal tenure and service may have been the last straw for a number of great lords.

Realising that at least tacit support for the plot of 1212 might have been widespread, John set about securing his position further in the months that followed. First, he had to ensure that there was not an outright rebellion. Things seemed to have calmed fairly quickly after the revelation of the plot, but to guarantee no further attempts, John progressed through northern England with troops in autumn 1212 – an explicit show of force designed to intimidate. He even ordered the castellans of the royal castles in the north to prepare for war, spending over £1,000 on enhancements to the fortifications in several places, including Scarborough, Durham and Newcastle in the north-east, and Bolsover, Newark and the Peak in Nottinghamshire and Derbyshire.

At the same time, though, three chroniclers – the Bury annalist, the Barnwell chronicler and the Dunstable annalist – commented that he changed some of his policies, promising to take advice from magnates rather than from foreigners, and reducing some of the financial exactions his agents had been making. The sheriffs were also instructed that the king wanted all those who owed Jewish debts to him to come to him because he wished 'by the Grace of God to relax their debts'. At the same time, John worked to secure the end of the papal interdict as soon as possible, under the banner of which Fitzwalter and Vescy had justified their position. Envoys were quickly sent to Rome to make peace and by May 1213 John and Innocent III were on better terms (though not without considerable concessions on John's part).

John again pursued a strategy in February 1213 of quickly rebuilding key relationships with individual lords, while punishing some others for their treachery. He extracted charters of fealty from those about whom he harboured continued suspicions, requiring them to pledge all their lands to prove their loyalty. In some areas he charged them huge reliefs to inherit lands from their fathers. John de Lacy, for example, was told in 1213 that his succession to the honour of Pontefract would cost him the huge sum of 7,000 marks. He was lucky: Robert Fitzwalter, despite being readmitted to the king's peace, found that John had completely destroyed two of his castles. This was characteristic behaviour: at the same time that John was cowing opponents by shows of force he was bringing others onside by indications of friendship or flexibility. For the nobles faced by this, John's tactics must have presented a continual dilemma: should they resist the at-times-monstrous near-tyrant, or should they welcome a fresh accommodation with him with a measure of relief and a modicum of hope for their future personal safety and prosperity? In this manner, divide and rule kept John on his throne and to a degree in command of events, but as resistance to his essentially hostile kingship grew year on year, and as John responded with repeated shows of force, his position was more and more compromised; crisis, should political space open up, became ever more likely.

Sensing an opportunity in John's domestic problems, and having already made an alliance with the Welsh, Philip Augustus swiftly ordered his son Louis to raise a force to invade England. In May 1213, just before the interdict was declared to be at an end, Louis overran Flanders with a view to launching the planned campaign across the Channel. John had been on high alert for such a campaign since late April, and had stationed his army in Kent ready for the possible assault from Louis. Among the nobility, despite tensions with John, there was still no desire for a French replacement and this defensive action had the support of virtually all of them. They were in Kent for the six-week period waiting in a state of readiness in case of French attack. Things soon began to unravel more generally for Philip and Louis. The latter's actions in Flanders, particularly the seizure of Saint-Omer and Aire, alienated the count of Flanders, and that in turn led the count to appeal to John for help. The loss of the loyalty of both the count of Boulogne (who had been allied with John since 1212) and the count of Flanders created a domino effect in the Low Countries, and a strong coalition at last began to build against the French king. John had in the meantime managed to recruit various lesser French lords, like the count of Nevers, into his pay. By late May he felt strong enough to despatch the earl of Salisbury across the Channel with a force. The earl and his allies, with a total of around five hundred ships, including on board the counts of both Holland and Boulogne, discovered the French fleet moored at Damme in Flanders, and Salisbury gave an immediate order to attack, destroying Philip's ambitions of a successful invasion of England.

Victory over Philip Augustus enabled John to step down from the defensive position he had adopted in Kent and to plan to take an army across the Channel instead. A campaign to recapture Normandy was resuscitated, with plans to set sail for Poitou in summer 1213, from where he intended to launch the southerly prong of his attack on Philip.

He therefore summoned the feudal army to appear at Portsmouth in July and readied for a sustained assault on the French king. And yet, when Normandy was tantalisingly close to being redelivered to him, John was thwarted yet again by lack of support from the English nobility. Despite all his concessions following the plot of 1212, many now simply refused to serve him: the six weeks that the nobility had spent together in Kent in late April and May 1213 may well have been crucial in this, enabling more discussions of rebellion to take place. When it came to the campaign, the chronicle accounts variously put forward three reasons which they say were given by the nobles for their lack of support: first, the king had not yet been absolved by the pope from his sentence of excommunication; second, the nobles apparently argued that they did not have the resources to campaign on the Continent because those resources had been used up in internal expeditions (by which they meant in Scotland, Wales and Ireland); third, the northern lords said that they could not be forced to provide military service abroad to John because it was not part of their feudal obligations.

There was no option for John but to abandon the campaign – a humiliating situation for a king who had only recently been similarly humbled by having to make concessions to the pope in order to secure his restoration to favour. The northern lords' argument that they did not owe service to the king overseas was a way of avoiding a charge of treason based on the strict technicality relating to when and where they owed feudal service; it was of course not the core reason for their failure to serve, but an excuse that gave their resistance legitimacy. Had they had a better relationship with John, he would probably have found himself in a different position. Now they were determined to use the only real lever they had over the king to wrest concessions from him. Angry, but determined not to cancel the campaign – instead deferring it to February 1214 – John promised general reform and made a series of deals with individual lords.

As summer 1213 turned to autumn, it became clearer and clearer to John that, despite all this, the north was going to be difficult to subdue, and in consideration of the gravity of the situation he set off there with every intention of inducing submission. Even the intervention of Stephen Langton, who pleaded with John that he could not attack any of his feudal vassals without legal judgement, could not halt the king's march north. It was only when Archbishop Langton went on to threaten excommunication if John proceeded to go forward without having first secured proper judgement that John climbed down from the nuclear option. In late October, he signalled a willingness to negotiate. What provoked this change is unclear, but initially the ensuing talks were constructive, and on 1 November it seemed like a settlement had been reached. However, by 7 November John, fickle as ever, had revoked the concessions he had made less than a week earlier, and began to threaten force against his northern opponents. This was made possible by a combination of his promise to others of general concessions, and the deals he had managed to do with individual lords elsewhere, especially in eastern and southern England. Perhaps he had only ever been playing for time.

Though the northerners remained steadfastly in opposition to the king's plans, with Eustace de Vescy continuing to offer the most entrenched resistance, by early 1214 John had gathered enough lords to accompany him to Poitou and he finally set sail in February, leaving the northern castles in a state of readiness in case of attack by his domestic opponents; he was not to return until October. At the same time, the earl of Salisbury took another force to Flanders to attack Philip on the other flank. John quickly took two of the fortresses held by the Lusignan brothers and moved northwards towards the Loire. In June he went on to seize Ancenis, on the border of Brittany and Anjou, then suddenly marched on the port of Nantes and defeated the French garrison who, together with citizens of the town, had attempted to prevent him crossing the bridge into it. However, although he began to besiege castles around Angers, John knew that to defeat the great powerbroker, William des Roches, his former ally who had defected back to the French king in 1202, would be an enormous undertaking and he feared he lacked the troops to do it. With the Poitevins refusing to provide support, he fell back to La Rochelle, where he attempted to raise more men. From there, he wrote to the home government in England that 'we earnestly entreat those who have not crossed with us to come to us without delay, being assiduous for our honour, to help in the recovery of our territory . . . Assuredly, if any of you should have understood that we bore him ill-will, he can have it rectified by his coming.'

The king's plea met with no response. Meanwhile, to the north-east of Normandy, a further delay occurred while the earl of Salisbury awaited the arrival of the Holy Roman Emperor, Otto of Brunswick, meaning that the ideal of concerted action against Philip, which would split his forces and potentially defeat them, could not be realised. Instead, the delays gave Philip and Louis the space they needed to raise the French feudal army and prepare for the battle to come. By the time the northern alliance had assembled its forces for battle, Philip was ready. The armies met on 27 July 1214.

Although Philip was well prepared for the clash, the battle might still have gone either way – both armies were large and well organised, and fought fiercely. Under great pressure in the centre from the crack Flemish infantrymen, the French king was at one stage himself unhorsed and had to be rescued by his bodyguard. But the capacity of the French to soak up the assault on their centre and remain ordered told overall. Philip's cavalry succeeded in forcing the Flemings into retreat and then the two wings of his army closed in on the Imperial centre. Otto of Brunswick, too, was unhorsed, and in the end only narrowly escaped the field. The earl of Salisbury and count Renaud of Boulogne fought fiercely to the end, but finally the Flemish infantry formations were broken and both were captured under a sustained attack from several thousand regathered French troops. The battle was over. The French victory resulted from good preparation, effective control on the battlefield and stalwart fighting both in defence and in attack. It represented a major triumph: in one fell swoop it decimated the alliance and left John critically exposed in Poitou. With Philip marching south to take advantage of his enemy's isolation, John was deserted by those Poitevins who had hitherto supported him, and was forced to make a truce with the French king in September 1214. By October he was back in England, his great plan of reconquest in tatters.

There is no doubt that John could have succeeded in 1214. The alliance he had constructed was carefully planned and very well funded, and the battle was closely fought. But there is no prize for coming second in war, and having failed in his dream of reconquest, John would also now pay a high price at home. It is easy to understand how things had become so bad in England: even after the plot to kill him in 1212 and further opposition in 1213–14, the years and months immediately before February 1214 had seen John, with his great continental alliance in his sights, place on his nobility some of the greatest financial impositions they had ever experienced. He had gambled everything on the hope of regaining Normandy, and with it an imperious authority that none would dare to challenge in England.

The Road to Magna Carta

When John's gamble on regaining Normandy failed, the volume and scale of opposition in England inevitably became louder and greater than ever. The king was so concerned about the situation that he sent messengers home in advance of his arrival to give secret orders to the justiciar, as well as commands to the royal castle-holders throughout England about both the guardianship of the castles and, interestingly, the guardianship of 'our person' – the king himself. John knew the position he was in; his very survival as monarch was in the balance. Despite his efforts, within just weeks of his return in October 1214 the severity of the situation had increased. With resistance spreading, it was not from the north but from the eastern and southern counties that the leadership of the rebellion came. A further rising took place in the West Country, which the loyal earl of Salisbury struggled to put down. Only in the Midlands and the south were John and his mercenaries able to hold out.

The rebels confronted John with concerted demands for concessions. First, he was asked to confirm the laws of Edward the Confessor and the laws and Charter of Henry I. John played for time. He had spent the winter preparing for war, bringing mercenary forces over from Poitou, placing royal castles in their custody and ordering work to be done on castle fortifications in several places, but war was the last resort. Both parties – king and rebels – sent envoys to the pope, with John cleverly taking the cross, an undertaking to go on crusade, on 4 March – a move that bought him favour with Innocent III. The northern opposition were then given safe-conduct for talks with the king's representatives and Archbishop Stephen Langton in February, and another meeting was planned in Oxford in April. But John did not attend to answer the rebel demands, and they renounced their allegiance to him on 5 May 1215. Within a week of this John had in turn ordered that their lands be seized. Civil war had begun, and the early advantage lay with the king's opponents, who managed to take London on 17 May, having gained entry after being admitted by friends in the city. The rebels went on to appoint their own sheriffs in a number of counties to shore up their control of government. In May and June they went on to work out the demands that were to coalesce to become Magna Carta.

Fundamentally, Magna Carta as it was drafted in 1215 (and subsequently confirmed) enshrined one central and general principle: the king should be subject to the same law as everyone else, and therefore should not be able to do as he wished to his subjects. Article 39 stated:

> No freeman shall be taken or imprisoned or disseised [dispossessed] or outlawed or exiled or in any way ruined, nor will we go or send against him, except by the lawful judgement of his peers or by the law of the land.

The king had previously been able to take such action at will when a lord had either refused or been unable to pay the often extortionate sums demanded from him. In the next article, it was also established that the king would not sell, delay or deny justice to any freeman of the realm. The rebels who drafted the Great Charter knew that to establish that the king was subject to the law that granted his subjects due process in respect of the taking of any property – lands or money – was key. It would mean that they would have a decent chance of resisting such arbitrary exploitation in the future, and so articles 39 and 40 lay at the very heart of their demands.

But in its sixty-three articles Magna Carta also went into great detail about many issues of principle. Some related to the king's feudal rights and dues: the payment of reasonable 'reliefs', the good management of the lands held in wardship when heirs were too young to inherit, the just treatment of widows and debtors whose debts came into the king's hands. Some of this was not straightforward: for 'reliefs', there were precedents and £100 was quickly alighted on as a good limit for the king to charge, but where there were not such precedents the nobles in Magna Carta ended up settling instead on the vague term 'reasonable' – which would cause them difficulties later. But 'reasonable' was a start, at least. The delivery of justice was also the subject of a number of articles: the court of Common Pleas, the Charter said, should not follow the king around the realm, but should be held in a fixed place, and two justices should also be sent to the counties four times a year to hold the assizes. No sheriff or other local official was to hold pleas of the Crown; they were reserved for the royal justices. The royal forest too, a source of regular complaint as the Angevins had sought to expand the boundaries of it and its law, was to be subject to regulation, and newly afforested land was to be cleared. And, in a likely response to John's levying of taxes, particularly that of 1207, it was clearly stipulated that 'aids' could only be given if the king had obtained the 'common counsel of the realm'. To be clear, said the Charter, this meant summoning archbishops, bishops, abbots, earls and greater barons individually 'by letters' to appear at a fixed date, with forty days' notice. The rebels pushed even harder on the issue of scutage, the payment made to commute military service, attempting to make that similarly subject to 'the common counsel of our realm'. This though was an innovation and not one the king was likely to be at all content with: scutage had never been in the same category as aids and it was blatantly an assumption to attempt to make it so now.

Where the Charter was also innovative was in its attention to lesser land-owners in particular. In addressing its articles to 'all freemen of the realm', it set out that it was freedom rather than rank that determined rights. In so doing, it addressed the wider realm, not simply the nobility. It meant that the articles on 'reliefs', wardships, widows and debts applied auto-matically to all freemen, as did the general stipulations about justice, the royal forests and taxes. But more local grievances of lesser men were also addressed specifically in other articles. Sheriffs, the Charter said, were to be qualified men, and were not to take the possessions of any freeman without agreement. Increments were not to be charged on the ancient 'farms' (the levies) of the counties to the Crown, and no town or man was to be forced to build bridges on riverbanks. Moreover, purveyance for troops had to be paid for, not simply taken. Merchants, too, were protected in the Charter's stipulation that only ancient and rightful customs should be levied, not new 'maletotes' (literally 'bad tolls'). The rights of the Church were to be preserved intact and there were also clauses relating to the just treatment of the Scots king, Alexander, and Welshmen, including Llywelyn. In other words, the Charter was an attempt to secure a broad range of support for the rebels' cause; it might even be described as a manifesto.

In that sense, while many of the articles of the Charter addressed long-standing issues or grievances that had become magnified during John's reign, some also directly addressed John himself. His mercenaries who had come 'to the hurt of the realm' were to be removed from the realm, and a number of his hated courtiers from the Continent were listed by name – 'we will dismiss [them] completely from their offices', it said. In conceding the Charter, John also promised to restore hostages and charters taken 'as securities for peace or faithful service' and to remit all fines 'made unjustly and contrary to the law of the land'. Indeed, the final few articles almost read as a list of direct indictments of John, and they make for a compelling picture.

From a contemporary standpoint, much of what Magna Carta demanded might seem entirely sensible: the king's subjects should not be faced with ever-changing and unpredictable demands they had no power to resist, particularly for money. But it is arguably because of Magna Carta that our modern conception exists in the first place. This was the very first time that people in England sought to introduce such extensive rules about what the government could and could not demand of them (what belonged to the royal prerogative and what did not), and they did so by reference to a vocabulary of subjects' rights and the law, a vocabulary given to them originally by the Angevin kings themselves.

To King John the demands of the Charter were anathema. Under what possible circumstances could it be advantageous for him to agree to restrictions on his freedom of action? Indeed, from his perspective, the situation was even worse than that, because the Charter not only stipulated what would happen in the future, it also sought redress for what had happened between John's accession in 1199 and the crisis of 1215. The rebels demanded that lands, liberties and rights that had been seized 'unjustly by the Crown' should be given back. The definition of this 'unjust seizure' alone was to prove to be immensely knotty, and a major sticking point for both parties, to say nothing of the ill-feeling and potential violence that would be provoked in the process of taking lands back from those who had received them in good faith. In June 1215, however, John had no real alternative but to agree to the Charter: accepting the status quo was the only way of bringing an end to the civil war that had lasted months; he was certainly not strong enough to defeat his opponents militarily. (For their part, once he signalled his agreement, the rebels promptly undertook to renew their homage to him.) But John's was undoubtedly a pragmatic climbdown, surely intended to be a temporary one allowing him to play for time and build up support. Given what we know of his attitude to authority, he could never have lived with the concessions demanded of him. Furthermore, with the opposition having appointed their own sheriffs in various counties in May 1215, John probably quite legitimately feared the permanent dismantling of his own governmental system if he agreed to the baronial demands. The rebel lords in turn could not be sure that John would honour his word; he had failed to do so on so many previous occasions, and this settlement was manifestly to his disadvantage. However much it might have seemed, then, as though both parties had withdrawn from the brink with the agreement of Magna Carta in June 1215, the reality was that they remained as irreconcilable as ever.

The Rejection of the Charter

In the coming weeks, despite the best efforts of both the archbishop of Canterbury and the bishops to bring about a long-term settlement with which both parties could live, it was therefore almost inevitable that the civil war would be renewed. For the situation to have produced peace would have required one side to make significant compromises on the assumption that the other side would not abuse its position, and neither believed that would happen: neither side trusted the other. In any case, how they were likely to define 'abuse' differed, a situation permitted by the vagueness of Magna Carta's terms.

In the stalemate of this period, there is no doubt that John played the more effective political game. He was a skilful and wily negotiator, and as king he inevitably continued to hold the best cards. The lords' renewal of their allegiance or 'homage' on 19 June, for example, could be construed as meaning that they accepted their feudal obligations to the king as their overlord: to provide him with military service for the protection of his person, his realm and his kingly rights. And John, who was not one inclined to miss an opportunity, quickly sought explicit confirmation of this detail from them. Their refusal to give it (they must have seen acceding to his demand as surrender, given that he had not yet implemented any of the promised concessions of the Charter) immediately meant that John could paint them as wholly self-interested and disloyal rather than having legitimate grievances. By the same token he could portray himself as reasonable. This was not simply diplomatic semantics. For many of those who had so far remained neutral in the dispute, the refusal on the part of the opposition lords to recognise the king's authority meant that they simply could not support the opposition. It was one thing to question the king's policies and seek amendment and reform; it was quite another to oppose the king himself. Where resisting royal policies was acceptable, resisting the person of an anointed, God-given king was not. Within weeks of 19 June John had therefore secured an important political victory, which took him closer to being able to fight and win a civil war.

Things were also difficult for the opposition in other ways. Their ability to get the Charter agreed had been due in part to its vagueness. It could mean different things to different men. Putting the settlement into effect, however, required definition, certainty: what exactly did 'unjust dispossession' constitute? What was 'lawful judgement'? Moreover, it had been agreed that John had to fulfil the demands made of him by 15 August. But what would happen if he did not meet the deadline? The rebels' answer was that they would decide on all these things.

In the coming weeks the imprecision of the Charter on various matters was used by both sides to argue that the other had failed to observe its terms, as positions became more and more entrenched. By early July it was clear that the peace was in jeopardy, and although negotiations led by the archbishop and bishops continued, John began to prepare for war. He also continued to work hard at the propaganda battle, stating explicitly in August that he was in fact the wronged party; if anyone had acted contrary to good faith and the law, it was the opposition. He had 'surrendered many things as he had agreed', he told his agents to say. The rebels, however, had given nothing back 'except the grave injuries and tremendous damages which had been inflicted on him and which no one was ready to amend'. John made himself out to be the victim of a determined and personal attack, under the guise of righteousness. Around this time he probably also wrote to Pope Innocent III asking him to annul the Charter. The pope, characteristically hostile to rebels and disturbers of the social order, in reply issued a sentence of excommunication on all 'disturbers of the king and the realm' and appointed commissioners chosen by John himself to investigate. Unsurprisingly these commissioners were to go on to criticise the behaviour of the baronial opposition:

> The dignity of the king has been filched, since they [the lords] grant out lands, a thing unheard of, and nullify the approved customs of the realm, and establish new laws, and destroy or alter all that has been prudently ordained by the king, their lord, with the advice of the magnates . . . They have gone as far as they could in despoiling the king of his royal dignity.

This was not just an attempt to right the wrongs John had committed, but almost to usurp his government and certainly to diminish the king's rights. The Charter was therefore illegal and undermined the very essence of kingship. This verdict made the baronial opposition traitors, a critical development in the argument that was not lost on them. They hastily realised that the only option left to them was to prepare for battle, and to secure more powerful support if they were to have a chance of winning. It was in this climate that they proposed the deposition of John and the installation of a new king. They called a Council to enact their will, but, unsurprisingly, given the king's recent victory in the propaganda war, found no support for the proposed course of action; the opposition nobles simply looked more disloyal and self-serving than ever. Those remaining opponents of John who wrote to Prince Louis of France in autumn 1215 inviting him to come to England were an isolated group who could no longer claim with any conviction to occupy the moral high ground. Within just two months of the original issue of the Great Charter, then, both sides were mired in a bloody civil war.

Why, given the gravity of John's undoubtedly tyrannical behaviour and the number of lords who opposed him late in 1214 and early in 1215, did they seek first to negotiate with him and not simply to remove him from the throne? The first and most obvious answer to this question is that it would be easy to imagine that opposition to John was unanimous among the nobility; it was not. William Marshal and Walter de Lacy, brought back into the fold in 1213, are two prominent examples of men who remained by the king's side during the crisis. There were others, too, with whom John had achieved reconciliation by concession after the plot of 1212. In addition to this, even if the opposition could be confident of overcoming the king's supporters (and they could not), the king of England was powerful in a way that many other European monarchs of the age were not. One in two castles was now a royal castle, a testimony to John's energy and vigour – at his accession it had been only one in five. Moreover, the king's governmental reach extended across the country – his subjects looked to Henry II's great common-law system to guarantee their property rights, and royal personnel on the ground might be relied upon to enforce loyalty (albeit some of his sheriffs had been replaced by opposition supporters). For magnate opponents of the king, the continued absence of the sorts of large territorial blocs that were the reality in France at the same time, whose tenants could be deployed en masse against the king's forces, also rendered them impotent, relatively speaking, in the face of this.

Besides, if this system of government could be made to work, its benefits were tremendous for the nobility as well as for John's other subjects. The lords wanted to make use of the common law, and when they were consulted about royal policy, government could work effectively to the benefit of all. Deposition was therefore not the first item on the agenda in 1215. It was only contemplated when John gave the opposition nowhere else to go; even then, the proposal was only to replace him with another king, not to dismantle the structure of monarchy. So much in England depended on the effective operation of royal government that going it alone for an individual magnate, with lands strewn across the country, was inconceivable. A king was essential.

Therefore, in producing Magna Carta in spring 1215, the nobles had not only to accept but also to embrace the nascent English state so greatly developed by the Angevin kings, and seek to negotiate a basis on which heightened royal power could operate fairly. In so doing, they wanted to remove prerogatives the king himself thought of as untouchable, prerogatives that attached not to his public rights as king, but to his feudal rights as the ultimate overlord. The reason he could charge whatever relief he chose to a lord wishing to inherit his father's lands was because those lands were granted as a royal gift; they were not something to which the tenant-in-chief had a right protected by law: the common law did not regulate the king's relationship with his own tenants. What the rebels now asked was that that relationship should come under the auspices of the same law as that which governed most other relationships, with fixed reliefs and the removal of threats of arbitrary dispossession by the king. There was great irony in this: not only had the nobility learned to deploy a vocabulary of rights effectively, but they had in fact been taught it by the Angevins.

On one level, England in this period was not so very different from many other countries. All over Europe, the Angevin kings' counterparts had been strengthening their public authority in the twelfth century, aided by the Roman law- and canon law-fuelled propaganda produced by political theorists employed by the pope and the Holy Roman Emperor (as well as other princes in their battles with each other); by greater literacy and in consequence access to ever-increasing numbers of men who could act as royal officials; by developments in accounting; and by growing notions of office. All these things had changed government in twelfth-century Europe as dramatically as the computer and the worldwide web have changed the modern world. And across Europe, as kings failed in war, their subjects came to extract concessions from them, which defined the terms on which public authority would operate. In 1183, the Emperor Frederick Barbarossa had already been forced to grant the towns of the Lombard League a number of liberties, and just seven years after Magna Carta the Golden Bull was forced on the Hungarian king by his nobles, imposing constitutional restrictions on his freedom of action too. Only the Capetian kings of France kept on winning and staved off the inevitable crisis until the fourteenth century.

Yet England was not just one example among many. It was different, too, in being far more centralised than most of its European counterparts; the existence of the common law also gave the king more practical power than any other European king, no matter what their pretensions. The English rebels of 1215 sought to regulate royal government, not to dismiss it from their lands. They embraced the English state, but the conversation about the terms on which it should be run, and about what form royal government should ultimately take, was to be a long and tortuous one. 1215 was only the beginning.

Civil War Rages

In the months after Magna Carta, the outcome of the civil war hung in the balance. John for his part not only commanded the theoretical high ground in his capacity as God's anointed king, but also outclassed his opponents in physical power: where John had possession of around 150 castles across England, the rebels commanded only sixty. Crucially, though, the rebels had control of London, as well as Cumberland, Yorkshire and eastern England. Consequently, victory was far from inevitable for John. With a keen sense of this, he characteristically wasted no time in trying to weaken his opponents militarily. He ordered a muster of forces at Dover in late September and he waited there for the soldiers to arrive, while at the same time his superior financial resources enabled him to bring over significant numbers of foreign mercenaries from the Continent to assist him.

If they were to have any chance of winning this war, it was essential for the rebel lords to prevent the royalist reinforcements moving up from Kent into the rest of England. This meant focusing their efforts on taking the great twelfth-century castle at Rochester, which dominated the River Medway crossing and held the key to one of the main routes by which troops might move from Dover to London. They prepared for a siege, but when they got to Rochester the constable of the castle simply opened the gates for them to enter and take control. While the castle was safe, it was crucial to raise more troops, and this required continued negotiations with Philip Augustus and Prince Louis, whom the rebels hoped would lead an army to England. Negotiations were initially hampered by the fact that John was simultaneously trying to make his own peace with Philip Augustus, but in the end French ambitions across the Channel prevailed, and by late 1215 Philip had decided to allow Louis to invade.

While the rebels waited for their French allies, John's own mercenaries gave him the momentum, and finding Rochester blocking his way north through Kent, he embarked on an immediate siege. In November 1215, after seven weeks, the Rochester garrison surrendered. John's forces had dedicated all their resources to the siege, deploying five siege engines and using pig fat to start a fire underneath the castle, burning the bridge over the Medway and cutting off the rebels' reinforcements from London. With characteristic brutality, John is said to have wanted to hang the entire garrison, only being persuaded not to do so by arguments that this would set a precedent of which he did not himself want to be a victim later.

Following this victory, the winter months saw a steady stream of royalist mercenaries arriving on the south coast and travelling up through Kent unchallenged to reinforce John's armies. The rebels by contrast had only a token force of French knights sent at the end of November to sustain them: the promised French invasion had failed to materialise. As 1215 drew to a close, the scales were beginning to tip firmly in the king's favour. Sensing this, John decided to split his forces in order to launch further attacks elsewhere: he left one group under the command of the earl of Salisbury to hold the rebels in London, while he set about attempting to break up rebel strongholds, one of which was at Belvoir Castle in Leicestershire, which he besieged, again forcing the rebels to surrender. This gave him an unchallenged area of royal control based around the east Midlands, specifically Nottingham, Newark, Sleaford and Lincoln. Attacks ordered by John on Hanley in Worcestershire and Tamworth in Staffordshire quickly subdued those centres of resistance too. By the time the king reached Pontefract, John de Lacy, earl of Lincoln, and a key rebel, was ready to submit without a fight. Finally, King John set his sights on King Alexander of Scotland, who had succeeded William the Lion at the end of 1214, and had led an army into the north of England in support of the rebels – a bold attempt to shift the border and annex parts of the north to his own kingdom. Faced with the direct wrath and military might of the king of England, Alexander quickly decided that discretion was the better part of valour, however, and returned to Scotland.

Such was John's show of force in rebel territories that even his arch-opponent, the plotter of 1212, Eustace de Vescy, was brought low and sued for peace. So much for 'Softsword'. One chronicler wrote that several rebels sought 'the mercy of the merciless one, or fled before his face', while another reported that by the time the king had finished only one rebel castle was left in the north. But the campaign had been punishing for John and his army too. It took place in the freezing depths of winter, between November 1215 and February 1216, a time when the weather was so bleak that military campaigning would ordinarily have been suspended. John was no ordinary military commander, though, and it was his almost reckless willingness to fight through the winter that shifted his position dramatically: when he left the north in the early months of 1216, its rebels were critically weakened. Even then, when he must have been exhausted by his efforts of the past few months, he took no time to pause for breath: in February and March he progressed to the eastern counties, where he again achieved notable surrenders.

Only London held out, and by early 1216 John had both money and forces enough to contemplate action there in a way that had been impossible in the latter part of 1215, a harsh reality that had probably determined his tactics that winter. But the rebels had in the meantime finally been boosted by the arrival of large numbers of French troops who had reached London in two waves, in December 1215 and January 1216. By April 1216 Philip Augustus and Louis had decided to follow that with a full-scale invasion. Just when it had seemed that only London stood in his way, John had suddenly to think about defending the very borders of his realm; it was a staggering shift in circumstances. In response, he tried one last diplomatic effort with the rebels, but it was futile. What could they hope to gain by making peace when victory was seemingly possible? John was never going to change. The pope, too, tried to persuade the French king not to intervene in England, to no avail. This was a situation that could only be resolved militarily, and in preparing for outright war, John gave orders to his sheriffs to consider all rebels who remained to be disinherited. He then moved quickly, marching straight to Kent, having already ordered the navy to convene ready to sail to Calais and try to prevent Louis's departure. But the action was a disaster, with bad weather putting paid to John's plans and destroying his fleet, leaving the way clear for Louis to land in England unopposed in May 1216.

Flushed with his early success, Louis quickly made significant gains in the south, first in Kent, including the critical Rochester Castle, which fell easily in the wake of John's defeat, and London, already sympathetic to the rebels, then in Surrey and Hampshire, forcing John further and further west. The king began to look very vulnerable, and the Angevin dynasty teetered on the brink of failure. In the face of this, many of those whom John had cowed with his show of force across the winter unsurprisingly deserted and joined Louis's forces. Some former loyalists, too, believing that John's cause was hopeless, submitted to Louis, one of the most famous being William Longespée, earl of Salisbury, whose lands in the south of England must also have had some impact on his decision to join Louis, given the prince's relatively easy passage through the region. William had previously enjoyed exceptionally good relations with King John, receiving several gifts and favours. He had been a loyal commander on the Continent, too, and was still with John after Magna Carta, having been entrusted with the command of the force John left to hold the rebels within London in winter 1215. His defection is a sign of the situation's ominous progression. This was a matter of survival; if Longespée was to hold on to his lands, he had to support the winning side.

But John's cause was not yet completely lost: he retained the support of around a third of the nobility, along with his mercenaries and vital castle constables – and while Louis was able to move through the southern counties quickly, he found it impossible to make progress in the Midlands. Military stalemate ensued, during which time cracks began to show in the rebel alliance: on the one hand, the French lords who had accompanied Louis in the hope of territorial rewards across the Channel became increasingly worried about the number of English lords who were also siding with Louis; the prospective spoils of victory were becoming fewer and fewer, and the incentives to fight were in turn diminishing. The result was a strained relationship with their English counterparts. On the other hand, to those English lords who had recently, and pragmatically, defected to the rebels, it began to look as though the French prince would not be able to make more progress. Men who stood to lose their inheritance if they were caught on the wrong side when the war was finally settled could not afford to be fixed in their loyalty. They had to bet on likely outcomes and some, including the earl of York, made the judgement that it was expedient to return to the king's side. 'Day by day adherents of the Frenchmen dwindled,' wrote the Dunstable annalist, and it began to look as though John might be the first of the two parties to be able to go on the offensive again.

When he realised the situation, John, with his customary energy, lost no time in taking advantage of his unexpected change in fortunes. In September he began a new offensive from the Cotswolds down the Thames Valley and towards the eastern counties, where the situation was so bad that Alexander of Scotland, having taken advantage of Louis's gains in southern England, had got as far south as Cambridge with his own army. Nonetheless, John was able successfully to deflect a rebel siege of Lincoln and take refuge in Lynn (now King's Lynn) in Norfolk, where he received the support of the townsmen. He then remained in eastern England, working to consolidate his position. As he did so, though, his fortunes began to turn again. First he lost his baggage train, including the Crown jewels, in quicksand in the Wash. Further woes followed – at King's Lynn, John fell ill, and in subsequent months that illness, probably dysentery, worsened, leaving him unable even to sit on his horse. The worst fears of the king's supporters were realised in October 1216, when John died at the age of forty-nine. He was not much lamented. 'Foul as it is,' wrote the chronicler Matthew Paris, 'Hell is made fouler by the presence of John.' There were probably few men (or women) who would have disagreed with that judgement. His left in his wake a realm in turmoil, a child-heir, and the eldest son of the French king ensconced with his army on English soil. Even the Angevin inheritance of England hung in the balance.

The Lessons of John's Reign

If we are to understand how power and authority fluctuate, King John's reign is instructive. No matter how able, any leader or would-be leader must build relationships in order to secure critical support – coalitions are crucial. In this regard, both John and Philip Augustus made mistakes: it is impossible to please all people all of the time, as they found with some of those from whom they hoped to garner support. However, John's ability to alienate allies far outstripped that of his Capetian opponent: to paraphrase a famous verdict on John, never did a king make so certain that those who were not for him would be actively against him as he did. Most of his mistakes were rooted in his inconstancy, paranoia and volatility. John fundamentally lacked the ability to discern who to trust, and the steadiness to be trusted. When he chose to, he could turn on the charisma or personal appeal (as is amply demonstrated by some of the alliances he did build, particularly the coalition he amassed in advance of Bouvines in 1214, whose result was by no means a foregone conclusion), yet he was not a man to inspire widespread, lasting or deeply felt loyalty or support.

Regardless of how many people John had alienated in England, however, had his allies prevailed on the Continent in 1214, the crisis that ensued across the Channel would have been averted. It is virtually impossible successfully to challenge a winner: all the momentum remains on their side, as it would have done with John, for a time at least, had he managed to humble Philip Augustus. Failure, though, meant something completely different: John immediately lost political momentum and with it a degree of authority. This left political space in England that could be occupied by the disaffected, and in which they could raise their concerns; the king could not hope immediately to silence them by a show of force, and even more than this, he now needed their active support to rebuild any semblance of a continental strategy.

The opposition was itself, despite all this, not as extensive as it might have been, a result of the fact that John had not been foolish enough to alienate everyone: the charm he had deployed had had an impact. So, while John's personality must have been widely known and understood among a questioning nobility, he continued to have active supporters (and too few opponents to constitute a critical mass). This suggests that, even in the face of such a personality, most people were pragmatic, and continued, quite understandably, to think about the best way to guarantee their own survival or advancement. Benefiting in that moment from his goodwill would have discouraged most men from taking up arms against him, and some even actively to fight for the devil they knew. Others, meanwhile, perhaps seeing the far from universal extent of the opposition, effectively absented themselves from the political dialogue, waiting, presumably, to see what happened before committing themselves one way or another. Betting on fighting the king, with all the authority and patronage he could command (and which John so effectively emphasised in the public relations battle), even in this humbled state, was a high-stakes gamble, in which one's entire inheritance could be lost; betting on fighting a king who still had several powerful supporters among the baronage was an even bigger gamble. Better to wait things out until the likely outcome became clear. It was mostly only those who felt that they had nothing to lose, or for whom the status quo would mean personal ruin, who took up arms against him once he had rejected Magna Carta. There were enough such men to make a civil war of it, but at the point when John died in the midst of the fighting, it was still far from obvious who would prevail, not least because of the complicating factor of the presence of the French dauphin.

Even if the royalist cause ended up triumphant, which it did, the occurrence of the civil war after John's rejection of Magna Carta itself nonetheless enshrined an important and novel political reality: no matter how far theoretical right was on the king's side, the need on the part of the Crown for extraordinary sums of money to prosecute war meant that John's successors would either have to accept the need for dialogue with the nobility and the principle of seeking their explicit consent before taking money from them, or face political crisis. A savvy king would do well to find constructive ways of working with what we might term an embryonic political community.

How far was a crisis like that of 1215 unavoidable, given the cost of warfare and the Angevin tradition of exploiting the king's position above the law in order to access their subjects' property? To suggest that some sort of political impasse was at some point inevitable is possibly too much: a highly able ruler or series of rulers might have entered into constructive dialogue with their subjects and created structures and processes to navigate the treacherous waters in which they found themselves. Or else they might simply have continued to win on the field of battle, as did the Lionheart, leaving no political space for opposition to occupy. Both outcomes were conceivable, but they were unlikely to be sustainable in the long term. Crisis was always possible, and by extension probable, across a long enough timeframe. What actually occurred in 1215 was a combination of this wider backdrop, the nature of Angevin kingship, political events and King John's own agency. The entwined circumstances, structures, ideas and personalities made politics in 1215, just as they have throughout history. In the autumn of 1215, with civil war raging, the political community could only hope for peace somehow to be restored and to be gifted a future king with sufficient ability successfully to lead and manage the realm to a new political settlement.

HENRY III, 1216–72
'Vir Simplex – A Simple Man'

An Inauspicious Inheritance

King John left to his son Henry one of the most difficult inheritances imaginable: at the point of his accession, despite the gains John had made recently, his son still only had the allegiance of eight out of twenty-seven barons. Worse, Prince Louis of France and the rebels held London, and Alexander of Scotland had taken Carlisle and done homage to Louis for the northern counties of England. To add symbolic insult to injury, the English crown itself had been lost in the Wash, so there was nothing even to put on the new king's head at the coronation, which had itself to be moved to Gloucester because London was in French hands. During the coronation itself, news came through of a Welsh attack by Llywelyn of Gwynedd on Goodrich, which was less than twenty miles away.

Even to retain the English throne would be a success in these circumstances, but there is another crucial point still to be mentioned: Henry was only nine years old in October 1216. The pope, through his representative legate in England, Guala, took responsibility for the young king's safety, but the vulnerability of his charge was evident for all to see. As Henry was led away from the safety of Corfe Castle – where he had been left by his father only months before – to begin his new role, it is impossible to imagine how he was feeling, but the gravity and danger of the situation were not lost on him: when he was delivered to the safe custody of William Marshal, his guardian, he is said to have wept. At the coronation itself, Henry's youth was again emphasised by the fact that he entered on the shoulders of nobles, attired in child-sized royal robes. Emphasising the paucity of his inheritance, a gold circlet took the place of the lost royal crown. Writing for him in a proclamation from this period, his advisers struck a plaintive and innocent tone, which might easily have issued from the mouth of the nine-year-old himself: 'We hear that a quarrel arose between our father and certain nobles of our kingdom, whether with justification or not we do not know. We wish to remove it forever since it has nothing to do with us.' It was an important statement of good faith: an attempt to sweep away the divisions of the last few years. But it would take more than a statement to transform the situation.

What was urgently needed before anything could be done to try to salvage the child-king's inheritance was a regent to take control of the government in his stead. Luckily there had been no debate about the best man for this role: William Marshal, although nearly seventy, remained a powerful landowner and commanded wide respect. At a time of deep divisions among the nobility, the latter was crucial. Marshal had accepted the role of guardian of the kingdom following entreaties from Henry's supporters, having initially been reluctant to step forward for fear of appearing to covet power for himself. Once established, Marshal quickly judged that the febrile situation called for a combination of military prowess and political skill, and within only a few weeks of his appointment as regent in November 1216, he reissued Magna Carta jointly with the papal legate. It was an important show of good faith to the rebel barons. This was a time for attempts at reconciliation not recrimination; the safety of the throne itself was at stake.

Military campaigns, on the other hand, while necessary, were more difficult to plan because there were limited financial resources available to the regime. So bad was the situation that Marshal bluntly remarked when he took on the regency that 'the boy [Henry III] has no money'. The only option was to pay soldiers with jewels and expensive cloth, the remains of John's treasure held at Corfe and Devizes. It did not help that, despite the general respect for Marshal, the royalist party was riven internally, with Earl Ranulf of Chester even threatening to abandon the cause and depart on crusade. Some of this seems to have been pique at being overlooked himself for the regency: at one point, he wrote to the pope to say that he thought Marshal was too old for the job and advised the pope that he himself should be appointed Marshal's colleague. Guala, to whom the pope forwarded the request, ignored it. Others in the royalist camp simply disobeyed government orders: Brian de Lisle, who was supposed to have handed the High Peak in Derbyshire over to the earl of Derby, had failed to do so, and tensions over that rankled.

Fortunately the rebel forces were in no better position, and, faced with an impasse, both parties saw the value of entering into talks with each other. These took place in December 1216 and January 1217, and the result was the agreement of a temporary truce until April 1217. For the royalists the truce was essential because of their lack of money. But Prince Louis, too, needed some time to regroup, rushing back to France to recruit reinforcements for his military effort. While he was away, the truce expired and the royalists made a number of gains, both through retaking castles and by some notable defections from the French prince's cause. But the rebels were far from beaten: on his return to England with a fresh force of soldiers from France, Louis quickly took Farnham in Hampshire and retook Winchester. If anything, the initiative was passing back to the rebel side.

Why did most rebel barons remain so entrenched in opposition, given that death had removed King John from the equation? The answer to this question lies not in a principled objection to Henry III's kingship per se, but in something much more difficult to overcome: by 1216, the conflict had developed an internal momentum that affected allegiances. Put simply, many of those who were in Louis's camp had unsettled claims against royalists, and vice versa: Peter de Dreux, duke of Brittany, is a good example of this. He was part of the invading army, and claimed the right to the lands and fees belonging to the honour of Richmond in Yorkshire that John had granted to Earl Ranulf of Chester in 1205. At the same time Gilbert de Gant's claim to the earldom of Lincoln, which had been agreed by Louis, was at odds with the earl of Chester's own claim to it. Elsewhere, Alexander of Scotland stood to keep the northern counties if Louis won the civil war and honoured his promise to him, while Robert de Vieuxpont, a royalist, claimed that Westmorland belonged to him, not the Scottish king. It was a tangled web of claim and counter-claim, and it was difficult for men, once committed, to change sides, or, if they did, for their action not to have ramifications for others. The earl of Salisbury's decision to return to the royalist cause, for instance, may have been given some impetus by the offer to him of Sherborne and Somerset, but in the event Peter de Maulay, also a royalist, and the current holder, refused to surrender them, and tensions arose between the two men as a result. Manifold private struggles were therefore subsumed within the wider national conflict. What this meant was that only a military victory for either side would be decisive for the future governance of England, and even after that the smouldering conflicts would in all likelihood take years to resolve.

An opportunity soon presented itself for the royalists to retake the immediate initiative. When Louis returned to England, he decided to divide his forces, sending the earl of Winchester and the count of Perche to Mountsorrel and then on to Lincoln, where the castle was still holding out for the royalists, while he renewed the siege of Dover Castle. Splitting the rebel forces was Louis's big mistake: although it only gave the royalists the very narrowest of openings through which to advance, that and William Marshal's skill as a military commander were to prove enough to allow a decisive victory at Lincoln; Marshal mounted an assault on it by opening a previously blocked-up gate on the west side of the town. Ordering the main body of his forces to concentrate on the gate, Marshal arranged a diversion tactic to draw the French forces to the north gate by sending a small sortie there. The royalist forces then flooded in on the west side, relieving the siege of the castle, and imprisoning many of the rebel leaders in the process.

With a large number of his forces having been destroyed at Lincoln, Louis was now in Dover in command of a siege that was showing no signs of ending in success. He quickly decided that it was time to negotiate, withdrawing to London, then still a rebel stronghold, from which he travelled on to Brentford to negotiate with Marshal. The negotiations came to nothing, but in the meantime many rebels, sensing that the initiative was now with the royalist forces and defeat was imminent, opted to return to the king's side. Nonetheless Louis, hearing that French reinforcements raised by his wife were on their way, decided to fight on. It was a mistake. On 24 August Hubert de Burgh, constable of Dover and a loyal servant of King John, took the opportunity provided by Louis's earlier abandonment of the siege of the castle to sail out of Dover and join battle with the French troops off Sandwich, destroying the French fleet in the process. Hearing of the rout, Louis knew that his ambitions, which so depended on the safe arrival of those forces, had been finally thwarted. In the Treaty of Kingston–Lambeth in September he surrendered his claim to the English throne and retreated to France. Many more rebels, having lost their leader, and presented with an olive branch by the royal government in the form of another confirmation of Magna Carta, began to drift back to the king's side. Most of them formally renewed their allegiance to Henry in November 1217. In return, the regency government under the victorious William Marshal maintained its earlier good faith and issued a new version of Magna Carta, together with a Charter of the Forest by which they committed to look afresh at the boundaries and administration of the royal forest, a contentious issue for decades. A new era had begun.

Rebuilding Royal Authority, 1217–25

Civil wars leave in their wake a mess of bad feeling, unresolved animosity and governmental weakness. For those representing Henry III, undoubtedly the most important task was somehow to restore genuine peace. But before they could do that, they had to secure what Henry was entitled to as king. One of the problems they faced in this regard was with castellans and sheriffs. These were the king's lieutenants in the localities, the former as holders of castles, and the latter as governors and guardians of the counties. Many of these had been loyalists to John, and had remained in the service of the Crown after his death. In the face of the government's demands, they refused to resign their positions, saying that they had taken an oath not to do so until Henry came of age in October 1228.

Up to a point it is true that these men represented Henry's authority rather than challenging it, but at the same time many of them had seized land and possessions from rebels and were refusing to return them, which went against the spirit of amnesty that the government was seeking to create. At the same time, they were often withholding significant sums of money that should have been going to the royal Exchequer, and had taken control of some royal lands. For a government desperately short of money, this was extremely problematic. Finally, their castles and sheriffdoms had sometimes become more like personal fiefdoms than royal offices, which represented a threat to the integrity and impartiality of royal authority. If the king, or those acting in his name, did not take control at this moment, they might never do so; the centralised, strong kingship established so securely within England in the preceding centuries would begin to be compromised and royal authority would be at risk of fragmenting. So, in 1218, William Marshal toured England with an army, removing some of the castellans from office. He followed that with a new judicial general eyre to hear legal cases across England in November. The Great Council also provided Henry with his own seal. Royal government was beginning to operate again.

This initial recovery was thrown into confusion in April and May 1219 when William Marshal resigned the regency in ill health, before dying only a month later. With him went the personal authority he had commanded, an authority that had imposed itself on many of those who otherwise would have remained recalcitrant, or had brought into the fold men who respected Marshal's integrity. In the aftermath of his death, government was taken over not by another regent – that was impossible, because there was no obvious or uncontroversial candidate – but by a group of men appointed formally by the Council. This consisted of Pandulf, the new papal legate, Hubert de Burgh, as justiciar, a role he had occupied since 1215, and Peter des Roches, the king's tutor.

Pandulf provided the formal leadership of the group as 'first counsellor and chief of the kingdom' until 1221 when he left England, but in practice he deferred to de Burgh. The latter was a long-standing official, whose fortunes had, like many, been made in royal service. Hubert was born in Norfolk in around 1170. His parents' names are unknown but he inherited at least four manors, so he was probably from knightly stock. Like many in his position, though, he needed to make his way in life, and the growing royal government offered a route for doing so. Hubert was talented and he progressed quickly: he was in the service of John as prince in 1198 and continued to serve him after he acceded to the throne, acting as chamberlain of his household, ambassador to Portugal, and sheriff and custodian of various counties and castles. He also campaigned overseas in Poitou in 1202 and returned there as deputy seneschal and then seneschal in 1212. During the civil war he remained loyal to John and then Henry, imploring John to sign Magna Carta; he was made chief justiciar in 1215. Naturally a conservative, Hubert was also a realist: he understood that royal government after 1215 was operating in a changed world. From his position as justiciar he ran royal government after William Marshal's death, while Peter des Roches, as guardian of the king, managed Henry's household, and sometimes deputised for de Burgh in government. Des Roches was a very different character: born around the same time, he was originally from Touraine and was fiercely proud of his continental origins; he had become bishop of Winchester in 1205, having previously been in Richard I's service in France. Like de Burgh, he fought for John and Henry in the civil war and was decidedly loyal. But he was also much more direct and bullish than de Burgh, and was widely distrusted, having been closely associated with King John's style of rule in a way that de Burgh had not.

Despite their differing personalities, the triumvirate was a perfectly capable grouping. What it lacked, though, was the personal gravitas Marshal had possessed. They faced an uphill struggle in asserting their authority, and, by extension, that of the child-king. Several castellans simply refused to obey the orders of the government to surrender their castles. If the deadlock were to be broken, authority would have to be attached to the person of the king himself: those who were refusing to submit needed to be forced to recognise the stark reality that defiance of those who acted for the king was defiance of the king himself. Pandulf duly arranged for Henry to be re-crowned at Westminster Abbey in 1220 and the magnates took a solemn oath to resign their castles and provide accounts to the royal Exchequer. Henry and de Burgh then journeyed to the Midlands, entering royal castles as a gesture that the king had resumed formal control. It was a start.

But the momentum had to be maintained, and after this initial success a great deal of care was taken to ensure that it was: in 1220, de Burgh managed, after a short siege, to regain Rockingham Castle in Leicestershire from the count of Aumale, and in 1221 the count also surrendered the castle of Bythorn in Lincolnshire. In the following year a government resumption of Crown land took place which increased the king's income by almost 100 per cent. And in 1223 Hubert de Burgh, who had by then taken control of government, had Henry confirm Magna Carta and the Forest Charter before the Council while at the same time pursuing an inquiry into royal rights. De Burgh also looked to deal with Llywelyn the Great's resurgence in Wales by supporting the campaign against him by Marshal's son, William II, earl of Pembroke, in the south. In the same year, de Burgh and Stephen

Langton, who remained archbishop, and to whom de Burgh had also made positive gestures, managed to secure letters from the pope (who had been a firm advocate of the need for royal authority to be restored in the face of recalcitrant castellans and sheriffs) declaring that Henry III was of age, and should therefore have his own seal. The pope urged that castles and sheriff-doms be given back to the king. Langton and de Burgh were subsequently able to come together to enforce the papal mandate at the end of that year, with the archbishop adding legitimacy to de Burgh's leadership. At last, sheriffs and castellans were made to surrender their offices and castles. The sheriffs appointed from early 1224 onwards were also required to deliver their stipulated annual revenues as well as fixed increments (the same that had been resisted in Magna Carta) to the Exchequer. The result was that between 1224 and 1229 most counties came to be placed in the hands of men who were described as custodian sheriffs, an echo of the policy John had experimented with in 1204, whereby sheriffs were told to deliver all the money they collected from the county to the government in order to increase royal revenues from the localities.

However, in the uneasy atmosphere of the early 1220s, and with the king still not ready to take active charge of government, there was a limit to what could be achieved to steady the royal finances. There was no desire on the part of de Burgh's government to impose heavy demands on local society and create resentment, not least because divisions and antagonism still existed between some in the upper echelons of the nobility and the government. This also meant that de Burgh needed to ensure that he had in place loyal and relatively powerful sheriffs to represent (and defend if required) the king's authority. The minority government could not yet afford to dispense with powerful courtiers, *curiales*, as sheriffs, and had to accept the significant financial and other rewards they demanded for their service. While there was so much dependence on these men, the royal finances did not improve dramatically, but the changes Henry's representatives had made at least meant that the royal government had broadly re-established the king's authority in the localities, and regained access to some revenue from the counties of England.

The events of the years from 1219 to 1223 also resulted in significant factional fallout among the nobility, and created disputes which, in the absence of a king to adjudicate, remained entrenched even after several years of 'peace'. Almost inevitably, with no one able to claim authority equivalent to that of the king, there were major rivalries between various men involved in government: one of de Burgh's own key objectives was to remove Peter des Roches, the king's tutor, who bore significant antagonism towards him, from the inner circle of Henry's advisers. He was only able to effect this in 1221, and the move against his rival inevitably created tensions. An obvious conclusion to make is that this was just factional politics between two men who were both eager to control royal government and not willing to share that control. Certainly there was no love lost between the two of them.

But aside from that, and underlying their rivalry, there were clear and important differences in how each of them saw royal authority and Magna Carta that made their approaches incompatible. Alongside personal antipathy, there consequently existed a more fundamental dispute between the two men about the way forward for the minority government. While des Roches had been a loyalist to King John like de Burgh, he had campaigned hard to have the pope nullify Magna Carta, and his actions in the early 1230s, when he was to gain a degree of control over royal government, demonstrate quite clearly that he did not think the king should be subject to the sort of controls and limitations of prerogative that Magna Carta imposed. De Burgh's acceptance of the new political status quo inevitably placed the two men at odds. Furthermore, there is no doubt that there had been problems with the behaviour of many of those who held sheriffdoms and castles in the years between the victory over the rebels and the changes of 1223, many of whom were associated with des Roches rather than de Burgh.

Des Roches was not alone in having issues with the justiciar. De Burgh's actions in relation to officeholders almost inevitably alienated other powerful men, a number of whom would never be reconciled to his government, something that was to have serious repercussions immediately, and later in the decade too. In late 1223, as the resumptions of castles and sheriffdoms were under way, there had been a confrontation involving de Burgh and, among others, Earl Ranulf of Chester, in which Ranulf accused de Burgh of wasting the king's treasure and oppressing the kingdom with unjust laws. Ranulf and des Roches were natural allies, and the tensions between them and de Burgh created a situation so bad that the pair attempted to seize the Tower of London in November 1223. Although the archbishop of Canterbury negotiated a truce, the two sides were in dispute again early in December, and the rebels were only brought to terms by the threat of excommunication. Castles and sheriffdoms were surrendered, but relations between the groups remained so strained that two rival Christmas courts took place.

Fundamentally, the men associated with Ranulf of Chester and Peter des Roches were concerned about the confiscation of castles and offices from men associated with them by de Burgh's government as part of its bid to restore royal authority. Despite being assured by Archbishop Langton that any redistribution would be fair and equal, they remained bitter about the policy. It is difficult to see what else de Burgh could have done, but the opposition his approach generated meant that as time went on his control became more tenuous. The events of the second half of 1223 were not the end of the story. They were followed by an outright rebellion in 1224 led by Fawkes de Bréauté and his brother William. Fawkes and William had been allied with Ranulf of Chester and des Roches in late 1223 and were members of the group who were refusing to give up the castles (and income) they had seized in the process. The rebellion meant that de Burgh had to send forces to Bedford to besiege the castle, where William had kidnapped and imprisoned a royal judge. De Burgh emerged triumphant from the siege, but the fact that it was necessary at all was a sign of how fragile his control was. For the moment the opposition had been quashed, but it would not remain that way.

The atmosphere more widely remained tense, too. In 1225, the first grant of tax since 1207 was made for a campaign in France by a large assembly convened at Westminster that included the archbishop of Canterbury, eleven bishops, twenty abbots, nine earls and more than twenty barons. But the debate preceding the grant lasted a week, and it was made contingent on the reissue of Magna Carta and the Forest Charter. In the reissues, vital new concessions were made in relation to the Forest Charter that enabled some major deforestations. The gesture was an important one for the knightly class in particular, as this edition of the Great Charter also retained a chapter first introduced in 1217 that sought to address their concerns about the burdens placed on them by sheriffs. And so, while the direction of travel was not all in their favour – the Council did not at the same time reinstate a chapter dropped from the 1216 Charter that had prevented the government exacting revenue that exceeded the established local county returns – clear steps forward in relation to the grievances of the knightly class had been made under the king's own seal. One other notable point about the 1225 Charter is that its provisions no longer included the stipulation that twenty-five barons would be empowered to enforce it; presumably it was felt that this was too much of a surrender of the king's prerogatives at a time when Henry was not far off coming of age. While in theory this change left the Charter vulnerable to royal abuse, it is also fair to say that had any such abuse taken place, it was bound to be met with vocal and entrenched opposition, as would occur only a few years later in 1233. For the moment peace and, to a great extent, goodwill prevailed, but it was brittle and might fracture at any moment.

The Struggle to Assert Royal Authority, 1227–30

By 1227 and aged twenty, the king could reasonably have been expected to have at least begun to emerge from the shadow of the highly factionalised minority years, and Henry's majority was declared in that year, slightly earlier than was the norm. However, where he might have begun to stamp his unique kingly authority on government, authority that had been impossible to replicate during his minority, he instead made a series of costly mistakes. As a result, the events of the late 1220s create an emerging picture of a young king with poor judgement and a lack of financial acumen who was susceptible to bad advice, faults that would become leitmotifs throughout the rest of his reign.

Problems were almost inevitable when Henry decided first to leave de Burgh largely in control of royal government. In one sense, this was not necessarily a bad political decision. De Burgh's positive record was unarguable: he had presided over a significant increase in annual royal revenues from around £8,000 at the start of the reign to around £24,000. While this was only about two-thirds of the income John had enjoyed, it was still a great improvement. However, in making this progress, de Burgh had also benefited hugely at a personal level from grants made by the king following the assumption of his majority in 1227, and that meant he had created enemies – according to the Dunstable annalist, 'the princes of the kingdom were indignant' about Hubert's aggrandisement. There was bitter resentment in particular from a number of influential people who had suffered under the redemption policy. His closeness to Henry therefore undermined the king's own impartiality in the eyes of those who had been disenfranchised by de Burgh's regime.

One episode in particular highlights the extent of Hubert's control and the animosity it was causing. In May 1227, Henry's brother Richard, who was now eighteen, had returned from the Continent. Henry was delighted to see him, and quickly promoted him to the earldom of Cornwall. Richard promptly seized eight of the manors that belonged to the earldom from Waleran the German. In the face of such a provocative move, Waleran had no choice but to appeal to the king, who commanded Richard to return the manors. But Richard had no intention of doing so, and demanded that his fellow magnates be asked to judge the case. What Richard intended was to force his brother's hand, but it was a blatant challenge to his authority that Henry could not ignore, and he ordered Richard either to submit or to leave England. Ignoring this, Richard moved to Reading, where he established an alliance with both the earl of Chester, Hubert's old adversary, and Walter Marshal, who had succeeded his father as earl of Pembroke following his death in 1219. Soon the earls of Gloucester, Surrey, Hereford, Derby and Warwick were all involved, blaming de Burgh for what had happened and demanding that Henry grant the eight manors to his brother. Worryingly, they also sought wider backing by supporting the complaints of men of the localities about the ever-controversial royal forest boundaries and the behaviour of sheriffs. The king was forced to call a muster at Northampton in August to fight off the challenge.

In reality, both sides really wanted a settlement, not war, and a deal was soon struck. Concessions were also made in relation to the royal forests, and the localities were appeased by the king indicating his willingness to hear complaints against the sheriffs. The situation shows not only how much resentment existed (or at least might be readily stoked) about de Burgh's position, but also how quickly, despite all the progress of recent years, royal authority might begin to break down. It also marks the emergence of Richard of Cornwall on the political stage as a man who was quick to defend his interests and a force to be reckoned with. At the same time, while the grievances of the men of the localities were not yet a pivotal factor in politics, the readiness of the magnates to adopt their concerns indicates the extent to which the knights were felt potentially to be able to bring some influence to bear on events. For now, Henry and Hubert got away with limited concessions to them in 1227, some of which they even successfully avoided the following year; this was not to be the case in the 1240s and 1250s.

Despite the crisis of 1227, Hubert de Burgh remained firmly in control of government. The following year he worked hard to placate magnates while continuing to gain personally from the king's patronage. The status quo seemed to have been firmly re-established, and he and Henry turned their attention to matters in Wales, where Llywelyn had embarked on a siege of Montgomery Castle, the latest in a series of acts of defiance of the English king's authority. An army was summoned to muster at Montgomery, bringing out a powerful force of English and Marcher magnates. In the event, the only action was a series of skirmishes: the king showed little inclination to lead a campaign against Llywelyn. While a settlement was made, no one was under any illusion that it had been an edifying episode for the young king. He was already quite clearly not a martial figure.

The early years of Henry's majority were similarly far from compelling across the Channel. In the mid-1220s, the forces that went to Bedford Castle to deal with the rebellion of Fawkes and William de Bréaute in 1224 were those that had been destined for France to defend Poitou, which had been attacked by the recently crowned Louis VIII. The attack was part of his bid to reclaim Poitou for the French Crown, itself a facet of the Capetian dynasty's continuing campaign for dominance in France. The siege of Bedford and the failure to send the planned forces left the door firmly open for Louis, and had disastrous consequences for the English position in France: not only was Poitou lost, but much of Gascony too was overrun by Hugh de Lusignan.

Following this, de Burgh was under urgent pressure to put together a campaign to save Gascony. It was to this that he and the royal Council turned their attention. The latter quickly approved a grant of a fifteenth on movable property, which yielded around £40,000, enabling an impressive force to be sent to Gascony in 1225 under the command of the stalwart earl of Salisbury, who took with him Richard of Cornwall. Luckily, Louis VIII's premature death in November 1226, in robbing the French of leadership at a critical moment, meant that the expedition of 1225–7 proved successful in securing Gascony. Henry's government could follow that by beginning to build relationships with the counts of Auvergne and Toulouse. Richard of Cornwall, showing early diplomatic prowess, at the same time negotiated a truce with the new King Louis IX, which averted further military action for two years, something that suited Louis's advisers well given that the French king was only thirteen in 1227. Louis would become a force to be reckoned with in adulthood, and one of Europe's great monarchs, but for now, thankfully for Henry, he posed no threat.

No one anticipated that the truce with France would continue after 1229, and Henry's advisers began to make preparations long before that date for the inevitable resumption of hostilities. It is this that explains the decision to declare an end to Henry's minority in 1227 when he was twenty, a year earlier than the norm. This enabled him to make grants in perpetuity so that his advisers could take forward a policy to 'buy' rivals to Louis IX in the king's name, most notably the Breton duke, Peter de Dreux. Securing this alliance meant that when the truce expired the English king would have a base from which to launch campaigns into both Normandy and Anjou. As it stood, the nearest port to England that was under Angevin control was Bordeaux, an indication of the extent to which the king's position in France had been critically weakened in the last fifteen years.

In 1229, when the truce duly ended, Henry initially sent representatives to France to try to secure a permanent peace. The proposals made by his representatives during the ensuing negotiations give an indication of the direction of his thoughts: he offered to abandon his claims to Normandy other than the dioceses of Avranches and Coutances, in return for the rest of the Angevin lands taken by the French king in the last twenty years. This may have been because he and his wider group of advisers were of the view that regaining Normandy was simply not feasible, and that the best starting point was the other Angevin lands. What is particularly interesting, however, is the deal Henry offered Louis as an alternative to this, which suggests that his priorities actually lay elsewhere: he suggested that his sister Isabella would marry Louis and take Maine and Anjou with her as her dowry. If she and Louis had children, they would inherit Maine and Anjou (in other words, those territories would be lost to the English Crown), and if they died without children the lands would revert to the English Crown. The one place missing from the offers to cede territory that had already been captured by the French was Poitou, which suggests that Henry was not willing to surrender his claim to it under any circumstances, perhaps not a surprise given that his mother was Isabella, who heralded from Angoulême in the heart of Poitou.

In the end the negotiations came to nothing and it was clear that Henry would need to lead a campaign to France in 1230 if he were to have any real chance of securing his interests. There was much support for him. Despite the domestic divisions, a large force of English nobles turned out to accompany their young king across the Channel. Several of the ports of Normandy also sent ships in support and a number of Norman lords offered to join Henry's army, suggesting that they thought an attempt at reconquest was on the cards. Such an ambition would not have been ludicrous: while Henry was in Brittany at the start of his campaign in France, Louis's army itself was riven by serious in-fighting, opening up an opportunity for Henry to make an assault on Anjou and Normandy. In fact, Louis even began a tactical withdrawal to Paris, and a group of Norman barons came to Henry to ask for an expedition.

But instead of heading for Normandy, Henry set off at speed to campaign in Poitou. An early predisposition for the sartorial was on display here as Henry set off in new clothes, the centrepiece of which was a robe made of white silk, together with new sandals and gloves. Once there, he avoided any conflict, giving out money in order to buy allies in the county. When he returned to England in autumn the same year, he had achieved virtually nothing across the Channel – the capture of the Île d'Oléron off the west coast of Poitou was the single conquest – and he had spent around £20,000. It is difficult to be sure what Henry should have done in 1230. It is true that the door seemed open for a potentially successful assault on

Normandy, but the terms he offered to Louis in 1229 had indicated explicitly that Henry did not feel that the recovery of Normandy was viable in the long term. A year later, it may therefore simply have been the case that Henry and those around him felt that their efforts would be better focused on trying to recover Poitou. At the same time, though, Henry had shown at the very least that he lacked drive and an appetite for military endeavour. It was already not the first time and would not be the last time these flaws would be on display.

The Return of Peter des Roches and the Fall of Hubert de Burgh

For many, the ignominy of the 1230 campaign in France was at least partly attributable to the counsel of de Burgh. If Henry thought this himself, however, he did not show it, continuing to reward his justiciar handsomely following their return. Yet with the bestowal of more patronage on de Burgh, antipathy from others was inevitably growing, something Henry ought to have been made alert to by the crisis of 1227 involving his own brother. One of the most significant gains Hubert made in this period was the wardship of the Clare earldom, which was resented by William Marshal and Richard of Cornwall, both of whom had a better claim to the wardship than the justiciar, Marshal because he had been married to the earl's sister and Cornwall because he was the king's brother and still without a title. For Richard, the situation was easily rectified. He swiftly married the earl's widow without the king's permission. Henry was livid, but, as would become the pattern of their relationship (and would ultimately help turn Richard into a valuable ally to his brother), his initial anger was replaced by a stronger desire to mend the relationship with his brother. Enabled by the sudden death of William Marshal, Henry granted Richard the Briouze wardship, which had been in Marshal's hands, instead. The brothers were again at peace, but not for long: when Llywelyn took advantage of Marshal's death to move in on the Briouze lordships and other lands in Wales, Henry and Hubert took the Briouze wardship from Cornwall and de Burgh himself took possession of it. Little was yet again achieved in the subsequent campaign against Llywelyn, and while another reconciliation was achieved with Richard of Cornwall, few were impressed by Henry and Hubert's showing in Wales.

This act alone demonstrates that Henry was clearly under de Burgh's influence when he should by now have been taking more direct kingly responsibility for policy, and that Hubert's personal interests were having an undue effect on royal patronage. Henry's actions did nothing to dampen the ire of those who felt abused by the justiciar; if anything the king himself fanned the flames of faction and resentment in the late 1220s. Yet the incidents with Richard of Cornwall also demonstrate other facets of Henry's character, as well as his devotion to his brother. If Richard showed fixity of purpose and a determination to ensure that his own interests were duly recognised, his brother was a man with whom it was hard to remain at odds for long. Henry might be susceptible to poor advice, but he was quick to amend his mistakes and seemed never to bear any animosity towards his brother. Matthew Paris described Henry as loving Richard and desiring 'above all to enrich and pacify him'; chroniclers were always quick to report on family division, so this observation of brotherly love is particularly telling. For his part, there is no sense of disloyalty to Henry from Richard, more frustration at the extent to which de Burgh's interests were wrongly allowed to take precedence over his own. Fundamentally, the two brothers' relationship remained strong, a far cry from the bitter feuds between Henry II's sons, and a reminder of how dysfunctional was the family world in which King John had grown up. It is perhaps no surprise that his own character was so difficult.

His son was quite a different man, but in some ways no less problematic. It was clear that he was warm-hearted, but easily influenced and overly generous; he was quick to anger, but equally quick to forgive; he was capable of ideas and of intense focus and purpose (in 1231 he had thoughts of a campaign to attack Llywelyn's stronghold of Gwynedd), but these were momentary (the idea of the campaign was rapidly abandoned). He also demonstrated poor judgement: one of his first ideas for marriage (influenced by de Burgh) was that he should wed the Scottish king's youngest sister, an idea that the magnate members of the royal Council baulked at, it being so obviously an unfitting match for a king. They need not have feared intransigence on the matter from Henry, though. He readily abandoned the idea and turned his attention to visiting his sister Isabella at Marlborough and to the new suit of clothes he (and Isabella) would need for the occasion, as well as a new bed. Comfort was from the outset high on his list of priorities. It should not be assumed that Henry was entirely lacking in intelligence, though. That would be unfair. Perhaps it is best to point to the simplicity of his character, as contemporaries did: he was a man often unsure of his own judgement and willing to bow to the advice of others. That susceptibility to the influence of persuasive characters was soon to provoke another significant crisis.

Problems began when Peter des Roches returned to England from crusade in 1231. After regaling Henry with stories of his adventures on crusade during the Christmas festivities, des Roches wasted no time in telling Henry that it was de Burgh's fault that there was no money for the campaigns in France that Henry still wanted to mount, and that the sortie in 1230 had been a disaster: Henry had been induced to give so much away, he said, particularly to de Burgh himself, that there was next to nothing left in the coffers for the crucial business of government. Henry had been particularly embarrassed when the duke of Brittany arrived in February 1232 to ask for more money, because he had nothing to give; in order to secure loans to make payment to the duke, he had to trust the Crown jewels to the Hospitallers and Templars. So des Roches's argument must have rung very true to Henry at that moment. It seems to have been enough to convince him to grant control of elements of government at the centre and in the localities to his former tutor. In March 1232, des Roches and his allies also managed to secure the rejection by the Great Council of de Burgh's request for taxation on the king's behalf.

While these events were taking place, Henry remained loyal to de Burgh with new favours, but the latter's influence on both the business of government and the king personally was beginning to wane. De Burgh's almost final throw of the dice was to persuade Henry to swear an extraordinary oath in July 1232 to maintain the private charters given to Hubert, while de Burgh simultaneously gave an oath that he would do everything in his power to prevent the king from overthrowing the Charters. Des Roches had never believed the king should be subject to Magna Carta and the Forest Charter, and de Burgh was clearly anticipating action he might take if he continued to gain influence over Henry. But de Burgh's attempt to put safe-guards in place was to no avail: the pope quashed the oath and both des Roches and his nephew Peter des Riveaux continued to be promoted to office. In June des Riveaux was made keeper of the wardrobe and keeper of the privy seal. This was followed by grants to him of the custody of wards, escheats, coasts, ports, the mint and the exchange. In a spectacular and unprecedented move, des Riveaux was given custody of the royal forests and all the sheriffdoms for life. Des Roches then succeeded in attaching blame to de Burgh for attacks on foreign clerics appointed by the pope in England.

Henry was convinced of de Burgh's guilt, and by the end of July 1232 he had dismissed him from office. In an ignominious end to his career Hubert was imprisoned in the Tower of London and forced to give up all the grants he had received during his time in power. At one point the king even ordered his banishment from the realm, only to rescind the order so that de Burgh could be subjected instead to a very public trial: Henry's adoration of his great servant had quickly turned to ire and even, it could be said, to hatred. However loyally Hubert had served Henry, his own gains had been immense, had compromised his position and had brought with them many enemies – there were few who were prepared to stand up for him when des Roches and des Riveaux launched their attack. No doubt Henry's brother Richard in particular was glad to see the end of de Burgh's influence over the king.

But with the rise of des Roches to the position of Henry's chief adviser in late 1232, the financial situation got worse, not better, despite some early successes. Under the auspices of a new regime promising better gov-ernment, a colloquium of lay and ecclesiastical magnates at Westminster was persuaded to agree to make a grant of taxation in 1232. This was a volte-face from the earlier decision in March to refuse a tax to help with the king's war debts from the 1230 campaign in Poitou, when the magnates had said that Henry had wasted his money and they had already provided the military service they owed. By September, enough of them had been persuaded to change their minds to enable the king to prevail: the tax was to be spent not on war with Llywelyn, with whom Henry negotiated a three-year truce, but on fees to the king's allies in Brittany and Poitou to whom he had granted pensions, the latter being much more in line with des Roches's own interests given his lands in France. This was followed by an attempt by des Roches to reinstate his friends and supporters to offices. Many of these had been John's over-mighty sheriffs and castellans – men like Earl Ranulf of Chester, Engelard de Cigogné, and Peter de Maulay, along with his own family, particularly des Riveaux. This was never going to yield benefits for the king's finances. Instead it was to be costly both financially and politically.

Moreover, to give something to one man almost inevitably meant depriving another of it, and that is what happened between October 1232 and February 1233. This is illustrated best by the famous case of the manor of Upavon in Wiltshire, which ultimately helped spark rebellion. Peter de Maulay had been given it to hold for King John by the king himself during the civil war, and in 1223 he had been asked to show his warrant for holding it, as part of the general policy of redemption of royal lands. He had to accept that he only held the manor temporarily, from the king's goodwill, and to surrender it. The manor was then given permanently via a royal charter to one of de Burgh's supporters, Gilbert Basset, who was a household knight. This was part of a more general campaign against close associates of des Roches at that time – Maulay had in 1221 been accused of treason by de Burgh, who, together with his allies, had visited Maulay at Corfe Castle, where he was custodian, and had him put in chains and dismissed him from his post, a vignette that indicates the brutality of the despatch of de Burgh's enemies. In 1233, under the new regime, Maulay was back with des Roches and demanded to have the manor back. Appealing directly to Henry III, he was successful in inducing the king to confiscate the manor from Basset. But Basset had a royal charter granting him the manor in perpetuity, and the king's decision to dispossess him in favour of Maulay was directly in contravention of Magna Carta. In depriving him of it, the king had therefore done the unthinkable: he had placed himself above the law. What might he go on to do? Which of des Roches's enemies would be targeted next? The Bassets revolted. They were soon joined by others, included their patron Richard Marshal, earl of Pembroke, and war erupted in the Marches, the south-west and the south Midlands.

For several months fighting continued, with Henry having to deploy his forces against several of his own magnates. In the midst of this a number of magnates refused to attend peace councils in late summer 1233 unless des Roches and des Riveaux were removed, and even made a threat that they would begin to think about creating a new king. For his part, Henry remained immovable in his defence of the Peters, and with no prospect of compromise a number of bishops desperately moved to urge Henry to make peace with the magnates. In the face of this des Roches remained defiant. How could the magnates demand judgement by their peers when no peers existed in England?

Amid the realpolitik and the factional fighting, the legacy of Magna Carta had become very clear. In 1216, 1217 and again when tax was granted in 1225, the Charter had been confirmed, and with it the property rights of the king's greatest subjects. Henry III could not hope to run or finance his government successfully by engaging in the sorts of policies towards his subjects' property that John and his Angevin predecessors had believed to be their right. It was the principle that rights to property were protected by the law that was directly cited by the opposition to des Roches in 1233. At one level, this was standing on ceremony, finding the most helpful way to defend and justify rebellion against the faction dominating the government by citing unjust seizure of property contrary to the provisions of Magna Carta. But at the same time there is no doubt that although des Roches's allies had previously held some of the property at issue, what they had not had, as the case of Maulay demonstrates, was a royal charter granting it to them for ever. The legitimacy of their claim to it was therefore tenuous at best, and so the arguments about Magna Carta were far from just technical. Des Roches's group was also attacked with the argument that they were foreigners, 'aliens', who should be ousted from England by the English, a distinction that was convenient even if it was not entirely a true reflection of the composition of the two parties in 1233. Not for the first or the last time in history, national identity was being used as a way of defining and exiling 'outsiders'. Henry should, it was said, 'adhere to the counsels of the native men of the kingdom'.

The strength of the opposition to des Roches was so great that by early 1234 both a succession of Councils, and, crucially, the new archbishop of Canterbury, Edmund of Abingdon, had made it clear to Henry that peace could only be restored if he were to disown des Roches and those associated with him. The archbishop had quickly and shrewdly deduced where the source of the biggest problems lay. Thankfully, shocked by the seriousness of the situation, Henry was finally inclined to listen. Within weeks of the warning des Roches had gone from the royal court and Henry had been forced to apologise for breaching the terms of Magna Carta in relation to the judgement of magnates by their peers and the removal of property at will. His immediate ambitions in France were at the same time brought to a swift end: having paid a pension for an alliance with Duke Peter of Brittany since 1230, Henry saw the urgent need to retain that alliance in the face of a possible French onslaught in June 1234 when the truce with the French was due to expire. However, the small force of household knights and Welsh foot soldiers he was able to deploy as a consequence of the crisis at home had no chance of preventing Louis IX of France from forcing Peter's submission to him. While the inevitable end of the pension that followed on from the loss of Duke Peter brought some small hope for the depleted royal finances, the turn of events represented a bitter blow. Domestic crisis had again exerted a pivotal impact on foreign policy. Henry was to look back on these early years of his kingship with profound regret. Writing to his brother-in-law Emperor Frederick II in 1235, he said that he had behaved in ways that had endangered his very soul, and that he had failed to fulfil his kingly obligations. Crucially, he seemed to see his sin as being against the very principles of Magna Carta, writing that he had thought that his acts of 'will' were justified by his royal power. His subjects could only hope the lessons had genuinely been learned.

Vir Simplex: England's New King

Henry's subjects had had a taste of the new king's personality in 1233–4: there was no doubt that he possessed a mind of his own, as his commitment to the maintenance and resumption of at least some of his continental inheritance shows, but he had not so far shown signs of being a natural and authoritative leader, and he was relatively malleable, particularly when he was promised things that appeared to be to the benefit of his own priorities. His lack of political nous and financial acumen, and his poor judgement, meant that he did not have the ability to discern which of these promises were likely to be false or undeliverable, or would lead him into avoidable conflict. What more can we understand of the young heir to John on whose shoulders lay so much responsibility? Unfortunately, information about him, other than that he had few around him who could shape his kingly personality positively, is limited. John had died before Henry reached a formative age, but in any case could never have stood as an exemplar of kingship. Henry was said to be close to his mother, who remained alive until well into Henry's reign, but, having returned to her native France to remarry in 1217 following John's death and not visiting England again until 1230, Isabella, too, did not play much of a role during Henry's formative years. The prince spent most of his time first with his wet nurse and then with his guardians. This meant that during the late 1210s and 1220s Henry was exposed only to the influence of the councillors around him, in particular William Marshal, Peter des Roches (his tutor in the early years) and Hubert de Burgh.

By the time he reached adulthood Henry was not an especially imposing figure physically: although his build was solid, he was not tall as his son Edward I would be: Henry stood at around five feet six inches in height, the same as his father. According to the royal justice, Nicholas Trevet, he had a drooping eyelid on one side. Of course, not being the tallest of men had not stopped King John from maintaining an imposing presence, but it did not naturally create one. Where John had amply compensated for this with the sheer force of his personality, Henry did not. Contemporaries referred to Henry as a *vir simplex*, meaning a man who was uncomplicated, perhaps naive, a reputation that lived on in fourteenth-century chronicles, in which he was noted to have been as unworldly in adulthood as he had been as a child.

At the same time, Henry was a relatively inactive king compared with his father and son, preferring to rest at royal palaces in the south of England than to tour the country or travel to the Continent, and he made it a priority to increase the comfort of those palaces, even in respect of the toilet facilities. This sedentariness meant that, unlike John and Edward I, Henry's sense of England as a whole, and to some extent of his own subjects, was limited. This was accentuated by the fact that in his adult reign he was, again unlike John and Edward I, relatively uninvolved in the detail of government and the law. Furthermore, having not excelled in his knightly training, he never promised to be one of England's best soldier-kings. In hindsight his unwillingness to take military action when gifted with a golden opportunity in France in 1230 is not surprising given that he had hitherto shown comparatively little interest in tournaments (in which military skills were usually, and crucially, practised) and hunting. All this underscores his peace-loving nature, but that was rarely a winning characteristic for a king, and the consequent avoidance of battle wherever possible, together with his preference instead to appease opponents, was to lead to considerable problems during the reign.

There was a wry sense of humour to accompany all of this, demonstrated by an episode recorded in the royal fine rolls detailing a joke he played on one of the Poitevins travelling with him back from France in 1243. The king apparently had his officials make a list of imaginary debts Peter owed to the Crown, including for large quantities of wine. When Peter saw them, he panicked and the joke was revealed, no doubt to general hilarity. People were apparently still raising Peter's fictitious debts in jest with him many years later. Henry is, however, much better known for his seriousness and piety. Matthew Paris, the great chronicler of the reign, wrote that even by the age of nine Henry had spoken with 'unusual gravity and dignity'. In adulthood, he was probably the greatest patron of the friars of the age and seems to have been heavily influenced by the Dominicans. He is known for having heard several masses a day (after 1234 he also increased the number of days each year on which the royal choirs chanted ceremonial hymns invoking Christ's aid for the king) and for his love of pilgrimage. He would prepare for feasts of St Edward the Confessor, to whose cult he became devoted from the 1230s onwards, by dressing in plain woollen clothes and consuming only bread and water. In 1229, after hearing complaints from men who dwelt on royal manors, Henry issued his first order to clothe paupers, and thereafter his charity extended to the provision of food for paupers every day.

Despite his piety, Henry's wider interests tended to favour luxury. First, he exhibited a love of expensive art and objects. The use of Italian marble and the creation of statues on shrines in precious metal and windows of coloured glass in Westminster Abbey, renovated by Henry at huge cost from the 1240s onwards, evidence this very clearly, but Henry also amassed a collection of jewels, clothes and regalia, much of which ironically went on to be pawned in the 1260s. Henry's courts were known for their pageantry and extravagance. A Poitevin satirist wrote of him: 'white bread, chambers and tapestries . . . to ride like a dean on a docile mount. The king likes better all that than to put on a coat of mail.' Henry coupled this taste for luxury with the patronage of artists and scholars, though he cannot be said to have been an intellectual – the most elevated literature he possessed was a great book of romances.

What attitude did Henry have to kingship? It has sometimes been thought that he was in many way the lineal heir to John in attitudes as well as blood. In 1248, Matthew Paris has Henry state very clearly that 'vassals' should never judge their prince or 'confine him to their conditions'. 'Inferiors', he said, could be directed 'at will' by their lord. A decade later, in 1258, the baronial rebels were also to argue that Henry had been surrounded by men who told him he was not 'subject to the laws'. These do not sound like the attitudes of a man who had accepted the restrictions of Magna Carta. Quite the opposite. Henry sounds like a king on the verge of a somewhat absolutist approach to kingship. But when we place the remarks in context, the picture looks much less compelling: the first statement was made in defence of Henry's right to choose his own ministers, and the second was a suggestion about those around him, not about the views of the king himself. In fact, actions and words that can be attributed to him with certainty indicate that he had a much more moderate attitude. In 1235, his letter to Emperor Frederick II shows a man deeply regretful of breaches of Magna Carta and desperate to treat his subjects according to his kingly obligations. As he took up the reins of power properly for the first time in 1234, and despite the events of 1232–4, it was not authoritarian tendencies his subjects needed to be concerned about. Henry's reign would not be an echo of his father's.

Recovering the Angevin Inheritance

In 1234, having dismissed Peter des Roches and admitted denying magnates judgement by their peers, Henry began to direct policy for himself.

In the ensuing years, he remained committed to the retrieval of the Angevin inheritance, pursuing a number of policies aimed at undermining the French king's position. In the short term the defection of Peter of Brittany to Louis of France meant that Henry had little choice but to come to terms in a five-year peace with Louis in 1235. However, this did not stop Henry making diplomatic efforts to forge alliances that might at some future point be deployed against the French king. With that in mind, attempts were made to preserve good relations with the count of Toulouse, and Henry sought through his own marriage plans to sustain his position in France in 1235.

Eleanor of Provence, whom Henry married in 1236, was the second daughter of Raymond Berengar, the count of Provence, and the niece of the count of Savoy. At only twelve years old, her alliance with Henry III is another example of the diplomacy of marriage in the period. Through his wife, Henry would have a stake in southern and south-eastern France, which might in due course enable him to put pressure on the French king, the principle being that the more the French king's resources were divided, the better it was for his enemies.

What the twelve-year-old girl herself thought about being uprooted from her home in order to be married to a man of nearly thirty whom she had never met in another country is unknown; like Henry she had no choices – she was a child thrust suddenly into the adult world. Yet amid the politics of the match, one of the strengths of Henry's own character is clear. Awaiting her arrival with 'ardent desire', he was from the outset the most devoted admirer of this beautiful girl from Provence: he rushed to meet her when she reached Canterbury in January 1236 and married her that day. With her were three uncles from Savoy whom Henry also welcomed and with whom he forged close friendships. The marriage of Henry and Eleanor became a model of devotion. The two would spend much time together, their mutual love clear for all to see and celebrated in painted images and other art commissioned by Henry during the course of their long marriage. Henry's unwavering and unusual faithfulness to Eleanor, in stark contrast to his father, is also well testified. He is said to have viewed the two of them as a team, and she in turn was to build up more independent power than many of her predecessors, with Henry's explicit blessing. She was a formidable woman with a strong and powerful personality, which would be demonstrated perhaps most forcefully in the 1250s, when Henry depended on her first as regent during his absence in France and later to raise an army for him while she herself was across the Channel.

In diplomatic terms, while much was hoped for from the match, in reality, since Louis IX was already married to Eleanor's elder sister, the benefits were limited, especially given that Eleanor came with no dowry – the ten thousand marks originally promised were never forthcoming. Henry had not secured an advantage over Louis by marrying Eleanor. A far bigger potential boon to Henry's position on the European stage than his own marriage was the surprise announcement in 1234 by the Holy Roman Emperor, Frederick II, that he intended to marry Henry's sister Isabella. The suggestion for this had come from Pope Gregory IX, who wanted to promote a fresh crusade, for which European peace was critical. Frederick himself, on the other hand, was facing revolt by his own son Henry, and the prospect of a large dowry to accompany his new wife would be a very convenient source of funds for securing assistance in defeating the rebels. He duly demanded some thirty thousand marks from Henry. For Henry, an imperial alliance was attractive: if the emperor were to go on to support Henry in his conflict with Louis IX there would be an opportunity in respect of the lost Angevin lands. He therefore lost no time in agreeing to the match and the huge dowry – in typical Henrician fashion, there was little thought about where the money would be found. While the marriage was another diplomatic manoeuvre, Henry nonetheless hoped for happiness for Isabella, his dearest sister. It was not meant to be. Frederick was known for his hard-living personality and little changed in that respect following his marriage to Isabella in 1235. Her English attendants were soon sent home by the emperor, and Isabella herself died only six years later. She never saw her brother again after she left England.

On the diplomatic front, the marriage was not to provide Henry with the hoped-for counterbalance to Capetian power. Frederick clearly had no intention of undermining his own relationship with Louis IX, writing to him in April 1235 to let him know about the wedding and asking for a meeting sometime soon. By June 1235 he was asking both Henry III and

Louis IX to meet him together on the borders of France and the Empire at Vaucouleurs. Henry made his excuses for the meeting, probably so as not to seem to spurn the emperor's likely attempts at a Plantagenet–Capetian reconciliation, but, undeterred, Frederick rescheduled it for 1237. This time, Henry promised that his representatives, who included Richard of Cornwall, would attend, but when they reached Dover, Frederick sent word to postpone the meeting, possibly because of problems the emperor was himself facing in Germany and Italy at the time. In the end, the meeting never took place, but Frederick II's attempts to arrange it suggested quite clearly that he had no intention of lending support to Henry in a campaign against Louis. Instead, he wanted to achieve peace between the two kings. The likely motivation for this was to secure the support of both for the pope's crusade, because Gregory IX was in turn putting Frederick under pressure to bring about renewed efforts in the Holy Land. Gregory was hoping, in all probability, to achieve a three-way alliance of the kings of England and France and the emperor, with the emperor using all of his influence with the two kings to broker a lasting peace between them. Frederick's marriage to Henry's sister was therefore far from the fillip to his cause that Henry had hoped for.

Henry's desire to regain his lost inheritance was further thwarted when Louis achieved diplomatic success in marrying one of his brothers to the heiress of the count of Toulouse and another of his brothers, Robert of Artois, to the daughter of the duke of Brabant. Both were lords with whom Henry III had attempted to create alliances. In fact, in a pattern that would become typical, by the latter part of the decade Henry had spent a great deal of money on his alliance projects but had made absolutely no material gains. And in Louis IX, he had an unenviable adversary. In 1241, the situation worsened further when Louis announced that he intended to invest his brother Alphonse as count of Poitou, as set out in Louis VIII's will. To Henry III this was an act of provocation and a clear usurpation of his own claims to authority as overlord in Poitou, while the Poitevin lords themselves, on the other hand, recognised no overlord at all. Henry and the count of La Marche quickly entered into a counter-alliance and Henry began to make plans for an expedition, but he was unable to secure a tax in support of the campaign. In fact, even before Parliament had met to consider the king's request for tax formally in January 1242, several lesser and greater magnates mutually agreed with each other that they would not give their consent.

Once it convened, Parliament's justification for the refusal was that Louis IX had not officially violated the truce between the two kings. Henry was urged to come back again when or if Louis breached the truce – when the magnates said they would be willing to help. Parliament's position was understandable: without explicit provocation, it is hard to see how a tax could have been justified; first, it would have set a dangerous precedent at an early stage in the development of a system of taxation, and second, more practically, it is hard to see how collection could have been enforced in these circumstances. Military service was another matter. In theory, the king's major nobles were obliged to provide service to him as their feudal lord, but they may well have had legitimate concerns regarding safeguarding the truce with Louis IX that Henry had to ameliorate; this was certainly the case for Richard of Cornwall, who was persuaded to join the campaign once he had been given reassurances about the truce. After the January Parliament, Henry called several earls to court for individual meetings. Whatever the content of their conversations, the king's words must have been persuasive and reassuring, because when he set sail for Poitou in May, he was accompanied by a heavily pregnant Eleanor and seven of his earls – almost a full complement, once those who were incapacitated were ruled out. But it was not enough: by the time Louis did formally violate the truce, Henry was stranded on the Continent with an inadequate force to combat the full might of the French feudal host. The outcome was inevitable and Henry returned to England in autumn 1243 defeated and humiliated, and having been forced to conclude yet another ignominious truce with his Capetian rival.

Tensions and Discord, 1234–42

The refusal of tax in 1242 says something about the principles guiding decisions about whether to grant the king taxation in these early years of Parliament; comments made in Parliament in early 1242 point too, though, to the wastage of the 1237 tax by the king, and complaints were also made about both breaches of Magna Carta and Henry's financial impositions. The complaints spoke volumes about ongoing issues with Henry's kingship since the crisis of 1234.

Yet the period had actually begun in promising fashion, with a prevailing mood of co-operation and conciliation after the fall of Peter des Roches. Henry and his magnates had met in Great Councils and oversaw the promulgation of a series of reforms, both governmental and legal, between 1234 and 1237. They ranged in subject matter from the abuses of local officials to the rights of widows and the provision of new common-law remedies. But it was not long before new persuasive and charismatic personalities again came to the fore to replace de Burgh and des Roches as royal advisers, causing tensions and division at court. The queen's uncle, William of Savoy, who arrived from the Continent after the king's marriage in 1236, and Simon de Montfort, regarded by the wider nobility as a parvenu, who had also come from the Continent, were the two most prominent. Matthew Paris referred to the latter, who was famously to go on to fight against Henry III in the civil war of 1258–65, as one of Henry III's 'infamous' and 'suspect' councillors. Between 1235 and 1237, de Montfort had manoeuvred himself into such a position of trust with the king that he was sent to negotiate with the Scots in early 1237, while in June Henry would not engage in peace negotiations with the Welsh leader without Richard of Cornwall, William of Savoy, Simon de Montfort and other key men.

It was William of Savoy, though, who became the king's chief adviser. William was one of the younger sons of the count of Savoy and was already bishop-elect of Valence in southern France. Having played a key role in restoring the finances of the diocese of Valence, he was a man of business and ideally placed to exert similar influence in Henry III's court. His emergence was sudden – within months of his arrival in England early in 1236, he had been promoted to head of the king's Council – and prompted immediate issues with the wider nobility. The problem was not that William lacked ability; in fact he was one of the most talented advisers Henry had at any time in his reign. He immediately realised that Henry's financial issues, particularly the need to pay the remainder of his sister Isabella's dowry to Emperor Frederick II in spring 1237, necessitated urgent reform. The problem was how it was carried out: something of what would be

William's modus operandi was revealed when attempts were made to force out some of the king's existing advisers. These included the chancellor, Ralph Neville, who in the face of pressure refused to hand over his seal. By the time of the scheduled Council in late April 1236, tensions were running so high that instead of going to Westminster for the Council, Henry headed straight for the Tower of London. He was expecting trouble. The impasse did not last long: the magnates insisted that Henry meet them at Westminster, to which the king characteristically succumbed. Once there, they raised their objections to Savoy. There was obviously great fear that yet again Henry had fallen prey to an adviser whose intentions were at best unclear. Memories of the des Roches and de Burgh years must have remained very prominent in people's minds.

In the event, those who assisted Savoy, particularly William de Raleigh, a lawyer-administrator who had risen to become a member of Henry's Council, and Alexander Swereford, a baron of the Exchequer, made several very constructive and uncontentious reforms to the king's finances. One element of their work was in relation to the sheriffdoms, and was arguably much needed. The sheriff's farm had been outdated for some time and it was known that the king was not receiving as much in the way of revenues from the localities as he might have done. Following a careful review of revenues by de Raleigh and Swereford, twenty-two of the twenty-seven sheriffdoms in England were placed in the hands of lesser-status men than the courtiers who had preceded them. These new sheriffs, appointed between April and October 1236, were to account at the Exchequer for all they collected and in return were to receive an allowance, a significant departure from the tradition of sheriffs paying a fixed sum to the Exchequer, and taking any excess they collected for themselves. This was an echo of a policy King John had tried in 1204, but which he had quickly abandoned in order to continue to promote his own associates to office. Unlike in 1204, the new sheriffs of the 1230s remained in office for the next few years and the policy led to a substantial rise in royal revenue.

But despite this, the magnates' initial concerns were not all without foundation. While the change in the sheriffs seems not to have caused extensive pressures on local society, other reforms, in a faint echo of 1233, flew in the face of what the nobility thought was now protected by Magna

Carta, prompted anger and opposition and led to another crisis. One of the most controversial of these reforms was in relation to the royal (so-called 'demesne') manors. These were taken out of the hands of the sheriffs and given to special custodians, and it is clear that the king's officials began as a result even to take back manors that had been formally granted out for the holder's life by royal charter. Connected with this in the autumn of 1236 was the decision to extend the resumption policy in relation to the demesne manors to the forests, meaning that the king's officials began to take back 'woods and parks' belonging to the demesne.

Faced with opposition, Henry relinquished this rather energetic interpretation of the original commission in relation to the royal demesne manors, but by then panic had set in and by late 1236, only months after Savoy's appointment, there were widespread fears that the king was planning to dispossess a much wider group of people. This was exacerbated by the fact that in December 1236 sheriffs were also instructed to look into all the lands in England that had been held by Normans, Bretons and other foreigners, the *terre Normannorum*, which, strictly speaking, belonged to the king. Would he suddenly be requiring the *terre Normannorum* to be summarily reclaimed by his officials, as had happened with many demesne manors? Fears were at fever pitch when Henry, despite all the financial reforms of the last year, gave notice that he still needed money and requested a grant of tax in mid-October 1236. In the negotiations that followed, the well-trodden ground of arbitrary dispossessions was traversed again.

Whatever the king's strict theoretical rights in all these areas of tension, the magnate view was the same in 1236 as it had been in 1233: all landholding should be, they believed, protected by the due process of the law; that had been the great achievement of 1215 in their eyes, and Henry and his advisers had again strayed too far into territory they regarded as beyond bounds in 1236. They demanded the abandonment of the *terre Normannorum* inquests, the royal demesne resumptions and forest policy, as well as the reconfirmation of Magna Carta. They also insisted on the exit of William of Savoy (which they did not achieve) and the appointment of three members of the royal Council by Parliament. This was the price extracted in return for the grant of taxation agreed in early 1237. The king's initial promise that the tax would be put aside for 'the necessary uses of the kingdom', and that it would be spent under the supervision of anyone the magnates wanted to act as representatives for them, had simply not been enough. Only careful and diplomatic negotiation by skilled royal councillors, led in all probability by de Raleigh, had secured a grant for Henry in a tense situation.

Further problems followed in 1238, when Henry's favouritism of de Montfort in particular, but also of another man, John de Lacy, earl of Lincoln, was to bring about a significant crisis. In that year a number of armed earls confronted the king at Stratford-upon-Avon, protesting against the king's decisions to marry his sister Eleanor to de Montfort in secret, and to allow the marriage of de Lacy's daughter to Richard de Clare, earl of Gloucester, who was still a boy. The latter match threatened to change the balance of landholding power significantly, while the former was bizarre given the differing status of the two parties. Such was Henry's secrecy that even Richard of Cornwall was caught completely unawares by the clandestine marriage of his sister, and was enraged both by his brother's secrecy and the match itself. In the currency of the time, royal sisters were a valuable asset, and while de Montfort was the king's favourite, he had little wider significance.

The initial reaction against Henry in early 1238 was led by Richard of Cornwall and Gilbert Marshal, earl of Pembroke, and the effect was to cause the king to flee again to the Tower of London (it was becoming something of a pattern). The match involving Eleanor and de Montfort could not by then be undone, but Henry seems to have placated Richard with a payment of around £4,000 (at that stage Cornwall was seeking to amass sufficient funds to launch a crusade) and presumably promised that nothing similar would happen in the future. De Montfort then humbled himself before Cornwall and left England temporarily, bringing to an end what might have become a much bigger crisis of authority for Henry. The problematic nature of de Montfort's personality in particular was exposed when, taking advantage of the king's favour a year later, he named Henry as security for the payment of a significant loan without any prior consent from Henry himself. This resulted in an outburst by the king in which he attempted to have de Montfort put in the Tower of London, this time as a prison rather than a place of sanctuary. Ironically, only the intervention of

Richard of Cornwall calmed matters, and de Montfort and Eleanor took themselves abroad at some speed.

Henry's style of government in the mid-1230s, the first time he had taken control for himself, was far from a positive step forward from the faction of the minority; the rebellion of 1238 as well as de Montfort's own behaviour both amplify our existing sense of Henry's lack of judgement. De Montfort may have been a wise military adviser, but Henry had given him favour over and above what his rank should have entitled him to, and de Montfort had wasted little time in taking advantage of his relationship with the king. Meanwhile, although William of Savoy was undoubtedly an able leader, with the king's best financial interests at heart, his rapid promotion and some of the policies with which he was associated prompted suspicion and fear; his subsequent decision to depart from the realm in 1238 must have prompted much relief. None of this boded well as Henry's adult reign advanced.

After the problems of 1237 and 1238, Henry seems to have tried hard to avoid directly antagonising his subjects. He had some success in this, but his continuing sense of the need to shore up the royal finances and his new desire also to accumulate funds in the Tower of London meant that he and his advisers increasingly focused on short-term policies to provide the extra cash he needed. Initially, this did not provoke opposition because the policies themselves were relatively uncontroversial, with the magnates at least. The imposition of greater financial demands on the Jews was one example. In 1239, they were ordered to pay a third of all their chattels to the Exchequer. When the proceeds were disappointing, the Council ordered an inquest into the wealth of all Jews in England, following that with a tallage (a tax) of around £14,000, the burden of which was so great that only a small number of the wealthiest Jewish financiers could bear it. Henry had in so doing begun the process of stripping England's Jewish community of its wealth. The tallage also had an impact on lesser landowners, many of whose debts to Jewish lenders were called in as the Jewish community came under pressure to produce funds for the king. At the same time as this, the general eyre's exactions on local society, which again placed burdens on local knights that Henry would later regret, were proving lucrative for the king. In the ecclesiastical arena, the exploitation of vacant bishoprics also brought in significant revenue for the Crown in these years, though there is no indication that Henry did anything other than profit from already vacant episcopacies.

Yet for all that he was not provoking opposition among his magnates and had broadly good personal relationships with many of them, in governmental terms Henry was becoming more physically removed from his subjects in the late 1230s. This situation was most immediately brought about by the changed composition of the Council after 1239. In the early 1240s, hardly any of its members were of the high status the Council had hitherto boasted. Some of this was accidental: the deaths of several nobles and the higher than usual number of episcopal vacancies meant that where the Council of the few years before 1239 contained five earls (or claimants to earldoms) and three bishops, now it contained only two earls, one bishop and the archbishop of York. The new councillors Henry chose came almost wholly from his own household, many of whom were recent immigrants to England and owed their positions to him personally. Ironically, this was in all likelihood a reflection of an attempt by Henry to be free of the controversy of earlier years by creating his own group around him, but it missed the point that what the king really needed to do was to choose counsel wisely and from a broad base, not a narrow cabal. Taken together, the absence of a justiciar and chancellor (both offices were now vacant) and the lack of nobility and bishops among the king's closest advisers made his formal lines of communication with the political community of magnates, knights and ecclesiastics increasingly circumscribed.

The result was that tension built and fault lines quickly began to open up. The first issue to arise was with the Church. In the late 1230s, Henry had attempted to force the electors at Winchester to have William of Savoy as their bishop, speaking out angrily against their preferred candidate, William de Raleigh. Ironically this was the same de Raleigh who had previously been one of Henry's most useful servants. Of the latter, the king said that he had killed more men with his tongue than Savoy had with a sword. Other issues were beginning to emerge, too, such as forcing clerics to plead in secular rather than ecclesiastical courts via writs of prohibition (literally writs prohibiting a case from being pleaded in a particular court), which created tension. For the bishops, these actions violated Magna Carta and in

1240 they came together in London to demand a remedy. The archbishop of Canterbury even issued a sentence of excommunication against some of Henry's advisers. For the moment, Henry could ignore these complaints with a degree of impunity, as there was little the bishops could do, but some years later he was to live to rue such a stance.

Much harder for Henry to ignore was the strong lay opposition to his foreign policy that was voiced in response to his request for tax in 1242. This was probably not a result of any sort of breach between the king and the nobility: while consultation on foreign policy had been limited, to say the least, Henry's personal relationships with key figures, particularly Roger Bigod, earl of Norfolk, and Humphrey de Bohun, earl of Hereford, had been very good in recent months. Both men had been at the royal court late in 1241, and Bohun had joined the king for the Christmas celebrations. The objections of the greatest nobles to the campaign and the tax were probably mostly confined to the existing truce with Louis IX. For lesser landowners, though, the issues were probably fundamentally quite different. Henry's recent impositions on local society – the Jewish tallage and the general eyre being two examples – had fostered resentment, which was now being aired.

The Emergence of Parliament

One momentous outcome of the king's need for money in the decades after Magna Carta was the rise of a forum in which formal negotiations took place for taxation. In 1237 it was referred to for the first time as 'Parliament'. It could little have been imagined then that the institution would endure even seven centuries later. This title seems to have originated in a legal case in November 1236, which was deferred until the next 'Parliamentum', the assembly of January 1237. The word 'Parliamentum' was not new: it had been around since at least the middle of the twelfth century and had been used as a descriptor for several types of meeting. Its adoption in 1236 to describe a national assembly in which discussion and debate of matters concerning the whole realm would take place was probably more than a chance occurrence, though. It may well have been carried across the Channel from France, where it had first been used in this particular way in the 1220s. Cross-currents of ideas between the two realms were always common, even after the collapse of the Angevin empire, and kings and their subjects frequently looked to what was happening in each other's realm. Once used, the term 'Parliament' became the norm in England (and in France); from this point on, chroniclers regularly used it to refer to large assemblies charged with the conduct of a wide range of important governmental business, and it appears in the government's official records from 1242. Custom in turn rapidly came to establish that an assembly of representatives of the king's subjects, known as Parliament, would be convened if the king wished to secure a grant of taxation; if debate was to be had in respect of funding foreign policy, it therefore took place in what was from then on known as Parliament.

If the terminology to describe it was novel, the assembly that took place in 1237 was far from an innovation. There was in fact a tradition stretching back to before the Norman Conquest of kings consulting with their subjects on various matters in some form of gathering. After the Conquest the fact that England was vulnerable to invasion, together with the need to arrange for the defence of lands held on both sides of the Channel, gave rise to regular consultation with the king's greatest subjects, especially at times when it was envisaged that national resources should be used. At the same time, the fact that the throne itself was often subject to rival claims in the period between 1066 and 1135 meant that kings became used to engaging their magnates and sometimes offering concessions in order to establish their own authority. This gave an early prominence, well before 1199, to what might be termed public counsel in England: Henry II, for example, made most of his legislation with baronial counsel at such assemblies, and in 1177 he called a Council to meet at Winchester when he was planning to sail to Normandy; following the advice given there, he made the decision to delay his crossing so that he could await the arrival of his envoys who had travelled to the French court. In other words, Parliament evolved out of an established tradition of gatherings of the king's magnates in which they were consulted on matters of policy. These assemblies to discuss the business of the king and the realm, and even to witness the creation of laws, included magnates from across the country and could in that sense be said already to be truly national.

In the thirteenth century, it was natural that it should be these noble assemblies that considered requests from the king for new types of taxes. During John's reign, the king claimed to have secured meaningful consent to a tax of 1207 – the writs for its collection referred to the common advice and consent of the Council – but that is doubtful: John was not averse to bending the truth to suit his agenda. Concern about the issue was one of the main reasons for the demand in Magna Carta for aids to be given only by 'common counsel of the realm', and for the explicit definition of 'counsel' that followed and the stipulation of a process by which consent could be achieved. 'Counsel' was to include not just the greatest lay and ecclesiastical lords, but all those who held their land directly from the king, and this wider group was expected to be summoned by the sheriffs if taxation was being requested. The clauses on representation were dropped in reissues of Magna Carta, and when aids were given in 1225 and 1232, the assemblies that made the grants simply claimed explicit authority to act on behalf of 'everyone in our kingdom'. But it was clearly the case that the principle of wider consent had struck a chord, and from the 1220s there is evidence that even lesser tenants-in-chief, some of whom were knights, were present at the assemblies where tax was requested – the minority government could not afford for it to be otherwise. These men could be said more broadly to give a voice to gentry grievances, and sowed the seeds of an expectation that the king would always consult fully if he wanted an extraordinary grant of money from his subjects. The mechanism for the negotiation of grants of money to the king had quietly but firmly been established, an abiding legacy of Magna Carta's protection of property rights from the arbitrary will of the king, which has prevailed into the twenty-first century.

The Ghost of Magna Carta, 1242–4

Parliament was not, though, to give Henry III much succour as his reign progressed. In the 1240s, the king seemed to stumble from one crisis to another. When he returned from his ill-fated campaign against Louis IX in 1243, Henry had debts amounting to some £15,000. Over the course of the next year, he managed largely to pay off those debts, but he was living from hand to mouth financially, partly as a result of his increasingly lavish spending. In addition, the marriage of Richard of Cornwall to Queen Eleanor's sister Sanchia had cost £3,000, and a campaign to Scotland to respond to a false story of invasion had cost £4,000. While, with the benefit of hindsight, royal revenues in this period were in quite good order, this was not so clear at the time, partly because of the confused state of central accounting. The result was that Henry saw no alternative but to ask Parliament for another grant of taxation in autumn 1244. However, his actions towards his subjects in the previous two years in particular had hardly been of a type to rebuild a positive relationship; quite the opposite. Soon after his return in 1243, he had launched yet more of the supposedly abandoned inquests into the *terre Normannorum*, and some of the people holding these lands had suffered confiscations as a result. The aim underlying the inquests was simple: to secure land that Henry had promised to provide to his wartime Gascon and English supporters. But he was short of money, and that too played its own role. Henry seemed to have learned nothing at all from the events of 1236–7.

The inquests were just one of several provocative policies: inquests into sergeanties (feudal services owed to the king) alienated without the king's licence were also initiated. These led to confiscations of landholdings, which people often felt were unjust. To add insult to injury, the holdings were then returned to those from whom they had been taken in return for an annual rent, yet another financial obligation. Meanwhile, a new series of inquests into the royal forests was begun, Henry being convinced that royal rights had been violated in them in recent years, again to the detriment of the royal finances. The result was a growth in the size of the royal forests, in direct contravention of the Forest Charter, and the concessions made in 1225. In April 1244, the royal government also issued a proclamation that from now on no liberties of any sort would be recognised without a royal warrant or proof of a warrant from Henry's predecessors or of ancient tenure since before 1215, meaning that those who claimed liberties would suddenly need proof of their right to exercise them. This was another reflection of Henry's concern about lost royal rights and the financial implications. Finally, there were attempts to increase the number of people who were qualified as a result of the property they held to become knights, and increased fines were imposed in the general eyres when they visited the localities. Many of these new policies affected local society well beyond the nobility.

When Henry made his request for taxation in Parliament in November 1244, this backdrop, which had seen the king increasing the financial demands he was making of both the greater and lesser nobility, and a wider group of his subjects in the localities, was critical to the opposition that followed. The laity were not alone. Clerics were concerned about various matters – the Crown's use of ecclesiastical vacancies for financial gain, the influence Henry was exercising over things like elections to bishoprics, and the ever-reducing jurisdiction of the ecclesiastical courts. As if all this was not bad enough, Henry added insult to injury in his request for tax by basing it on the debts he had incurred in Gascony, a campaign which, he *said*, he had undertaken on the advice of the barons, alongside the costs of recent Welsh and Scottish campaigns and money he owed for 'the necessaries of life', whatever those might be.

The result was that the king was met with a barrage of complaints and demands. Allegations were made that Henry had violated Magna Carta, that previous grants of taxation had not 'profited' the realm and that the absence of a high-ranking chancellor and a justiciar had led to the issue of unjust writs. A committee of twelve bishops, earls, barons and abbots was nominated by Parliament to bring about the appointment of new officials before they would consider Henry's request. They wanted government to return to the form it had taken in the minority, and for Henry to honour his commitment to Magna Carta. At around the same time, another set of demands, which was probably never presented to the king, was drawn up in a document known as the 'Paper Constitution'. Its writers sought to re-establish the Great Council as the body that appointed some of the king's leading councillors, including the chancellor and justiciar, and to fully restore those offices. It also referenced the impositions of sheriffs and the general eyres. From these concerns, it is likely that it was drafted by the knights in Parliament rather than by the magnates, who judged it too radical to present to the king. But its existence is evidence that the voice of the men of the localities was making itself heard in the early 1240s. In coming years, that voice would only get stronger.

In the face of the demands that were put before him, Henry adjourned Parliament until February 1245 to give himself time to take advice. Unlike in 1237, however, there was no skilful politician like William de Raleigh among Henry's councillors and advisers whom the magnates trusted and who was capable enough to negotiate successfully on behalf of the king. In fact, when Simon de Montfort had earlier been attempting to make the case for a grant to the nobility, Henry, unwilling to await the results, had gone to the chapel of St Katherine in Westminster Abbey, where the discussions were happening, and interrupted proceedings to tell the magnates that he could not live without them and they could not live without him. Such browbeating was not effective then and it would not be later when Henry took the lead in negotiations. The opposition was determined that while a deal might be done, it had to come at the price of concessions from the king, and without these he was bound to fail. So, while in November 1244 Henry subjected Parliament to days and days of pleading, and even secured a letter from the pope supporting his request for taxation, citing the Welsh war as justification, the inescapable reality was that when they all returned in 1245, he was going to have to be willing to agree to changes to both his policy and the personnel of his government. What actually happened was that Henry showed no sign of conceding on either question, and consequently he walked away from the negotiating table with only the scutage his subjects were obliged to grant him for the marriage of his eldest daughter, Margaret.

What had happened in 1244-5 can classically be summarised as a crisis inevitably created when an unstoppable force meets an immovable object. Yet it seems clear that Parliament did not set out to block the king come what may: it was prepared to negotiate and even agree a tax, provided the outcome of those negotiations was satisfactory. His subjects were not making unreasonable demands on Henry. Positions became entrenched because of the king's own unwillingness to compromise. This does not mean that his attitude to kingship had shifted in recent years. He was repeatedly to stress in royal writs in the 1240s and 1250s that he did not wish to dispossess any of his free subjects without judgement or unjustly, and his commitment to justice was further reiterated on more than one occasion. His view in relation to the landed tenures his action targeted in the early 1240s was simply that they fell explicitly outside Magna Carta's remit. Strictly speaking, he was correct. As usual, however, Henry missed the point, and his need for at least some financial support from his subjects for most of his major governmental projects, namely war and military endeavour, meant that it was their view of the situation that was most likely to prevail. This was realpolitik.

In the end, the crisis of 1244 passed and a more serious breakdown was avoided not because the opposition gave up, but because Henry, having failed to obtain the tax he had requested, opted not to continue to press for it. Nonetheless, what had happened had made more explicit than ever before the central points of contention for both the king himself and more than one group in the political community. With none of these issues resolved, it is unsurprising that it was not to be the last crisis of the reign. In fact, the problems Henry encountered in 1244–5 were as nothing compared with what he was to face fourteen years later in 1258, when a crisis of such magnitude erupted that it was to usher in more than seven years of conflict and turmoil.

A Fresh Start, 1244–58

While it might seem from this that the crisis of 1258 must have been an inevitable continuation of that of 1244, it was in some ways not so at all. Although he had been unwilling to compromise on what he saw as matters of principle in 1244, and while he lacked the intellectual capacity or political acumen to understand the origins of the crisis, it seems very likely that Henry regretted the disunity with his subjects that had been exhibited in that year. There is no reason to think his outlook had changed since his letter to Emperor Frederick in 1233, in which he had reflected that he had suffered because he had separated himself from 'the hearts of our faithful subjects'. In fact, the evidence indicates that he remained keen after the immediate crisis had passed in 1244 to build good relationships with the greater magnates. In 1245, following the death of Walter Marshal, earl of Pembroke, he took great care to distribute the landed resources from the earldom to other earls in the same area. And in 1247, when Henry introduced his Lusignan relatives from Poitou to England, he still attempted to bring them together with nobles in harmony at court by keeping both groups close to him and encouraging marriage alliances. By and large, the personal relationships between king and individual magnates were good in the late 1240s and early 1250s, though all his efforts did not prevent deep and growing resentment of the Poitevins, and disputes between them and the queen's Savoyard relatives. Similarly, Henry sought to rebuild bridges with the Church. Here fortune assisted him in not providing many episcopal vacancies in the late 1240s. And although the king's candidates for these tended still to be royal clerks, there were no particularly contentious elections. At the same time, he made genuine attempts, though ultimately without success, to limit the burdens of papal taxation.

There were other positive developments, too. His obligations in relation to justice and the maintenance of local order rose up Henry's personal agenda in the late 1240s following a particularly violent attack on merchants on the Alton Pass, a famous route through Hampshire, in which the merchants involved were robbed of a large sum of money. Having heard about this and about the failure of local men to come forward and suggest who might have carried out the robbery, Henry travelled to Hampshire to address the men of the county directly. His anger about what had happened seems to have been genuine: he even went to the trouble of making special arrangements for those who were robbed to be compensated from the takings of the Hampshire judicial eyre.

This was not the first time Henry's government had shown a direct interest in the question of local order: in 1242, when Henry departed for Gascony, his regents made careful provision to try to preserve local peace during his absence, bringing back more substantial courtiers as sheriffs, appointing central justices rather than local knights as assize justices (who heard property disputes in between visitations of the general eyre), and making it temporarily easier to bring pleas before the central courts. The regents also spent five weeks in East Anglia, where they had concerns about disorder, hearing pleas in person. However, Henry's personal interest in the late 1240s seems to have prompted further and more permanent reform and action. There followed several interventions in individual counties in relation to trespasses (a special writ of trespass was developing in this period, yet another common-law innovation) and felonies that had not occurred on this scale before. From 1249 his government furthermore increased significantly the number of writs *de gratia* (writs issued by the king's special grace) to transfer a case into a higher court, which enabled people to have cases heard by the king's courts rather than locally. These writs had to be paid for, and people did so in huge numbers, but the wider context of Henry's worries about the state of order suggests that this was perhaps not just a revenue-raising exercise. The result of all this was a dramatic shift in the provision of justice from the local courts to the central courts. Where the county courts had dominated in relation to litigation between local landowners in the 1210s and 1220s, by the 1250s the ease of transferring cases to the central courts saw pleas before the royal courts double almost overnight.

It is hard to overemphasise the importance of this change: the decline in the status of the county court was never to be reversed, and by the time Edward I came to the throne, cases before the central courts were increasing exponentially as growing numbers of litigants rushed to access the 'king's justice'. While it meant that royal justice was available to many more of the king's subjects than before, this in turn made those same subjects even more dependent on royal government at the centre and, ultimately and critically, on the king's ability and commitment to the provision of justice. This was one reason why Henry's failure to appoint a chancellor was so keenly felt, because it was the chancellor who very often provided a conduit through which petitions might be channelled and common-law writs accessed by people in the localities. People could always get a writ, even without a chancellor in post, but they could not so easily convey to royal government what problems existed on the ground. With central government taking on greater responsibility for the maintenance of local order, that dialogue was arguably becoming crucial. One of the great achievements of Edward I thirty years later would be to realise this in a way that his father never had. The Plantagenet state had to deliver on its promises.

What Henry had done in relation to justice was nonetheless an important start. He also took a personal interest in misbehaviour by royal officials and magnates in the localities during these years. In October 1250, he made a speech in which he spoke against magnate oppressions and required the sheriffs to investigate their behaviour. Those same sheriffs were furthermore themselves told to treat people justly. From 1246, the eyre justices, too, were asked to make inquiries into official misbehaviour when they visited the localities. And from 1249, Henry appointed two commissioners to tour the realm investigating trespasses with the help of local juries, a tour that lasted into the early 1250s. While criticism can be made of the limited achievements of all these measures – accusations were made, but very few people were punished – Henry's various inquiries had set a precedent of direct royal interest in local justice on which both Edward I and Edward III would build. It was another sign of the growing state.

But despite the notable positive developments in Henry's rule in these years, many of the same traits and errors as had been on display earlier continued to bedevil it. Events in Wales demonstrate this perfectly. In the early 1240s, Henry had continued to work to impress both his and the English Marcher lords' authority on the region in the face of the increasing assertiveness of many Welsh lords, particularly the princes of Gwynedd, first Llywelyn the Great, who had been such a thorn in King John's side, and then, after his death in 1240, his son Dafydd. In May 1240, having allied with Welsh lords who were resistant to Dafydd's claims of dominance, Henry refused to recognise him as a prince, depriving him of the homage of the Welsh barons. The English Marcher lords then moved in to undermine him further, while Henry worked hard to bring local rulers in Wales firmly on to the English side with a mixture of rewards and threats. By August 1241 Henry's forces had managed to bring Dafydd to heel through a military campaign that lasted just a week, so the situation looked stable.

But it was not to last. During the summer of 1244, border raids in England by a number of Welsh lords began, and by the autumn they were allying with each other to launch attacks on the lands held by English Marcher lords and on two royal castles currently under construction, at Dyserth and Deganwy. Henry sent assistance to the Marchers from his household forces, but it was not enough to subdue Dafydd. In early 1245 Henry was forced to announce an intention to launch a campaign in the summer, but crucially no date was given. It was hardly a decisive move. In March, John Lestrange, one of the Marcher lords, lamented in a bold letter to the king himself that the tardiness of the response meant that a campaign that might have cost £1,000 would now cost ten times that amount.

It would finally take place months later, in August, and the army he raised would be the largest Henry ever deployed to Wales. Yet the army was not triumphant: far from it. While a trade embargo enforced by the English, together with a lack of money and supplies, and starvation, had brought about the surrender of native rulers across South and mid-Wales, Henry did not secure the submission of Dafydd. The Welsh leader had studiously avoided pitched battle, though his forces had repeatedly attacked Henry's army, and Henry himself had focused all his energies on building a new castle at Deganwy. The castle had strategic importance in North Wales, and decades later Edward I would emulate the policy of castle-building to consolidate the English position in Wales. But the truth was that few martial kings would have avoided the opportunity to defeat Dafydd given the size of the army that had turned out for service in 1245. Nor, following Dafydd's death in February 1246, did Henry take the opportunity with which he was then presented to conquer Gwynedd. What he wanted to do instead was to reach a settlement with Llywelyn and Owain ap Gruffudd, who had succeeded Dafydd in the absence of direct heirs. The policy was successful in the short term because Llywelyn and Owain themselves were in no position to challenge the English king. It suited them to make a temporary (as they saw it) peace in April 1247. In the long term, though, Henry's preference for negotiated settlement stored up trouble: the undefeated Llywelyn would resurface in the 1250s when he was in a stronger position, and present Henry with a major challenge.

The only thing to conclude from this showing was that Henry was not interested in military campaigning, as had been the case in France. This was a problem not just because the Welsh situation remained unresolved, but also because a king's willingness and ability to lead his people in war in the national interest was as fundamental to kingship as was his proclivity to ensure that justice was done. The interconnection between the two was epitomised by the king's great seal, which portrayed him riding in manner of war on one side and sitting in judgement on the other. For contemporaries there was a clear connection between the king pursuing justice in international relations by the sword and his provision of peace to his people internally. By the late 1240s, Henry had shown himself again and again simply not to be interested in the business of war. It did not have an immediate cost in terms of his security on the throne, but it was far from what his subjects could have reasonably expected.

What might be called half measures were also on display in relation to justice and local order. While the end of the 1240s and the early 1250s saw access to royal justice significantly expanded, in other ways Henry was reluctant to make good on his promises. Complaints grew in the same years about the behaviour of the king's favourites among the native magnates and his foreign relatives, Lusignan and Savoyard. And there were instances of Henry being asked to intervene but refusing to do so, in some cases even preventing action against them. Anger over this would be strongly expressed in the serious crisis that enveloped the realm in the late 1250s.

In policy terms, Henry was far from an abject failure in this period; he clearly understood and practised some of the fundamentals of good kingship, and he tried hard to build bridges with his nobility at least. Where the great Angevin legal system was concerned, his reign, no less than those of his predecessors, saw a significant expansion in its and consequently central government's role in his subjects' daily lives. Yet despite all this, fundamental flaws remained with the way in which he approached kingship. The most immediately problematic of these was his continued failure to take counsel from his subjects and offer channels through which they might feel heard in the form of the justiciar and chancellor. *Plus ça change, plus c'est la même chose.* This would represent a critical backdrop to crisis in 1258.

A much more serious problem in this period, though, was the growing financial cost of novel and more highfalutin notions and grandiose schemes that Henry developed in the late 1240s. What were the grand ambitions that were to form a new ingredient in Henry's kingship and to turn out to be so problematic? And why did Henry embark on them? The question of motivation is always difficult, but with Henry III it is relatively easy to make conclusions. Across the Channel in Louis IX he was faced with a king who was famously one of Europe's great leaders, not just in the thirteenth century but across the Middle Ages. Like his Capetian ancestors, Louis was determined to emphasise and express his authority across France. By the 1240s he had not only already made considerable gains from Henry's crumbling Plantagenet inheritance, he had also spent a great deal of effort on the image of his kingship that he wanted contemporaries, and posterity, to embrace. He was a pious, even saintly, crusader, a lawgiver, a magnificent patron of the arts and culture. What made it possible for him to express and cement that image was the wealth of his kingdom and his own personal gravitas. As a result, under Louis, the Capetian dynasty was in its pomp.

It was against this foil, perhaps consciously, perhaps not, that Henry sought to express his own vision of kingship. Monarchy should be majestic, it should be opulent; it should be saintly, it should be revered. If Henry were to take his proper place on the European stage, he had to live up to those expectations. During the 1240s and 1250s he sought to ensure just that. This is exemplified by the scale of his spending on food and drink for his increasingly lavish court, which had risen from around £6 per day in the 1220s to around £20 by the late 1240s. Henry also became even more focused on finding new ways to express his piety. As a result, the number of meals he was giving to the poor increased dramatically (on an average day after 1240 Henry was providing nearly five hundred meals, to compare with around a hundred given by his French counterpart).

But this was not enough for Henry to achieve what he desired, and his ambitions ratcheted up in the second half of the 1240s when he embarked on one of his greatest projects, the rebuilding of Westminster Abbey, in honour of Edward the Confessor. It was to cost around £2,000 a year and take nearly twenty-five years. The plans for the abbey were characteristically ambitious: it was intended to become a great celebration of gothic architecture, to rival Reims Cathedral, Saint-Denis and the Sainte-Chapelle together. Henry was also determined not to be outdone in the acquisition of precious relics and by 1247 he had secured a phial of Christ's blood from the religious community at Outremer, celebrating the acquisition with a grand and extremely costly ceremony at Westminster in October. This placed him on an equal footing again with Louis, who had himself acquired relics from Baldwin II of Constantinople. By the late 1240s, Henry was even looking to fund his own crusade, first in the form of an English expedition that was preached from 1247 and which Henry encouraged Guy de Lusignan to lead, and later a campaign to be led by Henry himself, mirroring Louis IX. Matthew Paris wrote in 1250 that the king was amassing treasure with this end in mind: 'The king knew that he was to go to the eastern parts where gold is used as money and reward for serving on an expedition [and so he desired] to collect gold.'

At the same time, with the Angevin inheritance in mind, Henry continued to build up financially expensive alliances that could remove the balance of power in Europe from Louis IX's hands. One such alliance was that made in 1246 with Count Amadeus of Savoy, from whom he accepted homage for a number of castles and routes across the Maritime Alps in return for a no doubt very welcome payment of around £1,000 per year. The idea was that the count would take Henry's side in any conflict; accepting the grant, Amadeus explicitly committed to damage Henry's enemies as much as he was able to. While Louis was away on crusade, Henry aimed to make further alliances that seem to have been geared towards achieving the recovery of some of the Angevin lands, such as the plan to marry his eldest son, the Lord Edward, to one of the daughters of the duke of Brabant, which, although it ultimately failed, speaks to this wider strategy.

Henry's ambitions found an even bigger, grander stage with his acceptance of the kingdom of Sicily from the papal legate in 1254. Had it been successful, this would have made him Europe's foremost monarch. However, it came with a major and insurmountable catch: Pope Innocent IV wanted Henry to wrest Sicily from the hands of the German Staufen dynasty, whose head until his death was Henry's brother-in-law, Frederick II. When Frederick died in 1250, Innocent had quickly focused on replacing the Staufen dynasty in Sicily, Germany and Jerusalem, with the hope of installing more pliant kings. If Henry were to be successful in taking Sicily from Frederick's illegitimate son, Manfred, it would be placed in the hands of Henry's second son, Edmund. In itself, the conquest of Sicily was an almost impossible ask – Manfred was an unenviable opponent and the English would have to travel large distances, including through France, where the reception might not be friendly, just to get to Sicily. But in 1256 Innocent's successor Alexander IV added even more terms to the deal: Henry had to repay the huge papal expenses of nearly £100,000 in order for the pope even to release the throne to Edmund. If, having promised to do this, Henry failed to pay off the debt, he would be excommunicated. While it is true that there were some papal concessions along the way – by 1255 it had been accepted that the demands of reconquest were high enough to justify the commutation of Henry's crusading vow – the task remained unattainable. Nonetheless Henry had become fixated on the Crown of Sicily and, whatever the folly of it, would not be dissuaded from the course he had taken: he saw before him a potentially glittering trophy. In agreeing to the deal with the pope, Henry therefore sent a strong message about his own conception of his status in Europe to his counterparts: the Angevin empire had been lost, but the Angevins remained a force to be reckoned with on the European stage. He sent the same message to his English subjects, lay and ecclesiastical, who were to be the ones to pay for their king's grand designs – and they did not like it.

The English 'Milch-Cow', 1244–58

As the 1240s progressed and the king's commitments expanded, the financial situation steadily worsened. Henry was forced to turn to new expedients to fund his escalating costs. Some of these were uncontroversial, like the re-coinage which Parliament approved in April 1247 (re-coinages always brought in a windfall for government), or even popular, like the expansion in the number of judicial writs. But other measures created resentment and increased tensions. The sheriffs were ordered to pay more and more to the Exchequer as each year went by. Their costs were passed on to the men of the shires through a whole host of often unjust extra charges. The judicial system was also made to yield additional funds. One example of this was in relation to the procedure for coroners' inquests: when the eyre visited a county, the established tradition was that if a person had been found dead, the reeve and four men from each of the four neighbouring villages would represent their villages at the inquest, but in the 1240s the justices began to require far more villagers to appear, and to fine those who did not. This and other similar measures contributed to a significant increase in the government's revenues from the general eyre: in the three years from 1246 it raised a staggering £22,000 at a time when the ordinary annual revenues of the king only amounted to £24,000. These increases were a breach of the spirit of Magna Carta: the king had been refused tax, so he was exploiting the judicial and governmental systems instead in order to acquire the money he needed. To his subjects, it felt very unfair and arbitrary, and precisely what Magna Carta was meant to prevent.

But this was only the start. Towards the end of the 1240s the financial demands rose even further when the situation in Gascony took a decided turn for the worse. A truce with Louis IX had been made for five years in 1243, but in 1248, with the peace about to expire, the king of Navarre began separately making incursions across the southern border of the duchy. It was clear that the English king needed to assert his authority robustly if he were not to lose his grip on south-western France. This prompted Henry to invite some of his Lusignan relatives to England in 1247, as he attempted to build an alliance with the family in order to shore up his position in northern Gascony in the face of a possible French assault that would leave him exposed on both the northern and the southern border.

This alone was not sufficient, and it was soon clear to Henry that more direct action was necessary. In February 1248 he therefore asked Parliament for a grant for a projected military campaign to Gascony. In return, however, it was again demanded that the great officers of state be elected, and both merchants and clergy made additional vociferous complaints; the king, again refusing to submit to what were clearly limitations on his prerogative that he felt went too far, had consequently to find the money elsewhere. Only by selling royal silver plate, using the money from the Jewish tallage and raising loans from Richard of Cornwall was Henry able to send a small expedition to the duchy in August under the leadership of Simon de Montfort, who was his newly appointed steward of Gascony. Further requests for tax in Parliament in July 1248 and in January and April 1249 also met with determined refusals.

As time went on, the costs associated with de Montfort's attempts to shore up Henry's authority within Gascony grew even further, well beyond what the king had anticipated. While de Montfort managed to extend the French truce in 1248 and reach peace with the king of Navarre, he took a particularly tough line on maintaining order in the duchy, and his harshness began to cause considerable disquiet, resulting in complaints to Henry in November 1249 about his style of government. The financial demands coming back to England from de Montfort were so high that Henry had to mortgage two years of his revenues from Ireland in order to provide his steward with money to spend on the castles. More money followed in 1250. This time Henry had been forced to borrow it from Italian merchants.

As costs spiralled, Henry began to lose confidence in de Montfort: when Gaston de Béarn, one of Gascony's most important lords, was captured and sent to England in 1250, the king immediately issued him with a pardon, a clear affront to de Montfort's authority. And in January 1251, when de Montfort made a plea in person for further funds, the king was so worried by the state of affairs in the duchy that although he gave him another £2,000, he also sent commissioners to Gascony to arbitrate in de Montfort's disputes with its lords. Still de Montfort ploughed on, seeking to impose order through the use of force, and by the end of 1251 he found himself in outright conflict with Henry about how to run the duchy. Commissioners were again despatched in January 1252, and this time they found serious civil strife, with Gaston de Béarn even besieging the king's castle at La Réole. The king-duke's subjects in Gascony had made it clear that they did not want de Montfort to continue as seneschal.

The result was that in May 1252 de Montfort was brought to trial in England before the king and magnates for his conduct. The Gascons wanted their day in court and argued that de Montfort had behaved in a way that was both brutal and high-handed, that he had extorted money and that he had made unjust arrests. In his defence de Montfort argued that his job as seneschal involved arresting traitors on the king's orders, and additionally stated that he had been forced by lack of money from Henry to fund some of his duties as steward out of his own pocket. He even explicitly criticised the king, calling into question his Christianity. In his defence he was supported by a number of magnates. Though most of them were either de Montfort's particular friends or supported him because they felt that the Gascons were untrustworthy, Henry felt impelled to give a verdict in de Montfort's favour; for his part, the earl undertook to return to Gascony to rule in a different style. But before he had the opportunity to do so, Henry, no doubt sensing that more problems would inevitably arise on his return, changed his mind. Instead of de Montfort, he decided that he or his eldest son, the Lord Edward, would travel to Gascony and personally settle disputes.

This was a decision that essentially neutralised de Montfort's power in the duchy, and it infuriated the earl, to whom it came as a humiliating blow. He proceeded to ignore the king's orders and intervene in Gascony, causing the situation to worsen and forcing Henry formally to dismiss him. Although he wanted to follow up by going in person to settle Gascony in October 1252, a failure to gain support and resources at home meant that it was not until the rebellion had become more serious that Henry could mount an expedition. Even then, his unwillingness to reinstate the office of justiciar and the status of the office of chancellor meant that the magnates in Parliament would only grant him an aid on the knighting of the Lord Edward (which they were almost obliged to do), rather than a grant of taxation, and in doing even this they insisted on another confirmation of Magna Carta. The Gascon campaign that Henry was able to launch in 1253 consequently necessitated raiding the gold treasure that he had been working tirelessly to accumulate for his projected crusade.

Ironically, just in order to have access to the force required to restore his authority in the duchy, Henry was forced to recall the military services of Simon de Montfort, for which he had to pay dearly in financial terms. The earl's military prowess proved crucial in cowing those who were in rebellion, a fact that might be said to vindicate his style of government in Gascony in the first place. However, before making this conclusion, it is worth considering the context in which de Montfort had established his position. In a region where there were competing claims to authority, taking any line in government, tough or lenient, was risky. At any point, alliances might be made with the French king, or the king of Navarre, or with other Gascon lords, to mount a rebellion. Above all, a successful seneschal needed to be able to command personal respect and good relationships with key lords, an area in which de Montfort had manifestly failed. Even with such respect, it would arguably still be hard to maintain order and control in the duchy either if the English king were seen to be weak, as Henry III is likely to have been, or if the French king or other claimants were seen to be strong, as Louis IX was undoubtedly felt to be. What de Montfort had succeeded in doing, however, was provoking outright rebellion which the king had no choice but to tackle with military force, at a time when that was the last thing he wanted to be doing or spending extra money on. Henry can reasonably be forgiven for feeling that leaving him in charge of the duchy was fraught with risk.

Costs mounted from the king's Gascon woes. The total extra cost of operations in the duchy between 1248 and 1252 was somewhere between £8,000 and £10,000. In addition, the 1253–4 expedition used up Henry's gold treasure to the value of around £19,000, as well as another £17,000 in cash. And this figure does not count the loans Henry received from Richard of Cornwall. Unsurprisingly, the financial situation prompted him to make yet another request for taxation, and Parliament met in January 1254 to discuss it. Henry was at that point still in Gascony and his decision to make the request from overseas indicates how desperate he was for funds. But resistance in England was by now growing, and the regents, Queen Eleanor and Richard of Cornwall, were forced to write back to Henry in February 1254 to say that 'many complain that the aforesaid Charter is not observed by your sheriffs and other bailiffs as it should be'. As a result, they told him, he would be unlikely to secure a grant from 'the other laity' (those below the noble ranks) without reconfirming the Charters. Henry was forced to order personally that Magna Carta be observed via letters to the sheriffs and public proclamation. But the regents knew this would not be enough; the situation was tense and the magnates no longer felt able to speak for the lesser men of the localities. The regents' answer to this was to make an innovation: they ordered that two knights from each county, chosen by their own counties, appear at Westminster in April to consider Henry's request for taxation. In the meantime the sheriffs were tasked with explaining the necessity of the tax in the localities, focusing on the threat of invasion from Castile. But deep dissatisfaction prevailed below the baronial ranks, and when Simon de Montfort returned from Gascony and told the April assembly that the statements about the Castilian threat were false, there was anger all round. The king did not get his tax and de Montfort had reaped some revenge for Henry's treatment of him.

Queen Eleanor and Richard of Cornwall had not, despite their best efforts, been able to counter the prevailing tide of politics with which they were faced. Discontent was by this time too deep-rooted to be overcome. It is clear, though, that their instincts were sound and they were undoubtedly good choices as regents. Cornwall stood firmly by his brother's side in rule, even when he knew the extent of Henry's limitations as king. Only under the most egregious provocation from threats to his own legitimate interests and the insult Henry had meted out to him by marrying their sister secretly to de Montfort in 1236 had he risen against his brother. Thereafter, Henry had been much more careful to treat Richard with the respect that was his due, and a close professional relationship had developed in which he had emerged as Henry's leading counsellor. In the 1240s and early 1250s, Richard's repeated advances of money to his brother demonstrated his unwavering loyalty, which was returned in kind by Henry. The bond between the brothers was further strengthened by the fact that Richard had married Eleanor of Provence's younger sister Sanchia in 1243. Theirs was a close-knit family, whatever Henry's failings as king.

Eleanor, too, was a rock on which Henry could depend. Now in her thirties, she had borne Henry four children, and had matured into a formidable character. Aside from her renowned beauty, she was notably intelligent and cultured (she was even a writer of poetry). At the time of Henry's departure she was expecting their fifth child, and while she had travelled with the king in the past while pregnant, this time it was decided that she should take control of government at home. Whether that was because of the pregnancy or because Henry depended on her for the management of affairs in his absence is unclear, but she was in many ways the senior partner in the regency, authorising more letters than Cornwall. For good measure, she found time to give birth to a daughter, Katherine, in the process, though Katherine was both deaf and mute, and, to the great distress of both Henry and Eleanor, died only three years later. It is testimony to Eleanor's physical and mental strength that she remained regent for the duration of her husband's absence in 1253–4.

Henry could not have asked for better regents to represent him. But it was to no avail. He returned from Gascony not only with his treasure wiped out, but also in considerable debt. In February 1255 he was forced to levy a tallage of £2,000 on London and borrow a further £5,000 from Richard of Cornwall just to enable payment of his household expenses. In April 1255 he followed that with another request for taxation, and was again refused. This in turn led to more financial pressure being placed on the knightly class in particular, through judicial revenues and the county sheriffs. Burdens like these, as so clearly indicated by the grievances raised in response to Henry's request for taxation from Gascony, were already causing very significant disquiet, and it was bound to increase. Other burdens were added by an increasingly desperate government: in order to raise money, all those with land worth £15 or more each year were ordered to take up knighthood, with those who wanted to be exempt forced to pay fines to the government.

All these expedients still did not raise enough revenue for the king's commitments. By 1257 the situation was so dire that Henry even went so far as to present his son Edmund, his chosen successor to Manfred in Sicily, in Apulian dress at Parliament as part of his request for taxation for the Sicily campaign. There was consternation in response and a list of objections was compiled to a plan of action in which Henry suggested that he himself would travel overland to Sicily across France. Such was his inability to see the impossible magnitude of his commitments and the extent of the problems developing in England in the mid-1250s that, even as late as 1256, he was also considering an expedition to North Africa with Alfonso of Castile as part of the crusade efforts, which he refused to abandon. It was all the magnates in Parliament could do to persuade their king, whom everyone knew to be a lacklustre military commander at best, that he should not set out for North Africa with neither troops nor money. Where Sicily was concerned, Manfred was a formidable opponent, and it had arguably been the height of foolhardiness for Henry to have taken on the project in the first place: in 1252, both Charles of Anjou and Richard of Cornwall had refused the pope's offer of Sicily, with Cornwall bluntly telling the pope that he might as well have asked him to climb into the skies and capture the moon. To be fair to Henry, the situation had improved somewhat by 1254, and his decision to accept the offer where others had regarded it as something to be avoided was not quite as bewildering as it would initially seem: anti-Imperial feeling had been growing in Sicily, and that made Manfred's position less impregnable that it had once been. However, it is still hard to view this as anything other than a foolish project, which was, given Henry's own record and limited financial resources, doomed to fail. By 1257, still doggedly focused on his grand scheme, it must have seemed that Henry was no longer living in the realm of reality. Around him, as his ambitions became more and more far-fetched, things inevitably began to unravel.

To compound the challenges facing the king, Wales was in rebellion again. In 1255, Llywelyn ap Gruffudd, referred to by a court poet as a 'lion of the warband', had demonstrated his prowess by taking control of Gwynedd (which Henry had declined to conquer in the 1240s when he had the opportunity). To do this, Llywelyn had overcome his own brothers, and he followed this success with the launch of a campaign to assert his authority more widely within Wales too. He enjoyed quick success: by November 1256 he had taken the Four Cantrefs of North Wales from the Lord Edward, which gave him overwhelming mastery of Gwynedd. He then invaded Ceredigion in the south, taking more of Edward's lands in the area around Aberystwyth on the west coast. In 1257, having met with no resistance to the expansion of his authority in Wales from the now heavily distracted English king, he had set about plundering large areas, making lords in South Wales uneasy. It was only in the summer of that year that Henry finally turned his attention away from the Sicilian project temporarily and responded with an attack on Llywelyn. But although the earl of Gloucester made gains in the south, Henry himself had limited success in the north and was forced to call a halt to the campaign before winter set in. He planned to return in May 1258, but that was not to happen, for a crisis was to envelop England that was more serious than anything seen since Henry's childhood.

Crisis Erupts, April 1258

The first Henry knew of the seriousness of the situation was in early April 1258, when he made a request for taxation for the Welsh campaign in Parliament at Westminster. The response was a sworn confederation among several magnates, followed by an armed demonstration: Richard de Clare, earl of Gloucester; Roger Bigod, earl of Norfolk, and his brother Hugh; Simon de Montfort, earl of Leicester; Peter de Montfort (no relation to Simon); John fitz Geoffrey, half-brother of the earl of Norfolk, and a long-standing royal servant; and Peter of Savoy, the queen's uncle. They had two fundamental demands: that the king's Lusignan relatives should be exiled, and that government should be reformed. To do this, they proposed the appointment of twenty-four men. They would choose half of these themselves, but would leave the king free to choose the other half. Henry was shocked by the suddenness and strength of the opposition, and given that they were armed, like his father before him he had little choice but to agree to their terms. On 2 May he accepted that the committee of twenty-four would convene in Parliament on 9 June to reform the realm. Crisis had broken like a wave upon the Henrician court. Was 1215 about to be repeated?

With a king so focused on Sicily and crusade, and making political decisions in respect of those commitments that plunged him into worse and worse financial jeopardy, it is easy to see how the magnates could not but question his wisdom. And while he had good personal relations with many, his professional relationships with them were not so strong. Again and again Henry had returned to Parliament asking for taxation in the last decade, and again and again his requests had been denied: in 1244, 1248, 1253 and 1254–5. He had repeatedly failed to accept demands for better government and to comprehend the fundamental problem with his kingship. The parading of Edmund through Westminster in Apulian dress was not just a piece of theatre: the ambition to which it testified was fantastical, and everyone knew it – everyone except Henry himself. And Henry would listen to the wise counsel of no one. While all this was happening, there were grave questions over his handling of the Welsh revolt, not least from lords with lands in the area that were under threat, perhaps the most important of whom was the earl of Gloucester.

But it was not just the nobility Henry had to face. As a result of the political education that those below the magnate class had received in recent decades, not least through the reading of Magna Carta in every marketplace in England each time it was reissued, and the inclusion of more of the laity in summons to Parliament, the active political community was considerably wider in 1258 than it had been in 1215. And it was very vigorously demanding action to deal with its grievances in a way that it had not before. This is not to say that the burdens the knights in particular faced from the king were new – King John had arguably imposed even bigger demands on them, in relation to the royal forests and the money extracted from them by the sheriffs – but they now had a much louder political voice through their presence in Parliament, as well as increased confidence to express it on their own terms, which was hard to ignore. Even if the nobility had not had their own grievances against Henry in 1258, other fires were therefore already burning.

The men of the localities were not just complaining about Henry himself, but also, ironically, the behaviour of members of the nobility and their officials. Henry's appeasement of magnate opposition in 1244 and beyond, in his bid to rebuild his relationship with them after the crisis of that year, meant that not only had he imposed his own burdens on local society, but he had also turned a blind eye to magnate misdoings, creating deep resentment. In addition, there were a number of usurpations of royal rights and liberties across England by magnates during this period, which enabled them to exercise power in ways that further burdened those beneath them. Justice, too, seemed to be difficult to secure in the face of noble oppression, a fact illustrated very explicitly by the words apparently uttered by an estate steward of the king's Lusignan relatives: 'If I do you wrong, who is there to do you right?'

In fact, the king's foreign relatives represented a further ingredient in what was already a heady mix: Henry's family and allies, invited to England by the king himself, seemed to garner privileges from him ahead of local men, so that a general problem of kingly indulgence of the magnates was amplified by the presence of 'aliens' who were being treated better than Henry's native subjects. The Osney Abbey chronicler summarised the situation in pithy style by saying that Henry 'loved aliens above all the English'. Tensions over this might not have been so severe if the king had been accessible to his own subjects and behaved even-handedly, and if he had not been in the business of extracting so much money from the men of the localities. As it was, blame for the wider situation attached to anyone who was, or at least seemed to be, benefiting from it while others were suffering.

At first glance, what happened in 1258 looks like a straightforward combination of a political crisis generated by Henry's poor kingship, and a constitutional one hingeing on issues of good government. The constitutional elements were in many ways the direct result of Magna Carta's stress on the maintenance of property rights in the face of arbitrary lordship. But there was another ingredient in the crisis that might even be said to have predominated over both the political and constitutional elements: faction. Rivalries at the royal court placed Henry's Lusignan relatives and their allies at odds with another group that included Queen Eleanor's Savoyard relatives and their allies. This was not a battle between factional 'ins' and 'outs', but rather in-fighting between courtiers, which resulted in one group demanding that their rivals be expelled from the realm. Understanding this is critical to explaining both the crisis of 1258 and many of the events of future years, as well as the behaviour of several of the protagonists, including the king's eldest son, Edward.

Those factional tensions came to a head in the fortnight leading up to the Westminster Parliament. The immediate issue was a dispute over the right to appoint the vicar to the church of Shere in Surrey. On 1 April, the forces of the Lusignan Aymer de Valence, bishop-elect of Winchester, had attacked those of John fitz Geoffrey, as tensions boiled over in the dispute. Fitz Geoffrey appealed to Henry in Parliament for justice in his case (Valence's servants having killed one of his men), and was told in no uncertain terms by the king that he did not wish to hear the complaint. In the scenes that followed, another Lusignan, William de Valence, weighed in, inflaming the situation by accusing some of the English nobles of conniving with Llywelyn in Wales. Henry was forced to intervene to prevent full-scale conflict. But still he would not hear Fitz Geoffrey's case. On 12 April, in response to this, a group of magnates – the earls of Gloucester, Leicester and Norfolk, Peter of Savoy, Hugh Bigod, John fitz Geoffrey and Peter de Montfort – made a compact in which they swore to 'help each other, both ourselves and those belonging to us, against all people, doing right and taking nothing that we cannot take without doing wrong, saving faith to our lord the king of England and to the Crown'.

When the king asked for taxation later that month, the magnates in the compact were given an opportunity to make their demands of him with a greater likelihood of success. The very first thing they asked for when they reached the king's hall was that he should 'let the wretched and intolerable Poitevins and all aliens flee from your face'. With Richard of Cornwall away in Germany working to claim the Imperial throne for himself, there was no one to mediate between Henry and the opposition, a role Cornwall had increasingly assumed, most recently as regent, and the king was forced to submit to demands for reform.

The confederation of lords who gathered around Fitz Geoffrey were not simply motivated by what was a blatant disregard on the king's part of his obligation to provide justice without favour, which had been so prominent in Magna Carta, or by the issue of royal favouritism per se. Ironically, many of them had been recipients of the king's patronage and goodwill in the previous twenty years, and remained so – in 1256, Henry had apparently given an order that the Chancery should issue no writs against a particular group of courtiers that included the Savoyards, the Lusignans and the earl of Gloucester. And the Savoyards were also 'aliens'. The reality was that tensions between the two groups had been building for several years, and the dispute over the advowson of the church of Shere was symptomatic of wider issues.

At the heart of these was the fact that Henry increasingly lacked the means to fulfil promises he had made to his growing court. Some of this was a result of the arrival of the Lusignans from Poitou in 1247, which created many more demands on his resources, as they had to be endowed with land and money to enable them to remain in England. Despite the later complaints about them, probably because they had arrived at a time when Henry had fewer resources to distribute, they never received as much from Henry as the Savoyards: twenty-six of the Savoyards were granted lands before 1258, including eleven who received very large estates, whereas, by contrast, only eight Poitevins received lands, and only five got very large estates. There were also more Savoyards who settled in England than their Poitevin counterparts: seventy as opposed to fifty. And most of the time the fees received by the Poitevins were actually lower than those the Savoyards were given. Competition between the two groups arose because of the lack of patronage in the 1250s, particularly as Henry's financial situation deteriorated. The king was often reduced to taking from one person to give to another, which was bound to cause conflict.

It was an unsustainable situation and in the years immediately leading up to 1258 it alienated, or helped to alienate, some key figures, prominent among whom was Simon de Montfort, earl of Leicester, who would emerge as the leader of the reform movement. He already harboured resentment towards Henry because of what had happened in Gascony and was owed large sums of money by the king partly from his time as steward there, and partly from his wife Eleanor's dowry as the widow of William Marshal, earl of Pembroke. De Montfort began to press for payment of these debts towards the end of 1256. At the same time as this, Henry was locked in obligation to the Lusignan William de Valence, who had helped finance the war with Wales in 1257. With the costs of the recent Gascon campaign and the departure to Germany of Richard of Cornwall, who had essentially been acting as Henry's main financier, the king found himself desperately short of resources. He managed successfully to provide land grants for Valence, but that mainly involved confiscations from others. De Montfort, angered by this and the failure to replace his own money grants with lands in the same way as for Valence, was deeply resentful of the latter's precedence over him. This no doubt amplified the resentment Montfort felt about the blame ascribed to him by Henry and the Lusignans for the revolt in Gascony earlier in the decade. Tensions between de Montfort and Valence were running so high that they argued both in 1257 and again at the Oxford Parliament in 1258. There, Valence accused both de Montfort and the earl of Gloucester of being complicit in attacks by the Welsh on his own lordship of Pembroke, and called de Montfort a liar and a traitor.

Once Henry had agreed to reform, it is therefore no surprise that de Montfort set about making sure that his own interests were protected: after agreeing on 2 May to the reform of the realm by the committee of twenty-four, Henry was also made to accept on 5 May that he would honour whatever the committee decided in respect of the assignment of land to de Montfort and the payment of royal debts to him. It would be a mistake to say that reform was merely a cloak for the pursuit of self-interest on de Montfort's part, as there is ample evidence to suggest that he was a great believer in governance for the common good for its own sake. He was also a leading light in the most productive period of reform of government at the centre and in the localities in the second half of 1258. But it would be equally naive not to note the determined prosecution of his own interests and claims from the outset. The reform movement was a convenient vehicle for the settlement of a number of personal scores and grievances, of which de Montfort's was perhaps the most high-profile.

The crisis of April 1258 was particularly challenging for Henry because it comprised a range of ingredients: fights between favourites at court, arguments over the king's foreign policy, concern about his style of government and grievances in the localities about his increasingly egregious impositions. All these combined with the legacy of Magna Carta to create the biggest challenge to royal rule since 1215. In 1258 it was a moot point whether Henry would survive it.

Reform and Division, 1258–60

When Parliament reconvened at Oxford in June 1258 to begin the process of reform, the rebel lords again came armed. Henry himself had been bringing foreign knights to England in the previous month, who he said were for the campaign in Wales. Undoubtedly and quite understandably the opposition feared otherwise, and they were taking no chances. A new Council, heavily composed of reformers, took control of central government, tightly defining the parameters within which the king's officials could operate, through a series of stipulations known as the Provisions of Oxford. These subjected the king to a Council composed of fifteen men. This new Council would choose a chancellor and a justiciar. Both officers would be answerable to the Council: the chancellor could only sign routine charters and writs; everything else would need conciliar permission. Under the Provisions, other new processes for government were introduced, too. Parliament was to convene three times a year to 'deal with the common business of the realm and of the king together', placing another brake on Henry's independence and formalising the role of Parliament in government.

The rebels also acted to neutralise some of the military force the king seems to have been planning to deploy by appointing their own constables to the royal castles. As a result of the measures imposed, Henry was essentially placed under the sort of conciliar control that had existed during his minority. At the same time, the rebels were determined to remove the Lusignans from the realm, and the situation became increasingly bitter and vitriolic, with one baron apparently telling William de Valence that 'either you give up your castles or you lose your head'. The Valence brothers soon had no choice and fled to Winchester, from where they were hounded out of England in mid-July 1258.

The fact that, coincidentally, the Parliament at Oxford was also the venue of the intended muster for a campaign against Llywelyn in Wales (in the end a truce made during the Parliament led to the cancellation of that campaign) meant that the assembly was much more socially diverse than expected, with knights present. That, and the rebels' own need to shore up wider support for the project, led to a broadening of the reform programme. In the first instance, the baronial reformers followed up the governmental changes with action to deal with local grievances. The new justiciar, Hugh Bigod, brother of the earl of Norfolk, was tasked with touring England to respond to complaints against officials and others; to make it easier to raise grievances, complainants were instructed that they did not need a formal writ to begin proceedings. Then, in August 1258, the first of the Provisions of Oxford was implemented with the creation of panels of four knights who were to collect complaints in their own counties, and it was decided that these would be brought to the Michaelmas Parliament rather than to Bigod. The vexed issue of local financial exactions was dealt with by reducing dramatically the sums demanded from sheriffs. In Parliament in October 1258 a new sheriff's oath was also created, and Henry promised to deal with grievances against the sheriffs in the localities. New sheriffs were then appointed across twenty-eight counties. All of them were local knights rather than courtiers and outsiders.

While all this was ongoing there remained the question of the situation in Wales and France. In Wales, the Lord Edward proposed to lead a campaign and the Council issued him with a cash advance to support his efforts, though with England in such a state of crisis, there can have been no illusion that this would be anything other than an interim gesture. In France things were still more complicated. Given the situation in Gascony and his wider priorities of crusade and then Sicily, Henry had judged it imperative to secure peace with Louis IX prior to the outbreak of crisis. A temporary truce between the two kings had been achieved in 1255, but in 1257 negotiations had begun for a more permanent settlement that would see Henry surrender in full his claims to Normandy, Anjou, Maine, Touraine and Poitou. Gascony would be retained, but as a fief of the French Crown, with the English king answering to Louis IX as overlord. A treaty, for whom one of the negotiators had been Simon de Montfort, already existed in draft form by 1258 and included a clause in which Louis insisted not only that Henry rescind his claims to French lands, but also that his sister and de Montfort's wife Eleanor and Richard of Cornwall do the same. Henry always maintained that de Montfort, who had been one of the negotiators in 1257, had suggested to Louis that the additional clause be put in so that he could use his and Eleanor's consent as a lever to wrest concessions of land and money out of Henry in England. Whether or not that was the case, it was certainly what de Montfort went on to do. Initially, though, he was stymied. In November 1258, the rebel lords would not permit Henry to leave the country, and when de Montfort attempted to resume negotiations himself on Henry's behalf, the French king refused on the basis that Henry needed to be present. Progress had stalled.

Back in England, the pace of reform dwindled in de Montfort's absence, showing quite how much personal energy he had injected into it and the extent to which the reform movement was already becoming closely and directly associated with him. In November 1258, the death of John fitz Geoffrey, whose dispute with Aymer de Valence had been the catalyst for the crisis, also removed a key figure; with de Montfort away, it left the earl of Gloucester to lead the movement. The earl was a late arrival to the English political scene − despite having been invested with his lands and earldoms in 1243, he had been little involved in politics before the crisis of 1258, preferring to concentrate on building up and managing his vast estates − but he was a hugely powerful figure. His two earldoms (Hertford as well as Gloucester), four honours and two great Marcher lordships (Glamorgan and Gwynllwg in the south) as well as other lands and lordships acquired in the 1240s and 1250s made him the richest magnate in England outside the royal family and a man to be wary of alienating. While he had joined the rebels in 1258, his personal ties with the royal family were strong: his widowed mother, Isabel, had married Richard of Cornwall in 1231, and Cornwall became close to his stepson in the ensuing years, despite Isabel's death in 1240. A conservative man by nature, whose commitment to reform was ambiguous at best, Gloucester's emergence as a significant figure in the opposition can be attributed in large part to Henry's failure to deal with the Welsh threat, which jeopardised the security of his own Marcher lordships. There could be fewer clearer demonstrations of the seriousness of Henry's political failings than the fact that a man who should have been one of the king's staunchest supporters found himself driven into opposition.

Gloucester was in many other ways too not a natural political bedfellow for Simon de Montfort, and when de Montfort returned to England to attend Parliament in February 1259, cracks soon began to emerge in the reforming group's unity, running along the fault lines of the differing personal priorities of the protagonists. In Parliament, probably under de Montfort's influence, the reformers and all the magnates agreed to limits on their right to demand suit of court and to place themselves under the same restraints as the king and his officers. This meant that the justiciar could hear complaints against them as well as against the king and the disgraced lords. But for the earl of Gloucester this seems to have been a step too far and he opposed it vehemently – unsurprisingly so, as he himself was to end up being the subject of many accusations.

It was not only Gloucester for whom personal interest was beginning to take centre stage in 1259. It seems that he was one of several people who had come to mistrust de Montfort's motivations in the French peace discussions too. When they went to France in March 1259 to continue negotiations on the king's behalf with Louis IX, the two men argued about de Montfort's wife Eleanor's refusal to rescind her claims to the lands to be covered by the peace negotiations. Despite his commitment to the principles of reform, there is no doubt that in the French negotiations de Montfort was placing his own interests ahead of the conclusion of a lasting peace. Gloucester did not manage to prevail in France, and Henry, already rendered significantly impotent by the appointment of the Council in 1258, was left with no choice but to attempt to placate de Montfort in Parliament in the spring in order to try to move the treaty plans forward. He paid his debts to the earl in full and granted him a number of manors in fulfilment of his long-promised land grant, the matter that had caused such tensions with William de Valence. Arbitrators were also appointed to investigate whether Henry had short-changed Eleanor and de Montfort in relation to her dowry. All of this was taken to France, where it was presented to the earl, and after some debate and further concessions, he and Eleanor agreed to renounce her claim to the French lands. This, together with the renunciation of his own claim by Richard of Cornwall, meant that back in England the terms of the peace treaty with France could be agreed by Henry and the Council. It seemed to be a breakthrough.

But progress was illusory: it soon became clear that de Montfort was still not satisfied. Writing to the arbitrators, he and Eleanor demanded a much higher annual sum in settlement of her dower than she had hitherto been in receipt of from the king, and in addition, the couple insisted on the repayment of the alleged deficit across the twenty-six years of their marriage. This was entirely beyond Henry's financial means, and de Montfort knew it; his aim was to extract as much as possible from the king, using the French peace for which Henry was so desperate as a lever to do so. Henry attempted to circumvent this obstacle by swiftly sending new terms to Louis IX in which the clause about Eleanor renouncing her claims to the lost French lands was omitted. He offered to indemnify Louis if she did try to pursue them. But it seems that de Montfort may have used his own long-standing influence with the French king to persuade Louis to reject even this. The result was that Henry's plans to cross to France to ratify the treaty in autumn 1259 had to be put on hold.

An unlikely ally for de Montfort around this time was the Lord Edward, who had his own reasons for opposing the French peace, namely that he felt it would jeopardise his hold on Gascony, which had been granted to him as an appanage only recently. His view was that too much was being surrendered to the French side in negotiations, and he had already attempted to have the earl of Gloucester represent his interests more vigorously in the spring talks, to little effect. On 15 October 1259, despairing of the direction of events, he went on to make a surprise pact with de Montfort, presumably prompted by the possibility of delaying further what Edward felt would be a humiliating peace. Another motivating factor for this agreement with de Montfort seems to have been the degree of control that the earl of Gloucester and the queen's Savoyard relatives, who had so despised the Lusignans, were exerting on appointments to Edward's household. These he resented, having himself been a staunch ally of the Lusignans in the previous year when William de Valence had helped him finance a response to the initial Welsh rebellion. This highlights quite the extent to which factional or personal divisions at court were driving political actors. Edward was bent on delaying the truce, while from de Montfort's perspective, Edward's agreement in the pact to help him enforce any judgements of the royal courts in his favour promised a further level of protection for his private interests.

What seems also to have united the two men, though, was the reforming cause itself. While Edward had refused to sign the Provisions of Oxford in spring 1258, by late summer 1259 his attitude seems to have shifted significantly. Initially this had perhaps looked to him like a wholly or mainly factional crisis, in which Edward's friends at court had been ousted by their rivals. But in 1259 he realised that there were wider issues at stake. On 21 August 1259, Edward showed his awareness of, and agreement with, reforming principles, writing privately to his own chief justiciar in Chester that 'if . . . common justice is denied to anyone of our subjects by us or our bailiffs, we lose the favour of God and man, and our lordship is belittled'.

Two months later, in October, he and the earl of Gloucester were the recipients of a protest from men calling themselves the 'community of the bachelors of England' which argued that the magnate Council had done nothing for the cause of reform. Edward seems to have sympathised with the sentiment. Whether his support made any difference is unclear. But an accompanying threat by a group of knights to use force if the Council did not take action on their behalf gave rise to reforms that resulted in the Provisions of Westminster in the same Parliament. These sought to deal with all manner of abuses in the localities, including the exactions of the sheriffs and the eyre justices, as well as wrongdoing by magnates. A new special eyre to enforce the Provisions of Westminster was also commissioned in November that year. Suddenly the grievances of those beyond the baronial ranks had been given an outlet as never before and the heir to the throne was at the very least sympathetic to their cause.

Simon de Montfort himself stayed aloof from the reforms of the Michaelmas Parliament, but he and Edward maintained their alliance. His support probably gave Edward the confidence to make a bid for independence from the reformers' control soon after the October Parliament of 1259, when he ousted the men appointed by the Council to hold his castles and replaced them with his own men. But he and de Montfort could not stop the French peace: when Henry travelled across the Channel in November he was able to persuade Louis IX to agree the long-awaited Treaty of Paris in the teeth of de Montfort and Eleanor's continuing refusal to renounce her claims to the ancestral lands in France, and his own son's opposition.

To say that Edward and de Montfort were angry at the course of the events that had resulted in the Treaty of Paris would be an understatement. Both men were livid, and in early 1260, with Henry still in France, they marched to London and demanded that Parliament should go ahead in February even though the king was absent from the realm. It was a clear bid to wrest control of policy from the hands of the conservative Gloucester. Henry, who was increasingly reasserting his independence, quickly sent orders forbidding the holding of the Parliament, but de Montfort and Edward were undeterred and proceeded to London to try to hold the assembly anyway. The result was an armed stand-off, with the justiciar, Hugh Bigod, adjourning Parliament in the face of de Montfort's opposition. Now there were tensions not only between de Montfort and Gloucester, but also between de Montfort and other reformers. In the ensuing weeks both Edward and Gloucester marched to London with their retinues, with rumours reaching Henry in France, probably from the earl of Gloucester, that Edward intended to remove his father from the throne.

With civil war looking ever more likely, Richard of Cornwall moved quickly to ensure that neither Edward nor Gloucester entered the city of London, and from France Henry ordered a summons for an army to assemble in London in late April. In the event, both sides withdrew from the brink and crisis was averted, but it was a sign of how high tensions were running. Henry knew he needed to make some concessions if he were to regain the initiative. His first act was to make a bid for magnate support by postponing the planned special eyre visitation to enforce the Provisions of Westminster. This gave them a welcome reprieve from investigations into their own behaviour. He also worked to try to detach Edward from de Montfort by reconciling with him, something that was managed and achieved by Richard of Cornwall and the archbishop of Canterbury. After that Edward was despatched abroad with instructions to take part in tournaments there (instead, the implication was, of making trouble at home).

The reconciliation was only partially successful: while in France Edward and de Montfort remained in touch, and Edward actively represented the interests of the earl in Gascony. Henry knew that there was no option other than for de Montfort to be humbled if he were truly to prevail, even over his own son, and so he attempted to neutralise the threat from de Montfort by putting him on trial. But the need for de Montfort's service after the fall of Builth Castle to the Welsh in July, together with the support de Montfort still commanded from Louis IX, who even sent the archbishop of Rouen to England to defend him, meant that the trial never went ahead. Unable to humble de Montfort, the king found the initiative beginning to ebb away from him. As summer turned to autumn, a reconciliation between Gloucester and de Montfort, possibly prompted by the deteriorating Welsh situation and Gloucester's continued frustration with Henry on that front, further strengthened de Montfort's position. At around this time it seems Edward had returned to England; whether he was hoping to resurrect his alliance with de Montfort is unclear, but it would have been an obvious reason for his arrival given the two men's continued communications over the summer. By the time Parliament convened in October, it was possible for de Montfort to manoeuvre to change the three great officers of state (the justiciar, the chancellor and the treasurer), so that they included men associated with himself or the Lord Edward, a move Henry was unable to resist.

But de Montfort did not have things all his own way. In a nod to Gloucester's conservatism, and possibly as the price of his and other magnates' support, de Montfort was forced to oversee a watering-down of the wider reform programme, which empowered magnates to investigate themselves rather than be subject to the eyre's judgement if they were accused of abuses. This resulted in the commissioning of a largely emasculated eyre, a far cry from what had been envisaged in November 1259. The planned annual change of sheriffs was also jettisoned. De Montfort may have prevailed over Henry, but at significant cost to a movement he purported to champion.

The fundamental tension between the original aims of the magnates who had opposed Henry in 1258 and those of the wider community, who had demanded co-option into the opposition, had been cleverly exposed and exploited by the king in summer 1260. The former were driven by a mixture of factional rivalry and concern about Henry's foreign policy and leadership. The latter wanted to see wider reform of oppressive government, and an extension of the terms of Magna Carta to include more that protected the king's lesser subjects against arbitrary exactions, hence the Provisions of Westminster. They also wanted to see magnates held to account for such behaviour in the same way as the king. For their part, it is unsurprising that many magnates resented and resisted such an intrusion into their own powers. Even though de Montfort had commanded the upper hand in Parliament, the changes he was forced to make to the wider reforming programme indicate clearly that it had been unpopular among the magnates. It is hard to see how these constituencies could remain allied for long. De Montfort himself sat uncomfortably in between the two: clearly committed to the wider principles of justice and good government, he was also a man with strong personal ambition who was bent on wresting what he regarded as his own and his wife's dues from the king. This had been most starkly exemplified in his actions in negotiations with France, which put him at odds with the notion of a speedy peace and therefore with a number of magnates, not least among whom was the earl of Gloucester. The two men may have been reconciled in late 1260, but Gloucester's instinctive leanings were more towards the king than the reforming movement, and the alliance, like the rest of the Montfortian coalition, was always unlikely to last.

Henry Resurgent, 1261–3

Having prevailed over Henry in late 1260, de Montfort's position was therefore by no means secure. He needed to consolidate his control if the programme was to have a chance of success, but instead he travelled to France, where a hearing was scheduled at Poitiers in January regarding a suit he had begun in relation to his wife's inheritance from Isabella of Angoulême. Gloucester, too, seems to have been elsewhere from early December onwards. His natural discomfort with reform may well explain his absenting himself from Council business. Without de Montfort and

Gloucester, there was very little the Council could actively do in government, and the result was that throughout November the Montfortian Council transacted less and less business; by late December, it had stopped acting completely. In the vacuum created by de Montfort's absence, Henry was able to tempt some of the councillors back to the royalist side, and was aided in this by the return to court of Richard of Cornwall from Germany. It is perhaps not a surprise that the Lord Edward took the decision to make a speedy exit to the Continent around this time.

By early in 1261, Henry was increasingly confident in his position, taking the bold step of sending John Mansel, one of his key councillors, to the pope to ask for absolution from the Provisions. Nonetheless, as Parliament itself approached, expecting the return of both de Montfort and Gloucester, he took no chances, summoning a number of minor barons to come in arms to support him. Once Parliament was under way he continued his work to undermine the reformers. He accepted the Provisions, he said, but the reforming Council had not done what it had promised, and his finances were in no better state than they had been when the crisis had erupted. In fact, he argued, the councillors had profited from their control of government, failed to represent his interests in foreign policy by abandoning the Sicilian project, not tackling Llywelyn in Wales and leaving the Treaty of Paris incomplete. He also resurrected his earlier bid to put de Montfort on trial. In March 1261, knowing that Mansel might soon return with papal absolution, Henry created a delay to proceedings by accepting arbitration on his grievances. He also agreed to arbitration by Louis IX in respect of his personal dispute with de Montfort.

This was all a prelude to a much bolder bid on Henry's part for a restoration of his power in May 1261, when he took control of Dover Castle and the Cinque Ports before returning to London and replacing the keeper of the Tower. By June Mansel had returned with the papal bull of absolution for Henry from the Provisions and Henry quickly went on to change the justiciar and the chancellor, at the same time dismissing the sheriffs put in place by the reformers. They were replaced by powerful courtiers and household knights, who were also given custody of the royal castles. The return of the Lusignan favourite William de Valence and his restoration by the king was a further signal that Henry simply intended to turn back the clock. In the meantime he awaited the arrival of supporting foreign mercenaries from the Continent; all the signs were that he might be about to make war on the reformers.

If Henry thought the rebels would be cowed, he was sorely mistaken. Clearly afraid of what the king intended to do, a measure of the levels of distrust that now existed, the magnate reaction, led by de Montfort, was swift. Soon the earl had Gloucester, Norfolk, Warenne, Hugh Bigod and Hugh Despenser on side to reject the papal bulls. They also appointed rival 'keepers of the counties', who were local men in stark contrast to Henry's sheriffs; this was an undisguised bid for hearts and minds. They had a willing audience, for in the localities, too, opposition was building to the king's plans to restore the status quo ante, with eyres in Worcester and elsewhere encountering opposition as local men feared a resumption of the fierce exactions that had characterised the 1240s and 1250s. While Henry tried to justify his sheriffs as men who would work in the service of his subjects, few were persuaded and rumours abounded about the king's intentions. Even the Lord Edward may have rejoined the opposition in this period, though he quickly absented himself from proceedings, this time by departing for Gascony in July. But even without Edward's opposition, the turn of events was decisively against the king, and he was forced to take refuge in the Tower of London and agree once again to arbitration. While in talks with the rebels, though, Henry was playing a double game, trying to bring in more mercenary forces from the Continent. He would not concede quietly. For their part, the reformers, too, were busy. Approaches were made to the new pope who had replaced Alexander IV following his death in May, as well as to Llywelyn in Wales, probably at de Montfort's instigation. De Montfort himself was meanwhile back in France pleading the baronial cause to Louis IX.

Despite their ascendancy, the magnates were very wary throughout of engaging in military conflict with the king; in letters to Louis IX in July they expressed concerns about 'the desolation, destruction and irreparable loss which threaten the whole land'. Several were deeply uncomfortable about the prospect of armed opposition to their anointed monarch and it was again hard to maintain the coalition against him. By the early autumn they had lost a key figure when Gloucester had returned to the king's side.

It is hard to know what prompted his decision: he had always been an uneasy royal opponent, and the approaches to Llywelyn, the enemy of the realm and his own enemy in Wales, cannot have pleased him. But equally, the earl was by this time very sick. Given the importance to him of augmenting his earldom during his lifetime, something that meant he had been very little involved in politics before the crisis, he may well have made the decision in his final months to prioritise handing on an intact inheritance to his son Gilbert.

Gloucester's defection, together with bribes given to a number of barons to bring them back to the king's side, may have been pivotal to the king's achievement of another effective victory over his opponents in late November 1261. Henry had worked hard on political diplomacy during this time too, engaging in talks with magnates whom he thought he might persuade (determined opponents such as Norfolk, Despenser and Peter de Montfort were notably excluded) throughout the second half of October and the first weeks of November. He seems finally to have accepted the need for a degree of compromise, and he committed to the continuation of negotiations on the Provisions and the governance of the realm. The treaty agreed at Kingston upon Thames that followed made some token concessions: six representatives, three for the barons and three for the king, would discuss the Provisions and the state of the kingdom. In the event of a failure on the part of the six to agree on a way forward, Richard of Cornwall would arbitrate; if he could not bring about a settlement, an appeal would be made to Louis IX. In the meantime, though, nothing was to change in respect of central officials, and in the localities each county was to elect four knights as possible sheriffs, from whom Henry would choose one. De Montfort was alone in refusing to agree to what he considered a false and ignominious peace in which there were decidedly few concessions to the reforming cause, and left for France in disgust at his fellow magnates.

For all de Montfort's moral outrage, it was perhaps inevitable that many should be so unwilling to continue in opposition to the king; few magnates were committed to the wider reforming cause in the localities, and several simply wanted to see the king commit to taking advice and governing without favourites. Probably no one other than de Montfort wanted to see the king permanently deprived of autonomy. At the same time, with the king seeming to agree to arbitration, there was simply no political space in which to oppose him, had more magnates wanted to. Most, it seems, chose passively to accept the new order, absenting themselves from politics. They cannot have doubted the reality that Henry's position had been political posturing. In the ensuing months, while he backed away from waging war on the reformers, the thing that had caused the most fear, he nonetheless worked to sweep away the reforming programme. By early 1262, there was already no longer a reforming Council and the eyre had been restarted. A few months later, with the help of Richard of Cornwall, who had been assigned such a key role by the Treaty of Kingston, Henry was effectively restored to full control of government. New papal bulls put the seal on his revival by giving him formal absolution from the Provisions, demonstrating his true feelings.

Once Henry was back in control, efforts were made by both him and Queen Eleanor to purge the Lord Edward's household group, which, together with their son, had caused problems for the king, and which they felt was exerting undue influence on Edward. The enactment of the purge was particularly swift and brutal, with one of the central figures in the group, Roger Leyburn, suddenly accused of fraud and his lands summarily confiscated, an example, presumably, to the others. What role, if any, Edward played in all this is unclear, but the effect was to detach him from the group of keenly reformist young men he had created in the late 1250s to supplant those the queen and his Savoyard relatives had put in place. In early June 1262 Edward was made to agree to hand over the bulk of his estates to the king for a period of three years, a move that further increased control over the king's 'wayward' son. Determined on an unassailed restoration of his authority, Henry made plans to go to France, taking the Lord Edward and his other son Edmund with him to argue his case, particularly against Edward's former ally de Montfort, whom Henry was determined to discredit and see humbled. While the king was away, orders were issued to Edward's former household grouping not to engage in tournaments or to travel about armed.

But while Edward had been emasculated, de Montfort could not be so easily brought to heel. He returned in Henry's absence in the autumn of 1262 to attend Parliament, where he produced a new papal bull that endorsed the Provisions. Henry was forced to write to the royal Council from France urging them to maintain the peace. In the short term he was given a reprieve from what might have become another serious situation by de Montfort's decision to return to France himself to pursue his own and Eleanor's interests in Angoulême after the Parliament, but the atmosphere was febrile. Edward's alienated group of young supporters, who were mostly Marchers and therefore acutely affected by the king's failure to deal with the latest Welsh rising that had taken place in November 1262, as well as by their deliberate exclusion from politics, were beginning to pose more of a threat to Henry's position. In the localities, too, there was anger at the abandonment of reform.

All this meant that by late 1262, there was a growing risk that the entrenched reformers such as de Montfort, the earl of Norfolk, the young Marchers and the men of the localities might come together again to threaten the king's position. The situation was so severe that Henry was persuaded by his councillors to reissue the Provisions of Westminster in January 1263 in order to try to stave off the threat of rebellion. This was posturing: the king intended never again to be subjected to the control of others, least of all de Montfort. The now quiescent Lord Edward's return with an army of mercenaries on his father's behalf showed the king's true colours: he still intended to fight. It was not long before a group of disappointed and disenfranchised nobles knew that war was again on the cards, and called on de Montfort to return. In April 1263 he made a triumphant re-entry to England. His arrival was to mark the start of civil war after five years of unresolved political crisis.

Fighting for the Kingdom, 1263–4

On his return, it was the enforcement of the Provisions that de Montfort made his rallying cry, appealing directly to the men of the localities; he again also commanded the support of a number of magnates, not just the diehard reformers and the young Marchers, but the new earl of Gloucester, Gilbert de Clare, too. Aged nineteen at his father's death in 1262, he had not technically been old enough to take full possession of his estates, and Henry had appointed keepers. In anger, Gilbert had demanded to see the

king, and even the Lusignan William de Valence, who had now returned
to England, intervened on his behalf. But Henry refused to meet him, and
even went on to order an investigation into alleged usurpation of liberties
by Gilbert's father, an act that was provocative in the circumstances. But
what proved most incendiary and drove the young earl into opposition
was the grant of dower Henry made to Gilbert's mother, which deprived
Gilbert of both the honour court of Clare, the administrative centre of
the earldom, and important lands in the March of Wales. Gilbert was so
incensed that he refused to do homage to the Lord Edward in March 1263
and joined the building opposition in May. Henry had pushed him straight
into the arms of de Montfort. In the early months of the rebellion it may
even have been that de Montfort was joined by Richard of Cornwall; if
this was the case, it signals quite how deep divisions ran and how much
alienation Henry's actions in 1262 had caused.

Throughout June and July 1263, in what was later called by a Chancery
clerk 'the first war of the barons', de Montfort and his forces raided the
property of many of Henry's leading supporters, and allied with the Welsh.
The rebels were organised and co-ordinated, and made rapid gains. Henry
for his part tried to fight back, by appointing military captains in Kent and
Sussex and the northern shires, and sent the Lord Edward to try to secure
Dover and the Cinque Ports, but to no avail. By the middle of July it was
de Montfort, not Henry, who had secured the loyalty of the Cinque Ports.
The earl's appeal to Londoners was similarly successful, based on deep
resentment in the city towards the royalist mayor and aldermen. When the
Lord Edward raided the New Temple in late June in desperation in order
to find funds to pay his mercenaries, these local concerns fused with the
national civil conflict to provoke major unrest. So dangerous and violent
was the situation in the city that when Queen Eleanor attempted to sail
from the Tower to the safety of Windsor Castle in the face of the approaching Montfortian forces, she was driven back by a mob that attacked her. By
the middle of July de Montfort had taken the city of London.

Thereafter, the rebels immediately sought to secure their position,
changing the royal officers, promising better oversight of the king's household and abandoning Henry's plans for what would have been a financially
exploitative general eyre. In the localities they attempted to deal with

widespread disorder by putting in place keepers of the peace alongside the local sheriffs. They also reiterated their commitment to the Provisions, and, resurrecting a key element of the cause from 1258, the expulsion of aliens. The latter was in part related to the army of mercenaries Edward had brought back from the Continent, who had engaged in plundering the local countryside while based at Windsor. But resentment also existed about other mercenaries brought in by Henry, and towards the queen's Savoyard relatives, who had so readily abandoned the reform programme. De Montfort was therefore cleverly appealing to something of a ground-swell of popular opinion among the laity, which was even echoed within the church, where alien clerics were a source of resentment. It is clear that de Montfort commanded the support of a significant group of bishops who, while they sought the promotion of peace between the parties, had genuine sympathy with the cause of reform, and concern about a return to past patterns of behaviour on Henry's part were he to be permitted to jettison the Provisions. In short, Henry's repeated shows of bad faith had prolonged the crisis and made it much more serious; order was now break-ing down in the localities as discontent grew.

But even despite his relatively wide base of support, it still proved hard for de Montfort to hold the opposition together: the rebels were initially united by a mixture of personal dissatisfaction with Henry III and general fear about what seemed to be the king's intentions to revert to his previous approach to government. The problem remained, however, that while they may have appealed to the Provisions, most of the magnates had never been committed to wider reform, and so, as before, de Montfort struggled to maintain the momentum of the movement without taking the ultimate (and unacceptable) step of replacing the king himself. The group could only proceed by consensus built on shared concerns and interests. Aside from preventing Henry from governing as he had before, it was hard to see what else really brought the rebels together. In fact, ironically, elements of the alliance, most notably the Welsh Marcher lords, were responsible for precisely the sort of disorder and plundering that the notion of good gov-ernment stood against. Similarly, the attack on the queen by the Londoners was to undermine seriously de Montfort's relationship with Louis IX, her brother-in-law.

Inevitably, the contradictions and divisions within de Montfort's movement created the political space for Henry to begin again to revive his own position. Initially de Montfort was able successfully to stymie his attempts to do so: when Henry appealed to Louis IX to intervene, de Montfort prevented him from leaving the country to meet his counterpart across the Channel. Instead it was de Montfort himself who travelled to France and persuaded Louis to support both the Provisions and government by natives, not aliens. But delay was all de Montfort could achieve, and work on the royalist side went on. In Parliament in October 1263, with the French king's support, Henry appealed for justice for those who had had their lands seized in the recent conflict. Meanwhile, Edward achieved a crucial settlement with his former household men, detaching them from the rebel cause. This robbed de Montfort of significant force in the Welsh Marches, and arguably the mainstay of his military strength, and followed on from the departure from England of Edward's unpopular foreign mercenaries. Henry himself worked hard to woo the young earl of Gloucester, to whom de Montfort had not yet restored the castles Henry had previously given to the earl's mother as part of her dower. For his part, Gloucester wanted his inheritance in full, and he probably did not much care who granted it.

By November, Henry had joined Edward in Windsor, where they had gathered together a large military force, and it was not long before it was Henry who controlled appointments to the major offices of state. At the same time, recognising his vulnerability in the localities, he sent out commands that restored the pre-eminence of his sheriffs over the baronial keepers of the peace. While he was not able to regain Dover, he did manage to instate Edward's friend Roger Leyburn as Warden of the Cinque Ports, and thereby manage to reclaim a degree of control on the south coast. For de Montfort, trapped outside London by a group of royalists who had blockaded the London Bridge gates, the situation looked dire. Nonetheless, he refused to surrender to what he called 'perjurers and apostates'. His allies in London, rushing to his rescue, managed to bring down the gates of the bridge, enabling Montfort to craft a slick escape into the city of London. Without a moment to spare, he had avoided capture.

But while de Montfort had not been taken and he seems to have retained the support of a substantial group of bishops, he had lost the initiative:

most of the lay magnates now sided with Henry, passively at least. De Montfort had no choice but to agree to submit his differences alongside Henry's to the French king for arbitration, and watch as the king engaged in the promotion and restoration of his own authority. In a bid for wider support, Henry signalled that he would honour his oath at Oxford in 1258 and uphold rights and liberties. As insurance he appointed royalist keepers of the peace across the country, though even when he seemed to be in the ascendancy he was careful to avoid Montfortian strongholds in the Midlands and eastern England. He had to tread carefully: recent months had shown how quickly the political sands could shift. For the time being the advantage remained with the king, but it would take very little for that to change.

The events of late 1263 were followed by the greatest body blow for de Montfort when Louis IX delivered his verdict on the reformers' and Henry's case in January 1264 in the so-called Mise of Amiens. He condemned the Provisions of Oxford and argued that Henry should be restored to full control, an outcome that de Montfort could not accept. It was a verdict that de Montfort might have influenced, given his relationship with Louis IX, but bad luck meant the earl had been left unable to travel to Amiens to plead the baronial case by a broken leg caused by a fall from his horse. The case that went before Louis had strengths: the barons had talked about Magna Carta, the failure of Henry to fulfil his crusading vow to the Holy Land (an element of the plea that was no doubt intended to appeal to Louis's own deeply pious crusading commitment) and Henry's preference for greedy and alien courtiers, as well as his bad faith in recent months. But it lacked the personal charisma and credibility of de Montfort to present it. Henry, in France in person, was able to press his own case unopposed.

If Henry had been anticipating that the verdict would immediately restore him to full power, though, he was to be disappointed. Some of de Montfort's support was entrenched, and Louis's verdict was immediately and roundly rejected by the Londoners and the men of the Cinque Ports, among others. A Mise that had aimed to settle the political conflict in England for good had simply succeeded in stoking the fires of rebellion and the scene was set for a resumption of armed conflict. The rebels' tactics were the same as earlier: they allied with Llywelyn to undermine the position of the Marcher royalists. This time, though, in Henry's absence Edward showed his mettle as a commander, capturing two of Humphrey Bohun's castles, as well as the castle of Gloucester and the town of Worcester. But the war was far from won. The rebel stranglehold on the coast of Kent prevented the king from entering England at Dover on his return from France, and Henry had to divert. Nonetheless he was able to raise a strong force, which he took to Oxford ready for further conflict. De Montfort meanwhile was boosted by the sudden defection to the rebels of the earl of Gloucester, who had remained largely neutral in recent months, but had never trusted Henry and may have been concerned that the king would threaten his own position should he prevail in the coming war. Yet even despite this defection, de Montfort clearly thought a royalist victory was imminent and offered to make a settlement with Henry – the rebels would accept the Mise of Amiens, he said, so long as Henry removed all foreigners serving in his government from England.

The king was not of a mind to compromise; like de Montfort, he thought he would emerge victorious. The early events of the next few months bore out that optimism. Despite the continuing loyalty of the Londoners to de Montfort, the royal army took Northampton, Leicester and Nottingham, while Edward moved to Derbyshire and Staffordshire to attack the lands of the rebel earl of Derby. Suddenly the word from London was that the city, too, would soon surrender, while in the meantime Henry besieged and received the submission of the earl of Gloucester's castle at Tonbridge. De Montfort again offered terms: first he asked Henry to promise to observe the Provisions, but agreed that a group that included bishops and others could arbitrate their terms. Regardless, he still wanted the removal of 'evil counsellors' from Henry's government and dwelt on the point of using natives in government. Finally, he offered £30,000 to compensate Henry for the spoliations that had occurred in recent months. It was in effect a capitulation. But, dissuaded from agreeing by the counsel of Edward and Richard of Cornwall, who could not be blamed if they felt confident of victory, Henry decided to fight on. In doing so, he made a costly mistake.

Winning the War and the Peace: The Battle of Lewes and Its Aftermath, 1264–5

Initially, Henry's decision to continue the fight left the Montfortians with only two choices: return to the king's side, or withdraw their homage and openly declare war on him. They opted for the latter, though it looked like an unwise gamble in the face of odds that were stacked heavily in Henry's favour. In May his forces reached Lewes in Sussex, where they planned to wait for the arrival of reinforcements, Henry at St Pancras Priory and Edward at Lewes Castle. Together their army, even without additional troops, was double the size of de Montfort's. At first, things seemed to go predictably the way of the royalists. Commanding the royal army's right wing and heavy cavalry, Edward charged the troops ranged opposite him, who included the baronial cavalry, which he outnumbered, and, behind them, a large number of mainly untrained Londoners. They quickly broke under his onslaught. But then he made a critical mistake: he decided to pursue the fleeing enemy for many miles. The consequent absence of the royalist cavalry from the main field of battle left Henry's infantry exposed, and they were pushed back towards Lewes by de Montfort's army attacking downhill. In the rout that followed, nearly three thousand royalist troops died, Richard of Cornwall was captured and Henry was forced to flee to the priory of St Pancras to seek refuge. After an interlude in which he sought the missing Henry at Lewes Castle, Edward rejoined him at the priory, but by this time the baronial forces had the king and his son surrounded and heavily outnumbered.

Despite his victory, de Montfort was reluctant to embark on a siege of the priory with the king and his son inside. He knew how bad that would look politically and how much support it would lose him; it would in all likelihood be seen as nothing other than a bid for the throne. A negotiated settlement was the only course of action if the king and his son, safely in the priory, were to be induced to surrender. The truce, the so-called Mise of Lewes, that followed was therefore to some extent a compromise, despite de Montfort's victory in battle. It contained an agreement by Henry to pardon the rebels, to uphold the Provisions and to remove all English and foreign 'traitors' from the Council. But it also contained concessions to the king.

Arguably the most important of these was the freeing of his Marcher supporters who had joined him in St Pancras Priory. Two groups of arbitrators were also to be appointed. One of these, comprising four English bishops or nobles, was to consider acceptable amendments to the Provisions. If they could not agree, the matter was to be submitted to Charles of Anjou and the duke of Burgundy. The purpose of the other group, comprising mostly French nobles and bishops, is less clear, though the chroniclers who commented seem to have thought that its task was to determine what action should be taken to address the question of the state of the kingdom. It was perhaps also expected to conclude a permanent peace settlement between the rebels and the king. The appeal throughout to French arbitrators may at the same time have been connected with a desire to supersede the Mise of Amiens and secure acceptance for whatever status quo emerged. In the meantime, Edward, Richard of Cornwall and his son Henry of Almain were to remain hostages as a guarantee of the Mise of Lewes, though the king himself was given a semblance of freedom.

De Montfort's victory at Lewes was like that of David over Goliath, according to a famous poem, the *Song of Lewes*, written by a member of the household of Stephen Berksted, the bishop of Chichester and a Montfortian, shortly after the battle. It was also a matter of God's judgement. The author denounced Henry's autocracy and his foreign favourites, while celebrating the common good that he argued had triumphed, with God's vindication, at Lewes. De Montfort was celebrated as a bringer of peace and justice to England. But despite the idealism of the song, in reality the victory at Lewes settled nothing, because the king had plainly and repeatedly shown that he would never consent to the sorts of restrictions that had been imposed on him in 1258. All de Montfort could do to maintain his control of government was to make the king effectively a prisoner, while somehow sustaining unity among the reforming party. He began by attempting to build a wider base of support for his regime by calling a Parliament in June which included representatives from the knights of the counties and the burgesses from the towns. In that Parliament he followed the Mise of Lewes with an ordinance for the governance of the realm, which was to remain in place until the Mise had been confirmed or replaced with other arrangements by the arbitrators. The Ordinance provided for royal councillors to be chosen on the king's behalf, and appointments of the most senior officers such as the chancellor, justiciar and treasurer were placed in the councillors' hands. This set of changes to the operation of government echoed and even went beyond the Provisions of Oxford of 1258. Reports by the Merton chronicler were that Henry only agreed to the Ordinance when he was offered the alternative of deposition and the perpetual imprisonment of the Lord Edward. In a step well beyond anything that would have been considered constitutionally acceptable, the threat was furthermore that Henry's successor would be elected. To place these stipulations in context, one historian has likened de Montfort to the head of an emergency junta by the time Parliament closed at the end of June 1264.

It was not a sustainable position and things were already beginning to unravel. Despite orders to people to behave peaceably, together with the appointment of keepers of the peace in early June, the Montfortian regime quickly found itself associated with widespread disorder. As Parliament ended, the keepers of the peace themselves were accused by the government of not only being implicated in, but promoting disorder. The recently appointed, probably locally elected, new sheriffs were told to pursue them. Meanwhile, there remained dissenters to the new regime, which in itself must have accounted for a good deal of the prevailing disorder. It would take until December to secure the surrender of royalists in Nottingham Castle, and the queen was known to be in France trying to raise an invading army to free her husband. By early July the threat from the invasion force was so feared that de Montfort summoned the feudal host in the king's name, as well as whatever extra forces the leading lords could raise – he made sure that the queen's army was depicted in letters to the localities as a mass of aliens. The Marcher lords whom de Montfort had been forced to set free in the compromise after Lewes also continued to pose a threat and had already refused to attend Parliament. After this, the risk from them was thought to be so great that the first thing de Montfort and Gloucester did when Parliament closed was to pursue them, allying with the Welsh prince Llywelyn to seize lands and castles. A truce was made with the Marchers in late August at Montgomery, in which they agreed to hand over hostages to guarantee their good behaviour as well as the royal castles in their possession. But de Montfort was so pressed by the queen's invasion threat in south-east England that he could not tarry long enough to ensure that either hostages or castles were actually surrendered.

In the event, the invasion was delayed, probably deliberately, by Louis IX and the papal legate, who wanted instead to negotiate with the Montfortian regime, though what they thought they might achieve is unclear, given that Louis wanted nothing less than Henry's full restoration and the annulment of the Provisions. Summer 1264 saw several unsuccessful attempts to broker a diplomatic settlement, and so new terms known as the Peace of Canterbury were drawn up by the Montfortian party in the middle of August; these were designed to place Louis under more pressure to engage in arbitration, and envisaged Henry remaining under the control of the councillors not just for a few months or years, but until the end of his reign. The restrictions would even continue when Edward succeeded him. Constitutionally this placed de Montfort on very shaky ground, and the attempt to force Louis's hand backfired badly. When the French king heard of it, he was said to have been outraged: he would rather 'break clods behind a plough than have this sort of kingly rule', he said.

By September, it was clear that the proposals would never be accepted in France, placing the Montfortians in an increasingly difficult position. A further complicating factor was the arrival of the papal legate in France in person. He, like Louis IX, was inclined to take the king's side, and insisted on a direct role in proceedings. While de Montfort's loyal party of English bishops attempted to mollify the papal legate, and promised that they did not believe the king's power had been drained by the actions the Montfortians had already taken, divisions were developing in the reform movement about what to do next. Initially, less radical and more compromising minds prevailed, and new proposals were taken to France in early September. These would see the appointment of four arbitrators to reconsider the Peace of Canterbury. But de Montfort, who still took a more extreme position, was within a fortnight able to manoeuvre to secure the rapid jettisoning of these proposals. They were replaced with a set of would-be peace terms that were much closer to the more radical proposals that had been put forward in July and which retained a great deal of power for the Council as opposed to the king, though they now reflected the need for the incorporation of the papal legate by giving him the potential to play the role of umpire.

A group of bishops took the proposals across the Channel to the legate at Boulogne. However, he was unsatisfied and demanded amendments to them, which included a greater scope for him to have the casting vote among the arbitrators, and removed the stipulation that royal councillors would advise the king on appointments as well as the need for officials outside the Council to be Englishmen. Perhaps critically, amendments failed to mention a return to the original Peace of Canterbury if the arbitration did not succeed, a move that cannot have been acceptable to de Montfort. The legate sent the bishops back to England, threatening excommunication of the baronial party if they did not accept the changed terms. The Montfortians played for time, but they were dealing with a determined opponent. Eventually, with no agreement forthcoming, the legate demanded both that he should be the main arbitrator and that the barons agree to these terms within fifteen days, or the bulls of excommunication that he had brought with him from the pope would be published. The barons refused to concede.

The Montfortian party now found itself still facing the threat of invasion and at what seemed to be a dead end in the diplomatic negotiations. Defiance would not secure the regime; some concessions would have to be made if the invasion was to be avoided. So, in desperation, while they were still in France, the bishops of Worcester and of London, who had been representing the Montfortians in negotiations, made a deal to free the Lord Edward in return for the cancellation of the invasion. Back home the resolve of others too began to wane; a number of lay magnates, including Gilbert de Clare, who was fearful of the threat of invasion from Flanders, started to waver, and the Montfortian 'royal' host began to face desertions in Kent. In the short term, enough people stood by de Montfort, who himself stood fast and refused to compromise, to enable him to hold the line into the autumn at least. He was also saved by two other developments: first, as autumn turned to winter, the queen's funds ran out and the much-vaunted invasion army dissolved. And second, the death of Pope Urban IV on 2 October led to the end of the determined papal legate's term of office. With a new pope might come a fresh start to negotiations; de Montfort could hope.

In the event, the reprieve created by the situation on the Continent was not to last because threats emerged elsewhere: in October the Marcher lords were boosted by a large group of knights from the Lord Edward's household and began their own campaign, besieging the earl of Gloucester's castle of Hanley in Worcestershire, and occupying Bristol. They took back the royal castles at Marlborough, Bridgnorth and Gloucester. An attempt was also made, probably at the queen's prompting, to rescue Edward from captivity in the castle of Wallingford in Surrey. The political sands were shifting once more. The Montfortians reacted decisively, moving Edward, his uncle Richard of Cornwall and Cornwall's son Henry of Almain to more secure custody at Kenilworth Castle, which lay in committed reformer territory. They then summoned the feudal host to Northampton to attack the Marchers, helped by Llywelyn, who moved against them from the west. It was an extraordinary situation: the feudal host for the defence of England was in alliance with the prince of Wales against the king's own subjects. It was too much for the Marchers and Edward's knights to resist, and by the middle of December they had submitted. But the inflamed political atmosphere and the uncertainty of the Montfortian position is revealed by the compromise the baronial party made, even in victory: if the Marchers would agree to go to Ireland for a year and a day and surrender their own and Edward's lands to Montfort's custody, Edward himself would be released. This was a dangerous gamble: de Montfort must have been very worried about a continuing rebellion to agree to Edward's freedom, because he must at the same time have known that releasing him itself brought a serious risk to the security of his regime.

Royalist Revanche, 1265–7

In the end, though, the decisive crisis that was ultimately to befall the Montfortian government was in significant part brought about by de Montfort himself. Throughout his career, the earl had always kept a close eye on his own interests, and in the years after 1258 his own affairs had already more than once been in tension with his reforming ideals and his allies. This was again the case late in 1264 when Gilbert de Clare complained angrily about his behaviour. Having prevailed over the Marchers and with the threats of invasion and the pope's censure having both dissipated, de Montfort had quickly moved to restart investigations into his wife's grievances in relation to her dowry. This came at the same time as he and his sons were benefiting hugely in material terms from the raft of confiscations of land and ransoms that flowed in following their victory against the Marchers in the autumn. As escheator north of the Trent, responsible for upholding the king's feudal rights, Henry de Montfort was able to benefit from the surrender of defeated royalists' lands after the battle of Lewes, though the records give few insights into exactly what he kept for himself. At the same time, the vast estates of Richard of Cornwall in Devon and Cornwall were surrendered to the Montfortian regime, and given in custody to another of Earl Simon's sons, Guy. It seems that Simon's own gains were so great that during this period he could afford to amass a military household that exceeded even the king's in size, and a fortune in cash: at his death his wife took with her to France eleven thousand marks. In late 1264 and 1265 the de Montfort family was awash with money, but in fact the defensive words of the *Song of Lewes* suggest that this self-aggrandisement (and de Montfort's favouritism towards his own family) had been raising questions even as early as June 1264 in the immediate aftermath of the victory.

In Parliament between January and March 1265, de Montfort tried to keep the focus on two things: first the terms of Edward's release from captivity, and second shoring up knightly support for the regime by continuing to address their grievances. One element of the latter was the issue of a summons for two knights from each county and two burgesses from every borough to give their voice to proceedings and to raise their grievances. This was a significant step and echoed the innovation by Henry III's regents in 1254 when they were attempting to gain approval for taxation during the king's absence in France. The decision to summon elected representatives followed on from a change of sheriffs in summer 1264 and the renewed publication of the Provisions in December. De Montfort had at all costs to maintain the local base of support for his regime. As part of the terms for Edward's release it was also required that all officials, whether serving the king or lords, agree to obey the Provisions. Those terms were otherwise punishing for the king's son: he was to give five royal castles to de Montfort as guarantee for his own behaviour and he lost many of his most important lands: once more de Montfort himself benefited disproportionately from this, receiving Chester and the Peak in perpetuity. The earl must surely have known Edward would never accept such humiliation in the long term, but he pressed on regardless, perhaps hoping that Edward would be so hobbled as no longer to be able to pose any real threat to the regime. If that was the hope, it was to prove futile.

For all de Montfort's efforts to shore up the support of his base, this Parliament at the same time acted as a forum for division and complaints about the extent to which de Montfort and his sons were benefiting from their position. These proved a significant distraction, and while they did not cost de Montfort large numbers of supporters, they did result in the loss of some vital allies, including the earl of Gloucester and the Marcher lord John Giffard. Under the guise of concern about Llywelyn's attacks on his lands, the former departed for the Marches in February. De Montfort was left with a rump of knightly support, but that of only a small number of magnates. By April Gloucester was accusing him of failing to abide by the Provisions and the Mise of Lewes – of essentially establishing an autocracy.

Sensing another rebellion in the Marches led by the disaffected Gloucester, de Montfort took the precaution of taking Henry and Edward with him as he proceeded west with his army. Although he and Gloucester went on to make a settlement in the middle of May, multiple fires were breaking out elsewhere, with John de Warenne, earl of Surrey, and William de Valence arriving in Pembrokeshire by sea with their own forces. Two weeks later Edward escaped with the help of Gilbert de Clare's brother Thomas, an ally of the prince over many years. The earl himself returned to the royalist side to join a powerful coalition of Edward and the Marchers. The revanche had begun. Soon lands and castles across Cheshire, Shropshire, Gloucestershire and Worcestershire were taken by the royalists, and the base of conflict had been successfully moved away from the heartlands of de Montfort's support in the Midlands and London. The earl found himself isolated beyond the River Severn. He desperately needed to get back across the river to link up with supporting forces, but the bridges had been destroyed and he had no choice other than to attempt to cross by boat near Bristol, with Llywelyn covering his retreat. Anticipating this move, Edward and Gloucester went ahead of him and destroyed the ships that had been meant to carry him to safety. While de Montfort retreated to Hereford to regroup, the two men advanced on his son at Kenilworth, who had foolishly not taken cover in the castle, and it was quickly taken.

De Montfort had no choice but to try to fight his way out of the crisis. He had at least some reason to be confident: his skill as a commander at Lewes had told against the might of the royalist forces. Edward, though, had different ideas. He had been humiliated at Lewes, and he was determined that there would be no repeat: catching de Montfort by surprise at Evesham with forces that outnumbered those of the earl, he secured an easy win. This time, no chances were taken with the peace either: de Montfort had been a powerful and charismatic leader for the movement, and had almost single-handedly held it together at times since 1258, despite his own mixed agenda and his frequent absences in France. He was a vital figurehead. If the king was to prevail permanently this time, there was no alternative but to remove the earl permanently from the political scene. De Montfort was cornered by Roger Mortimer and stabbed in the neck with a lance. Then, treated as a traitor, his body was dismembered, his feet, hands and testicles removed, and his head placed on a spear. De Montfort would never again humiliate the king.

Victory over the rebels at Evesham might have been followed by attempts to heal the divisions of recent years, but instead it inaugurated a bloody settlement that prolonged the conflict unnecessarily. While the rebels immediately released prisoners they had held since the battle of Lewes in a gesture of good faith, a royalist campaign of looting and temporary occupation of rebel lands was their reward. The campaign was so extensive across the country that within only weeks of the battle, more than a thousand estates and properties had been confiscated or looted by royalists. The resentment this generated was intense and bitter, creating the potential for serious unrest.

Even so, Henry was not inclined towards clemency. When Parliament convened at Winchester in September he secured approval for what amounted to the effective disinheritance of Montfort's supporters. Afterwards, still ignoring the pleas of some of the loyalists and even the recently arrived papal legate for a more conciliatory approach, he went on to redistribute the confiscated lands and estates to royalists. This itself was done unevenly, the lands of more than three hundred rebels being given to only around 130 people, with a smaller group including the royal family, household knights and royal officials benefiting disproportionately. Edmund, the king's second son, secured both de Montfort's lands and those of Nicholas de Segrave, another Midlands magnate and rebel; when he also received the earl of Derby's lands in 1266, his endowment amounted to a huge collection of estates. The way in which estates were distributed inevitably gave rise to yet more grievances and unrest. News at the same time that Henry was intending an attack on London, which had been a Montfortian stronghold, was met with consternation and fear. Desperate appeals were made by the mayor and other prominent citizens for clemency, but to no effect: Henry's forces attacked London, first confiscating and then redistributing property. A pardon for the Londoners was only forthcoming in January 1266 in return for a huge fine amounting to £13,000.

As the new year began, London may have been brought to heel, but problems of unrest and disorder generated by the civil war and the punitive settlement showed no sign of abating, and every indication of worsening. Having already had to take his forces to Lincolnshire to deal with a rebel stronghold there, Edward was soon forced to campaign against the Cinque Ports, which were refusing to capitulate. From there, a peace having been concluded in May, he had to proceed to Hampshire, where more rebels were defeated and the leader placed in custody at Windsor Castle with the earl of Derby, whose own forces had recently been subdued by Henry of Almain. The most intransigent opposition, though, was at the Montfortian stronghold of Kenilworth Castle, which the king was forced to besiege in June 1266. Those in the castle were determined to hold out, and their fortitude provoked a siege that lasted many months and necessitated the use of forces recruited from ten counties. The besieged even taunted their opponents. By the summer they, and another similarly determined group of rebels in the Isle of Ely, were showing no signs of surrendering.

It was clear that something needed to be done to promote harmony if the realm was to be able to move forward from the discord of the previous seven years. Moreover, the king could not afford to find himself engaged in protracted military conflict with his own subjects if he was ever going to be able to govern effectively. In August 1266 Henry was finally persuaded of this and agreed to the appointment of a committee comprising a mixture of bishops and lay nobles 'to provide for the state of the realm especially in the matter of the disinherited'. With the help of the papal legate and the king's nephew Henry of Almain, the committee proceeded, in the so-called Dictum of Kenilworth, to make a vital compromise: those who had taken the rebel side were to be permitted to reclaim their lands after paying fines. When it proved difficult for many rebels to raise the sums demanded without possession of their estates, income from which would ultimately provide the means to pay their fines, a further concession was given that they could resume possession of the lands before the fines were paid. It was an important step forward, but even so, it did not go far enough: rebels had to buy back their lands at a price that depended on the scale of their offences, and that left leading rebels owing huge sums of money. There was consequently little incentive for them to make peace, and pockets of resistance continued. The defiant rebel garrison continued to hold out at Kenilworth, though they only managed to do this until December, when, in danger of freezing to death and having run out of food, they finally surrendered.

There were also problems among royalists: those who had drafted the Dictum had warned Henry that he would need to make provision for people who would end up feeling that they had not benefited fairly from the redemption fines paid by the rebels. The committee's fear was serious: they added 'lest an occasion for a new war should arise' to the warning to indicate the risk they felt the king was running. But it went without heed by Henry, and this generated a further, unnecessary crisis. One of those who had received very little from the settlement, despite his instrumental role in the defeat of de Montfort, was Gilbert de Clare, earl of Gloucester. The earl had also been key to the confiscation of rebel lands in the immediate aftermath of the battle of Evesham, and had every reason to expect significant rewards for his efforts. That did not happen. Instead, Clare saw his rival in the March of Wales, Roger Mortimer, receive much more than he did, while Clare himself also remained locked in dispute with the king over the dower lands previously granted to his mother, which he had still not been able to reclaim. With his immense landed assets and his record of being critical to the success of whichever side he supported in the civil war, it was a mistake to alienate Gilbert de Clare so casually. In April 1267, he marched on London, where he joined forces with the Londoners. At the same time, he became the champion of the disinherited rebels who had still not been able to regain their lands from those to whom they had been granted after Evesham. He had succeeded in allying two powerful groups with his own private cause.

Gloucester's occupation of London was of a different order of magnitude from most of the risings to date, and required a much more serious response from the king. It would have been foolish to attack London, given the resources taken up by the siege of the much smaller Kenilworth, though it seems the Lord Edward briefly considered doing so before realising this. Compromise was the only way forward, and Gloucester's rebellion was the only one strong enough to force the king's hand. Finally recognising this, Henry sent Richard of Cornwall and Henry of Almain, together with Philip Basset, a rebel-turned-royalist and member of Edward's household, to negotiate. Both sides also came under pressure from the papal legate, who had himself taken refuge in the Tower of London, to reach a settlement. The solution was simple, as it had been throughout: Henry had to conciliate the rebels and hear Gloucester's grievances. The first of those things was achieved by improving the terms of the original Dictum of Kenilworth. On the advice of his negotiators, Henry finally conceded that he would 'ask diligently' those who held the lands of rebels 'by his gift to restore seisin of them to the said disinherited, on sufficient security for the ransom of the same'. Where this involved clergy, the papal legate promised them financial assistance in paying their redemption fines. Where Gloucester himself was concerned, with the legate's assistance, he was persuaded to submit his grievances to papal arbitration. In return he promised not to oppose the king again, pledging a sum of ten thousand marks as security for that oath.

After this, the attitude of the government became more moderate and flexible. In the end most rebels recovered their lands, and while many still had to pay a lot to do so, the situation gradually settled down. Three further things probably contributed to the calming of the situation. First, the special eyre, which toured the country between 1267 and 1272 and addressed the accusations against those who were arguing that they had not been rebels, was lenient and flexible in its verdicts. The second critical factor in the establishment of a more peaceful climate was the Lord Edward's willingness to make peace and not to bear grudges against rebels. Several men who had been rebels went on to become senior officials when he became king, and he showed every sign of that attitude in the late 1260s (often in contrast to his father). Finally, the creation of the Statute of Marlborough in Parliament in Michaelmas 1267 resurrected many of the Provisions of Westminster of 1259 which had grown out of knightly grievances, demonstrating that the 'bachelors of the community of the realm' had not been forgotten. In its preamble, the statute explicitly stated its aim of bringing peace to the realm. 'The lord king', it said, wanted to make 'provision for the amelioration of his kingdom of England', which had 'recently been brought low by many tribulations and the inconveniences of dissensions, [and] requires a reform of laws and rights by which the peace and tranquillity of the inhabitants might be preserved, for which it was necessary that a salutary remedy be provided by the same king and his faithful subjects.' Its terms were to be followed, it said, by all of Henry's subjects, 'both great men and lesser, firmly and inviolably for all time'.

It would be a mistake to imagine that these measures brought complete peace to England in the late 1260s – one reason why Henry did not depart on crusade to the Holy Land with Edward in 1270 was because his advisers considered 'it neither expedient nor safe that both of us should leave the kingdom'. But the situation was by no means as threatening as it had been just three years earlier. And in due course, Edward was to accede to the throne with no challenge. Even in 1270 Henry was able to secure a grant of taxation to support the costs of his son's crusade. As in 1215, however, the world had changed: the negotiations for the tax of 1270 took two years, and involved several Parliaments to which elected knights and, on one occasion, burgesses were called as well. They demanded a familiar act of good faith in return for the grant: the confirmation of Magna Carta, the now well-established talisman of English politics.

Henry III had triumphed. But the drawn-out civil conflict and the events of the previous nine years had left the king a shadow of his former self. He had never intended to be shackled by controls on his freedom to govern and he had prevailed in that sense, but he had had to accept and begin to address the serious grievances the men of the localities in particular had raised. And his great European ambitions had been extensively moderated. The remaining years of his reign were played out in a calmer and quieter tone than the preceding ones, with the elderly king no longer embarking on any major foreign policy commitments to provoke his subjects. There is some evidence that the Lord Edward took an increasing degree of governmental control once the civil war was over, with Henry's blessing, or at least with his permission. The Winchester Annals tell us that Edward was made steward of England in 1268, and that he was given custody of London and all royal castles in England at Christmas in the same year. While the annalist seems to have been mistaken about the stewardship (it was in fact given to the king's second son, Edmund, in May 1269, which was in keeping with tradition), Edward was granted the custody of London in 1269 and of a number of counties in 1268–9. As well as acting on the royal Council, there is indirect evidence that he was responsible for appointments of sheriffs in the late 1260s, and the Statute of Marlborough had, as we will see, all the hallmarks of Edwardian attitudes rather than Henrician ones.

In the main, the quieter years of the late 1260s were spent making preparations for Edward's departure for the East. There the plan was for him to join Louis IX and the crusader army he had taken with him to launch an attack on Egypt. In the event the army had been diverted to Tunis, where Louis had died, but once he arrived, Edward pressed on from there to Tripoli and Acre, soon to be joined by his brother Edmund. When he left England in 1270, Edward made careful provision for the appointment of many of his associates to sheriffdoms to ensure that should Henry III die while he was away, the localities would remain well governed and any vestigial rebellion would have no chance to break out, a risk that was by this point small. England was finally rediscovering peace.

State Growth and Holding the King to Account, 1216–72

In November 1272, Henry III died aged sixty-five. His death brought an end to one of the longest reigns in English history. Across his adult years, the personal failings of the king himself were at the heart of all the crises that took place in England. And his failings had a very significant effect on his subjects because of the power and reach of the king. Unlike John, however, it was the relative weakness of Henry's personality and his lack of intelligence and judgement, not paranoia and wilful volatility, that created many problems. This gave rise to a susceptibility to the influence of men who benefited unduly from the king's favour, and sometimes treated others with contempt, both of which generated personal discord and antipathy among the king's subjects. While Henry had plenty of ideas of his own, which were often ambitious, even grandiose, he gave these men, often outsiders to the English political scene, his ear and his favour, and failed to consult and take the advice of a wider group encompassing those who were best qualified to assist him. Like John, then, Henry failed to build relationships with a broad spectrum of leaders and representatives of the embryonic political community. Instead he frequently surrounded himself with a series of narrow and poorly chosen cabals.

Not a king to give battle – he did not even much like tournaments – Henry nonetheless harboured dreams of being remembered as one of Europe's most important rulers, and a critical backdrop to this was a degree of rivalry for status with Louis IX of France. His grandiose ambitions were coupled with a lack of military prowess and a failure to locate his own priorities within the wider context of the situation at home, and to make the necessary adjustments as a result. This created financial burdens that had to be borne by his subjects across the land. And yet here was a king committed to protecting the well-being of the poor, to the religious crusading ideal, even to the principles enshrined in Magna Carta, none of which was dissimulation; he, like Louis IX, genuinely believed in these things. He simply did not understand how some of what he did could counteract this commitment. He wanted everyone to abide by Magna Carta, yet his favourites and some of the magnates were repeatedly allowed to ignore it. He agreed to protect property rights, yet he could not see how for his subjects that included all property, including money, not just the areas covered by the strict letter of the Charter. This meant that he made critical political miscalculations, and his doing so reinforces an important *sine qua non* of good governance: policy should never be created in a vacuum; consultation is critical.

Henry's failure to achieve his grandiose ambitions meant that he lost the political momentum on several occasions and political space opened up for opposition to be expressed. It was the magnates, lay and ecclesiastical, who were most affected by Henry's policies in the first twenty years of his adult reign, and who were most vociferous. But in the late 1240s and 1250s when Parliament refused him tax, a lesser group of the king's subjects found themselves increasingly subjected to Henry's desperate and arbitrary financial exactions, and they began to make their discontented voice heard. This was the crucial backdrop to the crisis of 1258. The knights who in that year and thereafter demanded fair treatment by the royal government (and, ironically, by the magnates too) were the lineal heirs of the 1215 rebels, on whom the message of Magna Carta had not been lost. And the opposition of 1258 onwards came to eclipse anything John had encountered because of the number of people affected: Henry had expanded the active political community by making so many more of his subjects pay for his policies without securing their consent, and as a result the crisis he faced in 1258 was the century's most broadly based yet.

The ensuing civil war was bloody and bitter. As is so often the case in political crises, the situation quickly became muddied by personal enmities and rivalries, sight was lost at times of the principles that had been so strongly expressed in 1258, and faction played a major part, as did the king's own displays of bad faith and de Montfort's personal ambition. But that did not stop principles from becoming established, even in spite of the eventual royalist triumph in 1265. As in 1215, the fact that war had broken out when the king refused to compromise signalled in itself a changed world order. The king could of course continue to do as he wished thereafter, but if he wanted to be *successful*, in other words in this context to avoid political crisis, he had to acknowledge and embrace a new way of governing, one that involved the representation and consultation of his subjects both in general, and specifically when taxation was required. He needed to do so via the Council and in the nascent forum that had evolved during the reign: Parliament. This was broadly to be the achievement of Edward I.

EDWARD I, 1272-1307

'A Politic and Warlike King'

A Political Apprenticeship, 1254-72

In November 1272, when Henry III died, Edward was thirty-three years old, with considerable governmental and military experience under his belt. It is hard to imagine a more different accession from that of his father fifty-six years earlier. Unlike the child-king Henry, Edward's age meant that his personality was formed and known, and he had had plenty of time to frame his vision for royal rule.

Edward had emerged into politics properly in 1254. In that year, following a threat by Castile to invade Gascony, a diplomatic settlement was made with King Alfonso X of Castile that saw Edward, then fifteen years old, married to Alfonso's thirteen-year-old sister Eleanor. From then on the couple were rarely apart, even when Edward was on crusade in the early 1270s, and their marriage went on to produce no fewer than sixteen children. In line with her brother Alfonso's wishes, a landed settlement was made for Edward and Eleanor in 1254 that saw the young prince receive Gascony, Ireland and the earldom of Chester from his father, alongside lands in Wales and the towns of Grantham, Stamford and Bristol. Almost from the outset, as Edward asserted his independence, there were differences of opinion between him and his father over the governance of Gascony in particular. It also rapidly became clear that the finances with which the young prince had been provided were wholly insufficient, particularly when Llywelyn ap Gruffudd led a rebellion in Wales in 1256. In dealing with this, Edward received little support from Henry, and was heavily defeated by Llywelyn in 1257. While Henry did then raise the feudal host to assist him, the resulting campaign, led by Henry himself, was a shambles, with the king forced to retreat as a result of inadequate victualling arrangements for the host. In its aftermath, Edward decided that there was no choice but to plan his own campaign and turned to his Lusignan relatives for financial support. Those plans were quickly overshadowed, though, by the much bigger crisis that enveloped England from 1258.

Edward's behaviour between 1258 and 1267 has often been cast in a negative light. The author of the *Song of Lewes*, written in 1264, accused him of 'inconstancy and changeableness' like a leopard, while one twentieth-century historian described Edward as 'an irresponsible, arrogant and headstrong boy, treacherously selfish . . . incapable of self-discipline'. It is true that Edward changed sides more than once during the period, but it is also the case that there may have been good reasons for much of his behaviour. At the outset of the crisis, he may have made the judgement that it essentially constituted a factional attack upon Henry III's Lusignan relatives, to whom Edward had recently become close and who had helped him financially in dealing with Welsh revolt. In Parliament in early 1258 one of them, William de Valence, had even argued that the other English lords had been lacklustre in their prosecution of the recent campaign. This, and loyalty to his father, may explain Edward's initial reluctance to swear to uphold the Provisions of Oxford in summer 1258. Whatever the case, he soon changed tack: by October, he had willingly accepted the Provisions, and in 1261, when Henry regained control of government, Edward would not allow his own oath to uphold them to be annulled. At the very least he seems quite quickly to have come to understand the deeper principles to which many reformers were committed: in autumn 1259 he wrote that he was ready to die on behalf of the community of the realm and the common good.

Following the exile of the Lusignans, Edward seems to have accepted that it was futile to oppose the reforming earls. But he also entered into a formal alliance with Richard, earl of Gloucester in March 1259, which seems to indicate active rather than passive support. This too is relatively easy to explain. Gloucester was one of those tasked with creating a peace treaty with the French king and was shortly to begin negotiations. With Edward's extensive lands in Gascony, the prince would naturally have been well advised to keep close to the earl. The rapidly shifting political positioning in this period of crisis is demonstrated by a further alliance, in autumn the same year, struck between Edward and his uncle, Simon de Montfort, another of the negotiators, who would play a more senior role in the negotiations than Gloucester. Since Montfort had by now argued with Gloucester, it was impossible for Edward to steer a course between them, and the earlier alliance was abandoned. These events alone show how difficult it must have been for Edward to know which horses to back in order to preserve his own and the Crown's landed interests in France; his actions were arguably less the 'heedless pursuit of his own ends' and more a demonstration of an understanding of realpolitik and political pragmatism.

During late 1259 and early 1260, Edward was damaged by further rumours that he was planning to unseat his father from the throne while the latter was in France negotiating the peace treaty. It is impossible to know if the rumours had foundation; Edward was certainly strongly opposed to the peace negotiations that Henry was engaged in, and at the very least had been attempting to hold a Parliament during his father's absence. So relations between father and son were clearly tense, which is not a surprise given Edward's opposition to the peace negotiations and his concerns about his own lands. But the rumours of deposition were spread by the earl of Gloucester, by now Edward's enemy, and it is not hard to imagine that they were scurrilous, possibly deliberately fashioned to try to bring about a breakdown in relations between father and son. If that were the case, Gloucester was to be disappointed, as Edward and Henry were quickly reconciled – though it seems that Henry's trust in his son to provide him with unquestioning support was at least dented. Despite the reconciliation, it was decided that it would be for the best to remove Edward from England, at least for the time being, and he was sent to the Continent to build his military skills in a series of tournaments.

Henry's worries that Edward would not simply toe the line were not without foundation: on his return early in 1261, the prince re-formed his alliance with de Montfort. Possibly under duress (Edward's household would be subjected to a major purge by the king and queen), he seems to have been persuaded out of this by Henry, and left England again to travel to Gascony. He was back briefly in 1262, but it was only in early 1263, at roughly the same time as de Montfort, that Edward properly returned from the Continent. At that point the objectives of the two men diverged. Edward gave his immediate attention to Llywelyn ap Gruffudd's rebellion in Wales. Llywelyn, who had taken full advantage of the disorder in

England, had just overrun the middle March, and Edward was quick to lead a campaign against him in April. De Montfort, however, offered no support for his nephew, and instead launched his own attack on Henry III. From that point on, probably convinced that de Montfort had his sights on the Crown itself, and not forgiving him for his betrayal and willingness to see the English position in Wales destroyed, Edward never allied with de Montfort again. The prince went on to play an important part in Henry's ultimate victory in the civil war and restoration of royal authority, cutting his teeth in battles at Lewes in 1264 (where he lost, and learned the importance of proper battle discipline and communication), at Evesham in 1265 (where he joined forces with the new earl of Gloucester to defeat de Montfort's army) and at the siege of Kenilworth in 1266 (in which the remaining rebels were defeated). In the late 1260s the governmental control Edward seems to have achieved is a clear indication that the sands had shifted and that, in all probability, at least a degree of real power had been transferred to the prince several years before his father's death.

Before we embark on an exploration of his reign, what do we know of Edward as a person and as a political leader? His character, even from an early age, as the events of the years after 1254 testify, was notably formidable. Physically, he cut an imposing figure, being both very tall and long-limbed (he was famously called Longshanks in reference to his long legs). In addition, reports suggest that although he had a lisp he was a strong speaker. He was, crucially, known to be brave in battle, a king who gave real meaning to the phrase 'leading from the front': he was famously to fight at the battle of Falkirk in 1298 (aged fifty-eight) while suffering from broken ribs. Edward was not a man for opulence. Instead his tastes were relatively ascetic and his was not an extravagant court: he preferred ordinary clothes to purple or expensively dyed cloth. And his reputation for charitable giving surpassed even that of his father. Like Henry, he was deeply pious: during his reign he often touched individual subjects who came to him wanting to be cured of scrofula, or 'the king's evil'. Edward's commitment to crusading is also testimony to his piety: while it is true that such expressions were de rigueur for medieval kings, Edward, like his father, sacrificed much both to go on the expedition of 1270 and in plans to launch a repeat expedition in the late 1280s.

Edward was capable of great depth of feeling: his devotion to his wife Eleanor, for example, is well rehearsed. Following her death aged forty-nine in 1290, probably from a strain of malaria combined with congenital heart problems, he was to arrange for the building of an extensive and unprecedented series of monuments in her memory, the so-called Eleanor crosses. When his second wife, Margaret, fell ill with measles, he demanded regular updates from the royal physicians on how she was; and when her sister died, he instructed her confessor to break the news to Margaret gently, and to console and comfort her. There are numerous instances of Edward's warm relationships with staff in the royal household, and of strong and loyal bonds with the king on the part of nobles and senior advisers. The fact that he was a chess player suggests that he was of an intellectual mindset. Edward I had cultural interests too, actively promoting much architectural and artistic work.

He was not, though, a man to cross: he had a violent temper and did not forgive easily. The bill recorded in the Exchequer records for repairs to his daughter's coronet which Edward had damaged in a fit of rage testifies to this; and late in his reign his frustration with his feckless and incompetent son was so great that he physically assaulted the young Edward, tearing out his hair. It is possible to feel some sympathy with this: Edward senior was no doubt sorely tried by his son in the early 1300s, as the whole country would be after 1307. But while his fury with the future Edward II may be entirely understandable, in other instances Edward I's actions seem out of proportion: he famously banished Archbishop Winchelsey of Canterbury in 1305, an act of revenge for Winchelsey's leadership of opposition to the king's military plans and demands for taxation in the late 1290s. Moreover, at the wedding of one of his daughters, Edward beat a man so badly that he subsequently decided to pay compensation to his victim for the assault (the voluntary payment of compensation perhaps reflects well on him, but the original assault gives a measure of the king's temper).

For all his faults, Edward had the characteristics of a leader and soldier that Henry III had never displayed, and that was crucial. But it was going to take more than good leadership and military skills to bring true peace to England in 1272. Major fault lines had opened up across the thirteenth century between Edward's predecessors and their subjects. The rebellions and civil wars under King John and Henry III had established that there were a number of non-negotiable principles by which the king must now abide if he wished to remain at peace with his subjects. First, the rule of law was fundamental, and the king himself was now regarded as subject to it, and so he could not take the property of his subjects without due legal process, or alternatively their consent. He must therefore rule in concert with his subjects, not in spite of them. In 1272, it was by no means clear to his subjects that the new king would come voluntarily to accept this; despite his experience and early promise, he remained to some extent an unknown quantity.

The King in Command, 1272–94

Edward's subjects would have to wait some time for a resolution of the uncertainty they must have felt about their new ruler in November 1272. Edward was on his way back from crusade when his father died, and only learned of his passing when he arrived in Sicily. Still recovering from an assassination attempt while on crusade that had ended his campaign and left him badly wounded, he was in no position to rush home. Instead he took the opportunity to spend time with other European princes, allies who could be vital in the future, as he travelled – first in Italy, then in Savoy. Finally, Edward reached France, where he paid the necessary homage for Gascony to his French counterpart, the ignominious outcome of the Treaty of Paris of 1259 that Edward had so opposed. Only in summer 1273 could he begin to envisage his return to England. But further delay ensued when in August a rebellion suddenly erupted in Gascony. This forced him to divert to the duchy. It was therefore to be August 1274, nearly two years after his father's death, before he was able to cross back to Kent.

Edward's absence from England in these years has been much questioned. During that time, the situation was far from calm. Early in 1270, the archbishop of York wrote to the pope to say that he could not go to Rome because the country was still disturbed. He wrote to say that he remained worried a year later. Just after Henry III's death, concerns were raised about those who were promoting dissension in the realm, and Edward's swift return was requested. Meanwhile, the earl of Gloucester put down unrest in London, and beyond the capital, government documents suggest crime was an issue. Disputes between magnates were in some cases also creating their own violence and disorder. But with Edward unable to return quickly, those who were acting in his absence, who included his loyal cousin Edmund of Cornwall and his trusted adviser Robert Burnell, had to make the best of the situation. While it was clear that there was no significant threat to the king himself, there would be a lot to do when he took personal control of the reins of power.

The king's return to England was triumphant. He was entertained by both the earl of Gloucester and his long-standing friend Earl Warenne of Surrey on his way from Dover to London, and entered London with the atmosphere at fever pitch in anticipation of the first coronation since that of Edward's mother Queen Eleanor over thirty-five years earlier. For months, preparations had been under way for the ceremony itself and for the massive banquet that was to accompany it: Westminster Abbey, despite the extensive renovations that had taken place during his father's reign, needed some work in order to host the coronation, and over £1,000 was spent on it in preparation while orders were sent out across the realm for the huge variety of food that would be needed. It was deeply symbolic that Edward should be crowned in London, the civil war having prevented this for his father. As the day drew near, there were the usual disputes about precedence in the ceremony, perhaps inevitably between the archbishops of York and Canterbury, who did not get along. Less predictably, Edward's brother Edmund, who was denied the opportunity to carry the great sword, may even have boycotted the ceremony (though there is no evidence of any significant damage to the fraternal relationship afterwards). Yet despite all this, the ceremony was a triumph. As Edward swore his coronation oath, the realm delighted in its new king.

In the first half of Edward's reign, the hopes of his subjects for better governance and true consultation were realised in the most positive way. In fact, Edward's style of rule and his priorities differed so starkly from those of his father as to make him almost unrecognisable as Henry's son. As he reformed the realm, expanded the judicial system, developed and grew the role of counsel and Parliament, and his subjects' representation in it, completed the conquest of Wales and almost succeeded in launching a new crusade in the East, Edward set out his political agenda for the period. His kingship was characterised by deeply felt ideology, a level of ambition that was at least as impressive as the first great Angevin, Henry II, and a degree of energy and determination that was truly remarkable.

The reform movement of the late 1250s had provided a template for governance as the king's subjects wanted it. Few can have dared to hope for its implementation under a new king. But from the outset, Edward both promised much and delivered on his word, and in so doing followed the agenda of the movement almost to the letter. At the first Parliament of his reign in April 1275 he provided what can only be described as a manifesto for his rule based on his commitment to upholding the 'common good of the realm', directly echoing the Provisions of Oxford of 1258. To set out his ambitions Edward used a piece of legislation that became known as the Statute of Westminster I. In it, he stated that 'he had great zeal and desire to redress the state of the realm', because his subjects had been less well treated 'than they ought to be', 'the peace less kept . . . the laws less used . . . and offenders less punished than they ought to be'. The fifty-one clauses of the statute went on to detail reforms of local administration and new punishments for corrupt officials, as well as for lords who committed abuses of their authority. New arrangements were also put in place for dealing with disorder. These were all things demanded in 1258.

To witness the statute and to ensure it would be proclaimed far and wide in the localities, Edward invited to Parliament a bigger group of people than ever before – four knights from each county (normally there were only two), and between four and six burgesses from all the cities, boroughs, markets and towns. These two groups alone probably amounted to as many as eight hundred attendees alongside the magnates, and heads of religious houses. No king had ever engaged in the dissemination of what was effectively a charter of governance in this way or on this scale before. Edward meant the whole realm to know that his reign marked a new beginning, in which the grievances raised under Henry III had been heard.

Edward made good on his promises through a whole raft of other measures, too, some even before the promulgation of the statute. In October 1274, just two months after his return to England, the 'Hundred Roll' commission was issued, a central element of its brief being the collection of complaints about corrupt officials: 'sheriffs . . . who have oppress[ed] the people beyond measure', as well as other royal officials who have 'by the power of their office troubled any maliciously'. Commissioners traversed the length and breadth of the realm, and completed their job in a matter of months, between November 1274 and March 1275. They produced detailed returns that survive even today. The inquiries again took their example from the investigations into official corruption during the crisis of the late 1250s and early 1260s, when knights had been tasked with rooting out 'excesses, trespasses and acts of injustice' on the part of royal officials, as had the special eyre of 1259. Edward took no chances with the potential issue of undue pressure from local officials on possible complainants: in September 1274 he changed the sheriffs across England to ensure that sitting officeholders could not intimidate accusers. The incoming sheriffs of that month were also given a new oath to swear, emphasising their duty to treat the king's subjects loyally. They were not yet in large numbers the local 'vavasours' (residents) of their counties that the knights had demanded in 1258, but that too was to come.

Edward also swiftly built on positive elements of his father's own work in relation to royal justice, making it possible to bring more cases to the royal law courts by increasing the mechanisms for transferring them from local courts. Simultaneously he encouraged an expanded use of the informal complaints (*querelae*) that the reformers of 1258 had permitted in order to redress grievances. Under Edward people seem to have been encouraged to bring these petitions to Parliament, where they could submit either an oral or a written complaint; no writ was required. If it accepted the petition, the government would issue either a commission of inquiry, or oyer and terminer (essentially to hear and determine, which meant to inquire and then gather a jury to reach a verdict) if a judgement was required more swiftly. When they heard of the new procedures, people flocked to Parliament and the royal law courts with their pleas – so many were brought before Parliament that men had to be specially assigned to receive them from 1278, and by the early 1280s the plethora of petitions addressed to the king himself risked overwhelming Edward and his Council, and had to be devolved to ministers, with only the most serious reserved for Edward's attention. Nonetheless this important outlet continued, a positive long-term response to the grievances of the 1250s.

Edward not only received complaints and petitions, he actively worked to identify and target specific problems in these first years. Soon after his return Edward embarked upon a drive to tackle crime. The key mechanisms he used for this were commissions of inquiry and commissions of oyer and terminer – probably because they were very focused on the question at hand, and could be issued quickly, they were an ideal mechanism to deploy in the localities. Commissions were given to royal justices, sometimes together with local knights, whose local knowledge could be invaluable. In Kent, Surrey and Sussex, commissioners even included Stephen of Penshurst, the warden of the Cinque Ports (essentially the man responsible for the defence of the southern coast), who was paired with local justices to deal with 'vagabonds' committing felonies. Penshurst probably added significant military might to the commission. This notion of 'vagabonds' or 'malefactors' at large was echoed by commissions into 'evil doers committing homicides and evil crimes' in Devon, Dorset, Somerset, Wiltshire, Middlesex, Essex and Hertfordshire. Large numbers of commissions were similarly generated in Norfolk, Northumberland, Staffordshire, Suffolk and Yorkshire. Aside from commissions of inquiry and oyer and terminer, Edward began to appoint keepers of the peace on an ad hoc basis at times when he was particularly worried about the maintenance of order. One of these was in 1277, when he and his magnates were in Wales at war with Llywelyn ap Gruffudd. In that year an order was given for keepers to be elected in every county for 'the intercepting and arrest of malefactors'. The king was taking no chances. He would do the same in 1282 for the second Welsh war and in 1287 when he was away in Gascony.

Edward's appointment of commissions of oyer and terminer and inquiry in the period to 1277 echoed Henry III's innovations in the 1250s when he had been concerned about crime, while the appointment of keepers of the peace was a repeat of action taken by both reformers and the king during the civil war. Neither was a new departure. But what Edward did in the 1270s with the commissions of oyer and terminer and inquiry in particular involved their deployment on an unprecedented scale. It was characteristically ambitious and resulted in an immediate and fundamental expansion in the state's intervention in peacekeeping on the ground. It is clear too that Edward was personally engaged with at least some of what was done in his name: in Kent, he had even issued a commission himself from France as early as 1273 to inquire into vagabonds who had committed homicides and 'who propose to do worse things as the king hears for certain'.

The initial wave of activity following Edward's return was not simply a short-term gesture. More followed as the reign progressed, at the same unrelenting pace. After the first Welsh war of 1277, Parliament met in August 1278, and another statute was promulgated: the Statute of Gloucester, named after the location of the Parliament, was aimed, the king said, at 'providing for the betterment of his kingdom and for more fully doing justice, as the well-being of the kingly office requires'. It dealt with a wide range of concerns about the operation of elements of the common-law system that had been raised before the king or his justices, introducing a number of measures to make justice more effective. At the same time, though, the statute highlighted the risks of expanding access to royal justice as dramatically as the king had done in 1275, when it pointed out that the justices of the court of Common Pleas had begun to be overwhelmed by business. It had therefore been felt necessary through the statute to place some new limitations on the ability of the king's subjects to transfer local pleas to the court.

The impetus for the expansion of the royal judicial system in this period was clearly coming as much from his subjects as from the king himself. One of the major issues that the statute dealt with was the sheer volume of writs of trespass that were being requested by people to deal with a host of misdemeanours. A whole family of these writs had begun to be created in the mid-thirteenth century, in response to growing demands for legal remedies for wrongdoings beneath the level of the much more serious felony. But so many writs were being requested by the late 1270s that in the Statute of Gloucester the king had to stipulate that they would only be issued for the most serious offences. Non-violent trespasses involving claims of small value (less than forty shillings) would from then on be heard in the county courts, not the royal courts. So eager were complainants to access the king's central courts, however, that they soon found ways around this by alleging that the offence involved 'force and arms' and was 'against the king's peace'; the use of these phrases rendered the action serious enough to come before the royal justices. This legal nicety gave rise to a variety of incredible cases:

a series of complaints that horses had been injured by force and arms by people who were smiths, for example, was obviously a way of bringing shoeing accidents before the royal courts.

Although he had to attempt to reduce the business before the royal courts in 1278, Edward did make other remedies available to his subjects. After the Gloucester Parliament the general eyre was relaunched to take royal justice directly to the localities. Having been increasingly used by Henry III as a revenue-raising mechanism, under Edward it took on an almost wholly judicial role, with any money it raised being largely incidental to its core purpose. The justices were given several new duties as part of the commission. One of these was to reach judgement on the complaints about official corruption that had formed a key part of the Hundred Roll inquiries. They were also empowered to hear *querelae*, meaning that people could bring informal petitions to the eyre without having to leave their own county, as well as to Parliament. Finally, the justices were ordered to inquire into a source of disorder that was beginning to concern the king: 'confederates and conspirators who bound themselves by oath to support their friends in assizes, jury trials and recognitions, and confound their enemies'.

This was a foreshadowing of formal conspiracy legislation later produced by Edward in the 1290s, when his fears on this front had become considerably amplified. In direct contrast to his father, Edward clearly viewed the eyre as an opportunity to 'clear up' problems; he was later even to describe its visitations as 'medicine for the shires', a far cry from policy of the 1240s which had sought to wring what must have felt like every last penny out of the king's subjects via judicial fines and the like.

All this was complemented by a range of initiatives to increase the engagement of local society with royal government, and to empower government to better maintain order on the ground. In 1278, just as the eyre visitation was getting under way, the sheriffs were again changed almost wholesale. This time, instead of courtiers and administrators from outside the counties, it was local men who were appointed and who came to make up the bulk of those holding office. Their appointment marked an important start in increasing the local connections of royal government and addressing the long-standing grievances of the people of the shires about

outsiders exploiting them. These changes were accompanied by equally significant shifts in the staffing of gaol delivery commissions, which, between
visitations of the general eyre, tried those who had been arrested and
remanded to the county gaol, the most frequent of their alleged crimes
being theft, homicide, arson and rape. The men appointed to these commissions could, like their counterparts in the sheriffdoms, be very useful to
the government in helping to maintain order, not least because they could
be expected, given their remit, to have a sense of fluctuations in levels of
crime in each county year on year – or at least they might, if the same men
were appointed with any regularity to commissions. It was this regularity
of appointment that was established after 1278, meaning that where in the
first years of the reign the composition of commissions had been highly
volatile, regular groups of the same four men were now much more usual.
The scale of this change was huge: annual turnover in personnel halved.
The king was building a strong network of local officials to act as critical
conduits for effective royal government in the counties.

It is clear from these changes to the sheriffs and gaol delivery commissions that Edward and his advisers were very focused on major reform of
the personnel of local government and that they sought to deploy more
local expertise. But this could only be of significant benefit of the government and local society if the new men were well supervised. The reason
for making changes in 1278 rather than in 1274 is probably that the government was convinced that its new arrangements for the supervision of
local officials, in the form of an increased variety of outlets for bringing
complaints, meant that officials could be better held to account then than
previously. It was probably also the case that after four years the king's
advisers had an improved sense of how many men were available to serve,
and who were the most able personnel on the ground. Whatever the immediate triggers for action, one thing is certain: the scale of what was done
after 1278 means that it could only have been a deliberate government policy. At a stroke, these measures and the vast expansion in commissions of
inquiry and oyer and terminer meant that local knights became part of the
delivery of royal government on an unprecedented scale and in unprecedented ways. They became an integral part of the human infrastructure of
the emerging state.

If the pace in the first ten years of the reign had been unrelenting, there was no let-up as time went on. In 1284, Edward again returned to judicial reform, using his preferred route of Parliament as a forum to address deficiencies in the common law through legislation. The Statute of Westminster II and the Statute of Merchants were issued at the Easter Parliament of 1285, the latter providing remedies for creditors trying to collect unpaid debts, while Westminster II sought to remedy procedural problems facing both lords and tenants. These might sound routine, but they signalled that Edward's government was systematically working through a whole range of issues that had inhibited his subjects in making use of royal justice. In addition, the statute tried again to combat the high volumes of commissions of oyer and terminer that were being demanded, frequently over relatively minor issues. From then on, the statute stipulated, commissions would only be granted in cases of 'heinous trespass where it is necessary to provide speedy remedy, and the lord king has seen fit to issue it of his special grace'. This had an effect on numbers of commissions but it was only temporary – it was proving near impossible to stifle the ever-growing demand for access to the king's legal system. The statute also formalised a system whereby the justices of assize, who since Magna Carta visited each county twice a year, could hear cases that were due before the central justices at King's Bench or the court of Common Pleas if they reached a county before the case had come to either bench. While they could not give judgement this speeded up the initial hearing of a case and made the delivery of justice more efficient.

Edward similarly turned his attention to the question of crime, moving to issue a statute outside Parliament in the same year to introduce new measures to counter it. The Statute of Winchester resulted, he stated in the preamble, from his knowledge that crime was more frequent than it had been in the past and that it was more difficult than before to induce juries to put felons forward for trial. This was probably true, but the timing of the legislation also coincided with plans for Edward to be away from England for a prolonged period in the following few years. In his absence it seems that he wanted to put in place enhanced structures for the maintenance of order. To achieve this, the statute focused on placing more responsibility for crime prevention and the maintenance of order on the localities themselves. Whereas before, hundreds (subdivisions of the counties) had to produce before the royal justices those who had committed homicides when the justices came to a county, the statute extended that requirement to cases of robbery. Self-policing was concurrently more vigorously promoted. Each district, the statute said, was 'henceforth' to be 'so kept that immediately robberies and felonies are committed vigorous pursuit shall be made from vill [village] to vill and from district to district'. Novel arrangements for security in towns and cities in the hours of darkness were made through implementing a vigil called watch and ward, and in rural areas roads were to be widened so that robbers would find it harder to hide and jump out on unsuspecting travellers. Finally, the list of military equipment local men had to acquire and maintain, by way of enabling this self-policing, was updated. The people of the localities were now expected to play a more active role than before in keeping the peace and bringing felons to justice, and Edward was providing a framework within which this might readily be done.

Since his return to the realm in 1274, Edward had been the major force in government, and the pace of reform had been unrelenting. Later events in England in 1286–9, when the king was away from the realm in Gascony, show the momentum he generated in the years before his departure. Even though his cousin the earl of Cornwall was appointed regent in his absence (Edward's brother Edmund accompanied the king to France), the volume of public orders halved while the king was away. Oyer and terminer commissions were also scaled back by about two-thirds, and there were no major governmental initiatives during the period. The key role normally played by the king in resolving disputes at the highest level is further sharply illuminated by events that unfolded in the March of Wales. There, a dispute between the earls of Gloucester and Hereford about the castle of Morlais in mid-Glamorgan turned violent in the king's absence, and despite attempts at arbitration by both the archbishop of Canterbury and the regent, the two men remained engaged in armed conflict with each other. There was little anyone could do other than wait for the king's return, because no one else had the authority to enforce a compromise between two of the realm's greatest men. When the dispute continued after he returned, Edward settled the matter in one fell swoop, throwing both earls into jail temporarily to demonstrate his anger at their behaviour. They were subsequently bailed and ordered to appear before the king and Council in London, following which both were imprisoned again to make an example of them. They were swiftly released, but only after the imposition of fines large enough to make them think twice about resuming the conflict.

Convinced also that royal officials must have taken his absence as an opportunity to behave badly, on his return from Gascony in 1289 Edward immediately issued major new inquiries to gather complaints about official corruption. Unlike earlier inquiries of a similar nature, this time the returns brought major consequences, the so-called 'state trials', through which officials at all levels were subjected to the king's wrath. Following allegations against a number of key officers, even of the highest status, several high-profile sackings took place, including the chief justice of the court of King's Bench, Ralph Hengham. He was the man who had in all likelihood been the major drafter of the king's legislation since the start of the reign, and his disgrace shows that no one was immune from scrutiny.

After a further absence to deal with the dispute over succession to the Crown of Scotland in 1291–2, Edward also developed suspicions about gaol delivery commissioners in the localities (those panels of four knights tasked with emptying the gaols of those arrested in each county), and ordered further inquiries by the eyre justices into the behaviour of the commissioners to see 'whether those aforesaid justices assigned have delivered the gaols of any felons or prisoners, through a . . . suspect or rigged jury'. Those who had done so were to be sent to prison and made to pay a high fine. Having lost eleven members of the higher judiciary as a result of the complaints made in 1289–90 it is perhaps no surprise that Edward had fears that official corruption was inhibiting his drive against crime. These concerns must have been major because in 1293 he removed local knights from gaol delivery commissions and integrated them into the assizes, which were now organised into four regular circuits. In Parliament at Easter 1293 he then went on to issue a new writ of conspiracy and trespass. There were, he said, 'conspirators' who 'maintained' and 'sustained' pleas maliciously, and the writ of conspiracy could be used to bring pleas against them.

It was again not just corruption that concerned Edward in these years, but crime too. He took sweeping action to combat this in 1290, tasking Henry

Lacy, earl of Lincoln, with inquiring in every county of England 'touching the persons who have committed homicides, depredations, burnings and other offences by night or day, their aiders and abettors, and to arrest, imprison and do justice'. Between April 1293 and February 1294, Lacy was again appointed to investigate vagabonds and malefactors across a whole swathe of English counties. It was a highly unusual move to use a member of the nobility to oversee such inquiries, and presumably Lacy's appointment resulted from the fact that Edward remained unconvinced of his officials' probity.

Throughout the first twenty years of his reign, the king's appetite for reform had been unceasing. His subjects were given greater access to royal justice than ever before, crime and corruption were targeted and rooted out, and the desire of the men of the localities for greater representation in officeholding were met. When Edward had sworn to uphold the common good, he had truly meant it. He had set the agenda for implementing the demands of the reformers of 1258 and providing a type of royal rule that was almost the diametric opposite of his father's. It must have felt like a breath, or rather gust, of fresh air was blowing through England in these years, taking with it the ill-feeling and rancour that had set the tone of most of the preceding decades and replacing it with a sense of a king working in partnership with his subjects for the greater good of all.

Edwardian Rule on the Ground

It is hard to be sure how far the interventions Edward made in the localities from 1274 testify to an actual increase in corruption and disorder and how far to the king's own desire to root out these things. Where corruption is concerned, this is partly because of the caveats mentioned above about the developing sense of what corruption actually was. Disorder, meanwhile, is something historians have not studied systematically in Henry III's reign. However, it would be odd if there had not been considerable fallout from the recent civil war; not only had the war been prolonged, the settlement had been far from easy. And there are few instances of war in any period in which increased crime is not an offshoot. The king's words in the Kent commission of inquiry in 1273 suggest less general anxiety than very specific concerns. And in 1274, things were so bad that the warden of the

Cinque Ports was forced to appeal to the king to settle a dispute in the Kent port of Sandwich, which had resulted in the mayor and his followers assaulting 'sergeants and other ministers of Dover Castle' who had been sent by Penshurst 'to deal with various offences'. Edward was characteristically tough in response: he sent out royal justices to inquire with explicit instructions that if it were found that the attack had been made 'with the assent of the commonalty', the people of the town in other words, they were 'to take the town into the king's hands, the king being very much moved at their contempt'.

One reason why securing good intelligence from the localities about the situation on the ground was crucial to Edward was surely, therefore, because of his worries about crime. These continued, on and off, throughout the reign, but mostly with very specific remits, suggesting direct responses to individual problems. The issue of a number of general commissions to inquire into breaches of the peace, vagabonds and malefactors indicates that there were individual pockets of disorder in south and south-eastern England, as well as Norfolk, Suffolk, Lincolnshire, Warwickshire and Leicestershire in the late 1270s, and in Essex, Shropshire, Staffordshire and Northamptonshire in the early 1280s. The commission in Warwickshire and Leicestershire adds detail to this. It seems that the government was specifically concerned about homicides, depredations, arsons and burglaries. These concerns must have been serious because the commission was followed in 1282 by the government's appointment of a special under-sheriff, Richard d'Amundeville, 'to assist with keeping the peace in these troublous times'. Normally the appointment of the under-sheriff would be made by the sheriff – the government tended not to trouble itself with appointments at this level – and so this indicates a very particular level of anxiety and intervention. In Kent, where crime had been a major worry before 1278, the appointment of the warden of the Cinque Ports to the bulk of oyer and terminer and inquiry commissions in the early 1280s and the use of another local man, John de Cobham, who was also a senior justice of the King's Bench, as a gaol delivery commissioner at the same time, were also unusual moves. Not only was Edward making broad, sweeping reforms to government as a whole, royal government was highly targeted in its response to disorder in the localities.

A number of urban centres seem also to have encountered difficulties in the period. In London, the mayor, Henry le Waleys, was ordered by the king in 1281 to take steps to restore order to the city. He cannot have been successful, because in 1285 Edward appointed the treasurer, John de Kirkby, to head a special commission into disorder there, particularly focusing on crime. When city oligarchs objected to the incursion on their liberties that this represented, the king simply took the city into royal hands. In a clash between dealing with crime and respecting a city's liberties, there was no contest in Edward's mind. Canterbury and York were similarly taken into royal hands in 1280, though in the latter case even that seems to have had little effect: in 1286 things were so bad that the government had to issue a commission which stated that vagabonds in the city were allegedly committing homicides and other crimes 'so that the king's subjects dare not leave their houses without escorts of armed men'.

There is evidence, though, that at least in some places direct royal action had an effect. Numbers of both crimes and disputes seem to have begun to fall in some areas in the 1280s, and while it is impossible always to trace a direct connection between Crown action and outcomes, it is apparent that the situation in certain counties at least was becoming more settled and stable. People may well have been thinking twice about their behaviour in an atmosphere in which the royal government was so clearly inclined to take direct action. That direct action, itself a novel concept on this scale, consisted of Edward deploying the special and general commissions of inquiry, and oyer and terminer wherever there were problems, both proactively when he heard about disorder, and in response to petitions. The commissions were in many ways the perfect tool for this: they could be targeted at a specific problem and despatched quickly to a county or region. The innovation in their use, albeit prefaced on a smaller scale by Henry III, reflected a significant expansion in the state's ambitions to deal with disorder on the ground. It was very probably pivotal in the improvements that took place across these years, and made the king's subjects still more dependent on him for the day-to-day maintenance of order even at huge distances from the centre of government.

That reliance is perhaps best signalled by the fact that when Edward returned from France in 1289, he seems to have been deeply worried that a major deterioration had taken place in his absence. His concerns are reinforced by the evidence from a number of areas: in the March of Wales, it was not only the earls of Gloucester and Hereford whose dispute was causing problems, though that was bad enough. Several other lords seem to have taken the king's absence as an opportunity to assert their own position in relation to other lords and even to royal jurisdiction itself. Peter Corbet of Caus, who had already once been reined in from attempting to extend his lordship in the 1270s, had done so again in the late 1280s, bringing himself into conflict with numerous others, including in one case the whole town of Shrewsbury. We know this because the burgesses wrote to Robert Burnell to complain about him. The king's absence was surely too much of a coincidence in this case. In the early 1290s, another Marcher lord Theobald de Verdun was brought before the king to answer for 'various trespasses and acts of disobedience perpetrated against the lord king to the harm of his Crown and dignity'. Probably in part as a result of this sort of behaviour, Edward's assertion of royal authority in the Welsh March increased in its vigour.

In Warwickshire, a resurgence of problems shows in a different way the importance of both the king's presence in the realm and his active role in governance. There the situation was always teetering on the brink of conflict, mainly because land in some areas of the county had only recently been cleared for settlement, meaning that disputes about landownership were particularly intense. By the time Edward returned from Gascony in 1289, even the keepers of the peace seemed to be fighting each other as a result of being mired in land disputes: Robert de Verdun and Thomas de Garsale, both long-standing royal officials, were at such serious odds over land and crops that it seems to have resulted in a fistfight between the two men. This came to light in the inquiries of 1289–90, but the deterioration in the county must have begun very soon after Edward departed, because the regency government appointed an extra keeper of the peace there in 1287, and in 1288 they sent in an experienced king's clerk, a senior royal official, to be sheriff. The king himself went a step further, asking the earl of Warwick, William Beauchamp, to arrest trespassers against the peace, and ordering the sheriff appointed in 1290, a non-local, Stephen Rabaz, to assist him. Edward kept a close eye on what was happening, and when

Rabaz failed to follow his order to show no grace to anyone the earl arrested, he was sent to the Tower of London in 1293 at 'the lord king's pleasure'.

Numerous conflicts also broke out elsewhere while Edward was in Gascony – in Kent, for example, between the men of the port of Sandwich and the prior of Christ Church Canterbury; between the abbot of Faversham and the town of Faversham; and between the archbishop of Canterbury and the citizens of the city over rights relating to market stalls. In this dispute the citizens claimed to Edward in the early 1290s that the jury of the Exchequer court that had given judgement against them had been rigged. Like Stephen Rabaz, the sheriff of the county, William Chelsfield, about whom there were several complaints, was sent to the Tower of London as a result, while some of his colleagues were made to pay heavy fines.

None of this was irreversible. Royal action after 1289 can be seen to have had a clear positive impact on the state of order in Warwickshire and Kent, as it had earlier, with many of the most entrenched disputes settled by the time war broke out with France in 1294. And it is not the case that order across England completely broke down while the king was away. Very few of the accusations made against officials in 1289–90 resulted in a guilty verdict, and while that is not an absolute barometer, it does have some significance. At the same time, the volume of the rolls on which cases were recorded in King's Bench did not differ much from the period before 1286, suggesting that a widespread and significant rise in disputes had not taken place. Finally, the context within which Edward was governing in the early 1290s meant that the king may have been more likely to worry than at other times. His actions in those years have a tone of panic which had not been the case in the 1270s and 1280s. It is most likely that this resulted from several factors – looming war with France must have been a source of great concern; in addition Robert Burnell, Edward's erstwhile chancellor, who had been central to his government, died in 1292, while Edward's wife and mother died in 1290 and 1291 respectively. In other words, the early 1290s saw the king's personal and professional world turned upside down, and some of his most important anchors removed. A number of causes célèbres among the judiciary and in some localities, as well as returning from Gascony to a major dispute between two of his leading nobles, would understandably have made him doubly nervous in these circumstances.

But it is important also to step back from the events of these years and place them in another context. Concern about disorder and corruption was not only a leitmotif of Edward I's reign, but also the latter part of the reign of Henry III. In part, it reflected a wider trend of thinking, extending beyond England's borders, about the duty of the king to uphold the well-being of his subjects and protect them from oppressions by officials. But it was at the same time about the standards of behaviour that were increasingly expected from royal and private officials. This was arguably an indirect result of the growth of officialdom as royal government had expanded and lords' administration of their estates had become more centralised and systematic. Because of the ever greater need for appropriate training and guidance to create expertise among these new officials, professions began to emerge: by the mid-thirteenth century, there was already what we might call a legal profession in London. Surviving registers of legal writs and the so-called 'year books' of legal arguments evidence the proliferation of legal training in the second half of the century, which accompanied the learning on the job completed by trainee attorneys or sergeants-at-law (respectively, the medieval equivalents of solicitors and barristers within the present-day English legal system). While other professions were not yet so clearly defined, similar trends are observable: there was a plethora of instruction manuals for estate officials dealing with anything from accounting methods to arable husbandry.

As these professions, or at least a notion of professional or expert service, developed, so, almost inevitably, did a notion of what constituted appropriate 'professional' behaviour. There emerged a tension between the impartiality increasingly demanded of royal officials and their bonds with their community or personal connections, which over time became ever more acute. It is fair to say that this tension took time to resolve as the state and professions grew. Sensational trials, like those of 1289–93, involving at times lurid accusations, resulted in a number of justices being punished by the king. But many of the justices and officials in question probably suffered from operating in formative legal and administrative environments for which appropriate rules of engagement had not yet been worked out. Consequently, a focus on official misdoings does not necessarily mean that significantly more corruption now existed than previously. It may indicate that people were more likely to identify particular behaviours, such as a noble paying a fee to a member of the judiciary for legal advice, as inappropriate or problematic. In other words, major inquiries like those of both 1274 and 1289 were probably at least as much a reflection of state growth as they were of the existence of corruption or other fundamental problems.

Edward had made huge innovations and progress in the first twenty years of his reign. He had not only accepted the programme of the reformers from 1258, with all the goodwill and strengthening of bonds between centre and locality that this must have generated, but had also continued with state-building in the best tradition of his Angevin predecessors. He had made royal law more accessible to his subjects and extended still further the Crown's judicial reach with a significant expansion in the use of agile, ad hoc commissions of inquiry and oyer and terminer that had begun under his father. By 1294 these had already, and would again in the future, prove a powerful weapon in the royal armoury of measures to deal with crime and disorder. But they had also increased the dependence of the king's subjects on the leadership provided by their monarch, and in the years after 1294, the limitations of the system would begin to tell.

The Development of Parliament and Royal Finance

In 1258, the reformers had called for Henry III to summon Parliament three times a year, at set times, in response to his repeated failure to consult regularly and properly with his subjects. By contrast, Edward was responsive right from the outset. In the two decades after his return in 1274, not only did he recognise the need to consult, he also summoned Parliament every year. The only exceptions were when he was absent in Gascony in 1286–9, and in 1291–2, when he was dealing with the succession dispute (the so-called 'Great Cause') in Scotland after Alexander III and his heir had died in quick succession. The number of annual sessions was not quite in line with what the reformers had wanted: under Edward Parliament was called twice a year, at Easter and Michaelmas, rather than three times, possibly because of the challenges of travelling in January, which was when the third assembly would have taken place. If the letter of the reformers' demands had not been adhered to, the spirit most definitely had. Edward's actions were appreciated by his subjects, and real harmony prevailed across these twenty years, in stark contrast to Henry and John's reigns. This was doubtless helped by the fact that, where his father and grandfather had tended to rely on a narrow clique of often foreign favourites for advice, Edward sought magnate counsel on a sustained basis. Formal magnate representation on the royal Council expanded, alongside informal collaboration: nobles were frequently witnesses to royal charters, which indicates that they were very regularly present with the king at the royal court. Previously, they had, of course, complained about the disconnect between the royal court and the king's greatest subjects.

Under Edward, Parliament came to have a variety of critical functions. It was here that his impressive body of legislation was enacted. This was probably a formality, as statutes were likely to have been drafted by royal officers with input from the royal Council of magnates and ministers. But nonetheless the use of Parliament for ratification signalled that Edward saw it as having a vital role in government. He certainly saw its use for ensuring that his legislation was widely proclaimed in the localities: when knights were called to both sessions in 1275, the king doubtless had in mind the role they would play in disseminating the messages he wanted to give about the tone of his rule, not least the Statute of Westminster I, essentially his coronation charter. Similarly, Parliament under Edward operated as a significant forum for the redress of grievances, particularly through the bringing of petitions, which expanded so dramatically from 1275.

Unlike under Henry III, the first half of Edward's reign saw Parliament give consent to three grants of extraordinary taxation, in 1275, 1283 and 1290, all harmoniously. Two of these grants were not associated with a plea of urgent necessity (usually a defensive threat to England or English lands), but with special requests from the king for discretionary help from his subjects. In 1275, it was his crusading debts that were cited as cause for his financial need, and in 1290 it was debts from his time in Gascony and other expenses. On both of these occasions, the knights of the shires were summoned to Parliament alongside the magnates, in 1275 to 'treat together with the magnates the business of the kingdom' and in 1290 'to come with full power to offer counsel and consent to those things which the earls, barons and magnates shall be led to agree on'. The magnates remained the key decision makers but the wider representatives of the counties and boroughs were being meaningfully consulted.

When tax was granted, there were notable concessions by the king in each case. In 1290, the Statute of *Quia Emptores* was granted in response to magnate grievances about the actions of their tenants depriving them of revenues from their sublet lands. Knights, too, were heard. One of the key bugbears for them was the cost of their debts to Jewish moneylenders, and in 1275, in return for a grant, they demanded that new limitations were placed on Jewish moneylending, one of which was ending the charging of interest on loans. This was followed in the Parliament of 1290 by the condition that the Jews must be expelled from England, something Edward made good on, in the process destroying England's already significantly impoverished Jewish community. His actions are a reminder of how widespread and pernicious anti-Semitism has been throughout the ages. Like the knights, burgesses from the towns were similarly courted: in 1275, aiming to negotiate a new customs scheme to help meet the costs he had incurred on crusade and which were now owing to Italian bankers, Edward consulted the merchants and then offered, in return for the new customs duties, the abandonment of a recent embargo on wool exports. Negotiation and compromise were the order of the day.

Only the tax of 1283 was granted for military reasons, following the rebellion of Dafydd of Wales the previous year. In requesting money to help with his resulting campaign, Edward was careful to consult in the fullest way possible. Two assemblies were called (neither of them Parliaments, as the king was fighting in Wales at the time), one in York and one in Northampton, to enable full participation by knights from across the realm. At these, the knights were told that the Welsh rebellion disturbed the peace of the realm, and they agreed to a subsidy of one-thirtieth on movable goods, provided that, when the question was put to the magnates, they did the same. They duly did so with no demur.

When Edward returned to England from France in November 1289, one of the biggest issues he faced was again in relation to money. By that date, around £110,000 was owed to the king's Italian bankers, debts largely incurred during the last three years. Some of this related to the significant costs that had arisen during Edward's time in Gascony. These resulted in large part from his constant travels around the duchy as he sought to reform its government, and from the costs associated with the foundation of a number of urban centres, known as *bastides*, which it was hoped would bring in valuable revenues to the Crown in due course. Meanwhile, at home, an extensive programme of castle-building to cement the conquest of Wales had continued apace during Edward's absence, and the regency government had had to deal, at significant cost, with a rebellion there in 1287. Urgent action was needed, and Edward had begun by promising the revenues of Gascony to the bankers for the foreseeable future. Following his return, he was able to raise a feudal aid (a royal prerogative to which Edward was entitled) from the earls in April 1290 as a result of the marriage of his daughter Joan to the earl of Gloucester. But these measures were not enough, and it was this situation that prompted the request in Parliament for a grant of taxation in 1290, which Edward managed so skilfully with concessions.

It is plain to see why Edward's requests for lay taxation were so favourably received. First, when there was no military emergency, he was prepared to make concessions in return for the grants he received; he saw the value of compromise in a way that his father had not. The backdrop to the grants was a well of goodwill, generated early on by the fact of the accession of a new king, and later by Edward's own actions. His responsiveness to issues of corruption and disorder, and his good working relationship with the magnates and Parliament all served to make his subjects amenable to requests for help where Henry III had, by contrast, alienated and antagonised them. Moreover, in 1283, there was agreement on the necessity of the king's campaign in Wales, triggered as it was by a rebellion. This had never been the case under Henry, and his subjects had never been convinced that any money given would be spent on the causes for which they had provided it.

Another important element in the diametrically opposing responses to Henry and Edward's requests for tax was the stewardship of royal finances. Following his accession, Edward quickly embarked on reforms of the finances designed to maximise revenues. In 1275, for example, the royal lands were placed in the hands of three stewards as part of a bid to improve the collection of revenues from them, a move aimed at stabilising the Crown finances. Where similar initiatives under Henry had involved challenges to tenure, Edward carefully avoided provoking his magnates. In 1279, he also took the opportunity to engage in a long over-due re-coinage, which brought in much-needed profits for the Crown, as re-coinages always did. This was complemented in the same year by the issue of such extensive inquiries into landholding that historians have sometimes likened them in scale to the Domesday inquiries – the great survey of England and parts of Wales that had followed the Norman Conquest. Like William the Conqueror, Edward may have had taxation in mind when he launched his inquiries. The size of the population and the complexity of landholding in the late thirteenth century meant that, whatever the king's initial aims, the survey was never completed. But the extent of Edward's ambition is clear.

When, following the campaign in Wales of 1282–3, the gap between income and expenditure remained great, and it became obvious that even more reform was needed to make the royal finances go further, Edward did not hesitate to act. The Welsh campaign, one of conquest this time, had cost over £150,000, a staggering amount when compared with the £23,000 bill for the previous war in Wales in 1276–7. And while Edward had col-lected loans and gifts when the rebellion broke out, including £4,000 from London alone, it was not enough to ease the burdens on the treasury. This was the case even with the tax of 1283. So, in the years immediately after the second Welsh war, unpaid debts were chased with more vigour than ever before, and John Kirkby, the treasurer, was despatched to the localities in 1285 to make inquiries about debts to the Crown, as well as dues and rents, and who held knights' fees from the Crown. The additional money raised in this way, together with loans from Italian bankers, helped stabilise the situation in the short term.

The financial challenges Edward faced in the 1280s and early 1290s underscore both how dependent the king was on extraordinary taxation for the prosecution of war, and how carefully, even with such grants, he needed to manage his ordinary finances. Maximising revenues, though, was only one side of this. The other side of the coin was royal expenditure. It is perhaps salutary that Edward cancelled his father's costly Westminster Abbey renovations as soon as he came to the throne. At the same time,

Edward did not replicate the patronage that his father had given to his Lusignan relatives in particular. His policy was to give rewards only in return for good service, and in moderation.

Consultation and Counsel

Another key to Edward's success in the first decades of the reign can be found in his choice of advisers and his use of counsel. Where Henry had surrounded himself with hangers-on and sycophants, Edward instead chose his closest advisers from among the most able administrators, and from the ranks of the nobility, as well as his own family. He fostered close and loyal relationships and his court was notable for its harmony, a welcome change after decades of faction and discord. Robert Burnell, Edward's chancellor until his death in 1292, was his most trusted servant. Burnell heralded from Shropshire and probably came from a knightly family. He was about the same age as Edward, and had entered Edward's service during the 1250s (in all likelihood when the prince was in Wales and the March area), rising to become head of his Council in 1268 and chancellor of England in 1274. Apart from when Edward was on crusade in the early 1270s (when Burnell was made responsible for the management of his affairs as lord, and, after Henry III's death, as king), the two men were almost always together. The extent of Edward's devotion to Burnell is indicated by the fact that he campaigned with the papacy to have him made archbishop of Canterbury on more than one occasion, always without success. While Burnell undoubtedly did very well personally out of his service to the king, it is his steadfast, devoted and hugely able service for which he is best known. Such was his importance as Edward's 'right-hand man' that he was even trusted in the late 1280s to make an important speech on the king's behalf to the French court. It was similarly Burnell to whom men and women from across England wrote in large numbers with their requests, petitions and messages for the king: this included members of the nobility such as the earl of Gloucester, who, unable on one occasion to come to Westminster because of the illness of one of his children, wrote to Burnell asking him to inform the king, but to keep the matter private. If anyone had Edward's ear, it was Robert Burnell.

Among the nobility, unlike under Henry III, the fact that a vast majority of the senior figures were regular witnesses to Edward's royal charters indicates that they too were often with the king. While Edward has sometimes been accused of having had a 'masterful' approach to his nobility focused on appropriating their lands for members of the royal family where opportunity arose, this is in reality something that all kings did. It does not undermine the broader evidence of a largely harmonious, positive and constructive relationship. Two of the most frequent witnesses to royal charters were Henry de Lacy, earl of Lincoln, and Gilbert de Clare, earl of Gloucester. Born in 1249 and therefore just under a decade Edward's junior, Lacy succeeded his father in 1258, though he did not take possession of his estates until the early 1270s. During Edward's reign, he proved utterly reliable and dependable and was therefore one of the king's most loyal and trusted servants. In 1279, this was demonstrated by Lacy's appointment alongside Edward's cousin Edmund of Cornwall as lay lieutenant of England while the king was briefly in France. He accompanied Edward on many of his military campaigns throughout the reign, as well as to Gascony in 1286–9; he was to serve as Edward's lieutenant there in the 1290s. By the latter part of the reign, Lacy was established as the elder statesman among the nobility. A truly honest broker with a continuous record of unstinting royal service stretching back over four decades, he was a man to whom Edward could always turn for advice and support.

Gilbert de Clare, who was almost the same age as Edward had, by contrast, begun his career on the side of de Montfort in the civil war. After being driven into rebellion by Henry III's handling of his own inheritance in the early 1260s and then becoming disenchanted with de Montfort's own behaviour and switching sides to the royalists in 1265, he then seems to have been much with Edward and fought alongside him at the battle of Evesham. De Montfort was so unnerved by this that he is said to have commented that 'this red dog will eat us today' – 'red dog' was Gilbert's nickname, as a result of his red hair – in recognition of the earl's military capabilities. A falling-out with Henry after this, though, prompted Clare to change sides once again in 1266. Much of the explanation for the earl's behaviour in the period between 1262 and 1267 lies in Henry III's own actions, but Clare also enjoyed a difficult relationship with the Lord

Edward in the 1260s, the reasons for which are not clear. Despite this, there must have been respect for Edward on the earl's part at least: when Henry III died, he immediately swore to protect Edward's kingdom, and was the first to welcome the new king as he journeyed from the south coast to London on his return in 1274, receiving him at his castle of Tonbridge.

After Edward's accession, the two continued to enjoy a mixed relationship, probably always with the underpinnings of mutual respect, and perhaps even fear: Ralph Hengham, chief justice of King's Bench, was later to say that Edward was afraid of Gloucester. Certainly the king could ill afford to lose his support as a military commander – in 1277 in Wales the earl was thanked fulsomely for 'his immense labours and expenses'. But if Edward was afraid of the earl it did not stop him singling out his liberties for special inquiry in the late 1270s, and throwing him into jail temporarily in the early 1290s alongside the earl of Hereford. Instead of fear, it would probably be more accurate to say that Edward knew how much he depended on Clare militarily, particularly in Wales. He took the opportunity to remind him who was king when he felt it necessary, but tempered that by taking care to show due respect for the earl's rank and seeking his counsel. It is fair to say that, for his part, Clare was a hothead who vigorously pursued his own interests, and who was capable of being one of the king's most difficult and most loyal earls. Edward seems, through his careful management of him, always to have kept Clare within his close circle of advisers and to have been in command of his respect and loyalty right up to the earl's death in 1295. It must have been a difficult line to walk and it is a measure of Edward's diplomacy that he was able to do so effectively.

Perhaps the two lords who were personally closest to Edward were William de Valence, who styled himself earl of Pembroke in the 1280s and became recognised as such by Edward in the 1290s, and John Warenne, earl of Surrey. Valence, who was probably born in the late 1220s, had come to England as part of the Lusignan migration in the late 1240s. He and Edward quickly became firm friends, partly drawn together in the 1250s by lands each held in Wales. Although Valence was exiled in 1258, he returned in the 1260s and remained an ally, fighting alongside Edward at the battle of Evesham and taking the crusading cross with him in 1268. After his return from crusade, he went on to campaign for the king in Wales in 1277 and 1282, and travelled to Gascony with him in 1286–9. In the early 1290s he was involved in both the adjudication of a dispute between the earls of Gloucester and Hereford, and hearings relating to the Scottish succession in 1291–2. Vilified in Henry III's reign as part of the Lusignan faction, Valence had effected a transformation under Edward I, and at his death in 1296 the Dunstable annalist notably wrote that he was 'faithful to the kingdom of England'. His staunch loyalty and strong record of royal service amplifies the role that faction and division at court, and at the root of that the mismanagement of people by Henry III, played in the crisis of 1258; it was not simply about matters of principle. Edward built and maintained relationships where his father had sown discord and mistrust.

John de Warenne, who was eight years Edward's senior, and whose father had died in 1240 when Warenne was just eight years old, had been brought up at the court of Henry III as a ward of the king. Later that decade Henry arranged Warenne's marriage to the daughter of Hugh de Lusignan, and by the early 1250s he had joined the group around Edward that included William de Valence. Warenne remained much with Edward from that time onwards. He joined de Montfort briefly during the civil war, insisting on the implementation of the Provisions of Oxford, but later returned to the royalist side. He did not go with Edward on crusade, but was made one of the custodians of the realm after Henry III's death. Warenne was known for aggressively pursuing his interests and fiercely managing his estates, but he served Edward loyally throughout the reign, particularly in Wales and in Scotland, where he was again made custodian of the realm. On his death in 1304 Edward ordered prayers and masses for his soul on a scale only previously reserved for members of the royal family. Edward prized personal loyalty highly and, as with the earl of Gloucester, made it his business to manage the difficult personalities around him effectively.

Edward was also loyally served by family members in the form of his younger brother and his cousin. His brother Edmund, who became known as Crouchback (or crossed back) while he was on crusade with Edward in the early 1270s, was very close to his brother. The only significant row they are known to have had was over Crouchback's desire to carry the great sword at the coronation of 1274, which Edward rejected and may have led to Crouchback missing the event. But the argument did not last long and Crouchback was to serve Edward loyally, both as a military commander and a diplomat, until his death in 1296, by which Edward was devastated. He wrote of 'Edmund, our dearest and only brother, who was always devoted and faithful to us and to the affairs of our realm, and in whom valour and many gifts of grace shone forth . . . whose loss has devastated us and our whole realm'.

His brother's death followed hard on the loss of both Edward's mother and wife, and his loyal servant Burnell, in the years since 1290. It must have felt to Edward like everyone who was most important to him was being lost in those years. He went on to lose Valence in 1296 and his equally loyal cousin, another Edmund, son of Richard of Cornwall, would die just four years later, in 1300. Cornwall acted as regent for Edward twice, in 1279 and 1286–9, a measure of the king's faith in him, and when Edward was in Wales engaged in the conquest between 1282 and 1284, it was Cornwall he chose as his lieutenant in England. Like Edmund Crouchback, he was assiduous in his support of royal government, a reliable and sensible adviser.

The quality of Edward's government, his embracing of the counsel of his nobility, his willingness to negotiate and make concessions, and the care with which he managed the royal finances all created an atmosphere of goodwill. Unlike his father, Edward fostered good working relationships with his nobility and with his wider subjects. His requests for taxation had been few and far between, and where they were not prompted by military necessity, they had been accompanied by concessions on the king's part, in negotiated recognition of the sacrifice his subjects were making in agreeing to a grant. Even with abstemious management of the finances, though, the Crown was never awash with money, and it was clear that any significant military commitments could only be funded through taxation. This was something Edward had already realised was part and parcel of governing in this post-Magna Carta world in a way that his father had not. Discord and antagonism had given way to co-operation and harmony.

Defender of Crown Rights

In his coronation oath, Edward committed himself, like his predecessors, to bringing peace to the Church and his people, to preventing oppression and to providing impartial justice. But he also inserted a clause to preserve the rights of the Crown. In the new sheriff's oath of 1274 he did the same: alongside its stipulation that officeholders treat the king's subjects loyally, there was a new reference to maintaining royal rights. Within weeks of this, the 'Hundred Roll' commission of 1274, as well as focusing on official corruption, was tasked with inquiring 'by what warrant (*Quo Warranto*)' people were claiming to hold royal liberties and privileges in the localities – things like the view of frankpledge, which could be very lucrative. The system of frankpledge stipulated that all men over the age of twelve in an administrative unit called a tithing had to take joint responsibility for producing any man accused of crime in their tithing. Twice a year, through the view of frankpledge, the sheriff (or lord, if the view of frankpledge was privately run) checked that everyone in the tithing was present, and issued fines where they were not. The usurpation of liberties and franchises like this could be a significant drain on royal finances, diverting into private hands money that Edward and his lawyers believed belonged to the Crown. He was determined to end the drain.

This focus on the rights of the Crown was a direct echo of Henry III's general inquiry in 1255 into those who had usurped royal rights in the localities. But Henry had never followed up on the returns, making no concrete challenges to what had been unearthed. Concerns about the issue, and particularly the scale of new usurpations during the civil war, had clearly resurfaced in government before Edward returned from Gascony, because in early 1274 two men were commissioned to look into lost royal rights across eleven counties, though for whatever reason the commission was never performed. Perhaps it had been decided to wait for the king's return to lend more weight to proceedings. The inquiries Edward set in train in October 1274 did that and more, significantly expanding the number and remit of the commissioners and making provision for following the returns with full investigations. More than forty articles were included in the commission, with the commissioners divided into pairs and given responsibility for groups of counties. They acted quickly: having set out in November 1275, their job was completed just four months later. The returns they produced were huge in volume, so large that extract rolls had to be compiled in order to be able to make use of them. This affected the ability of the government to follow up on them: initially Edward planned for Parliament and the royal Council to do this by obtaining proofs of rights to liberties and franchises, but the volume of claims to be checked was simply too great. So in 1278 the recommissioned eyre justices were tasked with pursuing evidence of people's rights to what they held.

Despite this, the results were largely disappointing. It was hard for the king to make people surrender rights that, for the most part, they genuinely believed belonged to them, and the eyre justices had real problems knowing what verdicts to reach on claims that came before them. In one case those on the northern eyre circuit wrote to Ralph Hengham, chief justice of King's Bench, to ask for guidance in relation to a number of legal questions relating to *Quo Warranto*. He gave largely pragmatic responses that, if implemented across the realm, would have allowed for a reasonable indication of long usage to be accepted. But that was not the case, and confusion persisted, with some justices permitting retention of rights if the plaintiff could show continuous usage by their ancestors since time before legal memory (1189), and others refusing to accept this, leading to the postponement of many pleas. In the end, there were only a few who paid a particularly high price as a result of the inquiries: Gilbert de Clare, earl of Gloucester, is the most prominent of these. In his case a special roll was drawn up detailing all his franchises and challenging his right to them, and he went on to suffer significant losses in Kent. He was so incensed about his treatment that in 1278 he brought a petition to Parliament begging that the king 'allow him to enjoy the seisin of his franchises . . . in peace . . . he does not wish, if it please the king, that the king's will should be done to him contrary to the law of the land'.

There is no evidence that Edward was singling Gloucester out as a result of personal vindictiveness; he seems genuinely to have believed Gilbert and his father Richard had engaged in extensive usurpations, and hence his case received special attention. But Gilbert was the exception rather than the rule, and large numbers of postponements probably account for the fact that there was no concerted complaint about *Quo Warranto* in the 1280s.

However, in 1290, things changed dramatically when Gilbert de Thornton, a notoriously hard-line judge, replaced the disgraced Ralph Hengham. Thornton took a tough line in cases of *Quo Warranto*, refusing to allow continuous usage as a defence of claims. This prompted widespread complaints among the magnates, and with the king in need of money following his return from Gascony, they forced him to concede on the matter through the Statute of *Quo Warranto*. It allowed a claim to be vindicated by evidence of long usage, abandoning the requirement to produce a royal charter, which many, even with legitimate claims, simply did not possess. Even for a king as determined as Edward I, the issue of liberties and franchises was not one for which it was worth surrendering a grant of taxation. In any case, no matter how strongly Edward felt about rights that he and his lawyers argued could only be granted by the Crown, it was clear that reclaiming them on any significant scale was simply not achievable. There was too much confusion and too much debate about the rules that should be applied, and the volume of claims to be investigated was too high. After the compromise of 1290, there was little attempt to pursue *Quo Warranto* on any systematic basis.

With the Church, Edward was more successful in defending the Crown's position, despite facing a challenging and potentially incendiary situation. Problems began in 1279 with the appointment of John Pecham to the archbishopric of Canterbury. Pecham, who was determined to reform the Church, wanted, among other things, to rid it of pluralism, a practice whereby ecclesiastics held numerous positions leading inevitably to absenteeism, and to assert what he saw as the church's jurisdictional rights. In the case of the former there was the potential to affect often quite senior royal officials (Robert Burnell, who was bishop of Bath and Wells, was a case in point), and in the latter to create conflict with the Crown over jurisdictions that both the church and the state claimed for themselves. Pecham expressed his intentions immediately and forcefully when he assumed office, and while he initially retreated when challenged by the king, it was not for long. When Edward requested taxation from the church in 1279, he found himself presented in return with an extensive list of grievances in Parliament in the following year. Although the clergy's grant of taxation had not been made on condition that the grievances were addressed, the situation was nonetheless delicate. Edward handled it skilfully, agreeing to reforms of abuses, while carefully not giving ground on the fundamental lines between state and Church authority.

But Pecham's challenges did not go away. He continued to raise issues in the ensuing years, writing a long letter to Edward in 1281, in which he insisted that the king ensure that practices in England replicated those in Christendom as a whole. The archbishop somewhat provocatively accused Edward of setting himself 'to defend the iniquity of Hell' in relation to royal free chapels, which were, in the king's eyes, not subject to ecclesiastical jurisdiction. Further grievances were presented to Edward when he requested tax in 1283 after the second Welsh war, and this time the clergy initially refused to make a grant. They bowed to pressure from the king later in the year, but complaints were again raised in Parliament in 1285, now by the wider clergy, not Pecham. The archbishop had set the tone for resistance, and in his absence (he was conducting a visitation of Salisbury diocese at the time), emboldened by his example, the clergy spoke out about such things as the treatment of clerics in the royal courts. Luckily Edward was not asking for tax on this occasion, so concessions could be avoided, but the tone did not augur well and he was not inclined to enter into a major dispute with either Pecham or the wider clergy; in 1285 his eyes were firmly set on his departure for France the following year. On his way to Gascony in 1286 he therefore issued a writ, *Circumspecte Agatis*, which was designed to take some heat out of the situation by instructing the eyre justices to act with circumspection towards the church.

While Edward had met with little success in his bid to restore lost liberties and franchises to the Crown, he had managed to prevent a wider onslaught on royal rights from his equally assertive new archbishop of Canterbury. He had deftly steered a line between compromise and capitulation, and consequently avoided a major conflict with both Pecham and the wider Church. Elsewhere, the preservation of peace would not be so easy.

A New King Arthur? The Edwardian Conquest of Wales

Edward's commitment to the defence of royal rights was tested to the hilt by the Welsh prince Llywelyn in the early years of the reign, and tensions between the two leaders resulted in the invasion of Wales by Edward in 1277. The initial cause of the intervention in the principality was Llywelyn's failure to perform the homage that was due to Edward as the new king of England, something Llywelyn had agreed to as part of the Treaty of Montgomery in 1267. As with the homage due by the English king to his French counterpart for Gascony, which had been the key outcome of the Treaty of Paris of 1259, the new relationship was not straightforward and both sides mistrusted each other. After the Treaty of Montgomery, several English Marcher lords had worked to gain back territory they had lost to Llywelyn and his allies in the 1260s. Llywelyn believed they had tacit support from the English Crown in this, and that their campaigns were orchestrated. By 1270 he was complaining vociferously that the treaty was not being honoured, and shortly before Edward's return in 1274 he argued that his failure to pay the tribute to the English king (which he had also agreed to in the treaty) was his legitimate response to the fact that the Marcher lords had not restored lands to him that they had unjustly occupied. He failed to appear in 1273 to do his homage in Edward's absence.

His actions became all the more egregious from an English point of view in 1274, when he missed the royal coronation. Arrangements were subsequently made for a meeting between Edward and Llywelyn in November, but Edward was ill – still suffering the effects of the assassination attempt on him in the East (see p. 184) – which prevented this from happening. In any case, Llywelyn's suspicions of the English had by then been further aroused by a plot against him by his own brother Dafydd and another Welsh lord, Gruffudd ap Gwenwynwyn, the revelation of which led to the two men fleeing to England. In summer 1275, Edward, by then recovered from his bout of ill health, travelled specially to Chester to hold talks with Llywelyn, but the Welsh prince simply refused to attend, leaving Edward waiting. Edward was incensed at Llywelyn's failure to appear and declined to offer him safe-conduct for the Parliament of October 1275. For his part, Llywelyn again refused to appear. After that, tensions continued to mount: during the course of the winter of 1275–6, Edward confirmed the ancient liberties of the see of St Asaph, a favour to the bishop, who was an English ally. At the same time, he had Llywelyn's bride-to-be, Eleanor de Montfort, and her brother arrested when she was on the way to Wales for her marriage. This was not simply an act of provocation: Llywelyn's betrothal to Eleanor was, from Edward's perspective, surely meant to stir up Montfortian resentment against him. Llywelyn regarded Eleanor's capture as yet more evidence of the danger to him posed by the English king.

By early 1276, the positions of the two men were becoming increasingly entrenched: Llywelyn had failed to do homage on five separate occasions and was refusing to do so until his grievances were addressed, while Edward would not enter discussions with him without having already received his homage. Writing to the pope in summer that year, Edward expressed his frustration at the situation, saying that he had gone out of his way to enable Llywelyn to pay homage: 'We had so demeaned our royal dignity as to go to the confines of his land,' he said, referring to the fact that he had gone to Chester to try to meet with Llywelyn in 1275. Negotiations continued, but neither man would concede. Llywelyn remained deeply suspicious of Edward, while the English king in turn felt he could not be seen to tolerate a flagrant refusal to perform homage to him as a feudal overlord: this was a matter of legal obligation. On this the members of Edward's Council were in complete agreement with the king. This impasse made war inevitable, and it did not take long for Edward to act: in December 1276 orders were sent out for the host to muster at Worcester on 1 July 1277 for a campaign in Wales to discipline his recalcitrant vassal, the Welsh prince.

The muster Edward had ordered in 1277 was preceded by months of preparation. Forces actually began to be deployed during winter and spring 1276–7, long before the official muster, and by 1 July several Welsh rulers had already either joined the English forces or surrendered to them. The situation looked bleak for Llywelyn before the war had even officially begun, something that probably prompted him to send the bishop of Bangor to propose negotiations with Edward. The attempt was ignored; Edward had made his decision to act, and he could not now be seen to back down. Once war began in earnest, the main thrust of the action took place in North Wales, with Edward using Chester as his base. But this was not a war of pitched battle; medieval war rarely was. Key to the outcome was a more complex mix of the sheer size of the forces Edward sent into

North, South and mid-Wales, the relationships of native Welsh rulers with Llywelyn, and food supplies. On all three fronts Llywelyn was unable to match the English: even before the war the English commanders had managed to drive Llywelyn back into his patrimony of Gwynedd, native rulers either having already submitted to the English forces or soon to do so, or in a number of cases joining them. In addition Edward's army successfully cut off food supplies to Llywelyn in Anglesey. In November 1277, with winter setting in, the Welsh prince was forced to surrender and submit himself to Edward's mercy.

The terms imposed on Llywelyn in the ensuing Treaty of Aberconwy were humiliating: although he retained his title 'prince of Wales', he was forced to acknowledge Edward's lordship and had lost much of his own authority within Wales. He was fined £50,000 for disobedience (though Edward later remitted the fine), and was made to perform homage in London at the king's Christmas court. Llywelyn was also made to reinstate his enemies in Wales and provide ten hostages from the leading men of Gwynedd; he was additionally forced to accept his brothers' claims to their share of the Gwynedd patrimony, something he had vigorously resisted. Llywelyn could from then on only take homage from a limited number of Welsh princelings, as Edward had reserved the homage of most of them for himself. Some thought had also been given to keeping Anglesey in English royal hands indefinitely, though Edward decided in the end to allow Llywelyn and the heirs of his body to retain it; should there not be direct heirs, however, he stipulated that it would revert to the English Crown. Finally, the Welsh prince was told that he must pay five hundred marks a year to the Crown, signifying his outstanding debts under the Treaty of Montgomery. By 1278, Llywelyn had been truly humbled and the power he had built up in Wales redistributed in favour of the English king.

The systematic humiliation of the Welsh prince did not mark the end of the matter. Edward was determined he would not be challenged again, and immediately embarked upon an ambitious programme to settle matters permanently in Wales. As with government in England, he gave a great deal of personal attention to this, briefing leading officers directly and requiring that many issues were referred back to him personally for a decision. From November 1277, the Welsh rolls were created to keep a record of all official correspondence regarding Wales, marking the start of its integration into English government, and to promote military security Edward embarked on building and restoring a number of castles. Four new castles were constructed, three of which were at sites chosen by the king himself, at Flint, Rhuddlan (the king travelled there himself to inspect the works in September 1278), Aberystwyth and Builth. This was done with remarkable speed, with Edward bringing more than two thousand diggers from England to Flint even before the war had ended. The castles were built using the latest techniques that Edward had witnessed first-hand both in France and in the East on crusade. They were characteristically ambitious: a desire to ensure that Rhuddlan was properly accessible by sea, for example, resulted in the construction of a deep-water canal between two and three kilometres long. Simultaneously, a number of existing castles taken during the war were retained under royal control, even if the local territory had been given back to native rulers. Those rulers were ordered to repair the castles at their own expense where necessary. Looking towards any future problems, routes through forests were cleared and widened to enable troops and supplies to move quickly should they be needed.

To cement royal rule more generally, new personnel were put in place on the ground. In west Wales, all the royal estates were brought under the sole command of Bogo de Knoville, a household knight, as the king's justiciar, while in the north, two of the Four Cantrefs were given over to the control of the justice and chamberlain of Chester. Justices were also sent to hear land and trespass pleas; it was the English king's justice to which native Welsh rulers were now obliged to look. Even Llywelyn was commanded to come before the justices 'to propound the suits of himself and his men and to do and receive justice'. This represented a very significant expansion of the judicial role of the English Crown in Wales – yet more Edwardian state-building, in fact, only this time across the border in a land not used to such active and interventionist English overlordship. Welsh law was very different from its English equivalent.

The introduction of such extensive administrative changes after 1277 rode roughshod over Welsh tradition, and, together with Edward's assertions and those of his officials, quickly bred a significant degree of resentment among native Welshmen. Many came to feel towards him the same way they had done towards the equally assertive Llywelyn in his pomp. Several native princelings complained bitterly about their jurisdiction and authority being undermined by Edwardian officials and about English lords being favoured in disputes. Llywelyn ap Gruffudd Maelor, a ruler of northern Powys who had defected to Edward in 1276, found he was forced to defend himself both against Edward's constable of Oswestry and a host of claims to his lands. The king quickly shed many of the allies he had made among native Welsh rulers in the run-up to the war of 1277.

Edward's treatment of Llywelyn had inevitably alienated the Welsh prince. Although Edward had made some gestures of conciliation, permitting Llywelyn's marriage to Eleanor de Montfort, and even paying for the wedding banquet, saying that he would be 'benevolent and a friend to Llywelyn in all things', all was not well. Llywelyn paid his debts from the Treaty of Montgomery, but he quietly worked to rebuild alliances in parts of Wales and the March. Meanwhile Edward not only obliged Llywelyn to come before his justices, he turned a blind eye to the excesses of his officials in their dealings with the prince: two of Llywelyn's men were executed at Oswestry and goods that Llywelyn believed were his through the right of shipwreck were confiscated by the justice of Chester. Edward furthermore prolonged a dispute over Arwystli in central Wales between Llywelyn and Gruffudd ap Gwenwynwyn, in a way that the former found understandably infuriating. First the dispute, which initially came before the justices Edward had sent into Wales, was adjourned several times on technicalities. Then Edward became personally involved in a way that signalled to Llywelyn that he would not receive royal favour. When Llywelyn claimed that the plea should be judged according to Welsh law, Edward refused to concede, even though in a similar plea the Marcher lord Roger Mortimer had been told that Welsh land should be judged by Welsh law. Edward argued to Llywelyn that 'the magnates of Wales had of their own free will recognised that disputes which arose ought to be determined by the king's majesty by the king's writs before him or his justices'.

In the early 1280s Edward began to claim in more general terms that Welsh law could only be legitimate if it did not detract from his Crown or the rights of his kingdom. Throughout all this there was no resolution of the Arwystli dispute, and Llywelyn was becoming more and more resentful of his treatment by Edward, which seemed to ignore his own explicitly recognised status as a prince.

By 1282, just five years after the war, anger at the changes of recent years had welled up into the stuff of revolt, particularly in North and mid-Wales, both of which had been much less exposed to English rule historically than the South. On 21 March, a sudden attack on Hawarden Castle by Dafydd, Llywelyn's brother, previously Edward's ally, ignited rebellion, and thereafter it did not take long for the fire to spread. The following day Llywelyn ap Gruffudd Maelor, who had been provoked by the constable of Oswestry Castle, launched an attack on the castle. Then the princelings of Deheubarth seized the castles of Aberystwyth, Llanymddyfri and Carreg Cennen. Llywelyn, who seems not to have been aware of any initial plot against Edward, quickly saw his opportunity and joined the revolt, taking the lead. Primarily this was a rebellion of North and mid-Wales, and inevitably not all Welsh rulers joined the rebels, but the scale was nonetheless huge and called for a much more sustained and extensive response from the English Crown than 1277. The scale of the task in 1282–3 is emphasised by the fact that the campaign to put down the rebellion would eventually cost Edward around seven times the amount of the war of 1277.

Once again, Edward's response was swift. The king himself personally directed the campaign, vowing 'to repress the rebellion and malice of the Welsh'. He set up three military commands under Reginald Grey at Chester, Roger Mortimer in mid-Wales and Robert Tibetot in west Wales. He also brought in around fifteen hundred Gascon crossbowmen, more than forty ships from the Cinque Ports and provisions from as far and wide as France and Ireland. Two storage depots for these were set up in Whitchurch and Chester. By the end of May he had called a muster at Chester of more than a thousand diggers and around 350 carpenters 'for the king's works in Wales' – as he progressed with the campaign this enabled the repair of castles which secured the rear of the army. There was to be no respite for the winter weather: Edward simply arranged for the delivery of winter clothing for the army; he was determined to continue campaigning, no matter what. The English army met with sustained resistance from the Welsh, who engaged in guerrilla warfare, but the forces Edward was able to deploy were simply too large to resist for long: by the end of the summer the Welsh were defeated in the west, and in mid-Wales Edward's commanders were holding the rebellion at bay. North Wales proved more difficult to subdue and it took three months before the English forces made enough progress to enable an assault on Snowdonia in the autumn. With Anglesey already under control, by October the English forces were converging on Llywelyn from the south, south-east and east, leaving him with few options. Desperately he attempted to open up a new front in mid-Wales, where Roger Mortimer had died in late October, but a Marcher force descended on him and he was killed on 11 December 1282 near Builth, either during or just after a skirmish. His death prompted desperate laments by Welsh chroniclers, one of whom wrote that 'all of Wales was cast to the ground'.

But despite his brother's death and the increasing dominance of the English forces, Dafydd fought on. While he did so, Edward continued his own march, crossing the River Conwy into Snowdonia in January 1283, bringing about surrender after surrender in his wake. By the middle of March he had been able to move his headquarters west from Rhuddlan to Aberconwy. Meanwhile, in west Wales, the garrison of Castell y Bere surrendered on 25 April; it had been Dafydd's last major outpost. In June Dafydd himself was finally captured and put to death not by the English but by 'men of his own tongue'. Summer 1283 saw the total subjugation of Wales. The campaign of 1282–3 had been one of startling organisation, scale and determination, and celebrations of victory were similarly impressive: in July 1284, Edward invited English and foreign knights to a 'round table', after the legend of King Arthur, comprising jousting and feasting, at Nefyn in north-west Wales, which had been one of the Gwynedd dynasty's most cherished courts. He followed that with a progress around Wales in the autumn to celebrate the conquest. As part of this he was quick to turn Llywelyn's hall at Aberconwy into a palace for his future son who would become prince of Wales, and all the insignia of the former princes were stripped from Gwynedd. Through the conquest Edward had, he said, 'extinguished the poison'. For many of the Welsh a new poison would now be administered.

Edward was to spend almost the entire year in Wales in 1284, personally directing his officials there. Hostages were taken, and passes cleared as the king journeyed around the land affirming his conquest, flanked by bannerets and knights of his household and mounted crossbowmen. Work had already begun on cementing the conquest in North Wales as early as March, when new castles were begun at Conwy, Harlech and Caernarfon. Edward's great military architect from Savoy, James St George, was employed to design each one using the latest techniques, and the king's workmen moved at staggering speed: all three castles were in large part built by 1289. The Edwardian castles in Wales were imposing symbols of military domination towering over their localities; they were also to become the impregnable administrative bases of the new government. Caernarfon in its grandeur even emanated overtones of Constantinople in its design, deliberately reflecting the ties of the area with imperial Rome and the alleged discovery of the body of Constantine there in 1283. Bands of coloured stone in its walls were an invocation of one of the walls of Constantinople, while imperial eagles were positioned on the turrets of its main towers.

The symbolism and majesty of these outward expressions of conquest were accompanied by the confiscation of lands from native princes who had joined the rebellion. English law and the shire system were also introduced into Wales, English settlers encouraged and English justiciars appointed. Some concessions were made: there was no thoroughgoing disinheritance of those below the native princes, and the most far-reaching governmental changes were reserved for the (now extensive) royal lands. Partible inheritance was permitted to continue and some Welshmen were given important posts. Marcher lordships were initially left alone. Nonetheless, plenty of lands passed into the hands of English lords, particularly in central and northern Wales as part of the consolidation of English supremacy: there could be no mistaking the fact that this was a conquered territory, which was being subsumed into the English state. At times Edward was particularly inflexible, and that prompted resentment on the part of several individuals and communities. In 1287, the king's former ally among the native princes, Rhys ap Maredudd of Dryslwyn in the South, rebelled in opposition to what he understandably felt to be humiliation by the king and his representatives, and the privileging of another English lord, John Giffard, over Rhys in claims to land. But Rhys could not command much support – few felt able to resist the English king's might, having seen what had happened in 1282–3 – and the rebellion was crushed swiftly by Edward's regency government while he remained away in Gascony. Rhys lost all his castles and went on the run, remaining at large until 1292, when he was captured and summarily executed.

The treatment of Rhys ap Maredudd in the 1280s was classically robust on the part both of Edward and of those who represented him (who could surely be said to take their tone from the king himself, or at least to have been appointed as men in his own image). Edward remembered the humiliation of the 1250s and was determined that Wales, and particularly the Gwynedd dynasty, should no longer be a thorn in the side of English kings; he expressed his determination in characteristically ambitious style. The conquest and settlement of Wales were nothing short of masterful.

In the early 1290s, Edward also began progressively to challenge the status of the March and Marcher lords' privileges. This was partly provoked by the behaviour of some lords during Edward's absence in Gascony. But it is likely that this simply provided Edward with the justification for a more vigorous assertion of royal rights in the Welsh March now that Wales had been conquered. It is no accident that in the same period he claimed sole guardianship of all temporalities during episcopal vacancies in the March, and demanded taxes there for the first time in 1291–2. Later in the 1290s he would send his own commissioners to the March to raise troops rather than requesting them from the Marcher lords, as had been the practice previously. It was to the 'dignity of the Crown' that Edward was quick to appeal in instances where he was challenged; in other words, this was again a matter of royal rights, which he was determined to assert ever more forcefully.

The Edwardian conquest of Wales has been called imperious and perhaps even imperial, though it seems clear Edward did not start his reign with a desire to bring Wales under English control. His overriding priorities in his dealings with the principality were twofold. First there was the due recognition of his royal overlordship, which Llywelyn had repeatedly refused to give in the 1270s. Second, and directly connected with this, Edward wanted to prevent the princes of Gwynedd from overtly threatening English interests in Wales, as they attempted to expand their power. His interpretation, and it was probably correct, seems to have been that, without conquest, the situation was destined to remain deeply unsettled and challenging. Where Dafydd's rebellion of 1282 was concerned, he presumably saw no point in prolonging things when, given his vastly superior resources, he had the opportunity to settle the matter decisively in the English Crown's favour. His actions, which rode roughshod over local custom and practice, remain understandably resented in Wales even now. The surviving great chain of royal and lordly castles, built to cement the conquest, reminds us of the assertiveness, power and resource of the English conquerors.

Edward and the Scottish Succession Dispute

Edward's strong sense of the English Crown's rights was equally in evidence in the north. In 1286, Scotland's long-lived king, Alexander III, had died in a fall from his horse, leaving only one heir, Margaret, the so-called 'maid of Norway', his granddaughter, who was only seven years old. While Alexander had persuaded the Scottish lords to recognise Margaret as his heir in 1284, there was significant unease in Scotland about whether peace could be preserved, as there were other claimants to the Scottish throne. This prompted the appointment of six guardians who were to rule on behalf of the community of the realm until Margaret was able to rule for herself. While the composition of the panel of guardians reflected the balance of power within Scotland, fears of unrest made the appearance of the additional prospect of a marriage alliance between Margaret and Edward I's son a good one. Where the marriage idea came from is unclear, but it suited Edward too, who swiftly conducted negotiations that culminated in the Treaty of Birgham in July 1290, which provided for the marriage. The treaty made it clear that England and Scotland were to remain separate, and under their own administrations, and that the relics and muniments of Scotland were to stay in Scotland. But despite all this, Edward went on to act in ways that showed little inclination to respect the independence of the Scottish realm. On 4 June 1290 he claimed that the earl of Ulster had surrendered the Isle of Man to him and appointed a custodian – this despite the fact that the island was claimed by the Scottish monarch. Edward's bishop of Durham, Anthony Bek, went on to admit the warring residents of the Western Isles of Scotland to Edward's peace, a remarkable act in another sovereign realm. And in late July Edward appointed Bek 'to administer justice and set that realm [Scotland] in order' on behalf of his son and Queen Margaret. Although Bek was to work with the guardians, they were expected to be obedient to him. Edward's actions probably reflected his own sense that he was the feudal overlord of Scotland rather than an outright bid to begin to take over its government permanently, but none of this augured well for Scotland's continued independence once Margaret assumed the throne.

In the end, fate intervened and the maid of Norway was never to take her place as queen of Scotland: she fell ill and died on the journey from Norway in September 1290. As she was Alexander's last direct heir, her death left the succession open to question and potentially violent dispute. Within weeks of the news, more than a dozen people had made claims to the throne and the guardians feared a rapid descent into civil war. One of the guardians, the bishop of St Andrews, wrote to Edward I to tell him that, on hearing rumours of Margaret's death, Robert Bruce the Elder had come to Perth with a large following. The bishop asked Edward to come to the border to help prevent trouble and decide on the rightful claimant to the throne. It seems that another group of lords, at around the same time, also asked for Edward's assistance *against* the bishop.

In the event, the death of Edward's own beloved wife, Eleanor, from a type of malaria in November 1290 meant that he could not move north that year. The loss of Eleanor was a devastating blow to Edward. The couple had rarely been apart during the thirty-six years of their marriage, with Eleanor even accompanying him on crusade in 1270. Like Edward's parents, the couple were devoted to each other: when Edward was injured in the assassination attempt in 1272, it was reported that she was led from his side 'weeping and lamenting' when the surgeon cut the infected flesh from his arm. And when Eleanor died, Edward's creation of the 'Eleanor Crosses' was unprecedented. His grief for her loss was deep and lasting.

During this time Edward, nonetheless, did not entirely forget about Scotland: he sent Anthony Bek in his place to make attempts to induce the Scottish guardians and claimants to allow Edward to decide on the succession. In March 1291, letters were also sent to around thirty heads of monastic houses in England, asking them to provide any information they had from their chronicles 'touching in any way our realm and the rule of Scotland', clearly an attempt to find evidence for Edward's understanding that the English king was the overlord of his Scottish counterpart. By spring, it had been agreed that Edward should play a role in determining the succession, but on meeting the Scottish magnates at Norham in May 1291, he made it conditional on their recognition of his overlordship. There was real resistance to this, with the guardians protesting that they could not affirm Edward's overlordship in the absence of a Scottish king. Undeterred, Edward instead put the question to the claimants to the throne themselves, who gave their agreement – they were all presumably hoping he would support them and were therefore keen not to annoy him. This was probably doubly important given that whichever of them was chosen would be likely to need his support later in case of challenges to their authority within Scotland. With the issue of overlordship settled, the hearing could proceed. It was a protracted process, which became known as the 'Great Cause', and it was not concluded until November 1292 when Edward declared John Balliol the rightful claimant to the throne. There is little debate that his was clearly the strongest claim, whatever his nearest rival, Robert Bruce, thought.

But having been placed on the throne by Edward I, Balliol faced two problems. On the one hand, he needed to establish his authority in Scotland, particularly over those who had been his rivals in the bid for the Crown. On the other, he had to accept Edward's overlordship, which had the potential to undermine the very authority he was trying to build. Much would depend on how Edward himself acted, and it soon became clear that relations between the two kings were not to be straightforward. Within a month Edward was hearing appeals against the judgement of the Scottish courts (technically his right as overlord), in one case overturning the original judgement. When the Scots raised concerns that Edward was hearing these cases outside Scotland, his justice Roger Brabazon replied on the king's behalf that Edward was under no obligation to stand by the promises he had made when the throne was vacant. This was essentially a statement that the king of England had carte blanche to act in whatever way he deemed appropriate. Soon afterwards, this was followed by a statement that the Scottish king might even be summoned to appear before him in England if Edward judged it appropriate. Under a year later, in Michaelmas 1293, Balliol was duly called to England to appear before Edward in Parliament in connection with an appeal. The Scottish king managed to secure an adjournment of the case, but his summons and Edward's actions over the previous year were stark indications of how Edward viewed his relationship with him: it was Edward's right as overlord to hear appeals and summon his vassal to appear before him, and, regardless of the political impact, Edward insisted on his rights. The result for Balliol was that his position within Scotland was critically undermined right from the outset.

In Scotland, as in England and Wales, the first two decades of the reign saw Edward I determinedly pursuing what he believed to be the rights of the English Crown. His actions in Scotland might seem opportunistic, but they were underpinned by a very real conviction that English overlordship of the Scottish realm was an established fact. At a moment of acute political crisis for Scotland, Edward focused on ensuring that those rights were not overlooked or conceded. But here, as in Wales, his insistence on exercising his rights to the full overrode political pragmatism, and created deep resentment. In Scotland, it also undermined Balliol's attempts to establish his authority and contributed to growing political instability. Later events in Wales and Scotland were to rebuke Edward for his masterfulness.

Taking the Cross and State-Building in Gascony

Edward was a man both of principle and of strongly held ideas. There can be no doubt of his deeply felt sense of duty to uphold the common good of the realm or of his commitment to royal rights. Like Henry III, his piety and his crusading vow similarly meant a great deal to him. The notion of a new crusade remained in his mind throughout his reign, and in 1284, with the situation in England and Wales much more settled, and the Scottish succession dispute a thing of the future, he declared his intention to go on crusade again. If his ambition were to be achieved it would take a great deal of planning, and key to it was the establishment of peace within Europe. In early 1285, Edward concluded that he needed to travel to

Europe to intervene diplomatically in the wars raging between some of his most powerful counterparts. He initially contemplated departing for the Continent quickly, and travelled to Dover to make preparations for crossing the Channel. However, it proved too soon to hope for a diplomatic solution to the major conflict of the period, the continuing fight between the French and the Aragonese over Sicily (in which Edward, unlike his father, did not play a part), and Edward did not make the journey.

In the months that followed, foreign policy remained high on the agenda for different reasons: by the time Parliament was convened in May 1285 Edward had been summoned as duke of Gascony to provide troops to assist the French king in a likely war with the king of Aragon (feudal vassals were obliged to provide military assistance to their overlord as a core part of the feudal relationship, and the fact that Edward was a king himself did not exempt him from his ducal duties). During the course of the Parliament ambassadors were sent to France to discuss the matter, but the situation across the Channel was quickly transformed by the death of the French king, Philip III. This necessitated homage by Edward as duke of Gascony to the French king. The timing of this was convenient because issues of governance in Gascony itself also required attention from its duke. Both of these necessitated Edward's personal presence. However, his determination to get reform in Gascony right and, perhaps more importantly, to try to broker peace in the Franco-Aragonese conflict over Sicily so that the focus of his counterparts could be shifted to his longed-for crusade meant that he fixed on a longer trip. His decision signals not only that his priorities stretched beyond England's borders but probably too the fact that he felt that the situation domestically was settled enough to admit of his greatest ambition, to take the cross again.

In May 1286, when Edward crossed the English Channel, he was prepared for a long stay, taking with him eight ships of kitchen equipment and a thousand horses. He proceeded to Paris where he performed homage to Philip IV, though not before the chancellor, Robert Burnell, had made a speech to the French court in which he stated that the French had thus far not honoured the terms of the Treaty of Paris of 1259 and that he expected that would change hereafter. It was a thinly veiled shot across the new king's bows. The two kings then entered into negotiations about the situation in Gascony, particularly the number of appeals to Paris by Gascons unsatisfied with the verdicts of the ducal court there. Philip agreed that Edward and his officials in Gascony would from then on have three months to deal with appeals before he intervened. It was a positive start, but Burnell's speech is a reminder of the tensions inherent in the relationship between lord and vassal that had been established by the Treaty of Paris in 1259. Edward had deeply resented the treaty at the time and, as king, can only have regarded its terms as demeaning to him.

With the formalities of homage over, Edward could shift his focus on to the negotiations between France and Aragon. The initial results were successful, and he was able to bring about a short-term truce between the two until March 1287. But further negotiations, through which Edward incurred very significant financial costs, ultimately came to nothing. By the early 1290s, for all his efforts, the French and Aragonese remained antagonists. Edward himself, having taken the crusader's vow for the second time in his life in 1287, nonetheless reached an agreement with Pope Nicholas IV in 1290 that he would depart in 1293. In 1292, he began diplomatic preparations for his crusade, but events in Europe in the next two years, which were ultimately to envelop England in war, were to mean that the planned departure never took place. Edward's inability to fulfil his life's greatest ambition, to 'bear the cross to where Jesus Christ was born' according to the chronicler Peter Langtoft, was a source of great regret to him for the rest of his life: on his deathbed in 1307, it is reported that he asked for his heart to be sent to the East, and eighty knights with it.

More successful were Edward's attempts to make major reforms to the government of Gascony, which mirrored his state-building efforts elsewhere. As in England, he commissioned a number of large-scale inquiries as soon as he arrived in the duchy in 1286. But although the principles underlying the inquiries were the same as in England, Gascony was a very different place. Among the main problems were the limited systematisation in its administration, the lack of revenues generated from the duchy and the small number of castles under ducal control, which posed defensive challenges. For those reasons the reforms that followed in May and June 1289, once Edward and his officials had acquired their own wider understanding of the issues in need of attention, could not simply be a copy of English initiatives. First, administrative changes were made: the seneschal's jurisdiction over matters judicial, military and political was clearly separated from the constable of Bordeaux's responsibility for duchy finances. A stipulation was also made that the ducal officials were to be remunerated with fixed sums as a way of reducing graft and corruption. To lessen the incidence of appeals directly from the regions of the duchy to the French king in Paris, sub-seneschals were appointed in Saintonge, Périgord, Limousin, Quercy and the Agenais. In all except the Agenais – which was historically more independent, having only been returned to the English Crown in the 1270s – the sub-seneschals were to report directly to the seneschal. An appeals justice was permanently established in Bordeaux, and a proctor was appointed to have responsibility for duchy business in the *Parlement* at Paris. Defence was attended to via work on castles which had begun before Edward's arrival in 1286. Repairs took place to existing fortresses, and attempts were made to acquire or build new ones. By the time Edward left Gascony in 1289 the situation had improved, and around twenty major castles were in ducal hands, but lack of resources meant that a castle-building programme on the scale of that which took place in Wales was never going to be possible.

Revenues were also a focus, an especially urgent matter since, as they stood, they were not even adequate to pay for Edward's visit. One of the problems was the lack of estates in the duke's hands, which meant that land generated very little income for him; attempts were made to remedy this by acquiring more land following Edward's arrival. This financial imperative, and the need to increase his authority, had already led to the creation by Edward of a number of new towns well before his arrival in 1286, something that was also found in England and following the conquest of Wales. Some of these new towns, or *bastides*, were founded on ducal lands, meaning that the duke could derive direct profits from them. Many others were founded on agreements between Edward as duke and the local lord, with the duke providing protection and granting town liberties, and profits being divided between the two. This increased ducal revenues and created an informal matrix of influence and co-operation between the duke and local landholders. This was a sort of 'soft power' – the duke could never hope to control by force his fiercely independent

Gascon lords, who ultimately had recourse to the king of France if they were unhappy with their duke. He needed to foster good working relationships with them.

By the time Edward left Gascony in 1289, reforms had been completed that were intended to produce much more stability in its government. Following his return to England, he added another layer to Gascon administration by appointing a royal lieutenant above the seneschal, to give the duchy government more power. As in England, the Edwardian reforms in Gascony were wide-ranging, and were attuned to local circumstances – there was no attempt to create common solutions to problems of differing types. Hence it took three years for Edward, ably assisted in Gascony by chancellor Robert Burnell, to issue the Libourne Ordinances. However, the problems with Gascon government were difficult to fix. For the most part it had to operate in the absence of the duke, and that was never going to be ideal. The reforms instituted by the Ordinances made a great deal of sense, but their implementation without Edward's direct supervision was less successful, and he was soon ordering an inquiry into the behaviour of Gascon officials in his absence.

To make matters still more challenging, relations began to deteriorate with Philip IV in France. Part of the background to this was the fact that Philip had come to feel threatened by Edward. Philip's concern may well have resulted from the fact that Edward had acquired the Agenais on the border with Gascony together with the county of Ponthieu in 1279 and southern Saintonge in 1286. These were lands that had been promised to the English king in the Treaty of Paris, and which gave him more territorial strength and prominence in France: the Agenais was strategically important because it controlled access to Bordeaux from greater Aquitaine. Much of the tax on the wine trade was levied in the Agenais, so it was an important source of revenues too. When coupled with Edward's reforms in Gascony, partly designed to prevent so many appeals coming to the *Parlement* at Paris, and Philip's need to assert his own position in France, the mix was heady.

In this context, events that would at other points have had relatively little significance for the overall relationship between the two kings came to reflect the broader tensions that now existed in that relationship. A war between Anglo-Gascon sailors and French sailors from Normandy drew the French king's fire, and Philip wasted no time in writing to Edward laying charges against him in connection with it. Furthermore, the number of Gascon appeals being entertained by the Paris *Parlement* suddenly increased. Whether the appeals were genuine or not (and there is a strong likelihood that they were being deliberately engineered), this could be used by the French king to assert his position of overlordship of Gascony. By spring 1293 English embassies were travelling to France to attempt to negotiate with Philip over the war between sailors. They were repeated in July. By then the situation looked grave: the French were already reinforcing castles in Poitou and Saintonge, and in October 1293 Edward was summoned to Paris in person to answer accusations about the behaviour of his Gascon officials and the war between sailors. Attempts to broker peace continued throughout this time, but the scene had been set for the French confiscation of Gascony and the declaration of all-out war in 1294.

In the twenty years following his return to England in 1274, Edward had demonstrated remarkable qualities as a ruler. Reforms were undertaken with ferocious energy, ambition and pace both in England and, later, in Gascony. State-building had taken place on an immense scale: in England, the judicial system had been expanded, financial reform had been effected, Parliament had been developed, the use of legislation to bring about major change had become established, royal officialdom in the localities had grown exponentially, giving an enhanced role to local knights, and royal government had come to perform a still greater function in maintaining order. In Gascony, government administration had been reformed, and attempts had been made to put ducal finances and the security of the duchy on a surer footing. Within the British Isles, Wales had been conquered, and the conquest had been followed by one of the most far-reaching settlements imaginable. The string of castles built there at immense cost bore witness to the towering and imperious authority of the English king in his newly acquired principality: Edward's state-building ambitions had even been exported across the Welsh border.

Edward was clearly not responsible for the detail of all the reforms and developments that took place in his name, but he clearly provided the driving force: it is surely not a coincidence that changes in England began in earnest not in 1272, but when Edward returned in 1274, and that the scale and pace of reform in England slackened dramatically during his absence in France between 1286 and 1289. What Edward provided was the strategic vision and the charisma of a dynamic leader with an over-arching sense of purpose. What was that purpose? Most obviously, Edward embraced the aims of the reform movement of his father's reign, with his focus on good government, sound financial management, consultation, the delivery of justice and rooting out official corruption. Underpinning this was both political intelligence and good sense, but it would be a mistake to characterise Edward as simply politically pragmatic or, worse, cynical or self-serving. Nor, though, was he straightforwardly altruistic. At the heart of Edward's approach to kingship was an acute sense of his duty to uphold the 'dignity of the Crown', in which the maintenance of the common good was key. In a letter to his justiciar of Chester in 1259, long before he became king, he wrote: 'If . . . common justice is denied to anyone of our subjects by us or our bailiffs, we lose the favour of God and man, and our lordship is belittled.' It was a compelling ideology: the Crown, and therefore the lordship of men, had been bestowed on Edward by God, and that lordship had to be just. If it were not, both it and he as lord would be brought into disrepute, undermined in the eyes of his subjects and of God himself. As an ideology, it chimed perfectly with the spirit of Magna Carta.

This same powerful ideological drive can be seen in Edward's unerr-ing pursuit of royal rights. If he were the God-appointed steward of the Crown, he had to pass on all that belonged to it intact to his successor. He could not countenance the loss of the sovereign rights of overlordship that existed in Wales and that he believed pertained to him in Scotland too, or the liberties and franchises he felt had been usurped nefariously in England, or the jurisdiction over the Welsh March and its lords that some were abusing. Of course, rights were defined in a way that was conveni-ent to the king, but overwhelmingly there is a sense in these first decades that underlying Edward's drive to maintain or recover rights was a set of genuine beliefs: he referred repeatedly to the 'dignity' of his Crown in correspondence, particularly where rights were concerned. Underpinning all this was his deep sense of religious conviction, a piety that drove his decision to embark on crusade in 1270, and his desire to do so again, and which remained high on his list of priorities right up to his death.

Edward under Pressure

In the first twenty years of his reign, Edward had to a large extent controlled the agenda. There had been relatively little to test him. The opposite would be true in the years after 1294. Edward would face war on three fronts, with opponents in France, the Low Countries and Scotland who were not easily defeated, as well as rebellion in Wales. These cumulative foreign commitments would come at huge cost, both financial and political, for the king, and his abilities as a leader would be tested to the hilt. At times he was to be found seriously wanting, and relations with his subjects became strained under the burdens of his military commitments. Edward's management of the situation revealed the weaknesses of his personality: his intransigence, at times his duplicity, and his failure to listen.

Problems began in France. As 1294 opened, negotiations with the French were still frantically being conducted with a view to avoiding war, and it seemed initially as though they might succeed when Edmund Crouchback, who had been sent to negotiate on Edward's behalf, came to an agreement with the French king. It promised to preserve Philip IV's honour as overlord while enabling Gascony to be retained by the English: this would be achieved by Edward formally surrendering Gascony to Philip, and Philip in turn never actually enforcing the surrender. The latter point was to be kept secret; Philip's negotiators possibly confided to Edmund that their king was under pressure within France to take a hawkish approach. It was a solution to which Edward readily agreed as a way of avoiding war, and he duly handed over Gascony in March 1294. However, it turned out that both Edmund and Edward had been duped: Philip immediately reneged on the pact to give Gascony back to Edward and ordered him to come before the *Parlement* at Paris as his vassal. It was a humiliating outcome, the worst possible, and historians have tended to be critical of Edmund for entering into an agreement on the basis of an informal promise and with such an implausible outcome. But this fails to appreciate the difficulty of the situation in 1293–4. Everyone expected war, and anything that seemed to promise peace instead was likely to be seized upon by Edward, especially given his desire to mount a crusade in the East. Moreover, Edward and Edmund would never have expected such a show of bad faith from Philip IV.

Once Gascony had been formally confiscated, the course of events was inevitable: Edward refused to show up at the *Parlement* in Paris to answer for his alleged misdeeds, and Gascony was declared forfeit to the French king. That in turn led Edward formally to renounce his feudal homage to Philip and to declare war. On the very same day, English envoys were sent to Germany to try to arrange an alliance with King Adolf of Nassau in order to begin the creation of a group of allies (what would become known as Edward's 'Grand Alliance') against the French king that was to form the cornerstone of Edward's military strategy, in much the same way as his grandfather in the run-up to the battle of Bouvines in 1214. Edward's approach had to take this form because reconquering Gascony would be impossible if the French king and his army were able to focus their attention entirely on retaining it. A diversionary conflict was needed elsewhere in order to split the French forces, and the most promising avenues to pursue in relation to this were to the north and east of France, where other discontented feudal vassals of the French king might be prevailed upon to challenge their overlord. A concerted action on the part of a number of disaffected lords was more likely to bring success for all of them.

Edward's plan was to conduct a campaign in person against Philip in the north, fighting alongside the Flemings and others, while other English forces combined with anti-French Gascons down in the duchy. The embassy to Adolf of Nassau was therefore just the first in a number of approaches to other lords. It was followed by agreements with several lesser German nobles as well as with the archbishop of Cologne, who agreed to provide cavalry. The duke of Brabant, who was already married to Edward's daughter Margaret, and Count Florence of Holland were similarly quickly brought on side. These alliances came at great financial cost to Edward, just as they had to King John: Adolf of Nassau and the duke of Brabant were each given assurances that they would receive £40,000 by the end of 1294. The archbishop of Cologne was promised ten thousand marks, again by the end of the year, while £20,000 was offered to Florence of Holland.

The aim was to add the count of Flanders to this growing list of allies – because of its wealthy wool towns, Flanders was a key vassal to the French. But that proved to be a harder task: although the count had grievances against Philip, the latter, seeing the risk of rebellion by him, attempted to appease him. By early 1296, Philip had also been able to detach the count of Holland from the fledgling alliance, and it began to look as though the carefully constructed compact would collapse. It took painstaking negotiation and a lot of money in 1296 to reconstitute it, and by early 1297 Edward was consequently ready to conduct a major campaign.

While all this was happening, a somewhat piecemeal holding operation had been launched in Gascony itself. That in itself had been a challenge: troops had been ordered to muster at Portsmouth at the beginning of September 1294, but so few responded that it had to be rescheduled for later that month. In October a decision was taken to pay wages to those who would agree to serve, and although numbers remained disappointing, this at least enabled a force to set sail under the command of John, duke of Brittany, the king's nephew who was also earl of Richmond, and John de St John, one of Edward's household knights.

Another group had been due to follow them out in late 1294 under the leadership of Edward's brother Edmund. This army was to represent the vanguard of the English attempt to regain Gascony, but at the last minute Edmund and his troops were forced to divert to Wales, where a fresh rebellion had broken out at the end of September. In the previous three years, English impositions on the principality had grown exponentially. First, in 1291, Edward had requested an unprecedented grant of tax from Wales in order to help pay his outstanding debts from his time in Gascony. This was the same tax that was imposed on the Marchers. What followed was a protracted process of negotiation with communities across Wales, meaning that the tax was only finally assessed towards the end of 1292. It bore heavily on the native population and created deep resentment. In 1294 it was followed by another unprecedented demand, this time for feudal levies to campaign in Gascony. As overlord, Edward was entitled both to request taxation and to raise armies from among his vassals, but to do this so soon after the conquest in a land where resentment was already festering was to tempt fate. On the very day the levies were due to assemble at Shrewsbury ready for their journey to Gascony, the date of which coincided with the deadline for the final instalment of the tax of 1291, revolt broke out in the principality.

Unlike 1287, this was not a localised rebellion, nor one predominantly of the north. Rebels came from across Wales, under the leadership of several lords, and grievances were against a mixture of English lords and English officials. Documents were burned, officials were killed and several castles, including the king's impressive new castle at Caernarfon, were taken. A cadet of the Gwynedd dynasty, Madog ap Llywelyn, came to assume over-all leadership and like Llywelyn made a call to resurgent Welsh nationalism by titling himself 'prince of Wales'.

It is a mark of Edward's complacence about the settlement of Wales that he was caught unawares by the revolt. Once he was notified of events, he acted swiftly and with devastating effectiveness. Not only was the force that had been earmarked for the campaign in Gascony diverted to Wales, but some thirty-five thousand infantry were assembled to conduct a war on three fronts in mid-, North and South Wales, with the king commanding the northern forces in person. As in 1282, Edward brought in supplies by sea from as far afield as Bayonne in Gascony. Some of the captured cas-tles were quickly relieved, but stalemate ensued, with the rebels deploying guerrilla warfare against Edward throughout the final months of 1294. In the end, though, the sheer weight of the English forces proved too much, with key victories by the earls of Hereford in the south-east, and the earl of Warwick in mid-Wales. By April Edward was able to set out from Conwy to receive the submissions of the rebels; the revolt was over, and after three further months traversing the country to make sure of his success, Edward left in July 1295.

But despite his victory, this was a crisis that had an impact on both royal finances and on the planned campaigns in France. All told, Edward was forced to spend over £50,000 suppressing the rebellion and not far under £20,000 on repairs to damaged castles. At a time when he was desperately trying to devote large sums to continental alliances, it placed real pressure on cash flow. In addition, the redeployment of the force that was bound for Gascony meant that it was not until 1296 that reinforcements were sent there. This meant that the whole weight of Gascony's defence had been entrusted in the meantime to John of Brittany and John de St John, together with whatever forces they could raise in the duchy itself. In view of that, they did well, partly because of the unwillingness of many Gascons to be subjected to French rule: its own citizens even handed the town of Bayonne to the English. But the French nonetheless retained the upper hand, and quickly responded to these initial gains with an invasion led by Charles of Valois at Easter 1295. To Gascon fury, in the face of that the English commander John Giffard surrendered Podensac on the condition that the English forces were not pursued, leaving the Gascons at the mercy of the French. By the summer, the English presence in Gascony had been greatly reduced and the French were even confident enough of their position that they started attacking ports in the south of England, including a raid on Dover. Rumours of a French invasion quickly began to circulate and an atmosphere of hysteria set in. But Edward had known the French might seek to attack the southern coasts if they were permitted the upper hand, and had taken action in 1294 to build thirty galleys to protect the coast. Those that had been finished were now deployed, merchant ships requisitioned and coastal defences put on high alert. This quickly put paid to any repeat of the raids of 1294 and enabled the king to refocus on the war across the Channel.

The developing situation in Gascony made sending what had been envisaged to be the main army to the duchy urgent, and Edward made plans for English magnates to command forces under contract alongside his brother. In January 1296, after a delay caused partly by the illness of Edmund of Lancaster over Christmas 1295, a force set out under the joint command of Edmund and Henry de Lacy, earl of Lincoln. The addition of troops to the English forces in Gascony in January 1296 gave an important and overdue fillip to morale, but by then the French had regrouped and were waiting for them, and the English forces achieved little. Not only did they fail to take back Bordeaux and unsuccessfully besiege Dax in the south-west of the duchy, they also ran out of money. In late May 1296, this was compounded by the fact that Edmund of Lancaster again fell ill, this time fatally; he died in Bayonne early the following month.

Following Edmund's death, the situation in France went from bad to worse. In January 1297, the forces under the command of the earl of Lincoln suffered a heavy defeat that resulted in the capture of John de St

John and the death of large numbers of infantry. The difficulty of conducting a successful holding operation in Gascony underlined the desperate
need to get the alliance policy off the ground and mount a large-scale campaign on multiple fronts. A crucial window of opportunity on that front
opened in early 1297 in Flanders. Suddenly it looked as though Edward's
great scheme might have a chance of success. But in the end, thanks to
problems at home in England, it was not until August that he was able to
set sail.

To add to those problems, Edward faced a major rebellion in Scotland.
As in Wales, the backdrop to the Scottish rebellion was the way in which
Edward had exercised his overlordship in the previous few years. In January
1293 he had annulled the Treaty of Birgham on the pretext that the marriage alliance it had envisaged between Edward's son and the maid of
Norway had not taken place. But the treaty had also contained a number
of guarantees about how the independence of Scotland would be respected,
which were now declared null and void. Edward had gone on to insist
on his rights to military service from both John Balliol and the Scottish
nobility, demands to which they did not respond positively, showing their
resentment by failing to show up at the muster in 1294. It was an act of
defiance that marked the start of more serious problems: in 1295, unable
to assert his authority within Scotland, Balliol surrendered control of the
government of Scotland to other Scottish lords. It is not clear whether
Balliol was removed by those lords or appealed to them for help, but the
result was that in July 1295 the government of Scotland was placed in the
hands of a Council of twelve.

Soon after this, the Council sent an embassy to France, probably to
discuss the French trade embargo that was affecting the British Isles as a
whole. The embassy returned in February 1296 with a much bigger prize
than the opening up of trade between the two realms, though. They had
established a broad-ranging Franco-Scottish alliance of mutual aid against
Edward and the French king's other enemies. As part of this the Scots
promised to attack the English king while the French king was waging
war against him. The following month the Scots duly attacked Carlisle.
Edward responded with swift action. He brought in a force of Irish 'hobelars', or light cavalry, a novel category of soldier, under John de Wogan, the

justiciar of Ireland, to make a diversionary foray into south-west Scotland while the main army attacked the Scottish forces at Dunbar. The arrival of the hobelars, while low-key, marked the beginning of a significant shift in warfare in the British Isles, in which the value of light horsemen, who could make devastatingly quick raids in difficult country where conventional heavy cavalry struggled with the terrain, was established. In the early fourteenth century, Robert Bruce used such skirmishing forces to great effect, and a generation later, Edward III was to combine the hobelar with the longbowman to create the mounted archer – the most effective troops in European warfare for over a century. In 1296, with their help, the English were ascendant, and Balliol was forced to submit and sent to prison. Edward took full control of the Scottish realm, as he had done in Wales: the Scottish regalia, including the Stone of Scone on which Scottish kings were crowned, were removed, and English administration imposed. The Scots were now subjected to the vigorous collection of revenue for the king's wars by Edward's treasurer, Hugh Cressingham, and, as in Wales, opposition grew across the land. By early 1297 this had crystallised into outright rebellion under two men, Andrew Murray and William Wallace, who had each started their rebellions separately, helping ignite the simmering discontent across Scotland.

In the first two decades of his reign, Edward had largely controlled events, whether in England, Wales, Scotland or Gascony. But from 1294, all that changed rapidly. Philip IV's decision to engage in a show of force in relation to Gascony created the biggest threat to English control of the duchy in several decades. The situation developed at great speed, forcing Edward onto the defensive. His response, to construct a web of alliances designed to split the French forces and undermine Philip's authority across his fiefdoms, was characteristically forthright. But Edward had not reckoned on also facing serious problems first in Wales and then in Scotland. Their implications for the war in France were profound. Dealing with the Welsh revolt in 1294–5 critically undermined the initial English reaction to the seizure of Gascony by diverting Edmund of Lancaster's forces, preventing them from reinforcing the advance army that had set out under John de St John. The Scottish rebellion and the Franco-Scottish alliance had similar consequences. That Edward had faced such serious rebellions in both Wales and Scotland was the almost inevitable consequence of his harsh and unrelenting imposition of his feudal rights, culminating in demands for money and troops for wars which were far removed from either land. The English were seen, with justification, as oppressors by both the Welsh and the Scots, and this helped to mobilise nationalism in both countries. For Edward, on the other hand, his feudal rights were not a matter for negotiation, and there is no doubt that he needed troops and money in short order wherever they came from. In the end, though, his attitude cost him more than the benefits he derived. His entrenched ideas and lack of political pragmatism told against him in a moment when the soft skills of good political leadership were most needed.

Years of Crisis

The campaigns in Wales, Scotland, France and the Low Countries placed huge burdens on Edward's English subjects. In each year between 1294 and 1297, it was necessary to call Parliament to ask for grants of taxation, and on every occasion elected representatives of the counties were included in order to secure their consent. The writs summoning them made clear that they were expected to come with authority to agree to taxation on behalf of their communities. At those gatherings, Edward's representatives were careful to explain the necessity of war, stating that taxation was 'in aid of the king's war which the king waged against the king of France for the recovery of the land of Gascony'. In 1295, they also cited the defensive emergency created by attacks on the coasts. It seems clear, though, that despite the routine calling of a wider group of people Parliament was not yet expected to be a forum for debate: local representatives were essentially being asked to agree with the verdict of the magnates that the king's requests were justified. And this they did with no opposition, advancing the enormous sum of around £200,000 across the years between 1294 and 1297. In three years, Edward had succeeded in achieving what his father and grandfather never had: the agreement of not just one but several national taxes for a war that all agreed was the nation's conflict, not simply the king's.

The demands of war were not confined to direct taxation. Prises and purveyance (the compulsory purchase of goods for armies) on a vast scale, and a heavy sales tax on wool known as the 'maltolt', were also imposed, the latter prompting significant resentment among merchants. And as the king scrambled to find cavalry and infantry to serve in his armies, he repeatedly extended feudal military obligations further into the land-owning class than ever before, effectively re-militarising the political community: in November 1296, anyone with £30 of land was required to become a knight (obliging them to provide military service to the king), and in 1297, Edward ordered all landholders with £20 of lands to be ready to serve him without even a promise of pay.

The desperation of the situation is amplified by the fact that from 1294 Edward began to issue pardons to felons if they would serve in his armies, a move that provoked complaints from the king's other subjects, but which he repeated nonetheless: by the final years of the reign more than 1,700 pardons had been issued for homicide alone. In fact, Edward's decision to order a muster of Welsh troops for service in Gascony in 1294 was only made after he struggled to secure this in England, where there was simply a failure to respond to his feudal summons to serve overseas in his absence. The same urgency may have prompted similar demands on the Scots. In addition to all this, there were the costs of defence: in October 1295, Earl Warenne was ordered to force the people who lived north of the River Trent to take part in the defence of the north, while in southern counties commissioners were appointed to do the same for the southern coastline. In 1297 the people of the southern and eastern counties were even required 'to keep and maintain' ships to be used for this purpose. England was on a war footing on a completely unprecedented scale.

The Church, too, was asked, and at points forced, to contribute to the military effort, yielding around £130,000 between 1294 and 1297. In 1294 Edward took all the remaining funds that had been agreed for his crusade, and sent royal officers into ecclesiastical houses to investigate clipped and counterfeit coins. Later that year, he imposed a tax on half the clergy's income on the basis of 'evident and urgent necessity' at a time when clerics had limited ability to resist because the archbishopric of Canterbury was vacant. In 1296, however, with a new and tough archbishop in place in the person of Robert Winchelsey, the clergy refused to make a grant. This was justified by the argument that they were prevented from giving tax by a papal bull just issued by Boniface VIII, known as *Clericis Laicos*, in which royal taxation was made subject to papal consent. Edward himself, though, was in no mood to compromise and responded with outrage: if the clergy failed to meet their obligations to him, he would consider himself free of obligations to them, he said, and in March 1297 he placed them outside royal protection. Soon afterwards the situation was defused when, despite the archbishop attempting to prevent it, large numbers of clergy purchased pardons from the king by paying him a sum of money equivalent to what the tax would have been. But in July new problems arose when the clergy responded to another request for a grant by saying that they would need to ask the pope for permission before they agreed. Edward, who had pointed out to them that his enemies were 'thirsting for English blood', was utterly intransigent and forbade them from appealing to the pope, threatening to seize church goods by royal authority if they refused.

By early 1297 the opposition of the clergy to taxation was being echoed by more general concerns about the scale and nature of the king's demands. These had been building almost from the outset: the feudal muster for the first campaign to Gascony in 1294 was poorly attended, and in August 1295 the nobility raised questions about service in Gascony without the king. For these forces Edward had proposed contracts promising payment to them for their service in reflection of the fact that they were not obliged to fight in Gascony under the current circumstances. In the end, some of the nobility were broadly content to serve, but with the lesser barons and knights, it took a threat to collect in all their debts to the Crown to persuade them to agree, a move that no doubt provoked significant resentment.

In February 1297 problems arose again when a number of nobles, led by the earl of Norfolk and marshal of England, Roger Bigod, refused to serve in Gascony without the king. In the face of this Edward did not stop but instead pressed ahead with extensive demands for feudal military service, prompting still further opposition. Edward knew the summons was controversial: he did not refer to the fealty and homage that the magnates owed but instead 'affectionately required and requested' them to muster 'for the salvation and general advantage of the realm'. Several magnates, led by Bigod and Humphrey Bohun, earl of Hereford and constable of

England (both of whom had significant responsibilities for the organisation of armies as part of their roles as marshal and constable), raised questions about the summons. Bigod and Bohun refused to muster the host on 7 July on the basis that the summons was insufficient, meaning that they could not properly judge whether service was owed. The crux of their objections was that the writs requiring the muster did not say where service was to be given and that those with £20 of land were called to serve with no promise of pay. These were essentially breaches of custom, and demonstrated that the king was increasingly acting in a way that suggested that he did not see himself as accountable to his subjects and did not respect the importance of custom in his engagement with them. In other words, he was behaving in a typically 'Angevin' fashion, over seventy years after Magna Carta.

The result was that by the middle of July the situation had become very serious, with unrest in England threatening to derail the king's great plan to defeat Philip IV. In response, Edward remained firm. If the two earls hoped to gain support for their stance from Archbishop Winchelsey, Edward was determined to thwart them by effecting his own reconciliation with Winchelsey on 11 July. In negotiations with Winchelsey he promised that in return for a grant from the clergy he would confirm the Charters, and Winchelsey agreed to negotiate with Bigod and Bohun on the king's behalf. But the mediation was a failure. Realising that Edward had not listened to their complaints of 7 July and was instead determined to drive through his plan, Bohun made a speech demanding the restoration of laws and customs and the reform of abuses. It was followed at the end of July by a formal document of grievances known as the 'Remonstrances'. Edward always denied receiving this, but he knew the arguments, because they had already been rehearsed by Bohun in discussions with the king's representatives in late July. At that stage it had been made clear that the only concession the king would consider was the confirmation of the Charters. In the Remonstrances, the earls now demanded to know on what terms the military service he was requiring was owed. They also complained about the impoverishment of the king's subjects and the unfairness of some recent forms of taxation. And finally they questioned the reliability of the king's Flemish allies and raised concerns about what the Scots would do if the king travelled to Flanders. The rebels north of the border would, they argued, 'rise against him . . . in a worse way if they were sure that he had crossed the sea'. In view of what would go on to happen at Stirling Bridge in September 1297, on that last point they were correct.

But this was no longer just a rebellion of a small number of the higher nobility, serious enough though that was. The list of grievances relating to impositions that had particularly affected the king's lesser subjects in the localities, such as the much-resented prises and purveyance, and some of the recent forms of taxation – the wool tax in particular had generated great antipathy – was not a bid by Bigod and Bohun for support from them; it was a reflection of input into the document by the aggrieved men of the shires. What the motivations were for Bigod and Bohun's actions has been a matter of intense debate. That they did not represent the nobility more widely is demonstrated by the lack of other magnate names among the opposition. Many were elsewhere engaged in military or diplomatic activity on behalf of the king, and even the earl of Arundel, who had expressed concerns in 1297, had been brought round to the royal cause with financial help from Edward to address his fears of impoverishment. Arguments have been made that Bigod and Bohun had been alienated by Edward's earlier treatment of them, but there seems to be little substance to this. Both men, as marshal and constable, did, though, have a critical role in raising troops for the king, and in managing the armies, and they will have seen at first hand how much resistance was building in the country as a result of the scale of the impositions. In the absence of other leading earls in France or in Scotland, they may have felt it was their duty to speak up and attempt to restrain the king. It cannot have helped matters that Edward made things distinctly personal by attacking Norfolk and his family and working to destabilise Hereford's lordship in Brecon in summer 1297. If anything was likely to entrench opposition, it was a personal campaign like this.

Meanwhile, the clergy remained intractable. Edward assumed that his discussions with Winchelsey in July meant that he would be granted a clerical tax, but that is not how the clergy saw it. When asked, they again responded to Edward's request by saying that they needed to ask permission from Rome before agreeing to it. This prompted Edward to order a tax on all church temporalities, regardless of the clergy's position. He justified this in an ordinance on 20 August 1297 in which he stated that the clergy had acknowledged the necessity of the warfare and were therefore obliged to contribute for the common profit; they could not legitimately refuse.

This was the worst possible situation for Edward. After he had spent almost three years painstakingly building an alliance across the Channel, his masterplan was threatening to unravel in the face of rebellion north of the border and lay and clerical opposition at home. But he was determined not to be prevented from crossing the Channel. For him, the war had to be pursued at all costs, because the alternative was the permanent loss of Gascony, which he refused to countenance. On 30 July, he pressed on with his plans. First, he ordered the collection of a new tax, which seems to have been agreed in Parliament sometime between 8 and 22 July. However, it was a Parliament to which, unlike previously, representatives had not been summoned, and rumours abounded that the tax had been agreed by those standing in the king's bedchamber at the time. This was no doubt an exaggeration, but the basis of consent for the tax was dubious to say the least. In documents, Edwardian officials even described it as a 'gift' rather than a tax, and the men appointed to collect it were to be men 'who know how to speak to the people well'. It was an anticipation of opposition, as was the appointment of men from outside the shires to collect it, where previously local tax collectors had been appointed. On the same day, Edward ordered a new seizure of wool, which had not received approval in any forum, and stated that the clergy had granted him a tax – which they had not. Even when Edward promised them that he would confirm the Charters if the tax were paid, the clergy would not relent; they insisted on appealing to the pope before they did anything. When Edward subsequently attempted to levy the clerical tax anyway, he had no success.

What followed was further royal diplomacy designed to placate his subjects while still pressing home his agenda. Edward issued a detailed proclamation on 12 August setting out the necessity of the warfare he was proposing: he was acting, he said, 'to recover his rightful inheritance out of which he has been fraudulently tricked by the king of France, and for the honour and common profit of the realm'. He had only imposed just and necessary burdens on his subjects, he said, and argued that he could not defend himself 'or his kingdom' in the wars in Gascony, Wales and Scotland 'without the aid of his loyal subjects'. If he did not fight now, the land of England might itself come under threat again. He did not envisage continual taxation in the future; this sort of necessity was occasional, and would remain so. The war was, he said, 'for the honour and common profit of the realm'. In other words, faced with opposition Edward was rehearsing in a novel way arguments about the English realm and its well-being that had been common themes in his kingship since 1274. The war in Flanders was not an aggressive one, he argued, because England herself would be threatened if Philip IV were not contained, but he promised that he had no intention of making his demands perpetual and every intention of securing peace. He had no choice but to defend 'his realm and his people . . . against his enemies'.

Following this, Edward began to make preparations for a swift departure for Flanders at Winchelsea on the south coast. On 22 August, a delegation led by Bigod and Bohun went to the Exchequer to protest again. They restated the Remonstrances and complained about both the new tax and the seizure of wool. They refused to allow collection of either, accusing the king of reducing his people to a state of servitude. But while all this was happening the king weighed anchor and set sail. From the Continent, when advised of the latest protest, Edward again tried to defuse the situation by telling his officials to stress that he would not make a precedent of the tax, and pointed out that he was putting himself in the way of considerable danger in the campaign on the Continent. He had no intention of abandoning the campaign.

When Edward reached Flanders the situation was no longer anywhere near as promising as it had been in early 1297. In the time lost over the months between spring and late summer the tide of the conflict had begun to flow fast in the French king's favour. In the middle of June, the French had invaded Flanders, and there was uncertainty there about what to do given that the English king had not arrived. The result was that the alliance that Edward had so carefully assembled collapsed into confusion. On 20 August a group of his allies were defeated by the French lord Robert of Artois so that by the time Edward got to Flanders shortly afterwards, there was little he could achieve with his small force of 895 cavalry and less than eight thousand infantry. He hoped for reinforcements from the German king, but nothing came. In Gascony, while the earl of Lincoln had been able to launch a raid into France in the summer, there was otherwise stalemate. Edward must have been very relieved when Philip IV offered to negotiate a ceasefire in the autumn. The war was proving as costly for him as it was for the English, and for the French a truce would bring about a temporary dissolution of the Anglo-Flemish alliance at least, allowing their own forces the opportunity to regroup, while peace negotiations proceeded.

While Edward was on the Continent, the situation in Scotland went from bad to worse. In the king's absence, Earl Warenne had marched north, hoping to deal swiftly with the rebellion. But William Wallace and Andrew Murray brought their forces together against the English, and the English troops were overwhelmed in September at Stirling Bridge. Warenne himself managed to escape, having overslept on the morning of the battle (it seems that he was ill around this time). The defeat was a disaster, the worst for an English army on British soil before the infamous battle of Bannockburn in 1314, and those who remained alive retreated in haste. Rampant in victory, the Scottish forces even cut up the skin of the hated English treasurer Hugh Cressingham to make somewhat gruesome souvenirs. Wallace then followed the victory with savage raids into Northumberland, forcing people to abandon their lands in terror.

The defeat and subsequent threat to the north of England was precisely what Bigod and Bohun had predicted from the king's absence, and it solidified the opposition to Edward's demands, which had already been mounting after the king's decision to sail for the Continent. Across England, September saw several expressions of discontent, from plans for an opposition Parliament to meet in Northampton to refusals by the county community in Worcester to permit the collection of the eighth until the Charters were confirmed. Thinking that serious unrest might break out, the regency Council instructed the sheriffs to gather together forces and bring them to London. Parliament, this time pointedly including representatives from the counties, was summoned to meet at the end of September under the king's eldest son, Prince Edward. The aim was probably to obtain formal consent for the eighth, but the mustering of forces shows how worried the government was. It was right to be: following on, as it did, from the ignominious defeat at Stirling Bridge, Parliament simply ushered in a further, and much more serious crisis, not driven primarily by the earls (most of whom remained supportive of Edward) but by the knights and the church.

Finding themselves backed into a corner, the regency government had no choice but to withdraw the eighth and to issue a document called *Confirmatio Cartarum* – the Confirmation of the Charters, namely Magna Carta and the Forest Charter. The document added some additional clauses to the Charters, as demanded by the opposition: most importantly, it established that no taxes or prises were to be taken in future without consent and that the maltolt, the unpopular wool tax, was to be abandoned. The royal forests were also to be perambulated, to investigate increases in their extent that had taken place at the expense of the king's subjects. Once the concessions had been granted, Parliament was willing to agree a new tax to replace the disputed eighth.

This document of concessions in one sense drew a line in the sand like Magna Carta itself. Its content is an indication of how far England had come since 1215. Taking taxation and indeed the forced purchase of supplies for the army were emphatically now not matters of royal entitlement, but for negotiation and agreement: no king could take his subjects' property arbitrarily, however great the necessity he pleaded. The agreement that tax should not be levied without the 'common assent of all the realm' – and, importantly, that it had to be for the *profit* of the realm – were important gains for the opposition. They had succeeded in establishing that no king, despite the defensive necessity, could impoverish his subjects; nor could he take any resources, including prises, without their consent.

With the *Confirmatio Cartarum* issued, the regency government could turn its attention to organising a new Scottish campaign, successfully securing a grant of clerical tax in November, which would act as the main means of financing it. This time, in the face of the obvious threat of invasion, the clergy were entirely amenable to agreeing the grant. A new prise was also ordered, and although there was no mention of securing consent, goodwill for the moment prevailed in the light of the government's recent concessions and the situation in the north. A muster was ordered for December at Newcastle for a highly unusual winter campaign in order that no time would be wasted. In view of this, special contracts for three months' service were made with Earl Warenne as well as with several others:

Norfolk, Warwick, Hereford and Gloucester and the northern lord Henry Percy. In time, the use of such contracts would set a precedent for much more wholesale military reform under Edward III. The result in 1298 was that the army that set out for Scotland early that year was one the biggest ever raised by the English. It had little difficulty retaking Roxburgh and Berwick. But with supplies running short and the king ordering the army commanders to delay further major action until he could get to Scotland to lead the expedition in person, progress was halted. Edward clearly wanted to take no chances on a repeat of Stirling Bridge. And it was certainly better to wait and secure a decisive victory than to proceed piecemeal when food was running short.

The next steps were taken carefully. First, Edward's Council met in York in April 1298 to decide on plans, and after this the army was told to muster again in June. By then the king, returned from Flanders, could be at the head of the army. But as the summer campaign got under way, things became more difficult. Wallace had adopted a policy of withdrawing north, giving the English no option but to follow. As he retreated, his forces denuded the land of all crops and livestock, leaving the large English army short of supplies. Had Wallace continued to move north, these problems might have necessitated a withdrawal, but instead, possibly thinking that another major victory was in sight, he took his army to Falkirk and planned an outright attack. Hearing news of this, Edward marched his troops west, and made ready to join battle with the Scots. On the way he sustained two broken ribs from his horse, but despite what must have been agonising pain he proceeded to battle. There, Wallace deployed the Scottish army for the first time in schiltrons, vast infantry circles, each one several thousand men strong. In these formations, secured behind stakes and chains, the Scottish infantry wielded twelve-foot pikes that made them, as contemporaries said, as impenetrable as the spines of a hedgehog. But although schiltrons were extremely difficult for chivalric heavy cavalry to engage, they were vulnerable to arrow-fire, and it was by attacking them with his archers to break up their unity that Edward was able to render them prey to the heavy cavalry attack that followed. Wallace's forces were routed, and while he managed to escape, his authority as the commander of Scottish forces was completely undermined. It was a dazzling victory for Edward and a vindication of the strength of his military leadership.

Edward returned to England triumphant after the Falkirk campaign, but he was misguided if he thought that the promises he had made in the *Confirmatio Cartarum* in 1297 would be forgotten, as he quickly found. The clergy, led by Archbishop Winchelsey, had remained querulous in the aftermath of the *Confirmatio Cartarum*: in June 1298 while Edward was in Scotland, they had refused to pay the remainder of the tax that they had granted in 1297 for the Scottish campaign because, they argued, it had only been intended for a defensive campaign in England, not an aggressive campaign north of the border. Winchelsey seemed bent on further conflict with Edward when, also in 1298, he threatened the excommunication of any clerics who collected prises for the king that had not been agreed by common assent of the realm. In so doing he was making a continuing issue of a point the rest of the political community was, for the moment, not pressing. Deciding that discretion was the better part of valour, Edward opted to back away from conflict by not pursuing further clerical taxation. He probably also wanted to avoid a unification of the clergy's grievances with those that were festering at the same time among the laity: immediately prior to the campaign Bigod and Bohun had made the king promise that he would uphold the concessions made in the *Confirmatio Cartarum* if he secured victory over the Scots. The two earls were angered again straight after the victory by the king's grant of the Isle of Arran to an Antrim lord, when he had promised to consult them as marshal and constable before taking any action. As soon as the army reached Carlisle they told Edward that their men were exhausted and asked to be permitted to leave.

This was just the start of renewed problems. In Parliament in early 1299 grievances were raised about the king's failure to confirm the Charters, which he had promised to do in 1298. In the ultimate display of bad faith, instead of facing these grievances, Edward crept away from London secretly, simply refusing to engage. He was chased by some of the earls and forced to concede, but in so doing insisted on adding a clause that preserved the rights of the Crown. Complaints resurfaced again when Parliament met in May 1299. This time Edward was forced to promise the perambulation of the forests in Michaelmas. The domestic unrest, particularly on the part of the gentry, meant that Edward's plan for a campaign to Scotland in early summer 1299 never took place. Against this backdrop, Caerlaverock was lost to the Scots.

Amid the gloom, there was some good news. Peace negotiations with the French under papal arbitration that had been ongoing since late 1297 resulted in an agreement in June 1299 that the pre-war territorial position in south-west France should be re-established and the lands handed over to the pope in the meantime. The peace was to be cemented by the marriage of Edward to Philip IV's half-sister Margaret, while Prince Edward would marry Philip's daughter Isabella. The agreement over Gascony was to come to nothing when the French refused to hand over the lands to Boniface VIII, but the peace held for the moment and the proposed marriage to Margaret took place in September 1299. Money remained tight and Edward was even forced to borrow from a Florentine banking house, the Frescobaldi, to help finance the marriage celebrations, which took place over three days after a ceremony presided over by Archbishop Winchelsey at Canterbury. Forty years younger than Edward, Margaret was just twenty at the time of her marriage. It is difficult to gain much of a sense of her from the records but it seems Edward was quickly devoted and the couple conceived a child soon after they were married. Edward displayed tender concern for her during a subsequent illness with measles and seems to have indulged an extravagant temperament: by the early 1300s Margaret had built up debts from spending on fine cloth and luxuries, for the payment of which Edward undertook to make provision. She had great powers of persuasion over Edward and was regularly asked to intercede with him on behalf of others, most notably doing this in 1305 when Edward imposed a ban on the Londoners lending money to his extravagant eldest son. In response to her pleas, Edward relinquished the ban.

The king's marriage to Margaret of France provided a happy interlude in an otherwise difficult year. When Edward tried to respond to the Scots following the seizure of Caerlaverock that same winter, he again failed to secure the backing of his magnates. They felt a summer campaign was a much better idea, and as a result of their reluctance to support the king, and continuing gentry grievances, only 2,500 of the sixteen thousand-strong force he had made plans for turned up. While the Scots eagerly offered to do battle, Edward realised the futility of attempting to fight with so few men, and abandoned the campaign. In the aftermath, the Scots went on to retake Stirling, a vital staging post in the route through Scotland.

There was no choice for Edward but to regroup and make plans for another campaign to Scotland in summer 1300. But for this he would need tax, as none had been granted since 1297 and debts to Edward's Italian bankers, the Frescobaldi, were mounting. He called Parliament to convene in March to ask for a grant of taxation, ensuring that he included the men of the counties and boroughs in the summons. But in Parliament the opposition he had faced in 1299 quickly resurfaced, beginning with an insistence on the part of Archbishop Winchelsey and Roger Bigod on the confirmation of Magna Carta. This was followed by demands for compromises on the part of the laity and the clergy. Edward largely ignored those grievances presented by the church; it was clear in any case that they would not make a grant. But lay grievances were addressed in the *Articuli Super Cartas*, or Articles on the Charters. In these the king secured some concessions from 1297 for himself, particularly the introduction of the clause saving the rights of the Crown, the stipulation that complaints could only be brought against his ministers in a personal, and not their official, capacity, and that complaints about prises, as a prerogative right, were reserved for the king's special grace. In other areas, Edward's subjects made an effective and important stand on issues of principle. The Charters were confirmed and new procedures put in place for their enforcement. It was additionally conceded that sheriffs should be elected by the local community, and Edward assured his subjects that purveyances would be paid for, not simply taken. Aside from the Articles, the king was forced to agree to the inspection of the royal forest boundaries, and to submit to whatever reductions the commissioners prescribed – this affirmed that the boundaries of the royal forests were established and that they could not simply be expanded as the king saw fit, thereby restricting the hunting rights of others.

In return, Parliament gave a grant of a twentieth, on strict condition that what the king had promised would be delivered before it was collected. On the basis of a promise of tax and military service, and with the support of the magnates, Edward could proceed with his planned Scottish campaign in summer 1300. Four battalions mustered at Carlisle under the commands of the earls of Lincoln and Surrey (Warenne), the king and Prince Edward, his eldest son, who at sixteen was to act under the instruction of a key member of the king's household, John de St John. In total the battalions comprised around nine thousand men. The garrison at Caerlaverock, which the army advancing from Carlisle reached first, surrendered quickly in the face of the attack. Negotiations then took place with the Scots, in which the Scottish magnates demanded John Balliol's release and the return of their lands. Their demands were fruitless; Edward was determined to proceed and achieve submission. Yet despite its size and whatever the king wanted, the army achieved little. By late summer, desertions, including among magnates, were beginning to undermine Edward's ability to continue with the campaign. There was no choice but for him to withdraw and agree a truce until the following spring. As he did so, he issued a parting warning, telling the Scots chillingly that he intended to return and lay waste to the country from one coast to the other.

With this at the front of the king's mind, Parliament was recalled in January 1301. The tax of 1300 had never been collected and the need for money was growing increasingly urgent. Edward was by now even more heavily reliant on loans from Italian bankers for cash flow. Nonetheless, domestic resistance rumbled on, and was articulated in a bill containing a number of demands presented by a knight from Lancashire, Henry of Keighley, possibly the first of its kind from someone below the ranks of the magnates, and a sign of the growing voice and independence of the gentry. The result was that, while he managed to secure a fifteenth, it was at the price of yet another confirmation of the Charters and a promise to complete the forest perambulation. Edward was furthermore made to promise that he would address complaints of official corruption. The magnates themselves complained indirectly about Edward's treasurer, Walter Langton, who was associated with the prises that had proved so unpopular. Edward was livid, confronting the magnates and asking them why they had stopped there and not asked for their own crowns. But the compromise had been inevitable given Edward's need to launch a further campaign in Scotland, and even he could not row against such a strong tide of opposition. Trust that he would honour his promises was still running low: the grant was made on the basis that Edward had to carry them out before it could be collected. Most importantly, he had to accept the reports of the forest commissioners, reconfirm the Charters and promise payment for purveyances (provisions for the army bought at less than market value). The first of these in particular was a major concession.

The result of this was that Edward managed to mount a campaign north of the border in the summer. Again its outcome was indecisive: the Scots' skill at avoiding pitched battle and the consequent stymieing of English attempts to win a decisive victory meant that he achieved very little. Licking his wounds, and planning to return stronger again in 1302, Edward retired to England. For the moment his plans to subdue the Scots were on indefinite hold.

The fifteenth of 1301 was to be the last grant of taxation requested by Edward in his reign. Never again would he approach Parliament for funds. The reason for this was almost certainly his desire not to provoke further opposition that would oblige him to make concessions in relation to the royal prerogative. Where earlier there had been harmony between the king and his subjects, in the years from 1296 to 1301 the views of Edward and his lesser subjects in particular had diverged dramatically. While the opposition was given leadership by Bigod and Bohun, for the most part Edward had been able to persuade, cajole and in some cases intimidate most of the magnates into acquiescence. The gentry, because of the sheer weight of Edward's demands, were not so easily satisfied, and it was accordingly they rather than the magnates who drove opposition to royal policy. While they challenged what they saw as the arbitrary extraction from them of money, supplies and military service in contravention of the spirit of Magna Carta, Edward saw only incursions into his prerogative. The deft political touch or pragmatism he had demonstrated in the first two decades of his reign had latterly been overpowered by his desire to protect royal rights, over which he believed he had sole discretion. For him this was the logical corollary of his commitment to maintain the 'dignity of the Crown'. The reality was that, over the course of the last eighty years, the implications of Magna Carta had brought royal prerogative rights into question. Increasingly, Edward's subjects did not recognise the distinction between the principles enshrined in the Charter and royal prerogative that Edward was making. Their question was simple: why should it be that the law protected some rights but not others? Parliament provided them with a forum to express their opposition to the king's demands, and it is perhaps not surprising that these years saw the presentation of the first independent petition against royal exactions by a member of the gentry.

These ideas were not going to go away; the king's lesser subjects simply did not agree about the exceptionalism of the royal prerogative. They wanted protections against the idea that a recognised plea of necessity could be used to justify all manner of extractions and impositions without their express consent, even if it led to their impoverishment and ruin. They sought assurances that the notion of a common peril would not in future be used to justify undermining the common good. Like King John, Edward did not see it this way, and was too willing to renege on promises. This is why the road through the crisis was so bumpy and ultimately unsatisfactory for both parties. Renewed opposition was avoided in subsequent years when Edward decided not to request further grants of tax, but the issue had not gone away.

Enemies Defeated? France and the Scots, 1302–7

In 1302, a devastating defeat inflicted on Philip IV's forces by the Flemish at Courtrai rapidly altered the whole complexion of the Scottish conflict. The defeat left the French king dramatically weakened and consequently keen to put an end to other commitments. He agreed a new truce with Edward later that year, completely abandoning his Scottish allies. Edward was to waste no time thereafter: he launched a major campaign in spring 1303 to bring about the full submission of the rebels north of the border. With rumours rife at the time that the Scots themselves might invade England, this time the muster was successful and Edward took a large force with him. However, the key to victory was not in fact the defeat of the Scottish forces on the battlefield – that never took place – but the surrender of most of the Scottish leaders in early 1304.

This seems to have resulted partly from the fact that the English had spent the winter in Scotland in 1303–4, giving a clear indication that

Edward was not simply going to let the issue drop; this was for him the final push. On the Scottish side, with the French no longer offering at least tacit support for their cause, and a further blow, the recruitment of the earl of Ulster to the English with a force of 3,500 men, their position was being rapidly eroded. Yet despite Edward's advantage, it seems that he was ready to make accommodations to secure a lasting peace. This made practical sense: it was not possible to keep an army in the field on a permanent basis, so a settlement with some concessions, if not as desirable for him as for the Scottish lords, was the best outcome. Edward's commanders were clearly very actively pursuing talks in 1303: in September, Earl Warenne wrote to the Exchequer that he had commenced negotiations with leading magnates. In this atmosphere, although William Wallace remained in opposition, his continued rebellion was increasingly peripheral to the business of establishing a workable peace. To this it was the Scottish leaders themselves who were central. It did not take long for negotiations to result in an agreement. In 1304, both sides seemed reconciled to an arrangement in which Edward retained power, but committed to respect Scottish laws and customs as they had existed in the time of Alexander III and not to make any ordinances that would be to their prejudice. The Scottish lords stressed the need for counsel in any action he took. Tensions were not entirely dissipated: lords whose estates had been confiscated and given to their English counterparts had to buy back their lands, and those who continued to oppose Edward were made to do so on particularly unfavourable terms. But overall the settlement was a major step forward and created the basis for a more permanent solution to the relationship between the two realms than had seemed possible only two years earlier.

What remained was the rebellion of William Wallace and the garrison of Stirling Castle, which under its commander William Oliphant was still holding out against the English. The latter had fallen by summer 1304 under the pressure of the English siege, but Wallace, whose forces had been beaten in winter 1303, remained on the run. This, too, did not last long: when Edward put a price of forty marks on his head, he was soon betrayed. Taken to England to undergo a show trial, Wallace was sentenced to death. In a reminder of the brutality of the age, he was made to wear a laurel-leaf crown, then hanged, drawn and quartered, with his head placed on London

Bridge as an example for all; other body parts were sent to towns in northern England and southern Scotland. In autumn 1305, Edward created new arrangements for the governance of Scotland in Parliament, and, finally at peace with both the French and the Scots, must have hoped for a period of respite from the almost continuous warfare of the last decade.

It was not to be. The abdication of John Balliol had given rise to bitter fighting between members of the Scottish nobility about the succession to the throne. This may even be one reason why so many were keen to reach an accommodation with Edward I: Scotland was internally riven, whatever the English did. It was arguably this division rather than Edward's interactions with the Scottish lords after the settlement that produced further rebellion in 1306 by Robert Bruce, earl of Carrick, whose family had been one of several that expressed a claim to the Scottish throne. In February 1306, Bruce murdered John Comyn, lord of Badenoch, in a church in Dumfries. The murder resulted from an argument between the two men about Bruce's plan to rebel against Edward I in retribution for the lack of rewards he had received for supporting him since 1302. Once he had murdered Comyn, Bruce had no choice but to cloak the action – a murder inside a church was doubly heinous – in the robes of outright rebellion. By late March, he had managed to secure his enthronement by his faction of followers as Scottish king at Scone. Edward had to respond. Too ill to lead an expedition himself, he nonetheless wasted no time in sending an army north in July 1306 under the command of his eldest son, Prince Edward.

The campaign of summer 1306 was successful, and Edward set about meting out punishment to the rebels, including one savage act towards Robert Bruce's sister Mary and the countess of Buchan, both members of Bruce's court. The women were locked in cages and kept in Scotland as an example to others. Edward must have been furious about the rebellion and determined to quash it mercilessly. His son, however, had less fixity of purpose, and during the winter left Scotland instead of staying with the English forces, taking twenty-two knights with him to the Continent for a tournament. His father was so furious in response that he ordered his officials to seize the prince's lands as punishment. In the meantime Bruce, determined that Edward would not have the last word, managed to amass a force strong enough to relaunch his rebellion, and in May 1307 pulled off a major victory against Aymer de Valence, earl of Pembroke, and son of Edward's long-standing friend William, at Loudoun Hill to the south of Glasgow. This was followed by the defeat of the new earl of Gloucester further west in Ayr. Edward I had no choice but to prepare for a fresh campaign. This time the fates were not on his side: illness was again to take hold and he was to die in July 1307 at Burgh by Sands, north-west of Carlisle, before he had been able to challenge Bruce. Gripped, like his grandfather King John, by dysentery – for which the Middle Ages knew no cure – he was to fight no more.

Edward had been determined to subjugate the Scots following the rebellion of 1296, deploying some of the largest armies of the period to his campaigns there in his attempt to do so. Yet despite notable victories at Falkirk and Caerlaverock, he never succeeded in subduing the rebels. To some extent this was about the common cause that bound Wallace's armies together: they were fighting for the independence of the land of Scotland, and that made them the most determined alliance. The rebels were able to take advantage of English weakness, particularly at Stirling Bridge in 1297, but also later, either as Edward struggled to deploy armies to Scotland, or as his large armies found themselves hampered by the rugged terrain of the lowlands and their preference for pitched battle which the Scots assiduously avoided. It was hard for English forces to make progress in the face of this; they could not demonstrate their masterfulness and frighten their opponents by decisive victory in battle. What gave Edward the advantage in the end was not, then, his military superiority to his opponents, but a combination of the detachment of the Scots from their French allies, the loss of a papal ally when the French stopped promoting their cause at the papal curia after 1302, and the disunity of the Scottish magnates. Ultimately, enough of them saw a need for pragmatism to make a settlement possible, and Edward himself saw the value of making an accommodation with them. The rebellion of Robert Bruce in 1306 was against the grain of recent years, but in a deeply divided land, he was successful in stirring up enough people to reignite the 'wars of independence'. The settlement of 1304–5 had been all too brief an interlude, and conflict with the Scots would be a keynote of many decades to follow.

The Pains of War: Disorder in England

The impact on Edward's English subjects of the unprecedented scale of warfare that took place in the last thirteen years of the reign, and particularly between 1294 and 1304, was immense. A key reason why he faced the most serious political crisis of his reign in this period was because his subjects experienced enormous privations as a result of the myriad burdens that war placed on them. In addition the level of disorder with which those same subjects had to contend rose dramatically in the years after 1294. That the king was alert to and concerned about this is indicated by the action he took to try to deal with it: in 1300 keepers of the peace were appointed across England, and in the same year the steward of the royal household was ordered to arrest all malefactors. In 1302, Edward issued several commissions into vagabonds and malefactors, particularly in northern counties, where such behaviour, he said, might result in 'terror or danger' to Queen Margaret, or to soldiers passing through on their way to war in Scotland. He accused the bailiffs of the town of Newcastle of having been 'negligent in dealing with complaints' about such criminals.

When the Scottish war ended in 1304, Edward wasted no time in turning his attention fully to this outbreak of crime, and issued several commissions across the second half of that year, culminating in an order to investigate not only malefactors who were committing 'homicides, depredations, arsons and very many other injuries' and intimidating juries, but those who assisted them, who aided and abetted them, and who hired them 'to strike, wound, ill-treat and kill many of our kingdom in fairs, markets and other places'. In spring 1305, Edward issued still more commissions for a wider range of counties, resulting in the arrest of 'a great multitude' of malefactors. This led to the Ordinance of Trailbastons issued by the king in April 1305, so named after the clubs with which armed gangs were alleged to beat their victims. The new commissions were to investigate crime across the whole country, and had power to bring together juries and reach verdicts on those they arrested, speeding up the judicial process; previously commissioners had been mostly only empowered to make arrests. This was a major crackdown on crime and Edward was demonstrably angry: in private correspondence in that year he referred to the 'outrages' of these criminals, which he said 'flouted' his lordship and 'were like the beginning of civil war'. The idea was that these commissions would represent 'a drink before' the 'medicine' of the general eyre, which, after its suspension since the war began in 1294, Edward intended to restart once the trailbaston justices had completed their work. Together the trailbastons and the eyre were intended to represent a comprehensive package of measures to tackle disorder.

If Edward was angry when he issued the Ordinance of Trailbastons, he was to be angrier still when he received reports from the justices in Yorkshire that they were encountering large-scale and deliberate evasion of justice, through the concealment of felonies and trespasses. As a result, the king added conspiracy to the remit of the trailbaston commissioners. The outcome was the single most wide-ranging government action to deal with crime in post-Conquest England to date. During the first half of the fourteenth century, this new mechanism for bringing order to the localities and retribution on conspirators, including royal officials who were deemed to have acted in excess of authority, became established as a key judicial tool and a weapon by which royal authority could be emphasised and enacted.

We should make no mistake about Edward's personal engagement with this outbreak of disorder. In 1306 he wrote to the sheriff of Yorkshire that 'the king marvels [that] little or nothing has yet come to the king's attention concerning the sheriff's diligence or solicitude in the execution of his order concerning malefactors'. If the sheriff did not act now, he was told that Edward would treat him as aiding the malefactors, which would bring the full force of the king's law down upon him. The commissions were not universally popular, and large numbers of people found themselves accused of crimes. The *Outlaw's Song of Trailbaston*, a song of political protest to the commissions, probably written in the first decade of the fourteenth century, has as its subject a veteran of the king's wars who is now an outlaw living in the greenwood. The outlaw says he was falsely accused, 'indicted out of their false mouths / For wicked robberies and other misdeeds', and talks of violent retribution for his plight. 'Better', he says, 'to stay with me in the woods' than be imprisoned on the word of people of 'evil disposition'.

But the problem of disorder was real nonetheless. The judicial rolls produced by the commissioners reveal many more clues as to the nature and cause of the problems: most of the worst occurred where the greatest concentrations of troops had been, particularly in the north and in the southern coastal counties. Complaints were often about bands of armed men committing crimes. Soldiers needing food or other resources, on their way to war or recently demobilised, would have moved through the counties in large numbers; it would be surprising for there to have been no problems associated with such large-scale movement of people, let alone those who were heavily armed – a sense of the scale of movement is made clear by the fact that a local official, William de Hodnet, was required to muster three thousand men from Shropshire and Staffordshire alone in 1297 for the Scottish conflict. It is perhaps no coincidence that one band of men in Kent was accused of coming to a town in the county 'like an army' and in 'great terror'. They allegedly beat a man, broke his arms and took goods worth twenty shillings. In 1302, another commission in the south of England spoke of 'a multitude of armed men on horseback and on foot' who had 'escaped into other counties and are wandering about refusing to submit to justice'. While not all behaviour of this type would have been associated with soldiers – some would surely have been about criminals taking advantage of disorder – the sort of disorder that is described and the location of the worst problems together make it a compelling conclusion.

Other problems too can be linked to war. The bulk of accusations against people in these years were for things like theft and trespasses on the lands of lords, which may well reflect the purveyance that took place during the wars and which caused such resentment: in March and April 1296 alone, the sheriffs of twelve southern counties were ordered to collect 13,500 quarters of wheat and 13,000 quarters of oats. It may in addition reflect looting. When landowners were away fighting for the king, as many of them were, their lands were vulnerable. Equally, there were several fights over town governance in the period, control of which could critically affect how much tax one might pay. In an era of heavy taxation, that was probably worth fighting for: in 1306 in York, the trailbaston justices heard a complaint there that Andrew Bolingbroke and fifty-three others had conspired together to form a guild, which had allegedly interfered with appointments to town government in order to obtain an exemption from taxation for its own members.

With the burden of tax so high, landlords seem to have themselves been attempting to extract more money from their tenants, which led to a rise in disputes. In Kent, a significant number of cases related to conflict between ecclesiastical lords and the towns in which they had jurisdiction and where they were seeking vigorously to assert what they perceived to be their rights. In Shropshire, the abbot of Halesowen was called to court to respond to a claim that he had conspired with others to indict a man for trespasses against the peace in Shrewsbury. When the details of the pleading emerged, it seems to have been a dispute over whether the man, Richard Ordrich, was a free peasant or a villein, in other words a chattel of the abbot, someone who would have owed him labour services on his land. Labour services from villeins did not need to be paid for by their lords, and so having villeins to rely on was very helpful to a lord at a time of reduced cash flow. It is no wonder the question of Ordrich's status was such an important one both to him and to the abbot. These incidences amplify quite how much strain the king's subjects were being put under by the warfare of the 1290s and early 1300s.

War was therefore either directly or indirectly at the heart of many problems. The most recent time in modern history that Britain has experienced anything similar to this was during the Second World War, and the parallels between this period over seven hundred years ago and 1939–45 are striking. Much is made of the idea of a 'blitz spirit' during the Second World War, but in fact crime rose in the UK quite dramatically: there were around three hundred thousand offences in 1939, but by 1945 there were just under half a million. The nature of the crime was very similar to that in the late 1290s and early 1300s: looting was a major problem; in one case an entire house in Dover was stripped of its contents during an air raid, including its pipes and carpets. The war saw increases too in delinquency, murder, the black market and other petty crime. Industrial unrest – discord in relations between employees and employers – rose as well, just as did relations between the tenants and landlords of the 1290s. Of course, it made sense in the early fourteenth century for those engaged in disputes to dress their opponents in the clothes that the king was most concerned about: they were often described as gangs who broke the peace and conspired to pervert the course of justice, aiming to undermine the authority and imposition of the king's law. But the detail of accusations indicates that often quite different things were really at work.

Despite the king's increasing age, and the trials of warfare between 1294 and 1304, the trailbaston commissions of 1304–7 show that Edward I remained deeply engaged with internal rule. The commissions indicate that he was if anything even more ambitious than earlier in his attempts to find solutions to the problems that arose. Given the scale of those problems, he had to be, and in fact the impact of his actions is much debated. Did Edward actually achieve anything in relation to the disorder of the latter part of the reign, or did he hand on a crisis of an unprecedented order of magnitude to his son in 1307? The answer seems largely to have been the former: the bulk of the accusations with which the government was dealing after 1304 related to wartime, and while disputes could and did rumble on afterwards, soldiers largely (if gradually) returned home. With successive trailbaston commissions in 1305, 1306 and 1307, fewer and fewer complaints were brought, and cases in the courts from a number of counties fell in 1306 and 1307. This is not to say that the situation was entirely settled by 1307 – far from it – but considerable inroads had been made into disorder. The renewal of the Scottish war in 1306–7 was likely to create further problems, but that became the least of England's worries after Edward I died in July 1307; instead the king's subjects had to wrestle with a period of kingly inadequacy that placed its own novel strains on the polity.

The Aftermath of Crisis: Edward and the Political Community, 1302–7

Edward I's continued engagement with the issue of disorder in the early 1300s is a reminder that this was a king who retained a strong sense of his duties throughout his reign. But his simultaneous steadfast commitment to maintaining what he perceived as fundamental royal rights and prerogatives meant that in the years after 1302 he assiduously avoided requesting taxation again. In 1303, when he needed money for the new Scottish campaign, he decided to collect the feudal aid that had been granted to him in 1290 when his daughter Joan was married to the earl of Gloucester. This was an entitlement. In the same year, he imposed another similar 'prerogative' tax, a tallage, on the towns and boroughs and on those who held lands on the royal estates, and negotiated an increase in customs revenue by making concessions to merchants in England. He was able to avoid approaching the clergy for tax because Boniface VIII's worsening relations with Philip IV saw the pope give Edward half of the crusading tenth granted in 1301. On top of all this, and to plug the gaps between what he had and what he needed, Edward turned to the Frescobaldi, borrowing large sums of money in the final three years of his reign. The message was clear: he intended never again to be forced into making the sort of concessions his subjects had extracted from him in 1297 and 1300.

So strongly did he feel about the compromises imposed on him in those years that in 1305 he went as far as to banish Archbishop Winchelsey, who had been so important to the opposition to him in the crisis of the 1290s, from the realm. The archbishop's expulsion was cleverly achieved by Edward, but was also the product of Winchelsey's own intransigence and difficult character. Having made 'special' friends with Robert Ferrers, who had been disinherited from his earldom of Derby after the civil war of 1258–65 by Edward's brother Edmund, Winchelsey proceeded to challenge Edmund's heir, Thomas of Lancaster, over the earldom by appealing to the pope for its restoration to Ferrers. The archbishop demanded that Lancaster come to defend himself at St Paul's in 1301. Needless to say, Lancaster immediately secured his own protection from the king, who issued a royal prohibition against the hearing. The archbishop went ahead anyway, in defiance of Edward's order, with Lancaster then bringing a legal case against Winchelsey in the court of King's Bench. Ferrers was forced to back down. But the ramifications of the case went further: several members of the nobility were concerned by Winchelsey's attempt to intrude spiritual jurisdiction in an area they felt was for the royal courts only. If he was prepared to challenge Lancaster, who might he challenge next? Seeing the archbishop's isolation, Edward sent his erstwhile ally the earl of Lincoln to Rome to ask the pope to suspend Winchelsey from office. No one spoke up for the archbishop, who left the realm in disgrace.

In the same embassy to the pope, Lincoln also asked the pope to annul both the Confirmation of the Charters of 1297 and the subsequent Articles on the Charters, and Edward followed that in 1306 with a reversal of the disafforestations he had been forced to make. In the same year, he gave orders for Henry Keighley, who had brought the petition to Parliament in 1300, to be imprisoned, though with some moderation: Keighley should not be put in irons and should be well treated, and the imprisonment should not be attributed to the king. Edward was treading carefully, but he would not brook opposition and he associated Keighley with some of his most ignominious concessions. The humbling of Keighley followed on from an earlier deal made with Edward's former opponent the earl of Norfolk, Roger Bigod, in which the latter, heavily in debt, had in 1302 been persuaded to surrender his inheritance to the king in return for a life-time grant of his lands and rents of £1,000 per annum. There is no doubt that this represented a victory for Edward over the earl at a time when Bigod, given his debts, had little power to resist. Edward had had the last word. His other opponent, Humphrey de Bohun, had died in 1298, so it was only for Edward to foster a new working relationship with Bohun's heir, which he duly did by arranging the marriage of the young earl to his own daughter Elizabeth.

With the expulsion of Winchelsey and the annulment of the Confirmation of the Charters and the Articles on the Charters, as well as the humbling of Roger Bigod and Henry Keighley, Edward had prevailed over those who had led opposition to him in the 1290s. However, as in 1215 and 1258, the political horizon had again changed in a short space of time, and Edward could not stop the clock in the way that he would have liked.

Across the thirteenth century, the state had grown significantly, as had the king's subjects' desire for governmental accountability. The latter arose out of the demands of warfare and the way in which John, Henry III and Edward I interacted with their subjects in relation to those demands. In 1215, the barons established that the king could not simply take their property as and when he chose without recourse to the due process of the law, or their negotiated consent. In 1258, this was rehearsed in further civil crisis, but this time the knights of the shires, the men who would later be known as the gentry, forcefully asserted that the same principles applied to them too. In 1297–1301, Edward I's subjects, both noble and knightly, though mainly the latter, expressed in no uncertain terms that not only did they expect to be asked for their consent to the king taking their property in the form of taxation, purveyance and prises, they expected to have a role in the formation of foreign policy. Just because he had established defensive urgency, the king could not, they said, alight on any strategy of his choice if this meant impoverishing his subjects. In addition, he could not assume that consent to one grant of taxation automatically meant agreement to further grants for the same war, and he had to seek the approval of representatives of all those whom taxation would affect, not just a limited selection of his chosen subjects. The matter of calling representatives of the shires to Parliament was not so that they could engage in a rubber-stamping exercise of royal policy; it was to perform genuine consultation and increasingly negotiation. Parliament had begun to have teeth, and the principle of no taxation without representation had been established.

It should not be assumed that Edward was atypical in reacting as he did to the demands made of him in the late 1290s; many kings would have had similar objections to granting these sorts of concessions that were demanded of him – Edward III in 1340–1 is one such example. Where Edward I was different from his grandson was not in the fact that he went on to annul concessions later (Edward III did that too). Rather, it was in failing to find, via subsequent negotiation and the establishment of mutual understanding, a way forward that he and his subjects could live with. As a result, when he died in 1307 Edward I saddled his son and heir with significant debts, estimated by historians at a value of anywhere up to £200,000. While solvency in and of itself was not critical to royal security on the throne (far from it – Edward II was still deposed, despite having £60,000 in the Exchequer, because he had alienated the entire political community through his tyranny), what this shows is that the development of dialogue about the circumstances in which war taxation should be granted was inevitable. By borrowing heavily, Edward I was simply papering over the obvious cracks.

But the interaction between English royal government and the king's subjects was not wholly negative or conflict-ridden in this period. Government also expanded in ways people desired and welcomed. The legal system developed a momentum of its own in the face of ever-increasing demands for access to the king's law and for the king to intervene in problems of disorder facing the localities. This suited kings very well, partly because expansion could be a good way to raise revenue for war, and partly because of evolving notions of the practical remit of royal jurisdiction: Edward I believed that he, as king, was directly responsible for the maintenance of order and the common good of his subjects, and sought to achieve that. In practice, this meant an expansion of royal government and its personnel both at the centre and locally. When war within the British Isles on a scale never seen before, particularly in Scotland, brought with it widespread disorder in England in the 1290s, Edward therefore naturally felt that the solution should be provided by him.

By 1307, the majority of the king's subjects were interacting with the state in some way or other on a daily basis, and as a result the health and responsiveness of that state came to matter greatly to their daily lives. They had become more dependent on government and, because government in this period depended largely on the direction of the king, the engagement and ability of the king became crucial to the well-being of the nation. Like any leader, the king did not have to direct all policy and action personally; it would be a mistake to see his role in such crude terms. The key lay in the tone and agenda he set, and in the people with whom he surrounded himself. The ramifications of poor kingship had the potential to be devastating; the achievements that could accrue from good kingship could be equally dramatic, as Edward I's reign showed. Even a short absence from the helm or a temporary loss of focus could have significant effects, as demonstrated in both 1286–9 and the years of warfare between 1294 and 1304.

So leadership was crucial to the well-being of the polity. But in a post-Magna Carta world, even leaders with the best intentions had to consult with their subjects. Under pressure from all sides in the 1290s, it is here that Edward fell down. In his reign, never the twain shall meet, but in the future, accommodations would have to be made with their subjects if vital taxation was to be forthcoming. Edward I's approach speaks to his strong sense of royal authority and royal prerogatives, but it may speak to something else too, what we might call 'leader fatigue', a sense on the part of an experienced leader that they have seen more than anyone advising them and that in consequence they know best. Experienced leaders in any period and any arena can run the risk of failing to listen even where previously they may have been known for their consultative approach. In the case of Edward I, given the pressure he was under, an element of leader fatigue and an already strong sense of his own authority may well have combined to undermine his judgement in one crucial respect in the final years. This was to be as nothing, however, compared to the stupendous failings of his son, whose reign was to culminate in the first deposition in post-Conquest England.

EDWARD II, 1307–27
'Without Hope of Amendment'

The Personal Disaster of Edward II

Edward I had had huge strengths as a king, but his rule had not been easy, and when any long-standing regime comes to an end, change tends to be welcomed. Leadership fatigue affects not just leaders but also the people. Most legitimate political successors therefore enjoy an initial period of political grace in which they can seem to do no wrong. So it is telling that Edward II experienced no such honeymoon period. Political tensions surfaced almost immediately, and within months developed into full-blown conflict.

Conceivably, a difficult political inheritance might be blamed. It is true that Robert Bruce's renewed rebellion had to be put down. Equally, tensions in the relationship between England and France over Aquitaine were unresolved. Prolonged international conflict since 1294 had left the royal coffers depleted: debts stood at up to £200,000, more than three years of direct taxation. But if the Bruce rebellion required prompt action, if Anglo-French differences over Aquitaine were arguably unresolvable in the long term and if the Crown needed to re-establish its cash flow, none of these issues presented a severe challenge in 1307. Moreover, the role of the king was so fundamental, and his position ordinarily so unquestioned, that structural problems or difficult circumstances rarely caused comprehensive political breakdown. The internal political conflict that occurred during the early part of Edward II's reign can therefore only really be attributed to failure on the part of Edward himself. With government resting upon the secure foundations established by Edward I, crisis could have been avoided had his son merely applied political deftness and effort: a willingness to listen, to respond reasonably and to act. But even this was more than Edward II was able or willing to give. The new king was irresponsible, extravagant, lazy and stubborn. He was not wholly deficient in ability, as is evidenced by a celebrated satirical letter he wrote as prince to his kinsman Louis of

Évreux, in which he described his Welsh greyhounds as 'more than capable of catching a hare, if they happen to find it asleep', and by his apparent skill as a public speaker; but he was disastrously lacking both in application and political judgement.

The great nobles must privately have feared disaster from the moment Edward II became king, for he was well known to them. Born on 25 April 1284 at Caernarfon Castle, he was the first heir to the English throne to be proclaimed prince of Wales. Tall, strong and fair, and carefully groomed for rule, by his early teens he was representing the king in Parliament. On 7 February 1301, he was formally created prince of Wales and immediately travelled to the principality to receive fealty in person from many hundreds of his higher-ranking Welsh subjects. From 1300, he gained considerable military experience fighting the Scots. Here, he served key nobles as well as his father, exercising semi-independent command, but accomplishing no notable feats of arms. Although he was an excellent horseman, Edward was no tournament fighter and showed little appetite for the hunt. Tourneying and hunting were natural counterparts to warfare, vital to the honing of knightly skills, so soldiering was probably something Edward did by obligation rather than inclination. What was he naturally interested in? One interest was music. He retained a number of musicians, including his minstrel, Richard the Rhymer, whose tuition in playing the Welsh *crwth*, a new bowed instrument, Edward personally solicited from the abbot of Shrewsbury. He also kept an organ at his favourite manor of Langley. But his best-known interests lay elsewhere. The author of the *Vita Edwardi Secundi* or *Life of Edward II*, by far the best contemporary biography of the king, famously held that Edward was more concerned with the 'rustic pursuits' of planting hedges, digging ditches and boating than with providing justice for his people. While there is no documentary evidence for the hedge-planting and ditch-digging, we do know that Edward nearly drowned in 1315 when boating near Cambridge.

It was once fashionable for historians to associate Edward's political difficulties with such apparent eccentricities. No such esoteric causes of political friction, however, need be searched for. The real causes of Edward II's failure are obvious enough. His fecklessness, lack of application and poor political judgement were all recognised and acted upon by Edward I.

In 1305, he was banished from his father's presence for several months on account of a bitter row he had had with Walter Langton, the king's treasurer, who had been seeking to control the prince's reckless spending. While the prince attempted, in his letters to his friends and contemporaries, to play down the severity of the king's anger, further friction shortly followed. Prince Edward's savage treatment of ordinary and blameless Scots, including women and children, during his campaign to put down the Bruce rebellion in 1306–7, forced Edward I to rebuke his son. And in February 1307, the prince was required by his father to forswear all contact with his retainer and close companion Piers Gaveston, whom the king was sending into exile in Gascony 'for certain causes' (a phrase that recurs in the government records whenever kings wished to keep a matter confidential). Contemporary accounts attribute Gaveston's exile to the prince having unwisely requested of his father that Gaveston be granted the county of Ponthieu in northern France, though there is no hard evidence for this. Whatever the case, it is likely that Edward I sent Gaveston overseas in an attempt to end a distraction that he believed was preventing his son from fulfilling his responsibilities as heir to the throne.

When Prince Edward learned of the king's death, he hurried from London to the north, conventionally 'wept for his father' at Burgh by Sands and received the fealty of his English subjects at Carlisle, followed by that of his Scottish allies at Dumfries. He then took two actions that reversed key aspects of the late king's policy. First, he created Piers Gaveston, who had already been recalled to England, earl of Cornwall. Second, Edward had Walter Langton, his father's treasurer – whom he openly declared himself determined to discomfit if not destroy – arrested and imprisoned for alleged corruption. (Later, in January 1312, the king decided that he needed Langton's financial expertise and performed a complete volte-face, re-employing him as treasurer and describing him as a victim of false accusations. Such was Edward's inconsistency and the crassness of his self-interest!) His lightning action in the first few weeks of his rule demonstrates that, where his own interests were concerned, he could be energetic. But his natural inclination was the opposite: to indolence. During a royal visit to France in 1313 (when he was infamously entertained by fifty-four naked dancers), contemporaries remarked upon his tendency to lie in bed until the afternoon; and in 1319, amid one of his rare spells of political engagement, it was noted that he was now getting up in the morning and showing clemency, not severity, in his judicial decisions. From the late summer of 1307, the king's lackadaisical attitude to duty was to the fore, and this, compounded by serious concerns over royal favouritism and the Scottish war, led to political disquiet by January 1308 and outright confrontation by April.

The Causes of Early Political Opposition

The king's favouritism towards Piers Gaveston was a critical political matter, but not for the reasons historians have usually assumed. Gaveston was the king's closest friend and adviser – in Edward's own language, his 'brother'. There is no doubt that their relationship was excessive and immoderate. But it may not have been sexual – as today tends to be the assumption – and in any case that misses the point; so too does the argument that the nobles were hostile to Gaveston because he was a foreigner of modest estate: an esquire from Béarn in the Pyrenees. In fact there was no principled objection to the promotion of foreign-born members of the royal household in fourteenth-century England, even to positions of the highest authority – so long as they deserved it.

The first issue with Gaveston was that the other nobles regarded him as undeserving: a meritless distraction extracting vast patronage from the king while simultaneously preventing him from doing his job. There is no doubt that Gaveston was heavily overpromoted by Edward. The Gascon acquitted himself well in tournaments but was otherwise distinguished primarily by his remarkable capacity to offend people. At the coronation on 25 February 1308, his arrogant and ostentatious behaviour, 'so decked out that he resembled the god Mars', together with Edward's constant fussing over him, incited the disgust and enmity of the French courtiers there present in support of Edward's new queen, Isabella, daughter of King Philip IV of France. Later, Gaveston provoked the earls by labelling them with offensive nicknames: the earl of Lincoln was 'Burst-belly', Thomas of Lancaster 'the Fiddler', the earl of Pembroke 'Joseph the Jew' and the earl of Warwick 'the Black Dog of Arden'. Had Gaveston shown aptitude for administration, war or diplomacy, or had he somehow persuaded the king to do his royal duty, arguably there would have been less political disquiet about his closeness to the king, or his having received first the earldom of Cornwall, then marriage to the king's niece Margaret Clare and, finally and most controversially, the keepership of the realm – during the king's absence in France for his marriage to Isabella in the winter of 1307–8.

The second issue was that Gaveston was an impediment to noble access to the king, which restricted the magnates' ability both to counsel Edward in an effort to amend his behaviour, and to request his assistance with their own affairs. This was because the king relied upon Gaveston's advice in everything and would not speak with any other great lord unless his favourite was present. In this way, the too-exclusive relationship between Edward and Gaveston represented both a subversion of a key political norm and a defiance of good governance. While Gaveston's superciliousness and offensiveness rubbed salt into political wounds, and while the other earls were infuriated by his demeanour and behaviour, their mounting determination to set him aside was chiefly about practical politics and the demands of the common good, not jealousy or resentment. The fact that opposition, when it speedily came, was led by Lincoln and Pembroke, perhaps the steadiest and most committed noble servants of the Crown, indicates this.

Although Edward's inherited debts were significant, repaying them was not an urgent matter. What Edward II needed in 1307 was renewed cash flow. This was to deal with the continuing Bruce rebellion and to pay for both his father's funeral and his proposed marriage to Isabella of France. Parliament had been summoned straight after Edward II's accession, and in October it provided both lay and ecclesiastical subsidies to meet the king's financial needs. Cash flow having been provided, it was essential that it was properly spent. Setting aside the royal funeral and marriage, in 1307–8 the clear priority was the war against Bruce. Instead of pressing ahead with putting down Bruce's revolt, however, Edward prevaricated. He was naturally indolent, but at this time was also increasingly distracted by defending Gaveston against criticism and attack. Meanwhile the magnates were anxious about what was happening to the subsidy intended for the Scottish war. It was widely suspected that it was lining Gaveston's pockets – and those of other courtiers. While historians considering favouritism in Edward II's early years have tended to focus almost exclusively upon Gaveston, in fact there was a larger group of favourites apparently sucking money, land or other preferment out of the king at will. With the benefit of hindsight, the courtiers surrounding Edward in his early rule look like a rogues' gallery for the reign as a whole. They were an ambitious and acquisitive lot, standing in contrast to Lincoln and Pembroke – who led a responsible political opposition that sought only to steer royal rule into safer waters.

Who were the courtiers? Henry Beaumont and Beaumont's sister Isabella Vescy were kinsmen of the queen, friends with both her and Gaveston, and generally perceived to be on the make. In 1311 they were proscribed in the Ordinances – an attempt by the nobles in Parliament definitively to force Edward II to mend his ways. Closely associated with them was Queen Isabella. Isabella was initially neglected by Edward II, but after her father responded by condemning Gaveston and giving encouragement and money to the English magnates who opposed him, Edward realised he needed to break the anti-Gaveston alliance between the French king and his nobles, and accordingly granted Isabella his own French lands of Ponthieu and Montreuil. During Gaveston's absence in Ireland in 1308–9, Isabella (now emerging from precocious childhood into assured adulthood) built a strong connection with the king, who henceforth regarded her as an ally. She received huge grants of money and land. After Gaveston's return from Ireland, she and the Gascon seem to have enjoyed a positive relationship. There emerged a constructive modus vivendi, in which Edward, Gaveston and Isabella resided and travelled together, and in which the queen backed her husband, even when he was chiefly focused upon maintaining his relationship with his favourite. The queen, much brighter and more capable than Edward, was herself politically ambitious, status-conscious and extravagant. She rightly calculated that her own position was dependent upon sustaining and buttressing the king, who came increasingly to rely on her insight and application. That their relationship was personal as well as professional is attested by their having had four children together.

Other notable courtiers around the king and on good terms with Gaveston included Hugh Despenser the Elder, John Charlton, Roger Mortimer of Wigmore and, initially, Thomas of Lancaster. Despenser was a long-standing courtier-administrator and ruthless justiciar of the royal forest. The opposition magnates wished to exclude him from the king's Council. Charlton, a household knight soon to be appointed chamberlain, was notably litigious and inclined to fall out with people. Like Beaumont and Vescy, he was duly singled out for proscription in the 1311 Ordinances. Mortimer was a highly capable and ambitious Welsh Marcher lord. Working in tandem with Charlton, he backed the king resolutely until 1320–1, when Edward's support for the violent and rapacious Hugh Despenser the Younger in Marcher politics left him (and Charlton) with little choice but to rebel. Finally, Thomas, earl of Lancaster is now infamous as Gaveston's killer and the king's most implacable opponent. Few people realise that, until he fell out with Gaveston and moved into opposition in 1309, he was firmly in the courtier camp.

During 1307–12, concerns about the courtiers were manifold. Gaveston was seen as the arch-offender. He had received all the gifts that were presented to Edward by Philip IV in recognition of his marriage to Isabella, together with many high-profile and substantial grants, including the aforementioned earldom of Cornwall, and the royal castles of Wallingford, Berkhamsted and Knaresborough, on the last of which alone Edward spent over £2,100 – a vast sum, more than twice the annual income of an earl – on an elaborate (and unnecessary) reconstruction project, intended to present Gaveston in king-like splendour, framed by a grand arch of immense span and illuminated by a huge window in a new audience chamber. Just as serious were the consequences of Gaveston's influence in Gascon politics. Gaveston was wont keenly to pursue grants and positions for his relations and friends. He used his influence to procure in his homeland of Aquitaine the seneschalcy of the Agenais – one of the most strategically important provinces within the duchy – for his brother, Arnaud-Guillaume de Marsan. Gaveston and Marsan then alienated Amanieu, lord of Albret, the greatest Gascon nobleman, by confiscating his recently acquired lordship of Nérac, against which judgement Albret appealed to the *Parlement* of Paris in 1310. Albret's contempt for Gaveston and Marsan ('The gifts of land and offices made by the said seneschal and his brother lord Piers Gaveston displease me,' he said) was one of the reasons why he ended his hitherto steadfast support for the

English Crown and started to back the French in the region. (The other reason was the depredations of John Ferrers, whose short-lived tenure as seneschal of Gascony in 1312 was so tumultuous as to result in his murder in the duchy.) Albret's local authority and his knowledge of the terrain later facilitated the French invasion of the duchy during the War of Saint-Sardos in 1324. Had he not been driven by Gaveston into French hands early in Edward II's reign, the invading French forces in the mid-1320s would have faced a much more difficult task.

Turning to gifts to the other courtiers, there was concern about the extent of the Beaumonts' land grants in Lincolnshire, and especially over Henry's receipt of the Isle of Man, whose strategic importance was amplified by the Bruce rebellion. In 1309, John Charlton received the great Welsh Marcher lordship of Powys, whose value, both financial and military, was enormous. Charlton's ascendancy had significant local-political ramifications. His handling of his new lordship of Powys was abrasive, and in 1311, he provoked his wife's paternal uncle, Gruffudd de la Pole, whose rights in Powys he had questioned, into staking a claim under Welsh law to the entire lordship. With Thomas of Lancaster choosing to retain and back Pole as a means to undermine the king by attacking his chamberlain, the dispute escalated horribly. Charlton found himself besieged in Powys Castle in 1312, and the business spun destructively on, with knock-on disorder across the Midlands, until it was finally resolved by a furious Edward III in 1331–2.

While all these issues were certainly worrying for the nobles, the compelling challenge in 1307–8 was the resurgent Bruce rebellion. Indeed, it was almost certainly the pressing need to back England's Scottish allies and put down the Bruce revolt before it gathered greater momentum that forced Lincoln, Pembroke, the earl of Hereford and others into political opposition by 1308. The problems of favouritism, seemingly incontinent royal spending, the inappropriate distribution of land and office, and lack of access to the king were all rendered critical by the Scottish context. In this way, removing Gaveston was less an end in itself than a first step towards re-establishing English (and allied Scottish) control in Scotland. Edward's focus on Gaveston and failure to move against Bruce allowed the latter to confound his enemies and embed his rule north of the border.

Bruce's murder of John Comyn in 1306 had rendered him a political pariah and cemented the alliance between the Comyns, their associates and the English. In the months that followed he had been reduced to desperate straits by his defeats at Methven and Dalrigh. But Bruce had revived his cause with his victory at Loudoun Hill – prompting Edward I's final journey north in 1307 – and it was now vital that the English stopped him in his tracks. Immediately after Edward I had died, it had been agreed that the summer campaign against Bruce should be postponed while the royal funeral and marriage took place. A sensible holding position, through the appointment of the experienced Pembroke as the king's lieutenant in Scotland, had been established. But then nothing material was done. It is important to stress that Bruce's position in Scotland remained vulnerable: he was fighting a Scottish civil war against bitter enemies as well as a war of independence, and despite his recent success, that winter he was arguably there for the taking, not least because he was gravely ill – possibly with the leprosy that eventually killed him. It was not until March 1309, and the St Andrews Parliament that formally recognised him as king, that his position began to stabilise. By failing to act, Edward II relieved Bruce of the problem of chasing two hares at the same time – to borrow an oft-used medieval analogy. Bruce was able make headway in the Scottish civil war against the Comyns and their allies because Edward II failed to hold him to account for his rebellion against English overlordship. His key triumph at this time was undoubtedly his vanquishing of the Comyns at the battle of Inverurie in 1308, immediately after which he denuded their highland power base by the brutal devastation of their lands.

None of this is to argue that dealing with Bruce was a simple matter, let alone that a long-term solution to the problems of Scottish independence and English overlordship was readily achievable. (As Edward III of England and David II of Scotland later demonstrated in the Treaty of Berwick of 1357, the closest thing to a solution that could be provided to the Anglo-Scottish problem was sustainable pragmatism, involving both kings conceding nothing fundamental while simultaneously agreeing to stop fighting one another via an extended truce.) But the particular challenge posed by Scotland to the English in 1307 was by no means insurmountable. It did, however, require action.

The 'Boulogne Agreement', the Fourth Coronation Oath and the 'Declaration of 1308'

The dearth of action against Bruce produced the first, guarded statement of political opposition on 31 January 1308: the so-called 'Boulogne Agreement'. It remained the case that the transformation of political disquiet into practical action required political actors to have time together to formulate positions. This is one reason why Parliament was so important, but any gathering in which leading figures could exchange and develop views could (and did) serve the same purpose. It was at their gathering in Boulogne-sur-Mer, for the wedding of Edward and Isabella, and for Edward's performance of homage for Gascony to Philip IV, that Lincoln, Pembroke, Hereford, Bishop Antony Bek of Durham and others publicly avowed that they would preserve the honour of the king and the rights of the Crown, and would do everything in their power to redress past challenges to the king's honour and to protect the realm and people against oppression. The Boulogne Agreement is worded with sufficient opacity to allow historians to put quite different spins on it. While some have argued that it was fundamentally a statement of support for Edward, this seems hard to sustain in the light of the '1308 Declaration', made only three months later and clearly a development of the Agreement.

The Declaration, formulated at Lincoln's castle of Pontefract between meetings of Parliament in early March and late April, and presented in the second meeting, deployed the so-called 'doctrine of capacities' to justify the magnates' opposition, explicitly drawing a distinction between the office of the Crown and the person of the king, and arguing that homage and allegiance were owed by subjects to the Crown as opposed to the individual who happened to be on the throne. This meant (the Declaration said) that, if the person of the king were not guided by reason, to the detriment of the Crown, his subjects were bound to 'reinstate the king in the dignity of the Crown' by 'constraint', the nature of this being indicated by the fact that the earls appeared at Parliament in arms, accompanied by their retinues. Restoring the king's dignity involved removing 'the evil' that had misled him, namely Gaveston, who was 'judged by the people' to be 'robber and traitor', 'disinheriting and impoverishing the Crown' and 'withdrawing the king from the counsel of his realm'. Meanwhile, in February, between the Boulogne Agreement and the 1308 Declaration, and in a sense progressing from the former while anticipating the latter, a fourth clause had been inserted into the king's coronation oath in which the king had sworn to 'uphold the laws that the community of the realm would decide'. Friction between the political community and the king was clearly expected.

Together, the Agreement, the fourth clause and the Declaration indicate rapidly escalating political resistance in the winter and spring of 1307–8 – a situation so serious by March that, in the aftermath of the first parliamentary meeting, Edward had begun to prepare for war against the magnates, issuing commissions against assemblies and 'malefactors', placing key castles in the hands of trusted new custodians, and putting the Tower of London and Windsor Castle – to which Edward and Gaveston retreated, breaking the Thames bridges at Kingston and Staines behind them – in a state of defence. The contrast between this focused attempt to take control of the realm and the king's usual disengagement from the day-to-day business of running the country is striking. While he was unwilling to take up arms against Robert Bruce, confronting his own subjects appears to have been a different matter. Such was the degree to which his kingship was already turning the political world upside down.

Edward initially refused to accept the 1308 Declaration, and in particular staunchly resisted the demand of the earls that Gaveston be exiled for a second time. But the near unanimity of his greatest subjects (Lancaster remained for now on the king's side), backed by renewed pressure from his father-in-law the king of France, forced the king to yield. On 18 May, he agreed that Gaveston should go into perpetual exile and that his lands as earl of Cornwall should be returned to the Crown.

This was no more than a tactical retreat, however. Edward immediately replaced Gaveston's confiscated Cornish lands with grants of Gascon territory and income from English estates, and, in a last-minute decision, clearly intended to provide Gaveston with both status and safety from his English and French enemies, he despatched him to Ireland (rather than Gascony, the destination originally envisaged) as king's lieutenant or governor. Gaveston's conduct as lieutenant in Ireland seems to have been unproblematic, and in the meantime the king set about building bridges with his opponents with a view to having his favourite's exile rescinded. In a sense this had already begun with the aforementioned grant to Isabella of Ponthieu and Montreuil, but Edward now devoted himself to completing the job, all the while seeking reconciliation with individual earls – Gloucester, Hereford, Lincoln, Warwick and Pembroke – by showing them favour. That they responded positively was consequent not, as the author of the *Vita* suggested, upon their fickleness or lack of principle, but upon the fact that the chief obstacle to their enjoying a more positive relationship with the king – Gaveston – had been removed. For the great lords, their being with the king was a matter of natural order. Gaveston was anathema precisely because he disrupted this. With the favourite out of the picture, it was right and expected that Edward and the earls should reconcile. A close and productive working relationship built around the king's leadership and the magnates' counsel would strengthen the polity and thereby the realm.

Perhaps it was because of the inherent attractiveness of this symbiosis, together with the lords' relief that things seemed to be getting back to normal, that Edward was eventually successful in persuading them (with one notable exception) that Gaveston might be brought back. Although the Parliament of April 1309 rejected the king's entreaty that Gaveston should return and be fully restored to the earldom of Cornwall, that assembled in July acceded to the request – partly because Edward formally renewed the Crown's commitment to limiting the burdens on the realm imposed by prises and purveyance, a great and continuing concern to Parliament, and partly because the king had already persuaded the papacy to overturn the sentence of excommunication that had been placed over Gaveston's head as a deterrent to his returning without warrant. Thus, through a mix of charm offensive, behind-the-scenes manoeuvring and political concession, Edward got what he wanted.

Thomas of Lancaster and the Ordinances

While some earls were evidently more optimistic than others about the prospects for the future, one figure stood out in opposition. Thomas of

Lancaster's earlier support for a problematic regime had, by early 1309, been transformed into implacable opposition. The reasons for this are uncertain. The *Vita* held that the exclusion of a Lancastrian retainer from office at Gaveston's instance was the cause. But recent research has suggested that Lancaster's change of sides had its origins in a dispute between one of his retainers in Yorkshire and the escheator north of the Trent – the royal official responsible for checking whether landed inheritance fell to the king or another party. It seems likely that tensions in Lancaster's Yorkshire territorial heartlands were indeed the cause of the earl's volte-face. The grant of Knaresborough Castle had provided Gaveston with a high-profile and lavishly upgraded platform adjacent both to Lancaster's existing territories and to others he anticipated inheriting from his father-in-law, the earl of Lincoln; and the accompanying appointment of Gaveston's associates to royal offices in the county may have been regarded by Lancaster, a proud and volatile man, as provocative. Competition between the king and Lancaster over local office also seems to have commenced in 1309 in Staffordshire, another Lancastrian heartland. Depending upon when exactly Lancaster moved into opposition, this may have been contributory cause or early symptom of the new hostility between the king and his greatest subject.

All now depended upon Gaveston's post-return behaviour and the king's engagement with royal duties. So far as the former is concerned, Gaveston could scarcely have played his hand worse. This was the period when he invented offensive nicknames for the earls, and although his influence upon patronage was exercised less blatantly than hitherto, it continued to cause serious concern. In short, he remained as odious as ever. At the same time, prises and purveyance continued, despite the king's undertakings. Purveyance on a grand scale for war in Scotland that never transpired had been ordered in both 1308 and 1309, and insult was now added to injury as Edward mandated further purveyance, this time for royal forces in Ireland. Meanwhile, government in the shires was characterised by lack of action. There was little proactive judicial engagement, reflected in rising numbers of petition-driven judicial commissions as the politically connected responded to the absence of Crown action for the maintenance of order by seeking legal redress outside the standard framework of justice. It is unsurprising, therefore, that, when the king summoned Parliament to assemble in February 1310, nominally to discuss the question of how to deal with the 'enemy, rebel and traitor' Robert Bruce, the earls refused to appear until Gaveston, 'their chief enemy, who had set the kingdom and themselves in uproar', was removed from the king's presence. If the king insisted that they had to appear nonetheless, they would do so in arms, for their own protection. The king despatched Gaveston to a place of safety and, three weeks late, Parliament proceeded.

Its principal outcome, agreed only after the earls had accused the king of breaking his coronation oath and threatened him with deposition, was the appointment of the Ordainers, sometimes called the Lords Ordainer. This group of twenty-one prelates, earls and barons received full powers to reform the kingdom and the royal household, for the honour of the king and people, and in accordance with reason and the king's coronation oath. The Ordainers' period of authority was to extend for exactly a year. Those appointed to the office included the archbishop of Canterbury, Robert Winchelsey, whom Edward had recalled from exile shortly after his accession, as well as the senior earls and a representative cluster of barons. A range of attitudes was represented, from individuals essentially hostile to Edward and Gaveston, among whom Lancaster was now the most forthright, to those, such as John of Brittany, earl of Richmond, who had tended towards neutrality. Having been elected and sworn in on 20 March 1310, the Ordainers set about their work – to draw up a plan for the amendment and right governance of England. Their preliminary Ordinances, promulgated by the king on 2 August, sought to impose basic financial and patronage controls on the government, to protect church liberties and uphold Magna Carta, and to establish London as a base for the Ordainers' work, where they could access expert legal and financial advice, and the records of the Chancery and Exchequer. Historians do not know how exactly the Ordainers proceeded, but access to lawyers and to government clerks must have been critical to their work, as the king's proposal to remove the Exchequer, King's Bench and Common Pleas to York from Westminster in October 1310 provoked outrage, and the threat on the part of the earl of Lincoln, then acting as keeper of the realm during the king's absence in Scotland, to resign.

The king was in Scotland at this point because he had finally responded to the demand that he take action against Robert Bruce. Why the change of heart? He was partly impelled by a Council meeting in June in which a number of the English Crown's Scottish allies had stressed that, without an appearance north of the border by the king in person, the anti-Bruce alliance in Scotland would be imperilled. But the matter had been urgent before and the king had done nothing. The real difference this time was the work of the Ordainers and the need to keep Gaveston away from them. A Scottish campaign would enable this to be done under a cloak of honour. What is more, as the chronicler Walter Guisborough recounted, if Gaveston were to enjoy notable military success against Bruce, this would considerably reduce his vulnerability to criticism. While many of the earls declined to participate in the campaign, because of Gaveston's expected presence on it and because of their continuing work as Ordainers in London, the king was nonetheless able to assemble a decent force of Welsh infantry together with cavalry assembled from among English and Scottish magnate retinues and the royal household. The English army entered Scotland in September 1310, sweeping to the Forth before retreating just inside the English border to winter, during which time limited diplomatic contact with Bruce, some of which was mysteriously confidential, was made. It was rumoured that Edward was seeking an accommodation with Bruce in which Gaveston would be granted safe haven north of the border. After Christmas, a second sweep went further, with English commanders, including Gaveston, establishing themselves in allied towns and castles north of the Forth, including Perth and Dundee. But Robert Bruce was too wise a general to risk his hard-won position in Scotland by needlessly engaging with an English army, and he stayed safely out of the way. Nothing permanent was achieved and when, in late July 1311, a combination of mounting political pressure and exhaustion of supply forced Edward to return to Westminster, Bruce took the opportunity to pour across the border into England on a devastating plundering raid that refilled his treasury's depleted coffers. There was already acute concern on the part of the polity about deficiencies in the realm's defensive policy in respect of Gascony and Ireland as well as Scotland. To this was now added positive proof that Edward could not defend England itself.

Parliament met at the end of August and spent most of September wrangling with the king over the 1311 Ordinances – the Ordainers' scheme for the government of England. Their preamble succinctly describes the Ordinances' background and purpose:

> Through bad and deceitful advice, our lord the king has everywhere
> been dishonoured and his Crown in many ways debased and ruined;
> his lands in France, Ireland and Scotland are on the point of being lost;
> and his realm of England has been brought to the point of rebellion
> through illegal taxes and other oppressive and destructive measures.
> These facts are known and proved.

Accordingly, at the heart of the Ordinances lay provisions against Gaveston – to whose evil counsel the troubles of the king and realm were attributed – and in favour of enhanced financial control and retrenchment. Those who had misled the king and siphoned money from him were to be expelled. In addition to Gaveston, who was ordered to abjure the realm on 1 November, a host of other courtiers were proscribed, including Henry Beaumont, Isabella Vescy and – in later provisions – John Charlton and more than twenty lesser individuals mostly related to or associated with Gaveston. Prises in particular had remained a major worry and were now prohibited. The Italian bankers the Frescobaldi, believed to be linked with Gaveston's associates, were to be arrested and were to have their assets seized. This was to prevent the king from running up further debts. Grants were to be annulled and appointments reviewed, and the king's actions guided by the barons in a range of other ways. References in the Ordinances to Magna Carta, the Forest Charter, the Articles upon the Charters and various questions of financial and judicial management that had emerged in earlier reigns spoke not of inherited political problems but of the inclination of medieval manifesto-writers to recapitulate pre-existing concerns. The Ordinances were ultimately about Edward II's delinquency and profligacy, and about Gaveston and his friends; they would never have been promulgated otherwise. They were about the English constitution only in so far as they were framed by the constitutional difficulty of managing a delinquent king in medieval England. They were not an abstract political manifesto.

The king fiercely resisted the imposition of any constraints upon his behaviour, but in the end pressure told. Revealingly, Edward offered to accept any constraint upon his kingship as long as no 'persecution' (his term) of Gaveston took place. He was forced, however, to accept his favourite's exile on this, a third occasion, though this time with the ominous and striking proviso that any return to England would render Gaveston an enemy of the king and people. A distinction between the office and person of the king was again evidently being drawn. For Edward, however, the very fact that he had been compelled to agree to the limits imposed upon him gave him a potential way out. In theory, kings were at liberty later to repudiate any concession that had been extracted from them under duress. What exacerbated the situation in 1311 was Edward II's determination to bring Gaveston back as quickly as possible and to confront his opponents from the relative security of the north of England. That this was always his intention is indicated by the fact that, unlike in 1308, in 1311 little financial provision was made by the king for Gaveston's absence, presumably because he believed his friend would not need it for long.

Gaveston's Murder

In the event Gaveston quit the Continent and came back to England – returning from exile for a third time – as early as January 1312. The pace of Gaveston's return may have been hastened by the fact that his wife, Margaret, was heavily pregnant. Shortly after he rejoined the king at Knaresborough, the two proceeded to York for the birth of Gaveston's daughter. In the meantime, Edward was engaged in politics entirely out of kilter with sense and realism. He formally overturned the exile and confiscation of Gaveston, who received a pardon. In March, arguing that he had consented to the Ordinances only under duress, he wrote to Archbishop Winchelsey, asking him to receive royal lawyers who would discuss with him aspects of the Ordinances that particularly irked the king. Predictably, once the earls had received this unwelcome news, they formulated a plan to capture Gaveston. Gathering under the cover of tournaments, so as not to warn Edward or Gaveston prematurely, and led by Lancaster following the death – in February 1311 – of Lincoln, they severally undertook to secure different parts of the realm, allotting Pembroke and Warenne to hunt down and arrest the hated favourite. Edward and Gaveston, together with Queen Isabella, who was also pregnant (one wonders whether the king and Gaveston were so concerned about their futures that they had resolved to father children before it was too late), retreated as the earls advanced and then divided – with Gaveston taking refuge in Scarborough Castle, from which flight by sea was possible, and Edward and Isabella returning to York to confront their opponents. Edward was now certainly contemplating the possibility of his own as well as Gaveston's demise, and when – in May – Pembroke, Warenne, Henry Percy, he and Gaveston agreed terms under which the latter could conditionally surrender, he must have been relieved. Gaveston was to be protected by Pembroke, Warenne and Percy on pain of forfeiture, pending renewed baronial negotiations with the king concerning the magnates' demands.

If Edward and Gaveston anticipated yet again somehow wriggling out of their opponents' clutches, Thomas of Lancaster and the earl of Warwick were determined to stop them from doing so. Perhaps they believed Pembroke had exceeded his brief in agreeing Gaveston's surrender on terms. In any case, as Pembroke escorted Gaveston south he temporarily absented himself to visit his wife, leaving Gaveston attended only by his guards. Informed that Gaveston was lightly guarded and that Pembroke was absent, Warwick seized his moment, dashing with an armed retinue to Oxfordshire to snatch Gaveston and abduct him to Warwick Castle. He was promptly joined there by Lancaster, Hereford and Arundel. The four earls agreed, quasi-judicially, that Gaveston should be put to death. He was an enemy of the realm who had been proscribed by the Ordinances. The pariah had been well warned of the risk he ran, should he return to England from exile a third time. They swore an oath of mutual assistance. On 19 June Gaveston was taken by Lancaster out of Warwick Castle and on to Lancastrian lands at Kenilworth, some two miles to the north. There, atop Blacklow Hill, he was run through with a sword and then beheaded by two Welshmen in Lancaster's service. The earl of Warwick kept away, and Arundel and Hereford followed the killing party at a distance. It was Lancaster who presided over Gaveston's death and took upon himself the chief responsibility. This was, the author of the *Vita* said, because he was the king's cousin, the greatest and most powerful of the earls, and believed that he should therefore bear the heaviest burden. That might be right. But Lancaster was also an arrogant, confrontational and stubborn man, with no more political sense than his liege lord the king. There was a question about the technicalities of Gaveston's legal status at the point of his killing. Was he a traitor and outlaw, the Ordinances being in force? Or, Edward having at least partially repudiated them, and Gaveston having been restored by the king and having been promised protection by Pembroke et al. pending negotiations, was he an earl entitled to trial by his peers? Whatever the technicalities, in the world of realpolitik the killing was politically disastrous. A nobleman whom the king called 'brother' had been killed without proper legal process and in cold blood. Arguably a grim precedent had been set for future years and certainly the political die was cast for the next decade. As the *Vita* makes clear, politics in England would henceforth be hamstrung by what amounted to a blood feud between the monarch and the wealthiest and most territorially powerful nobleman in the realm – until, that is, one destroyed the other. England in the period 1312–22 can be properly understood only within the context of this dominating and desperate reality.

Piers Gaveston's murder produced significant political realignment in England in two ways. First, it rendered the hostility between Edward II and Thomas of Lancaster implacable. Second, it allowed most of the magnates who had opposed the court since 1308 to return to their natural place at the king's side. They had been kept away from the king by Gaveston and that obstacle had now been removed – even though the manner of its removal had been turbulent in the extreme.

The speed with which an individual magnate who had been in a position of opposition was able to realign with the king depended upon the extent of his involvement in Gaveston's fate. Most lords rejoined the king quite quickly. But it took a full eighteen months for a formal peace settlement between the king and Lancaster to be agreed. This was because neither party was interested in settling on terms acceptable to the other. Indeed, they did not really want to settle at all, but were finally forced to both by circumstances and by pressure exerted by the wider polity. What the king actually wanted was justice for Gaveston and revenge upon his killers. Lancaster sought the king's subjugation and cast-iron guarantees of his own safety. None of this was politically realistic. But it took eighteen months for realism to materialise – when the personality-led politics of Edward and Lancaster were finally suppressed by a political community acutely aware that political structures and circumstances both demanded compromise. Government and the law could not operate effectively unless the king and his greatest subjects worked together, and the Scottish crisis similarly required a concerted English response, not one undermined by internal division.

Political Impasse and Nominal Settlement, 1312–13

Having re-established himself in London, the king's initial instinct was to gather an army to destroy Lancaster, Warwick, Hereford and Arundel. But, anticipating the danger, by August the earls had gathered in arms just outside the capital. Their forces were perhaps twice as strong as those at the king's disposal. Among the king's captains was Pembroke, outraged and mortified by the seizure of Gaveston from his protective custody. He was accompanied by Warenne. At this time Pembroke emerged as the king's pre-eminent counsellor, though the courtiers Hugh Despenser the Elder and Henry Beaumont were evidently important too, as was Queen Isabella. The earls of Gloucester and Richmond remained loyal, and acted as mediators in the ensuing negotiations.

If the king's urge was to seek to destroy his enemies, wiser counsel prevailed. The rebel earls' forces were strong. Plus there was the matter of defending the north of England. If Edward and his magnates fell to civil war, what would Robert Bruce do? The Scottish king had already harried Northumberland and extracted from its people devastating amounts of protection money. So a war of words ensued. The king's opening gambit was to demand that the Ordinances should be overturned as illegal, on the grounds that they had diminished the king's rights as well as his revenue. This was a strong technical argument (as the judgements of the French king and the pope on the baronial reforms of 1258 and on the Articles upon the Charters of 1300 had indicated, and as the Statute of York of 1322 went on to show). But it was not a politically realistic one. The polity wished to see the king and the rebels reconciled, which was in the best interests of the realm. The king was going to have to compromise.

The opening position of the rebel earls was similarly unsustainable. They wanted terms little short of a royal surrender: the Ordinances confirmed and enforced and all offences pardoned save those committed against the Ordinances. In other words, they demanded that they be absolved of all responsibility for Gaveston's death, on the grounds that Gaveston had been a felon and traitor, having returned to England in contravention of the Ordinances. (This argument required that the king's pardon of Gaveston of January 1312 should be ignored, but the rebels maintained – rather unconvincingly – that the pardon was illegal because agreements such as the Ordinances could only be overturned by the king, prelates, earls and barons acting in concert.) Accepting that Gaveston was a traitor was not something that Edward II was ever going to do.

During extended negotiations in the autumn and early winter, a settlement emerged, agreed for the two sides principally by Pembroke and Hereford, supported by mediators. It represented a classic solution to what was effectively an insoluble problem, in the best traditions of medieval negotiations: the intractable issues were side-stepped. There was no mention of the Ordinances or comment on Gaveston's status at the time of his death. Royal pardons were to be issued for all offences committed against Gaveston and his followers. No action was to be taken against Gaveston's associates. The king's and Gaveston's goods, seized by Lancaster and his allies when Edward and his favourite had fled before them, were to be returned. The king would provide an appropriate quittance. Justices would be appointed to hear the grievances of Lancaster's (newly acquired) retainers Gruffudd de la Pole and Fulk Lestrange against the chamberlain, John Charlton. Parliament would be summoned to discuss the Scottish war and to provide funding for a fresh campaign against Bruce. In the end, with tweaks to the wording in respect of the pardon and the quittance, the treaty was agreed – but only after another eleven months of negotiation. Why was there such a delay?

Lancaster and Warwick had not been personally present during the negotiations, and in January 1313, Lancaster declared himself dissatisfied by their outcome. In respect of the wording of the pardon, his dissatisfaction was understandable and in a way legitimate. The wording had to be got right to preclude the possibility that the king could afterwards repudiate it on the grounds that it had been extracted from him by force and against his will. Turning to the quittance, Lancaster insisted upon a statement in respect of returning the seized goods that described them as having belonged to a felon, implying that Gaveston had been outside the law at the point at which they had been seized and, by extension, at the point at which he had been killed. This was precisely what the king would not concede. In this way, Lancaster doubtless sought additional technical protection against future charges of homicide. But it is clear from the actions of Hereford in particular, who by now was working hard to try to persuade Lancaster and Warwick to accept the king's terms, that others who had been in the rebel party believed the terms on offer were acceptable. And Edward II was in no mood for further compromise. His political position had, on account of Gaveston's murder, improved dramatically. First, Pembroke and Warenne had come back into the royal fold. Now Hereford was detaching himself from Lancaster and Warwick. Plus Edward found himself backed afresh by the French king – just when he needed it.

The reason for this was the birth, on 13 November 1312, of a son and heir, the future Edward III, which gave the king great joy following the deep depression into which he had sunk after Gaveston's death. It seems also further to have cemented his now close relationship with Isabella – commented upon and celebrated by French chroniclers during a visit made by the royal couple to France at the invitation of King Philip in May–July 1313. For Philip IV, both of these developments were happy. He now faced the prospect of having a grandson upon the throne of England and as king-duke of Aquitaine at Bordeaux. And his beloved daughter Isabella was finally being accorded the status, position and political influence that he believed her lineage and intelligence merited. So far as Gascon affairs were concerned, Philip's new-found benevolence towards his son-in-law and the marked détente in Anglo-French relations that it brought could scarcely have come at a more expedient time. The alienation of the great Gascon lord Amanieu d'Albret and the general tumult and unrest generated in the duchy by John Ferrers's highly aggressive and uncompromising governorship had produced a tidal wave of judicial appeals from Edward's Gascon subjects to the Paris *Parlement*. Such was the disorder in the duchy that a state of civil war now effectively existed, which was threatening to escalate into international conflict between the English and French Crowns. The French king's resolve to ease jurisdictional tensions effectively got Edward out of the Gascon jail in which his favouritism towards Piers Gaveston in the duchy had landed him. Philip helped especially in respect of the lord of Albret, who now received compensation of £20,000 from Edward, at Philip's urging – though it did not undo the alienation to which Albret had been subjected between 1310 and 1312. But for now, the crisis was over. In the meantime, in the March, May and July Parliaments of 1313, little progress had been made in finalising the terms of the proposed treaty between Edward and the rebel earls. But the passage of time – perhaps as the king intended – succeeded in wearing down Lancaster's and Warwick's resistance, and following Edward's return from France, a new Parliament was summoned for late September with a view to bring the negotiations finally to a conclusion.

A series of proclamations in Parliament and beyond ended the impasse. The pardon and quittance were reworded to satisfy some of Lancaster's concerns. He was forced to back down, however, over demands he had made in March that Gaveston's followers should not be pardoned; indeed, the chapter of the Ordinances proscribing Henry Beaumont and Isabella Vescy was, by contrast, overturned. The rebel earls and their associates were received back into the king's grace and pardoned. Edward and the earls symbolically dined with one another on successive nights. Thus the end of hostilities between the king and the great lords was formally marked. But if the main body of the magnates was now clearly aligned with the king again (Hereford, for instance, tellingly remained in the court after the end of Parliament in November 1313), and if the hot war between Edward and Lancaster was over, a cold war had set in. Following the Gaveston murder, the king had forbidden conventicles and assemblies in Worcestershire, for example, and had begun to manoeuvre trusted men into official positions in Warwickshire, where previously the earl of Warwick's associates had tended to be appointed. This was in an attempt to thwart one of his enemies in his own back yard (Worcestershire and Warwickshire both being shires in which the earls of Warwick were usually pre-eminent). This sort of manipulation by Edward was to continue for most of the 1310s. In 1312–13, neither Edward nor Lancaster had been strong enough to crush the other. Furthermore they had been restrained by the political rump of great lords who sought a rapprochement between the king and his cousin. At the time of the settlement in the autumn of 1313, though, there was a moment of outward political calm in which the other dominating issue for the realm – Scotland – could be addressed.

Disaster at Bannockburn

It is traditionally held that Edward II's disastrous Bannockburn campaign of 1314 was launched to relieve the fortress of Stirling. Its commander – Philip Mowbray, a Comyn-supporting Scotsman – had agreed to surrender the castle to the besieging army of Edward Bruce (Robert Bruce's brother) if it were not relieved by the English by midsummer 1314. Stirling, which controlled the lowest crossing point over the River Forth and was thereby a gateway between lowland and highland Scotland, was strategically vital, and in May and June 1314, the English army certainly hurried northwards in an attempt to relieve Stirling before it was handed over to the Bruces.

But the campaign's inception pre-dated the investment of Stirling by many months. From 1312, with the relaxation of the English hold on lowland Scotland that had been precipitated by the final crisis over Gaveston, Bruce had been besieging and taking, one by one, the Anglo-Scots strongholds in Scotland that had hitherto provided the strategic framework for continuing opposition to his kingship. The great Bruce raid into Northumberland of 1311 had resulted in the men of the county buying the Bruces off with local truces and substantial monetary payments. This money was then used to fund armies to besiege the Anglo-Scottish fortifications within Scotland or on the border. In December 1312, only the warning bark of an alert dog had saved Berwick-upon-Tweed from succumbing to a night-time Scottish assault. During 1313 and early 1314, Perth, Dumfries, Linlithgow, Roxburgh and Edinburgh all fell, mainly to escalade, or night attacks by ladder-equipped scaling parties. The Bruces then reduced the captured fortifications to rubble, to denude the English and their Scottish allies of future strongholds. It was imperative for the English to put a stop to this systematic reduction of their Scottish assets.

There was another reason, however, why the English had to move decisively against Bruce now. This concerned the increasingly precarious position of their Scottish allies within Scotland. In October 1313, Bruce declared that his opponents had a year in which to enter his peace, recognising him as king, and forsaking their allegiance to the Comyns and Balliols, and their English lands. Otherwise they would be perpetually disinherited in Scotland. This would draw a cordon sanitaire between the Scottish and English Crowns, repudiating the cross-border landholding and related allegiances to both Crowns that had characterised the Anglo-Scottish nobility and high politics in Scotland hitherto. Scotland and England would be perpetually divided, not the separate but conjoined entities that they had previously been. If Bruce kingship were unacceptable to a cadre of Scottish lords – still loyal to the Balliols and Comyns – and if Scottish politics were complicated by the Scottish nobility's lands and family connections south of the border, both of these problems could be eliminated. Such scorched-earth radicalism would kill the Anglo-Scottish political settlement of 1304 and, indeed, change Anglo-Scottish relations forever.

In November 1313 Parliament granted Edward II a subsidy with a view to his leading a great army into Scotland. Bruce's ultimatum to Edward's Scottish allies meant that the English king had to act decisively to back them; otherwise they would be left with little option other than to settle with Bruce and accept his governance of an independent Scotland that rejected both English overlordship and landed connections with the English Crown. Yes, there would be some – the Balliols and Comyns, and those closest to them – who would never recognise Bruce, and others whose lands in England were too extensive to be abandoned. But many of those who adhered to the Comyns and continued to regard the Balliols as rightful kings of Scotland would have to weigh that commitment against their other powerful obligation – to their names, estates and heirs, which were in most cases fundamentally Scottish. Many would choose political compromise, even with a man whom they had recently regarded as a pariah, in order to preserve their inheritance. As the abortive conspiracy led by

William Soules to remove Bruce from the Scottish throne in 1320 was to show, some of those who did settle with Bruce in 1314 continued privately to adhere to the Balliol–Comyn cause. But, for all that, Bruce's decision to make the Scottish political community choose in 1313–14 was a political masterstroke. Those who still refused to back him would lose their Scottish lands, releasing to him, especially in all-important lowland Scotland where the pull of the Balliol–Comyn party remained strongest, a vital stock of estates that he could – and did – use to endow his strongest supporters. In this way he embedded them in the borderlands, where they provided local political leadership sympathetic to his kingship; he also gave them a genuine stake in fighting to maintain his right, because if Bruce were to fall, not only would they fall with him but they would also lose their newly acquired lands and status. By 1313–14 this process had already begun, with the grant in 1312 to the talented Thomas Randolph – created earl of Moray, and Bruce's right-hand man – of a great swathe of lands, with vice-regal powers, right across central Scotland. It now accelerated, and the families of Balliol, Comyn, Strathbogie and Soules were to lose their lands to endow the rise of Stewart, Murray and Ross, as well as many others of more modest origin. The value of this policy was arguably recognised by Edward III in the mid-1330s, when he sought to engineer pro-English loyalty and a personal stake in the Scottish lowlands by the creation of a new network of Anglo-Scottish Marcher lordships, in the hands of his household men as well as those of the Scottish lords – or their sons and heirs – who had lost out to Bruce. In this the English king duly failed, one might argue precisely because of the scale and impact of Bruce's land redistribution in the 1310s and 1320s. It was by no means the only way in which Bruce's once-fragile kingship was transformed, but it was surely a major factor in its transformation.

In any case, the danger was all too apparent to Edward II and those advising him in late 1313 and early 1314. But for the king a third reason for acting had emerged. As we know, in 1311, he had seen the potential value of campaigning in Scotland for his domestic political purposes; in 1313–14, he saw it again. But whereas in 1311 the aim had been for Gaveston to win credit and breathing space in England through victory over the Scots, now Edward's objective was the vanquishing of his comital enemies. Leading a campaign against the Scots provided him with an unarguable reason for raising an army. Only in time of war was the king likely to be able to raise a force sufficient in size to match (or ideally overawe) that which an earl or earls could raise from their private resources – especially through their powerful Welsh Marcher lordships. The author of the *Vita* makes it clear, lest we doubt it, that Edward's dream scenario involved vanquishing Bruce before, bathed in the glory and approval of God-given victory, redirecting his troops to England to deal with Lancaster. If Lancaster and Warwick joined the campaign, perhaps it would be a simple matter of arresting them after the battle. However, they – together with Arundel, who was also still out in the cold – declined to serve in person, sending the minimum legal requirement of troops in response to the royal summons. Their excuse, that the campaign had not been formally agreed in Parliament, was painfully thin, Parliament having been summoned the previous year explicitly to put in place measures to deal with the Scottish problem. Doubtless they feared arrest or even assassination on the field of battle. Warwick lived only one more year, but Lancaster was never to permit himself to be in close proximity to the king on campaign again, not even when he was finally shamed into participating in person outside the walls of Berwick in 1319: his retinue remained always at some distance from the royal army. Earl Warenne, perhaps surprisingly, also refused to serve in person in 1314, though this may have been because of his rapidly deteriorating relationship with Lancaster – his immediate neighbour in both Yorkshire and the northern March of Wales. It is possible that Warenne feared for the fate of his lands there if he quit them to fight the Scots while Lancaster remained south of the border.

Although the refusal of Lancaster and others to serve in 1314 reduced the size of the Anglo-Scottish army, the force that mustered at Berwick in June was nevertheless large – at perhaps twelve to fifteen thousand strong, the largest English army to penetrate Scotland since Edward I's Falkirk campaign. It departed Berwick with about a week to spare before Philip Mowbray's 24 June deadline for surrendering to the Bruces. This necessitated the setting of a cracking pace for Stirling, such that the author of the *Vita* described the king as proceeding at a speed more appropriate to the St James pilgrimage than to leading a field army. By the time the English and their Scots allies reached the approaches to Stirling, on 23 June, both men and horses were exhausted and the formations were strung out. But almost immediately they had to fight.

The Battle of Bannockburn

It should be stressed that, in common with those for many medieval battles, the sources for Bannockburn are contradictory and unclear. Some of this is about the nature of any pitched battle, in which eyewitnesses, located as combatants in different individual locations in the thick of a fight, typically had little idea what was going on elsewhere on the battlefield. Just occasionally, an eyewitness with a clear overarching sense of the battle, perhaps positioned behind the lines at some vantage point, might report, but here the tendency of the medieval mind to attribute all to providence can leave the historian none the wiser. In the case of Bannockburn, the most detailed medieval account is that of Barbour, but this was not compiled until the 1370s, and Barbour was not working from first-hand descriptions. The English knight Sir Thomas Gray's *Scalacronica* was written in the 1350s, when he was a prisoner-of-war of the Scots, but derives in part from his own father's eyewitness account of the first day of the fighting. The *Vita*, as ever, seems well informed and clear thinking, and was contemporaneously compiled. But it is difficult to tie these accounts – and others of the battle – together to make a coherent whole, and it is no surprise that, across a century of debate, historians have identified the battlefield in no fewer than six different locations. Nonetheless it is possible to describe and explain what seems evident about the rout of the English without giving a false impression of certainty.

The Scottish army, led by Robert Bruce, was positioned just short of Stirling in a wood straddling the road from Berwick. Like William Wallace before him, Bruce's political platform within Scotland rested upon military victory. Even one major defeat might jeopardise all he had built up. This meant that he usually avoided pitched battle against superior enemy forces, resorting instead to hit-and-run tactics. But with securing Stirling at stake, this time he was anticipating a head-to-head confrontation. Victory would depend upon neutralising the usual English advantage in heavy cavalry by choice of battlefield and careful troop positioning – on a narrow front with protected flanks, where English warhorses and weight of numbers could not easily be brought to bear. Imparking his army in a wood provided his men with natural protection against unexpected attack, and made it harder for the English scouts to ascertain what his plans were. As at Loudoun Hill, he also dug trenches around his position, which were then hidden, to catch the English men-at-arms unaware and bring down their horses.

As the fatigued Anglo-Scots approached, Bruce's soldiers were spotted retreating into the woodland. The English vanguard under Gloucester, Henry Beaumont and Robert Clifford, by now some miles ahead of the centre and rear guard, immediately moved into attack. Gloucester's men pursued the Scots into the wood, Clifford sought to prevent their escape through the other side of the trees with a flanking manoeuvre and Beaumont apparently pressed ahead to reconnoitre the situation beneath the castle itself. All three divisions met with fierce resistance and withdrew in some disarray. Whether this was a deliberate Scots trap is uncertain. That it was not is perhaps suggested by an incident early in the fighting. A young English knight, Henry Bohun, spotted Robert Bruce mounted on a palfrey, not his warhorse, only lightly armoured in a jack (or reinforced jacket) and in an isolated position. Bohun immediately charged him with his lance. At the last moment, Bruce deftly evaded Bohun's thrust and cleaved his helmet and head in two with a single blow of his axe. This must have provided a great morale boost to his men.

Retreating to a safe distance as their centre and rear guard came up, the English encamped for the night on a marshy plain, fearful of night-time attack. A heated debate then ensued about what they should do the following morning. Gloucester and others, mindful of their discomfit that day at the hands of the Scots, counselled delay, so that men and horses could be properly rested and fed, and so that the army could be put in its best order. The king, who seems throughout to have underestimated an enemy he referred to only as a 'rabble', exploded with anger, unreasonably accusing Gloucester of lies and even treachery. Gloucester was already in dispute with Hereford about who should lead the vanguard into battle and Edward's outburst seems to have led directly to Gloucester's over-hasty engagement with the Scots the following day, during the battle's decisive phase. For now, the earl replied hotly that the morning would witness who was or was not a traitor and liar.

The English duly rose early, advancing across the Bannock burn, the tributary of the Forth from which the battle now derives its name, around nine in the morning. From within the woods emerged Bruce's roughly six thousand-strong force, deployed in three schiltrons, or axe- and pike-armed infantry squares, with a modest – perhaps five-hundred-man – supporting division of light cavalry. The Scots were well rested, fed and briefed by the Scottish king, and as the battle unfolded, it became clear that Bruce's rectilinear schiltrons had up their sleeves a capability that William Wallace's circular schiltrons at Falkirk in 1298 had lacked: namely, rather than being static formations, they had been drilled to advance as a body in fighting order – a significant tactical advantage. Overnight, Bruce had been persuaded by Alexander Seton – a Scottish knight allied with the English, who had decided to switch allegiance and had come over to the Bruce cause during the hours of darkness – that the English were in disarray and low in morale, and that therefore they were there for the taking. Once out in the open, the Scots bowed to pray, which Edward II, with characteristic complacency, initially understood as a gesture of surrender; but the Scots then quickly advanced on their enemy. Gloucester rushed to meet them, and, left isolated too far ahead of his fellow knights, was cut to pieces. It is possible that the English, at this stage, were still arrayed for the advance, rather than being in battle array, because it seems obvious from the chronicle accounts that their forces – perhaps two thousand heavy cavalry, three thousand archers and up to ten thousand infantry – were inappropriately configured to meet the Scottish attack. At Falkirk, Edward I had broken up Wallace's schiltrons with massed archery, to enable his cavalry to penetrate the Scottish shield-wall. But at Bannockburn the English archers evidently found themselves wrongly placed to be able to do this. As it became clear that their cavalry were being defeated by the advancing 'thick-set hedge' of Scottish pikes commanded by the earl of Moray, they sought to fire over the heads of their own horsemen into the Scots infantry, but this indirect fire was ineffective. Equally, the English rear guard or reserve, nominally commanded by the king, could not manoeuvre on the restricted battlefield. Moreover, the English men-at-arms in the front line were too closely packed to be able to fight properly. Edward II's obtuseness, overconfidence and marked lack of tactical control are clear, for all our uncertainties about the details of the battle. What makes his failure of command even worse is that the English were fully apprised of the potential threat posed to them by the Scottish army: earlier in the year the king, through his officials, had spoken about the Scots amassing a great infantry army, and of their intention to ambush the English on ground not easily penetrable by cavalry.

Seeing the English line collapsing, the earl of Pembroke grabbed the king's reins and forced him from the field. The highest priority for the household knights was ensuring that Edward evaded capture. It is for good reason that the game of chess is won by checkmate, not by the killing of the king. A medieval king being captured represented disaster not just because of the economy-breaking ransom that would be required for his release, but also because of the political concessions that would be demanded in return for his freedom. Had Edward II been taken by Robert Bruce, it is obvious what the Scottish king would have required of the English for the safe return of their king – nothing less than recognition of his right and Scottish independence. Edward, Pembroke and the household knights around them made first for Stirling Castle. There they found the drawbridge up and the gates closed. Perhaps, like Alexander Seton overnight, Philip Mowbray had already resolved that his future lay with the Bruces. Or perhaps, as the author of the *Vita* implies, he knew that admitting Edward was more or less a guarantee of the king's capture, once the victorious Scots had besieged the castle rock. So Edward belted for Dunbar, where the castellan, Patrick, earl of Dunbar, still a keeper of the Balliol–Comyn faith but shortly to change sides, received him. Thence Edward took ship to Berwick – England's command of the seas made this a safe option, barring the intervention of Neptune – and from there proceeded to York, to counsel, and into forced negotiations with Thomas of Lancaster.

The English soldiers, meanwhile, found themselves forced back and down into the killing ground of an 'evil ditch', probably the shallow gorge through which, at one point south of Stirling, the Bannock burn runs. Other fleeing soldiers were apparently drowned trying to cross the nearby Forth. What saved the English was the imperative for the Scots to capture

301

knights and ransom them, rather than kill them. For the Scottish realm as well as individual Scottish soldiers, high-ranking captives were much more valuable alive than dead. Some politically important figures were killed – not least Gloucester and Robert Clifford – but many more were taken, including the earl of Hereford and a multitude of knights – even in the service of the king and the earl of Pembroke, showing just how narrow was their escape. The English left huge quantities of arms, armour, baggage and money behind in their flight. This was enormously costly – the author of the *Vita* estimates the loss at over £200,000, or more than three years' subsidy. The greatest cost, however, was arguably political – to the king's reputation.

Contemporaries reflected upon the meaning of this great victory of infantry over mounted knights, comparing it to the rout inflicted upon the flower of French chivalry by Flemish foot soldiers at Courtrai in 1302. The year after Bannockburn, pikemen of the Swiss Confederacy annihilated an invading army led by Duke Leopold of Austria at Morgarten. This trinity of victories in the early fourteenth century of rank-and-file infantry over elite cavalry marked an end to the hitherto assumed superiority of the mounted knight in battle, and paved the way for Edward III's military revolution of the 1330s and 1340s. The latter saw English mixed formations of dismounted men-at-arms and longbowmen, fighting on the defensive, achieve a supremacy in Western European warfare that lasted for a century. How far Robert Bruce had consciously learned the lessons of Courtrai before his own remarkable series of military successes is an open question. The awareness on the part of the author of the *Vita* of the parallels between Bannockburn and the Flemings' victory suggests that the Scottish king must have been alert to Courtrai too. But his adoption of a new way of fighting was also driven by force of circumstance, as have been so many fundamental shifts in military policy across the centuries. For socio-economic reasons, he could not hope to match the elite heavy cavalry of the English, so he needed, like William Wallace before him, to rely in war upon infantry formations and upon choosing his ground well. His military successes to come, and those of his disciples like Moray, would in time add devastating mobility to the mix. Courtrai 1302, Bannockburn 1314 and Morgarten 1315: three battles in which the urge for self-determination in the face of over-reaching monarchy – inspired or even impelled by emerging European ideas of sovereignty, masterfulness and state-building – led subjects to combine, face up to and defeat, through a new method of war, their would-be overlords.

Responding to Bannockburn

There is ample evidence in the shape of their own changed tactics that the English political and military community quickly began to learn the lessons of this new sort of war. But if they were already reflecting on the meaning of Bannockburn, they had more immediate concerns in mind. In particular they needed to defend the north of England against the rampant Scots, who penetrated Northumberland with seeming impunity once again as early as August 1314. They also had to prepare a fresh expedition to Scotland to attempt to reverse the major setback they had just suffered. Because of the king's material and financial losses at Bannockburn, because of the need to pay the ransoms of the many hundreds of English captives – in most cases a private matter for the families of the captured men, but one by extension likely to denude their capacity to help fund any future campaign – and because of his vast wealth and his territorial importance in the north of England, it was imperative that the king's chief enemy Thomas of Lancaster was somehow brought back into the political fold – ideally now as a partner, not an opponent, of the king. Given the blood feud that existed between Lancaster and Edward, this was unrealistic. But the political community had no other option. The interplay of circumstances and personalities demanded that they deliver the impossible.

Lancaster, for his part, could not stand aloof from political engagement. In the end, a point-blank refusal to aid his countrymen and play his proper role within the political community was tantamount to treachery. Furthermore, involving himself in the business of the realm on a conditional basis might allow him – by a process of bargaining and negotiation – to re-establish the defensive lines he had tried to erect in 1312–13. These centred on the idea of the 1311 Ordinances' inviolability. The reason the Ordinances mattered so much to Lancaster, and why he pushed for their implementation at every opportunity, was that they provided a technical justification for his killing of Gaveston, and thereby a defence against some future reckoning for the homicide. It was physical might rather than technical right that would ultimately render Lancaster safe or otherwise from the king's retribution, as the earl recognised. But he had no other defence, and, beyond the king's failure to implement the Ordinances, nor did he have any serviceable excuse for refusing to approach the king, join his Council or defend the realm against its enemies – all actions that he needed to be able to minimise if he were to maintain the physical isolation that he evidently believed made him safe.

Lancaster had showed his unprincipled true colours early in the reign, choosing to side with the court rather than the well-intentioned opposition. He changed sides not because the scales fell from his eyes, but because he fell out with the king. His apparent principle in respect of the Ordinances was matched by no discernible principle anywhere else. He was happy to subordinate the realm's interests to his own, and sacrifice its safety and good order to the cause of self-preservation. His repeated retreats to the safety of his strongholds at Kenilworth and Pontefract show that flight was a core instinct, but equally, he seems to have wished to take political control at the centre – without having the courage or ability to remain in office once he had done so. His desire for high political power may have been born of his arrogance or his desire to check courtiers whom he feared might assist the king against him. His ambition was either in tension with his fear, or bred of it, or both. Where local politics were concerned, there was a sort of blundering nihilism about Lancaster's inclination to pick fights with the king's friends – or, indeed, anyone else – in the shires. His backing of Gruffudd de la Pole in Powys in 1312 against John Charlton and his attack on Walter Langton at Thorpe Waterville in Northamptonshire in 1313 served only, in the end, to undermine his position in his Staffordshire heartlands, where the courtiers and their associates were able to bring pressure to bear on members of his affinity, who abandoned Lancaster's lordship and took the king's side. All things being equal, the monarch, with his control over legal office and the distribution of land, had a natural advantage in such contests for local control. Nonetheless, Lancaster singularly failed to back his people in the shires, and his lack of strategic vision in local as well as national politics, together with his inability to defend his 'country' once he had stirred up local conflict, rendered him self-defeating and vulnerable in the localities as well as at the political centre. All of this combined to make the task of the nobles who sought to build political consensus and promote reconciliation even more challenging. In no fewer than six separate attempts to re-involve Lancaster in politics and reconcile him with the king during the period 1314–19, the political community sought to exploit his ambition in an effort to get him to overcome his fear of, and scorn for, the king. That the magnates kept trying, despite repeated failure, reminds us that they had no alternative – until, that is, Hugh Despenser the Younger changed politics altogether at the end of 1320.

Pembroke and the courtier-administrator Bartholomew Badlesmere were critical to the efforts to bring Lancaster back into government, and Hereford evidently continued to co-operate with the king to the same end, despite his earlier role in Gaveston's demise. Initially they may have been assisted by the earl of Warwick, which we might find surprising, given that he had been the king's most consistent opponent and latterly Lancaster's only real ally among the earls. But it appears to have been Lancaster rather than Warwick who was principally responsible for the foot-dragging that had delayed a settlement with the king in 1312–13, and in the aftermath of the Bannockburn debacle, Warwick seems to have committed himself to trying to get government and politics back on track. This would fit with the judgement of both the *Vita* and the Chronicle of Lanercost that he was the wisest and most principled of the magnates. From autumn 1314 until late June 1315, when he retreated to Warwick Castle, presumably beset by the illness of which he was to die in August, he was highly active, alongside Pembroke, Hereford and others, as a witness to royal charters – a sure sign of close engagement in government and proximity to the king. The contrast with the position of Lancaster during the same period is clear. Lancaster was also involved with government for a short period after Bannockburn, but withdrew from Westminster into seclusion in the spring of 1315. It is notable that Warwick was sent by the king to discuss the defence of the north with Lancaster in May. Conceivably he was playing a mediating role by this time, akin to that played by Hereford in 1313. If so, Lancaster's political isolation following Warwick's death may have been prefigured during the final months of the latter's life.

Turning to government, it is evident that, although the king was not politically emasculated after Bannockburn, a coalition of lords had to step in to help run the country. On the face of it, the confirmation of the Ordinances in the Parliaments of September 1314 and January–March 1315 might seem to suggest that the king's opponents had triumphed and that Edward was under the cosh. But such an impression would be false. The Ordinances' confirmation was undoubtedly Lancaster's price for political co-operation. That the wider polity backed the policy was probably a matter of practical utility as well as political expediency. Confirming the Ordinances required the replacement of royal officials at the centre, the appointment of new sheriffs in the counties and the resumption of royal grants, all of which are likely to have been useful in controlling the expenditure of a bankrupt Crown. That the king retained power is indicated by his success in resisting the removal from the court of Hugh Despenser the Elder and Henry Beaumont, and in re-granting many of the resumptions in the spring of 1315. Furthermore, most of the new officials appointed were established royal servants, entirely acceptable to him – good examples being John Sandal, the new chancellor, and William Melton, the new keeper of the wardrobe. Perhaps tellingly, in December 1314, Edward granted Gaveston's former castle of Knaresborough to Roger Damory, an otherwise impoverished household knight who was to emerge in 1316 with two other household knights, Hugh Audley and William Montagu, as new favourites of the king. One wonders whether Lancaster's withdrawal to his estates early in 1315 may have been prompted by the rise of such individuals in court. Another withdrawal, in April 1316, was certainly prompted by his hostility to, and fear of, Edward's courtiers. Nevertheless, his retreat on both occasions may equally have resulted from his inability to dominate government in the way that he wished, or from his unwillingness to engage in the grunt work of administration. Lancaster seems to have been even less of an administrator than the king.

That the nobles were now substantially in control of government is indicated by its sense of purpose – not something that it had ever shown when Edward II had been personally in charge. Both the September 1314 and January–March 1316 Parliaments were primarily focused upon rebuilding the royal finances and remedying the situation regarding the war with the

Scots, though the former concluded that it could do nothing definitive while key members of the polity remained in Scottish captivity – not least the earl of Hereford and the entire staff of the privy seal office (another indicator of how narrow the king's escape at Bannockburn had been). Thus far in the reign, petitions had not been received in Parliament – a critical governmental omission; and in the Parliament commencing in January, the huge backlog that had built up was finally heard and remedies proposed. Many of the petitions concerned essentially private and local matters that had proliferated in the shires in the absence of active royal justice. The period 1315–20 saw a huge rise in the number of judicial commissions being issued, as petitioners requested, and the Crown resorted to, ad hoc and individual investigations ('special oyer and terminer commissions') in an attempt to provide solutions to matters that ordinarily should have been kept at manageable levels by the routine operation of royal justice. In addition to dealing with judicial issues, Parliament granted lay and clerical subsidies, which supplemented a loan scheme previously agreed by the church to provide the king with sufficient cash flow to enable the defence of the north, now under the military command of the earl of Pembroke. Such provision was urgently needed, as the Scots were besieging both Berwick and Carlisle, at opposite ends of the border; and although the Scots' inexperience in siege warfare was to tell against them, with both towns surviving in English hands for the time being, this was a most worrying period.

So it was that government, under the direction of the nobles who had taken charge of it, engaged with the proper business of rule for the first time since the death of Edward I. It is hard to gauge the extent of Edward II's personal involvement in this. There are clear indications in the form of grants, for instance, that, where his own interests or those of his friends were concerned, he was active. Although the three new favourites, Damory, Audley and Montagu, emerged at court in 1316–17, Queen Isabella remained close to the king. Her importance in government had already been underlined in spring 1314, when she had been sent to France to continue the negotiations with her father, Philip IV, over Gascony that had commenced during her visit to France with Edward the previous year. In spring 1315, another embassy departed for France, with the objective of having the new French king, Isabella's brother, Louis X, confirm the commitments made to the English by his predecessor in 1313 and 1314. It is hard to imagine that Isabella was not instrumental in the despatch of this mission. Certainly, her capacity to intercede with the king and more generally to influence government was by now significant. Foreign petitioners to the English Crown were, in this period, more likely to approach Isabella in their quest for assistance than they were the king – and understandably so, given that the queen was much more likely to respond. Famously, her candidate Louis Beaumont was triumphant in a fiercely contested election to the see of Durham in 1316–17, despite opposition from candidates backed by her husband and especially Lancaster. Given Edward's natural waywardness and indolence, it seems likely that he was more than happy to rely on Isabella to fulfil the aspects of his role as king in which he had no real interest. That their personal relationship remained strong is indicated by Isabella's having borne further children in 1316, 1318 and 1321.

Disorder, 1315–18

However, for all that government and the king were being corralled by the magnates and the queen, the continued absence of proper kingship and the ongoing hostility between Edward and Lancaster produced a steady breakdown of order in the country. This marked the beginning of an extended period of continuous unrest that was only to be brought to an end by the forceful and decisive kingship of Edward III in the 1330s.

Some of the disorder was consequent upon the failure of the Crown to defend the realm. It is scarcely surprising that, without effective defences, and against a backdrop of regular incursion and the destruction of both property and income, the rule of law in the north began to collapse. (The devastation of the region is compellingly evidenced by a wealth of surviving government inquisitions into the value of lands held in Cumberland, Westmorland, Northumberland and even Yorkshire. By the 1320s estates were overwhelmingly being assessed as 'worthless, on account of depredations and burnings by the Scots'.) To disorder and acute hardship caused by defensive failure in the north were added the same in Ireland. But elsewhere collapsing order was the result of mismanagement, oppressive lordship

King John hunting, from the fourteenth-century illuminated manuscript
De Regne Johanne in the British Library

Isabella of Angoulême, tomb effigy in Fontevraud Abbey

King Henry III, depicted in Matthew Paris's *Short Chronicle of England*

Eleanor of Provence, in the Muniment Room of Westminster Abbey

Edward I (presumed), contemporary portrait in Westminster Abbey

Eleanor of Castile, tomb effigy in Westminster Abbey

Magna Carta, one of only four surviving original copies,
in Salisbury Cathedral

Parliament under King Edward I, as depicted in the sixteenth century.
Edward is flanked by Alexander, king of Scotland, and Llywelyn,
prince of Wales. Before him sit the lords spiritual and temporal,
and the judicial and administrative officers

Edward II, tomb effigy, Gloucester Cathedral

Edward III, tomb effigy in Westminster Abbey, believed to be the first accurate portrait of an English king

Westminster portrait of Richard II, *c.*1390, which is unusual in showing the king full face rather than in profile. Hitherto, formal portraiture had tended to portray only Jesus Christ full face

Richard II and Anne of Bohemia, tomb effigies, Westminster Abbey

The Peasants' Revolt, 1381. Wat Tyler is killed in a depiction from the late fourteenth century

The sublime *Wilton Diptych*. Saints Edmund King and Martyr, Edward the Confessor and John the Baptist usher Richard II forward to receive England from the Christ Child, the Virgin and the heavenly host, the latter extraordinarily bearing Richard's badges of the broomcod collar and the white hart

Henry Bolingbroke, portrayed in a miniature from 1402

or warlike behaviour, especially on the part of the king and Lancaster. Disorder was compounded by appalling harvest failures and cattle murrains. The harvest failures were a result of prolonged summer rainfall in 1314, 1315 and 1316. 1317 saw some improvement, but dreadful weather produced another disastrous harvest in 1321. The loss of livestock came partly from starvation through lack of fodder and partly from what the *Vita* terms a cattle 'plague'. The consequences were grave, demographically, economically and in other ways. The population may have been reduced by as much as 10 per cent. Shortages produced a seemingly exponential rise in prices, which the government sought to combat via price controls. In turn this led to suppliers withdrawing goods from sale, exacerbating the shortages and increasing starvation. The loss of sheep seriously depressed the wool trade, taxes upon which were so essential to healthy royal finances. The Crown had to borrow in order to buy grain in the Mediterranean to supply its garrisons along the Scottish marches. For contemporaries, all this, after Bannockburn, was another judgement of God.

In May 1315, the Scots invaded Ireland. The prime mover was Robert Bruce's sole surviving brother, Edward Bruce. The latter was a bold soldier and strongly committed to the Bruce cause, but the family trait of ambition ran strongly in him. The chroniclers hold that he sought a share of his brother's power within Scotland, and perhaps even a division of the kingdom. A factor in this may have been the bouts of illness by which Robert was now regularly being crippled. But Edward lacked political judgement and, as contemporaries put it, moderation. While King Robert was content formally to recognise his brother as his heir (until such time that Robert's wife bore a son), he would not appoint him regent in the event of kingly incapacity, which honour fell to Moray. (It was the able Moray who was the king's true right-hand man and chief lieutenant, and it is no accident that he had been raised to the peerage a year earlier than the king's brother, and under notably more generous, vice-regal terms.) Edward Bruce's ambition found an alternative outlet across the Irish Sea. The Scots had long been conscious of the cultural, historical and linguistic connections between Scotland and Ireland, and in 1315 Edward Bruce sought to exploit these by claiming the throne of Ireland on a prospectus of opposing English lordship, building an alliance on this basis with the native Irish, some of whom had already requested assistance against the English. In 1316, he audaciously tried – with limited success – to extend the principle of a pan-Celtic, anti-English alliance to encompass the Welsh.

His efforts in Ireland, fighting from an Ulster base and periodically assisted by Robert Bruce and Moray, certainly discomfited and alarmed the English and their Irish allies. His strategy was repeatedly to raid out of Ulster, threatening but essentially avoiding Dublin, before withdrawing to Ulster again to regroup. Although he overran large parts of Ireland, his resources were insufficient for territory outside Ulster to be permanently occupied, and his most ambitious and far-reaching raids required fresh assistance from Scotland, as did his taking of Carrickfergus Castle in August 1316. Moreover, forced to live off the country, his soldiers caused great devastation and hardship. This steadily ate away at his Irish support, which had only ever been partial. In October 1318, seemingly spurred on by the impending arrival of yet another fresh army from Scotland, he fatally over-reached himself and was killed attacking a much stronger Anglo-Irish force at Faughart near Dundalk. His death brought an abrupt end to the Scottish adventure in Ireland, which, with the benefit of hindsight, was a flawed and doomed effort. Bruce won a number of clear-cut, if relatively small-scale, victories, and the English Crown was seriously alarmed about losing control of Ireland in late 1315 and 1316. But without the assistance of Robert Bruce and Moray, Edward Bruce was unable to make much headway against the English, and this drew the Scottish king and his chief lieutenant away from the principal theatres of the first Scottish war of independence, and stretched thin the Scots' scarce military resources. In the summer of 1315, Bruce's invasion of Ulster must have seemed to amplify the danger posed to England by the sieges of Berwick and Carlisle. But in due course, the armies of Robert Bruce and Moray that had invaded Cumberland and Northumberland were transferred to serve on a second front in Ireland, where victory was significantly less likely to ratchet up pressure on Edward II. One might go so far as to say that losing Ireland to the Bruces was never going to persuade the son of Edward I to give up his overlordship of Scotland. In other words, by intervening in Ireland, the Scots either speculatively backed an ambitious man's private adventure, or followed a faulty strategy intended to dissipate English military resources, but which in fact chiefly dissipated those of the Scots. Nonetheless, to the English, Ireland in 1315–16 had the look of a looming disaster to set alongside the realm's many other problems.

The abject failure of Edward II's kingship and the continued impairment of government resulting from the king's blood feud with Thomas of Lancaster – as well as problems caused by Lancaster's own self-absorbed and irresponsible lordship – now really began to tell. The cluster of outbreaks of serious disorder in the period 1315–18 is quite extraordinary, and together they illustrate precisely how the characters and behaviour of Edward II and Lancaster fed into the realm's difficulties.

The first major outbreak of disorder occurred in south-west Lancashire late in 1315. The origins of Sir Adam Bannister's revolt are obscure. But the revolt evidently involved Bannister and a number of other Lancashire knights disavowing the lordship of Thomas of Lancaster, whose lands dominated the locality, probably because of his promotion of the highly ambitious Robert, Lord Holland, his steward and right-hand man, to the disadvantage of Bannister and his associates. Whether Bannister had been denied justice by Holland, who was his neighbour and a local rival, or whether he rebelled pre-emptively, having committed homicide (as the *Vita* holds), is unknown, though the fact that Holland was, in 1328, apparently murdered by friends of Bannister in a revenge attack suggests that misrule by Holland lay at the root of the business. Bannister and his associates raided the lands of a number of Holland associates and attacked Halton and Liverpool Castles, seizing and displaying the royal standard – doubtless in reference to the king's hostility to Lancaster. They were eventually cornered by a force led by the deputy sheriff, and Bannister and other leaders were summarily beheaded. The revolt evidences Lancaster's harsh and inflexible lordship, the contempt in which he was held by leading subjects in his own 'country' and the extent to which the background of his dispute with the king provided a context in which rebellion against him was 'justified' in national as well as local terms. Such unrest on the part of the social elite against a great lord in the heart of his territory was extremely unusual in medieval England. It speaks volumes about Lancaster.

At the same time in Glamorgan, in lands controlled by the king, a strikingly similar rebellion, but with greater destructive consequences, was brewing. The Welsh leader Llywelyn Bren of Senghennydd was a learned and capable figure who had been a confidant of his overlord Gilbert Clare, the late earl of Gloucester. Custody of Gloucester's lands, including the lordship of Glamorgan, had fallen to the king, and in July 1315 Edward had erred in appointing Payn Turberville of Coity, an English lord in Glamorgan, their keeper. Turberville removed Llywelyn Bren and a number of other trustworthy men from office, replacing them with his own friends, whose governance was harsh and unyielding. In an affair reminiscent not just of the Bannister rebellion in Lancashire but also of the alienation of the lord of Albret by Gaveston in Gascony, hostility towards the regime erupted among hitherto loyal men. The king's mismanagement of the business was not restricted to his appointment of the wrong keeper of Glamorgan, however. When Llywelyn Bren directly approached Edward II to seek his assistance in resolving the situation, the king reacted angrily, threatening him with hanging and summoning him to appear for trial before Parliament in January 1316. This was precisely the sort of intemperate and hostile response to an appeal for intervention that a wise monarch would not have made. Fearing for his life, Llywelyn Bren responded by rising in rebellion. He was joined by some thousands of co-rebels in Glamorgan, who attacked and plundered Cardiff and Caerphilly before retreating to the hills. The fear that a local rebellion would become a national one in a country only recently conquered, and subject to anti-English overtures from the Scots, was significant. Accordingly, an army under the earl of Hereford was raised to suppress the disorder, prompting Llywelyn Bren to surrender in an effort to spare his followers. Llywelyn was well respected by the Marcher lords, and the honour and courage he displayed in his surrender ensured that his captors interceded on his behalf with the king. He and his family were imprisoned in the Tower of London, but the influence of Hereford in particular may be seen in the replacement of Payn Turberville that quickly followed, as well as in the placing of Llywelyn Bren's confiscated lands in the hands of Welsh, not English, keepers. A year and a half later, however, Hugh Despenser the Younger, who had married the late earl of Gloucester's eldest sister and co-heir Eleanor Clare in 1306, was formally recognised as lord of Glamorgan. In a move that portended the tyranny of the 1320s, in November 1317 he arbitrarily seized Llywellyn from the Tower and took him back to Glamorgan, where he had him condemned for treason, and hanged, drawn and quartered. This judicial murder technically allowed Despenser to seize the 'traitor' Llywellyn's lands. There was no immediate consequence for Despenser. He was already a royal favourite, though not yet the pre-eminent favourite he was shortly to become, and the king let the affair go. The Marcher lords, though, would not forget it.

Meanwhile, across the Severn estuary, another mishandled dispute had resulted in violent disorder. The town of Bristol was accountable to the Crown-appointed constable of Bristol Castle, Bartholomew Badlesmere, for its customs and other dues, and, as no one loved a tax collector, this led to friction. Bristol was also internally riven between an elite group of burgesses and the remainder of them, allied to the townspeople. Badlesmere and the elite faction evidently became associated with one another, and this appears to have undermined his capacity to exercise his authority as castellan. By March 1312, he had enlisted the earl of Gloucester – the dominant local nobleman – to help settle the various dissensions in the town, but this attempt failed and, in November 1313, the town had to be taken into the king's hands, such was its disorderly state. Matters came to a head shortly thereafter, when royal commissioners were sent to the town both to levy tax and to inquire into felonies and trespasses apparently committed there. The commissioners, who were mistrusted, were violently resisted, and in the ensuing riot a number of people were killed and many injured. In March 1315, the earl of Warwick offered arbitration to the parties at Warwick Castle, but this too achieved nothing. Ensuing attempts by the government to arrest the suspected leaders of the riot were repelled. With the town in a state of outright rebellion against Badlesmere and by extension the king, and non-violent channels for settling the unrest seemingly having been exhausted, Edward ordered that Bristol be returned to obedience by force. In July 1316, an army led by Badlesmere, Roger Mortimer of Wigmore and Maurice Berkeley invested the town, which rapidly surrendered. By December the burgesses were pardoned, in return for paying a fine of two thousand marks to the king, with the exception of the three ringleaders of the rebellion, who abjured the realm. While the outcome was not disastrous, the tortuous journey to it, involving two attempts by magnates to settle a matter that the king's officials could not, demonstrates how acutely the king was failing in his duty to maintain internal order. Once the monarch had involved himself directly, a resolution should have rapidly been reached. Instead, a lack of confidence in the king's justice to provide a fair outcome, combined with a sense that the king lacked resolve and therefore could simply be ignored, resulted in a four-year running sore. The idea that Edward I, Edward III or Henry V would have allowed this sort of thing to endure would be laughable. But Edward II's culpability goes even further than that, because twice during the dispute, late in 1311 and in 1312, having essentially sided with Badlesmere as the official representative of royal authority, he temporarily undermined him – first, by removing him from his office of castellan, and then by taking the anti-Badlesmere burgesses under royal protection. This occurred when the king was focused upon his dispute with the magnates over Gaveston and when those associated with opposition to Piers – at that time including Badlesmere – were subject to having their lives made as difficult as possible by the king. It is striking, and absolutely no coincidence, that in 1321, when Badlesmere had fallen out with Edward irrevocably by opposing the Despensers, the king pardoned the three riot leaders, who were allowed to return to England and Bristol.

The following years, 1317 and 1318, saw disorder reach a new nadir, for two reasons. First, the king's persistent failure to defend the north resulted in an insurrection against his rule in Northumberland. Second, Edward's dispute with Thomas of Lancaster escalated and spilled forcefully into the localities. The Northumberland insurrection is chiefly remembered for the cause célèbre of its attack on two papal cardinals who were en route to Scotland to negotiate with Robert Bruce. But this element in the revolt was essentially an accident. The cardinals happened to be travelling with the newly elected bishop of Durham, Louis Beaumont, and his brother, the courtier Henry Beaumont, the real targets of the rebels. Having captured the Beaumonts with a view to ransoming them, the rebels freed the cardinals, but not before they and their retinues had been assaulted and robbed. It was a matter of national shame that the king of England could not protect the Holy Father's emissaries, and that the incident was actually perpetrated by members of his own household.

Led by Sir Gilbert Middleton and Sir Walter Selby, both of whom had celebrated Christmas day with the king in 1315, as well as Sir John Lilburn (afterwards associated with Thomas of Lancaster), the rebels were northern household knights exasperated by Edward II's disregard for the defence of the north. Through famine and the depredations of the Scots, and in the absence of effective royal support, they had been driven to take defence and the maintenance of order into their own hands, extracting local funding and supplies to maintain their garrisons at the castles of Mitford and Horton Peel. Such behaviour, nominally in defence of the borders, seems to have rendered them, from the people's perspective, increasingly indistinguishable from the 'schavaldors' (or mounted plunderers) against whom they were supposedly providing protection. Their attack on the Beaumonts was sparked by Edward II's decision, at the urging of the influential Queen Isabella, to ask the pope to supplant the locally elected bishop of Durham with a despised outsider, Louis Beaumont, whose brother, Henry, had a reputation for having repeatedly raided the public purse for his own profit. For northern knights left to their own devices to protect their region against the Scots, the grant of a bishopric that encompassed responsibility for defence and justice in the palatinate of Durham to a grasping courtier family was anathema. Their rebellion continued until at least January 1318, when Middleton was captured, despatched to London and speedily convicted of treason. Walter Selby may have temporarily taken refuge with the Scots, who now exploited the chaos in Northumberland to seize Mitford, among other strategic targets. Whether installed by the Scots as 'their' new castellan of Mitford, or having subsequently retaken the castle from them by stealth or force, by 1321 Selby had returned the fortress to the king's hands. Edward II would not pardon him, though, and it was only with the accession of Edward III that he was released from imprisonment in the Tower. Like so many knights apparently involved in the 1317–18 insurrection, he went on loyally to complete a second career in the royal service as an MP and regional commander under Edward III. These were not men of inherently dubious ethics. On the contrary, they were hard-pressed individuals trying to defend their people and community under terrible circumstances, and feeling abandoned and betrayed by their leaders. That under such pressure their moral compasses may at times have flickered is unsurprising.

Thomas of Lancaster was also reputed to have been involved in the Beaumont kidnap plot. He was certainly associated with the Middleton circle and was clearly kept informed about the intrigue's progress, rushing, once the news of the unintended assault on the papal legates reached him, to escort the cardinals to safety – presumably in an effort both to limit the damage to his already tarnished reputation and to ensure that he escaped any papal sentence of excommunication issued in response to the attack. In any case, a new outbreak of disorder in which Lancaster was patently the prime mover rapidly eclipsed the Middleton treason. Characteristically, Lancaster's actions toxically mixed the political, the personal and the paranoid.

It was Joseph Heller in *Catch-22* who famously said that being paranoid does not mean that people are not out to get you. In 1317, Lancaster's persecution mania was stoked by reports that certain of Edward II's counsellors, in particular Roger Damory, were encouraging the king to take decisive action against him. Matters having come to a head at the end of September, when Edward appeared to have been on the point of mounting a direct assault on Lancaster's fortress of Pontefract, the earl took drastic action to secure his strongholds and take 'vengeance' (as the *Vita* puts it) on his enemies. Damory was the keeper of two castles adjacent to Lancaster's heartlands: the royal castle of Knaresborough in Yorkshire and the late Theobald Verdon's castle of Alton in Staffordshire, which was in the king's hands. In October both castles were seized for Lancaster. The earl almost certainly personally ordered the taking of Alton: Theobald Verdon had been a member of his affinity and the king was now seeking to bring the Verdons into the royal circle. Knaresborough was occupied in Lancaster's name by the former household knight John Lilburn, one of Gilbert Middleton's associates; but whether his action was actively commissioned by Lancaster or whether Lilburn, knowing of Lancaster's hostility to the king, proceeded on his own initiative as part of the ongoing northern insurrection is unclear.

At the same time, Lancaster embarked upon a sustained campaign against John, earl Warenne. It is no coincidence that the royal castles Lancaster occupied were those whose possession was likeliest to shore up his military position. Where Warenne was concerned, Lancaster's chief objective was similar: to strengthen his defences. He was mainly interested in Warenne's Yorkshire castles of Sandal and Conisbrough, and his Welsh

Marcher lordship of Bromfield and Yale. Sandal and Conisbrough both lay within half a day's march of Pontefract, Lancaster's principal stronghold; and Bromfield and Yale lay to the east of Lancaster's Marcher lordship of Denbigh. Nonetheless, the Lancastrian assault on Warenne's possessions was also a response to a personal affront, because in May 1316, Lancaster's wife, Alice Lacy – the heiress of her late father, the earl of Lincoln, through whom Lancaster had inherited the vast Lacy estates – had fled her marriage, being granted sanctuary by Warenne at Reigate Castle. In conventional medieval parlance she had been 'abducted', allegedly by an esquire in Warenne's household called Richard of St Martin, but it seems clear that her childless marriage to the oafish and argumentative Lancaster had been a miserable failure, and there can be little doubt that flight rather than abduction was the order of the day.

This nominally private war was in reality primarily a political matter, certainly in respect of its outcome. Warenne was forced to cede Sandal and Conisbrough, together with extensive Yorkshire estates, as well as Bromfield and Yale in its entirety, in return for a limited exchange of lands and a thousand marks yearly (far less than the value of the lands Warenne surrendered). Moreover, Warenne acknowledged a debt to Lancaster of £50,000, which was never collected, and which was counterpart to similar 'debts' acknowledged to Lancaster by others among his enemies at around this time. (These nominal debts were presumably bonds of good behaviour towards Lancaster.) The fighting around the castles and between the Lancaster and Warenne affinities was hugely disruptive. In late 1317 and 1318, the Crown ordered Lancaster to cease his attacks and issued wide-ranging judicial commissions against troop-raising, confederacies and vagabond gangs; and, if local ballad tradition is to be believed, the local blood feuds set up by the warfare in Yorkshire were still being acted out as late as the 1350s.

What had been the tune and tempo of high politics as the realm descended into disarray between 1315 and 1318? The principal lines in the counterpoint were the Edward–Lancaster feud and its crippling effect upon politics, the demands of the Scottish war and northern defence, and the grindingly repeated and ultimately fruitless endeavours of the political community to encourage Lancaster into the governmental fold. Indeed, such was the constancy of the political music that individual years seem almost interchangeable. In every year, Parliaments and military campaigns were repeatedly postponed or cancelled because of the Edward–Lancaster feud, and time and again Lancaster was cajoled into political engagement only to retreat from it post-haste, seemingly terrified of the king and his favourites. They in turn became increasingly fearful of Lancaster. In this way, the depressing parade of disorder in the realm was both driven and mirrored by a groundhog day of political paralysis and dysfunctional rule – the latter mitigated only by the sterling efforts of Pembroke, Badlesmere, Hereford and other magnates to keep some semblance of government functioning, despite it all.

Attempts by the Magnates to Engage Lancaster in Government, 1315–19

During the short-lived political consensus imposed by the disaster at Bannockburn, Pembroke and others had sought to bring Lancaster into government, only to see him quickly retreat to his estates in spring 1315. But later that year, the pressure being exerted by the Scots on Berwick and Carlisle prompted a second effort to bring the earl back on board. In August, Lancaster was appointed 'superior captain' of the royal armies in the north, superintending the forces led there by Pembroke, Badlesmere and others; this unusual office may have been granted to massage his ego, or because he insisted upon it as a condition for participation, or both. But Lancaster took no action, instead withdrawing from government once more, this time to deal with the Bannister revolt against his lordship. He returned to government only briefly in December – for further discussion of the Scottish crisis. Nonetheless, the king's officials continued regularly to write to him on governmental business, and as events were shortly to prove, it was evidently the hope of the magnates to bring him on to the Council. At a time when, owing to the losses at Bannockburn, the Crown's finances could stretch only to funding a holding operation in the north, Lancaster's wealth and his access to men and material made this highly desirable.

Parliament was summoned to meet in January 1316, with Scotland again at the top of the agenda, but Lancaster failed to show. The king and the lords papered over the cracks by dealing first with the myriad petitions they had received, and when Lancaster finally appeared, in arms, a fortnight late, there was further delay as he sought repeated reassurance that the king was not hostile towards him. As soon this obstacle was overcome, the earl was asked whether he would accept the role of head of the king's Council. After a short prevarication, he accepted, but on conditions: namely that the 1311 Ordinances be maintained and that, should the king not follow his advice and that of the Council, he could immediately withdraw from his position without incurring any ill-will or rancour. That this represented no Lancastrian political triumph is indicated by the composition of a commission for royal household reform that was appointed in accordance with the Ordinances: members included the earl of Hereford, whom Lancaster trusted, but otherwise consisted largely of existing royal councillors and loyalists, men such as Pembroke and Richmond. For the lords the new arrangement was a hopeful accommodation, not a surrender to the Lancastrian will, and Lancaster did not preside over a reforming government in his own image. Rather, as in early 1315, elements of reform in accordance with the Ordinances suited the magnates because of the close financial control they entailed – which was still much needed, for the royal finances remained desperately thin.

Lancaster seems not to have sat as head of the Council until mid-March 1316, having retreated to Kenilworth Castle in the interim; before the end of April he had returned to Kenilworth again, and if the implication in the surviving records is right, he did not rejoin the Council thereafter. Evidently he had abandoned his chairmanship of the Council within at most ten weeks of being appointed, and after having led meetings for as few as three. He was later to argue that he had withdrawn so quickly because the king would not accept the implementation of the Ordinances or the proposals of the reform commission, instead gathering around himself new favourites. It is hard to believe that foot-dragging by the king in the face of reform would have been readily tolerated by Pembroke and Hereford, who had been instrumental in Lancaster's appointment as head of the Council in the first place, but it is certainly the case that Damory, Audley and Montagu had now emerged as holders of the king's confidence. Moreover, there is evidence that, in the Midlands at least, the king was attempting to manipulate local officeholding to his own advantage: following Warwick's death he sought active control of the Worcestershire shrievalty and in 1316 removed the Lancastrian Sir William Trussell from the Leicestershire and Warwickshire shrievalty, replacing him with the royalist Walter Beauchamp, on the recommendation of Damory. Furthermore, Lancaster's principal retainer in Staffordshire, Sir Roger Swynnerton, had already been driven into the royal camp through pressure exerted on him by followers of John Charlton and the Mortimers. So Lancaster's throwing-in of the towel in all likelihood related to his fear of the king. Meanwhile the main business of Parliament – Scotland and defence – had rather fallen by the wayside, as the pressing distractions of the Llywelyn Bren revolt and the Bristol dispute both took up valuable parliamentary time and required the withdrawal of a number of key magnates to deal with them. In the autumn a fourth concerted attempt was made to bring Lancaster back on side. This time it foundered when Lancaster (who was promoting his own candidate) took offence at the election of Louis Beaumont as bishop of Durham. There was now no chance that a Scottish campaign might be mounted in 1316.

Instead, an embassy was despatched to the new pope, John XXII. Led by Pembroke and Badlesmere, the mission departed England with three objectives in mind: to have the pope overturn the Ordinances, which were now primarily serving the purpose of providing Lancaster with an excuse for opposing the king; to ease the terms under which the king's financial debts to the papacy had to be repaid; and to obtain papal sanctions against the Bruces. The first of these aims was obviously the closest to Edward's heart, but Pope John was no fool and he was not going to be drawn into taking sides in a dispute between the king of England, of whose limitations and weaknesses he was well aware, and his greatest subject. He declined to absolve Edward II of his promises in respect of the Ordinances. But there was better news on the money front, and the pope took a tough line against the Scots: it was in the interests of Christianity and a much-needed crusade that the war between the English and the Scots should end; therefore Robert and Edward Bruce must desist from attacking England and the English lordship of Ireland, and agree a settlement. A papal truce was to be promulgated on the warring countries. Should the Bruces refuse to co-operate, they would be excommunicated.

While Edward was doubtless disappointed by the pope's firmness regarding the Ordinances, otherwise this was a successful mission. But the embassy had a sting in the tail, for Pembroke was taken captive in the county of Bar (on the French border) on his way home and held to ransom. (Exactly why he was taken is unclear.) This delayed Pembroke's return until the summer. The earl – assisted by Badlesmere and Hereford, probably by Isabella and possibly by Warwick until his death in 1315 – had been providing a reasonably steady hand on the governmental tiller while continuously seeking an accommodation between the king and Lancaster. While the realm had nonetheless suffered severely on account of Edward's and Lancaster's misbehaviour, the basics of everyday government had continued. With Pembroke out of the country for the best part of six months, it is little surprise that the political situation markedly deteriorated.

Councils to consider the war with the Scots were summoned for February and then April 1317, but Lancaster failed to appear at both. It was difficult to plan a campaign without him, and the king became ever more irritated by his refusal to participate. In the spring Edward fanned the flames of conflict in resolving the vital but potentially controversial question of the vast inheritance of the late earl of Gloucester – hitherto put on ice because of the difficulty of coming up with a politically acceptable solution. He did this by awarding the highly advantageous marriages of the second and third Gloucester co-heiresses (Margaret and Elizabeth Clare) to Audley and Damory respectively, the eldest heiress (Eleanor Clare) having already married the younger Despenser. In May tensions were compounded by Warenne's 'abduction' of Lancaster's wife, which Lancaster evidently believed was part of a courtier plot to dishonour him. Rumour and counter-rumour swirled in an increasingly febrile political atmosphere. As the *Vita* reveals, some of those around the king counselled him to move decisively against Lancaster with a view to exile or imprisonment. We can readily guess their identities, and in June the two Despensers, Damory, Audley and Montagu entered into recognisances of £6,000 with one another by way of a contract of mutual self-defence. They clearly believed that Lancaster had them in his sights. Others of the royal counsel urged caution in the national interest: a direct approach by Edward to Lancaster might dissolve tensions and permit the construction of a peace treaty between the two men. But reports reached the earl's ears, to which he readily gave credence, that if he came within the king's reach he would immediately be taken and executed or imprisoned. In short, by the time Pembroke was back in England, in late June, the realm was closer to civil war than it had been at any point since 1312. As historians have commented, the records of government speak of real relief at Pembroke's return. Clearly this was the man who had been running the government in the effective absence of the monarch, and who it was again expected would help talk the king and Lancaster back from the edge.

A Great Council having been summoned to assemble at Nottingham in July 1317, for a third time in succession Lancaster failed to attend. The king wrote to him to remonstrate – not only on the issue of his repeated non-appearance but also about his gathering armed retainers 'to disturb the peace'. Lancaster's reply is revealing. He admitted that he had been raising troops, but said that this was only in anticipation of the muster against the Scots scheduled for August. So far as his non-appearance was concerned, he looked back to 1316 and his withdrawal from the chairmanship of the king's Council. The Ordinances had not been observed, the reform commission's recommendations had been ignored and grants had been made to inappropriate persons. But according to the *Vita*, an oral message accompanied his written reply, and this told the real story of his non-appearance: he was in fear of plots by royal favourites who, having already shown their animosity towards him, had now humiliated and disgraced him by abducting his wife. Without Lancaster, the Great Council was a non-event, and the government was left with little option but to put back the muster. Yet again, conflict between the king and his greatest subject had stymied the war effort.

Pembroke and Hereford promptly set out on a peace mission to Pontefract Castle, where Lancaster had taken refuge. After what seemed positive discussions with the dissident earl, they concluded that the differences between him and the king might be patched up. But in a situation in which every step forward was almost immediately followed by two steps back, the king's decision to advance northwards from Nottingham to York was met by Lancaster with military manoeuvring: once Edward, who had proceeded via a circuitous route to avoid passing through Pontefract, was ensconced in York, Lancaster broke the bridges to the south of the city and instituted a blockade to prevent the royal army from being reinforced.

For this action he concocted a new justification of remarkable inadequacy, claiming that, as hereditary steward of England, he had the right to be consulted before the king raised arms against his enemies. The potential implications of the Middleton–Beaumont outrage seem to have shocked him back into receptiveness, however. During mediation presided over by Pembroke, Hereford and the newly released papal envoys, Lancaster agreed to attend Parliament when summoned, the king having already declared that he would take no action against the earl. The fingerprints of Pembroke are all over the ensuing safe-conduct issued to the Lancastrians later that month. Yet between this small but potentially significant advance and the king's journey south in late September 1317 (the proposed Scottish campaign having, again, been cancelled), Damory and perhaps others among the favourites convinced the king that he should be belligerent. As the men-at-arms and archers of the royal household, accompanied by a significant body of troops from Warenne's Yorkshire lands, passed Pontefract, they formed up as if to attack, while Lancaster and his men mocked them from the battlements. Only the desperate intervention of Pembroke, who managed to calm the king, prevented fighting from breaking out. If the *Vita* has it right, this extraordinary episode illustrates the rampant paranoia now afflicting both the king and Lancaster. The king expected to be ambushed by Lancaster as he passed Pontefract. Lancaster worried that the king's armed manoeuvres in the north, while nominally part of the anti-Scottish muster, were in fact aimed at attacking and capturing him. Who is to say that, without the restraining influence of Pembroke, both sides would not have acted as their opponents feared?

Lancaster having been so directly threatened by the king and his favourites, his reaction – the attacks on the Damory and Warenne castles and lands detailed above – was in a way understandable, even if his taking the law into his own hands was unacceptable and destructive. Perhaps this helps explain why, yet again, and for the sixth time since Bannockburn, Pembroke and Badlesmere sought to defuse the political situation. First, in October and November 1317, they and many other magnates offered reassurance to the king by contracting to serve him with specified numbers of men-at-arms in peace and in war. If need be, they would stand by Edward – as, under present circumstances, was right: he was, after all, the king, and Lancaster had gone too far. Second, Pembroke and Badlesmere moved to deal directly with the difficulty that, while the king could be persuaded by their counsel to moderation, he was prone to swinging back to aggression under the counsel of others. What Pembroke and Badlesmere needed to do, therefore, was to persuade Edward's other counsellors also to advise him to be moderate. The most influential of the favourites was Damory, and Pembroke and Badlesmere evidently took him into their confidence, for in November he signed an agreement with them in which they promised to protect him, and in which he undertook to persuade the king to follow their counsel and swore not to profit excessively from the king's generosity – or permit others so to do. (Clearly Edward's inclination to have money sucked out of him by the unscrupulous had not abated with the passage of time.) Damory had been brought on side. This still constituted the application of a sticking plaster to a gaping wound, but it at least involved a strategic approach to the problem of Edward's hostility to Lancaster, his fear of the earl and his tendency to be swayed by provocative counsel. Pembroke and Badlesmere had clearly worked out that Damory and the other favourites felt as threatened by Lancaster – whose repeated calls for the resumption of grants endangered their recently acquired status and wealth – as he did by them; and that the way to reduce political tension was therefore to provide them with clear reassurance.

In a situation reminiscent of that in 1312–13, the next twelve months involved torturous negotiation that brought little more than nominal progress. Yes, another agreement was eventually reached between the king and Lancaster, but it was one that barely concealed their continued mutual fear and hostility. In the meantime it remained impossible for Parliament to meet or for a campaign against the Scots to be sent, and in consequence the situation in the country and especially in respect of defence declined still further. In late autumn and winter 1317–18 there continued to be grave concerns about troop-raising, armed confederacies, the depredations of vagabonds and the state of the peace more generally: in November, for example, the royalist sheriff of Leicestershire and Warwickshire, William Beauchamp, was also appointed 'superior keeper of the peace' in the two counties, and early in 1318 two other royal associates, John Hastings and John Pecche, were complaining about attacks on their Warwickshire lands. One wonders whether something close to insurrection was now breaking out across the Midlands as well as the north. Proposed Parliaments in January and March were postponed at the last minute. A meeting then took place between a negotiating team led by Pembroke and representatives of Lancaster. At that meeting it became clear that the central issue in resolving the situation with Lancaster remained the question of the royal favourites.

On 2 April 1318, meanwhile, Berwick had fallen to the Scots, after a soldier in its garrison had succumbed to a bribe and enabled a night-time Scots assault party to scale its walls. This represented a major strategic loss for the English. The port of Berwick was the largest urban settlement in Scotland – despite its location on the border with England – and a strong garrison town. In English hands it had acted as a secure point of departure for armies entering Scotland and a safe point of return, much as Calais was to do in France after its capture by Edward III in 1347. Berwick's loss at this time is a measure of how dysfunctional English politics had become. The Edward–Lancaster dispute had prevented Parliament from meeting or a campaign from being launched since early 1316, during which time Scottish forces had been dancing a jig around the English in the north. Following their capture of Berwick, the Scots had swept south, overrunning large parts of Northumberland and raiding deep into Yorkshire – indeed almost as far as Pontefract. It was probably on account of this raiding that Parliament was finally cancelled and a summons for military service for July 1318 issued instead. Given that, during June, Lancaster was attacking Warenne's Welsh Marcher lands, it is hard to believe that any real campaign against the Scots was feasible; but in any case the plan was overtaken by events – as the prospect that a settlement might be reached between Edward and Lancaster emerged during further talks in June and July.

The result was the so-called Treaty of Leake, agreed on 9 August 1318 – two days after Edward and Lancaster had exchanged the kiss of peace in the presence of the prelates, earls and barons on the road between Loughborough and Leicester. Quite how agreement was reached, when Lancaster had continued to maintain that Damory and Montagu were plotting to kill him, is unknown. The *Vita* suggests that it was the king himself who recognised the need for compromise, in light of the loss of Berwick, the continued dep-redations of the Scots and the vast time and money that had already been expended on seeking a settlement. But an examination of the terms of the treaty, and indeed its confirmation in the Parliament of October–November 1318, suggests that it was not the king who compromised – but Lancaster. Having insisted throughout upon the removal of the favourites from court and the resumption of all grants to them, he now took them into his peace, and neither their removal nor the wholesale resumption of their grants fea-tured in the treaty. The Ordinances were to be maintained, and a limited reform of the household, together with a modest review and resumption of royal grants, was to be led by Hereford. A new standing Council, consisting largely of prelates and courtiers, but including one of Lancaster's banner-ets, was to help guide the king's decision making. All this was eminently tolerable for Edward. Damory and the others promptly acknowledged significant monetary debts to Lancaster, which has led historians to sug-gest that the earl allowed himself to be 'bought off'. But this seems hard to credit. First, pecuniary gain was not a major political consideration for Lancaster (though he was certainly a grasping and mean-spirited landlord). Second, the sums involved, though significant, were (in the grand scheme of Lancaster's wealth) relatively small. The one very large sum, £50,000 of debt acknowledged to Lancaster by Warenne in a technically separate but clearly connected deal, was never called in. Moreover, at various points in the nego-tiations the discussion had focused upon how to establish trust between Lancaster and the favourites; at one stage it had even been suggested that the Despensers might join his retinue as a sign of their mutual confidence. So it seems likely that the favourites – fear of whom had kept Lancaster out of government for so long – now provided the earl with assurances, underpinned by financial undertakings, sufficient for him to agree to attend Parliament and serve on campaigns once more.

If Lancaster was bought off, it was probably done by leaving Warenne – who had appealed in vain for royal assistance against Lancaster's aggression – to his fate. As we know, Lancaster kept hold of Warenne's castles and vast estates in Yorkshire and the March of Wales in return for a modest transfer to Warenne of some Lancastrian estates and a yearly payment of a thou-sand marks. While Lancaster benefited financially from the arrangement, this was not its point. His objective in attacking Warenne had always been to strengthen his territorial and military position, thereby obtaining the greater sense of physical security that he craved. So, if this was a buying-off, it is likely that it was more focused upon practical security and territorial integrity than upon money or the satisfaction of avarice. Whatever the case, this, the sixth and most sustained attempt to realign Lancaster with the court and government since Bannockburn was, like its predecessors, doomed to failure: the hostility between the king and the earl could be eased temporarily but was too deep to resolve. Nonetheless it was more successful than any previous effort: it lasted longer – nearly a year – and it enabled, finally, a significant expedition to be mounted against the Scots, now directed towards recapturing the fortress town of Berwick.

The Berwick Campaign, 1319

At the time of the Parliament in October–November 1318, the signs regarding this new expedition may have seemed propitious. In September the papal envoys had excommunicated Bruce and his supporters for their attack on Berwick and their continued pursuit of war, and in October the English enjoyed their first real military success against the Scots since 1306 – at Faughart in Ireland. A further Parliament in May 1319 completed the planning for the proposed expedition, confirming Berwick as its initial objective and completing a comprehensive package of taxation, grants and loans to fund the campaign.

But the Berwick campaign turned out to be yet another military disaster for Edward II. With the exception of Sir Andrew Harclay, the middle-ranking commander of Carlisle, no English war captain seems to have had the talent or experience to be able to meet the Scottish generals on equal terms. After a shaky start, Robert Bruce had developed into an outstanding all-round commander, adept in mobility. His chief lieutenant, Moray, was a formidable tactician. In September 1319, as an English army of perhaps ten thousand men assaulted Berwick by land and sea, Bruce and Moray comprehensively outmanoeuvred their enemy. Anticipating the English attack, Bruce had despatched a diversionary force under Moray before Berwick had even been invested. Bypassing Carlisle, Moray advanced towards York under cover of darkness, with the aim of drawing the English off Berwick by attacking Edward II's northern capital. (The chroniclers hold that the Scots also hoped to capture Queen Isabella, whom they suspected would be waiting for the king at York.) Successive English assaults on the walls of Berwick had been beaten back by the hard-pressed garrison when news reached Edward II that a scratch militia of townsmen, clerics and peasants, under the command of William Melton, archbishop of York, had in the meantime been routed by the approaching Scots at Myton-on-Swale. The archbishop had retreated with the remnants of his army to York, where he now anticipated a Scottish assault.

The Scottish diversionary stratagem worked. Harclay was immediately sent from Berwick back to Carlisle with a substantial force of hobelars and archers in the hope that he might cut off the Scots' retreat, and after a brief and bitter debate among the other English commanders about whether to seek to confront Moray or continue with the siege, Lancaster promptly withdrew, redeploying his substantial forces for the protection of his own lands. (Because he had declined to accept the king's wages, the Lancastrian troops had remained under his independent command.) If the chroniclers are to be believed, his rapid retreat may have been prompted by rumours that the king had declared his intention, after the siege was over, of meting out justice to those he held responsible for the death of Gaveston. Whatever the case, with Harclay and Lancaster gone, the siege was broken. Moray escaped and the English were left with little option but to sue for a truce, agreed for two years just before Christmas 1319. The Scots retained Berwick as well as the strongholds they had taken in Northumberland. The Treaty of Leake, essentially agreed in order to permit an English expedition against the Scots, lay in tatters. No trust had been established between the king and Lancaster, even if sufficient semblance of it had been created to allow a campaign to go ahead. Lancaster again eschewed the king and government, and criticism of the earl at court was rife. No further attempts were made to reconcile Lancaster with the king. It was surely clear to everyone that this was unachievable. Rumours of Lancaster's false dealings with the Scots circulated widely. According to the *Vita*, the earl had supposedly received a payment from Robert Bruce of £40,000, his men had made no attempt on the walls of Berwick, and both he and they had allegedly crossed paths with the Scots in Yorkshire without either side laying hands on the other. Furthermore, the two-year truce with the Scots meant that there was no pressing need to bring Lancaster's military resources into play.

The Rise of Hugh Despenser the Younger

Hugh Despenser the Younger – a man vastly more rapacious and violent than any previous close associate of the king – now emerged foremost among the courtiers. His rise to dominance in 1320 changed politics fundamentally. Stalwarts of the court were driven for the first time into implacable opposition, and by the middle of 1322, Despenser's energy and ruthlessness had brought the febrile stagnation in which politics had been mired since the death of Gaveston to a shocking end. At the end of 1319 many people surely thought that the state of the realm could deteriorate no further. Such belief was to be undone with alarming swiftness.

The Despenser political earthquake was not exactly devoid of foreshocks. He had murdered Llywelyn Bren in 1317 in order to grab his lands. In 1315 he had seized Tonbridge Castle, and in 1316 he had assaulted Sir John Ros in Parliament. In December 1318, shortly after being elevated to the office of chamberlain, he had forced Hugh Audley to grant him the Welsh lordship of Gwynllŵg (or Newport), which had previously been assigned to Audley as the husband of Margaret Clare. By February 1319, he was regularly acting as a royal charter witness, and his constancy in the king's presence, necessitated by his new office, had produced a situation by the middle of the year in which he seems to have been as close to the king as anyone, rivalling Damory in Edward's affections. It was in 1320 that the latter was eclipsed by Despenser, as he too became a target of Despenser territorial ambitions, having inherited the Welsh Marcher lordship of Usk, which neighboured Gwynllŵg.

What were Despenser's aims? He clearly sought to reassemble the Clare inheritance – split between the late earl of Gloucester's three co-heiresses and their husbands – in the hands of just himself and his wife, the eldest co-heiress. But his aspiration to replace Gloucester must have been informal in nature, because he made no attempt to secure the Gloucester comital title for himself when – later – he might have done. Or maybe his ambitions were cruder: merely to make himself 'rich and attain [his] ends', as he put it in a letter to an associate. Exercising political power was clearly a component in his ambitions, whether for its own sake or because it was his willingness to do the king's work for him, and thereby absolve Edward of the responsibility of leadership, that was central to his attractiveness to the monarch. His career from 1322 was characterised by a resumption of the brutal land grab he attempted in 1320–1, but now conducted even more threateningly. Around that time he was obviously paranoid, though up to 1322 his behaviour was more anti-social than unhinged: highly ambitious, violent and tending towards illegality. Like Gaveston he was accused of dominating the king, but unlike Gaveston he shared his position of favour with almost no one – only his father and a compact group of Despenser insiders. It was this royal monopolisation together with the threat that he posed in the Welsh March that doubtless drove those hitherto constant courtiers Roger Mortimer and John Charlton into the opposition camp for the first time in late 1320. Damory and Audley took the same path at the same moment for the same reasons. Queen Isabella and the Beaumonts lasted a little longer, but they too were duly forced out of the court circle.

The occasion of the fundamental political shift that occurred in 1320–1 was Despenser's pursuit of the valuable lordship of Gower, which, like Usk, sat adjacent to Glamorgan. The lord of Gower was the impecunious and elderly William Braose. In the absence of a male heir Braose had promised Gower to his son-in-law, John Mowbray. But he havered about this decision and seems unscrupulously to have entered negotiations to sell the lordship to a number of other Marcher lords, including Hereford, Mortimer and the younger Despenser. By the end of 1319, it looked increasingly likely that Despenser would secure the lordship, and, in 1320, Mowbray occupied it to assert his claim. Behind the scenes Despenser worked on the king, persuading him to confiscate Gower from Mowbray on the grounds that he had entered into his inheritance without a royal licence. The application of this rule in the March of Wales was unprecedented, and this issue of principle, together with the king's allocation of Gower to Despenser as keeper, outraged the Marcher lords. The king's action was of highly dubious legality and undermined Marcher rights; furthermore it was clearly the king's intention to grant the lordship to the rapacious Despenser – who was also believed to have further designs on castles and lands in Wales, including some in the hands of Mortimer. Plus there were other compounding factors, foremost among them Despenser's treatment of Llywelyn Bren and his declared desire for vengeance on the Mortimers, whose ancestors he blamed for the death of his grandfather at Evesham in 1265.

In the face of this tumult Edward sought to shore up his political position by reaffirming the possessions of Damory and Audley, and by pardoning Damory a debt of £2,300, but he would not budge on the central issue; indeed when the matter of the law and custom of the March was raised with him by Hereford, he and Despenser dismissed it out of hand. By February 1321, almost all the major Marcher lords had retreated to their lands to raise troops and put their castles in a state of defence. The most notable exception was the earl of Arundel, whose lands were exclusively in the northern March of Wales, well away from those of Despenser, and whose rivalry with the forceful Mortimers probably pushed him into the royal camp, once they had vacated it.

The Despenser War and the King's Triumph

Receiving intelligence of planned attacks on the Despenser lands, Edward and Despenser advanced on Wales in March 1321, confiscating and occupying rebel property as they went. But in May the rapid occupation and despoiling of Despenser's Welsh holdings – led by Hereford, the Mortimers, Charlton, Damory and Audley, and facilitated by Despenser's Welsh tenants, who hated him for his oppressive lordship – left the king and his favourite with little choice but to retreat. Assaults now commenced on Despenser lands in England. Meanwhile, having first reached an agreement with Hereford, Lancaster had sought to build a coalition against the king and the Despensers between the northern magnates and the Marcher lords. In May this attempt failed, with the northerners agreeing only to an alliance of mutual defence, but at a subsequent meeting in June at Sherburn in Elmet, a manifesto against the Despensers was decided. This was to be presented at Parliament in July, which had been summoned by the king in an effort to establish a forum in which accusations against the Despensers could be legally heard and, ideally, defused or at least moderated. At Sherburn the chief representative sent by the king to address the gathering, Bartholomew Badlesmere, probably through alarm at the younger Despenser's behaviour and the extent of his influence, abruptly changed sides and joined the rebels. With Pembroke abroad – securing a new marriage in France following the death of his first wife in September 1320 – and Hereford taking the lead in the opposition camp, this left the king without the counsel of any of the experienced, moderate advisers among the magnates, upon whom he had previously depended in his negotiations with his political opponents.

In July 1321, as Parliament proceeded at Westminster, Hereford and the other Marcher lords approached London in arms and issued the king with an ultimatum. In essence, they insisted that the Despensers be exiled and disinherited, the principal charges against them being that they had usurped the royal power to the dishonour and peril of the Crown and realm, that they had given the king evil advice, that they had monopolised the king so that the lords could not provide him with counsel, and that the younger Despenser had murdered Llywelyn Bren. Edward would not entertain these charges, refusing even to meet with the lords; nor would the lords back down. But the stalemate was broken when Pembroke returned to England at the end of July; according to the *Vita*, he advised the king to 'consider the power of the barons' and to recognise that his throne was in danger. In the face of this advice, Edward reluctantly acceded to the lords' demands. In Parliament in August sentence of perpetual banishment and disinheritance was pronounced on the Despensers. In this judgement by notoriety, to which no reply was allowed, a precedent was set for the trial of Thomas of Lancaster in 1322 and Roger Mortimer in 1330. This novel process was essentially required by the king's refusal to accept that the Despensers were guilty of treason, or to concede a statute against them. But while the lords had little choice but to proceed as they did, one wonders whether they worried about establishing a dangerous precedent. Nevertheless the needs of politics and the realm overrode any such concerns. The lords then received pardons for their attacks on the Despenser lands and appropriation of Despenser goods. Shortly afterwards, the elder Despenser departed, probably for Aquitaine; the younger Despenser had already left England's shores, as a precautionary measure to protect him from the Marcher lords; but in a scenario characteristic of the man and almost beyond parody, he remained in the English Channel and the Cinque Ports to engage in piracy – as the *Vita* puts it, he was a 'sea-monster' preying on passing merchantmen.

While Channel piracy sat nicely with Despenser's natural inclination towards violence and illegality, it also allowed the king – who made several trips to the south coast in August and September – to maintain contact with him for plotting purposes; plus the piracy was probably intended to bankroll the revenge they planned: in 1336, Edward III assessed the compensation owing to the Genoese for their loss of a ship and its cargo to Despenser in 1321 at the huge sum of eight thousand marks. The royal counterstrike, which quickly came, was brilliant in conception and effective in execution. There can be little doubt that Despenser finally provided Edward with the cutting edge against his enemies that he had lacked. They had three targets in mind: Badlesmere, whom they regarded as an unspeakable traitor following his change of sides at Sherburn; the Marcher lords, who had moved so ruthlessly against the Despensers; and Lancaster. They resolved to defeat their enemies in detail and took action against them in precisely the right order.

Badlesmere came first. His power base in Kent, centred on Leeds Castle, was geographically isolated from the Marchers, and Lancaster hated him and would not countenance his being provided with assistance. So he was vulnerable. Moreover he had vast wealth, which meant that, if he could be pushed into treasonable behaviour, his money could be confiscated and used to raise a large army against the king's other enemies. (The disastrous Berwick campaign had left the royal finances again exhausted in 1319.) Alert to the threat the king and Despenser posed, Badlesmere put his castles in Kent into a state of defence and urged his people, including his wife at Leeds Castle, to permit entry to no one. In October Edward and Despenser exploited this by sending Queen Isabella, ostensibly on pilgrimage to Canterbury, to Leeds to ask for admittance and shelter for her retinue. Badlesmere's wife followed her husband's instructions to the letter and refused the queen entry. In response to the insult, Isabella ordered her men to force the gates. They were violently repelled and several of them were killed by arrow-fire. This gave Edward the perfect excuse to move against Badlesmere, and he promptly besieged

Leeds. By the end of the month the garrison was forced to surrender and its members were summarily hanged. Badlesmere had walked straight into the Despenser trap. Some nobles and many of the prelates were already of the view that the Marcher lords had behaved excessively in their action against the Despensers, especially in respect of attacks upon their English (as opposed to Welsh) lands and their disinheritance, and the Leeds Castle affair completed the restoration of the king to the moral high ground – ground that had seemed lost when he had backed Despenser over Gower in 1320–1. He was able to persuade a Council of prelates to declare the sentence against the Despensers illegal, and in addition to the support of Arundel, he could now count on that of Pembroke, Warenne and Richmond. Crucially, he also had at his disposal the full apparatus of royal government, which he tweaked in his favour by fresh appointments in the shires. A move against the Marcher lords was viable.

By the end of the year the king had recalled the Despensers and, having mustered a substantial royal army at Cirencester, advanced up the Severn, seeking a river crossing into the March of Wales. The bridge at Worcester was well defended and that at Bridgnorth burnt to destruction, likewise part of the town, by the retreating Marcher forces. But by the time the king reached Shrewsbury, the alliance of those opposed to him – the 'contrari-ants' – was collapsing. First, the Mortimers, Roger Mortimer of Wigmore and Roger Mortimer of Chirk, decided to surrender and seek terms. Their decision, like so many they took, was driven by self-interest. Royal forces under the Welsh sheriff of Merioneth, Sir Gruffudd Llwyd (who held the Mortimers in disregard as oppressive lords), had overrun their lands behind them, and their appeals to Thomas of Lancaster for assistance had fallen on deaf ears. The two Marcher lords were imprisoned rather than pardoned – as the reported terms of their conditional surrender, apparently agreed with Pembroke, had specified. Shortly afterwards, Maurice Berkeley suffered a similar fate, and in light of this, Hereford, Damory and Audley escaped north with their armies to rendezvous with Lancaster.

Lancaster was already in arms but had been wasting time besieging the royal castle of Tickhill in south Yorkshire. Towards the end of February, in the company of Hereford and the other remaining contrariants, he advanced south towards his castle of Tutbury in Staffordshire and the crossings of the

River Trent at nearby Burton, which he intended to defend. But the decision of his foremost retainer, Robert Holland, to defect to the king with a substantial contingent of the Lancastrian army weakened the rebels' position, and after three days of fighting at the river crossings, Lancaster and Hereford fled northwards. Inside Tutbury Castle was found the injured Roger Damory, who shortly afterwards died of his wounds, having been judged a traitor. Meanwhile, intelligence was received via the archbishop of York that Lancaster had entered into an agreement of mutual aid with Robert Bruce. Afterwards it transpired that Hereford had also been driven to this exigency. With the long-standing rumours of Lancaster's treacherous dealings with the Scots confirmed, the rebels were publicly declared traitors and the royal army continued in their pursuit. At this juncture Queen Isabella intervened to prevent the contrariants' escape. Writing to Andrew Harclay, she urged that the royal forces he had raised to counter possible Scots intervention in support of them should hasten south to head Lancaster off.

Closely informed by royal spies and his scouts, on 16 March 1322, Harclay intercepted the rebels where the Great North Road crossed the River Ure at Boroughbridge in Yorkshire. Dismounting his strong force of Cumberland and Westmorland militia, he divided his men to defend both the bridge and ford over the Ure, had the hobelars form up in Scottish-style schiltrons and reinforced them with large numbers of archers. At the bridge it was the hobelars who did the damage, killing Hereford and repelling his men-at-arms, whereas at the ford Lancaster's cavalry were defeated by a fierce arrow-storm. In this way, Boroughbridge both provides the earliest indication of how the best English war captains were responding to the lessons of war with Robert Bruce and prefigures the manner of the great English victories of the Hundred Years' War. Lancaster agreed an overnight truce with Harclay, apparently holding that he had resisted the Despensers, not the king, and believing that his consanguinity with Edward would protect him. This seems extraordinary, given his long-standing fears of the king's retribution, but who knows what was going on inside his head in the face of such palpable and immediate danger? In the morning, having been reinforced by the high sheriff of Yorkshire, Harclay advanced from the river crossings and arrested Lancaster in Boroughbridge town. Within days the earl was despatched to Pontefract Castle, which in the meantime had surrendered to the king, and where Edward now awaited him. On 22 March Lancaster was convicted of treason by the royal record. Like the Despensers in 1321, he was allowed no defence. Spared a traitor's death on account of his royal blood, he was beheaded before a jeering crowd on a hill outside the castle. As the *Vita* says, 'Having once cut off Piers Gaveston's head, the earl of Lancaster now lost his head on the king's orders.' Other contrariant leaders were quickly caught. John Mowbray and Robert Clifford were taken at Boroughbridge and hanged at York. Although he initially escaped, Badlesmere was later arrested in Lincolnshire, and hanged, drawn and quartered in Canterbury. The Mortimers, Hugh Audley and Maurice Berkeley were imprisoned. The lands of all these men and those of many of their followers were declared forfeit. While, from July, lesser individuals among the contrariants began to be permitted to buy their lands back, the payment schedules left them under heavy financial bonds to the Crown.

Lancaster's career in the final year of his life largely reflected his career in general. His capacity to attain his political ends was fatally compromised by his political obtuseness, inability to think ahead, obvious self-interest, tendency to bear grudges and unwillingness to venture beyond the ostensible safety of his strongholds. These factors all contributed to the failure of the contrariant defence in 1322. Three key moments stand out: first, Lancaster's refusal to assist Badlesmere; second, his failure to come to the Marchers' assistance on the Severn; third, the defection of Holland. While contemporaries attributed Lancaster's downfall to the last of these, Holland's betrayal of his lord and patron was in fact part of a wider Lancastrian collapse, consequent upon Lancaster's habit of picking unnecessary local fights without being willing or able to protect the retainers he exposed in the process. This deleterious local leadership meant that Lancaster's Midlands heartlands were lost long before Holland decided to throw in his lot with the king. The disloyalty of those around Lancaster reflected his unreliable, sluggish and bullying personality.

So far as his fellow magnates were concerned, Lancaster had rarely done anything other than burden them further as they laboured under the weight of an incompetent king. In 1321–2, this was truer than ever. The contrariants could do little without the powerful Lancaster and scarcely more with him – given that he consistently refused or failed to act. If one struggles to sympathise with the resulting plight of the self-aggrandising Mortimer, Charlton and Damory, the opposite is true of Hereford and Badlesmere, who had worked tirelessly to resolve the political divisions in the realm between 1312 and 1320, only to die violent deaths in opposition that they had generally sought to avoid. Although Badlesmere's mishandling of the Bristol dispute, sudden defection to the rebels at Sherburn and naive management of the Leeds Castle affair make him difficult to respect fully, Hereford enjoyed the conspicuous loyalty of his many Welsh tenants and seems to have been mistrusted by no one – save perhaps the king and the Despensers. Of the other major political actors, only Pembroke and Queen Isabella now remained in place. In little more than two years, however, Pembroke would be dead and Isabella alienated.

While the king had ostensibly swept all before him by the end of March 1322, his strength was more apparent than real. His misgovernment continued to undermine royal rights and rule in Scotland and Gascony, and to imperil northern England. Internal order was already collapsing for want of good governance – even before the king's campaign against his enemies had devastated the nobility, and dismembered the local social and administrative networks over which they presided. Although Edward's campaign of 1321–2 had been highly effective, it had depended for its execution upon his being able properly to mobilise the apparatus of royal government – administration and finance at the centre; the royal household, local officials and the wider royal network in the country – that had provided supplies, recruitment of troops, command in the field, key information and military intelligence. The king's access to such resources was unique, providing him with a substantial natural advantage against any opponents. But he could only fully deploy them when he was in the right. At the end of 1321, thanks to his enemies having overstepped the mark, Edward essentially had right on his side – despite the political community's well-founded reservations about the Despensers. Plus the king had triumphed by following the younger Despenser's plan, which was an excellent one – helped by the king's opponents being divided and hesitant, and by their mistakes. However, neither Edward nor Despenser had a track record to suggest that keeping to the moral high ground would come easily; quite the reverse was true. Moreover, whether the younger Despenser had the temperament, judgement and self-control to enable an incompetent king to keep government going and protect a severely damaged realm from further fracture was decidedly questionable, not least because, of the four people who had effectively steered the country since 1312, Pembroke, Badlesmere, Hereford and Isabella, two were dead and the others shortly to be marginalised.

An Illusory Tyranny

The rule of Edward II and the Despensers, between Boroughbridge and the king's capture by his would-be deposers on 16 November 1326, is habitually referred to as a tyranny, and with good reason. On the face of it, Edward and the Despensers held England in an iron grip as, by threats, menaces and illegal or dubious means, they shamelessly appropriated the king's subjects' money and estates. For historians this epic plundering raid and the undermining of the law that it entailed substantially explain why Edward was deposed in 1327. In addition to defending the realm against external enemies, the purpose of the office of king was to protect property and maintain internal order by upholding the law. Any king who chose to bend or ignore the law, especially in his own interests or those of his favourites, risked subverting the kingly role and making himself the opposite of a king – a tyrant. From late 1320 onwards – when he backed the younger Despenser over Gower against law and custom – Edward was conspicuously guilty of doing this. But while explaining why Edward was deposed has been straightforward, historians have not always found it easy to comprehend how deposition actually occurred, given that the king vanquished his enemies in 1322, and that the ruthless and seemingly well-organised Despensers had carte blanche in government and the country from that point. Why did a regime whose power seems to have been absolute collapse so quickly and comprehensively in late 1326?

Part of the answer is that the regime was both narrow and brittle. Some historians have argued that the Despensers failed to insert enough of 'their' people into strategic positions in the shires. The tight control historians have perceived they exercised at the governmental centre was only partially echoed in the localities, with fatal consequences in 1326: the Despensers should have packed local offices with their followers to shore up their situation, it has been said. But recent work has shown that after 1322, Edward and the Despensers effectively ran out of people to appoint to local office, having too few trusted associates to fill too many empty positions. It is striking that in 1325 and 1326, when the regime sought to respond via fresh commissions to clear dangers of rebellion and invasion, the same handful of over-stretched, trusted individuals was appointed to key offices again and again. The loyal inner circle comprised the former Lancastrian lawyer Roger Bellars, the royal clerks Walter Stapledon and Robert Baldock, the royal sergeant-at-arms Simon Reading, the younger Despenser's wife Eleanor Clare and the earl of Arundel. Surviving papal correspondence with England indicates that the pope regarded the younger Despenser, Stapledon and Baldock as especially influential with the king. Then there was a group of trusted solider-administrators and lawyers, including Ralph Basset of Drayton, Oliver Ingham, John Sturmy, Thomas Ughtred, Geoffrey Scrope and John Stonor. But these men were government loyalists rather than Despenser loyalists, as their subsequent careers were to show. Otherwise the regime was largely regarded with a mix of contempt, hatred and fear, even among its own appointees and retainers. It seems likely that Edward and the Despensers knew this, which explains their decision to concentrate critical positions in so few hands. When invasion came in 1326, the wider Despenser affinity, which historians have assumed made the tyranny so powerful, either sided with the invaders or sat on their hands. Might the regime have recruited a greater number of associates invested in its survival? It is hard to see how. Any self-interested, brutal and untrustworthy regime will naturally struggle to recruit even the unscrupulous to its service. The gains that any follower might make are outweighed by the potential loss to be suffered if he or she should fall into disfavour or if the regime should be toppled. Certainly by 1325, and probably by 1323, it was clear that the Despenser regime was only superficially strong. In desperation the king and his favourites tried to broaden their power base from late 1325 by pardoning contrariants and restoring their lands, but of course this attempt to buy support was completely transparent and came far too late: to generate any political capital, such mercy would have needed to have been exercised in the aftermath of Boroughbridge. That said, had mercy – rather than vengefulness – been exercised in 1322, any credit then built would in any case have been squandered in the subsequent foreign-policy disasters of 1322–3 and 1324–5. In other words, this was bankrupt rule fatally lacking in support and with no prospect of recruiting more. One hates to talk of historical inevitability, but if ever a regime was destined to fail, this was it.

Since the political platform of Edward and the Despensers was so rotten and creaking, was their supposed tyrannical power in fact illusory? It was, but it is easy to see how the Despensers have seemed powerful to historians.

First, there is no doubt that they made themselves immensely rich. The king seems to have been determined never again to find himself without access to money. He had inherited war debts of up to £200,000 from his father, and his military failures as well as his financial incontinence had left him periodically unable to pursue his objectives for severe want of funds. His victory over his opponents in 1321–2 had to be bankrolled by piracy, and by looting the lands and possessions of Bartholomew Badlesmere. From 1322 Edward demonstrated both a consistent interest in amassing money and a new-found and marked disinclination to spend it. (His obsessiveness in this regard is beautifully exemplified by two judicial commissions he issued, amid mounting disaster, in May 1325, to investigate the disappearance of the carcasses of an orca and a porpoise from the coastline of his lands in Yorkshire. He valued these at £10 and sixty shillings respectively.) His major streams of income derived from the management of royal lands and the forfeited estates of contrariants, and from judicial fines, the customs, and various clerical and lay subsidies. All were fully exploited by officials at the king's urging, and at the point of his removal in 1326, nearly £62,000 in cash and treasure – well over a year's subsidy – sat in the royal coffers. Contemporaries remarked that he was the richest king since William the Conqueror. Similarly, the Despensers – who probably encouraged Edward's acquisitiveness and parsimony – became vastly wealthy, though in their case the patchiness of surviving records and the complication of their affairs render making an accurate assessment of their wealth much more difficult. But we know that they must have derived a huge income from the immense estates they now controlled.

Control over land was the second element in the regime's apparent power. At the York Parliament in May 1322 the elder Despenser was made earl of Winchester and was granted substantial English lands to maintain his new status – as well as Thomas of Lancaster's forfeited Welsh Marcher lordship of Denbigh. His son received what was effectively a reconstituted earldom of Gloucester, retrieving all the Welsh lands he had claimed, and obtaining much more besides, such that he dominated South Wales. Their ally Arundel received the justiciarship of Wales formerly held by Roger Mortimer of Chirk, as well as his Marcher lordship of Chirk together with its castle. The king, the Despensers and Arundel now controlled some two-thirds of Wales. The land grab did not stop there, however, and the intimidation, judicial manipulation and chicanery by which it was conducted have further persuaded historians of the regime's terrifying power.

The Despensers infamously terrorised Alice Lacy and Elizabeth Clare, respectively the widows of Thomas of Lancaster and Roger Damory, into handing over vast estates. Alice Lacy was imprisoned in York and threatened by the Despensers with being burned alive if she did not transfer a large part of the Lacy inheritance in England and Wales to the king and the two Despensers, which she duly did in the summer of 1322. Elizabeth Clare's case provides perhaps the most complete illustration of the Despenser modus operandi. Arrested in March 1322, she was kept captive in Barking Abbey until she agreed to grant her lordship of Usk to the younger Despenser in return for his lordship of Gower, despite the latter being of lesser value than the former. Having been released, she was rearrested later the same year and imprisoned in York, this time being forced to quitclaim all her Welsh lands to the king. But the regime went further. In 1324 it persuaded William Braose, formerly lord of Gower, to sue Elizabeth Clare for false possession of the lordship, and rigged the ensuing legal hearing to ensure that he won the case. Braose then granted Gower to the elder Despenser, who in turn granted it to his son. Both Usk and Gower, with which Usk had been 'bought' from Elizabeth Clare in 1322, were now in Despenser's hands, and Elizabeth Clare was left with nothing – and no legal means of redress other than to petition the king, which she repeatedly did in vain. These are the two most notorious cases, but there were myriad others across the country. In 1322–3, for instance, members of both the Somery and Swynnerton families found themselves imprisoned by the Despensers and forced to sign over lands and goods, despite having recently backed the Crown against Lancaster in Staffordshire. After the death of the earl of Pembroke in 1324, Despenser was given custody of his Marcher lordship of Pembroke, and the earl's widow and heirs were pressured into surrendering control of extensive lands in South Wales, Herefordshire and Gloucestershire. In 1325, when the younger Despenser was still acquiring lands at an incredible rate, the Pembroke kinswoman Elizabeth Comyn was denuded of her inheritance by threats of violence. These examples show the wider picture.

The fourth reason why historians have believed that the regime was powerful relates to the Despensers' apparent hold on government and the administration. The period 1320–6, coinciding with the Despenser ascendancy, saw significant reform of the chamber, wardrobe and Exchequer, led by Stapledon, Baldock and Bellars. While it was once held that the younger Despenser was the architect of this reform, we now believe that it began before Despenser's rise and was essentially driven by an organisational dynamic internal to the medieval civil service. In other words, it was a normal dimension of state formation. Doubtless Edward and the Despensers encouraged it, valuing its financial benefits, and as chamberlain the younger Despenser continued his predecessor John Charlton's policy of presenting the chamber as an alternative to the Chancery and Exchequer, less susceptible to unwanted oversight. But theirs was not a reforming administration other than in respect of maximising revenue.

There are better grounds, however, for seeing Despenser as having been active in the conduct of government business. The records are full of instances of his issuing orders in the king's name or appending his own instructions to royal commands, especially during the War of Saint-Sardos; and, like Isabella during the 1310s, he was frequently petitioned by those seeking royal redress or action. Clearly his hands rather than Edward's were on the governmental tiller. This reality has augmented historians' sense that there was an all-encompassing Despenser clientele in the administration and the shires, informing and delivering the regime's business. It is certainly true that the younger Despenser in particular retained many men, but in practice this did not translate into support. This was partly because of the odiousness of his rule but it was also because of the nature of his connection. Most of Despenser's retainers were professional administrators or lawyers who habitually served the government of the day. They became part of Despenser's clientele in order to establish a professional link with a man prominent and influential in government. They were not his partisans. A good example is the aforementioned Oliver Ingham, a highly capable household banneret who successively served Edward II and the Despensers, Isabella and Mortimer, and Edward III, in each case with dedication and distinction.

If historians recognise that Despenser's links with administratively capable officers could do nothing to save the regime in 1326–7, should they assume that such connections contributed to its strength before it collapsed? While having access to a cadre of capable administrators at the centre can have done Edward and the Despensers no harm, neither does it seem to have done them much good. Their foreign and military policy was calamitous and contributed significantly to their demise. Yes, the younger Despenser engaged in governmental firefighting in the national interest (as an extension of his own interest) during the Saint-Sardos crisis, but to little positive effect. In general, the evidence of the government records points to his having been chiefly interested in acquiring yet more land, otherwise promoting Despenser interests and pursuing those suspected of being responsible for the many attacks on Despenser and royal possessions. So far as Despenser agency in the localities was concerned, contemporaries held that the Despensers had agents and spies everywhere, and the author of the *Vita* commented memorably upon the king's 'harshness' and the failure of the nobles, through fear, to resist him. Plus we have seen how the regime could apply great pressure to individuals. But if Edward and the Despensers intended a police state, this was not what was achieved: the Despenser network patently failed to prevent political opposition and unrest, both of which were in fact widespread.

Indeed they were present throughout the tyranny. Although historians, distracted by the Despensers' apparent tyrannical power, have arguably underestimated their significance, there were attacks on the Despensers' and the king's lands throughout 1322–6, as well as more generalised disorder. This is scarcely surprising. The tyranny's effective commencement at the end of 1320 had sparked what amounted to a civil war, and no matter how complete was the king's triumph at Boroughbridge, it was not going to bring such fierce opposition to an abrupt end. Rather, the harsh treatment of the contrariants in the battle's aftermath, accompanied by the Despenser land grab, gave it extra impetus: in addition to the executions, imprisonments and confiscations, commissions of arrest were issued for more than a thousand suspects. Large-scale attacks on the earl of Winchester's lands resulted, leading in September 1322 to the issuing of multiple judicial commissions against well over a hundred alleged offenders. Among those suspected of leading the attacks was John Maltravers the Elder – a contrariant associate of the incarcerated Maurice Berkeley and Roger Mortimer. Likewise, a realm reduced by incompetent kingship to significant disorder since at least 1315 had been further unsettled by the fighting of 1321–2. One might think that this problem would be largely confined to the March of Wales and the Midlands where the war had been fought. Sure enough, the Midlands were to remain notably disorderly into the 1330s, but in 1322 there seems to have been unrest everywhere. The townspeople of Cambridge attacked the colleges of the university, for example, and Hanseatic merchants suffered many assaults in the ports of the east and south coasts. The confiscated lands of the contrariants were extensively looted. Doubtless such widespread disorder resulted from the king's continued failure to provide effective local rule, as well as being a side effect of civil war.

As is implied by the above, the Despensers' greed for land almost certainly exacerbated their difficulties. The same is true of the king's appetite for money. In the end, both the land and the money had to be appropriated from the king's own subjects: in the words of the Articles of Accusation against Edward II, promulgated in 1327, the king and his favourites 'stripped the realm'. This produced not only broad political opposition but also a cadre of losers, naturally invested in the regime's demise. Furthermore, this was not simply a matter of personal or familial loss. Because late medieval English society was based upon local and regional networks centred upon landholding, the removal of the king's greater subjects who headed such networks and the appropriation of their lands seriously disrupted the local connections upon which people depended for protection and promotion. The losers were many. These were the people attacking the Despensers' holdings in the shires and Wales. Together with the operation of the common law that harnessed them for public purposes, the local networks also brought stability to the localities. Accessing and nurturing them were therefore fundamental to the management and defence of great estates, in an age when self-policing was a vital element in the machinery of justice and order. By seizing so much land, the Despensers both stretched themselves too thinly and made holding on to the land harder, since, with each fresh seizure of land, they broke another network. The younger Despenser in particular nonetheless carried on greedily acquiring land well into 1325, even as the regime began to collapse. Nor did their money or that of the king help. It could not buy local order or local acceptance of tyrannical rule – even had the miserly Edward II been inclined to spend it. Plus the people knew all too well that the money had been stolen from them in the first place, and all the treasure in the world would not buy an army to defend a morally bankrupt and rapacious regime, once reckoning forces were massed against it.

The Statute of York and Further Disaster against the Scots

In the aftermath of Boroughbridge any reckoning surely seemed far away. But Edward II immediately began to surrender the political high ground gifted to him by the opposition in 1321, thereby embarking upon the road to downfall. His and the Despensers' outrageous land grab was, as we know, fundamental to this, but equally important was governmental failure, which unfolded spectacularly and disastrously for the regime straight after its apparent triumph. In short, Edward quickly engineered a foreign-policy calamity in Scotland and northern England that eclipsed even Bannockburn. Moving decisively against the Scots was central to his plans directly that he had eliminated Lancaster, summonses for military service being issued on a grand scale from Pontefract on 25 March 1322. It is unlikely that his motivations for taking the fight to Robert Bruce had changed in any way. His detestation of, and contempt for, the Scottish king remained undiminished, and it is probable that, despite his recent successes against his internal enemies, he continued to see victory against the Scots as a prime means to build political capital and so proof himself against future challenge. As it was, the tendency of human behaviour to repeat brought precisely the opposite outcome, as Edward was again humiliated by Bruce and his lieutenants.

Before that could occur, however, he had to validate both the outcomes of the civil war and his plans for renewed war against his Scottish foe, which he did at the York Parliament of May 1322. Although the records of this Parliament do not survive, we know from contemporary accounts and the Statute of York that its purpose was firstly to annul the sentence on the Despensers of 1321, secondly to endorse the process and judgement against Lancaster and the other contrariants, and thirdly to prevent any further attempt to impose constraints upon Edward's conduct in the manner of the 1311 Ordinances – by legislating against such constraint. The resulting Statute of York was definitive: it declared the 1311 Ordinances null and void, as detrimental to the power and estate of the king, and thereby brought to an end the Ordainers' experiment in formalising kingly constraint in the national interest; and it stressed that any matter that touched upon the power and estate of the monarch had to be agreed by the king in Parliament, not imposed upon him – whether by Parliament or anyone else. In this way the great central weakness of the English post-Magna Carta constitution was inadvertently emphasised: faced by a king determined upon inappropriate rule short of tyranny, strictly the realm could do nothing; technically the king could not be restrained.

Parliament also approved the king's plans for war against the Scots, while delaying the start date for the proposed Scottish campaign to allow better preparations to be made. A plundering raid led as far south as Preston in early July by Robert Bruce himself – presumably during one of his periods of reasonable health – enraged Edward II, and it was with something close to maniacal zeal that the English king entered Scotland on 10 August at the head of an army larger even than that which had fought at Bannockburn. Among its contingents were crack infantry from the northwest of England and Wales led respectively by Andrew Harclay – recently ennobled as earl of Carlisle in recognition of his outstanding military service – and Gruffudd Llwyd, both of whom had fought so effectively for Edward against Lancaster and the Marchers. But yet again, the English were comprehensively outmanoeuvred by the Scots. Bruce withdrew north of the Forth, denuding the Lowlands of supplies – in Edward's own words, he saw in Scotland 'neither man nor beast' – such that the English quickly began to starve and succumb to illness, being forced back to England within a month. The king had been conscious that providing for such a large army on the march in Scotland would require both extensive purveyance and ample seaborne supply, and had planned accordingly, but Flemish pirates in Scottish service fatally disrupted English shipping and this, together with Bruce's scorched-earth policy, rendered the plans ineffective. What is more, as the English straggled home they were severely discomfited by pursuing Scots troops under James 'Black' Douglas; the Scots then proceeded to harry Northumberland. Once back in England Edward had little choice but to allow his army to disband in order that it could spread out to obtain food and forage, but he resolved to remain in the north to defend against an anticipated Scottish attack. Now the Scots threw an audacious counterpunch, as Bruce advanced rapidly into Yorkshire in the hope of catching the English king unawares and capturing him. Although English intelligence warned Edward of the Scots' proximity, and although in response he ordered an army to assemble in the vicinity of Byland in Yorkshire, he was almost taken at nearby Rievaulx Abbey when, on 14 October, the English forces under Pembroke and Richmond were routed by the Scots under Moray, ferociously attacking up the one-in-four gradient of Sutton Bank and taking many captives. The defeat at Byland and Edward's ignominious flight to safety in York – the second of his reign – capped a catastrophic campaign that had uncovered the king's martial incompetence again. An even more humiliating coda saw Queen Isabella, who had been left cornered in Tynemouth Priory by the speed of the Scots' advance, fleeing by sea and only narrowly escaping drowning.

The critical outcome of this debacle came at a meeting of the royal Council at Bishopthorpe near York on 30 May 1323. Edward confirmed a thirteen-year truce with the Scots negotiated earlier that month. Henry Beaumont, once one of the king's confidants, protested so violently at the abandonment of English and allied Scottish interests north of the border implied by the truce that he was removed from the meeting and for a time imprisoned. The peace was regarded as a disgrace. What made it all the more disgraceful was that, earlier the same year, the king had had Andrew Harclay stripped of his newly awarded earldom and executed for treason after he had learned that amid post-Byland recriminations, his key northern commander had privately entered into negotiations with the earl of Moray. Harclay had concluded a provisional treaty with Moray to end the Anglo-Scottish war by agreeing that England and Scotland should henceforth be ruled independently of one another. His objective had been to protect his beloved Cumberland and Westmorland, having faced up to the reality that the king neither could nor would defend his realm against the Scots. (Nor was Harclay the only magnate to think in this way: the archbishop of York sanctioned northern prelates to negotiate with the marauding Scots by way of protecting their houses, and Louis Beaumont, bishop of Durham, entered into direct negotiations with the invaders, much to the king's disgust.) Although after Byland Edward had requested and received a grant of taxation to fund a further campaign against the Scots, and although he remained deeply hostile to Robert Bruce, there was no reason to believe that a fresh attempt on Scotland would result in anything other than further defeat. In agreeing to such a long truce with the Scots Edward effectively acknowledged his inability to pursue English interests in Scotland or even defend his northern border. Overall, Byland was even more calamitous for Edward than Bannockburn – despite the prominence of the latter in historical accounts. The battle and the truce that followed stripped him of any remaining political credibility and fully exposed the vacuity of his kingship.

The Regime's Failure

From this point onwards – that is, just a year after Boroughbridge – the government of Edward and the Despensers began to fail. The combination of mercilessness against opponents, internal misrule by outrageous misappropriation and incompetence in external defence would have been undermining enough. But the regime was also imploding. Harclay – arguably the regime's best military asset, who ought to have been prized, not cruelly condemned – was the most spectacular victim of this, but he was neither the first nor the most important.

The first was Pembroke, who had been forced in June 1322 publicly to pledge loyalty to the king. (This was presumably a hangover from his having advised the king to accede to the Marchers' demand for the Despensers' banishment in 1321.) The earl – so vital to maintaining a semblance of good government between 1312 and 1320 – was now politically side-lined. His marginalisation undoubtedly weakened the king's position. Edward had repeatedly benefited from his good counsel, framed by a devotion to the realm's interests, and this was now in scant supply. When he died suddenly, on an embassy to France in June 1324, the political impact was slight. This speaks not only of the intractability of the diplomatic situation then pertaining in respect of Gascony, but also of the extent to which Pembroke had ceased to be a political player in England.

The most important victim of internal collapse, as events demonstrated when she was instrumental to the king's deposition in 1326, was another valuable counsellor: the queen. Like Pembroke she had mediated the king's relationships with others – especially those from overseas – sometimes to critical effect. An abhorrence of the younger Despenser was at the heart of the breakdown of her relationship with Edward. Isabella's loathing of Despenser appears to have developed between late 1321, when she willingly participated in the entrapment of Badlesmere at Leeds Castle, and the autumn of 1322, when she repudiated military assistance at Tynemouth because it was led by Despenser. We can only speculate as to the nature of her antipathy. An element may have been personal or even sexual: Edward's relationship with Despenser was alleged at his deposition to have been sexually deviant, and Edward was undoubtedly also close to Despenser's wife, Eleanor Clare, who appears to have been placed in proximity to Isabella as a spy once suspicions about the queen began to mount. But Isabella was notably conscious of her status and power, and the decline in her influence as she was side-lined by Despenser surely infuriated her. Her anger must have reached fever pitch in September 1324, when Despenser used the excuse of the danger of a French invasion to sequestrate her estates without compensating her. He also detained the French members of her household and removed her three younger children, John, Eleanor and Joan, from her supervision, placing them instead in the custody of Eleanor Clare. Nevertheless Isabella evidently had the self-control to maintain outward equanimity, and even to feign goodwill towards the younger Despenser before her fateful departure for France in March 1325.

In this way, with the encouragement and help of the Despensers, a king whose platform had long been held up by the greater ability and dedication of others actively sawed away at the stilts that had hitherto prevented it from sinking into the mire. Meanwhile the mire rose up. The first manifestation of this came with the rebellion of Robert Ewer, a king's yeoman whom the Ordainers had demanded be removed from the court in 1311. Ewer had spectacularly fallen out with the Despensers in 1320 but was subsequently rehabilitated, playing an important role in the victory over the contrariants in 1322, in command of the royal infantry at Bridgnorth and Burton. Although he served in Scotland later that year, his hostility to the Despensers resurfaced and in September he secretly withdrew from the king's presence and thereafter attacked the Despensers' and the king's manors in southern England, pointedly including those confiscated from executed contrariants. It is worth noting that Ewer's depredations fitted into a wider pattern of attacks on the Despenser estates at this time, and coincided with reports from Oliver Ingham of unrest in the Welsh Marches. Ewer also mounted an assault on the royal castle of Odiham, of which he had formerly been constable, and, if the *Vita* is correct, planned to capture the earl of Winchester, who consequently took refuge in Windsor Castle. The king issued commissions of arrest against him right across the kingdom, and in December Ewer was recognised and taken in Southampton as he prepared to flee the country. As he remained silent in the face of the charges against him, he was sentenced to so-called *peine forte et dure*, the only use of torture permitted under the common law. Defendants could only be tried if they entered a plea. If they remained silent, feigning muteness, they were tortured by being forced to lie down under a wooden board, on which were piled heavier and heavier weights until they could no longer stand the pressure and agreed to plead. In Ewer's case fortitude or stubbornness triumphed, and he held out for several days until the weights or starvation killed him.

In some of the commissions of arrest directed against him, Ewer was associated with partisans of Roger Mortimer, probably the surviving contrariant most feared by Edward and the Despensers. Among Mortimer's closest allies was Maurice Berkeley, who had been imprisoned in Wallingford Castle. By 17 January 1323 – only a month after Ewer's capture, and little more than a week after the king had learned of Harclay's negotiations with Moray – the king had been informed of an escape attempt by Berkeley, which came close to succeeding and which required a military response when the cornered Berkeley and his accomplices took over the castle. In February Berkeley was interrogated as the king sought to get to the bottom of his escape plan and root out other potential plots involving imprisoned contrariants, and in March members of two contrariant families, the Trussells and the Zouches, attacked the Despenser lands in the Midlands. By the summer, the publicly displayed corpse of the executed contrariant Henry Montfort had become the centre of a miracle cult in Bristol, echoing that already established around the tomb of Thomas of Lancaster in Pontefract. And on 1 August Roger Mortimer escaped from his prison in the Tower of London, conspiring with the deputy constable and heavily drugging the constable and guards. His escape was made across the Tower's roofs and down a rope ladder to the Thames, where accomplices, seemingly from among a London merchant community alienated by the king's hostile behaviour, spirited him away by boat, horseback and finally sea to the relative safety of France.

There followed rumours that there would be a Mortimer-inspired uprising against Edward and the Despensers in Wales, and that Mortimer would descend from the Continent on Ireland, where he held great estates and where he had once been king's lieutenant. Attempts were made to prevent communications passing between Mortimer and his suspected allies in England. Inquisitions into his escape against the wider context of plots against the regime were obsessively pursued, and by November 1323 the king was convinced that the attempted flight of Berkeley from Wallingford had been simply one element in a comprehensive conspiracy to seize royal castles including Windsor and the Tower, and to free Mortimer. The regime's paranoia is apparent in the surviving governmental records from late 1322 onwards: commission after commission sought to head off conspiracies, including suspected murder plots against the king and his favourites. Whether the manifold references to attacks speak more loudly of reality or suspicion matters little: the government clearly believed itself assailed from every direction, and even if the scale of that assault was in fact less than the language of judicial commissions or the chroniclers implies, it still speaks of a teetering regime. The distraction of so many internal challenges coming on top of one another – attacks on the Despensers' and the king's lands, wider unrest in the country, hostility to the truce with the Scots, and dangerous conspiracies woven by both contrariants and disaffected courtiers – blinded Edward and the Despensers to a fresh threat, and one that eventually was to prove fatal to them: from France to the security of Gascony. That their paranoia, especially in the aftermath of Mortimer's escape, was severe enough to destabilise their government is shown not just by their suspicions and alienation of their own supporters, and their failure to see the War of Saint-Sardos coming, but also by the younger Despenser's patent conviction, by 1324, that he was being targeted by necromancers. This belief produced an extraordinary correspondence with the pope, who advised Despenser to turn to God with his whole heart, no other solution being necessary, as well as judicial charges against alleged magicians who had made waxen dolls of the king, Despenser and others, with the intention of killing them.

The War of Saint-Sardos, 1323–5

The War of Saint-Sardos had its origins in an outrage committed by the king-duke of Aquitaine's Gascon subjects against the French Crown in the person of an unfortunate royal sergeant, sent to Saint-Sardos in the Agenais to enact the establishment of a French *bastide* – a commercial town – on French-held land deep within the king-duke's territory. This had been authorised by the new French king, Charles IV, who had succeeded his brother, Philip, on the latter's untimely death in 1322. On 15 October 1323 the sergeant erected a marker post bearing the French royal arms at the proposed site, but in the night the place was attacked by angry locals who hanged the poor sergeant from his own post. Their fear, shared by many in the locality, including the dominant local lord, Raymond-Bernard de Montpezat, was that the creation of a French *bastide* with the usual commercial privileges would be to the detriment of their own economic prosperity. Hostility to the plan was exacerbated by a conviction that the

French king had no jurisdiction outside the walls of the French priory of Saint-Sardos, which, under its parent house, the abbey of Sarlat, was sponsoring the *bastide* and proposing to share its profits (in the customary manner) with the French king. We might ask why a French priory was sited so far into Gascon territory. The answer is that this reminds us both how patchy and how involved jurisdiction in south-west France was, and how compromised were the territorial gains ostensibly made by Henry III in the Treaty of Paris of 1259. Blaming Lord Raymond-Bernard for the atrocity, Charles IV confiscated his castle of Montpezat. But the garrison refused to hand it over and was backed in its defiance by the English seneschal of Gascony, Ralph Basset of Drayton – a politically obtuse act that served only to confirm the French king's (probably erroneous) suspicion that Basset had been implicated from the start. On 7 December – nearly three months too late – Edward II wrote to Charles IV to express his consternation at the incident and stress that he had only just learned of it; his words rang true and Charles believed him. His failure to have noted that a grave situation was developing might partly be attributed to the everyday difficulty of obtaining speedy communications from distant Gascony – and partly to Basset's inclination to bury bad news. But any king remotely worth his Crown should have been avidly attentive to developments in Gascony at this time. With Charles IV's accession. the period of détente in Anglo-French relations since 1303 had ended, and French policy towards Gascony was again hawkish: while the Flemings' momentous victory over the French at Courtrai in 1302 had seen off those arch-promoters of 'forward' French foreign policy, Pierre Flotte and Robert of Artois, their ally Charles of Valois now emerged as one of the new French king's chief advisers; and he had unfinished business both with the Plantagenets and in Aquitaine. Instead of keeping a close eye on Gascon affairs, however, Edward II and the younger Despenser had been engrossed in rooting out conspiracies at home.

As 1323 came to a close, and as Charles IV took the unusual step of advancing on the French south-west to take action against the perpetrators of the Saint-Sardos outrage, Edward and the Despensers were forced into action – characterised by incompetence. First, they failed to act promptly to reinforce the duchy. Men, money and supplies did not reach Bordeaux at all until the autumn of 1324 – by which time the Agenais had already fallen to the French – and substantial reinforcements arrived only in May 1325. Although the king spent £65,000 on the War of Saint-Sardos, he did not deploy his resources effectively. Second, because they were increasingly fearful of leaving a realm on which their hold was insecure, Edward and the Despensers repeatedly sought to postpone Edward's travelling to France to perform homage for Aquitaine to Charles IV. In September 1323, before the Saint-Sardos incident, the French had asked that Edward perform homage at Amiens by Easter 1324. In response to a request from the English king for more time, they had moved the deadline to 1 July. But during diplomatic negotiations intended to resolve the impasse over Saint-Sardos in spring 1324, Edward's representatives – led by his half-brother, Edmund, earl of Kent – sought yet another postponement of the act of homage. This convinced the French that Edward was determinedly playing fast and loose with his obligations as a vassal. Third, the English embassy handled the negotiations ineptly, first agreeing to hand over the confiscated castle of Montpezat and then shortly afterwards changing their minds. It is little wonder that Charles IV, who was probably in the business of seeking grounds on which to declare Aquitaine confiscate but who nonetheless acted with restraint for many months, began active preparations to invade the duchy as soon as the discussions with the English were aborted.

When the French invasion came in August 1324, it quickly overran the Agenais as far as the strategically important town of La Réole on the Garonne, which the earl of Kent, now Edward II's lieutenant in Gascony, had made his base. The ease with which the French were able to seize so much of the region owed a great deal to their alliance with the lord of Albret, the great Gascon noble and dominant local lord alienated by Edward II and Gaveston in the 1310s. The French commander, Charles of Valois, besieged La Réole, and on 22 September, Kent surrendered the town and castle in return for a six-month truce. If the French had aimed to occupy all of Gascony they were disappointed: although the duchy had been seized by a degree of panic at the French invasion, in fact it remained largely secure in Anglo-Gascon hands, the French having lost both men and momentum during the siege of La Réole. But the Agenais, which had only been in English possession since the Treaty of Amiens of 1279, was a great prize in and of itself, and it is evident that negotiating its long-term retention was henceforth central to Charles IV's purposes.

For the English, negotiation was equally imperative if they were to get the Agenais back; and here the question of homage again loomed large, since there was no prospect of obtaining a satisfactory settlement from the French unless homage was performed. Managing this and securing the Agenais without Edward II having to leave England's shores involved the king and the Despensers in making two fatal decisions: first they sent Queen Isabella to France to negotiate on the English Crown's behalf, and second they permitted Prince Edward, the heir to the throne, to be invested as duke of Aquitaine in his own right, and to follow her overseas. This was so that he could perform homage for the duchy in his father's stead.

During the winter of 1324–5, negotiations between the English and the French were deadlocked. The suggestion that Isabella might travel to France to negotiate personally with her brother Charles IV as a way of breaking the impasse came from the papacy. Charles IV indicated that he would be receptive to overtures from his sister. Edward and the Despensers needed a settlement and the king continued to trust his wife, so Isabella embarked for France on 9 March 1325. Although Charles negotiated hard, her presence eventually helped procure the best settlement that the English might have hoped for under the circumstances: Aquitaine was to be temporarily surrendered into the hands of a French seneschal acceptable to the English, to be returned once homage was done. The exception was the Agenais, which would be retained and over which the French king promised to do Edward II justice. The English were also to pay the French a substantial war indemnity. If Charles resolved to keep the Agenais, the indemnity would be cancelled. It was clear that the French intended to hold on to the Agenais, but when faced by the prospect of both renewed war in Gascony and – according to intelligence reports – a simultaneous French invasion of England, probably backed by the Scots, Edward had little option but to settle. His next challenge was to wriggle out of performing homage in person.

Papal nuncios had already raised the prospect that Prince Edward might be granted Aquitaine and swear fealty to Charles in place of Edward II. Indeed, the peace settlement anticipated this ploy by allowing alternative arrangements for the completion of homage to be made if either Edward or Charles fell ill. The need for a convenient illness duly to afflict the English king was made all the more compelling by a renewed bout of disorder in England and Wales over the summer. Whether this was prompted by the spreading news of the unsatisfactory peace settlement with the French is unknown. Whatever the cause, July saw an explosion of unrest: commissions were sent to investigate the beating and blinding of a royal deputy keeper of contrariant lands in the March of Wales, assaults on the king's parks at Conisbrough, raids by confederates in Essex, and conspiracies and extortions in Norfolk and Suffolk. Further commissions were issued nationally against disturbers of the peace, and captive contrariants were secretly moved from castle to castle to thwart any attempt to rescue them. Clearly the state of the realm meant that Edward could not leave England, even for a short time. As the Despensers put it, in his absence where would they find a place of safety? Feigning illness in Kent en route to France to perform homage, the king suggested that his son should receive Gascony and perform homage in his place. This proposal was accepted by Charles IV and in early September Prince Edward was made duke of Aquitaine. Crossing to France, he swore fealty to Charles for the duchy before the end of the month.

The Road to Deposition

At this point everything changed. Although Edward and the Despensers had worried about the threat presented by Roger Mortimer to Prince Edward in France, and had accordingly assigned Walter Stapledon to accompany the prince, they evidently did not foresee the danger posed by Isabella. In October 1325, she publicly revealed her hand, informing Stapledon that she would not and could not return to England while the younger Despenser, who had come between her and her husband, remained there. Prince Edward stayed with her. By sending the prince to Isabella, Edward and the Despensers had unwittingly played into her hands: now she could present any attempt against them as an act on behalf of her son, the future king. That month the king pleaded in Parliament for assistance in persuading her to return, claiming that there had been no sign before she left that she hated Despenser: on the contrary, she had shown Hugh great favour. Hugh bore her no ill will and never had, Edward held. 'Someone' – unnamed but undoubtedly Mortimer – must have 'changed her attitude'; 'someone' had 'primed her with inventions'. Meanwhile disorder continued in the shires. Commissions of mass arrest were issued and fresh rebel attacks investigated, including assaults by John Maltravers in Dorset and on the king's constable of Conisbrough. John Sturmy and Thomas Ughtred were sent on internal secret missions. A pardon was issued to the contrariant and former Mortimer adherent Hugh Turplington, the first of many pardons and re-grants of confiscated lands that stretched into 1326 and were evidently intended – in vain – to buy much-needed political support at a critical time.

What was going on in and around the French court? Traditionally Isabella and Mortimer are identified as the prime movers against the Despensers. Certainly they led the invasion of England from Dordrecht on 23 September 1326. But they had substantial help: their force of around 140 ships and 700 mercenaries had been supplied by William, count of Hainault, whose wife Joan was both Isabella's and Charles IV's cousin and who reintroduced Mortimer to the queen in Paris in December 1325. A central objective of the count and countess of Hainault, and one promoted by Charles as early as January 1326, was to negotiate a marriage between the heir to the English throne and one of their younger daughters, Philippa, which was agreed. In addition to promoting the Hainault marriage, Charles underwrote his sister's financial commitments as she hired Hainaulter sailors and troops using her Ponthieu revenues. Indeed, until the last moment, Edward and the Despensers believed that the main invasion threat they faced was from Charles and France. Beyond the four major parties of Isabella, Mortimer, William of Hainault and Charles IV, various English lords and prelates were privy to the anti-Despenser plot. Sir William Trussell was a long-time enemy of the Edward–Despenser regime. He was joined in Paris by Bishop John Stratford of Winchester and the earl of Kent, who declined to return to England having accompanied Prince Edward to France in September 1325. The prince's personal perspective is hidden from us. He is usually assumed to have fallen under his mother's influence in France, and at age thirteen he surely relied heavily upon her guidance. But the future Edward III was an immensely strong character and the prince was believed by contemporaries to detest the younger Despenser. Despite his youth, his refusal to return to England must have involved an element of personal choice. This was exercised in the face of many letters from his father, entreating him to come home. So far as Isabella's relationship with Mortimer was concerned, the two were suspected of being lovers by March 1326, when Edward II referred to Mortimer being in the queen's company 'within and without house' in a letter to Prince Edward. The pope – prevailed upon by the English king – requested that Charles IV should expel them from his court as adulterers in the summer of 1326. By that time the two were in any case about to leave for Ponthieu en route to Hainault and the endgame of Edward's reign. They may not have been lovers – although historians generally believe they were – but they were unarguably the closest of political partners.

In England, fear of invasion and rebellion now dominated. In December 1325, coastal defences were boosted and in the new year commissions were issued to intercept letters being carried abroad. As riotous assemblies proliferated in Kent, on 19 January 1326, the regime suffered arguably its most disturbing attack yet, with the murder in Leicestershire of Roger Bellars, chief baron of the Exchequer and a member of the Despenser inner circle. Although his killing was partly motivated by local issues, its perpetrators the Zouches were longstanding contrariants. They fled to join the king's opponents abroad. Security measures were stepped up: in February new constables were appointed in royal castles and commissions against foreigners and contrariants assigned. More pardons were issued to former rebels. In March the king again raised concerns about contrariants, who were said to be moving freely in and out of the country. By May Edward was anticipating that Isabella would invade from France. That this threat remained foremost in the king's mind thereafter is shown by his allocating the bulk of his realisable forces, some 130 ships and 1,600 troops, to an amphibious raid on Normandy in early September. This was just before Isabella landed near Walton-on-the-Naze in Essex. The objective of the Normandy action is obscure. It may have been intended to capture and retrieve Prince Edward, whom faulty intelligence reports had placed there, or may simply have aimed to disrupt suspected

French military preparations. But as we know, the real threat came not from France but from Hainault, and on 24 September Isabella invaded unopposed. She was accompanied by Prince Edward, by Kent and, in the background, by Mortimer, as well as by her Hainaulter troops. Although Edward II had taken the precaution of instructing two thousand soldiers and a dozen ships to assemble at Orwell to protect the east coast, this force never materialised.

Deposition

Isabella immediately received support: first from the East Anglian gentry; then from Thomas Brotherton, earl of Norfolk, the king's other half-brother; and shortly thereafter from Henry of Lancaster, earl of Leicester, Thomas of Lancaster's brother and heir, who now assumed the title earl of Lancaster. Already Isabella headed a weighty coalition. It was rendered complete when the great northern lords Henry Beaumont, Thomas Wake of Liddell and Henry Percy joined it at Gloucester in October. All had seen their Scottish landed interests abandoned in the Anglo-Scottish truce of 1323, and their backing of Isabella reflected the north's disgust at Edward II's miserable labours against Robert Bruce. To the support of great nobles was quickly added that of London, the allegiance of which was vital to any revolution in medieval England. Isabella wrote to solicit the assistance of the Londoners immediately after landing. The king also sought their support, but they made their disdain for his rule clear on 30 September by shouting down royal pleas for help. Afraid for his safety, Edward, loaded with a war chest of £29,000 and accompanied by the Despensers, Arundel, Baldock, Simon Reading and a troop of men-at-arms, promptly quit the city and escaped west. The Londoners then mobilised against the remnants of the regime in their midst. The Tower was stormed and its prisoners released, and a mob seized and summarily beheaded Bishop Stapledon, who sought sanctuary in St Paul's in vain. Order was subsequently restored by the election and appointment of two Mortimer associates as mayor of London and constable of the Tower.

Isabella was now firmly in the ascendant. With her forces in hot pursuit, Edward and his associates split up in an attempt to maximise their chances of securing support. The earl of Winchester took refuge in Bristol, to whose burgesses the king had shown friendship in 1321, but the castle garrison delivered him to Isabella's troops after a short siege. On 27 October, he was tried in a parody of the proceedings against Thomas of Lancaster, and sentenced to be hanged and beheaded for robbery, treason and misdeeds against the church. Arundel chose to trust in his Shropshire heartlands, but was repudiated by the townsmen of Shrewsbury and arrested by his Welsh Marcher neighbour, John Charlton. He was taken to Hereford and, apparently at Mortimer's insistence, beheaded – by an incompetent executioner who took twenty-two strokes to finish the job. Meanwhile Edward, the younger Despenser and the others entered Despenser's Marcher lordships in the hope of receiving backing there, the Welsh having fought for the king against the Mortimers in 1322.

While Isabella and Mortimer waited at Hereford, the pursuit was continued in Wales by Lancaster and, symbolically, two of Llywelyn Bren's sons. With their hoped-for Welsh support having failed to materialise, Edward and Despenser set sail for Ireland. But adverse winds kept them in the Bristol Channel and after several days they made land at Cardiff. Initially retreating to Despenser's great fortress of Caerphilly, they later rode west to Margam and Neath, again seeking to rendezvous with anticipated Welsh allies. By the time they were arrested in the countryside near Llantrisant on 16 November they were heading back towards Caerphilly in rain-sodden disarray, the only Welsh supporter to have reached them in the meantime being the household esquire and Mortimer opponent Rhys ap Gruffudd. Accounts of their capture vary but it seems that Edward was surprised on the road; the others were subsequently rounded up in nearby woodland. As Edward was secured in the castles of first Monmouth and then Kenilworth, Despenser et al. were taken to Hereford for trial. In Despenser's case speed was of the essence, since he tried to beat the executioner by starving himself to death. On 24 November he was convicted by notoriety of myriad crimes against the Crown, queen, nobles and clergy, and hanged, drawn and quartered. Initially he bore his ordeal with fortitude but finally he let out an inhuman howl. Simon Reading was hanged, and Robert Baldock, who pleaded benefit of clergy, was handed to the bishop of Hereford for imprisonment. Baldock was afterwards extracted from the bishop's custody by the citizens of London and incarcerated in Newgate gaol, where he died.

Isabella's public platform from the moment she landed had been anti-Despenser rather than anti-Edward II. This was a matter of political calculation: rebellion against a lawful king, even one as atrocious as Edward II, was anathema. Nonetheless, removing the king as well as the Despensers was clearly in the minds of the leading rebels. In this regard Edward played into Isabella and Mortimer's hands by fleeing to Wales. This enabled them to argue that he had abandoned his realm of England and justified their taking control of the government by appointing Prince Edward keeper of the realm, which they did on 26 October. Under the prince's privy seal, Parliament was summoned for 15 December, but a month later writs issued in the usual form – the great seal having in the meantime been obtained from the king at Monmouth – prorogued the gathering until 7 January.

The January Parliament assembled under the gaze of the Londoners, massed in Westminster Hall, and their expectation that Edward II would be removed from the throne impelled agreement on the king's fate among the assembled lords, prelates and commons, the bishops in particular being divided. On 12 January, after several days of debate, it was reported to the assembly by Mortimer's associate Adam Orleton, bishop of Hereford, that the king, having been asked to attend Parliament, had vehemently refused to appear before people he considered enemies and traitors; Orleton then asked the assembly if they wished Edward II to remain king. Agreement not being forthcoming, Parliament broke up until the following morning to permit further consideration to take place. At this point, writing to the magnates and prelates, the Londoners asked them to join them in swearing allegiance to Isabella and Prince Edward, and in deposing Edward II. That evening the so-called Articles of Accusation against Edward II were finalised – stressing Edward's loss of lands in Scotland, France and Ireland, his denial of justice, his greed, his stripping of the realm, his weakness, cruelty and lack of character, and his incorrigibility – and something close to consensus was reached among the prelates. The following day in Parliament, Mortimer and the Lancastrian Thomas Wake led the way in proposing that the king be deprived of his throne and the prince crowned in his stead.

Orleton spoke to the biblical text 'where there is no governor the people shall fall' and the bishop of Winchester chose as his theme 'my head aches', arguing that the failures of the king as head of the kingdom had brought evil upon the realm. With Wake again orchestrating the debate, the archbishop of Canterbury, Walter Reynolds, proceeded to the text 'the voice of the people is the voice of God', whereupon the assembled Londoners were asked if they unanimously approved of the deposition. With one voice they proclaimed that they did, and so it was that Edward II was deposed – nominally for inadequacy rather than tyranny, though the reading out in Parliament of the Articles of Accusation, with their charge that, out of greed, Edward had denied justice and stripped the realm, clearly implied that he was a tyrant as well as a gross incompetent.

Deposition Becomes Abdication

The deposition was a joint-stock enterprise of the whole community of the realm. (Only a handful of prelates, including Archbishop Melton of York, silently dissented.) But straight afterwards it was reconstructed and propagandised as an abdication. On 21 January a representative deputation led by Orleton and William Trussell browbeat Edward II into abdicating at Kenilworth. They did this by threatening to disinherit his son if he refused to stand down. In floods of tears Edward agreed to go, and the following day the delegation formally withdrew the realm's homage. Thereafter all governmental references to the end of Edward II's kingship cited his abdication, not deposition. The opening of Edward III's first formal statement as monarch is characteristic:

> Whereas lord Edward, recently king of England, of his free will and by the common counsel and assent of the prelates, earls, barons and other nobles, and of the whole community of the realm, has abdicated the government of the realm; and whereas he has granted and wills that the government of the realm should devolve upon his eldest son and heir . . .

This attempt to minimise and spread the responsibility for Edward II's removal was a matter of self-interest, as well as self-deceiving propriety, for the king's subjects. Above all, the abdication provided a belt to supplement the braces already holding up the new king's legitimacy. Edward III's title had been popularly acclaimed in Parliament on 13 January, and as a medal struck to commemorate his coronation said, 'The will of the people gives right.' To this the abdication added hereditary legitimacy, with Edward II having resigned the throne in favour of his eldest son. For different reasons, both Mortimer and Henry of Lancaster – represented at the abdication by Orleton and Trussell respectively – particularly sought to bolster the young king's legitimacy, Mortimer because he needed Edward III's kingship to be beyond question if he were to rule through him (which he intended to do), and Lancaster because he was already worried about Mortimer's ambition and intentions.

The Kingship of Edward II

In many ways the years 1307–27 were a hiatus between periods of extraordinary governmental and national growth under Edward I and Edward III. This was not just about the complete absence of state-building agency in the rule of Edward II: circumstances partly beyond the king's control presented him with challenges from Robert Bruce and the French Crown against which even a leader of greater ability, responsibility and application might have struggled to make progress. But it is unarguable that it was Edward II's indolence, deleteriousness and malignancy that were chiefly responsible for governmental stagnation and reverses between the death of Edward I and Edward III's assumption of personal rule: much of the time, Edward II's government was completely hamstrung by problems stemming from the king.

Perhaps Edward II was unlucky to have been faced by an opponent in Thomas of Lancaster whose selfishness, disregard for the common good, incompetence and paranoia were matched only by his own. But under a competent king, Lancaster's emasculation of government in the 1310s would simply never have occurred; indeed it is notable that before 1307, he created no difficulties beyond his own estates, and participated fully in the king's wars. A summary of Edward's faults provided by the lords in the Articles of Accusation identifies where culpability lay. Edward's cruelty and lack of character, his unwillingness or inability to recognise the errors of his ways and accordingly accept guidance, his greed, his failure to defend the realm, and above all his incorrigibility stand out. He was also lazy and had a lackadaisical attitude towards duty, which doubtless accounts for his acute vulnerability to the ministrations of favourites who offered to complete his obligations for him; beyond this there was his stubbornness and repeatedly poor political judgement: in respect of the latter, one thinks especially of his treatment and condemnation of Andrew Harclay – his one really effective military commander – so quickly after Harclay had delivered to him the defining victory of Boroughbridge. Edward's willingness and capacity to act when it suited him is striking: in his tit-for-tat (and damaging) manipulations of local officeholding, for instance. Nor, as has been argued, did he completely lack cognitive ability. His delinquency was therefore at some level a matter of choice.

That said, from a structural perspective, the reign of Edward II is instructive. First, it demonstrates the limitations of Magna Carta as a protector of the people against a tyrannical king or even a determinedly incompetent one. While the Charter subjected the king to the law, for practical reasons he also had to stand above it. He had to be impartial in the political fray, and since politics and the law were inextricably linked in a system of royal rule now dominated by the common law, the king being under the law was not politically straightforward. Moreover, the judicial system required that the king, as the fount of natural justice, was not strictly bound by the letter of the law. This was because he had to exercise the equity or mercy that was needed to soften, in the interests of justice, the written law's inevitable angularities. So while certain of Magna Carta's articles, for example in respect of arbitrary taxation or imprisonment without trial, retained real utility, it could provide no general restriction on royal action: in too many areas, royal action needed to be largely unconstrained to be effective. The inherent contradiction between Magna Carta's assertion that the king was subject to the law and the practical requirement for royal independence is illustrated by the 1311 Ordinances and their rejection in 1322 in the Statute of York: in the end the king could always argue, as he did in 1322, that constraint, even constraint in the correct legal form, infringed his rights and was therefore unacceptable. This was a difficult argument to resist and could only ever be gainsaid in the short term when political factors obliged the king temporarily to give way. The solution to the problem of the king being simultaneously both above and under the law was, of course, provided by the compromise of politics, in which a competent and well-meaning monarch, governing for the common good, could be given carte blanche in respect of certain aspects of the law on the implicit understanding that he was not going to overstep the mark and start behaving tyrannically. But since this solution depended upon the interface between the accident of heredity and a successful upbringing it was not one to rely on. That the next king of England turned out to be so successful may have rested upon the genes he inherited via Isabella from his French forebears St Louis and Philip the Fair, to say nothing of his genetic inheritance from the English grandfather whose rule he so admired. But it may also have derived – equally accidentally – from a childhood spent largely in isolation from a father and mother neither of whom was exactly a model for monarchy.

The second lesson from the reign of Edward II relates to his deposition, the first in England since the Conquest. Rather than threatening to destabilise the very foundations of monarchy, as historians once contended, the deposition in fact confirmed exactly the opposite: the extent to which the king's subjects depended on him. By the fourteenth century, royal authority reached so far in England that the realm simply could not allow a tyrannical or useless king to remain on the throne.

EDWARD III, 1327–77

'So Loved and Feared'

Edward III's Character

Edward was born at Windsor on 12 November 1312 and was aged just fifteen when he succeeded his father on 24 January 1327. For almost four years, he was overshadowed as monarch by his mother, Queen Isabella, and her political and personal partner, Roger Mortimer, who sought to dominate government. But on the night of 19 October 1330, he seized both the formidable Mortimer and the reins of power in a lightning-fast and violent coup d'état at the royal castle of Nottingham.

The Nottingham coup was not just a critical turning point in politics; it also arguably encapsulates the essence of Edward III's approach to rule, even though it occurred when he was not yet eighteen years old. Faced by urgent need, and despite the considerable personal risk involved, Edward took bold and radical action in the interests of the realm – in consultation with, and assisted by, a group of hand-picked, closely trusted colleagues. The chroniclers, Edward's surviving letters and above all the government records tell us that this was his natural modus operandi as a political leader. The historical record also communicates his forcefulness, his insistence upon fast and effective responses from his subordinates, and his tempering inclination to grant mercy and admit weakness or error where appropriate. He was charismatic but thoughtful, regarded – contemporaries tell us, albeit reductively – with such love and dread by his subjects that no one would do other than as he asked. His direct political interventions and aspects of his personality leap from the pages of the chronicles and the official records alike. Where the latter are concerned, dry documents, in which the monarch can often seem a cypher, positively crackle with his presence.

From his surviving death mask, from the effigy on his tomb at Westminster Abbey (believed to be the earliest accurate portrait of a medieval English king) and from contemporary descriptions we know that Edward was of middling height, with a broad brow, high cheekbones, an aquiline nose and a 'berry-brown beard', according to the Middle English poem 'Wynnere and Wastoure' ('Winner and Waster'), written in 1352. His face was variously described as 'comely' and 'like that of a god'. He was physically fit, keeping good health until late in life, and brave – fighting alongside his men in the front line of battle at Halidon Hill (1333) and Calais (1350), and taking a crossbow bolt in the thigh at the naval battle of Sluys (1340). He was literate in English, Norman French and Latin. His surviving handwriting is the earliest of any English monarch. Historians have tended to assume that his first language was French, but the evidence provided in 1354 by his cousin, friend and trusted lieutenant Henry of Grosmont (1310–1361), first duke of Lancaster, in his devotional treatise *Livre de Seyntz Medicines* (*Book of Holy Medicines*), suggests another possibility. Grosmont describes how, when he was younger, he found French difficult to learn, showing that the greatest nobleman in England in the fourteenth century spoke English as his mother tongue. Edward was certainly the first English king to employ mottoes in English. While his most celebrated motto – *Honi soit qui mal y pense*, the motto of the Order of the Garter – was in Norman French, his lesser-known English mottoes are equally intriguing: the philosophical 'It is as it is', the touching 'Constant as the woodbine' and the baffling and fabulous 'Hey, hey, the white swan, by God's soul I am your man'.

Tournaments and chivalry were important parts of Edward's life: he famously founded the Order of the Garter, England's pre-eminent knightly order (of two tournament teams, under the command of the king and his son and heir, the Black Prince) in 1348. But that other training for arms, the hunt, was probably his strongest personal interest, avidly pursued, especially in Sherwood and Rockingham forests. He was a great falconer and fisherman as well as a keen horseman. He was also a renowned builder – at Windsor, Westminster and other royal residences – and was interested in art, music, books and university education. He was conventionally but sincerely pious, with a focus upon the Virgin, as witnessed by his regular pilgrimages within England and his intense reflections on the Black Death (1348–9). He enjoyed a close and loving relationship with his wife, Philippa of Hainault, with whom he had thirteen children. They remained together whenever they could, and when separated by political circumstances, the couple corresponded devotedly, sending each other many gifts. Husband and wife alike were doting parents (the burdens of office did not stop the king from dining with his children, even as toddlers), and Edward maintained strong and affectionate relations with all his offspring throughout his life. While family was very important to him, he also enjoyed close friendships with powerful lords and ladies, as well as with the less exalted members of his household. But in his largely positive relationships with the great men of his realm, business was prioritised over pleasure: duty came first. He behaved with real commitment to the people who merited his trust but was also capable of sustained hostility towards those he believed had behaved inappropriately and excessively, or who had otherwise (in his view) transgressed against the king and his people – a phrase he repeatedly used. Certain dimensions of his charisma stand out. Like the grandfather whom he so admired, Edward I, and St Louis, king of France, from whom he was descended, he employed the royal touch to 'cure' thousands of people of scrofula – 'the king's evil'. But his mingling with the common people also reputedly involved many incognito visits among his ordinary subjects to ascertain their perspectives and opinions. He certainly fought incognito – as a humble esquire – in tournaments and once even in battle, at the action to defend Calais in 1350. He was a great wearer of fancy dress, often satirical or comical in nature, in court celebrations or at tournaments. This included appearing as the pope, surrounded by 'cardinals', at the Smithfield tournament of 1343, and in a pheasant costume, complete with flapping wings, at the Bury St Edmunds tournament of 1348. The celebrated opening section of the great Middle English alliterative poem *Sir Gawain and the Green Knight* describes the court of King Arthur at Christmas, but is believed to have been inspired by the court of Edward III. The king is depicted as playful, curious, enigmatic and insistent.

Edward was something of a dandy, with a particular penchant for hats. The beaver-skin hat he wore, with a black velvet doublet, at the naval battle of Winchelsea or *Les Espagnols sur Mer* in 1350, was remarked upon by contemporaries as especially suiting him. At that battle, as at his most celebrated military victory, Crécy, in 1346, he commanded from a vantage point behind the front line, without donning his armour. This calm detachment in command was typical of the man, though on occasion he could also be impetuous in battle – as he was at Calais in 1350, over-reaching himself in the face of the enemy and having to be rescued by the Black Prince. As a war captain and diplomat he was possessed of great strategic vision as well as tactical shrewdness; and that capacity to see clearly, and win and build alliances for the future, characterised his entire political programme. He repeatedly created effective political and military teams, and delegated well, without surrendering capacity to intervene personally. His interventions could be obsessive: for instance, his determination to attribute blame for the surrender of the Perth garrison and for the erroneous plundering of an enormously valuable Spanish ship, the *Taret* (for the loss of which Edward had to pay its owners vast compensation), in 1339 resulted in many years of aggressive judicial investigations. Such obsession was rarely gainsaid, though the king characteristically exercised moderation in respect of punishment once guilty parties had been identified – especially if guilt (actual or otherwise) had been admitted and the king's grace humbly beseeched. It is easy to see why, after his death, he was described as 'the flower of kings past, the pattern for kings to come', and 'with his enemies as grim as a leopard, but with his people as merciful as a lamb'. Never defeated in battle, he was the 'English Maccabeus' – a king whose sustained victories marked him out to contemporaries as especially pleasing to God. This was a driven, demanding, hard-working person, with the cognitive ability, emotional intelligence, courage and acute sense of duty that have characterised great political leaders across time and geography.

He also arguably personifies a riposte to the tendency of historians to search in the childhoods of destructive political actors for the 'causes' of their harmfulness. It is scarcely possible to imagine a childhood – on the face of it, at least – more challenging than Edward's, caught between his tyrant father Edward II, the disturbed Hugh Despenser the Younger, his forceful mother, and her ambitious and unscrupulous partner, Roger Mortimer, who (as we shall see) was responsible for Edward's father's death. As the great Welsh poet Iolo Goch put it during Edward's life, the king's youth was 'hard'. But he seemingly emerged largely unscathed: well adjusted, stable, secure and reasonable – once his periodic outbursts of anger had subsided. Perhaps the genes of Edward I and St Louis trumped a difficult upbringing.

Or perhaps the nurture that the young prince received, not from his immediate family but from his beloved wet nurse Margaret Chandler and then his tutors Richard Bury and Henry Beaumont, neutralised the psychological damage he might otherwise have suffered.

In the Leading Strings of Isabella and Mortimer

Edward's powerful personality, application to duty and interventionism make it all the more striking that, in the years before the Nottingham coup, the chronicles focus predominantly upon the behaviour of Mortimer and those who resisted him, and the governmental records primarily reflect the political control exercised by Isabella and Mortimer. Evidently the king was not yet in control. How was it that someone who came to dominate government so quickly after 1330 was seemingly so subdued before that time?

Part of the answer is that there is a world of difference between a fifteen- and an eighteen-year-old, no matter how strong their character and penetrating their intelligence. We should remember that more than four years passed before the determined boy who had refused to return home from France in 1326, despite his father's entreaties, became the adult who dramatically asserted his authority and power over England in 1330. In that time Edward grew as a person and a politician. Another dimension of the answer involves the young king's location in the same court and government as his assertive mother and her daunting partner. The domination of Isabella and Mortimer emerged organically. At the beginning of Edward's reign (indeed, before its beginning), the boy-king was perceived as a cure to the realm's ills not in his own right but in combination with the wronged Queen Isabella: the untainted fifteen-year-old and his politically experienced mother were naturally seen as a single political unit – and his remaining in her custody for the time being was deemed appropriate. Because of Mortimer's close political and personal partnership with Isabella, in practice it was straightforward for him to become the co-director of government, though he was careful to do this mostly through informal channels rather than formal appointments, so as to avoid provoking political opposition. His power base was twofold: the court, in which he was treated as if he were a member of the royal family, and his vast Marcher lands, quickly reclaimed and dramatically increased by bold appropriation. Where he and Isabella could not themselves be present in particular areas of government, he ensured that allies such as Adam Orleton, the bishop of Hereford, or the courtier-administrator Oliver Ingham represented their interests – for example, on the regency Council that was appointed to guide the king in January 1327.

Their domination was something that Isabella and Mortimer evidently strategised. They generally kept the court physically away from Westminster, mostly in the Midlands, Mortimer's heartland, and in royal castles that they directly controlled – especially Nottingham and Wallingford. This was presumably so that Edward, through whom they ruled, was more isolated from the wider political community than would otherwise have been the case. Mortimer and his closest associates – Hugh Turplington, John Maltravers, Simon Beresford, Thomas Berkeley and John Wyard – remained constantly with the king (and rewarded themselves for so being with substantial grants of money), or enlisted government loyalists like Ingham or Bartholomew Burghersh to accompany him when they could not. Isabella and Mortimer presumably persuaded, emotionally blackmailed or browbeat the boy-king who was effectively their captive – as he later put it – into political acquiescence. (Edward remained emotionally close to his mother throughout, which must have been a factor in his subjection.) Direct pressure was embodied by the increasing presence of Mortimer's and his allies' Welsh retainers in the court, and was progressively applied the longer their regime endured, and the more Edward matured and sought to assert himself. Historians have tended to assume that, because of his youth, Edward was essentially subsumed by the self-serving machinations of his mother and Mortimer until the eve of the Nottingham coup. But the governmental records tell a more complex and compelling political story: of Edward's creeping assertion of his independence in the face of his mother's and Mortimer's greed, ambition and political insistence – as we might expect of a highly intelligent and responsible political actor, emerging into adulthood under involved and potentially dangerous political circumstances.

While the first eighteen months of the reign of Edward III saw Isabella and Mortimer establish their grip on power at the political centre, and acquire immense land and wealth, they also witnessed considerable political collaboration – a continuation of the politics of the revolution of 1326–7.

It was Isabella, rather than Mortimer, whose extreme acquisitiveness was initially to the fore. On 2 February 1327, the day of the king's coronation, she was granted vast lands, raising her income to twenty thousand marks yearly, a huge and unprecedented sum, fourfold higher than a queen in England might ordinarily expect. Isabella's motivation is unclear. She may, with an eye on uncertain politics, have wished to make herself financially very secure, having previously been stripped of her wealth for political reasons by Edward II and the Despensers. But it is hard to set aside greed as an impetus. She kept an exceptionally close eye on her income, assiduously securing additional grants for relatively trifling sums to make up the deficit when she identified that there was a slight shortfall in respect of the twenty thousand marks she had been promised, and carefully extracting full compensation in land and rents when the emergence in 1330 of Queen Philippa as a political force in her own right demanded the transfer of Pontefract from Isabella to Philippa. In March 1327, she lent the Crown ten thousand marks to meet an urgent need in respect of Gascony, but insisted that the sum be repaid within two weeks. Mortimer was more circumspect – for now. He retook control of his historic lands in late 1326, and around the same time acquired custody of the former Lancastrian Marcher lordship of Denbigh, latterly in the hands of Hugh Despenser the Younger, and appropriated the great Marcher lordship of Chirkland, painstakingly carved out in the late thirteenth century by his late uncle, Roger Mortimer of Chirk. If the latter – involving the deprivation of his cousin, the rightful heir – was outrageous, it was also substantially a family matter, for which no one else was going to go to the wall. Mortimer's rapacious greed, ironically akin to that of Hugh Despenser the Younger, was only satisfied later, after a breakdown in relations among the political elite negated the need for caution.

For the time being, those relations seem to have been workable. Henry of Lancaster and his associates, including Thomas Wake of Liddell and William Trussell, had played an important role, alongside Isabella and Mortimer, in the revolution. The balance of power between Lancaster and Mortimer had at that time been important and for now remained so. It was also politically important that Isabella and Mortimer should embrace the king's uncles,

Edmund, earl of Kent, and Thomas Brotherton, earl of Norfolk. This was reflected in the composition of a regency Council to guide the young king, set up under the presidency of Lancaster during Edward III's first Parliament, which straddled his coronation in January and February 1327. Lancaster's right-hand man, Thomas Wake, joined him on the Council, and while Mortimer, playing a circumspect hand, was not included, his representatives Adam Orleton and Oliver Ingham were. A similar balance between Mortimer and Lancaster was struck in respect of some key official appointments. Mortimer was made justiciar of Wales, for example, but Wake became keeper of the forests south of the Trent and constable of the Tower of London. Although tensions between the two camps must have existed – over the fate of Denbigh, for instance, or the rehabilitation by Isabella of Thomas of Lancaster's former steward, Robert Holland, who had abandoned the earl to his fate in Staffordshire in 1322 – it does seem that government proceeded with input from all. Mortimer was obviously in pole position with Isabella and in the court, and his creatures Thomas Berkeley, John Maltravers and Hugh Turplington were, by April 1327, being very extensively used on commissions. But Lancaster, Wake and their fellow Anglo-Scottish lord Henry Beaumont, with whom Lancaster had co-operated during the revolution, all exercised influence in government, as, to a lesser degree, did Norfolk and Kent – the latter witnessing a great many charters throughout 1327. On 28 February, Lancaster received a grant for service to Queen Isabella. By the end of the year, however, the government records were also reflecting the emerging influence of the young king's own household men: especially the knights William Montagu and William Clinton, the yeoman Thomas Bradeston and Edward's former tutor, the cleric and administrator Richard Bury. Edward was evidently starting to exercise independence where he could.

Consensus clearly existed around the need to settle the severe disorder in the realm that was the result of Edward II's deleterious rule, the Despenser land grab and the local insurrections that erupted in response. In the January–March Parliament, forty-two common petitions promoted by the Lords and Commons together sought, perhaps definitively, redress for people of all estates – genuinely the community of the realm. Contrariants, their descendants and others, deprived of their lands by Edward and the

Despensers, were now largely restored, and verdicts against them – including against Thomas of Lancaster – were overturned. (Intriguingly, the verdict against Mortimer was not reversed until July.) But the various judgements against the Despensers and the earl of Arundel were confirmed, partly because Mortimer was already benefiting so handsomely from the confiscations of their lands – now his. It was not until early 1331, after Edward III had himself seized power, that a much-needed repair of the established landed fabric, and of the all-important local socio-political networks connected to it, was properly attempted. But in the meantime many pardons – for example, of the garrison of Caerphilly Castle, who had resisted the revolution – were symbolically issued. From February through until May an enormous number of special oyer and terminer commissions was issued in an attempt to settle disputes caused, or left unresolved, by the disastrous politics of 1307–26. Amid these, from 8 March 1327, the Crown began to appoint new commissions of the peace right across the country. Further special oyer and terminer commissions were then issued on a grand scale between August 1327 and May 1328. The government's response to urgent judicial need arguably lacked imagination or strategy in that it was reactive and run of the mill. But it was at least a response – after many years in which Edward II had blithely ignored unrest and judicial need.

Beyond the turmoil in the localities and the political tensions at the centre, three pressing problems confronted the regime as it sought to establish itself early in 1327: first, the threat to Aquitaine; second, the threat of Scottish invasion and the question of Scottish independence; and third, plots to free Edward II from captivity.

The Threat to Aquitaine, Scottish Independence and the 'Shameful Peace'

Although the War of Saint-Sardos, which had effectively petered out in 1325, had nominally been settled in negotiations in the same year, no definitive peace had been established. This was because the Anglo-Gascons could not accept a situation in which the French retained the all-important Agenais, and Gascon lords, loyal to the English king-duke, remained displaced from their lands by the French invaders. At the same time, the hawkish Charles IV and his advisers wished to confirm the French Crown's hold on greater Aquitaine – the territory beyond the broad coastal strip running from Bordeaux to Bayonne. In 1326, under the seneschalcy of the highly able courtier-administrator Oliver Ingham, Anglo-Gascon forces had recovered significant lands from the French following the local collapse of the 1325 peace settlement. In February 1327 news reached the ears of the new regime in England that Charles IV was planning to re-invade the duchy. Faced by a simultaneous threat from the Scots, who had just broken the Anglo-Scottish peace of 1323 by attacking Norham Castle in Northumberland, the English government was in no position to go to war in Gascony. Though it took measures to strengthen the duchy's defences, it also immediately sued for peace. The settlement that ensued in the 1327 Treaty of Paris was exacted from a position of strength by Charles IV and was wholly to the disadvantage of the English. The French were to retain the Agenais, and much of the Bazadais and Saintonge. Oliver Ingham's recent reconquests were returned. The English were required to pay additional war reparations of fifty thousand marks, and perhaps most seriously, many Anglo-Gascon lords were banished from France – including Oliver Ingham, who had to surrender his seneschalcy. Henceforth English diplomatic efforts would focus heavily upon persuading the French to rescind the terms of the treaty.

The English resisted being provoked by the Scottish attack on Norham. Instead they took defensive precautions while seeking by negotiation to ensure that the Anglo-Scottish peace of 1323 was maintained. But this proved impossible. Robert Bruce, ailing though he was and little more than a year from death, was determined to exploit the fragility of the new regime in England, to draw from them a recognition of his right to the kingship of a wholly independent Scotland. To this end he descended upon Ireland around Easter 1327. Ireland remained unsettled and insecure – a considerable worry to the English. Bruce may also have calculated that government in England was being steered by a man – Roger Mortimer – whose landed interests in Ireland were extensive. Rumours abounded that Bruce sought to invade England from Ireland via Wales. In the event, his apparent attempt to build a joint Scottish–Irish–Welsh alliance against the Isabella--Mortimer regime foundered, and Bruce duly turned his attention to exerting pressure on the English directly – in Northumberland in the autumn. The opportunity for Bruce to do so was created, meanwhile, by the Weardale campaign of July–August 1327, in which the boy-king Edward III first experienced military action.

Anglo-Scottish negotiations having collapsed in June, with an impasse over Bruce's royal rights and Scottish independence, both the English and the Scots prepared for war. Edward III's army, nominally under the command of Henry of Lancaster but in practice commanded by Mortimer, mustered at York on 1 July but was delayed from departing for Scotland by serious disturbances – essentially xenophobic in character – between the king's Hainaulter mercenaries and his English archers. This delay allowed the Scots to invade England before the English could invade Scotland, and by mid-July the English were in pursuit of highly mobile and elusive Scottish raiding parties under the overall command of the formidable earl of Moray. A fortnight of fruitless searching in and around Weardale left the English and their horses exhausted, and they resolved instead to try to cut off the Scots' retreat home. The confident Scots now allowed themselves to be located, at Stanhope Park, and in early August the two armies confronted each other. A stalemate ensued, with the Scots in a very strong defensive position, and showing no inclination to mount a frontal attack on the English. Stalemate was broken temporarily on the night of 3–4 August, when a surprise Scots attack on the English camp led to heavy English casualties and the near-capture of the young king: Edward was left tangled in the remnants of his pavilion in the dark, when its guy ropes were cut by the marauding James Douglas. On 7 August, the English awoke at dawn to find that the Scots had outflanked them and slipped away in the night. The king is said to have wept tears of vexation.

No further pursuit was attempted, as the campaign had already exhausted the English Crown's coffers as well as its army and supplies. The government resolved to consider next steps at a Great Council at Lincoln on 15 September, but little more than a week after the Council commenced, Robert Bruce invaded Northumberland again, seemingly intent upon annexing that county to Scotland, which historically had claimed it. Norham Castle now fell, and Bruce was known to be granting extensive lands in Northumberland to his followers. Unable to respond militarily at this time, the English appointed negotiators to agree a final peace, which was formally approved at Edinburgh on 17 March and then at Northampton on 4 May. In the Treaty of Edinburgh–Northampton, Isabella and Mortimer essentially bought away the Scottish problem by abandoning the rights of both the English Crown and the Anglo-Scottish lords. Bruce was recognised as king of a fully independent Scotland, owing nothing – other than twenty thousand marks in war reparations, which were pocketed by Isabella and Mortimer – to the English king. Bruce's infant son and heir, the future King David II (1324–1371), was to be married to Edward III's sister, Joan of the Tower. Edward was so disgusted by the peace that he refused to attend the subsequent wedding. The Anglo-Scottish lords – who had crucially backed the Isabella–Mortimer invasion partly because of their great anger over the Anglo-Scottish peace of 1323 – now found themselves sold down the river for a second time. Although Robert Bruce made noises about considering their claims to lands in Scotland, he had already granted most of these lands to his followers and there was effectively no chance that restitution would be made. It was therefore for good reason that Henry of Lancaster, Thomas Wake, Henry Beaumont and many others – as well as King Edward – termed the treaty the 'shameful peace'. It represented a pragmatic betrayal of the realm on the part of Isabella and Mortimer, and from this point forward political collaboration between them and the Lancastrians essentially ceased. Conflict was quite quickly to ensue.

Plots to Free Edward II – and His Murder

Plots to release Edward II from captivity emerged as early as March 1327. They were essentially twofold: a cluster of schemes involving Dominican friars and other lesser clergy from Warwickshire, and another led by Rhys ap Gruffudd, a Welsh lord hostile to Roger Mortimer and now linked to the Bruce regime in Scotland. In both cases the leaders were close associates of the former king.

The clerical plotters were the brothers Thomas and Stephen Dunheved, the former a Dominican friar and the latter a valet, both lately in Edward II's household; two clergymen both called William Aylmer; and another

Dominican friar named John Stoke. These men and a wider group of alleged accomplices were suspected of plotting to release Edward from Kenilworth Castle in March and April, occasioning both Edward's removal from Kenilworth to the more remote Berkeley Castle, where Thomas Berkeley, a close Mortimer associate, now replaced Henry of Lancaster as Edward's custodian, and the issuing of commissions of inquiry and arrest to Lancaster and other commissioners. Edward's removal from Warwickshire to Gloucestershire evidently did not work, however, because at some point in early summer 1327 the same plotters penetrated Berkeley Castle and succeeded in temporarily releasing the former king from his cell. How and exactly when Edward was re-imprisoned and what happened to his would-be rescuers is uncertain, although it is clear that he *was* re-imprisoned, and that Thomas Dunheved was arrested and later died in captivity. From this point, Edward was regularly moved between Berkeley Castle and the royal castle of Corfe in Dorset, so that those seeking to release him could no longer be certain where he was located.

It was the second plot, led by Rhys ap Gruffudd, the Welsh lord and household esquire whom Edward II had vainly hoped would bring troops to his rescue in South Wales during the revolution in 1326–7, that unnerved Mortimer to such a degree that he ordered that the former king should be killed. Mortimer was warned about the plot by his deputy justiciar in North Wales, William Shalford, on 14 September 1327. Shalford, in seeming panic, urged Mortimer to take measures to ensure that the king might never be freed again. The plot was understood to be dangerous because of both its timing and the political position of its leader. It occurred at the height of the Scottish invasion scare, and Rhys ap Gruffudd was a substantial figure, loyal to Edward II and hostile towards Roger Mortimer. Rhys had recently accompanied Robert Bruce in Ireland, when the Scottish king was seeking afresh to build a pan-Celtic, anti-English alliance. It is no coincidence that another Welsh lord with a record of loyalty to Edward II and opposition to Mortimer, Gruffudd Llwyd, was arrested on suspicion at this time. Edward II's status was now being linked to wider political threats – both national and international in character.

Mortimer's response was decisive. He instructed his retainers Thomas Gurney and William Ockley to take 'speedy action to avoid greater danger'.

According to the chroniclers, on the night of 21 September, at Berkeley Castle, they smothered Edward under a huge weight of feather pillows, and then, to ensure that he was dead without leaving a mark on his body, inserted a red-hot iron into his intestines via a horn introduced into his rectum. So expired the former king, violently and alone, a victim of the broken politics that his own self-absorption, irresponsibility and cruelty as king had engendered. His son Edward III was informed of his death – nominally of natural causes – at Lincoln on the night of 23 September. The young king must surely have been distraught and perhaps suspicious, but immediate attention was now focused upon the urgently anticipated Scottish invasion of Northumberland. It was only after English envoys had met with the Scots to discover their proposed peace terms, in late October, that Edward II's body was moved to Gloucester for public display. He was buried, with great ceremony, in Gloucester Abbey (now Cathedral) on 20 December 1327, and in the 1330s a magnificent Gothic tomb was commissioned by Edward III to memorialise him.

In recent times Ian Mortimer and other historians have maintained that Edward II was not in fact murdered in 1327, but escaped before he could be killed. In this alternative account, Edward spent the next eighteen months at Corfe Castle and then nine months in Ireland, before travelling right across Europe – visiting the pope at Avignon en route – and finally becoming a hermit in northern Italy. The basis for the account is a letter, discovered in archives in France in the 1870s and written to Edward III in the 1330s by a high-ranking Italian cleric named Emanuele Fieschi. Fieschi claimed to have met Edward II in Italy, following the latter's alleged escape from his captors in England. The purpose of his letter to Edward III is unclear. It describes Edward II's apparent deeds and peregrinations at length, including details – for example, relating to his flight to Wales during the revolution in 1326–7 – that are probably correct, but others that are probably wrong.

The problems with this alternative fate of Edward II are manifold, but the most important are as follows. First, it was overwhelmingly agreed by contemporaries that Edward II had died in 1327. Second, the account in the Fieschi letter of Edward II's alleged adventures is inherently implausible, starting with his highly dubious eighteen-month sojourn, immediately post-escape, at the royal castle of Corfe. (Why would he go to Corfe, effectively straight back into the hands of his captors, and how did he remain there undetected and unrestrained for so long?) Third, the tale of his survival as a hermit abroad is part of a fantastical European tradition, stretching across many centuries, in which numerous monarchs and other celebrated individuals, the precise circumstances of whose deaths were uncertain, were reported to have lived on in obscurity. It is certainly true that, on the Continent in 1338, Edward III was introduced to a man named William Walsh who claimed to be his father. (This was not an unusual scenario in medieval Europe: Edward II had experienced something analogous in 1318, when John Powderham of Oxford had claimed to be the rightful king of England.) No action was taken against this presumably unfortunate and confused individual. It is possible that this was the same person whom Emanuele Fieschi had interviewed before writing his letter to Edward III, though there is no hard evidence of this.

Given the extraordinary circumstances of Edward II's death, it is unsurprising that his fate has been periodically questioned. But today, as in the late 1320s and 1330s, the evidence points strongly to his having died on 21 September 1327.

Political Conflict

The first eighteen months of Edward III's reign had witnessed considerable political collaboration, but the next two and a half years were characterised by political division – as the ambition, acquisitiveness and ruthlessness of Isabella and Mortimer took overt form. The consequences included political rebellion and local unrest, reminiscent of the dark days of Edward II and the Despensers. Nonetheless, Edward III – on the verge of adulthood, as was symbolised by his marriage to Philippa of Hainault, at York Minster on 26 January 1328 – was able steadily to build his own political platform. It was from this that the Nottingham coup of October 1330 was duly launched, ending the effective tyranny of Isabella and Mortimer and marking the beginning of his own, independent rule.

The turning point between collaboration and division was the summer of 1328, when Henry of Lancaster emerged as Mortimer's leading opponent. The cause of the shift was the 'shameful peace' of Edinburgh–Northampton, the terms of which were even less acceptable to the northern lords and the wider political community than those of the Anglo-Scottish truce of 1323. Since Mortimer's political rivals had moved into opposition, he no longer needed to keep them on side by exercising the political moderation that had characterised his behaviour in the first few months of Edward III's reign. Instead, he now compounded the grave foreign-policy error of Edinburgh–Northampton by celebrating his political and social ambitions in grand style. With open greed to match that of Isabella, he had himself granted vast lands, money and honours, additional to the substantial holdings already in his possession – including the Irish lordship of Trim, almost all the Arundel lands in the March of Wales, all the goods and chattels lately belonging to the earl of Arundel and Hugh Despenser the Younger in the same region, the justiciarship of Wales for life, an additional five hundred marks of annual income drawn from Wales 'for his labours serving the king', and, most dramatically, the title earl of March. This honour, granted in the Salisbury Parliament in October 1328, was unprecedented in England – where earldoms were traditionally named after counties. It reflected Mortimer's status as the greatest Marcher lord there had ever been, with Welsh lands surpassing even those assembled after Boroughbridge by an unconstrained Hugh Despenser the Younger. In public, Mortimer now arrogantly walked alongside, or even ahead of, the young king whose society and decision making he sought to dominate. The supposedly natural death of the hitherto strong and healthy Edward II in the autumn aroused widespread suspicion, and contemporaries began to speculate that Mortimer might seize the throne. It is no surprise that Mortimer's own son, Geoffrey Mortimer, referred to his father as the 'king of folly'.

Despite his offensive self-aggrandisement, high political moves against Mortimer proved abortive. Perhaps the rebellion led by Henry of Lancaster and supported by a coalition of great lords – including the king's uncles Edmund, earl of Kent and Thomas, earl of Norfolk – in the winter of 1328–9 came too soon, before the young king had established enough independence from Isabella and Mortimer to act other than as they advised. Lancaster had voiced his opposition to the government at a Council in

Worcester in June and had refused to attend a Great Council at York in July, from which point onwards his name ceased to be attached to royal charters. Tensions escalated dramatically on 15 October, when Robert Holland – the infamous former Lancastrian steward – was murdered in Essex on his way to meet his new patron, Isabella. His head was apparently sent by his killers to Henry of Lancaster. The following day, Lancaster and his right-hand man Thomas Wake refused to attend the Salisbury Parliament in protest at the failures of government. With the onset of winter, Mortimer's long-time ally Adam Orleton moved into opposition, and Wake presided over meetings in London in which Lancaster's rebellious coalition was assembled. Meanwhile the court retreated to Mortimer's power base on the Welsh borders, where Isabella and Mortimer evidently prepared a bold response. When Lancaster advanced on London from his heartland of Leicester in January 1328, their forces seized and sacked his Midlands estates, and shortly thereafter Kent and Norfolk returned to the court, presumably having been persuaded by Mortimer. Lancaster, who had advanced from London to Bedford, had no choice but to surrender as his army melted away. In February he and Wake were obliged to deliver bonds of £30,000 and £15,000 respectively for the return of their confiscated lands, and their allies Henry Beaumont and William Trussell were forced into exile, accused of complicity in the Holland murder. The northern lords had been comprehensively outmanoeuvred – for the moment.

Trouble was next manifested in the localities. The approach of Isabella and Mortimer to justice had hitherto been largely reactive. Many special oyer and terminer commissions had been issued in response to judicial petitions, especially during Parliaments, and this continued in the autumn of 1328. Tellingly, the government now also ordained commissions of inquiry into conspiracies – including in London, where Lancaster's rebel alliance had been built – and repeatedly reissued peace commissions. Royal appointments were dominated by Mortimer associates. Isabella and Mortimer were clearly worried about resistance in the country.

The legal records offer the historian intriguing – because inconclusive – insight into the progression of the political struggle between Isabella, Mortimer and Lancaster at this time. From early May until late July 1329 Lancaster secured a large number of judicial commissions into incursions into his lands, especially in Staffordshire, Derbyshire and Lancashire. This indicates either that partisans of Isabella and Mortimer were still attacking the Lancastrian estates, or that Lancaster was now seeking judicial retribution in respect of the plundering his lands had suffered during his recent rebellion. What is unarguable is that Lancaster had already recovered sufficient sway within royal government – presumably with the king or his close associates – to be able to obtain the judicial commissions he wanted. Indeed, Isabella and Mortimer were obliged to issue general pardons to many of their partisans to protect them against prospective prosecutions. Lancaster received a number of other royal grants and licences, and in September a letter of legal protection while going overseas on a diplomatic mission that was to keep him away from England until the spring of 1330. On this assignment he was accompanied by Edward III's confidant William Montagu, whose influence in government at this juncture the records make very clear. It was during the same period that another of Edward's most trusted men, Richard Bury, agreed with the pope that letters from Edward III would indicate the king's personal wishes – as opposed to those ascribed to him by Isabella and Mortimer – when they included the code 'holy father' (*pater sancte*) – written in the king's own hand. Evidently, Edward was now significantly asserting himself, and this included affirming his political relationship with the Lancastrians. The contrast between the diplomatic personnel despatched in the autumn of 1329 and those who had accompanied the king to Amiens to do homage for Aquitaine to the new French king, Philip VI, in June is striking. Montagu had been present then, but so had Mortimer's spies, John Maltravers and Hugh Turplington.

If anything signified a shifting political order as the end of 1329 approached, it was a series of judicial commissions issued into attacks on the lands of Isabella and Mortimer in the late summer and autumn – in Wales, Gloucestershire, Somerset, Surrey, Berkshire and the Isle of Wight. There are other indicators that order in the country may have been breaking down more widely, including an effort to restart the general eyre (the Crown's most powerful local judicial commission, suspended nationally since 1294) in Northamptonshire and Nottinghamshire in August 1329 – an endeavour repeated a year later in Bedfordshire and Derbyshire. Isabella and Mortimer were evidently now the targets of local insurgency in a way they had not been since the revolution. The timing of the attacks on their holdings implies a link to high politics, though there is no hard evidence that Henry of Lancaster lay behind them. It could be that, for the first time, a sense was emerging in the country of their vulnerability, which emboldened those who opposed or resented their immense landed acquisitions. The parallel with the local assaults mounted from 1322 on the lands seized by the Despensers is obvious. A sense that power was starting to slip away from them, combined with their inclination to act boldly, perhaps explains the extraordinary plot they now initiated to entrap and intimidate their enemies.

The Earl of Kent's Conspiracy and the Nottingham Coup

In late 1329, rumours began to circulate that Edward II had not in fact died, but remained alive and in captivity. The archbishop of York was one of the people who believed these rumours, and so was Edmund, earl of Kent, the late king's brother. Whether Isabella and Mortimer initiated the rumours, or whether they merely responded creatively to rumours that had naturally emerged as their political power began to decline, we cannot know. But on the basis of the chronicle and parliamentary evidence, it seems likely that, early in 1330, Kent was actively duped into believing his brother remained alive. He may also have found himself subject to approaches from other anti-Mortimer conspirators. Kent certainly sent a letter to Corfe Castle, addressed to the former Edward II, encouraging him to be of good cheer as he was going to be rescued. Arrested by Mortimer at the Winchester Parliament in March, Kent sensationally confessed all – blaming a devil for having seduced him – and was convicted of treason against Edward III. He was beheaded on 19 March, after a day's wait in his shirtsleeves while an executioner was, with great difficulty, enlisted. No one wanted Kent's blood on his hands, and in the end, only a condemned felon was willing to accept the job, in return for escaping the noose.

While it seems doubtful that the hapless and ineffectual Kent was actually at the centre of a grand plot against Isabella and Mortimer, the two rapidly made intimidating accusations against a plethora of actual or perceived enemies, via multiple commissions of inquiry into conspiracies and rebellions issued between March and August 1330. This sustained judicial assault on their opponents is starkly reminiscent of the end-of-days paranoia displayed by Edward II and the Despensers in 1325–6. Alleged adherents of the earl of Kent were sought everywhere, and a number of leading political figures were forced to flee the realm and had their lands seized, including Rhys ap Gruffudd, Richard Fitzalan, the heir to the last earl of Arundel – who had been executed on Mortimer's orders in 1326 – and Thomas Wake, Kent's brother-in-law. Wake joined his fellow Anglo-Scottish lord, Henry Beaumont, overseas. Whether or not a conspiracy to invade England and oust Isabella and Mortimer had existed before March 1330, one certainly emerged now, as men hostile to the regime found themselves together in exile. In July, the duke of Brabant warned the English government that conspirators had gathered in his duchy with the intention of descending on England and attacking Mortimer's lands. The extent to which Kent's fate had caused outrage is indicated by a government order issued in Wales in April, mandating punishment for all those who said that Kent had been killed 'other than for treason and evil-doing, or that Edward II [was] still alive'. But the outrage in the country did not stop Isabella, Mortimer and their associates from shamelessly grabbing for themselves Kent's confiscated lands, which can only have exacerbated the hostility they faced.

In September 1330, the court relocated to Nottingham, whose great royal castle had been a favoured haunt of Isabella and Mortimer since 1327, with a view to a Great Council being summoned there in October to discuss the ongoing problem of Aquitaine. By this time, however, Edward III – who on 15 June had become father to a strong and healthy heir to the throne, Prince Edward, known to posterity as the Black Prince – was ready to take decisive action against his mother and her partner. The revolution they had led in 1326–7 against Edward II and the Despensers had been prompted by many factors: severe foreign-policy failure in Aquitaine and Scotland, the betrayal of the Anglo-Scottish lords, outrageous greed and the illegal or semi-legal appropriation of land on a vast scale, the domination of the March of Wales by one rapacious lord, the hijacking of the judicial system for partisan purposes, and the execution and disinheritance of great nobles. All these offences had been repeated by Isabella and Mortimer across the intervening four years, in some cases *a fortiori*. Likewise, the low-level insurrection in the country that had been a consequence of the Edward–Despenser tyranny had essentially re-emerged by the end of 1328. The realm desperately needed legitimate, authoritative and effective rule in the non-partisan interests of the Crown and people. Only good and unfettered kingship could now provide this. Moreover, Mortimer's ruthless despatch of Kent had shown, had it not already been evident, what the man was capable of; and, cornered as he now arguably was, and increasingly afraid when in Edward III's physical proximity, he represented an active danger to the king. As William Montagu reportedly remarked to Edward, 'It is better to eat the dog than have the dog eat you.'

With the tacit backing of Henry of Lancaster – billeted, like Edward's household knights and yeomen, in the town not the castle of Nottingham, at Mortimer's apprehensive insistence – Edward plotted boldly and secretly to outflank Mortimer's numerous court followers and seize their lord in what we would now term a special-forces operation. Assisted and encouraged by his household bannerets William Montagu, William Clinton, Robert Ufford, Edward Bohun and John Neville of Hornsby, together with other, more junior household men such as Thomas Bradeston and John Molyns, Edward arranged that, on 19 October, his personal retinue would be seen riding away from the castle but would return under cover of darkness clandestinely to penetrate the fortress via a secret passage – which survives today – leading from the cliffs beneath the castle walls to the dungeon area. The fifteen or so heavily armed men under Edward's captaincy were guided through the passage and up to the royal chambers (where Mortimer was meeting with his principal counsellors) by William Eland, who was responsible for the castle's fabric and knew its layout intimately. Once outside the royal chambers they rendezvoused with the king, who then directed their assault on Mortimer and his men from the safety of the rear: protecting the king was essential if the coup were to be successful. In the sudden assault, Hugh Turplington and two of Mortimer's other retainers were slain; Turplington was killed with a mace, at the hands of John Neville, albeit Montagu, Clinton and the others also duly received pardons for his death; and although Mortimer hid behind a curtain, he was quickly discovered and arrested, together with his surviving confidants.

Queen Isabella, who instinctively knew her son commanded the coup, but who could not see him from within her chamber, apparently cried out, 'Fair son, have pity on noble Mortimer.' For the king's enemy, as he was now described, no pity was afforded and none was deserved. Instead, in the morning, Henry of Lancaster broadcast the happy news of the revolution, and the king and his retainers embarked for London with their prisoners, having first carefully apprised the sheriffs of every county of what had occurred. Two days later, after overnight sojourns at Castle Donington and Lancaster's principal seat of Leicester, Edward III arrived at Westminster – and his rule proper began.

Internal Challenges and External Needs

The Nottingham coup cleanly and definitively ended the misrule of Isabella and Mortimer. By courageous, cool-headed and decisive action, Edward III, still not yet eighteen, had resolved the immediate problem bedevilling the polity. But its resolution merely brought to the fore the deeper problems – internal and external – that had afflicted the realm since 1307, and which Isabella and Mortimer had seriously exacerbated. These needed prompt attention. This the king determinedly gave them – while proceeding consultatively, and tempering with appropriate moderation his inclination to work at pace.

Where internal rule was concerned, Edward first needed formally to draw a line under the Isabella and Mortimer regime and its actions, while simultaneously allowing his mother the space to be politically rehabilitated in due course. This would enable Edward to continue to have the close relationship with her that was clearly important to him and would permit her to re-enter the court, where her contacts, experience and intelligence had been so useful in the past in respect of international relations. In addition to rehabilitating Isabella, he needed to lead a wider process of political reconciliation – contrasting with the political vengeance wreaked by Edward II and the Despensers in 1322–6, and Isabella and Mortimer in 1326–30 – so that leading figures from all the great political families of England could be reincorporated into the political community, and their historical landed inheritances largely restored. This was likely, in turn, to make repairing the socio-political fabric in the localities more achievable, with positive knock-on effects in respect of order and justice. Where the latter was concerned, judicial commissions needed to be provided to deal with great and persistent unrest in the country, especially in the Midlands, which the government records indicate were especially disordered. This disorder was consequent upon the myriad failures of England's political leaders since 1307, which had led to highly damaging feuds and warfare across the localities. Finally, the royal finances – reduced almost to nothing by the sustained depredations of Isabella and Mortimer – needed to be protected and ideally rebuilt.

The realm's external needs were arguably even more pressing. Both the Treaty of Paris of 1327 and the 'shameful peace' of Edinburgh–Northampton of 1328 had left English interests and allies very seriously undermined, and it was self-evident to contemporaries that neither could be allowed to stand in the medium term. In both cases a heady mix of Crown 'rights' and practical politics was involved in a dispute that was technically over sovereignty and jurisdiction, but was really about geo-political power, national integrity and local rivalry.

In France, the accession of Philip Valois as King Philip VI in 1328 had supercharged an already forward and insistent French approach, akin to that seen in the 1290s, which had re-emerged with the accession of Philip's predecessor, Charles IV, in 1322. While Charles had shown patience with the English during the Saint-Sardos crisis, under his kingship the arch-champion of French royal rights, Charles Valois, had reattained prominence and influence in government, following a period of détente in Anglo-French relations that was not to Valois's taste. Philip VI was Charles Valois's son and inherited his father's perspectives. Where French royal rights were concerned, there could be no compromise: the French king was the greatest Christian monarch and it was therefore right that he should exercise sovereignty effectively without restriction wherever he was suzerain or overlord – including in Aquitaine. The English Crown's repeated attempts to renegotiate the 1259 Treaty of Paris, in which the English had conceded French overlordship over Aquitaine, were offensive. The French government must insist upon its rights and should wherever possible seek to extend its practical, day-to-day hold on the duchy, as had been done in 1324–5 – with justice on the French side – and 1327. In diplomacy over Aquitaine, the French king's overlordship over the English king-duke meant that the latter should be treated as a vassal rather than an equal, and that disputes should be settled by French adjudication, not negotiation. Even had Philip wished to adopt a less inflexible stance over Aquitaine – and, indeed, other aspects of international relations – he would have been hard pressed to do so. This was because his accession to the French throne, in 1328, had not been uncontroversial. His claim, via a cadet line as nephew of Philip IV, was not especially strong, and he had acceded to the throne primarily by effective political positioning upon the death of Charles IV, and because the alternatives – one of whom was the young Edward III, a direct descendant of Philip IV via Isabella, the French king's daughter – were politically compromised. Philip was seen as a safe pair of hands. But in practice his relatively marginal legitimacy weakened his authority as king, and he was consequently forced to take a very robust line where French interests were concerned or risk being accused of betraying the French Crown. In other words, his power within the French polity was limited, and this meant that he was captive to a bellicose foreign policy (of which he happened to be the lineal heir) deemed by the polity, whether wisely or not, to signify strong and appropriate French kingship.

Philip also lacked the political intelligence (though in certain respects he was no idiot) to be able to manage events, the French court, and French nobles and officials in such a way as to build political capital and create room for manoeuvre. In short, inflexibility in respect of the English was something he was essentially stuck with. In the list of causes of the Hundred Years' War, Philip VI's enforced inflexibility born of French exceptionalism – combined with a tendency to bombast and overconfidence in his dealings with his international neighbours – looms large. The French king's situation and stance meant that improving the Anglo-Gascon position in the south-west of France was going to be very challenging for Edward III.

Where Scotland was concerned, the challenge was more practical than theoretical. Although abandoned royal rights – English sovereignty via overlordship over Scotland – were a real issue, they were arguably less fundamental than the visceral reality that a murdering usurper, Robert Bruce, had been formally recognised by the English as the rightful king of Scotland, and that, in the recognition, the English had simultaneously abandoned their anti-Bruce Scottish allies, as well as the land rights of the 'disinherited' Anglo-Scottish lords who had formed such an important political grouping in English politics since 1322. Although the great and terrifying Bruce had died in 1329, to be succeeded by an infant son, David II, Bruce's formidable right-hand man Thomas Randolph, earl of Moray had immediately been installed as guardian of Scotland. Whereas in Aquitaine the English had generally been able militarily to hold their own against the French, even while losing territory, in Scotland they had been repeatedly and disastrously routed by Moray. So while it was evident to the English that it was their responsibility to reassert the primacy established by Edward I in their relationship with the Scots, how and when they should seek to do so was much less clear: great risk was potentially involved. A political opening had to be awaited.

The Post-Coup Parliament and the French Threat to Aquitaine

That Edward – despite his youth – hit the ground running as an independent ruler is strongly evidenced by proceedings in the Parliament of November 1330. Although the hand of Henry of Lancaster can arguably be seen in some of the Parliament's provisions – those relating to his rebellion in 1328–9, for instance – it is the king's voice that speaks most clearly through the records.

Parliament first tried and condemned Mortimer. He was deemed 'notorious' and was therefore not permitted to speak at his trial, though he was reported to have admitted that the earl of Kent had been wrongfully killed. The key charges against him were that he had usurped the royal power, had had Edward II murdered, had entrapped and executed Kent, knowing all along that Edward II was dead, had sown discord between the former king and his wife, Isabella, and had plundered the realm of lands, money and treasure. Convicted of treason, felony and evil-doing, Mortimer was promptly hanged on the common gallows at Tyburn. His close associate Simon Beresford was similarly convicted and executed. Also condemned in Parliament were John Maltravers and certain others involved in the killings of Edward II and Kent, but this group had all fled – several, including Maltravers, apparently escaping overseas via the tiny Cornish port of Mousehole – on hearing of the Nottingham coup. Rewards were offered for their capture – or their heads. In the end only Maltravers was pardoned and permitted to return to England – in 1351, after years in which, of his own volition, he had laboured to advance the king's diplomatic interests in the Low Countries, where he had taken exile. The others died in obscurity. Thomas Berkeley, the Mortimer associate in whose castle Edward II had died, was tried by twelve experienced knights and found not guilty of the former king's death. He may have been accorded more generous treatment than the others because his relationship with Mortimer had been less close and because his younger brother, Maurice Berkeley, was a household knight who had fought for the king in the recent coup. That other close Mortimer associate Oliver Ingham, who had served with such distinction in Gascony in 1325–7, was rapidly pardoned and reappointed as seneschal of Aquitaine. Edward recognised that he was guilty primarily of being a loyal government servant. It was characteristic of the king's political intelligence to see the benefit of retaining, rather than punishing, Ingham – who was to perform brilliantly in the duchy for another twelve years: his ability to manage Gascon political relationships well and thereby mount a stout defence against the French, despite thin resources, essentially sustained the Anglo-Gascon position in the duchy until a substantial army could be sent there from England in the mid-1340s. Isabella was deprived of her recently acquired lands, had her income drastically cut to a level congruent with the status of a dowager queen, and was placed under loose house arrest at Berkhamsted Castle. But she was back in the court by Christmas, was released from supervision in 1332 and assumed the life of a normal dowager queen – comfortably flitting between her main residence of Castle Rising in Norfolk and the court in London, where her advice remained highly valued.

Reconciliation was the order of the day in the November Parliament more generally, though with a twist that we now recognise as classic Edward III. Lancaster, Kent and their actual or alleged adherents were all pardoned for their rebellions in 1328–30 and had their estates restored, so far as doing so suited the king's purposes. (The great Marcher lordship of

Denbigh, for example, to which Lancaster could conceivably have mounted a claim, was reserved for William Montagu as a thank-you, approved by Parliament, for his service in leading the king's soldiers at the Nottingham coup.) Richard Fitzalan, the *de jure* earl of Arundel, saw the 1326 verdict on his father overturned (as contrary to Magna Carta) and his ancient lands accordingly restored. The Londoners, burdened by Mortimer's judicial inquiries following Lancaster's rebellion, saw the proceedings against them ended. But Arundel was expressly forbidden from seeking vengeance against John Charlton, who had arrested his father in 1326; Charlton in turn was ordered – together with his opponent Gruffudd de la Pole – to end their long-standing and destructive dispute over Powys; and the Londoners were strictly instructed not to pursue justices or jurors who had brought in verdicts to their detriment. Here was Edward III's authentic voice: the king listens; the king gives; but the king also requires – in the interests of the common good. Edward was pursuing a policy not just of mercy and rehabilitation, but also of universal reconciliation – which was demanded, not just enjoined. Equally authentic was Edward's transparent and self-effacing reference to his conscience, when Parliament agreed to his reducing the sum – from £50,000 to £5,000 – required of Eleanor Clare, the widow of Hugh Despenser the Younger, to purchase re-entry to her former lands of Glamorgan and Morgannwg. Throughout his reign, his conscience was something to which the king would repeatedly refer when communicating decisions to his people, especially when he was unveiling a change of mind.

The final major commitment Edward made in the November Parliament was to justice and the preservation of order. Having invited and heard petitions seeking judicial redress and amendment, Edward determined to end the recent and retrograde reintroduction of the long-absent general eyre. Instead he replaced all sheriffs and ordained trailbastons, or general oyer and terminer commissions, to inquire nationally into oppressions against his people since 1307 – the last time a regime committed to justice had held sway in England. Altogether, the manifesto shared by the king with his people in the November Parliament was strikingly mature and assertive.

When Edward III had performed homage for Aquitaine to the new French king, Philip VI, at Amiens in June 1329, he had performed only simple homage, not the liege homage – involving swearing an oath of fealty to the French king – which Philip, ever his father's son, had demanded. Philip was dissatisfied by this and chose, as the king-duke's overlord, to set a series of deadlines for liege homage to be completed. The English, who disputed the necessity to perform liege homage under the terms of the Treaty of Paris of 1259, dragged their feet and the deadlines passed. So Philip decided to increase the pressure. At the beginning of 1331 he accordingly despatched an army – under his brother, Charles, count of Alençon – to re-invade and confiscate the duchy. The invasion may also have been a response to the Nottingham coup, reflecting a recognition on the part of the French that, in the near future, England was likely to become a much more formidable opponent than had been the case for many years. In short, this was the moment for the French to strike. Attacking the duchy's north-western approaches, Alençon quickly took and sacked Saintes, the capital of Saintonge.

Philip's stratagem worked. Newly established in power and with empty coffers, Edward was in no position to resist – certainly not at this juncture. He responded in March by writing to Philip to concede that the homage he had performed in June 1329 should be considered to have been liege, not simple, and to agree to meet with Philip in France to confirm the matter, though on the condition that the meeting should be kept secret. He then travelled to France incognito, disguised as a merchant, in April, and he and Philip had a positive encounter at the French king's hunting lodge of Saint-Christophe. Philip did not insist on the act of liege homage being physically performed, and agreed to pay reparations for the destruction of Saintes, which he advised he had not authorised. Justice would be done, he said, in respect of the Agenais and the other lands that the French retained following the War of Saint-Sardos. Edward declared his willingness in principle to accompany Philip on a crusade to the Holy Land. After Edward had completed further discussions in England, including in Parliament in September, he resolved to seek a solution to the Gascon problem by further negotiation, through the 'process' (or negotiation) of Agen – named after the capital town of the Agenais, where the diplomacy would be conducted. Although events would prove the process of Agen a blind alley – because the aims of the English and French were fundamentally incompatible, and because Philip, ultimately, did not really want a settlement – conflict in Aquitaine was effectively put on hold until the later 1330s.

The New Nobility

Edward's decisions to seek diplomatic solutions in south-west France and behave cautiously in respect of the Scottish question allowed the king space, in the first two years of his personal rule, to establish not only new working relationships with individual great lords and their families – whose dealings with the Crown had latterly been so troubled, in many cases – but also a novel and radical paradigm for how government and the nobility should work together. This was an important aspect of state growth.

From late 1330, by melding established nobles with other men of high ability whom he ennobled, Edward rapidly created a service nobility in his own image and employed them to deliver his rule. By this means he was able to harness – as never before – private landholding and socio-political networks to the government's purposes. Royal patronage was boldly leveraged to increase the Crown's capabilities both internally against disorder and externally against foreign enemies. Talented and ambitious men saw their personal stock and status rise (though not necessarily their wealth, as serving the king was an expensive business), and identified with duty and travail for the king and the common good.

While previous kings – such as Edward's admired grandfather, Edward I – had enjoyed political success by ruling *with* the nobility, Edward III ruled *through* his nobles. What was the difference? The king ruling with the nobility involved nobles at the political centre enjoying ready and appropriate access to the king so they could provide him with counsel. In the localities their social networks, based upon their landholding, generally supported royal government by providing enforcement to underwrite the operation of the common law. Individual great lords served the king as military commanders and diplomats, and were occasionally commissioned to deal with particular tasks in the shires. Edward III took this much further. He ruled through the nobles in that he overtly shaped the nobility as government agents. Under his clear direction, they were given considerable military and diplomatic responsibility as his formally contracted lieutenants, and were systematically charged, as royal officers, with delivering key dimensions of his internal rule in localities or regions where they already held significant lands, or where Edward positioned them among the landed elite. He did the latter either by restoring former magnates to lands their families had forfeited, or by promoting talented and trusted new men to the ranks of the nobility through the grant of lordships, manors or marriage, sometimes supplemented by financial grants.

Where ancient houses were established in a locality or could be re-established through restoration, ruling through them was Edward's favoured modus operandi. Deep-rooted local socio-political networks, headed by established lords, could be hitched to the delivery of the king's rule. Excellent examples of nobles restored by Edward are Richard Fitzalan, whom he restored to the earldom of Arundel in 1331, and Roger Mortimer, grandson of the Roger Mortimer executed by Edward in 1330, whom the king restored to the earldom of March in 1354. Both played key roles in his government. Arundel, for example, quickly reactivated his family's historical connections with Welsh political society, with positive results for order in both Wales and the neighbouring March. He was also a highly effective financier and logistician, and a trusted diplomat. In the 1350s the young earl of March emerged as an outstanding military commander and in Wales was praised for his political wisdom by Iolo Goch. Where there was a dearth of high-level local socio-political leadership, however, highly able and meritorious individuals well known to the king could be endowed in a locality as his favoured men. While the monarch endowing new men in a locality could sometimes generate local friction, witnessed in the early 1330s by attacks on the lands of William Clinton in Kent, overall, it was a highly successful way of providing local leadership to implement and support royal rule.

Edward's radicalism regarding government and the nobles was rooted in the politics of the 1320s in several ways. First, in the late 1320s he had built around himself a cohort of highly able and trustworthy men, the group – visible in the surviving government records – that enabled the king to establish and maintain his own political space amid the noble rivalry and rancour of 1326–30. It comprised knights and yeoman from a diver-sity of backgrounds, who acted with true unity under the king's leadership, as exemplified by the Nottingham coup. The coup and the team that delivered it – which included scions of ancient noble houses such as Edward Bohun and Maurice Berkeley – were definitive in that they provided a model for how Edward might tackle the wider challenges of royal rule he was destined to face. When he was confronted by bigger and more complex governmental problems, his natural response from November 1330 was to forge a bigger and more diversely talented team, central to which, in a hierarchical world, were members of the nobility – whether hereditary or created. In short, Edward's formative political experience led him to embrace and own the nobility as a dimension of his government, rather than merely recognising and accepting them as arguably the most important element in political society.

Second, Edward was lucky in that noble fatalities and confiscations since 1322 both cleared space in the polity into which gifted and hard-working men could be promoted, and left in his hands a much greater stock of patronage, especially in respect of land, marriages and wardships, than was ordinarily the case. This was used to endow and support the newly promoted. In other words, he arguably had more scope to take radical action in respect of the nobility than any of his predecessors since the Conqueror. As he put it when he raised a cadre of men to a dukedom and a clutch of earldoms in 1337, nobility in England had been unusually depleted, allowing and demanding that he replenish it.

Finally, his personal political stock was high, which further permitted radicalism. This was partly a consequence of Edward's own deeds: the lightning strike of the Nottingham coup; the political maturity, leadership and deftness of touch he demonstrated in its aftermath; and the martial success he was shortly to enjoy. But it also concerned his political inheritance. Historians once argued that Edward III had to tread very carefully because of the gross errors of his immediate political predecessors. But this is to misread politics and collective psychology. On the contrary, Edward's rule was such a manifest and dramatic improvement on that of his father, Isabella and Mortimer that he was naturally cut considerable political slack: caution was not something he especially needed to exercise.

In short, Edward ruled through nobles – established or newly made – whose ability and trustworthiness he rated. He was also a loyal man, which meant that those who had served him well earned political credit that tended to endure, though not without qualification. One of the things that is so striking about his management of the nobility is that he regularly renewed his team, repositioning or resting men in whom he had placed great trust but whose records of delivery were clouded, and replacing them in the governmental front line with new men of high talent. Perhaps the best example of this is the supplanting in military command of William Montagu by William Bohun in the early 1340s, only for Bohun to be supplanted in turn by Thomas Dagworth and Roger Mortimer in the late 1340s and 1350s. First Montagu and then Bohun, despite their undoubted talents, eventually disappointed the king in the field. (A modern analogy would be Churchill's replacement of Auchinleck by Montgomery in the Western Desert in 1942.) The king's practice of active team renewal goes some way to explaining the unprecedented scale on which he raised men to the ranks of the nobility. It has been estimated that, over the course of his reign, Edward granted some 140 men noble status – defined by their receiving the title of duke or earl, or being summoned to Parliament in their own name among the Lords (as distinct from the shire representatives who constituted the Commons). Among the sons of established houses in whom he placed the greatest trust across his long reign were Henry of Grosmont, son of Henry of Lancaster and later duke of Lancaster (1310–1361), Thomas Beauchamp, earl of Warwick (1314–1369), Richard Fitzalan, earl of Arundel (1313–1376), William Bohun, earl of Northampton (1312–1360) and Roger Mortimer, earl of March (1328–1360). Edward actively shaped even this hereditary group of nobles: Grosmont and Bohun were raised to earldoms when the heads of their great houses – Henry of Lancaster and Humphrey Bohun – were prevented from playing an active political role from the early 1330s by progressive blindness and physical disability respectively; and the king restored Arundel and March after their families were disinherited. Favoured household knights raised to the highest noble status included William Montagu, earl of Salisbury (1301–1344), William Clinton, earl of Huntingdon (d. 1354) and Robert Ufford, earl of Suffolk (1298–1369). All were essentially gentry. Walter, Lord Mauny (1310–1372) was of humbler status still, having arrived at court from Hainault as a page in Queen Philippa's household. Broadly, such new men were as pre-eminent among Edward III's most extensively employed nobles as were hereditary magnates such as Warwick and Arundel. Edward clearly regarded all his nobles as one another's equals and allocated them responsibilities according to their individual abilities and skills, not their backgrounds – albeit he ordinarily appointed them to local commissions only in counties where they held land, as he sought wherever possible to marry royal appointment to the realities of local power and status. To the ranks of the hereditary and promoted men the king was in due course to add his most capable sons: Edward of Woodstock, the Black Prince (1330–1376); Lionel of Antwerp, duke of Clarence (1338–1368); and John of Gaunt, duke of Lancaster (1340–1399). A tier below these magnates in status, but just as vital to the delivery of Edward's rule, were court-based soldier-administrators such as Oliver Ingham (1287–1344), Thomas Ughtred (1291–1365), Bartholomew Burghersh (d. 1355), Reginald Cobham (1295–1361) and Guy Brian (1310–1390).

Edward typically employed his nobles in central government office (on the king's Council or as steward of the household, for example), in war and diplomacy (as theatre or divisional commanders, or as negotiators), and in all manner of local offices in the shires, Wales and Ireland. He often clustered local offices in the hands of a single individual to whom he was close, especially where that individual was able to draw on their local sociopolitical networks to gather information and provide enforcement.

Securing Wales was vital, after the turmoil caused by Edward II, the Despensers and Roger Mortimer, and against a background of hostile Scottish and French invasion plans; and Edward III's appointment of Arundel to a raft of interlocking offices in Wales and neighbouring Shropshire, underpinned by the addition of the Marcher lordships of Chirkland (1334) and Bromfield and Yale (1347) to the earl's ancient Marcher holdings of Clun and Oswestry (restored in 1330–1), was inspired. Arundel witnessed more royal charters than any other magnate during Edward's reign: he was very frequently with the king, to whom, of course, he owed his restoration. But he was also regularly present and extensively networked in Wales, Shropshire and the March, and was highly attentive to the needs of a region that was his family's historical power base. Surviving letters show that his understanding of Welsh society and politics was deep and nuanced. Having such a man as justiciar of North Wales and constable of Caernarfon Castle, justice and overseer of the peace in Shropshire, and life-sheriff of the same county gave the king direct access to local rule via an agent whom he rightly trusted but who was personally and immediately answerable to him – as was shown in the 1340s when the king's sergeants-at-arms, Edward's bodyguard, twice arrested Arundel's deputies and associates for alleged failures of duty. It also meant that the same royal agent presided over neighbouring though technically separate territories, which must have facilitated effective cross-border action against disorder: disruptive elements could not so easily take refuge in Wales or the March from the peace officers of Shropshire, or vice versa, because Arundel presided in all three jurisdictions.

Likewise, William Clinton was Edward's maid-of-all-work in strategically crucial Kent from 1331, receiving local offices of remarkable scope and extent, including the wardenship of the Cinque Ports and the constableship of Dover Castle, shrewdly interfaced with the admiralship of the west and a plethora of judicial, military and tax commissions. Clinton was accordingly burdened by an extraordinary amount of royal administration – sometimes thanklessly. In 1334 and 1335, for instance, the king wrote to him concerning a large fine levied in Kent, upbraiding him for his alleged 'lukewarmness and negligence' in collecting it. If the overdue sum was not immediately produced, Edward avowed, it would be levied in its entirety on Clinton's own goods and chattels. Nicholas, Lord Cantilupe (1301–1355) was one of the greatest landholders in the north-east Midlands, but in the late 1330s and 1340s he received so many royal judicial commissions in the region that he was to all intents and purposes a professional justice.

While the careers in royal service of Arundel, Clinton and Cantilupe reflect the typical core-noble pattern in that they also served the king extensively in war and diplomacy, and as counsellors, this should not mislead us into thinking that the king was undiscriminating in how he deployed people: not everyone did everything. We have already remarked upon the king's inclination regularly to refresh his noble team. He was also alert to his nobles' relative strengths and weaknesses. Arundel was one of the great men of business of his age but proved an unexceptional soldier. Accordingly, while the earl served on campaign whenever he was needed, as a second-tier commander, Edward used him in war primarily to head the home government in his absence, and to manage supply and logistics. In this Arundel was frequently accompanied by Clinton, whose greatest strengths were similarly administrative, though he also developed considerable diplomatic and naval expertise – hence his regular appointment to embassies and as an admiral. Cantilupe's regional and legal knowledge made him a natural judge in the north-east Midlands where his lands lay. John de Vere, earl of Oxford (1312–1360), on the other hand, was a willing but journeyman warrior, who served the king regularly in war but never saw an independent military command and was rarely used as an administrator or justice. Oxford may have been typical of the wider nobility, beyond the highly capable core: so far as the generality of nobles was concerned, Edward expected them to serve in war for the safety of the realm (as he put it), and took a distinctly dim view if they behaved sluggishly in this regard; but not all nobles served at the governmental centre, or received diplomatic or local commissions – only those whose capability and temperament suited them to the tasks.

Edward III's positive relations with his nobility stood in stark contrast to those of his predecessor and successor. During his reign the political community engaged together in international war on an unprecedented scale, the Second War of Scottish Independence from 1332 flowing seamlessly into the Hundred Years' War from 1337. Even during a nine-year hiatus in the Hundred Years' War, following the Treaty of Brétigny–Calais of 1360, English nobles continued to fight overseas – now in Spain under Edward's talented and charismatic son and heir, the Black Prince. This continual joint enterprise, together with Edward's celebrated chivalry – epitomised by his foundation of the Order of the Garter – and elaborate court celebrations, has led historians to characterise the king's dealings with the nobility as clubbable and even pliant. This is significantly to misunderstand Edward's character, the nature of the political community and the gravity of the political demands they faced together. Relations between Edward and his nobles were indeed good, but they were not straightforward. The king was an appealing and cordial character but he was also serious, determined, obsessive and at times ruthless. Working under his direct leadership – as the core nobles did – was exhilarating but could be burdensome, exhausting, dangerous and costly. This may be illustrated by briefly examining the career of one of Edward's most favoured noble lieutenants, William Montagu, earl of Salisbury.

Montagu was as personally close to the king in the 1330s as any noble other than the king's kinsman Henry of Grosmont. As we have seen, his pivotal role in the Nottingham coup resulted in his receiving the Marcher lordship of Denbigh together with £1,000 per year in land in England. In 1331 he was commissioned as a diplomat, worked extensively in central government and arranged a great tournament at Cheapside. In 1332 he was appointed to the peace commission in his home county of Somerset. From 1333 he was heavily committed to war against the Scots, which resulted in his receiving further extensive grants of land but also losing an eye on campaign and seeing his reputation as a commander tarnished by his failure at the siege of Dunbar in 1338. Meanwhile he received commissions in the Channel Islands and the royal palatinate of Chester, and was appointed to a number of fresh embassies. In 1337 he was raised to the earldom of Salisbury in anticipation of a continental campaign against the French that required greater comital representation among England's leading commanders. But he erred in command again outside the walls of Lille in April 1340, being needlessly captured alongside Robert Ufford, earl of Suffolk – with the result that, wounded, he suffered hard and close imprisonment in Paris at the hands of Philip VI. Burdened by a heavy ransom, he returned to England in time to play an emollient role in high politics during 1341, and then fought against the French once more, in Brittany in 1342–3 – though now without an independent command. Thereafter sent as an ambassador to Castile, he participated in the siege of the Moorish town of Algeciras, before dying of wounds received in a tournament at Windsor in 1344. Salisbury's financial affairs on his death were sticky. He was never able to secure all his grants from the king, who owed him some £11,700 when he died, much of which had to be written off by his executors. His less talented son succeeded him as earl of Salisbury but saw his inheritance significantly cut by Edward III in 1354, so that the king could redistribute the lordship of Denbigh to the brilliant, upcoming Roger Mortimer.

Although Salisbury's career in royal service was cut short by his premature death, it was otherwise broadly typical of the careers of his noble contemporaries. His strenuous work for the king transformed his status but not his financial circumstances, because the grants he received were more than cancelled out by the costs he was obliged to bear as a leading war captain. Granted, his being captured and ransomed hit him hard, but he was not alone in thus suffering. Nor was he alone in failing to capture enemy lords whose ransoms he might otherwise have received. A few nobles – such as Walter Mauny – profited in this way but most did not. This was because Edward III gave no quarter at Halidon Hill (1333), Sluys (1340) or Crécy (1346), and so no enemy soldiers were taken prisoner: if they did not escape, they were killed. Prisoners were taken at the fall of Caen (1346) and at Poitiers (1356), but even then, the number of English soldiers securing valuable captives was limited. Commanders could make significant sums out of plunder, but only if wealthy towns were taken by storm under circumstances where booty could be secured and transported home. This did not occur before 1346 and was less common thereafter than historians have tended to assume. Salisbury's financial struggles in war were echoed by those of so many others, the earls of Northampton and Oxford being two good examples. Likewise, the injuries Salisbury suffered were commonplace among Edward's nobles, a surprising proportion of whom lost eyes in combat, presumably because they wore open-faced helmets to optimise their vision and breathing in battle – two significant safety factors for knights in the field. The king himself was hit by an arrow from a crossbow at Sluys, which incapacitated him for a fortnight, and David II of Scotland took two arrows in the face at Neville's Cross (1346). David had to undergo gruelling surgery over several months. As it was, only one of the arrowheads was successfully removed, though the other apparently spontaneously emerged from his face on pilgrimage many years later. Salisbury's death at a tournament was unusual, but tournament injuries were not. Indeed, contemporaries valued tournaments as training for war precisely because they taught participants how to keep fighting when they were injured – 'as their teeth cracked and blood ran down their faces'.

Were Salisbury's continuous exertions on the king's business – and the exertions of other lords – worth it? Born to fight, like all English nobles, and inured to the idea of service, Salisbury must surely have regarded his life as well lived. But the king's undoubted affection for him did not stop Edward from shunting Salisbury sideways when it became clear that he was not the top-flight commander the king needed, nor from significantly disinheriting his son and heir for reasons of realpolitik in 1354. The earl of Arundel – who, across his career, probably spent more time with Edward than did any other magnate – was threatened with similar partial disinheritance in 1346. In that year the elderly earl Warenne entered into negotiations with the king for one of the royal princes to receive his vast estates after his death, which lands were otherwise due to be inherited by Arundel, as his nephew. The latter personally protested to the king about his apparent plans during the Crécy campaign, on which Arundel was serving as commander of the English army's vanguard. Tensions between the two men must have been heightened. In the event, Edward finally decided against proceeding, having considered the matter 'in the court of his conscience' (his words). Shortly thereafter, at the siege of Calais in 1347, Northampton found himself investigated by the king for sedition, having, in the face of unsustainable default of wages, warned Edward that he could not prevent his troops from withdrawing from the English lines.

So relations between the king and even his most favoured lords, rather than being comfortable, could be fraught, just as we should expect, given that highly able and strong-minded people were engaged in a dangerous and high-stakes war, under immense personal and collective pressure. Northampton was rehabilitated in time to be made a garter knight in 1349, but like Salisbury, whose place in military command he had taken, he then found himself side-lined to make space for other commanders whom Edward now rated more highly. He continued to serve as a counsellor, on campaign and in diplomacy until his death, following the arduous Reims campaign, in 1360. Salisbury, Arundel and Northampton must, at points, all have felt frustrated by, and even angry with, the king. They continued to oblige Edward III because he was a magnetic leader whose work fundamentally mattered; because they accepted that participating in affairs of state inevitably involved hardship and disappointment as well as success and affirmation; and because – most importantly – aiding the sovereign was central to their identity and status under a king who, from the beginning of his personal rule, had made royal service a defining characteristic of nobility.

Perhaps it was precisely because Edward placed his nobles under great pressure, charged as they were with ensuring that the king's urgent business was properly done, that they bonded so strikingly under his command. His active integration of established and new nobles in his government quickly came to be reflected in their own attitudes, as they witnessed one another's charters and, most importantly, negotiated marriages among their offspring. This remarkably successful integration of promoted men into the ranks of the ancient elite partly explains why almost no accusations of favouritism were made. The other reason why favouritism did not become a political issue is that the ability and merit of the promoted men was widely recognised, as was the appropriateness of the rewards they received. Montagu gained more than anyone, via royal patronage, from the Nottingham coup, but the rewards he received were proportionate to the service he provided to the Crown and were approved in Parliament. Contemporaries would also have known that the patronage received by the new nobles under Edward was calculated, circumspect and, most importantly, conditional. The king tended to make grants incrementally, building promotion as worth was proved. Arundel is a case in point. Grants were mostly for life only, and depended upon continued good service and behaviour. Edward was not averse to reducing them on later reflection: he did this to Thomas Ughtred in 1349. Equally, the king primarily used his temporary possessions – such as escheats and confiscations – to provide for his new nobles, leaving the royal patrimony undiminished. Contrast this with the grants made by Edward II to Piers Gaveston, which significantly thinned the Crown's resources.

While historians have in the past argued that Edward III's extensive patronage of the nobility was consequent upon his need to 'buy' noble political support, following the misrule of his father, or to construct his own political grouping in the early 1330s to counter existing groups of nobles that had emerged amid the internecine politics of the 1320s, we now understand that noble support naturally flowed to him as a competent and rational monarch, and that in 1330–1 he simply and straightforwardly took command of a noble class desperate for royal leadership, reshaping it for his kingly purposes. Rather than reflecting royal weakness, therefore, his grants to key lords – of land, marriages, money and above all offices

– radically strengthened the Crown, by enlisting the nobility as a division of government in a manner hitherto unseen. Rebuilding the nobility by restoration and promotion explicitly refocused nobles upon royal service while providing the king with administrative, military, regional and local leaders to take his vital purposes in hand, under his direction and with accountability built in.

The political height of Edward's policy regarding the nobility was arguably reached in the second and third decades of his rule, when magnates such as Lancaster, Warwick, Arundel, Northampton and March were the king's principal agents in their localities as great landholders, life-sheriffs and presidents of the peace commission, and when they simultaneously acted as chiefs of regional military recruitment, then leading their great contingents of uniformed men-at-arms and archers in war, either as the king's lieutenants overseas or as his divisional commanders within the royal army. Such a comprehensive melding of royal office with local landed power and networks, and the substantial increase in governmental capability – internally and externally – that it permitted, may not have been fully conceptualised by Edward when he embarked upon his programme in the early 1330s. He was aided, at that time, by Edward I's policy, two generations earlier, of remilitarising the English landed classes, which had re-engaged many noble and gentry families with an important dimension of royal service. He was also helped by the shifting nature of chivalry in Europe in the fourteenth century, in which an emphasis upon service to the state and the common good was now supplementing and broadening the traditional ideology of Christian service. (We see this exemplified in the *Book of Chivalry* by the great French paladin Geoffrey de Charny, who crossed swords with Edward III and the Black Prince, figuratively and literally, many times.) It is likewise true that, under Edward's father, some nobles (such as Pembroke and Badlesmere) had been significantly defined by service to the Crown, while household men of modest origin (such as John Charlton) had been promoted to the ranks of the nobility. But these caveats do not significantly qualify Edward III's radicalism or precocity. It was not until his personal rule that noble service and the promotion of new men were incorporated into royal policy for the provision of government. Equally, he undoubtedly saw from the very start that, by promoting and creating great lords, he could efficiently harness the considerable patronage at his disposal to the delivery of royal rule both at home and abroad. The long-term consequences of his approach were not only to strengthen the English state but also to raise the stakes for kings – whose management of the nobility for the collective profit now extended beyond taking their counsel, arbitrating their disputes and encouraging their military service to something much more active, comprehensive and demanding.

Internal Disorder and Judicial Intervention

In the first two years of his personal rule, Edward III's restoration and promotion of men like Arundel and William Clinton, and his placing them in key strategic positions in the localities, was central to his agenda to restore order and re-establish good governance in the country. Equally important was his direct intervention on the ground to quell the worst disorder and settle the most infamous disputes. This supplemented the general oyer and terminer commissions that had been announced in the November 1330 Parliament, as well as renewed peace commissions, issued nationwide alongside the oyer and terminers in late 1330 and early 1331.

The extent and the scale of disorder faced by Edward – after so many years of deleterious and partisan rule, which had reduced so many localities to a state bordering insurgency – is clearly indicated in the Chancery and legal records. Both peace commissions and determining commissions into oppressions committed by royal officials were layered upon one another in the winter and spring of 1330–1, as the king sought repeatedly to afforce the government's judicial provision. This was especially the case in the Midlands and neighbouring counties of eastern and southern England. Here the government clearly believed disorder was rife and opposition to judicial process significant – and with good reason. Although strict comparison is made challenging by patchy record survival, cases of homicide in the very early 1330s seem to have been especially numerous. That killings and other crimes associated with political conflict, such as the murder of Robert Holland in 1328 or the looting of contrariant lands and goods in 1322, feature noticeably among the accusations shows that the realm remained fractured by earlier clashes. Some justices certainly experienced resistance in undertaking their duties, as local pockets of defiance openly confronted the reimposition of royal authority. In such situations, action by the person of the king – whom even the wayward and recalcitrant could not readily ignore – was necessary to end conflict and restore order. A comparison may usefully be drawn with the situation in the north-east of England in the 1310s. There, Gilbert Middleton, Walter Selby and others had been driven by absent and incompetent royal rule, Scottish incursions and dearth into violent self-help – in which they effectively became indistinguishable from the lawless raiders from whom they were supposed to be defending their fellow countrymen. Likewise, in the heart of England in the 1320s men had been pushed by corrupt government and something close to civil war into behaviour in which the lines between political allegiance, the exercise of royal office and criminality were heavily blurred. In the localities as at the political centre, Edward III needed to assert his authority and insist – forcibly, if necessary – that everyone should enter his peace. Where fear on the part of his subjects obstructed reconciliation, the issue could be mediated by his noble lieutenants and through royal service.

In spring and summer 1331 Edward perambulated East Anglia, incorporating personal superintendence at key judicial sessions – for example, to settle a bitter and persistent dispute between the abbot and townspeople of Bury St Edmunds – into a programme of pilgrimage. At Bury the king's presence lent a force to royal justice that even the attendance of the most senior royal judges could not deliver. An extraordinarily detailed account survives of his intervention to settle an even more problematic dispute during the same period. This was the long-running and destructive Charlton–Pole dispute over the great Welsh Marcher lordship of Powys, which had re-erupted in September 1327 when John, Lord Charlton seized Deuddwr and Mechain, lands he alleged had been wrongly kept from him by Gruffudd de la Pole. In early 1331, following the fall of John Charlton's ally, Roger Mortimer, Pole approached the king's Council seeking redress. Edward ordered that the bailiffs of Moghnant, Oswestry and Cynllaith should inquire into the matter, and with the assistance of the newly restored earl of Arundel, Charlton was attached (or formally instructed) to appear before them on 3 July. But he did not appear, and in response the king arbitrarily fined him the colossal sum of £4,000 and ordered that he be arrested. A weightier royal inquest, held in October by William, Lord Butler of Wem and experienced local justices John Leyburn and Roger Charles, was also shunned by Charlton, but the pressure exerted by the king evidently told, and in the winter he surrendered himself to the Marshalsea prison. In February 1332 Edward ordered that a judicial hearing should proceed at Easter, which it duly did, finding in Charlton's favour – on the grounds that Powys was held under English rather than Welsh law. This was classic Edward III: a major dispute having been brought to the king's attention, he intervened forcefully to resolve it without overturning legal process.

Another legal intervention by the king the following year was just as forceful and is equally well documented, though in this case the extent and nature of the surviving records has rather seduced historians into mis-characterising the Folville and Coterel families – whom, among others, the king targeted – as criminal gangsters. In fact, they were out-of-control partisans in a turbulent region whose refusal to accept the new political order since October 1330 had rendered them pariahs.

The Folville and Coterel brothers – the former of knightly status in Leicestershire and the latter minor gentlemen in Derbyshire – had been drawn into partisanship by the tumultuous politics of 1322–30. The Coterels were associated with the contrariants in 1322 and the Folvilles were accused of complicity in the murder of the Despenser associate Roger Bellars by the Lancastrian Zouches in 1326. The two families' insurrection against the Despensers then morphed into partisanship for Isabella and Mortimer, as part of which they fought against Henry of Lancaster's rebellion and raided his Leicestershire and Nottinghamshire lands in 1328–9 – their Lancastrian sympathies having presumably been superseded by their connection with Isabella and Mortimer. Edward III's vanquishing of Mortimer in the Nottingham coup, backed as it was by Lancaster, left them out in the cold in a political situation that remained febrile, partly because Edward's kingship was not yet a known quantity and partly because 1322–30 had seen terrible political vengeance repeatedly wreaked on the defeated. When their arrest was ordered shortly after the coup, they disappeared and were outlawed.

In January 1332 the government was sharply reminded of their continued political alienation by a great cause célèbre – alluded to in Parliament by the chief justice of King's Bench, Geoffrey Scrope, and recounted by the chronicler Henry Knighton – in which they were strongly suspected of involvement. This was the kidnapping, on the Leicestershire/Lincolnshire border, of the royal justice Richard Willoughby, who was probably travelling from his manor of Willoughby-on-the-Wolds towards Grantham, having previously been appointed to oyer and terminer commissions to restore order in the region. Willoughby was allegedly hidden in woods by his captors, to whom he apparently had to pay a huge ransom to regain his freedom. Willoughby came from the same regional community as his kidnappers (Willoughby-on-the-Wolds stands only twelve miles from the Folville family seat of Ashby Folville) and the offence may partly have been locally motivated. But it was received by the king as a gesture of defiance akin to Gilbert Middleton's seizure of Louis Beaumont in 1317 or John Charlton's refusal to appear before the justices of inquiry in Shropshire in 1331, and he responded by ordaining a fresh oyer and terminer or trailbaston commission in March. This was issued to the steward of the household Ralph, Lord Neville, Scrope and other senior judges into breaches of the king's peace across the south and east Midlands. The commission proceeded the following month, with the king in attendance at the sessions in Stamford.

The seniority of the justices appointed and the king's personal presence indicate that Edward III proposed a show trial in the theatre of politics, and both the nature of the accusations brought, and the judicial and political outcomes that ensued, confirm this. The king and his justices arrived with predetermined political (and thereby judicial) objectives in mind, and were assisted in their work by co-operative local communities, represented by the presenting juries who drew up the indictments. Edward's first objective was to make it abundantly clear to the Folvilles, Coterels and anyone else still residing outside the king's peace in a disorderly locality that continued resistance was futile and that the only path open to them was to seek his mercy and a political accommodation. His second objective was to provide his subjects with an opportunity to bring accusations against government officials who might have been guilty of acting in excess of authority. Prominent among the government officials in the Midlands in 1332 were the former constables of the royal castles of Rockingham and Tickhill, Robert de Vere and William Aune, whose offices had placed them in positions of considerable local power. The king's third objective was to demonstrate his commitment to enabling victims to pursue notorious criminals.

This tripartite set of objectives was characteristic of Edward when he despatched powerful judicial commissions to flashpoint localities about which he was concerned. We see them recur throughout his reign, but especially when he returned home following extended periods of military campaigning abroad. At such times there was often a fourth objective: to strengthen the royal finances by extracting enormous fines from guilty or even allegedly guilty people of substantial financial means. The famous medieval adage, that poor men were hanged by the neck and rich men by the purse, was only untrue in Edward III's England because relatively few poor people were in fact hanged. Wealthy suspects were certainly seen as fair game, and if spectacular fines were levied by the king on great lords who had been bullying their neighbours, the people might celebrate. For contemporaries, justice and royal financial exactions were not necessarily in tension: justice could be well served by extracting fines from transgressors, and government costs were considerable. In the Midlands in 1332, however, Edward III did not have the profits of justice in mind: his overwhelming concern was forcibly settling a disordered region.

The judicial proceedings that began at Stamford in April 1332 also typified Edward's direct judicial interventions in the localities in that the indictments obligingly drawn up by the presenting jurors were aggressively targeted at individuals identified as problematic by the king. For this reason they should not be taken at face value. From our vantage point in free countries in the twenty-first century, we have a very particular understanding of justice. It should be non-conflicted, non-hierarchical, impartial and based on hard evidence. Personal relationships, considerations and impressions should not influence the judgement of the courts. But in medieval Europe expectations of justice were different, reflecting alternative social and political structures, ideals and circumstances. In England the king's courts ideally dispensed natural justice, but nature was understood hierarchically and only God was revered more than the king. Another of Edward III's show trials, ironically of the same justice, Willoughby, who was the kidnapping victim in 1332, gives us a sense of this. In 1341 Willoughby was charged with 'selling the laws like cows and oxen'. The presiding justices, led by Thomas, Lord Wake, took the view that whether Willoughby was guilty or innocent, the king himself had accused him and therefore the right thing for Willoughby to do was to throw himself on Edward's mercy. Willoughby mounted a spirited defence, in which he argued that the proceedings against him should cease because there was no formal indictment and because the court was legally inferior to the King's Bench where his offences had allegedly been committed. The reply came from the bench that Willoughby was technically correct, but that the king tried him 'by clamour of his people' and would do so, offended as he was by Willoughby's actions, in any court he liked. So, in 1332, when Edward III asked the presenting jurors of the Midlands to bring particular indictments against the Folvilles, Coterels and others, they did as they were bidden. If the king needed to bring recalcitrant and disruptive members of the political community to heel by deploying the law as a heavy weapon against them, so be it. Likewise, if he wished to correct the actions of his own officials through his courts, that was essentially his prerogative. In practice, the king could usually fine his senior officers heavily without encountering significant resistance, but his subjects were likely to feel differently if fines were levied collectively on a mass of minor royal servants, embedded in the local community. Resentment and even obstructionism might then result.

This does not mean that the king was subverting the law. Rather, justice was operating within acceptable contemporary bounds. Presenting jurors' indictments were accusations, not verdicts, a recognition that a case should be heard rather than a judgement of guilt or innocence. The trial jurors who brought in verdicts in medieval English legal cases were altogether more circumspect. Ordinarily selected from the locality where an offence or offences had allegedly been committed, they drew on their collective knowledge of the circumstances and individuals concerned, often in the absence of the hard evidence provided by the modern innovations of a paid police force and forensics, and delivered something close to community justice. Where charges were serious and the penalty death, they tended largely to acquit. This was not a sign that the judicial system was feeble, but that it was robust. Evidence was probably scant in most cases, and indictments were found unproven. Suspected offenders were not executed lightly. Where a criminal case was clear cut or where numerous accusations were brought against an individual over many years (in other words, where they were a habitual offender), convictions were delivered. What mattered was that order was broadly maintained or, where the king was directly intervening in a locality, reasserted. The latter happened in the Midlands in the early 1330s and it was primarily a question of politics.

All this is brilliantly illustrated by the judicial records surviving from the Midlands trailbaston of March–April 1332, and from other oyer and terminer commissions operating in the region in the same period. All manner of accusations were brought against people from a wide range of backgrounds, including many politically engaged men as well as common criminals. The overall impression conveyed is of a region still reeling from the long-term impact of high political conflict and partisan government. Dispute and lawlessness remained prevalent. While the general picture seems clear, however, care should be exercised when we consider the details. The indictments against the Folvilles, Coterels, Robert de Vere and William Aune in particular are far more descriptive and lurid than is the norm among medieval English legal records. Their very distinctiveness should make us cautious, but instead historians have tended to treat them as unbiased accounts of serious crimes repeatedly committed by men of superior social status, when in fact the indictments are best understood as politically driven declarations of royal intent, rooted in a local reality that was significantly amplified or even twisted to maximise their impact. It would not quite be fair to describe them as trumped-up charges, but they are certainly far from impartial or reliable. Historians have also erred in failing to recognise that many of the indictments were worded with the charge of conspiracy in mind. Having emerged in the thirteenth century as a means to prevent false accusations from undermining legal process, this had latterly expanded to prohibit any agreement to commit a wrong. It was especially useful to the king because it enabled powerful people who were allegedly complicit in a crime committed by others to be prosecuted, and because those convicted of it were punishable by having all their goods and chattels confiscated by the Crown, which made it highly lucrative. The 1332 charge sheets accordingly label Eustace Folville and James Coterel the 'heads' of their 'societies' and emphasise their alleged roles in planning crimes, while accusing many other suspects, including Vere and Aune, of being their confederates. It is this language of conspiracy, almost always seen in indictments when Edward III directly intervened in the localities, which resulted in the Folvilles and Coterels being identified as professional criminal gangs, representative of a wider group of nobles and gentry seemingly engaged in grave criminality during the reign of Edward III. All these individuals were prosecuted for conspiracy in high-profile trials under the king's explicit direction, and a critical examination of the evidence against them quickly raises serious questions about its reliability. This is a theme consistent in Edward's judicial inquiries of the 1340s, 1350s and thereafter.

The indictments relating to the Willoughby kidnapping are a case in point. Historians noticed their internal inconsistencies as long ago as the 1950s, but glossed over them then and have continued to do so since. In fact, the indictments presented by juries representing a range of legal districts tell us that Willoughby was kidnapped in no fewer than five locations across three counties, by five groups of kidnappers, variously including the Folvilles and Coterels, and many other people. (These significant discrepancies have previously been explained away by the argument that after he was kidnapped, Willoughby was taken from place to place. But the indictments explicitly say that he was captured in five different places, by five different sets of men.) One is tempted to be satirical and argue that Willoughby was either desperately unlucky with kidnappings, or that his kidnappers were staggeringly incompetent and kept having to recapture him after he had escaped. But in truth, what the indictments evidence is the Crown's grave concern about disorder and its determination to leave no stone unturned in prosecuting those whom it suspected had been involved in the kidnapping of a royal justice. It also shows the jurors' compliant willingness creatively and liberally to frame wide-ranging accusations against both named rebels and notorious criminal suspects. What the charges do not safely evidence is specific criminal behaviour: they are far too compromised by their political and legal context for us to trust them on the details.

The resolution of this drive to re-establish order in the Midlands by cracking down on rogue individuals and groups was fittingly political. Some of those indicted in 1332 were undoubtedly criminally inclined, and two of them, Richard Folville, rector of Teigh, and Anketil Hoby, were later executed for felony. (Around 1340 Folville was summarily beheaded in his own churchyard by the keepers of the peace, having just shot to death with a bow one of their men who was pursuing him. In 1360 Hoby was hanged for horse theft, after being repeatedly accused of crimes in the intervening years.) But neither was brought before a trial jury in 1332, and nor were any other Folville or Coterel brothers, or their alleged confederates – other than the Folvilles' (presumably long-suffering) mother, Alice, who, unlike her sons and most other suspects, had not gone into hiding. Alice was acquitted of the conspiracy of having received the Folvilles, knowing of their crimes. Nor did follow-up trials in the court of King's Bench in 1333 produce many convictions. Instead, the previously recalcitrant principals were politically rehabilitated in a regional extension to Edward's national policy of allowing previous political opponents to redeem themselves by entering his service. Beginning in 1332, and under the superintendence of William Bohun, whom Edward later made his regional leader in the south-east Midlands, the Folvilles and Coterels were pardoned in return for serving the Crown in war – initially in Scotland and later in the Low Countries. Eustace Folville and James Coterel also received commissions to arrest fugitives, and James and his brother Nicholas served Queen Philippa in her High Peak lands. William Aune was recognised by the king as a loyal servant and went on to perform valuable administrative work for the Crown as a castellan, surveyor and recruiter of troops in Wales. The parallels between Aune and, at a more senior level in government, Oliver Ingham, Mortimer's highly able, rapidly rehabilitated associate, are obvious. Other members of the gentry accused in the Midlands in 1332 were similarly assimilated back into royal service. Almost none ever faced criminal charges again.

That the Folvilles, Coterels and their alleged associates were being pardoned and taken into royal service almost as soon as the ink on the indictments against them had dried has been seen as flawed and corrupt. But this is a misunderstanding resting on a series of false and anachronistic assumptions: that the accused were gangsters, that the Crown was seeking a strictly legal solution and that only guilty verdicts were appropriate. For contemporaries, the ideal resolution of the sort of disorder experienced in the Midlands in the early 1330s was political, and depicted in the classic denouements of the ballads about Robin Hood and other outlaws: men driven to outlawry by corrupt politics were pardoned after the intervention of a good and wise king, whose service they entered or re-entered. This was the ideal being determinedly pursued by Edward III when confronted by local unrest in the 1330s. Almost everyone bar Mortimer and the killers of Edward II was permitted to redeem himself. The king was using the law not to produce legal outcomes so much as to drive universal acceptance of his new order, and to shock those who had grown accustomed to taking the law into their own hands into more appropriate behaviour.

Seen in that light, the outcomes of his direct judicial interventions in the shires in the early 1330s were broadly positive. Royal service not only provided the wayward with a route back into the political mainstream but often also involved their removal – for a time – from the locality in which they had been a disruptive force. Naturally, this is not to play down the extent to which people like the Folvilles and Coterels may have crossed the line, nor to imply that all was necessarily for the best. Richard Folville evidently remained wild and transgressive, Nicholas Coterel proved a problematic royal servant, and John Charlton, who was sent to Ireland as chief justiciar in 1337, lasted only a year before his actions were denounced by his own brother, the bishop of Hereford, who had accompanied him there as the lordship's chancellor. But it seems that such individuals were significantly outnumbered by others now willing to embrace less problematic behaviour.

In truth, given how uproarious the years 1322–30 had been, one judicial campaign was never going to be enough to restore order in the country. The Crown understood this, as its layering of legal commissions in the localities in 1330–1 indicates. But from 1332 the reality that repeated interventions were needed became fully apparent. New peace commissions were issued in February of that year, with enhanced trial powers in some shires where problems were perceived to be acute. March saw not only the powerful determining commission aimed at the Folvilles, Coterels, et al., but also the nationwide appointment of the 'keepers of the counties', nobles and other senior figures intended to assist the peace commissioners in their work. When the keepers of the counties were withdrawn in the autumn, in light of a likely military intervention in Scotland, the Crown blithely justified the withdrawal by saying that peace had been restored. It had not, and Edward III certainly remained concerned about unrest in England while campaigning north of the border. Another set of peace commissions was issued in 1335, followed by powerful commissions to arrest notorious suspects in 1336; the latter were quickly uprated with trial powers in some especially troublesome localities. The Crown then refreshed provision in 1338, as the king, with the outbreak of the Hundred Years' War, departed for the Low Countries. The latest peace commissions all included trial powers, as well as responsibility for the array of troops, and, in coastal areas, local defence. This was a special, wartime measure. Men of the most senior local rank, such as the earl of Arundel in Shropshire, were appointed the peace commissioners' 'overseers', in a move reminiscent of the appointment of the keepers of the counties in 1332. As had been the case then, concern that in some areas the peace commissioners had been unable to restore order was a factor, though the importance of the military element of the peace commissions' duties at this time should not be overlooked. Nonetheless the localities continued to experience significant levels of disorder, and the king's justices had real difficulties in apprehending suspects; and it was not until after the appointment of yet more oyer and terminer commissions – this time the super-powerful 'new inquiries' of 1340–4 – that disorder went into obvious decline.

The Outbreak of the Second War of Scottish Independence

When the Treaty of Edinburgh–Northampton had been agreed in 1328, Robert Bruce had made a token commitment to reconsider the position of the Anglo-Scottish lords who had lost their lands in Scotland. In December 1330 Edward III formally requested that David II's government should restore the Scottish inheritances of Henry Beaumont, Thomas Wake and Henry Percy, arguably the three leading 'disinherited' lords. No satisfactory reply was received, for no Bruce government could provide such a reply without betraying their own loyalists, to whom the lands of the disinherited had long since been granted. Although the eyes of Edward III and his government were directed in 1330–2 primarily towards disorderly Ireland as well as the disturbed localities of England, those of the disinherited remained focused upon Scotland, searching for an opportunity to take direct action to reclaim their lost rights. In early 1332 this arose with the news that the feared guardian of Scotland, the earl of Moray, was terminally ill. By this time the disinherited, among whom Beaumont had emerged as the leader, had acquired a vital figurehead in the form of Edward Balliol, eldest son and heir of John Balliol, king of Scots (1292–6), who now claimed the Scottish throne, proposing to remove it from the hands of his family's historic rivals, the Bruces.

Beaumont, Balliol and the other disinherited lords, supported by a wider group of knights, many of whom had fought in the First War of Scottish Independence, made clandestine preparations in the Humber estuary for a seaborne invasion of Scotland. This was intended to strike directly at the heart of Scottish political power in Perth while avoiding a lengthy approach through the Scottish Lowlands. The experienced heads among the disinherited had conceived a bold strategy, which sought to minimise the known dangers of potential failure of supply and debilitating skirmishing in the face of an enemy employing guerrilla tactics. But it was not without risk, not least because it would involve an amphibious landing. The disinherited anticipated employing equally bold tactics in mitigation, however, reminiscent of those used by Andrew Harclay at Boroughbridge a decade previously, in which a compact, highly trained army of dismounted men-at-arms and massed longbow archers working in close co-operation would outfight the vaunted Scottish schiltrons. Edward III must have known of the Beaumont–Balliol plan – he was close to Beaumont, his former tutor; and members of his household, such as Edward and William Bohun, were involved – and probably facilitated it in private. But officially he prohibited the gathering of troops in the north and east of England, maintaining necessary deniability – within the connected contexts of the continuing process of Agen and the Auld Alliance, reaffirmed at Corbeil in 1326 – in case the expedition failed.

In fact, the expedition was an extraordinary – if short-lived – success. Launched shortly after Moray's death on 20 July, its first engagement took place as the disinherited sought to disembark from their ships on the beach at Kinghorn in Fife, on 6 August. The devastating effect of massed English and Welsh longbow archery is a commonplace of set-piece battles in the Second War of Scottish Independence and the Hundred Years' War alike, but massed archery was arguably of even greater utility in landings and sieges, where its hail-like fire could be used quickly to clear the enemy from beaches or walls so that English or Gascon men-at-arms could safely advance. This is exactly what happened at Kinghorn. Faced by a substantial Scottish force opposing their landing, the disinherited used their archers to clear a bridgehead so that the men-at-arms could disembark in good order to confront the enemy. The defenders were routed and the invaders immediately marched on Perth. Five days later, as they approached the city, they met the main Scottish army, under the new guardian, Donald, earl of Mar, at Dupplin Moor. The result was a stunning victory for the heavily outnumbered disinherited and the first occasion on which the new English way of fighting – in a mixed formation of men-at-arms and archers, fighting dug in and on the defensive, with the men-at-arms in the centre and the archers to either side – was remarked upon by contemporary commentators. The advancing Scottish schiltrons were broken up by a withering arrow-storm that robbed them of momentum and left the Scots compressed closely together, disoriented and struggling for breath. By the time they reached the wall of English men-at-arms many were in no condition to fight and they died en masse, from arrow wounds, the savage blows of maces, war hammers and Dane axes, and most of all from suffocation, as men trapped in the front line were crushed by their comrades advancing desperately and blindly from behind. The Scottish dead in front of the disinherited men-at-arms were piled fifteen feet high, most of the bodies bearing no obvious sign of injury. The guardian and many other Scottish lords were killed.

While Balliol was crowned king of Scots by a group of supporters at Scone on 24 September, his kingship was destined to be little more than a chimera. The Balliol–Comyn connection and cause that had been mainstream in Scottish politics between 1292 and the mid-1310s, against which the usurper and (in many ways) outsider Robert Bruce had rebelled in 1306, was now essentially incompatible with political power in Scotland.

Bruce had remodelled the Scottish polity both by dramatically redistributing land and by successfully marrying his own dynastic ambition to the Scots' desire for independence and self-determination. By the mid- to late 1320s the only acceptable kingship in Scotland was Bruce kingship, and although the renewal of conflict in 1332 was in one sense a straightforward reanimation of the civil war over the Scottish kingship that had effectively emerged as early as 1286 and reached its height in 1306–8, in another and much more important sense it genuinely was a Second War of Scottish Independence. Acceptable Scottish kingship could no longer propose, as Balliol duly did, to recognise English overlordship, cede the border region to the English, and re-grant lands to the Anglo-Scottish nobles who had lost out under Robert Bruce. Without buying the English Crown's political and military support through concessions Balliol stood no chance of countering his many opponents within Scotland, and he was firmly embedded in the Anglo-Scottish political grouping that had just enabled him to retake the throne for his family. While such policies undoubtedly diminished his chances of survival as king of Scots, short-term realpolitik meant he had no alternative. This was clear even before the Bruce grouping in Scottish politics reasserted itself, retook Perth and, murderously attacking Balliol and his retainers in his ancestral lands at Annan in south-west Scotland, drove the new king back into England before the year was out.

In the meantime, Edward III had summoned Parliament urgently to consider the dramatically changed political situation. The Lords and Commons met at Westminster in early September, immediately agreeing that Scotland should be prioritised over Ireland and that the king should prepare to defend the northern counties in case politics in Scotland spun out of control. A subsidy was granted. Edward now determined to refocus all his efforts on re-establishing English hegemony in the north. The keepers of the counties were withdrawn from the shires so that they could be repurposed to fight the Scots, and the apparatus of government began relocating from Westminster to York, where it would remain until 1338. Further Parliaments at York in December and January declined to answer the king when he directly asked them whether he should support Balliol and reassert English overlordship, or claim the Scottish throne himself. The Lords and Commons were probably both nervous of the risks of a

renewed Scottish war and hesitant about advising the monarch on matters
that pertained to his own rights. In the event, Edward resolved on the first
of the two courses, raising a substantial army by the new method of issuing
military contracts to his great lords, who in turn recruited mixed retinues
of men-at-arms and archers, as well as by the traditional means of the
array. Edward's leading noble lieutenants – including Arundel, Montagu
and Henry of Grosmont – accompanied Balliol in re-invading Scotland
in March 1333, and in May the king joined them and took command at
the siege of Berwick. Berwick remained Scotland's largest and strategically
and economically most important town, had been taken by Robert Bruce
in 1318 and had remained in Scottish hands since. Under the pressure of
the siege, the garrison and townspeople were obliged to agree that, if they
were not relieved by a Scottish army by 11 July, they would immediately
surrender themselves, the town and the castle to the English king. When
that date was reached without the Scots surrendering, Edward ruthlessly
began to hang hostages the town had previously handed over, starting with
the garrison commander's teenage son. 'So we will teach them to break
their covenants,' he said. The Scots rapidly agreed a new deadline for surrender of 20 July, and it was this commitment that forced the new Scottish
guardian, Archibald Douglas, to meet the English outside the town in
pitched battle, in a near reversal of the circumstances pertaining before
Bannockburn in 1314. The consequence was Edward III's first great military victory, at Halidon Hill on 19 July.

Halidon Hill was in many ways a repeat of Dupplin Moor on a larger
scale. Again, the Scots outnumbered the English, but their numerical
advantage was negated by the dreadful carnage wreaked among them by the
English archers on the flanks as they advanced towards the men-at-arms in
the centre, dismounted in prepared positions. Their situation was exacerbated by having to cross marshy ground, which their scouts had failed to
spot and in which they became bogged down, to reach the English position on the hillside. As at Dupplin Moor, by attacking under devastating
arrow-fire they quickly lost the good order that has always been crucial to
any army's prospects of victory in battle. They had no choice but to attack
if Berwick were to be relieved, and this doubtless explains their falling into
the same trap as had their compatriots at Dupplin Moor eleven months

earlier. Commanding the central English division (of three), Edward III found himself faced by an opposing schiltron breaking and taking flight. Promptly mounting his warhorse, he led a cavalry charge against the enemy while the earl of Norfolk's adjacent division was still engaged in hand-to-hand combat. This broke Scottish resistance altogether and the slaughter was immense. The young Robert Stewart, who commanded the Scottish centre opposite Edward, somehow escaped death or capture, however. Nephew and heir to David II (though seven years older than the infant Bruce king) and in due course the first Stewart monarch (1371–90), his political leadership was to prove crucial to maintaining Scottish resistance and independence for much of his long life.

Indeed, while Edward III derived huge personal credit from a victory in battle seen by contemporaries both as providential and as retribution for Bannockburn, and which returned Berwick to English hands for the first time since 1318, Edward Balliol's position in Scotland was only provisionally improved. Although Balliol re-entered the country as nominal king of Scots and established an administration, in practice he struggled to govern. His restoration of the disinherited lords naturally deprived others of lands granted by Robert Bruce, and although he was able to obtain Scottish parliamentary approval for his commitments to Edward III, his cession of large parts of the Scottish Lowlands to the English king and his performance of homage to Edward in June 1334 were anathema to most Scots. Opposition to Balliol quickly re-emerged, and in August he was forced to retreat to safety in England for a second time.

The English king responded by backing Balliol militarily again. In the winter of 1334–5 he mounted a campaign in Scotland that recovered Roxburgh Castle, where Edward's excellent reputation among his troops was cemented by his sharing of their hardships. In the teeth of terrible winter weather, he insisted upon drinking from the same cup as the rank and file. In summer 1335 he led a much larger campaign in which he and Balliol advanced deep into Scotland via a west–east pincer movement that added garrisons in Stirling and Perth to those already in Anglo-Scottish hands. Such was the success of this that many of Balliol's enemies sought terms. Edward's aim was to confirm the reconfiguration of landed power in Scotland that he had envisaged since at least Dupplin Moor. While it is a commonplace that he learned military lessons from Robert Bruce, his political indebtedness to the great Scottish king whose legacy he aimed to overturn was probably greatest in his conception of how to secure his hold on the overlordship of Scotland. By redistributing land on a grand scale, Bruce had created a Scottish polity personally as well as ideologically invested in his survival. Anglo-Scottish lords such as Henry Beaumont, now determinedly clinging to his earldom of Buchan in the Scottish north-east, already depended upon Balliol's necessarily pro-English kingship if they were to maintain their inheritances north of the border. To their ranks Edward III added a number of his leading nobles, including promoted men such as William Montagu, William Bohun and Thomas Ughtred, who were granted very substantial lordships in the ceded Scottish Lowlands. Edward doubtless also had in mind the Welsh Marcher lordships established in central and northern Wales by Edward I, which had helped secure Wales after its conquest in the late thirteenth century. This high-level colonisa-tion amounted to a strategic vision for English overlordship that foresaw the long-term financial risk to the English Crown of having to prop up a puppet king of Scots, and sought to transfer that risk to a broad cadre of trusted great lords. The lowland lordships granted to these men would ideally both motivate and fund their support for a sympathetic Scottish king, and act as a buffer zone to protect England from Scottish raids, which had been such a scourge on the northern counties since 1297.

While Edward's Scottish policy was undoubtedly strategic, it was also probably unrealistic. What scuppered it, however, was less the realities of Scottish politics than the sudden and dramatic intervention of the French. In May 1334 Philip VI of France had David II and his queen transferred from Dumbarton Castle to the security of Chateau Gaillard, Richard the Lionheart's great fortress overlooking the Seine, whose loss by King John had precipitated the fall of Normandy in 1204. It is hard not to see the French king's choice of refuge as symbolic! The following month, at around the same time that news of David's relocation reached Edward III's ears, his diplomats were dismayed suddenly to be advised by their French coun-terparts that no resolution of the Anglo-French difficulties over Aquitaine could be reached without Scotland being incorporated into any settlement. The process of Agen was effectively finished. Such was the French king's apparent determination to deliver on his obligations to the Scots under the Treaty of Corbeil that he not only loosed French and Norman privateers to raid Anglo-Gascon shipping and attack English ports, which from the summer of 1335 they did, but he also envisaged military assistance to the Scots. An initial plan to send a modest army to Scotland developed by spring 1336 into one to invade England with a substantial force. A landing in north-east Scotland was resolved upon, whence, reinforced by Scottish troops, the French would advance south and cross the border. Edward's spies presently brought him news of this plan, and he responded to it – and to Balliol's latest losses, following the defeat of his forces at Culblean in late 1335 – with characteristic decisiveness. In June and July 1336 he raided throughout north-east Scotland, systematically destroying all food and fodder so that any French landing would be gravely at risk of starvation. This scorched-earth *chevauchée* or mounted raid, which he was to repeat to the same ends in 1356, had the desired effect of deterring the proposed French action. English forces, led by Montagu, Arundel, Ughtred and others, continued to campaign in Scotland – besieging Dunbar, for example, in 1338 – but without great success. For all their effort, Anglo-Scottish positions were steadily reduced. Perth fell to the Scots – to Edward's sustained fury – in 1339, followed by Edinburgh in 1341, and Roxburgh and Stirling in 1342. By 1341 it was safe for David II to return from France. While Scotland remained significantly ungovernable for many years – as the Bruce administration was unable to exercise clear control over the country – with hindsight it is clear that from 1337 the Anglo-Scottish position was in terminal decline, as the king of England was forced to divert first his gaze and then a large part of his governmental resource to France and the Hundred Years' War.

The Outbreak of the Hundred Years' War

The term 'the Hundred Years' War' was coined in the nineteenth century to denote a more intense phase of fighting, between 1337 and 1453, in wider conflict between the English and French Crowns. This was over lands held by the English king in France between the Norman Conquest – when a great French landholder (William the Conqueror, duke of Normandy) first became king of England – and the loss of Calais by the English to the French in 1558. First characterised by historians as a war over the French throne, the Hundred Years' War in fact began as an effective continuation of the War of Saint-Sardos (1323–5), albeit triggered by French intervention in Scotland. It was arguably only in the fifteenth century, under Henry V and Henry VI, that the English king's claim to be the king of France became more than just a useful diplomatic tool, bargaining counter and propaganda piece. Although Edward III and his political advisers privately discussed claiming the French throne for diplomatic and propaganda purposes as early as 1337, the king did not act on the discussion until January 1340. By this time the war was long under way and his proclamation took his subjects by surprise. Even after this point the French throne scarcely featured in Edward's considerations. In negotiations with the French his diplomats repeatedly and consistently offered to surrender his claim to the kingship of France in return for unfettered sovereignty in a fully restored Aquitaine. In this way Edward's war aims brought together England's long-term dissatisfaction with the legal status of Aquitaine under the Treaty of Paris of 1259 and the vexed issue of the Agenais, whose restitution following its loss to the French in the War of Saint-Sardos the English had hoped the abortive process of Agen would resolve.

Edward straightforwardly specified these grievances to his people, together with the added provocations of French assistance to the Scots and attacks on the south coast of England, when he carefully explained to them – in Parliament and via nationwide proclamation – why war was necessary in 1337. French raiding had multiplied in 1336–7 and was to reach a height in 1338–9, with highly destructive assaults on Portsmouth, Southampton, Harwich and the Channel Islands. While the English king has been characterised as a capable propagandist, he barely needed to propagandise the offences committed by Philip VI in 1337. Philip was certainly captive to French foreign policy that demanded he assert himself internationally, and nor can Philip fairly be blamed for having been mindful of French commitments to the Scots; he also resented that Edward III had provided refuge to the French magnate Robert of Artois, who had questioned Philip's legitimacy within the context of a wider dispute, and whom the French king regarded as his mortal enemy. Nonetheless, in his dealings with the English king and his plenipotentiaries, Philip had shown himself intransigent, bombastic and hectoring. His stance in the mid-1330s meant Edward had to prepare for war: the English king had no choice but to defend his lands in Aquitaine and England, and little choice but to look to his rights in Scotland. Such was Philip's self-righteousness that he even beat Edward to a declaration of war, which he made on 30 April 1337. Shortly thereafter he declared Edward a contumacious vassal and formally confiscated Aquitaine.

Edward had laid the foundations for his forthcoming campaign against the French in Parliament in March, where, among other initiatives, he had raised six of his noble lieutenants – William Montagu, William Clinton, William Bohun, Henry of Grosmont, Robert Ufford and Hugh Audley – to comital status in anticipation of their leading major contingents of troops on the Continent, potentially alongside overseas allies of comparable rank. After circumspectly mustering substantial forces for home defence on the English and Welsh coasts, and in the north of England and Scotland, he initially planned to raise a large expeditionary force, which he would personally lead to Gascony. But events quickly overtook this scheme. In an egregious case of biting off more than he could chew, in February 1337 – just as war with the king of England was looming – Philip VI provoked his neighbours in the Low Countries into hostility by clandestinely acquiring five castles on their borders, in the Cambrésis. This manifestation of French overconfidence opened up the possibility that Edward might re-create Edward I's grand alliance in the Low Countries of the 1290s, which he had already been considering and which he now pursued with alacrity. The princes of the German Empire – including the emperor, Lewis of Bavaria, the duke of Brabant, the marquis of Juliers and the counts of Guelders and Hainault – responded positively to his diplomatic overtures, and during 1337–8 an anti-French coalition was painstakingly assembled. Perhaps the greatest challenge herein was that – as in the 1290s – the princes of the Low Countries demanded the English Crown should cover their vast military costs, and in some cases also provide them with hefty annuities. The king would no longer go to Gascony, which was already under military pressure from the French, in person, but a smaller relief force would be sent.

The defence of Aquitaine was being managed with great competence by the seneschal, Oliver Ingham, Hugh of Geneva and other trusted royal servants, ably and strongly supported by Jean de Grailly, the captal de Buch, and many other loyal Gascon lords. The huge financial demands of building the northern alliance necessarily deprived the Anglo-Gascon administration of much-needed funds and in 1338 precluded the despatch of a larger relief army under the earl of Huntingdon. Ingham, Geneva and the Gascon lords were hard pressed. But this did not prevent a consistent and effective threefold strategy from being pursued in the duchy. Its first element involved the rebuilding, reinforcement and supply of strategic castles and towns key to Aquitaine's defence. Its second centred on incentivising Gascon lords and communities to retake other important castles and towns from the French by granting them rights there in anticipation. Finally, there was a focus upon bringing the most powerful Gascon magnate, Bernard Aiz, lord of Albret – whose father, Amanieu, had disastrously been driven into French hands by Edward II – back into the English fold. This was achieved – with Edward III's personal involvement – provisionally in 1337 and definitively in 1339, from which point the vast Albret wealth and connection underpinned the Anglo-Gascon war effort, rendering the duchy significantly more secure.

Edward's alliance policy sought to place maximum pressure on Philip VI by attacking France in the north, much nearer to the French political centre of the Île-de-France than could be achieved from Aquitaine. The inherent strategic sense of this was shown in 1339 when French forces in the duchy were largely withdrawn because they were urgently needed for the defence of northern France, now threatened by the English king and his continental allies. (This effect was successfully repeated by the English – though without a grand alliance – in 1346.) Given Edward's heavy commitments to home defence and the Scottish theatre as well as Aquitaine in the late 1330s, it is also fair to say that he was likely to struggle independently to raise the size and calibre of army deemed necessary to meet the vast French royal army in the field. His military resources were simply too stretched, and he therefore needed to buy in additional support – from the German princes. Nonetheless, while his focus upon a northern alliance was therefore understandable, like his strategy in Scotland it was also arguably unrealistic – or at best overly optimistic. To deliver the knockout blow of a great victory in battle over the French king, too many things had to go right. Edward needed to produce the maximum amount of money possible from the realm of England to have any chance of meeting his immense financial commitments to his allies. As was now standard practice for English kings in time of war, enormous loans were extracted from Italian banking syndicates. An innovative, though probably misconceived, attempt to manipulate the wool trade with Flanders leveraged further huge loans from the English merchant community, and a generous three-year subsidy was granted by Parliament in 1338. But both measures needed to deliver every single anticipated penny. Even then, the window of opportunity in which enough money was available to sustain the alliance in the field was likely to be very short. His allies would have to be corralled into the right place at the right time. Given their different motivations and disparate war aims, this would require vast attention and considerable luck. Most of all, the French king would have to agree to attack at a favourable moment for Edward. Since medieval commanders tended to avoid pitched battle because it was so risky, there was surely a fair likelihood that Philip, who was no military fool, would instead wait for Edward's costly and fragile alliance to fall apart first.

Everything going according to plan almost never happens in war, and the late 1330s were no exception for Edward III. Before he departed from East Anglia for the Low Countries in July 1338, he had taken great care to ensure that everything that reasonably could be put in place was in place. Provision for the maintenance of internal order and coastal defence in his absence had been made with the fresh appointment of commissioners of the peace and array, and their noble overseers. The realm's revenues and resources north of the River Trent had been hypothecated for the defence of northern England and military service in Scotland. Under the so-called Walton Ordinances, government was placed on a war footing in which Edward and the advisers accompanying him overseas – pre-eminent among them John Stratford, archbishop of Canterbury, and William Kilsby, keeper of the privy seal, in addition to the earls of Derby, Salisbury, Northampton, Warwick and Suffolk – were able to co-ordinate action with the government at home to prioritise the provision of money and supplies to the king and army in the Low Countries. The home government was left in the highly capable and trusted hands of the earls of Arundel and Huntingdon, and Ralph, Lord Neville. Arundel and Huntington were both skilled administrators – the former specialising in finance, and the latter in logistics and amphibious supply – and Neville was the greatest nobleman in the north of England. All three were also experienced military commanders, justices and royal counsellors. But such sensible and extensive provision for the management of the war and government of the realm was no proof against the unexpected, in a highly pressured situation.

As soon as the king arrived in Antwerp it became clear that his financial provisions were far from delivering in line with expectation. The shortfall was so severe that his allies, who awaited their promised payments, would not take the field. They also demanded that the king's authority to lead them in war as the German emperor's representative should be confirmed, which prompted Edward to make a flying visit to Koblenz. There, on 5 September, he was formally appointed the Imperial vicar-general by Lewis of Bavaria in a grand public ceremony. Theoretically this gave him the right to summon all the resources of the Empire in his support. But financial supply remained key, and it was almost a year before Edward's allies were persuaded that their payments were in train. Edward had been reluctant to accept that his existing financial plans were insufficient and to request a fresh subsidy from Parliament. He recognised that he was already making vast demands on his realm. His subjects were certainly heavily burdened by taxation, the evil effects of the misfiring wool scheme and the long-standing problem of purveyance for war. With the despatch of money to the king abroad being prioritised, his purveyors found themselves without cash to pay for the goods they were requisitioning. They were forced to issue effectively worthless IOUs in the form of wooden tallies. As the king 'marvelled' from Antwerp at the continued failure of supply, like his subjects he instinctively blamed official corruption. This was a perennial complaint, elucidated in a unique song of popular protest that survives from the reign of Edward I, when another grand alliance in Flanders imposed near-intolerable burdens upon the populace of England. 'Against the King's Taxes' alleged that the king received less than half of what he was due.

In August 1339, however, Edward III was finally persuaded that a new financial initiative was required, and sent Archbishop Stratford back to England to summon Parliament and request an additional subsidy. Stratford was tasked with raising a staggering additional £300,000 to meet the king's obligations to his allies. This news was enough to persuade the princes of the German Low Countries finally to enter the fray, and the resultant Anglo-Imperial army penetrated the Cambrésis on 20 September and France on 9 October. As they advanced, they burned and wasted in an attempt to force the French king into battle to defend his territory and subjects. At the head of the rapidly summoned but formidable French royal army, Philip VI cautiously approached the invaders. On 21 October he made camp at Buironfosse and shortly afterwards the Anglo-Imperial army took up a new position near the hamlet of La Flamengerie. On 23 October, in expectation of a French assault, Edward's army assumed battle order, his allies remarking approvingly on the novel disposition of his forces in the front line, with thousands of archers flanking the dismounted men-at-arms in the centre. The revolutionary battle order deployed at Dupplin Moor and Halidon Hill to such devastating effect was unsurprisingly now normal practice for the English, and remained so until another European military revolution in the sixteenth century led to the demise of the longbow as the decisive weapon of war. But the new English way of fighting had two connected drawbacks, both of which were factors in what happened next.

First, because English tactics involved fighting on the defensive, they depended upon the enemy attacking. Second, because the English habitually adopted such strong defensive positions, there was a good chance that the enemy would choose not to attack. In the event, when Philip VI's scouts reported that the Anglo-Imperial army was strongly situated, the French king changed his mind and resolved not to offer battle after all. The French host immediately stopped and dug themselves in against any surprise assault the allies might attempt. The Imperial troops were short of food, cold and wet. That evening their commanders resolved to await a French attack no longer and immediately returned home. Against all his hopes, Edward III's campaign was over. The French king had gained no credit by declining – some said through cowardice – to confront his opponent. But Philip had made a sound tactical and strategic decision, knowing that hunger and winter would drive the enemy out of France for him.

Edward remained convinced that one more push could deliver victory, however, and to this end the following months were devoted to raising new funds. In England, Archbishop Stratford, now effectively head of the home government, placed Edward's acute need before Parliament in October. The Lords and Commons immediately recognised the king's plea of necessity, obliging themselves to provide him with an aid, but could not agree on the form. Taking a position independent of the Lords and home Council, the Commons insisted upon returning to their communities to discuss how financial support might best be provided, given the existing burdens on the people. When they returned to a new session of Parliament in January 1340, they demonstrated continuing radicalism by offering the king thirty thousand sacks of wool, but only 'under certain conditions', outlined in the form of petitions to the king. These related to their concerns about corruption and their desire to prevent the king's subjects from being hit by arbitrary exactions in addition to grants agreed. Since the proposed conditions touched upon the royal prerogative, Stratford rightly held that only the king could agree to them, and in late February, with aid from the Commons still not forthcoming, Edward himself returned from Bruges to Westminster personally to present his case – in another Parliament, summoned for the end of March.

Meanwhile, on 26 January 1340, the king had formally claimed the throne of France for the first time, in Ghent marketplace. His proclamation was prompted by a specific diplomatic need. The townsmen of Ghent, Ypres and Bruges, the three great cloth-producing towns of Flanders, had long endured a difficult relationship with their overlords, the kings of France, with whom they argued over rights and territory. They also depended upon wool supplies from England. In 1339 they resolved to take up arms against Philip VI, alienated by his perceived intransigence and hostility – as had been so many others. Nonetheless they remained uncomfortable about rebelling against their liege lord. It was to help them overcome their discomfort that Edward claimed the French throne. If he were the rightful king of France, Philip of Valois could only be a usurper, negating the

Flemings' status as rebels. The prize for Edward was a revived grand alliance and the military assistance of the formidable Fleming militias.

In Parliament in April the Commons granted the king a ninth of corn, lambs and wool for two years, plus a new wool subsidy. In return Edward reassured his subjects by confirming that the realm of England would never be subjugated to that of France, despite his claim to the French throne. He also willingly accepted many of the Commons' petitions. Purveyance would be contained and official corruption investigated. Prerogative levies – including tallage and scutage, which the king's Council had already assessed as useful to the Crown only as bargaining counters in negotiations over tax – were suspended. While the king remained abroad, a Council of great lords, answerable to Parliament, would ensure that the king's campaigns and home defence were properly funded. Although the Commons had succeeded in associating the redress of grievance with grants of taxation, an important constitutional development, the king had obtained his aid. Moreover, he had conceded nothing he was not content to concede, maintaining the procedural position that the Commons made the king grants before its petitions were formally considered, not afterwards. This meant that the king retained control of the negotiating process.

Armed with seemingly revived finances, Edward prepared to return to the Low Countries. In 1339 Philip VI had intensified French naval raids on the south coast of England so that many ports between Harwich in the east and Plymouth in the west were attacked. But now Philip posed an even greater threat, amassing a huge invasion force of French and Genoese vessels (the French having hired Genoese mercenaries as crossbowmen and sailors) in the Zwin estuary off the Flemish port of Sluys. In June 1340 this fleet was tasked with preventing the English from rejoining their Flemish and German allies. According to the chroniclers, Edward III was advised against confronting the Franco-Genoese by his councillors, led by Stratford, but vehemently insisted that he would do so. He was right to have confidence. Although the enemy fleet was much larger than his own, medieval naval battles were rather like land battles fought aboard ships. Opposing vessels sought to grapple one another, using archery, crossbows, catapults and heavy stones dropped from masts to reduce the enemy, before boarding and occupying their ships in hand-to-hand combat. In such warfare the English, with their massed longbowmen and men-at-arms accustomed to fighting on foot, would be at a significant advantage. And while the English lacked the fast and manoeuvrable galleys of the Normans and Genoese, their tall cogs, with wooden 'castles' at either end, were well suited to the sort of naval fighting likely to occur. Moreover, Edward had developed and professionalised his naval forces as he had his army. He had invested in king's ships – vessels owned, rather than requisitioned, by the king – and their administration. In the earl of Huntingdon and Robert Morley in particular he had two experienced and skilled admirals among his nobles, whose command was underpinned by naval specialists of lesser social status, including members of the king's sergeants-at-arms, the royal bodyguard.

Having sailed on 22 June, the English fleet of around 140 vessels, commanded for the king by Morley, Huntingdon and the Flemish pirate and military engineer John Crabbe, confronted the Franco-Genoese on 24 June. The Franco-Genoese had chained their 220 or so ships together in the Zwin estuary to create a formidable barrier to English attack. Waiting until midday for a favourable tide to lend them momentum as they attacked the enemy, the English first feinted a retreat to tempt the French and Genoese admirals to abandon their fixed position and pursue them. The ruse worked, and when the English turned to attack, the French and Genoese vessels were already scattered and therefore vulnerable. Intense fire from the thousands of archers on the castles and in the rigging of the taller English ships cleared the enemy decks before the men-at-arms in smaller vessels boarded and captured their opponents. The English took ship after ship – more than 160 in all – and the slaughter, which went on until well after midnight, was immense. Perhaps twenty thousand French and Genoese soldiers and sailors were killed in combat or drowned attempting to escape. In the aftermath of the battle, Philip VI's court jester is reputed to have told the biting joke, 'How do we know that French knights are braver than English knights? Because English knights are afraid to jump into the sea.' Fighting in the front line, as at Halidon Hill, Edward III was hit by a crossbow bolt and had to spend a fortnight afterwards recuperating. But to his great delight, among the many captured vessels, he recovered his favourite king's ship, the cog *Christopher*, taken by the French off Flanders earlier in the war. More importantly, the great naval victory of Sluys swung the balance of naval power in the Channel decisively back to the English, immediately ended the threat of a Franco-Genoese invasion and cemented Edward's military and personal reputation. Strangely unknown today, Sluys was perhaps the greatest European naval battle before Trafalgar, and was celebrated by Edward in the minting of new coinage, showing the victorious monarch aboard ship.

As soon as he had recovered from his injury, Edward sought to exploit his advantage with another land attack on France. Parliament, summoned again in July, provided Edward with better cash flow by converting the biennial ninth into a grant of thirty thousand sacks of wool. Their willingness to help had doubtless been revived by Edward's victory at Sluys. This grant secured the immediate military support of both the Germans and the Flemings, and on 1 August the allies besieged the French city of Tournai, which the Flemings claimed. The English king's objective was effectively to repeat his successful Scottish strategy of 1333, in which the threat of his capturing a key municipality forced his enemy to meet him in pitched battle. But in 1340 it did not work. Although the siege lasted for many weeks, during which allied raiding parties wrought savage destruction across a broad swathe of adjacent France, Philip VI remained ensconced with his army first at Arras and then at Bouvines. As in 1339, he calculated that meeting Edward III in battle was too risky, and trusted that the English king's financial difficulties would before long result in his allies and their troops melting away. The French king was right. Edward's allies were politically divided as well as financially short. By late September it was clear that the alliance was going to break up. Indeed, it had probably remained in the field as long as it had only because of persistent rumours that Philip was approaching Tournai with his army. On 25 September Edward III reluctantly concluded a truce with the French at Espléchin, which encompassed his allies as well as the Scots. Fighting was suspended for nine months, with all sides retaining their present possessions. Prisoners who could raise their ransoms would now be released. This included the earls of Salisbury and Suffolk, who had been detained in Paris under harsh conditions, having through their own overconfidence been captured by the French outside Lille earlier in the year. Their liberty now needed to be secured, as did that of the earls of Derby,

Warwick and Northampton, all of whom were guarantors, and therefore potential captives, for the king's huge debts in the Low Countries.

For Edward III, the Truce of Espléchin was close to a disaster. He had probably spent £500,000 on foreign alliances, only for the resulting armies to break up for want of supply twice, in 1339 and 1340, without Philip VI being forced to fight. Edward had rebalanced naval power to England's advantage through his victory at Sluys, had secured the support of the lord of Albret in Aquitaine, and had reduced Philip VI's reputation by invading and wasting his territory without being stopped. But otherwise he had made no progress in respect of his key strategic objective of securing a restored Aquitaine in full sovereignty. He blamed the home government, for having twice failed to provide him with the money he had been promised, as well as his officials in the English localities. Like the Commons in Parliament, he had concluded that only official corruption could explain why he had received such a small portion of what the Commons had granted. While it is difficult to be sure why returns were so low, the reason was probably mass obstructionism and non-payment. There was certainly widespread and mounting popular grievance about the burdens imposed upon the people by the king's incessant financial demands, despite the equally widespread recognition that his cause was just (as had been the case in 1297–1301). Edward himself, in taking his allegedly corrupt officials to task in 1341, talked of his fear that '[his] people would be put to mischief against [him]' unless official corruption were dealt with. Doubtless brooding in Ghent after Espléchin, with poison about Archbishop Stratford seemingly being dripped into his ear by Stratford's rival officials William Kilsby and John Darcy, and receiving anonymous correspondence from England accusing his ministers of incompetence and even treachery, Edward resolved to take direct action to end the inefficiency and venality in England he blamed – largely incorrectly – for his military failure. In late November, under the guise of going on a hunting trip, he made a break for the coast with a small group of close advisers, including Northampton and Nicholas Cantilupe as well as Kilsby and Darcy, secretly took a small ship at Sluys, and at midnight on 30 November 1340 arrived unannounced at the water gate of the Tower of London to begin a dramatic and thoroughgoing purge of his government.

Political Crisis and the King's Government Redoubled

There is no evidence that Napoleon ever said 'give me lucky generals', though the sentiment widely attributed to the French emperor, that being lucky makes a difference, is one signally applicable to Edward III. The same might be said of the aphorism 'you make your own luck'. In late 1340 Edward's alliance policy was on the point of collapse, having singularly failed to deliver its objective of a definitive land battle with Philip VI. His coffers were empty, his people were impoverished, many of his allies were about to abandon him and there was no obvious way forward. His great political enterprise in the first decade of his rule had come to naught. His failure, however, had the effect of returning Edward to the task of governmental reform, upon which he had embarked in the early 1330s but from which he had subsequently been diverted – by both circumstances and choice in respect of international relations. In the 1340s and 1350s his revived radicalism handsomely paid off, and this is where he was lucky. Where he made his own luck was in seeing and successfully pursuing the opportunities that emerged amid the failure.

Historians have repeatedly stressed that Edward III's kingship was more successful after 1340 without properly understanding why. The traditional view is that, having consulted inadequately and pushed his realm too hard in the late 1330s, Edward found himself checked in a serious political crisis early in 1341. The shot across the bows he received from the polity at that time persuaded him to proceed more collaboratively and circumspectly henceforth. By this means he took his people with him and consequently enjoyed great political success.

The problem with this interpretation is that the evidence does not bear it out. It is true that, throughout the 1330s, the king made heavy and at times vociferous financial demands under pressure of war. Likewise, in 1339–40, desperate to bring Philip VI to battle, he began to lose some political perspective. But overall, his political approach had been broad and collaborative. Equally, his rule from 1341 is arguably best characterised as a continuation or even an intensification of what came before – though shorn of its policy of grand alliance. We see this in his creating what we might term a 'new officialdom' in the 1340s to add to his 'new nobility' of the 1330s, and in a revised military strategy that, unshackled from the demands of the Low Countries alliance, sought properly to exploit the benefits of the organisational and tactical revolution he was overseeing in English arms. We also see it in Edward's revived use of the common law, now enforced by his personal bodyguard, the king's sergeants-at-arms, as a weapon against elements within the polity he regarded as problematic or recalcitrant. In that respect his rule was certainly more demanding in the 1340s than it had been in the 1330s. The political unity initially created by Edward, which had begun to crack under the pressure of the alliance strategy in 1339–40, re-emerged from 1341 not because the king eased back on the political throttle, but because, after the understandable distraction of the Low Countries campaigns, his rule retook a more natural and effective – but still strongly directive – track.

High political crisis between December 1340 and May 1341 is sometimes called the 'Stratford crisis', and for good reason. This is because the king's treatment of the archbishop of Canterbury – the de facto head of the home government from late 1339 – became emblematic of wider concerns about the king's anger towards members of the political community following his dramatic return from Flanders. For Edward's most senior nobles and lieutenants, concern about his treatment of Stratford centred on the principle of the right of great lords to be tried by their peers in Parliament. The king's apparent desire to proceed against Stratford by royal accusation that permitted no response worried them. A wider uneasiness on their part about the king's determination to purge his officialdom is indicated by their collective declaration, when they agreed in December to preside over judicial commissions into alleged corruption in the shires, that this should set no precedent for the future. For contemporaries and historians alike the two strands of the row with Stratford and Edward's judicial assault on his men in the localities were and are intertwined. But while the latter is of real historical significance, the former was essentially a matter of accident. In short, the Stratford crisis occurred because the archbishop of Canterbury hid in his cathedral when the king demanded he account for his actions in government.

Stratford was by no means the only leading official the king called to account immediately upon his surprise return to a Tower of London that he found unlit and effectively unguarded, which must have confirmed his worst suspicions about incompetence at home undermining his struggle abroad. Other prominent officials and great lords were, like Stratford, summoned before the king and pursued through the night by the king's sergeants-at-arms and other trusted household men. They included the mayor of London, the constable of the Tower and career official Nicholas Beech, the great Lancastrian political veteran Thomas, Lord Wake of Liddell, the merchant-financier William de la Pole and John Molyns, household banneret (or senior knight) and steward of the king's chamber, who had participated in the Nottingham coup in 1330. What is striking about this group is that the men who immediately faced the king – like Wake and Beech – quickly rehabilitated themselves in his eyes and joined the ranks of his aides pursuing the purge in the country. It was the men who refused to face him – notably Stratford and Molyns, who fled into hiding – who attracted his special ire; and it is fair to say that Edward remained notably hostile to Pole for many years.

In Canterbury Cathedral Stratford seems to have fantasised about being a new Thomas Becket. Confronted by Edward's representatives, the archbishop refused to come before the king, instead issuing a clutch of public statements and letters denouncing the accusations against him in inflammatory, even hysterical terms: in one letter, addressed directly to the king by way of warning, he explicitly referenced Edward's father's tyranny as well as Edward II's eventual fate. In January 1341 Edward sent another representative, his steward Ralph, baron of Stafford, to summon Stratford for a second time. This provoked Stratford into making another bout of public denunciations, which by now had wider traction on the issue of ecclesiastical rights: the choleric Bishop John Grandison of Exeter, for instance, excommunicated the justices sent by the king to investigate alleged official abuses and other offences in Devon. In February Edward unwisely responded by issuing a vituperative letter against the archbishop, the *libellus famosus*. The following month, coolly and piercingly, Stratford publicly rebutted this point by point. His new calmness and confidence perhaps reflected support he may privately have been receiving from among the great lords as well as the prelates, as together they contemplated the Parliament that was surely coming, and which duly assembled in April.

The Purge in the Country

Meanwhile the king had been busy reforming his government. Declaring himself determined never again to have senior officials who could not be prosecuted in his own courts because of their clerical status, he had appointed the first lay chancellor, the lawyer Robert Bourchier. Bourchier and his successors Robert Parving and Robert Saddington, who were also lawyers, were to lead the king's administration until 1345. All three played a central role in the purge of justices, sheriffs and other royal officials that characterised royal rule throughout 1341 and into 1342. Chronicles and surviving judicial records bear witness to the scale and penetration of the purge, as well as the king's personal direction of it, symbolically administered from the Tower of London – the greatest fortress, arsenal and prison in the realm, from which Edward's rule continued to flow well into the 1340s. Over Christmas Edward went in personal pursuit of John Molyns, successfully searching his houses, lands and associates for allegedly stolen money and treasure, which the king found hidden under water in ponds and locked in the abbey of St Albans. Told by the abbot that no one had the keys to the abbey chamber in which Sir John's goods were kept, Edward responded that, by St Mary, he would make the keys himself. In London, Justice Richard Willoughby, who had led the king's drive against the Folvilles and Coterels a decade earlier, was subjected to a blatant show trial for corruption, presided over by the king's right-hand men, Thomas Wake and Robert Parving. When, browbeaten, Willoughby finally ceased mounting a legal defence and threw himself on the king's mercy, declaring, 'I will no longer plead with my liege lord,' Wake, who had been gazing out of the window, suddenly sat up. 'That, Sir Richard, is the wisest plea you have ever made,' he said. The energetic and politically connected sheriff of Essex, John Coggeshall, sought permission via his noble friends in the king's orbit to be tried for his alleged offences by the king's Council, rather than by the judicial commissioners in Essex. Edward agreed this and wrote to the Council members accordingly. But note his words: 'You must take no fine from Sir John unless it accords with his guilt – of which we have manifestly heard.'

The charges against Willoughby and Coggeshall were uncannily echoed by numerous others, brought right across the country, particularly against

the king's justices, sheriffs and purveyors of military equipment and supplies. Among the senior judges arrested and detained for months, in royal
and lordly castles across England and Wales, were John Stonor and William
Shareshull, the former famously incorruptible and the latter – who went
on to lead the king's great judicial drive of the 1350s – astonishingly able.
In the king's determination to root out corruption there is no doubt that
loyal and effective royal servants, as well as others who had perhaps been
less responsible and assiduous in the performance of their duties, were
freely accused. While it is hard to know with any certainty which royal
officers and ministers had actually oppressed the people (as the king put
it) and which had not, what the surviving records show is that, right across
the country, patently similar charges were brought, time and time again,
against men who, until late 1340, had been at the forefront of delivering
royal rule in the localities. In a way this is no surprise, because Edward's
drive for reckoning and the dramatic reassertion of his kingly authority
were carried out in uniform fashion across the country.

The mechanism he chose derived from the great judicial innovations
of Edward I, but as ever with Edward III's adoption of his grandfather's
instruments, it was taken to another level. The 'new inquiries' or 'great
inquisitions', as Edward variously termed them, were thoroughgoing general oyer and terminer or trailbaston commissions led by his key noble
lieutenants, accompanied by those justices whom he had not targeted in
his initial arrests. It was habitual for Edward III to appoint men as justices only in areas where they had a landed interest. (There are instances of
lords being nominated as justices in a particular shire while they temporarily controlled lands there, for example by holding the wardship of an
important minor, but ceasing to be nominated once the ward had reached
his majority.) This was fundamental to his harnessing the social fabric to
the delivery of his rule. The ideal was that the appointed royal officials
in a shire, while representatives of the king and attentive to the needs of
his rule, would also be regarded as acceptable by the local community:
knowledgeable about local circumstances and keyed into the local networks from which other commissioners and jurors were drawn. But in the
case of the new inquiries, many (though not all) of the magnates who presided over them were appointed outside the areas where their key lands lay.

This emphasises the king's determination not to allow local connection or interest to hinder the prosecution of his officers and ministers. Presenting juries of eighteen or even twenty-four men (rather than the usual twelve) were empanelled. Vast numbers of royal officials were required to present themselves and submit to fines: in Essex some two thousand officers and ministers queued together to submit to fines totalling in excess of three thousand marks, acting as one another's guarantors as they filed past the justices and their clerks. It is the huge scale of such fining – in respect both of number of men fined and total sums – that has led to the new inquiries being mischaracterised as mass fines on the populace. They were absolutely not that. But in a county like Essex few of the king's subjects can have failed to know someone whom the king had fined – and in the April Parliament in which Edward was resisted by the concerned political community and the Stratford crisis duly petered out, many of the protesting MPs had themselves just been heavily fined, in respect of their recent royal service as local justices or other royal officials.

Edward's personal obsessions stand out in the new inquiries' extant rolls: the loss of Perth for want of supplies and the plundering of the merchant ship *Taret* in 1339 are there, neither for the first nor last time; and it is no surprise that the commissioners in Buckinghamshire had John Molyns, who was still on the run, squarely in their sights. Most strikingly, in shire after shire, the sheriff, the Crown's key local administrative official, was accused of corruption. By the time the commissioners empanelled their juries, the king had systematically replaced England's sheriffs with new men. This made the former sheriffs' pursuit straightforward. Like Justice Willoughby, ex-sheriffs such as John Coggeshall (Essex and Hertfordshire), Gilbert Ledred (Lincolnshire) and John Oxford (Nottinghamshire and Derbyshire) found themselves targeted and scapegoated. It is not just because of the obvious nationwide patterns in the accusations against them that we can say this with confidence. It is also because so many of the charges were clearly brought by disgruntled men who had clashed with them in the legitimate prosecution of their duties – especially in the late 1330s, when they were under huge pressure from the king's demanding rule. In 1341–2 former sheriffs were almost universally accused of having seized men and imprisoned them on their own property until they paid ransoms for release. On the face of it, this seems like the most outrageous corruption. But in reality, it was a sensible commonplace for sheriffs arresting indicted criminals or intractable debtors to hold them securely in their own manors, rather than deposit them in the county gaol, which might be significantly distant (especially in the vastness of a county like Lincolnshire) or disturbingly insecure. (It would be fair to say that sheriffs also stood to make some additional income this way, by charging their prisoners for bed and board; in the Middle Ages prisoners always paid for their own upkeep.) Likewise, under the new inquiries ex-sheriffs were frequently accused of having stolen litigants' animals or crops, or having imprisoned mariners, in the late 1330s. Purveying on a grand scale for the royal armies in Scotland and Flanders, without making the required payments – in an environment in which supply of specie to the king overseas had been urgently prioritised – was a necessity demanded by the king of the cash-starved sheriffs. So was the impressing of ships, boats and sailors to carry soldiers and material to the royal army in the Low Countries. In some cases, long-standing local disputes intervened in the new inquiries' prosecutions.

In Lincolnshire, for instance, Gilbert Ledred was not only the former sheriff but also the steward, or chief legal officer, of Henry, earl of Lancaster. Alice Lacy, countess of Lincoln was Lancaster's former sister-in-law, as the widow of Thomas, earl of Lancaster. It was through her bad marriage to the rebel earl that the Lancastrian house had gained the great Lincolnshire holdings of her father, Gilbert Lacy, the last Lacy earl of Lincoln. Alice evidently resented this, and in 1341 brought numerous charges against Gilbert Ledred as Henry of Lancaster's steward, rather than as sheriff. Most vivid among them is a case relating to the alleged theft of a valuable whale, or 'great leviathan of the sea', which she claimed Gilbert had had hauled up the coast from her manor into the neighbouring manor of Henry of Lancaster, after it had been washed ashore. For the presiding justice, the king's friend Nicholas, Lord Cantilupe, this was the third time in as many years that he had found himself hearing this case, brought by the indefatigable countess. It is hard not to imagine him hunched over the bench and muttering, 'Not the whale again,' as he unrolled the indictment.

The former sheriffs and justices who paid the bulk of the mass fines on the king's officialdom (in Essex the king's great officers each paid fines of

£100 or more, whereas the minor ministers typically paid sixpence or less) frequently threw themselves on the king's mercy – like Richard Willoughby. This was probably because of political expediency. We know that at least one of the presiding magnates (Thomas Wake) regarded this as only right when one found oneself accused by the king. We also know, from notes in the roll of the new inquiries in Essex, that the king instructed that all accused officials found guilty should be fined at one level, all accused officials found not guilty should be fined at a second level, and every other official, even if they had not been accused at all, should be fined at a third level. Collective responsibility for problems in the country on the part of officialdom was assumed. As in the Midlands in 1332, this was more about the theatre of politics than justice. The seeming 'corruption' of officials like Willoughby, Coggeshall, Ledred and Oxford – who, on the strength of the new inquiries' charges against him, has even been erroneously identified as the model for Robin Hood's 'sheriff of Nottingham' – was, like the alleged criminal gangsterdom of the Folvilles and Coterels, more apparent than real. While this is not to say that justices, sheriffs and other royal officials never acted in excess of authority, or presided over a sympathetic hearing for a colleague or friend (because they surely did), the output of the new inquiries was mostly a product of the furious king once more banging very hard on the judicial table, and declaring an effective 'open season' upon his former officials – readily responded to by the resentful. It is no wonder that committed and competent royal servants such as Willoughby and Coggeshall were afterwards rehabilitated into royal service. This was not about cynical royal government, pragmatically re-embracing the genuinely corrupt. (Where corruption was proved, Edward III did not forgive.) What Willoughby and others were principally guilty of was finding themselves in the wrong place at the wrong time. It is notable that, where actual trials proceeded in 1341–2, Edward's officials were largely found not guilty of the oppressions with which they had been charged. It is only because some prominent officers took the political decision to make a plea bargain, by begging for the king's mercy, that the records provide any indication of corruption beyond initial accusation – the latter so easy to make.

The king's motivation for this most penetrating judicial drive seems to have been straightforward if manifold. First, he was convinced that corrupt and inefficient men had, as he put it, committed offences against both himself and his people – a characteristic formulation that reflects Edward's sense of the bond between himself and his subjects, and his duty to protect them. If he did not deliver on that duty, he said, there was a risk that his people would be put to mischief against him. Second, he was determined to retake control of government at every level, to prevent the corruption he perceived from bedevilling his enterprises again. Third, he desperately needed money – to rebuild his military position and, most urgently, to secure the release of key noble lieutenants (to some of whom he had made personal commitments) who were prisoners of war or to repay his debts in France and the Low Countries. The earls of Salisbury, Suffolk, Northampton, Derby and Warwick needed to be brought home. Given how much he had drawn from the realm for the war in the late 1330s and 1340, Edward could not raise all the money he needed through taxation, and certainly not with sufficient speed; hence the profits of justice needed to step in. There was a political bonus for the king in that heavily fining his leading officials publicly signalled a prioritisation of his oppressed people over his own servants. There was undoubtedly a degree of hypocrisy about this, because the person chiefly responsible – though with honest motives in time of war – for the oppressions had been the king himself, through the heavy demands he had made on the country, to which his seriously burdened officials had simply been responding. But this was a hypocrisy seemingly widely tolerated in later medieval England – even if it was also periodically satirised in songs and poems – such as 'Upon the King's Taxes' and 'Wynnere and Wastoure' – circulating among the political elite. Perhaps it was this general acquiescence, underpinned by forgiving deference to the king, that facilitated the political doublethink practised by Edward III in this period. It would be natural to characterise such behaviour as cynical, but the documentary record suggests that instead the king was sincere, if self-deceiving.

The Parliament of April 1341

On 3 March 1341 Edward III summoned a Parliament to meet at Westminster on 23 April. The king's purpose was to resolve the worst of his remaining financial difficulties by negotiating either revised terms for the collection of his existing taxes or, ideally, new taxes. He effectively did both. Lords and Commons reaffirmed their commitment to supporting the king's cause in war against the Scots and especially the French, and agreed that the remaining year of the ninth granted in 1340 should be replaced by a new, carefully constructed tax on wool, which duly generated the huge sum of £130,000 – more than twice the value of a normal subsidy. This instrument marked the beginning of an epoch-making phase in Edward's reign, in which, by negotiation, with a clear sense of shared purpose and without significant political tension, Parliament provided the monarch with sustained taxation on an essentially ongoing basis – in war and peace alike. At the heart of this new arrangement stood confidence on the part of the political community in a king whose requirements of his realm remained high, but who was open and straightforward to deal with, who listened, who was flexible where appropriate and, most of all, who delivered. During the course of the 1340s, 1350s and 1360s, Edward repeatedly showed himself willing to hear and act upon concerns raised by his subjects in Parliament as part of an increasingly established process of consultation and negotiation in which the king's financial needs were systematically recognised, adopted and met by the political community. At times this involved the king surrendering prerogatives – best exemplified by purveyance – that were no longer of practical use to him but which, historically, had led to friction in the country and periodically in high politics. What was critical about such surrender on Edward's part is that it was voluntary. He was effectively trading debased political stock for a vastly more valuable new asset: public finance on a scale, and with sustainability and predictability, hitherto unknown. The process of parliamentary negotiation involved the Lords and Commons recognising the king's necessity and providing him with the money he needed first, and Edward agreeing to certain of their petitions for change or redress afterwards. It was never the case that the king 'bought' war finance by 'conceding' royal rights. Parliament and king were mutually engaged in mature political dealings in which the common good, encompassing the Crown's as well as Edward's subjects' needs, was recognised by all parties as their central concern. Perspectives on the common good were shared.

The agreement reached in the Parliament of 1348 arguably best illustrates this: despite the Black Death, the worst demographic crisis the medieval world had seen, Parliament granted the king an unprecedented triennial subsidy to meet his and the realm's continuing needs in war; in recognition of this, Edward agreed that no financially burdensome judicial commissions should be despatched to the localities during the corresponding three years. This evolved relationship between king and Parliament over public finance and the common good, built by Edward III on the platform created by Edward I, was transformative in respect of state formation. It drew Lords and Commons into considering the needs of war as their needs as well as those of the king, and in this way changed foreign policy from being a royal matter into a national question and concern. Matters of state became matters for everyone and, by extension, everyone's responsibility. Responsibility brought practical commitment, which resulted in the English Crown having access, in the mid-fourteenth century, to financial resources unimaginable to Edward III's forebears.

The April 1341 Parliament witnessed Edward III's willingness to listen and compromise, even when he was at his angriest, and with it to defuse politics. As Parliament gathered at the end of the month, Archbishop Stratford, who had left his Canterbury sanctuary to take up his rightful place among the prelates, found himself blocked by the king's courtiers from entering the painted chamber at the Palace of Westminster, where the Lords had gathered. The venerable Earl Warenne, and the earls of Arundel, Northampton and Salisbury, argued that the archbishop should be admitted, and held that he should be tried by his peers, not summarily, on thirty-two charges of dereliction of duty that Edward wished Stratford to answer. In the face of this representative group, and after a period of negotiation, Edward conceded he had erred, and in early May he entered the chamber in company with the archbishop and agreed that his accusations against Stratford should be considered by a broad committee of peers. While he refused, in the face of the Commons' petitions, to accept that he should appoint his officials in Parliament, he did agree that they should be sworn into office in Parliament and that, in the continuing new inquiries, allowance should be made for men who were unable to defend themselves because they were unavoidably absent from the shires in which charges had been brought against them. He likewise agreed that future proceedings under the new inquiries should focus only upon the king's senior officials and tax collectors. In the event, the charges against Stratford were quietly dropped, although it was not until the following October that, in a fresh Parliament, Edward and Stratford formally exchanged the kiss of peace. At that time, following discussions with the great lords, the king repudiated the so-called Statute of April 1341, in which the political concessions he had then made had been summarised. Edward had remained concerned about the potential limitations on his freedom of action implied by the requirement that his officials be sworn into office in Parliament, and wished to reassert his independence. At the same juncture, he stated he would 'do his duty' in respect of any individuals who might find themselves subject to injustice because of the repudiation of the statute. Parliament accepted the change with scarcely a murmur. Normal political relations had resumed.

New Officialdom

This is not to say, however, that nothing had changed in the government of the realm. While Stratford was once more admitted to the king's Council, he and his close associates who had failed to deliver as ministers were never again granted high governmental office. Strikingly, nor were Stratford's chief accusers, William Kilsby and John Darcy. Side-lined administratively, they now pursued military careers. Instead, Edward promoted a new generation of exceptionally able government clerks. Within a handful of years, the king had retreated from the position he had adopted in 1340-1 of only employing lay (and therefore justiciable) officials as his chancellor. Laymen of appropriate experience were simply too few in number, and many of the clerics holding more junior positions in government were highly talented. In the mid-1340s, this new generation, untainted by the unedifying quarrels of their predecessors, began to hold prominent positions in the Westminster administration. Foremost among them were John Thoresby and William Edington. As keeper of the privy seal (1345-7) and chancellor (1349-56) the former showed great organisational ability. Although Edington succeeded Thoresby as chancellor (1356-63), it was in his earlier roles as keeper of the wardrobe (1341-4) and treasurer (1344-56) that he stood out. In addition to performing outstanding work financing the king's campaigns in Scotland and Brittany in 1341–3, Edington oversaw a raft of financial reforms at the political centre that witnessed increasing co-ordination between the Exchequer and the royal household, and placed the king's personal finances on a sounder footing than ever before. The result was vastly improved financial control and efficiency. Nor were Thoresby and Edington alone. John Winwick is an excellent example of a lesser-known clerk who played a key role in delivering governmental excellence. Trained in canon and civil law, he worked as an attorney in the court of King's Bench before taking holy orders and entering royal administrative service. Winwick played a key role in the purge of 1340–1 as deputy keeper (effectively castellan) of the Tower of London and as one of the king's sergeants-at-arms, before returning to a more conventional administrative and diplomatic career in the later 1340s and 1350s. As keeper of the privy seal (1355–60) and de facto chancellor (1359–60) he led the team that negotiated the vital Treaty of Brétigny (1360) on behalf of the king.

In the localities, as in central government, an older generation of officials, some of whom had sorely disappointed the king, saw themselves replaced by younger and more energetic men in whom Edward had greater confidence. This was an incremental process. Some shires, such as Essex, saw an immediate clean sweep of senior local office. In Shropshire, on the other hand, new blood was brought in across the course of a decade. The new men were characteristically lawyer-administrators who had served Edward's noble lieutenants, and it was presumably on the recommendations of the latter that they were recruited. Robert Tey in Essex, for instance, was a scion of a gentry family with a tradition of performing legal work, and an associate of the earl of Northampton. John Delves in Shropshire, the younger son of a gentry family in Staffordshire, began his career as an attorney in the court of King's Bench before working successively as steward for Roger, Lord Strange of Knockin and his close ally the earl of Arundel in their Welsh Marcher lordships, and then being transferred (at the king's direction) into the service of the young Black Prince in Wales in the late 1340s. It was in the 1350s that Delves joined the ranks of the Shropshire justices working directly for the king – while retaining his close relationship with the Black Prince. Delves is also an excellent example of how service was often multifaceted for middle-ranking royal officials, just as it was for the king's noble lieutenants: Delves served with Strange and Arundel on the Crécy–Calais campaign in 1346–7, and fought at Poitiers with the Black Prince in 1356.

In this way, the remodelling of government in his own image that Edward III had begun in early 1331 with the creation of his new nobility was extended to encompass royal service in the next social tier – among the government clerks at the centre and gentry lawyer-administrators in the counties. The connections between the magnates who were the king's regional lieutenants and the king's new local officials served to extend the effective reach of royal rule, a theme that was to continue in the early 1350s when, in the face of the Black Death, larger numbers of local lawyer-administrators were brought into the king's service. But Edward was not content to rely only upon locally embedded social networks to carry his rule into the country, even where those networks owed their renewal (in the case of that centred on the earl of Arundel) or even existence (likewise for the earl of Northampton) to his action.

We see this in his introduction into the localities, as an adjunct to the new inquiries, of his personal bodyguard, the king's sergeants-at-arms, from late 1340. The sergeants were a mix of English, Welsh and Gascon soldier-administrators, typically drawn from among the minor gentry or upper peasantry. Some enjoyed a close personal relationship with the king. They were sent from the Tower on numerous commissions of inquiry and arrest – beginning a new pattern of judicial and political intervention in which the king had notorious suspects, the recalcitrant or the tardy brought directly to him. There is no surer indication of Edward's probing interest in the mid-fourteenth century than the local work he allocated to the sergeants-at-arms. Travelling fast on horseback, and characteristically leading compact retinues of mounted archers, the sergeants could be despatched from the Tower on day one, arrest suspected pirates in the West Country on day two and have them in front of the king on day three. They carried some of his most pointed missives: the letters that explained that, earlier summonses having apparently been ignored, more peremptorily worded letters were now being brought by the king's sergeants-at-arms, so that the recipient, no matter how powerful, would know that, were he not immediately to respond, the sergeants would bring him. Where the king harboured doubts about the capacity of his magnate-led networks to deliver, he sent the sergeants in response. Twice in the 1340s, for example, associates of the earl of Arundel whose tax collecting in Shropshire was suspected of being lackadaisical were arrested by sergeants-at-arms. This pattern of Edward III reaching directly deep into the localities via the sergeants continued throughout the remainder of the king's reign. It was only in time of war, when the sergeants formed the king's personal bodyguard on campaign, that their activities in the shires of England reduced.

What were the effects of the purge, the revision of local officeholding and the introduction of the sergeants as agents of inquiry and justice upon the shires? Contemporaries undoubtedly felt the weight of the king's attention. 'Trailbaston lay upon the country,' ominously wrote one chronicler. The surviving records are imperfect as sources but also provide some indications. The collection of taxation and of supply for the royal armies seems to have been more efficient and effective in the 1340s than it had been in the 1330s. This is what we might expect within the context of central government reform, re-staffing in local government and a renewed consensus on war and finance forged by king and Parliament. So far as the state of the peace is concerned, the records of the court of King's Bench show a consistent, if undramatic, decline in the number of cases from 1341, following a prior decade in which there had been no change. A closer examination of the records in individual counties suggests that certain persistent litigants in the 1330s seem to have stopped litigating in the 1340s. Perhaps the hammer-blow of the new inquiries had persuaded some troublesome local figures that keeping a lower profile was wise when presented with a king seemingly determined to root out corrupt or disruptive elements. It is true that certain high-profile local disputants who maintained hostilities in the 1340s found themselves facing Edward III's wrath, on which the king was definitively to act in the early 1350s.

War Renewed

Although, during the course of 1341, Edward and his lieutenants planned for a return to Flanders and a resumption of their grand alliance against

Philip VI, events dictated a new approach to war, which quickly proved advantageous to the Anglo-Gascon cause and, in the end, decisive.

The critical dimension of this was the French king's early success, through more politically intelligent and accommodating diplomacy than he had practised in the 1330s, in detaching the princes of the German Low Countries from allegiance to Edward III. The natural political position of the princes – broad alignment with the French king – was restored. This essentially left only the townsmen of Ghent, Ypres and Bruges – an important but not strategically decisive grouping – as Edward's natural allies in the Netherlands. The English king would now have to look largely to his own military resources – from England and Wales, and in Gascony – to produce armies capable of confronting Philip VI in the field.

At the same time, a succession crisis in the neighbouring duchy of Brittany provided Edward with a new route into mounting a continental expedition that might lead to the decisive land battle with the French king that remained a central part of his strategy. The death in April 1341 of John, duke of Brittany, who had also been earl of Richmond in England, initiated a struggle for the dukedom and control of the duchy between two men, both of whom had been variously identified by the late duke as his favoured heir: his younger half-brother, John de Montfort, and his nephew by marriage, Charles de Blois, who happened also to be the nephew of Philip VI and who was supported by most of the Breton nobility. To their support was duly added that of the French king, after Philip was informed that John's court in western Brittany had received diplomatic representatives of Edward III. Philip backed Blois militarily, sending a strong force under his son and heir, John, duke of Normandy, to recover the city of Nantes and other parts of Brittany overrun by Montfort. Philip's decision pushed Montfort – who was shortly afterwards captured and imprisoned by the French – into formal alliance with the English king in October 1341, as part of which Montfort recognised Edward's claim to the French throne. This continued Edward's policy of placing the French king under political pressure by driving wedges between Philip and his vassals.

No immediate action could be taken by Edward in Brittany, however, because he first had to respond to renewed Scottish raids into the north of England, mounted by the seventeen-year-old David II of Scotland, who had returned from exile in France and taken direct control of the Scottish government in the summer of 1341. Edward wintered in the north in 1341–2, and while his own campaigns were indecisive, they did persuade the Scots to agree a truce, underpinned by the appointment of the highly able earl of Derby as Edward's lieutenant in Scotland. By early 1342 the Montfortists were beleaguered in western Brittany, but it was not until the summer that the English were able to send significant forces to their aid. Resources remained scarce and the Edwardian military revolution – which saw the recruitment and composition of armies, as well as their way of fighting, change radically – was only just under way.

While Edward was assembling his main army, a smaller expeditionary force under the earl of Northampton was despatched to stabilise the Montfortist position and test the enemy's strength. Northampton was contracted as Edward's lieutenant in the duchy, in an early example of the indentures or contracts characteristically agreed by Edward with his key commanders in his new way of making war. Captains appointed in this way agreed to serve in particular theatres for specific periods of time, recruiting their armies directly (though with the Crown's practical support where necessary) from their regional, landed bases in England and Wales, at approved rates of pay. The initial costs of recruitment and equipment were typically borne by the contracted commander, and the noble subcommanders or retinue leaders he had in turn engaged, on the promise of future reimbursement from the king – which could be long coming or (in some cases) did not come at all. In this way, Edward III leveraged the patronage with which he had provided his new nobles (such as Northampton) as well as the landed inheritance of the restored or established nobility (such as Arundel or Warwick) to modernise and supercharge military enrolment, and with it his armies in theatre. Forces raised under contract were more cohesive (because they emerged from regional social networks), fitter, better equipped and much better motivated than the troops previously enlisted via feudal means or royal commissions of array. At a time when English regional dialects could differ such that they were almost different languages – compare, for instance, the language in *Sir Gawain and the Green Knight* with that of Chaucer's *Canterbury Tales*, the former composed in the north Midlands and the latter in the south-east – contracted men were also likelier to be able clearly to communicate with one another in the field. Contemporary descriptions of Arundel's tight-knit Marcher retinues on campaign, uniformed in quartered green and white, are striking.

Northampton landed at Brest in mid-August and Charles de Blois responded by retreating to gather fresh forces. Northampton promptly pushed east in pursuit, besieging Morlaix. When Blois counterattacked, Northampton advanced to meet him and held off Blois's larger army, capturing his commander, the French paladin Geoffrey de Charny. This was the first occasion when the English used tactics learned from the Scots – including fighting dismounted, digging hidden pits to bring down the enemy's horses and using woodland as defensive cover – in France. At the end of October, Edward III arrived at Brest at the head of the main English army, having been delayed by lack of amphibious lift. The enlisted merchant fleet that had carried Northampton to Brittany in the summer had been instructed to return to England to pick up the king, but many of the ships had deserted because of pressing commercial commitments – an action investigated by the furious king via a host of judicial investigations after the campaign was over. Edward's army, though more than twice the size of Northampton's, was compact, at no more than a few thousand men, and the king had been obliged to leave his heavy siege equipment on the beach at the port of Sandwich, as there had been no space for it in the available transports. Towards the end of November, the combined English force embarked upon a winter campaign. Apart from in Poland and Lithuania, where frozen conditions better permitted crusading knights to penetrate swampy heathen territory, medieval armies usually ceased campaigning in the winter months, because of lack of forage and challenging environmental conditions. One of the many ways in which Edward III was an innovative commander was his willingness to sustain major campaigns through the winter. Here he was assisted by the professionalism of his new contract armies, whose comprehensive apparatus – typically including portable forges, corn-mills and ovens, prefabricated and demountable bridges and siege engines, and companies of sappers and miners for river-crossing and siege work – equipped them for a host of eventualities. As December approached, the English advanced in three widely spaced parallel columns – a method that was to become a strategic trope of Edward III

– towards the main Breton urban centres of Rennes, Vannes and Nantes, all of which were located in the Blois-controlled east of the duchy and all of which the English besieged.

Blois promptly sent to his suzerain and ally Philip VI for help, and around Christmas the French king led a large royal army into Brittany, where he rendezvoused with the duke of Normandy. Edward III now concentrated his forces outside Vannes, with its strategically valuable port, and awaited the French advance. Meanwhile, he appealed home urgently for reinforcements, a need already being responded to, through assiduous troop-raising in the March of Wales, by the earls of Arundel and Huntingdon, who had remained in England to manage recruitment and logistics. For the third time in four years, Philip VI declined to attack the English. He approached to within a day's hard march of their position but then halted, while papal representatives sought to negotiate a truce. This they managed in a fortnight: on 19 January 1343 the truce of Malestroit saw hostilities in Brittany come to a close, without any fundamental issue being resolved. Philip VI remained reluctant to risk pitched battle, while Edward III's position outside Vannes was compromised by the size of his army and the absence of large trebuchets (or boulder-throwing siege engines). Contemporaries judged the truce to be highly favourable to the English: they were to retain all the Breton territory they had occupied; Vannes was to remain in neutral, papal custody; John de Montfort was to be released by the French; and after capturing the commander of Vannes, Oliver de Clisson, a powerful Franco-Breton nobleman, Edward had in his hands an important member of the French polity whose commitment to Philip VI he promptly set out to weaken – another example of his ongoing diplomatic strategy, underpinned by military action, of driving wedges between Philip and his great feudal subjects. A number of Clisson's noble clients, including his brother, had already sided with the Montfortists. After Clisson was released by Edward III, having paid a surprisingly low ransom, and with rumours of his treachery swirling, the French king had him seized and executed without trial – together with other disloyal or suspected Franco-Breton lords. Alongside the loss of Breton territory to the English and his repeated refusal to confront Edward III in battle, Philip's immoderate action served only to undermine his personal position in the French polity. It was this weakness that forced him finally to confront the English king in the field in 1346, with disastrous consequences.

Peace Negotiations and Fresh Strategy

In the intervening three years, Edward III cemented the internal position he had established in 1341 and negotiated for peace, while developing and enacting what became definitive strategic and military stances. Parliaments, carefully consulted by the king in 1343 and 1344, confirmed the community of the realm's commitment to supporting the war, both materially, through continuing taxation, and morally. Edward formally set the political confrontation of 1341 behind him by having the accusations he had brought against Stratford publicly destroyed. But the new inquiries continued and were reinforced by fresh commissions, until the failure of peace negotiations under papal auspices at Avignon prompted revised arrangements for maintaining order in the localities, in anticipation of renewed continental warfare. The new arrangements saw peace commissions established in the shires in a new form, in which a mix of respected local gentry, many of them lawyers among Edward's new local officialdom, and the justices of the central courts appointed to hear assizes and deliver the gaols, would combine. The purpose of these commissions was to maintain ready access to justice and redress for Edward's people at home when he and his trusted associates were campaigning overseas. The papal peace negotiations of 1343–5 – in which Edward had been prominently represented by the earls of Derby and Arundel – failed because English and French objectives remained irreconcilable. The English again offered Edward's claim to the French throne in return for full sovereignty in Aquitaine, but this was something Philip VI would not – and, for internal political reasons, could not – concede.

It was clear before the end of 1344 that war was likely to be renewed, and detailed planning and preparation, presided over by Edward III himself, began in earnest. The king's radical reconceptualisation of how war should be fought, of strategy, tactics, organisation and support, was now complete. The tactical dimension had emerged in England gradually across the preceding half-century, but it was only under Edward's direction that it was fully realised in a form that was to dominate European warfare for the next hundred years. It combined the 'infantry revolution' of the early fourteenth century, in which – as at Bannockburn – well-organised and -equipped infantry armies defeated the cavalry that had hitherto tended to sweep all before them in medieval European warfare, with Edward I's innovative use of longbow archery and hobelars (or light skirmishing horse-men). To this mix, Edward III critically added mobility on campaign, as his mounted archers – who married the overwhelming artillery impact of massed longbows to the agility and tactical flexibility of the hobelars – and his men-at-arms alike travelled on horseback before fighting predomin-antly on foot, in formidable defensive positions on the field of battle, and in devastating assaults on town or castle walls, at river crossings or opposed amphibious landings. In such skirmishing scenarios, the capacity of Edward's longbowmen to lay down withering suppressive fire, under the cover of which his heavily armed men-at-arms could make rapid progress, was repeatedly decisive. The war in Brittany in 1342–3 had shown that Edward's professional contract armies, despite their modest size, could in practice more than match much more numerous French opponents. Their very compactness contributed to their tactical effectiveness: they moved faster than their opponents; were better able to exploit natural defensive positions; offered the enemy only a narrow front on which to fight, which turned his advantage in numbers into disadvantage, as his men impeded one another as they sought to engage; and were better co-ordinated in the heat of battle. With the now-established compact between the king and the community of the realm in Parliament over the necessity of war and the best means of financing it, and with Edward's continued injection of new personnel under his direction to make government more effective, the number and size of the contract armies he could raise, transport, deploy and sustain grew.

All this was potentially game-changing, but what turned potential into achievement was something for which Edward III was once decried as lack-ing: strategy. Edward's grand alliance strategy in the Low Countries, which he had inherited from his grandfather, had proved costly and ineffective, and had now effectively collapsed – though the king retained hope of bring-ing the townsmen of Ghent, Ypres and Bruges into play on his side as part of a new strategy. His fresh strategic approach was rooted in his long-held ambition to retake lost Gascon territory in practice as well as to regain it diplomatically. He could do this, without a grand alliance, if he could enact the way of war recently pioneered in Brittany on a greater scale. He would continue to rebuild and maintain strong relations with the great lords of Gascony whose loyalty had been undermined by the misrule of Edward II. Since the late 1330s, this had been supplemented by a clever policy of systematically granting towns, lands and rights to loyal Gascon subjects prospectively, in areas of Aquitaine – most importantly in the Agenais – currently under the control of the French. This provided the Gascons with a direct interest in helping deliver an Anglo-Gascon reoccupation of lost lands to their duke and king. Edward also continued his strategy of seeking to undermine Philip VI's political position by detaching key nobles from Valois allegiance. In Brittany he had deployed multiple armies to attack different Franco-Breton positions in co-ordination and simultaneously. In 1345–7 he took this principle and applied it on a national scale, fielding substantial armies in Gascony, Brittany and northern France at the same time, allying with local interests where possible, but not depending on them on a scale and in way that exposed each initiative to failure – as had been the case in the Low Countries in 1338–40. This multiple attack on exterior lines was henceforth Edward III's grand strategic signature, just as his operational strategic signature was high mobility – the *chevauchée* – and his tactical signature was mixed men-at-arms and archers fighting dismounted, on the defensive.

The king intended to unleash his new grand strategy on the French in 1345 – in Aquitaine, where the focus would be on reoccupying territory lost to the French during and since the War of Saint-Sardos; in Brittany, where recent gains would be consolidated, to the nuisance and political diminution of the Valois government; and in another operational theatre in northern France, the location of which Edward III kept secret, but where he would again seek to challenge Philip VI in person. While action in the first two theatres commenced, that in Aquitaine being prosecuted to a high level of success, the king's own campaign was delayed until 1346.

Aquitaine, Brittany and Flanders

An advanced force under Ralph Stafford, newly appointed seneschal of Aquitaine, departed for Bordeaux in February 1345, and in early summer made initial advances against the French. Heavily reinforced by Gascon lords and their retinues, Stafford besieged two strategically important towns: Blaye to the north of Bordeaux and Langon to the east. The Anglo-Gascon political community initiated action while they awaited the arrival of the king's lieutenant in Aquitaine, Henry of Grosmont, earl of Derby – Edward's cousin and most talented military commander. Grosmont had been contracted in March to represent the king's interests in south-west France with an army of two thousand men. The English had planned to send significant forces to Aquitaine at various points since the early 1330s, but this was the first time it had proved possible to implement that long-held ambition. After landing with his men at Bayonne in June, Grosmont advanced to Bordeaux, where Gascon troops at least doubled the size of his force, and local lords such as Bernard Aiz d'Albret, Jean de Grailly, captal de Buch and Alexander Caumont joined his command structure. By August he had suspended Stafford's sensible but cautious siege policy, intent instead upon a lightning campaign of attack that would catch the French unawares, push them off balance and drive them rapidly east along the main transport axes – the great river valleys of the Dordogne, Garonne, Isle and Lot – while loyal Gascons reoccupied numerous lost towns. Towards the end of the month his army arrived unexpectedly outside the French headquarters of Bergerac, at a key crossing of the Dordogne. The defending French panicked as they retreated first into the southern suburb and then north across the bridge into the town, where they were trapped by ferocious fire from English archers on sandbanks in the river. The town was subsequently taken by storm; hundreds of French men-at-arms were killed and many more were captured, while others fled; Grosmont secured vast sums in plunder and ransoms to sustain the next phase of the campaign; and the Anglo-Gascons were established in a new forward position.

This they promptly exploited. An advance into Périgord secured a number of strategic strongholds around the French-held regional capital of Périgueux. Placing the city under blockade, Grosmont returned to

Bordeaux to regroup, but was obliged urgently to reverse his plans when a large French force under the overall command of the duke of Normandy arrived in Périgord, and besieged the new Anglo-Gascon garrison of Auberoche. On 21 October, following a forced night march to maintain surprise, Grosmont attacked the enemy with a compact force of men-at-arms and mounted archers, while the French were eating their evening meal and were without arms or armour. Surprise almost carried the day, but, heavily outnumbered, the English had to rely for victory upon a sortie from the castle led by their Brabantian garrison commander Frank van Hal, who attacked the enemy in the rear at a critical juncture in the battle. Nonetheless, this stunning victory – in which Grosmont took prisoners and booty of greater value even than he had at Bergerac – produced a catastrophic loss of confidence in the French camp, which effectively allowed the Anglo-Gascons free rein in the duchy throughout the autumn and winter. As the duke of Normandy disbanded his forces and retreated, Grosmont and Stafford, now joined by the young and able Laurence Hastings, earl of Pembroke, took first La Réole, critical to controlling the Agenais and the approach to Bordeaux, and then Aiguillon, whose strategic position at the confluence of the Lot and Garonne rendered it almost as important. Flying columns of Gascons completed the work of reconquest so that, by the early spring, Edward III's forces had retaken more than a hundred towns and villages from the French and had all but overturned the losses suffered in the mid-1320s.

In Brittany and northern France, however, 1345 brought frustration rather than progress for the English. The second prong of their planned attack on France was commanded by the earl of Northampton, who resumed his position as king's lieutenant in Brittany, but became bogged down – despite attempting to fight a war of high mobility – securing northern Breton ports. (These stood to offer the English easier sea passage to the duchy than did Brest or Vannes.) Northampton returned to England in 1346, leaving Brittany in the highly capable hands of his brother-in-law and deputy lieutenant, the soldier-administrator Thomas Dagworth. The third English army intended for the Continent in 1345 was also the largest, under the king's personal command. It mustered at Sandwich in Kent; its original destination (though secret) was probably northern France, and its anticipated date of departure July. But it was delayed by both a sudden need for Edward to travel to Flanders to resecure his alliance with the Flemish towns of Ghent, Ypres and Bruges, which in early July was believed to be teetering, and by strongly adverse winds, which scattered the fleet. The transports then reassembled at Portsmouth, but by this time men and horses had been on board in cramped conditions for too long, and by the time they had been disembarked and rested, and were ready to re-embark, the season was too advanced for safety. Reluctantly, the government resolved to reassemble Edward's army in May 1346. But the king took the opportunity over the winter and spring both significantly to strengthen home defences on the south coast and in the March of Scotland, and to stiffen his judicial position in respect of allegedly corrupt justice and disruptive behaviour on the part of social elites. The Ordinance of Justices of 1346 forbade judges from receiving fees or robes, and disputing nobles or gentry now found themselves liable to be prosecuted for treason if they rode against one another 'arrayed in manner of war' – Edward's rationale being that, in time of war, internal fighting aided the enemy. The allocation to home defence of troops originally raised for continental service was wise, and reassured the king's subjects, but further set back Edward's departure from the spring to the summer. The king was also forced to resort to outmoded methods of troop-raising – specifically, the array – to produce the overall numbers he needed. This was because of the scale of his commitments in Aquitaine and Brittany, as well as to home defence, and also because a new scheme he had attempted in 1345, which sought to assess his subjects' duty to provide soldiers based on their possession of landed wealth, had had to be abandoned as too radical. This was the last time in his reign, nonetheless, in which substantial numbers of soldiers were recruited in the old way.

Crécy and Calais

The campaign led by Edward III in northern France in 1346–7 produced both his rout of Philip VI at the battle of Crécy and the capture of Calais, which the English then held as a permanent bridgehead in France for over two hundred years. The Crécy–Calais campaign represents the acme of Edward's personal military command.

His departure for France was heralded by the French response to Grosmont's capture of La Réole and Aiguillon in the winter. In spring 1346, the duke of Normandy was again despatched south to deal with the threat posed by Grosmont and to reverse his successes. As in 1345, he failed, partly because of the effectiveness of the English king's new strategy in dividing and defeating the enemy in detail, and partly because of the ability of Edward's commanders in Aquitaine. It was the latter — with Stafford and Pembroke in Aiguillon, and Grosmont (by now earl of Lancaster, following the death of his father, Henry of Lancaster) in La Réole. The duke of Normandy's first target was Aiguillon, which he attacked, failed to take and then besieged in April. Effective counter-attacking on Normandy's huge encircling army by all three English commanders meant that the blockade of Aiguillon was never complete; nonetheless the relief of its garrison was important, both strategically, so that the English recapture of lost Gascon territory could be cemented, and personally for Edward III — who had promised Grosmont that he would come to his rescue, should the latter's forces prove hard pressed. Edward's initial objective in France may indeed have been Aquitaine, but by the time he departed from the Isle of Wight, at the head of a fully equipped army of some twelve thousand English and Welsh troops, he had resolved on a landing in Normandy instead.

His selection of the Cotentin peninsula was probably influenced by the latest French lord to have recognised him, having been alienated by Philip VI. This was Geoffrey d'Harcourt, lord of Saint-Sauveur, who guided the English down the Cotentin after their barely opposed disembarkation on 12 July 1346 at Saint-Vaast-la-Hougue, just north of the Normandy beaches where the Allies would later land in June 1944. As in the Second World War, secrecy and a campaign of disinformation meant that opposition to the invading forces had been spread thinly and ineffectively all along the northern French seaboard. As soon as news of Edward's landing reached Philip VI, he urgently recalled Normandy and his army from the south-west to help defend the motherland against this greater threat. The duke immediately abandoned his siegeworks, leaving behind valuable tents and equipment. Despite making all haste to reach his father in the north before the French king and his English counterpart clashed, he and his army arrived too late to participate in the encounter. The English hold on Aquitaine was now secure. In the autumn, Grosmont raided deep into Saintonge and Poitou, capturing Saint-Jean-d'Angély and storming Poitiers, while the Gascons under Albret and Caumont consolidated the reoccupation of the Agenais and the Bazadais.

Edward III's army – commanded by the king, his newly knighted, sixteen-year-old son and heir, the Black Prince, the earls of Warwick, Northampton and Arundel, and Lords Reginald Cobham and Richard Talbot – reached Caen, the capital of lower Normandy, on 26 July – having taken Valognes, Carentan and Saint-Lô en route. Defended by the constable of France, the count of Eu, Caen was captured by archer-led storm. Eu and many other French knights were seized and despatched home to be ransomed. They represented potential political leverage as well as a source of war finance. After a few days' rest, the English advanced on the Île de France, while the French broke the bridges over the Seine in an attempt to constrain their movement. After rebuilding the bridge at Poissy and publicly dismissing Philip VI's invitation to join him in battle beneath the walls of Paris, Edward headed north towards the Somme, burning and plundering as he went, with the French in fruitless pursuit. There, his archers were again critical in forcing a crossing of the river at Blanchetaque, which both enabled the English to rendezvous with their supply fleet at Le Crotoy on the Somme estuary, and brought Edward home to his ancestral French county of Ponthieu. His army freshly restocked, Edward once more outran the pursuing enemy, before turning to fight on 26 August, on a south-facing ridge near Crécy-en-Ponthieu – a village he had visited once before, in 1329, when doing homage to Philip VI for Aquitaine.

By the time Philip VI's huge army approached Edward's lines in the rain that evening, the English and Welsh were well dug in, in three defensive divisions of mixed men-at-arms and archers: the vanguard under the Black Prince and Warwick; the centre under Northampton and Arundel; and the rear guard under the king, who commanded from a windmill and during the course of the battle never needed to don his armour. Although Philip was counselled to pause, rest his men and attack the English in the morning, he was unable to prevent his eager and ill-disciplined knights from advancing immediately. This absence of control betrayed a lack of confidence in their king on the part of the French nobility, who looked askance at his record of having previously avoided fighting the English king, and had been openly talking about his 'foxiness' or cowardice in the French court. Philip's reputation desperately needed a military victory at this point, and, seeing his soldiers advance, he abandoned caution and threw himself into the thick of the fray.

Philip's two thousand Genoese crossbowmen were the first division to fail under the firestorm laid down by the English archers. Although the crossbow was a dangerous weapon, its rate of fire was slow, and amid the chaos of the French advance, the *pavises* or large shields of the Genoese, behind which they reloaded their crossbows, had been left behind. Outnumbered three to one by the opposing longbowmen, whose rate of fire was also three or four times faster, and also fired upon by primitive cannon, used for the first time by an English army, they stood little chance. As they turned in retreat, they impeded the advancing French cavalry, who, accusing them of treachery, cut them down. The French knights quickly learned what the Genoese had suffered at the hands of the English archers. Advancing closely packed at a fast trot, each French cavalry charge was in range of the longbowmen for at least a minute before they reached the pits, stakes, chains and men-at-arms in the English front line, during which time they may have received between sixty and ninety thousand arrows. The shafts, which contemporaries described as falling like hail and darkening the sky, brought down many horses, killed or wounded knights whose armour was in some way deficient, and disoriented, slowed and sapped the strength of everyone. Fighting in the mêlée, as the French finally reached the English men-at-arms, was still intense, especially around the Black Prince; but as night advanced, and after many waves of French attack, Philip VI was led, wounded by an arrow in the jaw, from the battleground for his own safety, leaving several thousand French knights dead on the field. This included the flower of French nobility – among them John, the blind king of Bohemia, whose knights had led him on his warhorse into the heart of battle, Philip's brother Charles, duke of Alençon, Louis, count of Blois and Louis, count of Flanders. The unwounded state of many of the bodies indicated that, as at Dupplin Moor and Halidon Hill, many knights had been suffocated or crushed to death in the press. English casualties were slight. Early in the morning, another division of French troops, mostly infantry, who had presumably arrived too late to learn the news of the French defeat, blundered out of the mist only to be put to flight and killed in large numbers by a cavalry charge under Northampton.

Thus far, Edward III had fought an exemplary campaign. His army had been expertly assembled, equipped and supplied. His logistics had been sophisticated and effective. His military intelligence was good. He had maintained excellent communications among his divisions, with his government at home, with Grosmont in Aquitaine, Dagworth in Brittany and his lieutenant in Flanders, Sir Hugh Hastings, who had led a co-ordinated incursion into northern France by the Flemings. During the *chevauchée* between Caen and Crécy, his troops had been quick and agile in manoeuvre, and highly disciplined. His dispositions on the field at Crécy were exactly right and he had maintained tactical control throughout – ruthlessly holding his rear guard in reserve even when his son and heir had appealed for assistance. Contemporaries remarked that his men fought for him so steadfastly because 'they both loved and feared him'. Before the battle he had toured the ranks, cheerfully encouraging his men. Afterwards he addressed the warlike Black Prince, pointedly asking him, 'Son, now you have seen war, do you still think it good sport?' We are told that 'the prince looked down and was ashamed'.

The king now resolved on a radical next step. He would take and hold Calais, the great French port closest to England, as a permanent bridgehead in northern France, which he could use as a base for the projection of strategic power in the long term. This would make confronting the French in France, relatively near to the political centre of Paris and close to his remaining allies in Ghent, Ypres and Bruges, significantly easier. Calais was chosen not just because of its proximity to Sandwich, the other Cinque Ports and Flanders, but also because it was strongly protected and situated: with double walls and moats, and enclosed by marshes. Once taken it would be relatively easy to hold. But its very defensibility made it difficult to capture in the first place, and although the English attempted to storm it several times after they had arrived outside its walls on 4 September, they quickly settled down to what was clearly going to be a long siege.

In the eleven months before Calais surrendered, successes in war elsewhere strengthened the English hand, though not all their military endeavours proved profitable. Although they continued to enjoy the naval superiority in the Channel created by their victory at Sluys in 1340, they were bettered by French forces in certain naval actions relating to the maritime resupply of both the Calais garrison and its besieging army; and some English raids on neighbouring towns, such as Saint-Omer, met with fierce and effective resistance. But the triumphs they saw were, in the long term, definitive. On 17 October 1346, at Neville's Cross just outside Durham, King David II of Scotland was captured by the English knight John Coupland following his defeat in battle at the hands of Ralph, Lord Neville, William Zouche, archbishop of York and Henry, Lord Percy. The Scots had invaded England in force at the behest of their ally Philip VI. Their subsequent rout was consequent upon their choice of a difficult battlefield, divided and cut by walls and ditches, which broke up their attacks, as well as upon devastating English archery, and was testament to the effectiveness of the measures for home defence that Edward III had put in place before departing for the Continent. Many of Scotland's political and military leaders were killed or seized. The courageous Scottish king took two arrows in the face, but was still capable of knocking Coupland's teeth out with his iron gauntlet before he was taken. Surgeons summoned from York struggled to remove all of the second arrowhead, leaving him prone to headaches until the fragment spontaneously emerged from the wound some years later, which David attributed to divine intervention. His comfortable captivity in England, first in the Tower, and later in Windsor and Odiham Castles, lasted for eleven years. Then, on 20 June 1347, the English commander in Brittany, Thomas Dagworth, captured the French-backed claimant to the duchy, Charles de Blois, in a hard-fought battle outside the town and castle of La Roche-Derrien, which Blois was besieging and to the relief of which Dagworth had come. Blois now joined David II in the Tower, and Edward III had in his hands two prisoners of immense political value. Meanwhile, Henry of Grosmont's raid on Saintonge and Poitou, which the French feared might eventually threaten Paris, had helped prevent an early response to Edward III's investment of Calais, and had pressured the count of Eu – whose lands

Grosmont plundered – provisionally to recognise Edward as rightful king of France.

Maintaining the siege of Calais for nearly a year required high expenditure, and exceptional organisation and logistics on the part of the English. To minimise the effects of disease, the army's tents were quickly replaced by a carefully planned wooden town, named Villeneuve-la-Hardie. Regular supplies of food and arms came directly by sea or overland from nearby Flanders. Desertion for lack of wages – because the royal coffers were close to exhausted – threatened to weaken the besieging army, and created conflict between Edward and Northampton. (This conflict prompted the king to order investigations into 'scandalous accusations' that the earl had behaved seditiously. While 'the whole truth' was explored, no judgement against Northampton resulted.) But determined recruitment among older knights, who had remained in England for the purposes of home defence while their sons had served in France, swelled the Anglo-Welsh ranks to more than thirty thousand men – a huge army by medieval standards. Capturing a sandy spit commanding the entrance to Calais harbour in April 1347 enabled the English finally to enforce a blockade hitherto periodically run by French mariners. Meanwhile, the French were in serious difficulty. Recent high taxation, losses to English raiding and fear of Edward's armies remaining in France combined to persuade many French communities to retain scarce resources for their own defence rather than contribute to the central war effort. Division between the French king and his heir reflected widespread disillusionment with Philip VI's kingship, even if only a minority of French magnates openly discussed recognising Edward III. Desperate pleas for help from the governor of Calais, Jean de Vienne, finally resulted in the prevaricating Philip mustering a relief army – though a relatively small one – and leading it north. On 27 July the French reached the heights of Sangatte, only to look down on Anglo-Welsh and Flemish forces well entrenched around Calais, and outnumbering them at least two to one. Philip attempted to save face by opening negotiations through papal envoys, but his thin offering to the English – the restitution of Aquitaine in full, albeit as a fief of the French Crown – was immediately rejected. In the early hours of 2 August, he marched his army away. Left to their fate, the townspeople of Calais surrendered the following day. It is impossible to know whether the incident recounted by the great chronicler Jean Froissart and later celebrated by the sculptor Auguste Rodin in *The Burghers of Calais* – in which Queen Philippa interceded with the king to spare the lives of six men nominated by the townspeople to represent them at the town's surrender – actually occurred. If it did, it surely represented another conscious foray by Edward III into the theatre of politics.

The Order of the Garter

In need of financial and material respite, the English king promptly agreed an advantageous truce – to last until June 1348 – with a French king whose fiscal circumstances were even more pressing. Edward retained control of all the urban centres and territory his forces had occupied. He then spent two months putting Calais in proper defensive order before returning to England in October 1347.

His homecoming brought a combination of consolidation and celebration. Two Parliaments, in January and March 1348, saw his military and diplomatic policy affirmed by the political community, and the grant of an unprecedented triennial subsidy to sustain the king's financial position, despite the then state of truce, with Edward conceding in return that during the three years of the new tax, he would not send financially onerous judicial commissions into the localities. Celebration took the form of numerous tournaments across the winter, some attended by the captive David II of Scotland, with whom both Edward III and Queen Philippa quickly built up a relationship of marked cordiality and even friendship. Seemingly as part of a tournament at Windsor hosted in June 1348, the king either conceived or began to realise a scheme for creating an exclusive chivalric order, the Order of the Garter. Two tournament teams of knights were ordained, commanded by the king and the Black Prince respectively, and encompassing a range of social and national backgrounds. The Order of the Garter has been misunderstood as a mechanism for uniting the king and his nobles, but Edward's service nobility was already fully wedded to his rule and too many garter knights were men of minor political importance – such as John Chandos or Neil Loring – for this to have been the case. Instead, they were individuals of great chivalric merit, personally close to the king or the prince. Their enduring motto of *Honi soit qui mal y pense* is usually translated as 'shame on those who think badly of it', supposedly referencing either Edward's claim to the French throne or an alleged and obscure incident in which he picked up a garter dropped by the countess of Salisbury. But two near-contemporary references to the motto – in the poems 'Wynnere and Wastoure' and *Sir Gawain and the Green Knight* – make it clear that the contemporary understanding was the more philosophical 'shame on those who think evil'. In August, the king refounded the chapel at Windsor Castle as a collegiate home for the Order of the Garter, dedicating it to the Virgin, St George and Edward the Confessor. The first meeting of the order was delayed, however, until 1349, by the calamitous arrival in England of bubonic plague – termed the 'pestilence' or 'great mortality' by contemporaries, but known to posterity as the Black Death.

The Black Death and State Economic Intervention

News of a great mortality afflicting the world, spreading from the East, reached England in the winter of 1347–8, but it was not until July and August that the Black Death landed on its shores, carried in merchant ships to its southern ports, just as it had already been carried from Crimea to Constantinople, and thence to Italy, France and Spain. Genomic research completed on corpses found in gravesites associated with the Black Death has latterly underpinned the widely accepted theory that the pestilence was a mix of bubonic, pneumonic and septicaemic plagues. In England, judging by the recorded mortality among clergy, it seems to have killed between 40 and 50 per cent of the population in its first wave, which seems to have peaked in early 1349, was starting to decline by the summer and was largely over by the end of the year. Mortality may have exceeded 60 per cent following a second outbreak in 1361–2, and the population of England probably reached its pre-Black Death levels again only in the sixteenth century. The Black Death spread first to the West Country, then north-east to London and the Midlands by the autumn of 1348, and reached Norwich in early 1349. It extended throughout the north as the year continued, entering Scotland in 1350. Whole villages were eradicated by the disease, and everywhere the fields were left untilled and the crops unharvested.

Edward III had early and devastating experience of the mortality, when his beloved daughter, Princess Joan – who was en route to Castile to be married to Prince Peter, the heir to the Castilian throne – died outside Bordeaux on 1 July 1348. Edward wrote about her death, reflectively and movingly, to King Alfonso XI of Castile – who was later to die of the Black Death himself, in 1350:

> Your magnificence knows how . . . we sent our daughter [Joan] to Bordeaux, en route for your territories in Spain. But see, and with what intense bitterness of heart we have to tell you this, destructive Death (who seizes young and old alike, sparing no one, and reducing rich and poor to the same level) has lamentably snatched from us our dearest daughter, whom we loved best of all, as her virtues demanded. No fellow human being could be surprised if we were inwardly desolated by the string of this bitter grief, for we are human too. But we, who have placed our trust in God and our life between his hands, where he has held it closely through many great dangers, give thanks to him that one of our own family, free of all stain, whom we have loved with a pure love, has been sent ahead to Heaven to reign among the choirs of virgins, where she can gladly intercede for our offences before God himself.

Although Edward spent more time than usual in his rural retreats during 1348–9, distanced from the deadly miasma that contemporaries believed spread the pestilence, he still regularly visited Westminster, the Tower of London and the royal port of Sandwich. Devastating mortality meant that government could not continue as normal: Parliament was cancelled and the operation of the law courts was suspended for all of 1349. But the king remained resolutely focused upon national need. He considered the cause of the pestilence 'with intense concentration', writing to the bishops that he attributed it to an absence of due religious devotion, and urgently imploring them to encourage people to turn to prayer and fasting as solutions. Taxation was kept flowing. With concerns mounting about the rural economy and the soaring cost of employment, the king promulgated the Ordinance of Labourers (1349), later strengthened in Parliament to

produce the Statute of Labourers (1351), which sought through state regulation to ensure that all able-bodied adults worked, that wages remained
at pre-plague levels, that workers kept to their existing employment contracts and that food prices remained 'reasonable'. In March 1351 the peace
commission was significantly enlarged to provide the additional personnel
necessary to enforce the labouring legislation, though the new commissioners were subsequently separately appointed as 'justices of labourers'.
This was a new office in the shires, junior to the justices of the peace, and
generally staffed by gentry administrators of lower rank than the experienced local lawyers who tended to be appointed to the peace commission
alongside the justices of the central courts. The justices of labourers were
the sort of men whom the Crown had hitherto typically appointed as tax
collectors, or commissioners to survey and maintain sea walls, drainage
or bridges, and in 1357 they were also given responsibility for enforcing
legislation on weights and measures.

This was not the only way in which the Crown extended its regulation
of the economy. Price regulation continued and expanded, and under the
direction of Edward's brilliant new chief justice of King's Bench, William
Shareshull, and in the face of popular demand, a flexible and responsive
common law adapted and grew to encompass, with increasing sophistica-
tion and complexity, many commercial contracts and relationships. While
a degree of local resistance and workarounds, such as payments in kind,
meant that the labouring and price legislation was not always effective, the
consequences for the economy were mitigated, first by economic growth,
which was fostered by the king's effective liberalisation of the wool and
cloth trades following the Ordinance of the Staple in 1353, and second by
the reality that the economy remained coin-based and that the supply of
coin was efficiently managed and modernised by the Crown. Although the
population had been dramatically reduced in size, the total value of coin
in circulation remained broadly the same, which probably helped limit
the impact of rises in wages and prices. A novel scheme of 1352 allowing fines on peasants and other workers levied under the Ordinance and
Statute of Labourers to be offset against taxation also reduced the pressure
on taxpaying landholders generated by post-Black Death wage rises. In
some shires the effective subsidy this provided to taxpayers halved their tax

bills. By this means, the common people, whom market forces had made more prosperous because their labour was now in short supply, indirectly helped fund the nation's wars, a significant portion of the tax burden being shifted down the social pyramid. While the economy remained buoyant, the political consequences of this shift were slight – though they were to bite disastrously in the late 1370s and early 1380s, after the economy had entered decline.

Justice in the Localities

In addition to agreeing laws to counter economic disorder caused by the Black Death, the king and Shareshull now took determined action to stem other forms of disorder. Inappropriate and unacceptable behaviour on the part of great lords, their associates and royal officials was targeted, and common-law structures directed towards providing solutions or redress in the country for ordinary people who faced everyday disputes and crime were revised and rationalised. Neither of these complementary strands of work represented a new initiative, because both involved a resumption of approaches pioneered in the early 1330s and powerfully renewed in the 1340s within the context of war. But the Black Death undoubtedly lent them yet more impetus, and in the early 1350s, Shareshull presided over their co-ordinated implementation within a single, coherent judicial system, completing a systematic overhaul of legal provision on a nationwide basis. In county after county, the arrival of powerful, extempore judicial commissions, intended to deal with alleged oppressions of the king's people by nobles and officials, was underpinned by the Crown issuing a revised peace commission in the same locality at the same time. This was thoroughgoing royal justice, and in practice, the different judicial commissions worked together: in Essex, for example, ruthless judicial hearings conducted in the court of King's Bench into alleged wrongdoing by magnates and others were facilitated by the justices of the peace rapidly drawing up first drafts of the charges in advance. (Intriguingly, the JPs' clerks in Chelmsford still took their notes in Norman French, even though the discussion among the litigants they served would, by this time, surely have been conducted in English.)

471

Edward III was personally and openly determined to ensure that the great men of the realm, not just the common people, should (as he put it) look to their responsibilities in the face of the pestilence. This insistence was in many ways a continuation, reinforced by the disaster of mass mortality, of his established attitude towards the law and transgressors. From the beginning of his rule he had employed the law as a political weapon against elements within the polity he believed were acting against the common good; this had been especially evident in his pursuit of the Folvilles and Coterels via trailbaston and other interventionist judicial commissions in the early 1330s. Although the sheer vividness of the charges brought by the Crown against members of those two families had rarely been matched in judicial commissions since, the new inquiries of the early 1340s had been conducted on an unprecedented scale. While national drives for order had been seen before, especially under Edward I, no previous judicial commissions had charged so many royal officials with so many alleged offences, and in such a sustained way. Although the Commons had declined to endorse interventionist commissions of this sort as a potential solution to disorder after 1343, the king resolutely continued to employ them, though in a more targeted way than in 1340–2. While MPs were now tending to see such direct royal judicial intervention in the shires as a fiscal and political burden best kept away from their communities, the king saw only a means to ensure that ordinary people were protected and his great subjects who transgressed fined. The year 1346 had seen added to this Edward's decision that lords who fought private wars with one another should be charged with treason, and in the following two years the Crown deployed judicial eyres in the principality of Wales. This represented a novel extension, within the lands of the Black Prince, of the great inquiries that had been pursued in England in the early 1340s. The prince's eyres fitted into a wider pattern of investigations implemented throughout England and Wales in the late 1340s and early 1350s that sought to combine the redress of abuse with the raising of war finance by judicial means.

In 1351 Edward III again picked up the heavy judicial baton in England that he had laid down in 1348, when he had acceded to the Commons' request that no financially punitive royal commissions should enter the localities during the course of the triennial subsidy then granted. The consistency of his judicial approach either side of the hiatus of 1348–51 is shown not only by the comparability of the heavyweight legal commissions issued in the 1340s and 1350s, but also by the treatment of individual nobles who first came to the Crown's attention as problems in the mid- to late 1340s and were pursued in the courts from 1351. Prominent among the magnates targeted were John, Lord Fitzwalter, James, Lord Audley of Heighley and Thomas Lisle, bishop of Ely. Fitzwalter was identified by the king as a transgressor in the late 1340s, when he was accused of sedition because he had allegedly exported wool from his Essex manors without having paid the appropriate dues. Audley came under the baleful royal gaze a year or so earlier, having contracted to serve as a war captain in Aquitaine but having in fact sent a deputy in his place. The two received letters from the king requesting their attendance to 'discuss matters touching the safety of the realm', and Audley was also subject to the attentions of the king's sergeants-at-arms. Lisle had been involved in a high-profile legal dispute that had come before the king's Council in 1348, but does not seem to have been directly targeted by the king as a problem demanding decisive action until 1355.

In 1351 Fitzwalter was charged with a lurid catalogue of felonies and trespasses against his immediate neighbours in his Essex heartlands, especially the prior of Dunmow and the townsmen of Colchester. The accusations largely centred on abuses allegedly committed by Fitzwalter within the context of wider legal dispute: the disproportionate use of distraint, for example, or his deployment of the county coroner to investigate the killing of one of his men outside Colchester, where only the town coroner was supposed to sit. Some charges also probably related to requisitioning for war. The internal evidence in the indictments indicates that, had the process under which they were drawn up not been directed against Fitzwalter, they could have been spun in the opposite legal direction: there is no dispute that the prior's animals had destroyed Fitzwalter's crops, for example, or that one of Fitzwalter's retainers had been killed, and that men of Colchester were suspected of having been responsible. Relations between the Fitzwalter family and Colchester were historically fractious: the Fitzwalter manor of Lexden abutted the town, and both parties periodically brought legal cases against the other because of jurisdictional clashes over access to land and water, and over fishing rights. Perhaps the clearest indication that Edward III was again in the business of making examples through his courts of those he believed were not delivering on their obligations to the realm is the existence in the records of far-fetched, catch-all allegations that the various high-profile targets of his ire in Essex – including Fitzwalter, John Benington, steward of the earl of Hereford and Essex, and the wealthy knights John Farmer and Robert Marney – had formed 'coven and alliance' and had 'conspired together to do harm' to 'the king's good men of Essex'. Nonetheless, the charges against Fitzwalter were myriad, prominent among them the extraordinary assertion that he had twice besieged the town of Colchester for several weeks in the early 1340s – though how a lord whose retinue on the Crécy–Calais campaign appears to have numbered only eighteen men managed to besiege a large, wealthy and tough town for so long can only be guessed at. Fitzwalter was outlawed, surrendered to the king at the palace of Westminster, was imprisoned first in the Marshalsea and later the Tower of London, and had his estates confiscated. During his incarceration, royal auditors completed a valuation of his lands, and in 1352, he was released and pardoned in return for paying a colossal fine equivalent to the entire value of his possessions; confiscation to the Crown was the due punishment for conspiracy, which remained the king's indictment of choice against his political-legal targets. Sir John Farmer, another prominent Essex lord, received exactly the same treatment, as more than five hundred substantial fines were levied on major landholders, their ministers and royal officials in the county, in proceedings strongly reminiscent of those completed in Essex via the new inquiries in 1340–1.

It was another variety of conspiracy, oppressions under the colour of his office of sergeant-of-the-peace in the Black Prince's palatinate lordship of Chester, of which Lord Audley was convicted in trailbaston hearings conducted under the authority of the Cheshire eyre of 1353, which was led by Chief Justice Shareshull in his guise as the prince's senior legal officer. The prince stayed with Audley at Heighley Castle en route to Chester and the party travelled on together, before the political community in Cheshire bought off the eyre proper by agreeing to a collective fine of five thousand marks, and Audley was fined the huge additional sum of seven hundred marks in the subsequent trailbaston that was conducted in the eyre's place – in what appears to have been another act of political theatre. The Crown was evidently also taking a conscious stand in 1354–7, when Thomas Lisle, bishop of Ely – who had fallen into dispute with the king's kinswoman, Blanche of Lancaster, the widow of Thomas, Lord Wake of Liddell – was pursued through the courts by Shareshull and then the king in person. Lisle, who lacked political judgement, made the catastrophic error of accusing Edward III of being biased against him when the king offered personally to arbitrate the dispute. Edward managed to contain his rage, but when Lisle subsequently refused formally to submit to him after he had, nonetheless, brokered a settlement, he was incandescent, and the bishop was forced to flee the realm for the papal palace at Avignon in 1356. Although some senior clerics considered Lisle's behaviour to have been poor, bombastic and self-righteous, the judgements against him prompted John Thoresby's resignation as chancellor over the conjoined questions of secular jurisdiction and ecclesiastical rights. While the king derived significant and much-needed income from the bishop's confiscated temporalities, it is moot whether the point of principle, that great lords acting in excess of authority should be brought to book, was in this case worth the loss of such an effective government official as Thoresby – or the additional friction generated with the papacy at a time of challenging foreign-policy negotiation.

The Crown's mechanisms of choice for holding members of the social and political elite to account were eyres in the Black Prince's private lordships of Wales, Chester and Cornwall, and the central court of King's Bench in England. King's Bench, which was the highest court below Parliament, was despatched under Shareshull from Westminster in 1351 to perambulate the country as a court of first instance, in an unprecedented extension of the king's judicial reach. It was the King's Bench sitting in Chelmsford that brought Lord Fitzwalter to justice, and in its perambulations to 1354, it systematically toured south-east England, East Anglia and the west Midlands. We term this judicial innovation 'superior eyre' because of a comment made by Shareshull when asked by other lawyers what would happen if, theoretically, the new mechanism entered a county where the general eyre – the obsolescent but still-revered supreme judicial instrument of the Angevin kings – was acting. 'The eyre would cease, because the King's

Bench is superior to the eyre,' replied Shareshull. Both the prince's eyres and the superior eyre of King's Bench, which was to return to the localities later in the 1350s and 1360s, were supplemented by general oyer and terminer or trailbaston commissions: in England these effectively enlarged the scope of the king's and Shareshull's inquiries beyond the confines of the county in which the King's Bench was then sitting, without the entire apparatus of the court having to be transported to another location. While the King's Bench was in Warwickshire in 1352, for instance, its justices were appointed to conduct oyer and terminer proceedings across the shire boundary in neighbouring Leicestershire. In the prince's lands, the use of trailbaston enabled high-profile offenders such as Lord Audley still to be individually targeted where communal fines were being offered in return for the withdrawal of the eyre proper. The superior eyre, supported by general oyer and terminer commissions, remained a powerful division of the state for the purposes of asserting and re-establishing order, in the hands of a monarch focused upon the common good – as Henry V was twice to demonstrate during the course of his reign, in judicial campaigns modelled on those of Edward III.

The early 1350s also saw the king and Shareshull further rationalise and strengthen provision against everyday crime and disorder. While very serious or political disruption in the shires was best addressed by the king issuing powerful, ad hoc tribunals, most disorder, most of the time, was not of this nature. However much it afflicted the lives of the individuals it touched, it was ultimately run of the mill, consisting of routine property disputes and everyday criminality – theft, robbery, assault, homicide, rape and arson – of the sort that bedevils almost every society, irrespective of time and geography. Following the creation of the common law through Henry II's Assize of Clarendon of 1166, the general eyre had provided redress for this sort of everyday disorder during its perambulations of the realm. But because of the infrequency with which the cumbersome eyre was able to visit each shire (at best, once every four years), some of its core functions were also devolved to new judicial mechanisms: commissions of assize and of gaol delivery.

The justices of assize settled property disputes by hearing assizes like that of 'novel disseisin', in which a trial jury decided whether a plaintiff

476

or plaintiffs had been deprived of property, or access to property, that was rightfully theirs. The jurors frequently based their decisions on interviews with elderly locals of long memory, or agreed behind the scenes to regularise through their legal verdict a settlement or compromise that had been privately agreed by the parties in negotiations taking place parallel to the trial. The justices of gaol delivery 'delivered', or emptied, the county gaols of prisoners who had been arrested and imprisoned to await trial after being indicted for a felony: a crime punishable by hanging. The main felonies, in order of frequency of accusation, were serious theft, homicide, arson and rape. The justices delivered the gaols by presiding over jury trials that resulted in the accused being either acquitted and released without further punishment, or convicted, in which case they were hanged or, if they were a member of the clergy, delivered to their bishop for imprisonment. Acquittal was much the most common outcome, probably because of a lack of hard evidence, but it is likely that the high acquittal rate for felony was also underpinned by private compensation and settlement, taking place behind the scenes and with the jurors' knowledge. In such cases, a felony had probably been committed, or may even have been known to have been committed, but was regarded as an aberration or one-off on the part of an individual believed by the community otherwise to be of good character.

Trial before the justices of assize and gaol delivery was readily accessible to the king's subjects. To bring a plea of assize of novel disseisin, would-be litigants had to purchase a writ, but this was affordable, costing sixpence or around £250 in present-day terms. The vast majority of cases were brought by ordinary peasants or townspeople. Initiating a prosecution for felony was just as straightforward: it involved persuading a presenting jury that a crime had been committed and that a named person (or persons) might reasonably be suspected of having done it. The presenting or indicting juries were twelve-, eighteen- or sometimes twenty-four-strong panels of men of some social standing in a county or, more commonly, a hundred or wapentake – a subdivision of a county. At the so-called hundred court, presided over by the sheriff in each hundred or wapentake several times each year, alleged victims could bring their claims against the people they suspected of having committed a felony against them or of having killed one of their family members, friends or associates, either in person or (if they were wealthy) via an attorney. The presenting jurors then decided whether the accusation had merit. If they believed it did (applying a relatively low bar), the sheriff was ordered to arrest the suspects and imprison them in the county gaol until the next visitation by the justices of gaol delivery. The justices then heard their trials before a new, trial jury. A similar process could also be completed in cases of alleged homicide through the court of the coroner – a local individual appointed by the Crown to investigate violent or suspicious deaths.

Even before the suspension of the general eyre on a national basis in 1294, the commissions of assize and gaol delivery were in practice the Crown's key judicial offering in the shires, and they were certainly fundamental to the provision of justice for ordinary people after 1294. In the ensuing four decades, the commissions were professionalised and rationalised: appointments were restricted to the justices of the central courts of King's Bench and Common Pleas; they were set on regular, regional circuits; and finally they were merged, so that the same justices heard the assizes and delivered the gaols in every county, at least three times each year. The justices' regional visitations occurred during the vacations between the legal terms of Hilary, Easter, Trinity and Michaelmas, when they could be spared from their duties in the central courts, characteristically in the regions from which they originated or where they had latterly acquired estates. Having regional roots probably helped them better understand local circumstances and dialects, and may have helped build mutual trust between them and the local communities they served.

From the late thirteenth century, their routine partners in the provision of everyday justice in the localities were the peace commissioners, termed 'keepers' or 'justices' of the peace depending upon whether they were invested with powers of indictment and arrest only, or of indictment, arrest *and* trial. When the peace commissioners were not accorded trial powers, the suspects indicted before them were tried by the justices of gaol delivery at their next visitation, or sometimes by justices of trailbaston if the latter happened to be despatched to the locality before the justices of gaol delivery returned. The keepers of the peace had emerged under Henry III as a measure additional to the sheriff for maintaining local order and had further evolved under Edward I and in the reign of Edward II.

Suspected criminals might be indicted before, and arrested by, the keepers, much like the sheriff. In the early years of Edward III, at times when concern about crime and disorder was high, and expediting justice was a matter of urgency, the peace commissioners had periodically been granted trial powers, thereby becoming justices of the peace while their enhanced powers remained in place. In 1338 and 1344, when Edward anticipated being abroad for some time because of looming continental warfare, he again granted the peace commissioners trial powers because he believed it vital that order should be maintained in his absence. That imperative, however, was potentially in tension with another abiding concern of the king: that the provision of justice should be impartial and professional, especially where felony – which imperilled the lives of the accused – was concerned. His solution in 1338 was to appoint regional 'overseers' of the justices of the peace, drawn from among the magnates and justices of the central courts. In 1344, he required the justices of assize and gaol delivery to afforce the justices of the peace in the counties comprising their regional circuits whenever the latter presided over trials.

In the early 1350s, anticipating that the challenge posed to order by his absence from the realm through sustained continental warfare would be exacerbated by the effects of the Black Death, Edward III formally appointed the justices of assize and gaol delivery to the peace commissions within their circuits as a legally expert quorum who had to be present whenever felonies were tried. Commissioned alongside them were larger numbers of locally based lawyer-administrators: men who were still legally knowledgeable but who were also embedded in the locality and its social networks; in practice, these were the justices of the peace who did the bulk of the work. In many shires, an experienced local figure of higher social standing was also appointed to act as tribunal president. By this means, the king increased the number of royal justices in the shires available to deal with everyday disorder, now within a single, coherent judicial mechanism, without significantly compromising the quality of royal justice. The justices of assize and gaol delivery would provide a direct link to the central courts and the political centre, as well as the highest levels of legal expertise and impartiality. The local lawyers would also provide expertise, together with ready availability and local knowledge. The tribunal president would provide local political heft, and in many cases an additional link to the Crown at the centre – if he was one of Edward's regional lieutenants, such as the earl of Arundel or Walter, Lord Mauny, both of whom presided over the peace commissions in their 'country'.

This was a strong judicial and governmental combination, and its seamlessness in practice is indicated both by the surviving trial records – whether they are formally those of the justices of gaol delivery or the justices of the peace, they are strikingly alike – and the fact that many of the local lawyers built their own direct links with the central courts and administration. The local lawyers also tended to forsake personal ties when challenging circumstances and the king required that they choose between their local connection and the interests of the Crown – as was the case in Essex in 1351, when Lord Fitzwalter was ruthlessly prosecuted and his associate John Coggeshall led the JPs drawing up the charges. It was precisely the dual relationship with centre and locality characterised by the new-model JPs that made them genuinely effective royal agents: they represented both public authority and impartiality, and acceptability within and responsiveness to the local community. The reformed and enhanced peace commission was confirmed by statute in the Justices of the Peace Act of 1361, a decade after its practical creation. The Act confirmed the institution of 'quarter sessions', in which the justices of assize and gaol delivery and the JPs among whom they were included dispensed all manner of justice in the localities, four times each year. The transformation from the situation that had applied when the common law was created nearly two centuries earlier, when justice was available in the shires through the general eyre once every four years, could hardly have been more complete.

From 1346, within the context of war, Edward III had taken his realm under tighter control, and this position had been significantly reinforced in the face of the effects of the Black Death. There was certainly a degree of outcry against the labouring legislation among those adversely affected by it, and it was surely concern on the part of the political community about the king's use of the crime of treason as a weapon against elite disorder that led to the great Statute of Treasons of 1352, in which the scope of treason was dramatically narrowed. Treason was now confined to killing or compassing the death of the king or the heir to the throne, aiding the king's enemies in war or killing the king's justices while they were performing their duties. The specification that killing a justice was only treason if he was working as a justice at the time of the attack was a clear reference to a particular treason case of the late 1340s, where the justice concerned had been killed when not on duty. Similarly, the clarification in the statute that riding in manner of war with (heraldic) arms displayed when in dispute with a personal enemy was not treason was another clear reference to a recent case in which it had been held that it was. Otherwise, political concern about the force of the king's rule was manifested only in the clerical resignations that followed Bishop Lisle's flight into exile in 1356. Even those seem an outlier: while the king had taken a strong judicial line with Bishop William Bateman of Norwich in 1346–7 and Bishop John Grandison of Exeter – with whom he had previously sparred – in 1350, and while he had asserted English control over appointments in the Church via the Statutes of Provisors (1351) and Praemunire (1353), he nonetheless continued to enjoy a strongly collaborative relationship with his prelates: Bateman, for instance, acted as a key diplomat for the king throughout the late 1340s and until his death during a mission to Avignon in 1354.

Perhaps the key to this general amity in the face of heightened royal expectation was Edward's willingness to recognise, and respond to, his subjects' concerns. When he enacted the Statute of Treasons he also confirmed the liberties of the Church. In the same year, while receiving another triennial subsidy, he agreed that Parliament should henceforth be consulted about array and purveyance – royal prerogatives that had caused past friction, but which were of marginal utility following the Edwardian military revolution and the rise of the contract army. Although the legal records show that he remained obsessive and even intransigent about particular issues, his default modus operandi was to provide strong political direction and demand, moderated by accessibility and compromise. It should be recognised, too, that all this was underpinned by his flawless record and peerless reputation as a military commander and warrior. The 'English Maccabeus' had been repeatedly judged righteous by God, and this enabled him to act in ways that less exalted kings could not. The broad acceptance of his radical remodelling of landholding in the March of Wales between

1353 and 1356 contrasts starkly with the violent reaction faced by his father when he interfered in the March in 1320. Edward's reallocation of the lordships of Gower and Denbigh provided greater landed resource to support the work of his leading generals, the earl of Warwick and the precociously talented Roger Mortimer. The latter was the grandson of the same Roger Mortimer Edward had had hanged for treason in 1330, the legal verdicts against whom were annulled by the king in order to make the grandson second earl of March and restore him to the grandfather's lands in 1354. The noble families of Montagu, Mowbray, Talbot and Berkeley all lost heavily in these changes, and William Montagu, second earl of Salisbury, son of Edward's great favourite William Montagu, the first earl, who had been killed in a tournament in 1344, protested vehemently and publicly. He was never reconciled to the loss of the lordship of Denbigh, but continued to perform valuable military service as a captain in the king's wars, and, after peace was agreed in 1360, regularly served as a commissioner of the peace in the West Country.

The Resumption of War and the Battle of Poitiers

The exhaustion-driven truce of 1347 was inevitably extended by the catastrophe of the Black Death, which hit the French and Scots just as hard as it hit the English, Gascons and Welsh. But in the late 1340s and early 1350s, fragmented fighting resumed before a sustained, though wary and ultimately doomed, attempt was made to reach peace. The failure of diplomatic negotiations was rapidly followed by renewed warfare on a scale comparable with that of the mid-1340s, culminating in the game-changing English victory at Poitiers in the autumn of 1356.

As the Black Death receded, summer 1349 saw Henry of Grosmont lead an Anglo-Gascon *chevauchée* from Bordeaux to the walls of Toulouse and back, in response to emerging French plans for a fresh intervention in Aquitaine. Shortly afterwards, as the French advanced through Poitou, they were defeated by another Anglo-Gascon force under the captal de Buch. This fighting was relatively small scale: more than skirmishing but less than a fully fledged campaign. The same was true of a celebrated action at Calais at New Year in 1350, which further contributed to Edward III's stellar renown. The French commander of Saint-Omer, Geoffrey de Charny, had bribed Edward's Italian-born captain of Calais, Aimeric of Pavia, to open the gates of Calais, but Aimeric took passage to England to warn the king, who received the information during the Christmas revels of 1349. Assembling a compact but elite force from the royal household, including the Black Prince, Walter Mauny and Roger Mortimer, Edward secretly sailed to Calais, where, on 2 January 1350, his forces burst from hiding to surprise and confront the would-be French subjugators of the town, led by Charny and another renowned paladin, Eustace de Ribeaumont. In a dynamic action in the gate tower and on the sand spits outside the town walls, Edward fought incognito as a humble knight in the service of Mauny. Despite nearly being captured as he rapidly advanced on the French, the king personally subdued Ribeaumont – on whom he later bestowed the honour of having been the knight who fought most valiantly that day – as the French were defeated and taken. Calais was saved, though Pavia later paid a dreadful price for his double dealing, when Charny, now released after paying a substantial ransom, captured and killed him in revenge. Edward was again at the centre of the action when he led the Black Prince and all his leading noble lieutenants in a naval action off Winchelsea, named *Les Espagnols sur Mer*. Under their new king Peter the Cruel, the Castilians – traditional enemies of their near neighbours, the Gascon mariners of Bayonne – had recently aligned themselves with the French. Their great ships had attacked Anglo-Gascon merchantmen and also posed a potential threat to the coasts of England. On 29 August 1350, responding to intelligence reports, Edward and his captains ambushed a Castilian trading fleet returning laden from Flanders within sight of spectators gathered on the English shore. The battle was hard fought, not least because the Castilian vessels towered over the English cogs that intercepted them, but the combination of English longbow archery and the ferocity and skill of their men-at-arms triumphed as the two fleets grappled one another. During the long wait at sea for the Castilians to appear in the Channel, Edward III encouraged the young knight John Chandos to entertain him by singing, accompanied by guitarists brought along specially for the purpose. As fighting commenced, he positioned himself on the fo'c'sle of the cog *Thomas* and roared encouragement to his mariners and troops.

From 1350 until 1355, however, the king's primary foreign-policy objective was to pursue peace through diplomacy. Since his capture at Neville's Cross in 1346, David II of Scotland, in genteel captivity, had become something of a fixture in the English court. For different reasons, both Edward and David were keen for the English to negotiate a ransom and conclude a peace with the Scottish government under David's nephew and heir Robert Stewart, who was later to succeed him as king of Scotland. Edward was keen to obtain a substantial ransom by way of guaranteeing Scottish neutrality in his struggle with France during the years the ransom was being paid off. David wanted to buy his freedom. The sticking point was Edward's specification that he or one of his sons should inherit the Scottish throne after David's death, should the latter produce no legitimate male heir meanwhile. Although the precise terms of the proposed peace were adjusted several times during the first half of the 1350s, at no point would the Scottish government accept them. By 1354 they were looking to a hoped-for French revival against the English, which they intended to support. In the same period, Edward sought to reach terms with his other great captive, Charles de Blois, duke of Brittany. His hope was that Blois would be very heavily ransomed and would maintain a truce with the English king while the ransom payments remained extant, during which time neither Edward nor he would aid the other's enemies. Such a settlement would have involved ruthlessly leaving the Montfortists, Edward's erstwhile allies, to sustain their position in the duchy alone, from their own resources, though it is noteworthy that Edward's proposals would have left him free to support whom he pleased once the Blois ransom was fully paid. Both David II and Blois were temporarily released home to negotiate the acceptance of the proposed terms, but had to return chivalrously to England and captivity when they failed to secure domestic support for them. While the potential transfer to an Englishman of the Scottish throne was anathema to the Stewart-led government, in the case of the Blois party in Brittany, it was the sheer scale of Blois' proposed ransom that made the accompanying treaty non-viable.

In France, the death on 22 August 1350 of Philip VI might have ushered in a new political era, had it not been for the reality that his successor King John II's political judgement was yet more marginal. He began badly, by summarily beheading the count of Eu – who had recently returned from captivity in England to raise his ransom – without explanation, though it was believed John held Eu guilty of treason. Such brutal repression in the face of questionable loyalty, echoing his father's similar actions, served only to alienate members of the French nobility from the house of Valois. John compounded the situation in 1356, when he personally arrested Charles the Bad, titular king of Navarre, a great Norman landholder and a rival claimant to the throne of France, as well as other rebellious Norman lords, imprisoning Charles and immediately executing the others. Between these two bloody measures, he sought first to re-establish French military momentum, then desultorily followed the path of peace in light of renewed military failure, before reverting to the way of war again in 1355. His establishment, with Geoffrey de Charny, of the chivalric Order of the Star in 1352 has been seen as a response to the creation of the Order of the Garter, but was conceived on a vastly grander scale. A central vow of its members, never to retreat from the field of battle, was to prove disastrous at Poitiers in 1356; but it brought death and captivity to the French nobility much sooner at Mauron, near Ploërmel, in Brittany on 14 August 1352. A substantial army raised by John and led by Guy de Nesle, who was killed, was heavily defeated in a Crécy-like action by a much smaller force under the new English lieutenant in Brittany, Sir Walter Bentley (Thomas Dagworth having been ambushed and murdered in the duchy in 1350). This great setback prompted the French king to enter negotiations with the English under papal auspices, first at Guînes (a town eight miles south of Calais, captured by the English in 1352 as they extended their control of the locality) and later at Avignon, where Henry of Grosmont, who had been raised to the first dukedom of Lancaster in 1351, and Richard, earl of Arundel led the English delegation across the winter of 1354–5. Such was their fame on the European stage by this time that they struggled to cross the famous bridge to the papal palace in the face of a vast throng who had descended upon the city to catch sight of them. At both Guînes and Avignon the negotiations were doomed to failure as neither side could accept a position tolerable to the other. Supported by a carefully consulted Parliament, Edward III seriously sought peace. He instructed Lancaster, Arundel and their fellow diplomats to offer to surrender his claim to the

French throne in return for full, untrammelled sovereignty in an enlarged Aquitaine and Normandy; if necessary, claims to the further reaches of Aquitaine and Normandy might also be traded. Edward's central war aim remained as it always had been. But it also remained anathema to a French Crown wedded for so many generations to the notion that their overlordship of the English in France was non-negotiable.

The inevitable consequence was a return to war, accepted as a necessary evil by the political community in England and regarded in the French court as a fresh opportunity to erase the shameful stain of Crécy. The English king reanimated his signature strategy of a multiple attack on exterior lines, executed so successfully in the mid-1340s. In 1355, he planned for the duke of Lancaster to unite with the disaffected Charles the Bad in Normandy, for the Black Prince, newly made his lieutenant in Aquitaine, to *chevauchée* from Bordeaux deep into the French south-west, as had Grosmont in 1349 (though this time the prince would operate on a grander scale), and for himself to sortie from Calais towards Paris in an attempt to bring King John to battle. The Normandy expedition was stillborn, as the slippery king of Navarre reconciled – for the time being – with the French king. The Black Prince, however, saw striking success. Having crossed to Bordeaux with several thousand troops in September, in early October he departed the city at the head of a strong and well-equipped Anglo-Gascon force commanded by the lord of Albret and the captal de Buch, alongside the earls of Warwick, Suffolk, Salisbury and Oxford. The prince's twofold objective was by destruction and plundering to denude the French Crown of much of its valuable Languedoc revenue, while driving back and diminishing the French regional commander, John, count of Armagnac. During a three-month campaign, he marched on a broad front past Toulouse, where Armagnac and his army remained in safety, fired the outer town of Carcassonne (remarking that the old town and citadel were too formidable to be attacked) and besieged Narbonne, before returning via a similar route in a successful effort to avoid being trapped south of the Garonne by advancing French forces – though he failed to force the elusive Armagnac to battle. His objectives attained, he wintered at Bordeaux, consolidating and where possible extending Anglo-Gascon control in wider Aquitaine.

Edward III, meanwhile, had himself led the largest of the 1355 contingents – of perhaps ten thousand men, largely English and Welsh but including a significant contingent of Flemish and German soldiers of fortune – out of Calais and towards Paris in early November. Although John II advanced to meet him, he declined the English king's invitation to battle, remaining ensconced with his army in his regional headquarters of Amiens. Faced by a shortage of forage and hearing pressing news from home, Edward then retreated and promptly took passage back to England. The pressing news was that the Scots, encouraged by the French, had raided Northumberland, and had occupied the strategically critical town of Berwick and besieged its garrison in the castle. Preventing its loss and ending the renewed challenge posed by the Scottish government were high priorities for Edward. He advanced through England in December, celebrated Christmas at Newcastle and joined his advanced guard under Walter Mauny outside Berwick in the New Year. The Scots immediately surrendered and (according to chronicle account) the townspeople of Berwick begged his forgiveness for their foolishness in allowing the Scots in. To this, the king apparently responded mercifully, 'with his usual grace and good humour'. But he subsequently afforded no such grace and good humour to the Scottish government and people, perambulating in January and February through the Lowlands to Edinburgh, mercilessly burning and wasting on a wide front in the so-called 'Burned Candlemas'. This was part political intimidation and part foreign-policy pragmatism, a means to ensure – in response to intelligence and in an echo of 1336 – that no collaborating French military force could be sustained if it landed on the Scottish eastern seaboard. Edward completed this new initiative in respect of the Scots by effectively buying off the elderly Edward Balliol, purchasing his claim to the Scottish throne as a prelude to a renewed drive for a settlement with David Bruce and the Scottish leadership. That was to come in 1357.

It was finally secured by a stunning development in France in September 1356. This derived from the pressure exerted by another season of multiple attacks on exterior lines. Edward had intended the duke of Lancaster to campaign out of Brittany, but John II's renewed attack on Charles the Bad and his Norman allies reopened the possibility of a campaign in

Normandy. Diverted to Saint-Vaast-la-Hougue and allied with Charles's brother, Philip of Navarre, Lancaster embarked upon a typically dynamic *chevauchée* in the duchy, in which he advanced as far as Verneuil in the east, boldly outmanoeuvring the pursuing French king through June and July as he returned to safe territory in Montfortist Brittany, laden with booty and having seized more than two thousand horses. As Lancaster was retreating, the Black Prince was advancing from Bordeaux to La Réole. His Anglo-Gascon army was now large enough that he could afford to allocate almost half of it to the continued defence and extension of Aquitaine as, in August, he pushed north to the Loire. Once more he sought to waste enemy territory and thereby reduce both the credibility and capacity of Valois kingship, but now he also anticipated rendezvousing with Lancaster in anticipation of a direct confrontation with John II.

The French king urgently moved to counter the new threat. As French troops assembled across a wide front and descended on the Loire, the local garrisons broke many of the bridges to prevent the prince's forces uniting with those of Lancaster, whose co-ordinated foray out of Brittany saw some success on the borders of southern Normandy and Maine, but failed to find a Loire crossing. While, to the east, the prince lingered in the vicinity of Amboise in the second week of September, still hoping that he and the duke would join one another, John's forces advanced on either side of him from Blois and Tours. While the prince wrote shortly afterwards that he was now manoeuvring to draw the French king into battle, the details of his retreat towards Bordeaux, and his offer – in pre-battle negotiations initiated by papal nuncios accompanying the French – to surrender his booty in exchange for a truce imply significant concern on his part that he would find himself trapped and starved out by a much more numerous enemy.

When battle finally came, south of Poitiers on 19 September, the first French attack – a chaotic disaster rooted in noble disputes over command, reminiscent of the English at Bannockburn in 1314 – was probably prompted by their having spotted an attempt on the part of the earl of Warwick to withdraw the Anglo-Gascon baggage train. Nonetheless, the prince had chosen his ground well: undulating country broken up by woodland and hedgerows that provided excellent cover for the Anglo-Gascon archers and men-at-arms, while preventing the French from bringing their superior numbers fully to bear or even seeing clearly what was happening on the battlefield. Advancing on foot with shortened lances in an attempt to negate the grave danger posed by longbow archery to their horses, the French knights still suffered grievously at the hands of archers manoeuvred by the earl of Oxford to shoot obliquely into their vulnerable flanks. The first two French waves were routed in fierce hand-to-hand combat, and retreated in confusion only for the rear guard, under the king himself, finally to come into view. As soldiers around him despaired of their prospects, the Black Prince confidently ordered his men-at-arms to mount their heavy warhorses, or *destriers*, and charge the enemy front line, while the captal de Buch led a flying column in a mounted flanking attack on the French rear. The French lines broke under the double cavalry shock and King John was later taken, fighting bravely, by a Flemish knight in the prince's service. Geoffrey de Charny and Eustace de Ribeaumont, bearers of the Oriflamme (the French battle flag denoting that no quarter would be given) and the royal standard respectively, perished around their king. All three, and many hundreds of others, were victims of their membership of the Order of the Star, which precluded flight to safety. Realpolitik should have dictated that men such as Charny and Ribeaumont extracted their monarch from the field as soon as it was clear that the battle was being lost. Some two thousand French knights forfeited their lives and as many again were captured.

After attending to their wounded and assembling their prisoners, the Black Prince and his men returned in triumph to Bordeaux. The ultimate prize – the French king – had been captured through relentless strategic pressure, brilliant tactical command and professionalism in arms. By 10 October, messengers had brought Edward III the miraculous news. His vision and toil, as well as the brilliance of his son and heir, had delivered him into a formidable political position, from which he now strove to extract the peace on English terms for which he had for so long been fighting.

Peace Negotiations

Edward III was naturally determined to extract the greatest possible political profit from the capture of John II. Having previously agreed, in the contracts he had issued to the bannerets in the prince's Anglo-Gascon army, that any French prisoners could be ransomed by the captains of the men who had taken them, he quickly moved to purchase for himself all the French captives of political import, in order to maximise his leverage in the negotiations to come. He advised the Black Prince to conduct no negotiations with John until the French king showed his diplomatic hand and a truce was agreed. That point was reached in March 1357, and the following month the prince, King John and the other prominent French captives embarked at Bordeaux en route to England, reaching London in late May – where the French king was detained in the duke of Lancaster's palace of the Savoy. Charles de Blois had finally been ransomed the previous August and the two kings of France and Scotland stood out as Edward's pre-eminent captive guests, on great court occasions sitting either side of him as the three monarchs dined together. The English king was quickly able to progress an agreement with David II, signed at Berwick in October, which essentially set aside for the time being the vexed questions of Scottish independence and English suzerainty. Edward contented himself with, and David acquiesced in, a heavy ransom, payable over ten years, during which time a truce would be maintained between the two sides. The rights of the 'disinherited' Anglo-Scottish lords were theoretically maintained, and David II was now amenable to the idea that, if he remained childless, one of Edward III's sons might in due course succeed him as king of Scotland – though this naturally remained unacceptable to Robert Stewart and concerning to the wider Scottish political community. The intractable, interlinked issues of Scottish independence and English overlordship were simply ignored, which meant that everyone reserved his rights in a pragmatic triumph of peace-making that prefigured the Anglo-French twenty-eight-year peace of 1396 – where a similar approach to irresolvable differences was adopted. The Treaty of Berwick differed little from Edward's proposals of the early 1350s but was agreed by the Scottish government partly because of English military dominance and partly because the capture of John II precluded any possibility that an English setback against the French might improve the Scottish negotiating position. In truth, Edward III and David II shared a governmental vision as well as a personal connection, and had no desire to fight one another. Once David, a strong and effective king, was back heading his own government, there was effectively no prospect that England and Scotland would go to war with one another again while he and Edward III remained on the throne. That remained the case until the Scottish king's death in 1371.

Negotiating a permanent peace with the French was much more challenging because, while the same intractable issue of sovereignty lay at the heart of the dispute, this time the English were the party seeking guarantees of independence. The Scots, in a position parallel to that of the English in Aquitaine, had had little choice, in the face of English political supremacy, but to accept private assurances from the English that in practice they would not force the issue of their overlordship. The French were unwilling to provide similar assurances, and the long history of judicial appeal to the French Crown from unhappy litigants in Aquitaine meant that, unlike in Scotland, this was a practical political problem that could not be side-stepped. Moreover, overturning the Treaty of Paris of 1259 and ending the threat posed by judicial appeal to effective control in Aquitaine had remained the key English war aim since the beginning of the Hundred Years' War and had been a central foreign-policy objective since the reign of Edward I. The first formal agreement between Edward III and John II was proposed in 1358 and is now termed the first Treaty of London. It satisfied England's core war aim by prospectively delivering full sovereignty in a fully restored Aquitaine, plus Poitou, Ponthieu and Calais, in return for Edward surrendering his claim to the French throne, the whole being underpinned by the payment of a huge ransom by the French for John II. The proposal was duly rejected by the English Parliament because they believed it too generous to the enemy. By the time the Commons spoke out against it, Edward may also have begun to worry about having conceded too much, in light of the terrible difficulties being experienced by Charles the dauphin's government in France, which was beset by the urban rebellion of Étienne Marcel in Paris, the numerous peasant uprisings known as the Jacquerie and elite rebellion in Normandy led by the newly escaped Charles of Navarre. France was also bedevilled by the ravages of the 'free companies': groups of mercenaries, many of them English, who had emerged during the civil war in Brittany in particular, and who were now living off the country in France, following the effective collapse of

French royal rule with the defeat and capture of King John. The following year a second Treaty of London was provisionally agreed by the two kings: it proposed everything the first treaty had, but added English control of Anjou, Maine, Touraine and Normandy, and suzerainty over Brittany. It seems likely that John promised so much in order to prevent Edward from re-invading his stricken kingdom, which the English king was certainly contemplating, but in any case the second treaty was rejected by the French government as far too favourable to the English. The consequence was Edward's final continental expedition, the Reims campaign of 1359–60.

The Reims Campaign and the Treaty of Brétigny–Calais

After disembarking at Calais in October with a force at least ten thousand strong behind him, the English king made a long, straight march to Reims, where the kings of France were traditionally crowned, in a symbolic underpinning of his claim to the French throne and the threat he posed to the viability of Valois government. His comprehensively equipped army (including collapsible river boats for fishing, in anticipation of a long campaign that might extend into Lent, when only fish could be eaten) spread out in three divisions across a thirty-mile front under its commanders the king, the Black Prince and the duke of Lancaster, burning and wasting as it went. Thanks to effective military intelligence, the French had anticipated Edward's targeting of Reims, and the city was well defended and provisioned. Meanwhile, although the dauphin had no intention of leaving the security of Paris to face the English in a battle he was overwhelmingly likely to lose, the French had organised forces to harass the English on their anticipated passage, and throughout the long campaign the latter had to cope with small-scale, skirmishing attacks – in one of which, a then-unknown writer by the name of Geoffrey Chaucer was captured. Realising that he faced a siege potentially as long as that of Calais, and in the face of difficult winter weather and the looming exhaustion of locally available food and fodder, Edward moved into the independent duchy of Burgundy in January 1360, in alliance with local lords dissatisfied by what they regarded as the undue influence of John II on the government of duke Philip, a minor, whose stepfather John was.

As Easter approached, Edward and his forces advanced on Paris, which they loosely besieged in early April, but within a week the English departed west, driven to seek new supplies and still beset by harsh weather, as well as by disease that, among others, had killed the brilliant young earl of March and the veteran earl of Oxford. At this point the French approached the English king with proposals for talks, which Edward accepted. At Brétigny near Chartres, on 8 May, a definitive treaty for a final peace was provisionally signed. It essentially confirmed the terms of the first Treaty of London, though with Guînes added to Calais and modest enlargements to Aquitaine and Poitou. It overturned the Treaty of Paris of 1259 and satisfied English war aims, and in years to come became the touchstone for English foreign-policy objectives. However, there may have been reservations about how much had been surrendered on both sides, because at its ratification in Calais on 24 October, the 'renunciation clauses' were removed from the main treaty and placed in a separate 'letter'. These were the terms under which the two monarchs would definitively renounce their claims to, on the one part, sovereignty over Aquitaine, and, on the other, the Crown of France. The conditions for the renunciations being made were essentially that all ceded French territories were fully handed over to the English and all English troops withdrawn from France by November 1361 at the very latest. That timetable was extremely tight. It was in the long-term interests of the French for the Treaty of Brétigny–Calais to be compromised at a technical level, since this potentially provided them with a get-out clause in the event that they reclaimed sovereignty over Aquitaine at some future point – which they were likely to wish to do. Edward III may also have valued retaining his technical claim to the French throne as a future bargaining counter with which to lever French compliance, but the serious efforts of the English, led by the earl of Warwick under the king's instruction, to round up and remove their nominal troops, the free companies, from France, suggest that, following the death from plague of John Winwick, who was their key negotiator at Brétigny, the English may have been diplomatically outmanoeuvred at Calais. Whatever the case, for now at least, peace was finally attained.

Peace at Home

In the aftermath of the Treaty of Brétigny–Calais, Edward III took measures to ensure that the demobilisation of his army did not lead to disorder at home, as returning troops – traumatised or otherwise destabilised by military service – created difficulties. In addition to confirming, via the Justices of the Peace Act of 1361, the core structure for delivering the common law in the shires, which had pertained for a decade, the king appointed his personal bodyguard, the king's sergeants-at-arms, en masse in the southern counties of England to arrest malefactors. In 1364, as the situation in the country calmed, he reappointed the peace commission, contrary to the terms of the recent statute, with reduced trial powers, in the expectation that – as in the deeper past – the keepers of the peace would send the suspects who had been arrested after being indicted before them to the justices of assize and gaol delivery for trial. The broad structure of the quarter sessions, however, remained. In 1368, as the king again began to anticipate a renewal of war, the peace commissioners were recommissioned as justices, to expedite the provision of justice in time of national emergency – just as they consistently had been in the face of coming conflict since the 1330s.

Similarly unchanged, though on a lesser scale than in the 1340s or 1350s, were the king's actions against unacceptable behaviour among the social elite and royal officials. The ad hoc tribunals of earlier decades continued, with the superior eyre of King's Bench being despatched to the regions in 1362, 1363 and 1364, the issuing of trailbastons elsewhere, and a further judicial drive against official corruption in 1365 – when two justices of the central courts, the chief justice of King's Bench, Henry Green, and the chief baron of the Exchequer, William Skipwith, were tried and heavily fined for corruption. The surviving proceedings before the King's Bench in Essex in 1364 show that exactly the same process that had been brought to bear against Lord Fitzwalter in 1351 was now applied to Leo de Bradenham – a landholder and commercial agent who, like Fitzwalter before him, had fallen into jurisdictional dispute with the men of Colchester, his neighbours in respect of his manor of Langenhoe. In 1368, the heavy weight of royal justice was felt by Sir John Attlee, steward of the royal household, who had been accused of corruption by the Commons in Parliament. That this prosecution was initiated by the Commons rather than the king – though the king pursued it with alacrity – arguably speaks to the isolation the ageing Edward was starting to experience in relation to the wider political community towards the end of the decade.

That isolation was rooted not just in the king's seniority but also in the depletion of his trusted noble lieutenants. This had occurred during the Reims campaign – witness the deaths of the earls of March and Oxford – and continued afterwards, with a fresh outbreak of the Black Death in 1361–2 that saw the demise of the duke of Lancaster and the earl of Northampton, both of whom had been key lieutenants delivering royal rule since the 1330s, as well as other members of the upper nobility and senior officialdom. While Edward worked assiduously to replenish the nobility at baronial level, his capacity to endow earls or dukes was less than it had been in the 1330s. This was partly because available royal patronage was less extensive than at the start of his personal rule, and partly because he was garnering its stocks to ensure that his younger sons, Edmund Langley and Thomas Woodstock, received appropriate landed endowments. In the 1360s, he was surrounded by a smaller group of earls than had hitherto been the case. His third surviving son, John of Gaunt, whom he had made duke of Lancaster and heir to the vast estates of Henry of Grosmont (whose only daughter Gaunt had married), was foremost among his counsels. Beyond Gaunt, the earls of Warwick, Arundel and Suffolk, his surviving contemporaries, constituted his core connection in the court – with Arundel continuing to counsel him even after advancing age and declining health meant that the king had regularly to send a litter down to Arundel Castle to bring him safely to Westminster. The heavy blow of the renewed Black Death was rapidly exacerbated by a terrible storm in January 1362, which brought down many buildings and produced considerable hardship among the people. The weather in mid-fourteenth-century Europe was unusually poor, and in the 1360s it worsened economic and social conditions. Despite feeling his age, which he acknowledged, the king continued to exercise his considerable cognitive ability and emotional intelligence, as well as his directive leadership. This is shown by his refusal – until a third outbreak of the Black Death in 1368 made it economically unavoidable – to countenance the Commons' repeated suggestions that he should reprioritise enforcing the labouring legislation, which he had deprioritised in 1359. Edward recognised that a sectional interest was at play here, and stood firm in protection of the wider community. Likewise he rejected the Commons' pleas that he should cease to send powerful judicial commissions into the localities to investigate corruption, saying that, as king, he neither would nor could do so.

He showed similar focus, confidence and attention to detail in the great building projects he completed in the 1360s. His remodelling of Windsor Castle, to make it a centre truly fit for the activities of a great royal court, had begun in the 1350s with the building of the Garter Chapel of St George, and now extended to the royal apartments in the upper ward. Other royal palaces and lodges were extensively modernised with more windows, fireplaces and the provision of hot, running water, and at Queenborough in Kent Edward built a state-of-the-art fortress to defend the Thames estuary against raiders. Some of the costs were met from the vast ransoms he had secured from Charles de Blois, David II and John II, payments for which steadily came in, albeit often not to schedule, because of the challenges faced by his former captives in collecting them in Brittany, Scotland and France. But Edward also secured, by political appeal and by appropriate political concession, two triennial wool taxes, in 1362 and 1365. To receive six years of indirect tax in time of peace was unheard of. The king eased its agreement by issuing the Statute of Purveyors, which finally eliminated the frictional issue of royal purveyance, and by convincingly arguing the tax's necessity – burdened as he was by the costs of defending Aquitaine, Poitou, Ponthieu and Calais, and of securing English rule in Ireland. Between 1362 and 1366, Lionel of Antwerp, the king's second surviving son, was located in Ireland (where his marriage to Elizabeth de Burgh had brought him considerable landed wealth) to consolidate the English position there as the king's lieutenant. Appointed duke of Clarence to make him the senior Irish nobleman, he took effective military action against rebellious Gaelic chieftains and brought some order to the royal finances in the lordship – though this largely had the effect of confirming that royal rule there was only sustainable with subsidies from England. In 1368, Antwerp's untimely death in Italy – where he had been central to his father's alliance-building plans to counter a suspected anti-English bias on the part of the papacy, following his withdrawal from Ireland – may have contributed to Edward III leading a somewhat more withdrawn, less ostentatious life by the end of the decade. Another cause was surely the long-standing illness suffered by Queen Philippa, to which she finally succumbed in 1369. By this time the king was restricting his hunting to his southern English hunting grounds, eschewing Sherwood Forest where he had hunted so frequently in his youth. He now mostly remained in southern England even when he was not pursuing the chase. The days of a vast royal entourage were also evidently over: as Edward hunted in the New Forest, Berkshire and Northamptonshire, he was accompanied by many fewer men than had once been the case. But the need for retrenchment and economy, as continental war again loomed, probably also contributed to Edward's more compact life.

Peace Abroad and the Return of War

Edward III's key foreign-policy objective in the 1360s was to make his newly confirmed continental possessions secure and defensible in the medium to long term. His approach was twofold: to place Aquitaine itself – now much greater in extent and political complexity than in the past – on a sound political and governmental footing, and to reinforce its security by building wider European political alliances. Although intelligent action was taken on both fronts, neither approach was to succeed after 1367.

The king initially focused upon helping to ensure that the stipulations in the renunciation clauses of the Anglo-French peace treaty of Brétigny–Calais were met and the renunciations mutually completed. It was evident when the deadline for the renunciations of November 1361 was reached that some French land transfers remained to be completed and a significant number of English troops continued to reside in France, despite the seeming best efforts by both governments to deliver on their obligations. The deadline therefore passed without the renunciations being made, but the parties agreed that completing them remained highly desirable and that work towards that end should continue. No new deadline was set, however. Meanwhile, Edward was formulating a radical answer to the question of how greater Aquitaine, which now reached almost to the Loire in the north and into the western reaches of the Massif Central in the east, should be governed. His solution, which appears wholly to have wrong-footed the French, was revealed in July 1362, when he received the Black Prince's homage as prince of Aquitaine. After several delays, the prince departed for the duchy – accompanied by a large entourage including his new wife, Joan Holland, a widowed cousin with whom he had evidently formed a love match, as well as key officers and commanders such as the law-yer-administrator John Delves, raised to the bench of Common Pleas, and his right-hand men and duchy experts James Audley and John Chandos. Granted full vice-regal powers, he was to govern Aquitaine independently, with the power to make his own treaties, which in due course he did with his regional neighbours Peter I of Castile and John de Montfort, duke of Brittany. His regime in south-western France was to be self-sustaining rather than a draw on the coffers of England, and this may have been a real-istic prospect, had he been able to avoid ruinously expensive foreign-policy commitments. He underwrote his finances early in his rule by asking for a *fouage* or hearth tax. While this request was broadly accepted, some lords from the greater duchy, especially those unused to being subjects of the English, protested that their liberties meant it should not be levied within their lands. The prince and his new court spent many months touring Aquitaine, meeting and receiving homage from myriad Gascon lords.

The year 1362 also saw the young John de Montfort, claimant to the dukedom of Brittany, leave England for his duchy, where he took up his claim to the ducal throne. He was strongly backed by the English, despite Edward III having briefly toyed, in the early 1350s, with the idea of recognising the right of Charles de Blois, within the context of peace negotiations with the French. Talks between Montfort and Charles de Blois, presided over by the Black Prince at Poitiers, twice failed to reconcile the two rivals' claims, and a return to war in the duchy resulted. In 1364, this brought Montfort's definitive victory over his rival at the battle of Auray, where Blois was killed. Montfort's army had been commanded by the prince's great war captain John Chandos, and although the new French king, Charles V (John II having died on 8 April 1364), promptly recog-nised his right in Brittany as a fait accompli, Montfort remained strongly wedded to his English allies – until political circumstances changed signif-icantly in the 1380s.

In the mid- to late 1360s, however, Edward III's alliance building to help secure sovereign Aquitaine through pan-European connection proved abortive. The English king invested huge diplomatic resource over several years seeking to secure a marriage alliance with Louis de Mâle, the count of Flanders. Louis almost certainly always intended to ally with the French Crown, but skilfully exploited extended negotiations with both the English and the French to ensure that his own concerns about the relationship between Flanders and France were resolved to his satisfaction. He then finally showed his hand, agreeing that his daughter and heir should marry Charles V's brother, Philip, duke of Burgundy, in 1369. This represented a significant setback for English diplomacy, for whom alliances in the Low Countries and especially Flanders had been a constant since the 1330s – with a substantial and significant prehistory before that. Edward III's focus upon Flanders was mirrored by concerns over Castile, rooted in the power of the Castilian fleet and the potential boon it provided to French naval power projection in the Channel as well as the Bay of Biscay. In 1366, having been approached by King Peter I of Castile's half-brother, Henry Trastámara, who wished to depose Peter and usurp his throne, the talented and celebrated French military commander Bertrand du Guesclin agreed to lead a force of mercenaries and French troops into Castile in support of Henry. Guesclin's actions were backed by Charles V for strategic reasons – as a firm alliance with Castile was obviously to French advantage – and also because, by drawing so many mercenaries into Spain, Guesclin hoped to remove the scourge of the remaining free companies from French territory. (Foremost among his commanders was Hugh Calveley, a *condottiero* or mercenary originally from Cheshire, who – like the former Cheshire archer Robert Knollys – had established himself as a leading free-company commander during the extended civil war in Brittany.) The success of Guesclin and Henry led to Peter I seeking refuge with, and support from, the Black Prince in Aquitaine. Sympathetic to Peter's situation (albeit wary of his character) because he had been deposed by a bastard half-brother and, like the French, considering the strategic implications of a secure alliance with the king of Castile, Prince Edward – with the agreement of his father – made alliance with Peter to recover his kingdom.

Accompanied by John of Gaunt and, among other commanders, Hugh Calveley (who had changed sides to back the now-English cause with which he naturally felt most comfortable), he then led an extraordinary winter march across the Pyrenees in January 1367, before confronting and routing Trastámara and Guesclin at Nájera on 3 April. This was the third great battle – after Crécy and Poitiers – that the Black Prince had fought and won, and the second in which he did so as overall commander. His victory in Spain derived in part from the English staple of devastating longbow archery and partly from an audacious night-time manoeuvre on the eve of battle, which resulted in the prince being able to make a surprise flank attack on Guesclin from which the French commander was never able to recover. But the aftermath of the campaign was triply disastrous for the prince. First, Trastámara escaped the battlefield, returned to Castile (again with French backing) in 1369, defeated Peter in battle outside the castle of Montiel and then murdered him. Castile's alliance with the French was confirmed. Second, during the campaign, the prince caught the chronic illness or illnesses, probably dysentery and possibly malaria, that quickly reduced him to a sickly shadow of his former self and eventually led to his death. Third, Peter's promise to pay for the entire campaign, including, critically, the wages of Prince Edward's key commanders and their retinues, proved utterly hollow. Consequently, the finances of the duchy of Aquitaine, which already had to be carefully managed, were placed in jeopardy, leading to relations between the prince and some of his key Gascon subjects fatally breaking down.

The breakdown had arguably been coming for some time. At its heart lay a reluctance on the part of some of the prince's major subjects in wider Aquitaine to accept English rule, perhaps exacerbated by dimensions of ostentation and high-handedness in the prince's behaviour. One such individual was the count of Armagnac, against whom the prince had played a commanding hand during his great *chevauchée* to Narbonne in 1355. Another was Archambaud, count of Périgord. But Arnaud-Amanieu, lord of Albret, who joined Armagnac and Périgord in effective rebellion against the prince in 1368, was from a family of Gascon loyalists. Although his grandfather had switched to French allegiance in 1312, alienated by Edward II's officers in the duchy, his father Bernard Aiz had returned to the English fold in 1340, remaining steadfastly loyal until his death in 1358. What alienated Albret now was serious default of wages from the (hugely costly) Nájera campaign on which he had recently served, when he desperately needed the money to pay off a ransom consequent upon his having been captured in an earlier, local war over disputed land. In January 1368, the flashpoint that led all three lords, in alliance, to appeal to the French Crown's judicial oversight, which had applied between 1259 and 1360 but not since the Treaty of Brétigny–Calais, was the prince's imposition of a new and unprecedented, five-year *fouage*.

While this tax potentially provided a solution to his own dire financial situation, Armagnac and Périgord were by no means alone in the duchy in resisting the collection of the *fouage* in what they argued were their liberties; and Albret took a similarly dim view of direct taxation on this scale – especially when the prince owed him so much money for the military service he had completed. Charles V, who was the canniest of political operators, assiduously courted the disaffected lords and promised them financial support. For someone in Albret's situation, a debt-clearing annuity from the French Crown was hugely attractive. A secret alliance between the French king, Armagnac, Périgord and Albret followed in June. In the autumn, the prince fell seriously ill for the first time. Having taken extensive legal advice, and absolutely conscious that his proposed action amounted to a reopening of the Hundred Years' War, Charles then summoned Prince Edward to appear to answer the judicial appeal the French king had encouraged his three allies to submit. Issued in November, the summons requested that Edward present himself before the *Parlement* of Paris on 2 May 1369. By the time that date arrived, the French were already reoccupying parts of Aquitaine lost under the Treaty of Brétigny–Calais – by means of persuasion and financial incentivisation more than military action. This assault on the peace settlement of 1360 had been well telegraphed, and although, in response, Edward III had attempted to reopen negotiations about the renunciation clauses in an effort to save the gains he had made at Brétigny, the English king knew before the end of 1368 that the war would recommence. While both sides had appeared committed to peace in the first half of the 1360s, it was obviously in the interests of the French to overturn a settlement forced on them by military loss, which was fundamentally incompatible with their sense of French sovereignty. In the second half of the 1360s, the immense cost of the Black Prince's strategically driven campaign in Spain, the difficulty of Gascon politics and the prince's seeming limitations as a political (as opposed to military) leader permitted Charles V a route back into the war, for which the unfulfilled renunciation clauses provided technical cover: the French king could not easily be accused of breaking a treaty that had never been technically ratified.

The War between 1369 and 1375: French Progress and English Disappointment

The resumption of the Hundred Years' War from 1369 saw the French rapidly recover many of the lands they had lost under the Treaty of Brétigny–Calais. Then a sort of fluid stalemate set in, in which the English sought military revival through new initiatives and the French hoped to subjugate their enemy, without either side being able to make a decisive breakthrough. French success, after so many years of military failure, rested on triple foundations: first, a hearts-and-minds approach to retaking lost territory, in which an emphasis upon French nationality, which was a powerful ideological and psychological force in greater Aquitaine, was combined with local concessions in respect of rights and territory; second, financial incentives; third, Fabian military tactics under the command of Guesclin, in which pitched-battle confrontation with the Anglo-Gascons was avoided at almost all costs, its place being taken by lower-risk skirmishing, harassment and siege work – something more than guerrilla warfare but less than conventional campaigning. This negated the key dimensions of English success to 1360: effective alliance building, especially within Aquitaine, and tactical mastery. French financial strength also played a critical role. Ironically, the pressure of raising John II's huge ransom had produced structural changes in the French taxational system that effectively doubled its productivity, with the result that the English were now comprehensively outspent. At the same time, the taking of French captives, whose ransoms had reinforced English war finance from the mid-1340s, occurred much less frequently without the context of pitched battle and English conquest; and the campaigns the English did mount proved very expensive, such that Edward III's vast treasure, acquired by ransoming the enemy in the 1350s, had been spent on the war by 1373. The English then found themselves seriously short of money. Other factors in English underperformance included a dearth of effective commanders and bad luck. John of Gaunt was a skilled military leader, but otherwise the English and Gascons seem to have lacked top-flight captains in this generation, especially following the deaths early in the renewed war of James Audley and John Chandos, the former through sickness acquired on campaign and the latter in a skirmish, and the capture and subsequent demise of John Hastings, the young earl of Pembroke. That the Black Prince fell so debilitatingly ill just as his father was starting to age might be accounted bad luck, and it was certainly bad luck that, in 1369 and 1372, when the king was about to embark on continental campaigns, he was stopped from so doing, first by the death of Queen Philippa, and second by sustained contrary winds that prevented him from leaving England. After that, neither he nor the prince was well enough to lead military expeditions again.

Initially, both sides sought to play to their strengths, with the French concentrating on detaching to their allegiance those parts of greater Aquitaine more distant from Bordeaux, where acquiescence in English rule had been least willing. Edward III countered by extending his truce with David II of Scotland to 1384, by seeking afresh to find common ground with the Gascon nobility and by planning a major expedition in northern France, which was to fight out of Calais under, first, John of Gaunt and, later, himself. While Gaunt reached Calais by July 1369, the death of the much-loved Queen Philippa in August, and the need to attend to her elaborate funeral, prevented the king from following him. In northern France, as later, Gaunt could not draw the cautious French into meeting him in battle. In summer 1370, in Aquitaine, Gaunt, with his younger brother Edmund Langley and the earl of Pembroke, joined the Black Prince, who was now confined to a litter. They counterattacked against French advances very effectively, but with failing Gascon support, they were unable to retain the territory they had retaken. As castles and towns continued to turn to the French, the English found themselves pushed back even in the Agenais, whose recovery had been at the heart of the English war effort in the 1340s and 1350s. The Albret family had played a crucial role in English success there at that time, just as, alienated, they had in earlier English losses during the War of Saint-Sardos in 1323–5. The lord of Albret having been lost to the French again, it is unsurprising that English fortunes should have fallen as they did. By the end of the year, the Black Prince had recognised that he was no longer well enough to rule in Aquitaine and resigned his position. In January 1371, he was shipped back to England.

The summer of the same year saw Edward III's first period of serious illness. The king may have had an ulcer or perhaps the beginnings of cancer, which some contemporary references suggest. Or his illness in 1371 may have been a first stroke: it appears from the downturned mouth of his death mask that he was to die from a stroke or more likely a series of strokes in 1377. It was also in 1371 that serious concerns were raised in Parliament about war finance, especially in relation to credit operations, following a request from the Crown for £100,000 in direct taxation. The chancellor, William Wykeham, bishop of Winchester, was forced to resign, as were the treasurer and the keeper of the privy seal. Wykeham and his colleagues were supplanted by laymen, as the Commons sought to replace clerical officeholders at the centre with justiciable individuals, just as Edward III had done in the earlier crisis over war finance in 1340–1. The king's isolation in a narrow court was an increasing and understandable political concern. In particular, there was rising consternation about his relationship with his mistress, Alice Perrers, which dated back to 1364, but had only become a matter of public knowledge following the death of Queen Philippa. There is no doubt that Edward was deeply attached to Perrers, but her acquisitiveness and assertiveness won her few friends.

In 1372, the English sought to strengthen their international position via a revived alliance with John de Montfort in Brittany, but this proved counter-productive when it generated both French and Breton hostility, culminating in 1373 with Montfort having to flee his own duchy. English attempts to help him retake it were ineffective, though increasing concern on the part of his subjects about the duchy being absorbed into France enabled him to re-establish himself there in 1379. September 1372 also saw King Edward, recovered from his illness of 1371, seeking to take to the seas to counter Franco-Castilian naval power, which had dealt the earl of Pembroke a telling blow off La Rochelle in June, when French and

Castilian ships had intercepted the latest English expedition to Aquitaine. Both Pembroke and the vital war finance he was carrying to Bordeaux were captured. The king's letters to his sergeant-at-arms Walter Hanwell, who was supervising shipping at the port of Sandwich, show that he remained sharp and focused – and very concerned about the need to make progress. But adverse weather for many weeks meant that the fleet was able to progress only as far as Winchelsea before the expedition had to be abandoned. The following year saw the greatest English campaign since 1369, when John of Gaunt – now formally declared England's senior commander – led a grand *chevauchée* from Calais right across France all the way to Bordeaux. This was a powerful statement of continued English military power, tied up French defensive resources and, like the great raids of the 1340s and 1350s, hit the French tax base hard. Nonetheless, Gaunt's army, repeatedly harassed, took heavy casualties and again failed to bring the French to battle. It would be incorrect to describe this as a failed operation, any more than we would account the Black Prince's *chevauchée* of 1355 ineffective. But the Gaunt raid emptied the English royal coffers, and it was only the granting of successive triennial wool subsidies that kept the war effort afloat.

The Good Parliament

By 1374 the war was stagnating, and first the English and then the French looked once more to negotiation. Peace talks – as ever, under papal auspices – commenced in Bruges in March 1375, with Gaunt taking the lead on behalf of Edward III. Various creative proposals to solve the problem of Aquitaine and sovereignty by subdividing the duchy proved unacceptable to all parties, but on 27 June a one-year truce was agreed, and was later extended until 1 April 1377. By this time the English royal finances were in such a parlous state, however, that the truce brought no respite from urgent financial need, and Parliament was summoned to meet in February 1376, eventually assembling in late April. The atmosphere was febrile. Shortly after the truce had been agreed at Bruges, the long-standing English garrison of Saint-Sauveur-le-Vicomte, in Navarrese territory in Normandy, had been sold to the French by the garrison commander. This was a great scandal that inflamed pre-existing suspicions about corruption in government. These centred on William, Lord Latimer, the chamberlain, and Richard Lyons, a London financier: both were suspected of having made huge sums by manipulating the king's credit operations in 1372–3, and Latimer was also held partly responsible for the loss of Saint-Sauveur. Associated with them, and likewise targeted, was Alice Perrers. William Wykeham remained resentful after his governmental fall in 1371 and Edmund Mortimer, earl of March owed Latimer money and was hostile to Gaunt, partly because he believed he had been robbed of a significant military victory in Brittany by the truce Gaunt had agreed at Bruges. It was March's steward, the MP Peter de la Mare, who was chosen by the Commons as their first spokesman or 'speaker', as they sought to hold the courtiers and government to account, but Wykeham joined those making accusations against the courtiers.

The condition this Parliament – later termed the Good Parliament – placed upon its agreement to grant three years of much-needed indirect taxation (it refused to grant any direct taxation) was that the activities of the suspected courtiers would be thoroughly investigated. Since Gaunt, presiding and representing the Crown, was unwilling to initiate accusations against Latimer, Lyons and others, the Commons took it upon themselves to do so, through their speaker, thereby creating the process of impeachment, which remains central to modern-day politics in many jurisdictions. Latimer and Lyons were duly convicted, proscribed and imprisoned, and the ailing king was persuaded by Gaunt, at the urging of the Commons, to remove Alice Perrers from the court as a drain on the public purse. A continuous Council, including the earl of March but not John of Gaunt, was appointed to direct government. The Good Parliament was suspended in June when the anticipated but shocking news of the Black Prince's untimely death reached its ears, but later that month, its sessions resumed and John Neville of Raby, the steward of the household, was among a wider group of courtiers removed for alleged corruption and negligence. The Parliament finally closed on 10 July.

The drama of the Good Parliament and its creation of the legal process of impeachment should not lead us to overstate its importance. It occurred because the Hundred Years' War was perceived to be going badly, following so many years of Anglo-Gascon military success, because money was desperately short and was believed to have been squandered or stolen, and because, in the absence of an active king or adult heir to the throne, there was an authority vacuum at the political centre and a lack of direction in the war. (The Black Prince's eldest surviving son, Richard of Bordeaux, who was aged ten, had recently been recognised as his heir by Edward III.) At the same time, attacks on English shipping and the south coast by Castilian vessels in the Channel were occurring, and invasion fears were starting to mount. The political community was looking to hold someone accountable for the perceived failure. Within a handful of months, in a Council held at the royal manor of Havering, Gaunt led a court revival and a volte-face reminiscent of Edward III's overturning of the Statute of April 1341. This was not without an element of vindictiveness (de la Mare, Wykeham and March were all targeted by Gaunt), but the duke of Lancaster's reassertion of Crown control and his overturning of the judgements against the courtiers saw broad political acceptance. Gaunt himself was duly attacked by the Londoners and other rebels during the Peasants' Revolt of 1381, but blame for the poll tax, first instituted in 1377, which was the primary cause of the rebellion, should properly rest with the Commons, who again sought to spread the financial burden of war more widely across the community, at a time of rising hardship, following an economic crash in the mid-1370s.

The Death of Edward III

The great king finally passed away at his palace of Sheen on 21 June 1377, and was succeeded by Richard II. For contemporaries, there was an acute sense of loss, not just for a king they described as the flower of kings past and the pattern for kings to come, a terror upon England's enemies and a bringer of peace to his people, but also for a golden generation and a golden period in English history. They were not reflecting, of course, on structural change in the way that modern commentators, with historical hindsight, are. For the latter, the reign of Edward III brought critical legal change and growth, a revolution in foreign policy and arms that made England the pre-eminent power in Europe, and the emergence of national identity and mission, symbolised by national taxation on an unprecedented scale and an established debate in Parliament about the realm's interests and the common good, which drew the political community, writ large, together. For contemporaries, Edward III brought good government: responsible, fair, effective and accessible – all qualities that the person of the king possessed in abundance.

RICHARD II, 1377–99

'Where will reigns and reason has withdrawn, great peril threatens'

When Edward III died in June 1377, his grandson Richard II was just ten years old. The realm was in disarray and suspicion of elites and authority was at an unprecedented high. The nobility themselves were deeply divided over how to deal with the renewed threat from France. So, at a time when the country needed a monarch of almost unparalleled ability to restore peace and prosperity, a child-king ascended to the throne, surrounded by nobles who could not agree on the way forward. The king himself would rapidly show signs of having an extravagant, fickle and narcissistic temperament. Richard's reign was to become one of the most notorious in English history, and the next twenty years witnessed even more dire crises than those seen during Edward II's time on the throne.

At Richard II's magnificent coronation in July, none of this was apparent: the first in over fifty years, it was dominated by hope and joy, as huge crowds flocked to the streets to watch the king ride in procession, carried at various points, as Henry III had been, in his small-sized robes on the shoulders of members of his nobility and his tutor, Simon Burley, from the Tower of London to Westminster Abbey. His coronation marked a fresh start; perhaps the following years would even, God willing, be a period of renewed peace and prosperity, an end to some of the terrible trials of the last half-century. People might have been forgiven for thinking that things could not get much worse.

As the festivities of the coronation came to an end and the jubilant crowds dispersed, the king's Council turned rapidly to the business of government. Richard was far too young to rule independently yet, so decisions had to be made about how government would be organised during his minority years. The obvious solution was the appointment of a regent, as had happened before, but given events of recent years it was inconceivable that the most senior member of the nobility and Edward III's eldest remaining son, John of Gaunt, would be an acceptable choice to the Commons. It would have been an obvious slight to Gaunt to appoint someone else, so the only alternative was the nomination three days after the coronation of a Council to guide the king. The Council moved on to considering what action to take to counter the threat from both the French and the Castilians. The fleets of the latter were at that moment conducting raids on the south coast of England, endangering wool exports to Calais and making it hard to access Gascony by sea. Parliament was called in October to discuss what to do. But before proceedings even got under way, many new and increasingly wild rumours were circulating about Gaunt, including that he had designs on the throne itself. In response, the duke immediately sought to identify anyone accusing him of treason, an act that had the desired effect of subduing the Commons and forcing them to confirm him as their 'principal aid, comforter and counsellor' for this Parliament. While the Commons had been forced to profess their outward loyalty to him, Gaunt was still to be the scapegoat for governmental failures for many years to come. There is no evidence that he had any desire to rule himself, and every indication from his actions in the years after this that his main priority, however indelicately delivered, remained the preservation of the reputation of the Crown. But in the atmosphere of the late 1370s, and given his inflexible and overbearing personality, there was little chance of convincing the Commons otherwise.

Parliament instead approved the appointment of nine councillors who would deal with matters of state on Richard's behalf. The councillors were to sit only for a year, and the king's uncles, Gaunt, Edmund of Langley, earl of Cambridge and Thomas of Woodstock, earl of Buckingham, though not appointed themselves, were to ensure that the councillors did not take bribes – the Commons remained fixated on corruption. A large grant of taxation was then forthcoming. Accompanying it, though, was the stipulation that two of London's wealthiest merchants, representing a constituency fearful for their trading interests in Calais in the precarious military situation, should become treasurers of the tax, and an insistence that funds be spent only on war. The Commons even attempted to secure the nomination of the king's household officers in Parliament, a point on which they were overruled but which again indicates continuing suspicions of corruption, and divisions between them and the royal court. They also presented an extensive list of grievances, several of which seem to have been copied from the 1311 Ordinances, which nearly seventy years earlier had voiced very similar concerns about the misappropriation of royal funds, particularly taxation. By the time Parliament dispersed, there could have been no mistaking the Commons' focus on corruption and their determination to participate in any significant decision making.

With the tax agreed, those representing Richard moved forward with military planning. At the heart of the new strategy was a 'Great Expedition' to be led by Gaunt, the focus of which was initially on Brittany. This was key to enabling safe overland passage to Gascony as an alternative to the sea route on which the Castilian fleets had been attacking ships in recent years. However, this was just one element in English strategy: at the same time, the experienced commander John Neville of Raby was appointed to lead an army to Gascony with a view to moving south to assist the count of Navarre in his fight against the Castilians. Although he was never to resume his former position at court after his disgrace at the Good Parliament, this appointment marked Neville's re-entry into the military sphere, probably due to the influence of Gaunt, as he remained one of the duke's most important life retainers. Simultaneously, the plan was for Richard, who had recently succeeded his father as earl of Arundel, to provide a distraction for the French army by striking the French fleet in its own ports with a six-thousand-strong naval force.

These were huge commitments, and it was never realistic to imagine that even a double grant of taxation would suffice to meet all the resulting costs and to fund the existing garrisons as well. The strategy was doomed to failure for that reason alone, though in the event the plan collapsed well before the money ran out. While preparations were being made for departure, the Castilians unexpectedly attacked and burned the town of Fowey in Cornwall. Then, when Gaunt arrived in Saint-Malo in August, he suffered a disastrous defeat by the French, in part because his army was far too big to be supplied effectively – a fundamental error (though one the French were also to make later in Richard's reign). In the autumn of 1378, not only had the English failed to take Saint-Malo, they were forced to throw resources at the English garrison in Cherbourg, which was under attack by the French. In Navarre, the plan was also unravelling: the Castilians were overrunning the kingdom, and the count was forced to make peace not only with the Castilians themselves but also with their French allies. Arundel, having set out later than planned, similarly achieved little.

The Great Expedition had turned out to be a catalogue of disasters and the Council was forced to return to Parliament in October 1378 with nothing to show for its efforts other than an empty treasury and seriously damaged pride. Unsurprisingly the Commons declined to grant a tax, and the entire Council subsequently resigned. In spring 1379 a new Council recalled Parliament, but in the meantime the government was forced to resort to borrowing money from a mixture of wealthy individuals and corporations, particularly in London. Once Parliament reconvened, the chancellor accepted independent inquiries into the treasury accounts, which subsequently deemed them satisfactory. This is unsurprising: it is obvious from the Great Expedition alone that the main problem was overambition, incompetence and a singular lack of leadership rather than corruption, though none of those should be understated. In the light of the clean bill of health for the accounts, the Commons were induced to agree another poll tax – some goodwill remained for the new king, despite the wider failures of recent years. While the grant was reassuring, the proceeds would not start to come in until August, meaning that a new plan to challenge the French in Brittany, which had been formally taken into the French King Charles V's hands in April, was repeatedly delayed. This had significant consequences: eventually John de Montfort, by then one of several exiled claimants to the dukedom of Brittany, who was due to lead the expedition in the hope of establishing himself there in alliance with the English, decided he could wait no longer and set out independently in July with a small force. His progress was surprisingly good and rapid, and quite soon it seems he reached an accommodation with Charles V, which essentially left the English isolated. Unaware, the Council pressed on with its plans, but in a further setback, the force that eventually set out in December was devastated by storms, and hundreds of men died at sea.

It is hard to imagine worse management or a more dire state of affairs, short of invasion itself. To add to this, when Parliament met again in early 1380 to consider a new request for taxation, the chancellor declared that the king's government was bankrupt. In response, the Commons, many of whose members must by now have been wondering why they had agreed to serve in Parliament (and perhaps, given the government's insolvency, whether they would ever be paid for their efforts), demanded again that the Council be sacked. They furthermore sought the removal of the chancellor, and demanded that Richard II, now aged thirteen, take the reins of government; they were desperate for decisive leadership, and understandably so. Surely even a child could do better than what they had seen so far?

The demand for Richard to take over government fully was futile at such a young age, but the resulting changes in personnel around him promised a fresh start and temporarily eased tensions, and the government again approached Parliament for money. The king's advisers were now proposing an expedition to Brittany of five thousand men under the command of Richard's youngest uncle, Thomas of Woodstock. The aim was to bolster John de Montfort, who was safely established in Brittany and keen to assert his own independence against the French king by leveraging a new alliance with the English. Down in Gascony, John Neville's limited forces, which had never made their foray into Navarre, had been struggling with a lack of resources. They had retaken some fortresses from the French, especially in the Médoc, but the latter were bearing down on Bordeaux, and the need to send reinforcements had therefore become doubly urgent.

Persuaded by the arguments, the Commons agreed to a large subsidy on the condition that there would be no further Parliaments before autumn 1381. It was a forlorn hope. By November 1380, Parliament was already in session again to hear a request for additional taxation; proceedings must have begun to feel like an ever-revolving circle for the unfortunate MPs. This time money was needed for a force that would be despatched to Portugal the following summer under another of the king's uncles, this time to support the Portuguese in campaigns against the Castilians (though secrecy about the expedition meant that details were never revealed to the Commons). Funds were additionally required for Thomas of Woodstock's forces, which had quickly run short of money. The seriousness of the situation was clear, though the Commons hardly needed a reminder. To compound matters, the Castilians had all the while been inflicting repeated damage along the Kent and Essex coastline, further denting wider morale at home. Shocked by the lack of money the government was reporting, there was intense and fraught debate in the Commons. Finally, they granted another poll tax, the third in four years, but the rate was higher than before, at one shilling per head for all lay men and women over the age of fifteen, three times the level of the 1377 grant, and there was no grading, making it hugely unfair on the poorest taxpayers. While in Parliament there had been entreaties for the rich to help the poor, there was no obligation to do so, and in many areas there was no one wealthy enough to provide that financial safety net anyway. The Commons in Parliament were simply attempting to remove as much taxation as possible from their own shoulders and place it instead on to the shoulders of peasants who had been demanding higher wages since the Black Death. For many of the gentry the financial situation was particularly urgent in the late 1370s, as the economy had collapsed suddenly in the middle of the decade, critically affecting the grain prices and landlord incomes on which they depended, so they must have felt as though they had no choice.

Like the final years of Edward III's reign, the first three of Richard II's showed just how important the leadership of the king was in foreign policy. Without a king or, because of John of Gaunt's unpopularity, a regent, to steer a clear course, multiple voices prevailed at once. By the late fourteenth century, these included not only members of the nobility but factions in the Commons, too, where merchants and gentry, towns and countryside were all represented. This prompted confused, overambitious and disorganised military strategy and planning. The immense costs associated with the repeated endeavours to deal with the threat from the French and the Castilians weighed heavily on taxpayers, and the recurring failures provoked suspicions of corruption. Just a few years into the new reign, trust in government in the Commons was at a critically low ebb. Beyond Parliament, the situation was even more troubling.

The 1381 Peasants' Revolt

As more and more burdens were being pushed on to the peasantry and lesser men of the localities, and as less and less progress seemed to be made in defending the coasts and England's interests, politics on the ground unsurprisingly became increasingly combustible. This was amplified by the fact that the government moved forward the original plan to collect the latest 'poll tax' from June to April 1381. In addition, collectors in the localities, in order to find all the people who were liable to pay the tax, were making deeper inquiries into personal circumstances than ever before, prompting still more resentment. Even then, though, their progress was limited, and in March 1381, desperate for funds and believing the collectors to be negligent, the government set up commissions to investigate the issues with collection. This led to rumours that a new tax was soon to be raised which had not had Parliamentary approval. In the meantime, across the Channel, English hopes for progress were shattered in early 1381 when John de Montfort agreed to do homage to the new French king, the child Charles VI, for Brittany. Instead of allying with the English against the king of France, as he had promised to do, this meant that he had performed another volte-face. Consequently Woodstock had no choice but to abandon his campaign to join Montfort and return to England.

By then the domestic situation was becoming extremely dangerous: in April, the sheriffs of London were so fearful of violent reprisals that they refused to collect the poll tax, and by May it was clear that the situation in south-eastern England was very febrile. The spark that finally ignited rebellion was resistance to one of the commissioners sent out to investigate non-collection of tax in Fobbing, Corringham and Stanford-le-Hope in Essex. Angry and frustrated, peasants across the area rose against the commissioners and when the chief justice of the Common Bench, Sir Robert Belknap, was sent into the county with a commission of trailbaston (these were by now notorious for resulting in large numbers of fines), the rebels seized him and made him swear that he would never hold a trailbaston session again.

In Kent similar protests had also begun. There, the actions of another unpopular tax collector, John Legge, provoked an outcry, with the people apparently demanding only the taxes of their 'fathers and forebears', namely the fifteenths that had been the norm before the introduction of the poll tax. The Kent rebels came together at Dartford on 5 June, but they were no mob. Organised like an army, they represented a force determined to bring order and reform to a realm they believed had been brought to its knees by corruption. Their first action was to resolve that those who lived near the coast should stay in place to defend it while the rest moved on to Rochester, where they took control of the castle. From there, they went to Maidstone on 7 June and elected a leader, Wat Tyler. Since the revolt, Tyler has become part of popular legend, but the historical record tells us very little about him: his name suggests, and the chronicler Froissart stated, that he was a tiler, but there is confusion about whether he came from Maidstone in Kent or Colchester in Essex. Another chronicler notes that he was a disbanded soldier and there are hints that he was aged around forty at the time of the rebellion. Whatever his origins, one thing is very clear: Tyler was quickly recognised as a leader of men.

Following his election in Kent, Tyler moved the rebels on swiftly to Canterbury, storming the cathedral while mass was being said. They were looking for Archbishop Sudbury, who, as chancellor, stood at the heart of a government they felt was rotten at its core. At the time, however, he was in London. As they left to pursue him there, the rebels told the monks that he would soon be beheaded. By the middle of June, they were on the outskirts of London, planning, they declared, to destroy 'traitors' and 'save the king', and they demanded to speak to the king himself at Blackheath. Around this time, according to the chronicler Thomas Walsingham, Tyler was to tell the St Albans rebels that he would 'shave the beards of the abbot, prior and monks' of the abbey, but that the rebels had to follow his orders. They were apparently unsure at that time whether the king or Tyler had more power in England.

The government was now faced with the formidable combination of the Essex men camped out at Mile End and their Kentish counterparts at Blackheath. For forces like this to have amassed so quickly, contemplating such violence against those in authority, shows the depths of despair to which they had been driven in recent years. Even to contemplate the murder of the archbishop of Canterbury represented an outrage; it was not only a crime, but one of the worst mortal sins.

The Council seems to have decided swiftly that conciliation was the best route forward. This was the first rising of its kind in English history and it was unclear what the outcome would be, or the extent of the rebels' violence. They had petitioned for the heads of John of Gaunt and the chief officers of the state, and there must have been real fear that this would turn into a bloodbath, and perhaps even result in the overthrow of the government. No one wanted to make things any more incendiary than they already were. It was decided that Richard should set out along the River Thames ready to meet the rebels and hear their demands from the Tower of London, where he had been sent for safety. However, the crowds made it impossible for him to land, and he was forced to turn round and return to the Tower. Tyler responded by marching his men to Southwark, where they stormed the Marshalsea prison before burning the Chancery records at the archbishop's residence at Lambeth. From there the rebels moved to the Fleet prison, which they also stormed. At the New Temple they burned legal records and attacked houses belonging to the treasurer, Robert Hales.

In London, the rebels launched a savage attack on Gaunt's opulent Savoy Palace. Everything – clothing, furnishings, jewels – was trampled and burned, including the palace itself, which was razed to the ground. Foreigners similarly found themselves targeted and around 150 lost their lives in London alone during the rebellion, including a number of Flemings, with whom there had been recent trading tensions. Remarkably, though, there was little looting, possibly due to Tyler's leadership and insistence on the higher end of truth and justice which the rebels proclaimed. Richard watched on from the Tower powerless; it was essential to try once more to meet the rebels if calm were ever to be restored. The mayor duly ordered a proclamation that King Richard would hear their grievances at Mile End, and many of the rebels began to head east. At the same time, Richard issued a general pardon to those at Tower Hill, provided they retreated peacefully. But anger was high, and most simply ignored him and continued with the attacks on lawyers and the houses of those officials they regarded as traitors to the realm, as well as burning important documents.

Those who did congregate at Mile End, though, were rewarded with the promised audience with the young king, still only fourteen years old. Richard was accompanied by several members of the nobility, but he left behind the archbishop and others – the 'traitors' the rebels were railing against – advising them to try to escape. That advice turned out to be ineffectual: the archbishop-chancellor and the treasurer were both captured and beheaded, and their heads placed on London Bridge as an example to others. The savagery was unprecedented. At Mile End, while the rebels insisted on their loyalty to Richard, they demanded that 'traitors' be given to them to be 'punished', the meaning of which was by now entirely clear. They added a further petition for an end to all villeinage (unfree peasants who held land in return for labour services but did not receive wages) and for services to be on the basis of free labour. Richard, faced with no real choice, quickly agreed to the demands, and many of the Essex men began to leave the city in good faith, believing their aims to have been realised.

Elsewhere in London Tyler's Kent rebels were still at large and showing no signs of dispersing. Richard moved to Smithfield to face them and hear their demands. Like his Essex counterparts, Tyler wanted an end to villein-age, but he went further: there should be 'no lordship but that of the king', he said, and all men should be equal. The property of the church should also be seized and redistributed among the laity, with all bishoprics abolished. It was no less than a call for social revolution. The king again apparently met these demands with a calm acquiescence that was remarkable for his age, and asked the rebels to disperse, but a fracas ensued between Walworth, who was mayor of London, and Tyler, in which Tyler was killed. There is a hint in the sources that his death may well have been pre-planned to deprive the rebels of their charismatic leader, but if so, that would have been highly risky in its provocation. What defused the situation was an astute, and probably not pre-planned, response by the king himself that the rebels should follow him as their 'captain' instead, promising to pardon them all. In so doing, he slowly rode away, taking many of them with him, a move that undoubtedly dispelled much of their anger. Remarkably, the rebellion was over, and while problems continued for a short time in parts of England, by the end of the year most counties were settled.

The government had been taken completely by surprise by the 1381 rebellion; peasants had never come together on this scale before. Moreover, they were organised and targeted in their actions, and in Wat Tyler they had a particularly strong and effective leader. For a time, the situation had been about as dangerous as it could get; only the prospect of external invasion would have been worse. At a glance, the causes of the rebellion are obvious – high taxes on those who could least afford to pay them, military and governmental failure, perceived (and at times real) governmental corruption, and heavy-handed local enforcement. It was a heady and combustible mix.

But the revolt of 1381 had even more complex long-term origins than this suggests. Despite occurring over one and a half centuries after 1215, it owed a debt to Magna Carta too: those who were being subjected to arbitrary impositions by the government were demanding that their rights be respected and that they have a say in how the country was run. Like the many financial exactions made by King John under similar military pressure, the poll tax was arbitrary and unfair. As their social superiors foisted on to them the burden of economic collapse and wartime failure, the peasants had little or no voice, just as the barons had none in the seizures by King John. In the 150 years that followed the revolt of 1215, the Charter had become a touchstone of good governance, being read out in market squares regularly and alluded to in almost every subsequent political crisis. It is impossible that its central messages – that the common law should protect the property of all freemen from arbitrary seizure, and that the rule of law in general should prevail – had been lost on peasants.

Before the 1370s, though, they had never been subjected to the kinds of impositions that the barons and the knights had faced. In that decade the combination of the lasting effects of the Black Death, wartime failure, the dotage of Edward III and the politically troubled minority of Richard II, and sudden economic collapse, created a perfect storm provoking them to action. For the peasant rebels of 1381, as for the Commons in Parliament, abject military failure despite the high taxes that had been demanded again and again from the king's subjects meant that there had to be people who had appropriated the money – men who had behaved in their own, selfish interests, not those of the realm. They must surely be held to account. The truth, of course, was much more prosaic: without good leadership and with no one with the authority to determine a clear path forward, English government was divided and mired in confusion during one of the most challenging periods in the country's history. With so many voices now expecting to be heard among the king's subjects, the ramifications of governmental failure were always going to be far-reaching. There were also bound to be increasingly serious questions about the conduct of government, and major tensions between different groups of the king's subjects.

The other, more revolutionary demand made by the rebels, for an end to all villeinage, is confusing, because the vast bulk of the rebels were not villeins at all. They were free peasants, even men who had held local office. It will never be entirely clear why this demand was made, but it is possible that it was a bid for support by free peasants from their unfree counterparts, in the same way as the barons had appealed to 'all freemen' in Magna Carta. Or perhaps it simply reflected how freemen felt they had been treated in recent years. After all, the Statute of Labourers placed restrictions on both the movement and wages of free peasants that would have made them feel distinctly unfree. New sumptuary laws similarly regulated how peasants dressed, to increase social control and entrench class boundaries. And yet peasants were at the same time being expected to pay taxes in which they had no say, at higher levels than ever before. It is no wonder that they sought to have their voices heard in the most dramatic way.

Emerging from the Shadow of Revolt, 1381–4

In the immediate aftermath of the 1381 revolt, the government was reeling. The conciliatory approach taken during the rebellion itself had achieved its aim of persuading the peasants to disperse, but they could not be permitted to form the view that the brutal murder of government officers and the archbishop of Canterbury would be met only with concessions. In late June 1381 the sheriffs were ordered to proclaim the enforcement of the peace and were empowered to take all action necessary to put down any remaining rebellion. Those same powers were shortly afterwards given to Richard's uncle Thomas of Woodstock, and the new hard-line chief justice of King's Bench, Robert Tresilian. The latter had been promoted to the position of chief justice after the murder of the incumbent, John Cavendish, by the peasant rebels, and the chroniclers Henry Knighton and Thomas Walsingham commented on Tresilian's tough stance. They even pointed to the pressure he put on juries to convict and the brutal punishments he advocated for those who were found guilty.

It was high risk to appoint someone so hawkish, given recent events, but the government was determined, also issuing commissions across southern England giving military and judicial power to nobles and gentry. While many of these acted with restraint, the strong message from the centre was that the rebels were to be treated as traitors and executed: the commissioners were instructed to act 'according to the law and custom of England', and no mercy was offered in these circumstances. When, in spite of this, Essex continued to suffer disturbances, no time was wasted: the king was despatched in person to the county in late June, and when the rebels tried to negotiate confirmation of the concessions previously made in London, his attitude was both dismissive and entirely at odds with what it had been during the rebellion itself: 'Villeins ye are and villeins ye shall remain,' he said. There was to be no more discussion. When the rebels mobilised in resistance, Thomas of Woodstock and Sir Thomas Percy, earl of Worcester, an experienced soldier, were immediately tasked with putting down the rebellion by force. The result was a foregone conclusion: in effect an army (albeit small) under the command of two noblemen had been despatched to Essex, and the revolt was quickly suppressed. Tresilian then stayed in the locality presiding over the trials of rebels. Nineteen were hanged as a deterrent to any who might be tempted to think about resurrecting the rebellion. Following this, the government was inclined also to continue with its uncompromising position in relation to villein labour services, providing assurances to lords that they would receive support if they encountered resistance imposing them.

For many lords, Tresilian and the government's hard-line approach went beyond what they were comfortable with. Harmonious social relations depended on a degree of negotiation and compromise, and the brutal punishment of peasants was felt to have the potential to be counter-productive. In the febrile atmosphere of late 1381, remembering how many leading figures had been murdered by rebels in June that year, the local gentry and nobility in many areas were nervous about provoking further unrest, and they told the royal Council this in no uncertain terms. They were led initially by the men of Kent, where the leaders of local society felt so strongly that they themselves stood surety for the 'commons' of the county, persuading the government not to send in a commission.

While all this was happening, wider concerns about the direction of government continued to fester. By the time Parliament convened in November 1381, the Commons, still extremely nervous about the possibility of another rebellion, repeated earlier criticisms of the government and urged both restraint and reform. The result was the removal of the chancellor, William Courtenay, also archbishop of Canterbury, and his replacement by Richard, Lord Scrope. He was a Yorkshire knight who had been appointed to the baronage following distinguished military service, and in whom the Commons, importantly, had long-standing faith. They also renewed their focus on corruption and the management of the king's resources, specifically his household, with the result that the earl of Arundel and Michael de la Pole were appointed to 'attend the king in his household and counsel and govern his person'. Pole appeared to be a very good choice for the role: originally from a northern mercantile family with little money, he had made a successful career in royal service. He had served on campaign with the Black Prince in the 1350s, going on to make a good marriage with the daughter of a member of the prince's affinity, Sir John Wingfield. Later he was with Gaunt, too, and his advancement in the 1370s as well as his appointment with Arundel in 1381 probably owed something to Gaunt's patronage. Now nearing the age of fifty, he was no longer to play a role in military campaigns, but he was clearly highly regarded as he had also been tasked since 1379 with the negotiation of a marriage for Richard. He seemed like an ideal choice to counsel the young king.

Yet while the Commons' concerns about corruption were understandable in the context, the prevailing issue remained not misdoings but lack of leadership in foreign policy, on which resources were still being haemorrhaged with no positive outcomes. In the short term, only the prospect of a good royal marriage on the Continent offered some hope for breaking the foreign-policy impasse. The royal Council therefore focused on arranging the most advantageous union possible, between Richard and Anne of Bohemia, the eldest daughter of Charles VI of Luxembourg, and sister of Wenceslas, the Holy Roman Emperor and king of Bohemia. In an echo of Henry III's policy, it was felt that a strong alliance between England and the Holy Roman Emperor had the potential to drive a wedge between the emperor and the French which might work to England's advantage. Discussions over the marriage had gone well and the terms of the alliance had been settled in early 1381; this was celebrated with a lavish reception at Gaunt's Savoy Palace that March. Anne herself, who was fifteen (relatively mature by the standards of medieval royal marriages), almost exactly the same age as Richard, arrived in England in December 1381. She travelled to Canterbury and from there to Leeds Castle in Kent to celebrate Christmas. However, in what should have been a period of unadulterated joy, there followed an unfortunate argument between the new archbishop of Canterbury and the bishop of London about who should preside over the marriage and Anne's coronation. The archbishop, William Courtenay, who was newly elected, had not yet received his pallium – the vestment that signified his conferred authority – and the bishop of London, Robert Braybrooke, who had been among those who had conducted the marriage negotiations, claimed that he should therefore preside instead. Courtenay objected to Braybrooke's claim and others were forced to try to broker a settlement between the two men before the events could proceed. In the end a compromise was reached in which it was agreed that Courtenay would oversee the coronation and Braybrooke the marriage. On 18 January 1382 Anne was brought into London, and two days later she married the king in Westminster Abbey. Her coronation took place another two days afterwards.

There are few details of the royal wedding, because chroniclers gave it only the briefest attention in their writings, indicating their lack of regard for the match. Focus was given to the lamentable financial cost of the marriage. Not only was Wenceslas poor – the new queen came with no dowry, and Wenceslas even had to turn to Richard for a loan in the months leading up to the marriage – but he had so many problems in Bohemia that he never even arranged a coronation for himself in the Empire, despite his father having secured his election as Holy Roman Emperor. The English Council had banked on an alliance with an active emperor; what it got was a lame duck and something of a diplomatic farce, and the chroniclers were not inclined to see anything positive in the whole affair. The Westminster chronicler also delivered a particularly brutal verdict on Anne herself, calling her 'this little scrap of humanity'. On the tour of the realm that followed their wedding, Richard and his wife quickly became a devoted couple, but in diplomatic terms the marriage itself was simply another example of the minority government's failure.

By spring 1382 Richard was tall, handsome and married, but he was still fifteen years old. He could not be expected to lead policymaking, though the political community hoped that he would at least show signs of it. Instead, disagreements between members of the nobility, and between some of the nobility and the Commons, over immediate military policy continued and were hard to surmount. Gaunt pressed for resources to campaign in Castile, with the idea of removing the Castilians from the Channel waters as a consequence, but there was both a good deal of opposition to the strategy in Parliament and an unwillingness to fund it. This was accompanied by lingering suspicion of Gaunt, and fear on the part of the Commons about any major nobleman leaving the country in case there were to be a further peasant uprising. Instead Gaunt suggested that Richard should personally lead a large army to France, which might then proceed to Castile. However, this too was rejected by Parliament; if they did not want a nobleman to leave the country, they certainly did not want the king to do so. Divisions continued into autumn 1382 between, on one side, Gaunt, the king (who was becoming increasingly active) and some of the Council, and on the other the Commons in Parliament, with the former preferring the Spanish plan put forward by Gaunt. Things were complicated by the fact that at the same time the English position across the Channel was coming increasingly under threat: in the north, the French under the duke of Burgundy took control of Flanders in winter 1382 and the French government then ordered commercial relations with England to stop. There was panic among those whose livelihoods depended significantly on continental trade, and a desire for action, but nothing was happening.

During this impasse Henry Despenser, the bishop of Norwich, proposed what in hindsight (and to many at the time) was a ridiculous idea of leading a campaign to Flanders. It was not only the scheme that was problematic; the bishop himself also posed an issue. No stranger to violence, he clearly had something of an uncompromising temperament: in 1377, for example, he had been wounded during a riot in Bishop's Lynn that had resulted from his attempts to enforce his lordship in the town, despite a long-running dispute over the matter. The royal Council acting on Richard II's behalf had to intercede to calm the situation. He had also been quick to take an aggressive stance during the Peasants' Revolt, violently putting down rebels in North Walsham, Norfolk, where he was bishop, and hanging their leader. In early 1382, such was his unpopularity that a further revolt was planned in Norfolk with the aim of killing the bishop, though neither the revolt nor the assassination came to pass. Walsingham, who had briefly been prior of Wymondham in Despenser's diocese, described him in excoriating terms as arrogant, unable to make or keep friends, without discipline or discretion, and immature: a thoroughgoing condemnation.

For the Commons, in which some groups of merchants had trading priorities in the Low Countries, whatever the bishop's character, the Norwich crusade was a low-cost option. The Council, on the other hand, was understandably concerned at the turn events were taking; it was now, in effect, losing control of foreign policy. While a northern campaign was desirable given the French blockade on trade with Flanders, one led by a maverick bishop with little military experience was not. The Council desperately tried to secure support for an alternative campaign led by the king himself. However, they could neither persuade Richard to go nor produce funds on the scale necessary for such an undertaking: both fundamental obstacles to action. And for their part the Commons in Parliament remained reluctant to grant further taxation: suspicious of Gaunt and concerned about the Scottish border, the king's uncles, they said, should stay in England to watch the northern border; and, they added, they did not like the idea of the king leaving the country in these circumstances either. Gaunt stormed out of Parliament, such was his anger at the direction of the debate, understandably: anyone familiar with military campaigns would know Despenser's proposal was utter folly. While Gaunt may not have been England's most talented military commander, he knew abject stupidity when he saw it. But with the Commons adamant, there was now no choice but to sanction Despenser's campaign; without extra funds and royal support, the idea of an offensive led by Richard was hopeless. In a final insult to the lords, the bishop even rejected all pleas for a royal lieutenant to oversee the campaign.

In response, the best the Council could do was hastily devise a plan in which it was envisaged that when Despenser set out for Flanders in April 1383, Gaunt would secure the northern border with Scotland, where the Scots had already breached the truce more than once. They could only hope that Despenser might, against all the odds, succeed. Initially the signs were good: the campaign began well, with a successful attack on Gravelines. But from there things rapidly deteriorated: dysentery broke out among the troops and there was a shortage of the right equipment. At this stage, Despenser rejected an offer by the Council to send the earl of Arundel out in support, and the English position rapidly began to collapse in the face of the mobilisation of the French army. When news of this reached England, Gaunt and Buckingham were determined to take action to rescue the enterprise – concerns were mounting about the fate of English-held Calais if this turned into a rout. Both wrote to the king in Yorkshire to try to persuade him to lead an army across the Channel, and merchant ships were requisitioned in preparation for transporting more troops to Flanders. But after two weeks, despite the urgency, no reply had been received from Richard. Gaunt had no choice but to act, and swiftly prepared his own retinue to set sail.

On hearing that Dunkirk had been occupied by the French, Richard jumped on to his horse and rode to London from St Albans in the night to chair an emergency session of the Council. Why he had delayed for two weeks and why he suddenly acted in haste is perplexing, but in any case, by then, it was too late to organise a force strong enough for the king to lead; the only option was a rescue mission for the bishop's troops, led by Gaunt and Buckingham. In the event the position of the English forces across the Channel disintegrated so quickly that the bishop was home in England before the rescue mission could even depart. In Parliament in October 1383, the Commons demanded, somewhat ironically given their support for the campaign in the first place, that those responsible for the disaster be punished, and Despenser was subsequently impeached. Gaunt was swiftly despatched to France to negotiate the best truce he could out of the mess the bishop had left behind.

With nothing resolved, the situation was even worse than it had been a year earlier. In Parliament the chancellor spelled out that the king was at war not just with France and Castile, but with Flanders too. He asked for another subsidy to plan for a new campaign. To take the war to his opponents the government would need more money, he argued. In response, the Commons finally, and very reluctantly, gave a subsidy, but they made it conditional on war with France taking place (an undoubtedly optimistic caveat, as they probably knew); they also said that the second half of the subsidy could be collected only if peace with the French was not possible by Easter 1384. But England's problems no longer lay only across the Channel. The Scots raided into Northumberland while the autumn Parliament was taking place, and the border captains warned the government that their opponents were becoming more intensive in their activities, raising concerns for the borderlands in the north of England. The Council had to act quickly, and the immediate response was to ask local lords to defend the border. This was reinforced soon afterwards by Thomas of Woodstock, who embarked with three thousand men to hold the line until a more substantial campaign could be planned.

The only optimistic aspect in what seemed to be an interminably deteriorating military situation did not come from the floundering English government, but from France and an unexpected letter from the duke of Burgundy to the Council in October that included an extremely positive set of peace proposals. Philip of Burgundy was at that stage the leader of a minority Council governing on behalf of Charles VI, who had acceded to the French throne aged eleven – just one year before Richard II. In response, Gaunt hurried to France to participate in diplomatic discussions, and by January 1384 he had managed to agree a draft treaty. There was no doubt that this had all happened because it suited the French, but it provided desperately needed time. The draft treaty enabled a truce to be put in place until October to allow time for further discussions, with talks scheduled to restart in June 1384. This meant that the immediate focus could turn to the threat to the Scottish border area, and when Gaunt returned to England in spring 1384 he set off straight away together with his younger brothers, arriving in Newcastle towards the end of March.

The Beginning of Richard's Personal Rule

The years immediately following the Peasants' Revolt were full of confusion. It is hard to underplay the fear that must have existed following the rebellion – the brutal murder of government ministers and the prospect of renewed mob violence must have terrified many nobles and gentry alike. There was a very fine line between taking an approach to the rebels that was tough enough to dissuade them and others from future action, and exercising enough clemency not to provoke them further. For a while the government seemed to be steering only the former course, and the king himself in one of his earliest interventions displayed an attitude towards the rebels that itself had the potential to be incendiary, despite his promises at Mile End. In this, both he and his government were out of step with many of the gentry in the localities themselves, and local opposition forced the king and his advisers to soften policy somewhat. All the while, the fear of renewed violence remained high, and dominated attitudes to foreign policy. Even though the military situation on the southern shores of England, across the Channel and in the north remained serious, the idea of the king or members of his nobility leaving the realm clearly filled people with terror. It is this, as well as their own financial situation and recurring worries about corruption, that explains the Commons' unwillingness to grant taxation in the period. It also goes some way towards making sense of their backing of the ill-fated and poorly conceived Despenser 'crusade' in 1384. The unexpected French truce of 1384 gave a welcome respite from conflict, but in the north of England a full-scale campaign was much needed; Woodstock was only holding the line. At seventeen, Richard was now the same age as his grandfather had been when he had so decisively seized his throne back from Mortimer in 1330, and his subjects desperately needed him to begin to provide leadership and a sense of direction for government.

The reality, though, was that there were already worrying signs that the new king's personality was very problematic. In the late 1370s it had become clear that he was not using royal resources carefully, and was generous, perhaps overly so, in his giving to others. In March 1378, for example, his tutor Simon Burley was granted Llanstephan in South Wales at a time when revenues from lands that had come into royal hands were much needed. It was also very unusual to make a grant like this to someone like Burley, who, despite having a good record of military service to the Crown, and having acted as Richard's chamberlain before he became king, was nonetheless not from the ranks of the nobility. In 1382, the chronicler Walsingham went on to allege that Richard was extravagant and did not heed the counsel of the magnates. When the earl of March, Edmund Mortimer, died in December 1381, leaving a seven-year-old son, some of the profits of the wardship that came to the king were said to have been wasted on grants to people in his immediate circle. Richard also placed the administration of the estates in the hands of men from his household, who supplanted the established local and often long-standing family servants; profits were used by Richard for his household expenses rather than for those of the government. Given the state of government funds and the burdens that had been placed on the king's subjects in the form of taxation in recent years, this was worrying.

These grants might simply have been manifestations of an early immaturity, but the pattern continued as the king grew older. Following the death of the earl of Suffolk in early 1382 leaving no heir, Richard simply handed many of the lands of the earldom to Michael de la Pole. In the face of the king's actions, the Council and Chancellor Richard Scrope attempted to rein in Richard's generosity: in the six months leading up to July 1382 they granted portions of the Mortimer estates to Mortimer associates and reappointed long-standing members of the established administration of the estates to office. In July 1382, however, Richard summarily dismissed Scrope from the office of chancellor and replaced him after two months of searching with Robert Braybrooke, bishop of London. Not long afterwards, in March 1383, Braybrooke himself was replaced with Michael de la Pole, who was most definitely Richard's personal choice, having become friends with the king over the last two years.

Pole was not the only beneficiary of the king's increased largesse as he began to assert himself: late in 1382, Simon Burley was made justice of South Wales for life, while John Beauchamp of Holt, one of Richard's leading chamber knights and previously a loyal servant of Edward III, was given the custody of Conwy Castle. Notwithstanding the lack of wisdom of some of Richard's generosity, it is true that some of those with whom he was surrounding himself were established and broadly sensible men, Pole and Beauchamp, and to some extent Burley, being good examples – the former had apparently tried to stop the bishop of Norwich's ill-fated crusade and had a strong sense of the importance of obedience to the Crown, come what may. But many of the other courtiers around Richard would have been considered unsuitable company for the king. They were said to have encouraged him in indolence and the rejection of the usual kingly sports that fostered military skill and often served to build up an essential *esprit de corps* with the nobility. Richard was continuing to be indiscriminate in his dispensation of favour as well as lacking in judgement.

Furthermore, even chroniclers who were inclined to think well of him began to describe Richard as lazy and dissolute, with an unpredictable temper. In autumn 1382, the Commons asked outright that 'good governance be set in place around your honourable person so that you may live honestly and regally within the revenues of your kingdom, and that all kinds of wardships, marriages, reliefs, escheats, forfeitures and all other resources be kept for your wars, and for the defence of your kingdom, and not used elsewhere'.

Richard agreed to this at the time, but later, in November 1382, he ordered that all issues from the Mortimer estates that remained in royal hands should again be devoted to royal household expenses. He was also already growing increasingly sensitive, and took any criticism of his government very personally. When in February 1383 the Commons in Parliament made an attempt to control royal spending (in much the same vein as attempts had been made for the last twenty years), Richard, by then sixteen, reacted testily that he would take about himself such specific persons, lords and others, 'as seemed best to him for his honour and profit'.

Instances of behaviour like this inevitably had a negative impact on his relationship with his nobles, and in autumn 1383, as Parliament was taking place, reports began to emerge of open breaches between Richard and some of them, who claimed that the king was listening to unsuitable counsel. Complaints also began to grow about the behaviour of his confidants. The integrity of both Pole and another associate, Robert de Vere, was even questioned by Parliament itself. Five years older than Richard, de Vere was brought up in the royal household as he was still a minor when he succeeded to his earldom of Oxford – there are no records but it is very likely that he met Richard then. When he was still just fourteen, his marriage was placed in the hands of the earl of Bedford and he was duly married in 1376 to Philippa de Coucy, granddaughter of Edward III. This greatly aided the young de Vere in terms of his status, but he remained the poorest of all the earls when he acceded to his inheritance. Nonetheless (or perhaps because of this), it seems that in the early 1380s he somehow emerged as part of a clique of young courtiers around Richard, and by late 1383 he seems to have been singled out as a particular favourite. (Although rumours would later circulate about the nature of his relationship with Richard, there is no indication that they were anything other than close friends.) In his capacity as royal favourite, de Vere certainly exercised a great deal of influence over Richard – Froissart would claim that if he had said 'black was white the king would not have gainsaid him'. He also benefited hugely from royal patronage, which suited him well as he liked the high life; the opulence of his possessions found at Chester when he was later exiled from the realm testifies to this. There were no fewer than six different liveries for his valets and grooms and four for his minstrels, along with expensive tapestries and silver plate.

At the same time as Parliament was understandably raising questions about the king's associates in late 1383, the earl of Arundel and a group of other noblemen who had been custodians of the Mortimer inheritance in the March managed to wrest control of the inheritance back from the king – which meant an end to the insertion of household officials and in many cases a return to the more natural practice of appointing experienced local Mortimer family servants to estate offices. But Richard was stubborn and not willing to acquiesce. While he could do nothing about the Mortimer estates, it seems clear that he involved himself directly in business a number of times in the same Parliament, reflecting his increasing assertiveness. According to the chronicler known as the monk of Westminster, the interventions were not constructive: the lords claimed that they 'laboured to take the full burden of government on themselves'. None of this boded well for the future.

The effects were made clear when Parliament met again in April 1384. Pole put before it the draft peace treaty Gaunt had agreed with the French over the course of the previous autumn and winter. The terms of the treaty have not survived, so it is impossible to know exactly what was proposed, but it seems that the Commons were concerned about clauses in it that had the king paying homage for Calais and other territories secured during war. Otherwise, their only comment was that they preferred peace to war, which was a statement deliberately designed not to light the fires of controversy. They were in the most awkward of positions: it was unprecedented to have the terms of a treaty put before them for decision without a considered and united steer from the king and his nobility to accompany it, and so they were being expected to cast judgement in a novel way. This reinforces the emerging sense from contemporary views that the relationship between the king and the nobles was already very fraught. Faced with this, evidently the Commons did not know which way to turn – they were accustomed to asserting and defending their interests, but not to deciding strategy, and it was not a responsibility they wanted to bear.

The atmosphere in Parliament was fractious, and following more criticisms of the government from the earl of Arundel, who was against the Gaunt peace treaty and favoured a more aggressive policy, a quarrel broke out between the earl and the king. Richard reacted angrily to Arundel's criticisms, saying that if the earl blamed him for the parlous state of the English position in France, 'you lie in your face: go to the devil'. It was a bizarre outburst, and it was left to Gaunt to make a speech attempting to placate both king and earl. But in an equally bizarre turn of events Gaunt himself also came under suspicion, when a Carmelite friar who was saying mass before the king told Richard that the duke was plotting to murder him. Richard seems to have believed the accusations, for which there is no evidence, and Gaunt was forced to defend himself. Thomas of Woodstock, who as Edward III's youngest son had few landed endowments and must have already been concerned to see the elevations of Pole and Burley, apparently then stormed into Richard's chamber and declared that he would kill anyone, including the king, who accused Gaunt of treason. Although tensions subsequently decreased quite rapidly, these events and the king's reactions suggest a defensiveness that had in it a strong element of paranoia and irrationality, and relationships between key figures that were coming dangerously close to collapsing altogether. This marked the beginning of Woodstock's alienation from Richard.

The bitterness of Arundel's feelings towards the king may have arisen from more than a bellicose personality and the failures of foreign policy. From around 1383, Richard had been acting in ways that had the effect, if not initially the intention, of beginning to exclude Arundel from local government and power in the Welsh March. The most notable example of this relates to Thomas Mowbray, who was permitted by Richard to accede to his earldom of Nottingham as a minor in early 1383 on the condition that he marry Elizabeth, the daughter and heir of John Lestrange of Blakemere. The significance of this was that Lestrange's lands were in the north-west March, where Arundel was dominant. That Arundel was concerned by this move is suggested by the fact that when Elizabeth died prematurely shortly afterwards, he quickly secured the marriage of Mowbray to his own daughter without acquiring the necessary royal licence first. After the earl's outburst in Parliament in 1384, the king's actions became more deliberate. Arundel was removed from the Shropshire peace commission, and in June 1384 Richard also tried to detach a section of his lordship of Bromfield and Yale from the earldom, awarding it to his half-brother John Holland. Luckily for Arundel, Holland was soon in disgrace himself for the murder of Ralph, son of the earl of Stafford, and the grant was repealed. But this was not the end of Richard's manoeuvres: in August he sold the guardianship and marriage of the young earl of March, Roger Mortimer, to his other half-brother, Thomas Holland, from under Arundel and the other custodians.

While there is no evidence of other individual nobles being targeted by the king at this point, there were novel policies that suggested at the very least an unconventional approach to governance. Richard's promotion of his household knights to office in place of local men in Wales and the March, for example, meant that by 1383, the Marcher lordships of the earl of Warwick and the duke of Lancaster, as well as the Bohun and Despenser inheritances, were surrounded by offices and estates administered by royal household men. By the later months of 1384, it seems that Richard's policy had expanded significantly and chamber knights were increasingly being granted lands as well as local offices across the Marches. Knights of the royal household were also being appointed to sheriffdoms and peace commissions in several parts of England, including some areas where there was no dominant local lord: in Rutland, Robert de Vere was made life sheriff, and in Wiltshire de Vere's chamberlain was also appointed for life; when he was replaced in 1385, it was by another household knight. Placing household knights on the peace commission was an unusual policy that had been adopted for the first time by the Council to quell disorder in the immediate aftermath of the Peasants' Revolt. The fact that it was deployed by Richard later, as he began to assert himself, suggests that he was attempting to use his household to exercise royal power on the ground, an idea reinforced by similar action in respect of the sheriffdoms, as well as his use of his personal seal, the signet, in place of the great seal of state to effect commands. Since the norm was not for the king to be so closely engaged with local government, but rather for it to be overseen on a day-to-day basis by magnates and their affinities on his behalf, this must have been disconcerting. They must have begun to wonder what was in Richard's mind and what he was attempting to do.

Some of Richard's actions in the localities were ultimately to provoke major opposition, but for the moment they were a side-line to the major issues at the centre, and government went on as usual. Most immediately, Gaunt and Buckingham were sent back to France in August 1384 to negotiate a better peace for England. Their mission would arguably have been a poisoned chalice even had the state of affairs across the Channel remained similar to the start of the year, because it was hard to envisage a route forward that would satisfy everyone. But to make matters worse, Philip of Burgundy had succeeded to the county of Flanders (through his wife) on the death of the count, Louis de Mâle, and was keen to assert French control there. He was unwilling to surrender Calais and its dependent forts to England as had been promised in January, and the English delegation held equally firm in return. Despite managing to negotiate a further truce until May 1385, Gaunt and Buckingham settled nothing material. It seemed even more inevitable that a renewal of war would take place once the truce was over, causing serious concern back in England. In November 1384, Chancellor Pole approached Parliament for another grant of taxation, detailing the mounting threats posed by the French, the Spanish and the Scots; the latter was so serious that during the Parliament itself the Scots breached a truce made earlier in the year, seizing Berwick Castle. Just as government seemed to be treading water and it was hard to see a way forward that the Commons would support, positive momentum crept into proceedings when de la Pole suddenly said that Richard was keen to embark on a personal campaign across the Channel. The importance and impact of kingly leadership is demonstrated by the fact that this alone immediately prompted the Commons to make a grant. Trust in the king's intentions was clearly not high, though: the grant was in two parts, and the second part was made on the condition that Richard fulfilled an expedition to the Continent.

As Richard approached full adulthood, there were clear signs that his reign would be troubled. The military and economic situation he had inherited was unenviable, and the former was showing no sign of improving, not least because of the incoherent policies that had been pursued since 1377. That situation might have been ameliorated had Richard been the kind of leader Edward I and Edward III had been, but by the mid-1380s it was clear that the king's personality was going to introduce further difficulties into an already combustible mix, rather than solutions. He seemed vengeful, unreliable, violent, profligate and unwilling to listen to advice. At the same time, he showed signs of having no sense of the need to focus on government and the magnitude of his duties, and was favouring men who were unsuitable associates, most of whose priorities lay a long way from the business of the realm. In the vacuum created first by the absence of leadership during the minority and then by the failure of the young king to begin to engage constructively with matters of government, the leading nobles inevitably attempted to act on his behalf, just as they had done in Edward II's reign. In the same way as before, though, they could not replicate royal authority, partly because no single noble was pre-eminent, and because that was the very point of kingship: the king was not simply *primus inter pares*. Nor could Parliament act as a proxy for the king. Even by the 1380s, when their role was so much more developed than it had been even seventy years earlier, the Commons wanted only to influence debate, not to make foreign-policy decisions. His subjects needed Richard to lead, and they needed him to do so urgently.

The Road to Crisis, 1385–6

Despite the glimmer of hope provided by Michael de la Pole's announcement that Richard would lead an expedition to France, little improved thereafter: there was still no leadership on wider military strategy from the king, and in the face of French threats, no reinforcements were offered to traditional allies in the Low Countries. Policy was adrift again, and in February 1385, with rumours circulating of a French invasion of England, the king's Council met at Waltham wanting some urgent decisions. However, without any steer from the king, and with the nobility divided over what policy to pursue for the best – some wanted Richard to launch a campaign in France and the Low Countries, while others felt that at this stage the defence of England against invasion had become the priority – there was inevitably renewed deadlock. Ultimately, the situation was so bad that Gaunt and the king's younger uncles, the earls of Buckingham and Cambridge, walked out of the Council in protest at the unwillingness of Richard and his ministers to press ahead with a campaign. Clearly, whatever Richard had promised, there was no sign of delivery. For men who were used to getting things done, the constant delays and indecision were enervating, and as with Arundel in 1384, it was hard to contain tempers. The source of the catastrophic stall was the king himself, and he had to act soon if disaster were to be averted.

What occurred was something entirely different: Richard's friends at the royal court, possibly led by de Vere, devised a plan to have Gaunt arrested and brought before the Council. When this failed, they plotted to have him assassinated at a tournament in February 1385 at Westminster, though this was revealed to Gaunt, who wisely stayed away. It is hard to overstate how odd and out of proportion Richard's action was with the situation; many were aghast at what was unfolding. Later that month, the duke confronted Richard at the king's manor of Sheen, west of London, turning up armed and with members of his affinity for protection. He accused Richard of having been party to the plot, while the archbishop of Canterbury told the king in no uncertain terms that it was heinous to plan to assassinate his own uncle. Richard's immediate response was deeply defensive: he abused the archbishop and threatened to confiscate his secular possessions; he even drew his sword on Courtenay and had to be restrained from attacking him. This time it fell to Richard's mother to restore calm. These events are the earliest indication that Richard's developing approach to kingship was seriously pathological. His actions suggest that his focus may have been entirely on what he saw as Gaunt's insubordination in walking out of Council, rather than on the fundamental issue at stake, the seriousness of the military situation.

The country could ill afford such abject dereliction of kingly duty, and while all this was going on the military situation inevitably continued to deteriorate. By summer 1385 it took the form of an outright emergency: the Scots together with the French were threatening a massive invasion of the north of England once the current truce expired on 15 July; the French fleet destined for Scotland had already assembled on the coast to the north-east of Bruges at Sluys. The royal Council met in June 1385 in Reading and immediately decided to send an army to Scotland to prevent the imminent large-scale invasion. By the next month one of the biggest armies of the fourteenth century, totalling around fourteen thousand men and including every important magnate as well as – remarkably, given recent events – the king himself, was marching north to deal with the threat. Among the largest retinues was that of John Neville of Raby, who, since returning from Gascony in the early 1380s, had done very well for himself. Appointed as one of the wardens of the Scottish Marches, he had been able to continue to build up his position in the north of England, fortifying two of his castles and even constructing a grand new gateway at his manor of Raby bearing his shield and that of his wife. Most importantly, he seems to have flourished financially too, meaning that he was able to lend the king a much-needed two thousand marks in 1386, and take two hundred men-at-arms and three hundred archers to the Scottish expedition, a force with which only a few of the nobility could compete.

But when the campaign commenced, much to the king's frustration, the superior numbers of the English did not enable them to dominate because the Scots simply deployed the established tactic of declining to do battle. After only two weeks of this, Richard grew restless. He rejected Gaunt's pleas to continue the campaign, again accusing his uncle of treason, and retreated back to England, while the Scots, spurred on by the king's departure, proceeded to ravage Cumberland and Westmorland, with Carlisle only just managing to hold out in the face of the attack. The sole thing the English army had achieved was to lay waste to the Lowlands, though Richard had still taken the opportunity to lavish titles on a number of people. He promoted his two younger uncles, Edward of Cambridge and Thomas of Woodstock, to the dukedoms of York and Gloucester, and made Michael de la Pole earl of Suffolk, and John Neville earl of Cumberland. Luckily, while all this was unfolding, the French were forced by problems of their own across the Channel to postpone the planned invasion until

1386, or disaster might have ensued. As it was, Richard had been spared full exposure of his catastrophic failures of leadership, to which he seemed personally oblivious.

Crisis at home was nonetheless bound to follow. The debts from the failed Scottish campaign were high, and there was no choice but for Chancellor Pole to ask Parliament for help in October 1385. In response, outright criticism of the king began for the first time. The Lords issued articles of 'advice' to Richard that he should attend Council more often, so that he could begin to learn 'what pertains to the government of him and his estate', and not countermand its decisions. This was highly unusual, to say the least. The Commons were similarly angry at the patronage dispensed by Richard in Scotland, and demanded that limits be placed on further largesse; the Westminster chronicler tells us that Parliament refused to ratify John Neville's promotion to the earldom of Cumberland as part of the protest against Richard's excessive patronage. A number of other stipulations were also put forward by the Commons, including that the king should agree to an annual review of the royal household and that he should make no further grants from royal revenues for the next twelve months. A separate commission was appointed to review the king's estate. Richard refused to accept all of the detailed requirements put forward by Parliament, but was somehow persuaded to make enough concessions to secure a grant of taxation. That grant came again with an important caveat: it could not be used to pay off debts from previous conflict; it could only fund future warfare. That would have been acceptable if there had been plans for how to deal with the continuing threat of invasion, but there was still nothing to set before the Commons.

Meanwhile, nearly one thousand miles away in Portugal, events occurred that would play a significant part in changing the tone of Richard's reign: in August 1385, the Portuguese defeated the Castilians at Aljubarrota. When news of this reached Gaunt, he proposed to Parliament in November 1385 that he lead an expedition. With the English position in Flanders having disintegrated following the duke of Burgundy's assertion of control there, and the king of Portugal having already despatched six galleys to the Channel to assist his English allies, it seemed to make sense to attempt to strike at Castile. There were by now no other remotely attractive options on the table. Having secured a generous grant of taxation for his proposed campaign, and probably anxious to be out of England given the king's obvious disdain for him and the political tone, Gaunt began preparations for his departure immediately. His plans were nearly scuppered early in 1386 when peace talks were resumed between the French and the English, as part of which the French demanded that Gaunt abandon his ambitions in Castile, but in March the Council held firm to Gaunt's expedition and rejected the French proposal. There was sense in this: the only return offering from the French was a temporary truce, while success for Gaunt in Castile had the potential to dent French ambitions massively and for a long time to come. The predictable result was that the French immediately renewed their plans for invasion, this time of England from the south by sea, and the English focused their energies on a mixture of defensive preparations and investment in the Castilian expedition. In early July, a window for departure opened when rumours began to circulate that the duke of Burgundy, without whom a French invasion was impossible, had died. With his own ships and forces already prepared, Gaunt did not delay in setting sail, no doubt breathing sighs of mingled relief and concern as he did so. It was not clear that he would return.

Unfortunately for the English, the rumours of the duke of Burgundy's death were unfounded, and it soon became obvious that the threatened invasion was merely delayed, not cancelled. A small Council was called in August 1386 in Oxford to consider what to do. Money supply from the last grant was running dangerously short and panic had begun to set in: Walsingham describes the Londoners as behaving like frightened hares around this time, as they began to be fearful of an attack from France. Richard apparently wanted to cross the Channel and attack the French transports, but in August and again in September the nobles who were present at the Council argued that the threat was now too serious to contemplate that; all resources had to be focused on shoring up domestic defences. As in 1383, the king's sudden desire to act had come too late to be useful. On 6 September the Council ordered all the nobility and leading knights to meet Richard at Westminster at the end of the month for defensive duties; this resulted in a force of nearly 4,500 men being stationed within a sixty-mile radius of London ready to face the attack. By then the

Council had found out that the invasion plan was centred on Orwell on the Suffolk coast and had taken steps to defend this area of coastline. Their informants told them, correctly, that the planned embarkation date was the end of October.

There was no time for delay. Parliament was rapidly summoned in early October, and Pole addressed the assembled Lords and Commons at Westminster, arguing for a royal expedition and a grant of four subsidies – an unprecedented sum. In a bizarre codicil to the request, Pole also pointed out that the king wanted to go to war to dispel the slander that he did not want to labour in his own person, slander by which he had, Pole said, been hurt. Presumably this was in answer to rumours that had been circulating since at least August that Richard was idle and cowardly. Aghast at the desperate state of government finances, and the scale of the sums being requested, and furious that the reforms to the king's household instituted in 1385 had not been implemented, Parliament responded with outrage. The Commons demanded that Pole be sacked, with a thinly veiled reference to impeaching him. For a king as sensitive and defensive of his prerogative as Richard, this was the ultimate provocation. He responded angrily that he would not dismiss so much as a scullion from his own kitchen at Parliament's request and immediately withdrew to Eltham, leaving both houses to consider the request for taxation.

But Lords and Commons would not be subdued. When Richard told them to send a delegation to discuss their demands, their suspicion of the king was so intense that the Commons refused to send anyone for fear that they would be arrested and imprisoned. Finally Thomas of Woodstock, duke of Gloucester, and Bishop Arundel, brother of the earl of Arundel, represented both houses. They made it clear to Richard that if he did not return to Parliament, it was free to disperse after forty days, to which Richard allegedly retorted that it was clear to him that Parliament was plotting against him and that in the face of this he intended to appeal to his kinsman the king of France for assistance. It was yet another peculiar outburst: the king of France had at that very moment amassed huge forces at Sluys with which he intended to invade England, and the English king was threatening to request aid from those same forces against his own subjects.

With Gaunt gone, those who remained to lead the nobility, the duke of Gloucester and the earl of Arundel – men with notorious tempers whose patience was exhausted – were an unfortunate duo to be entrusted with such a delicate situation. It was Gloucester who had threatened his nephew in 1384 in defence of Gaunt, against whom de Vere and others among Richard's friends were at that time plotting, and Arundel and Richard had almost come to blows in Parliament in the same year. When Richard talked about turning to the French king in 1386, then, it is not surprising that Gloucester responded by invoking the memory of Edward II's deposition as evidence of the mechanisms available to the political community, should he continue to refuse to engage with Parliament's demands. It was a threat Richard would never forgive or forget, but in October 1386 it left him no immediate alternative but to return to Westminster and dismiss Pole, who was impeached in early November. The king had been forced to submit, but it would not last long.

While Richard and Parliament were at loggerheads, the French invasion had still not materialised. Luckily for Richard, Charles VI's regents had their own problems across the Channel. In the first place, the size of the forces that had been amassed, the largest ever seen, meant that they were unwieldy, and in an echo of what had happened to Gaunt's forces on the Breton coast, provisioning was a major challenge. Similarly difficult was transporting them across the sea to England: there simply were not enough ships to do so. Early in November, the French were even making discreet diplomatic approaches to the English about a truce, with the winter weather further delaying any departure. On 16 November, the invasion was postponed for a second time, and then disbanded entirely for the winter, news of which reached the English via informants about a week later. But by now England was in the throes of a political crisis so serious that the lifting of the invasion threat had no impact. Following Pole's impeachment, a continual Council had been appointed for a year by Parliament, taking power out of the king's hands, and instituting a series of reforms designed to bring the royal finances under control. Powers as extensive as this had never before been granted to a parliamentary commission, but so serious were concerns about the king's intentions that it was even feared that he might rescind the grant of a commission as soon as Parliament dissolved. The novel step was therefore taken of enshrining the appointment of the commission in an Act of Parliament.

Yet despite the bitterness of politics in late 1386, the commission was never intended to be punitive, and while it included Gloucester and Arundel, it was largely made up of people with strong records of service to the Crown to whom Richard can have had no sensible objections. In the coming months it would work hard to institute retrenchment and sound financial management in the royal household, much to Richard's chagrin. He quickly showed his contempt for the serious concerns that had been raised about his household and associates by joining Pole for Christmas celebrations at Windsor, where the duke had been 'imprisoned'. During the festivities, it is alleged that Richard allowed Pole to recline at table dressed in a toga and made no effort to change the group of courtiers around him, whom Walsingham witheringly described as 'more knights of Venus than of Bellona, worthier in chamber than in field, sharper in tongue than in lance'.

By contrast, the Council, under the influence of the earl of Arundel, devoted a good deal of its own attention to the war with France, adopting the aggressive stance that Arundel had been demanding for several years. In December the earl was made admiral in the north and west and began amassing a naval force to attack the French fleet. In the spring he managed to rout ships from the French invasion fleet that had been to collect the wine harvest from La Rochelle after being stood down in November 1386. The earl returned with a significant loot of eight thousand tuns of wine. He followed that on 26 March with a major attack on the remaining French fleet at Sluys, and another expedition to relieve Brest in May 1387. Although the threat of invasion remained thereafter, Arundel's victory and events unfolding independently in France itself had rendered it a greatly attenuated risk. The main threat to England now came instead from Richard himself.

If the king's subjects in Parliament had been unsure about Richard's character before 1385, they were under no illusions a year later. He had abandoned a crucial Scottish campaign after only two weeks, allowing the Scots to devastate parts of northern England. Seemingly oblivious to this, he had then recklessly and provocatively distributed patronage. If John of Gaunt were not actively driven to Spain by Richard's hostility and obstructiveness towards him, he may have escaped there with relief. Subject to wide accusations of cowardice and idleness, in Gaunt's absence the king attempted to treat Parliament with the same contempt he had displayed towards the peasants in Essex after the revolt of 1381. But this time he was not able to do so with impunity. The political crisis that broke out in 1386 was much more serious than any since the reign of Edward II. Richard's ability to govern, which previously had surely been privately debated in the political community, was now being openly questioned, as the king responded to demands that he rule appropriately by blatantly abdicating all responsibility to do so. In a time of national emergency, the king seemed neither to realise nor to care.

Richard Attempts Revenge, 1386–7

The restrictions placed on him by the Council and the humiliation he had suffered at the hands of Parliament in 1386, as well as the threats of deposition made to him by his uncle and Bishop Arundel, left Richard embittered and enraged. While the earl of Arundel was busy seeking to neutralise the French threat in the spring and early summer of 1387, the king himself was otherwise occupied. Rumours had begun to circulate as early as winter 1386 that the group around the king was plotting to murder the duke of Gloucester and others, but from February 1387, when Richard abruptly left London and embarked on a tour of the Midlands and the north lasting several months, a much fuller plan of revenge was formed.

From August onwards, he systematically began to retain men under his own badge (a sun with silver crowns) as he moved around the country, in ways that cut across existing relationships: one of the earl of Warwick's most important retainers in Worcestershire, Sir John Russell, was directly selected from the earl's retinue: Richard was taking advantage of a dispute that was probably in train between Russell and another of Beauchamp's retainers at the time. But the aim was not, or at least not simply, to create upheaval in areas where established nobles had their landed base. The king was trying to raise an army. In East Anglia, where one royal agent was sent, this was not successful: the agent was arrested and thrown into prison in Cambridge for his trouble. And when Richard asked the local sheriffs in

Nottingham and a party of Londoners what support they could provide if there were to be an armed confrontation with the Council, the Londoners havered, while the sheriffs told Richard that since most of the Commons were on the side of the Lords, they would not be able to contribute. In Cheshire and North Wales, Richard had more luck. Here the existing royal lands made it a potentially more fertile ground for raising an army against his 'enemies'. Richard began by vastly increasing his friend Robert de Vere's powers in the area, making him justice of Chester in September and justice of North Wales in October. Badges were also offered to anyone who was willing to take up arms for the king.

For the king to raise an army with the obvious and at points explicitly stated intention of silencing his internal critics was in itself frightening; it was doubly so when accompanied by an attempt to extend the scope of the law of treason. This seems to have first occurred to Richard in August 1387, at the same time as his attempts to recruit an army began in earnest, when several of his chamber knights and household men apparently suggested to him that he should look for legal grounds on which to dismiss the Council. Richard's friend, Robert Tresilian, the uncompromising head of King's Bench in the aftermath of the 1381 rebellion, then arranged for consultations with a number of judges at Shrewsbury and Nottingham, known by historians as the 'Questions to the Judges'. They concluded that the commission of 1386 was damaging to the royal prerogative, that the impeachment of the king's men was illegal, and that the judgement against Pole was consequently invalid. Those responsible were 'traitors', they said, although they stopped short of saying the actions were treasonous (the named individuals were guilty, they stated, of 'accroaching the royal power', which was not in itself classified as treason in the statute of 1352). Nonetheless, the suggestion that his critics were traitors was a dangerous weapon to place at the angry king's disposal. The judges were sworn to keep their conclusions to themselves for the moment while Richard amassed his forces. He was now equipped with the beginnings of a legal justification for wreaking the ultimate revenge, and the army that would enable him to put it into effect was taking shape.

The duke of Gloucester, the earl of Arundel and their allies were acutely aware of the king's feelings towards them – the former had even felt compelled to leave the Garter Feast (the annual grand event to bring together the Knights of the Garter created by Edward III) in April 1387, because he found the attitude of the king's friends so menacing. In October, Richard made another attempt to be sure of the Londoners' loyalty before he took his next steps, sending Pole and Archbishop Alexander Neville of York, John Neville's younger brother, to whom Richard had become close in 1385, to ask whether the Londoners were willing to stand by the king. They gave the reply that that they would do so in all that his royal majesty demanded, which was in fact ambivalent, but Richard took it as a gesture of positive support. He re-entered the city on 10 November, and immediately summoned Gloucester and Arundel to his presence. By this time, though, the answers the judges had given to Richard's questions had been leaked and, fearing for their lives, Gloucester and Arundel refused to meet the king, saying that he was surrounded by their enemies. Both were acutely aware that Richard had treason in his mind, and that the penalty for that was likely to be their death; they presumably had no intention of walking straight into a trap. But in responding as they did, they were ignoring a royal order, opening the way for Richard to have them arrested anyway. He wasted no time, immediately giving the command for the earl of Northumberland to seize Arundel at his castle of Reigate. Arundel, though, was not going to make it that easy; if the king had had months to plan his revenge, his opponents had themselves been furnished with plenty of time to contemplate their defence. Arundel moved with his forces to join those of Gloucester and Warwick at Harringay and then to Waltham Cross, where they waited for the king to act.

Warwick's decision to join the leaders of the opposition requires some explanation. It is hard to date the precise moment at which it happened, and we can only speculate on the earl's motivations, but various issues must have given him serious pause for thought between 1385 and 1387. First was the murder of Ralph Stafford, who was both Warwick's nephew and the son of his local ally the earl of Stafford, by John Holland in 1385 en route to the campaign in Scotland. Richard's subsequent failure to expedite, and perhaps even deliberate action to delay, the judicial process in the case against Holland cannot have helped. The chroniclers say the case was pursued by Earl Stafford and Warwick together; if that was so, it would have made the king's behaviour an outright affront to the latter.

These events followed hard on the disastrous campaign to Scotland, which can only have increased Warwick's unease about Richard's temperament and capabilities, especially given the spectre of a French invasion. Warwick was from a distinguished military family, and while he did not boast the martial talents of his father, he would clearly have been conscious of the contrast between the glittering victories of Edward III and the ignominious indecision of his grandson. The poaching of John Russell, who had only signed a life indenture with Warwick in 1383, from the earl's affinity in 1387, prompting Warwick to cut off Russell's fee immediately, must have added insult to injury. At the same time, Richard made an attempt to ensure that the custody of the lands of the Warwickshire lord Sir John Pecche, who had died in 1386, came into royal hands rather than remaining with the earl, who had undoubtedly held them with Pecche's explicit blessing at the time of the latter's death. As it happened, the local grand jury found in Warwick's favour in summer 1387 despite the apparently brooding presence of the king himself at the verdict, but Richard's willingness to side-line justice in pursuit of something he desired must have been disconcerting to say the least. Chroniclers certainly noted that rumours may even have reached the earl that Pole was encouraging the king to bring about his death.

By autumn 1387, Warwick had seen at first hand the king's approach to judicial process, and particularly his willingness to subvert it. He had directly experienced Richard's disastrous military leadership and fits of temper; he had himself been a victim of the king's attempts to promote his own interests and those of his friends at the expense of others; and he had witnessed, through the loss of one of his own retainers, Richard's thinly disguised attempts to raise an army against his critics that summer. When news of the Questions to the Judges reached him – highly likely, given how quickly it leaked and his geographical proximity to it – the earl was bound to be deeply worried about the thought process it betrayed; it was clear, after all, that he was not favoured by Richard, and there was every indication that in his mind Richard had him in the enemy camp already. If Richard was already equating opposition and criticism with treason, the outlook was bleak. It is no surprise that Warwick made the decision to join Arundel and Gloucester.

From their base at Waltham Cross, Arundel, Gloucester and Warwick sent a message to the Londoners to say that five men, Robert de Vere, Michael de la Pole, Archbishop Neville of York, Chief Justice Tresilian, and another of Richard's associates, Nicholas Brembre, the former mayor of London, who was a rich merchant representing one of the city's factions, had caused the king to disturb the realm. This had, they said, created a fissure between him and 'the lords of his Council, so that they were all in doubt and peril of their lives'. The statement pulled no punches and had the desired effect of bringing more followers to them, leaving Richard shaken. With the lords' forces outside London ready to attack, several nobles and courtiers, including many who had been on the commission of 1386, tried to mediate – Archbishop Courtenay of Canterbury, together with several others, pleaded with the lords to lay down their arms and meet the king. At last, on 17 November, there appeared to be a breakthrough when a meeting took place at Westminster in which Gloucester, Arundel and their allies agreed to make a formal accusation against the five 'traitors', and the king referred it to the judgement of the Parliament that was to take place in February 1388. This was followed, somewhat bizarrely, by drinks in the king's chamber.

But like his opponents, Richard was not going to be easily defeated. He ensured that the accused were not kept in custody and de Vere was sent at speed to Chester with secret orders to the constable to raise a force on behalf of the king. Richard furthermore issued a proclamation in London that no one was to defame the five by calling them treasonous, and at the end of November he again asked how big an army he could raise in London; the response was muted. Later in the month he issued writs of summons to the Parliament that was to take place in February 1388, but an additional clause had been added that the elected had to demonstrate 'indifference to recent disputes', a way of keeping associates of the appellant lords out of Parliament, and making it clear that the king did not want anyone in Parliament who would be critical of him or his friends.

News of all this quickly reached the rebels, prompting Gloucester and Arundel to be moved to depose Richard immediately; they were only talked out of this by the earl of Warwick, who highlighted the need to defeat de Vere's force first: his troops were moving south from Chester to join

Richard in London. The earls had every chance of success, their ranks now being swelled by two younger nobles, Gaunt's son Henry Bolingbroke, earl of Derby, and Thomas Mowbray, earl of Nottingham and earl marshal. The latter was possibly motivated by rivalry with de Vere for royal favour, but perhaps more likely his family connection with Arundel through his marriage to the earl's daughter had persuaded him to act. Bolingbroke's decision to rebel, on the other hand, is more difficult to explain given his father's propensity to be steadfastly loyal to the king. Without evidence it is reasonable to conclude that having seen his father's life threatened and plotted against, Henry may have had fewer scruples. Together with Arundel, Gloucester and Warwick, the forces of Nottingham and Derby blocked the route via Northampton and de Vere was forced west. In mid-December at Radcot Bridge in Oxfordshire he was then met by Bolingbroke, and his forces were attacked from the rear by the duke of Gloucester. De Vere abandoned his army and fled in terror to Queenborough Castle in Kent. From there Richard, apparently somewhat forgiving of cowardice on the battlefield, smuggled him out of England and took refuge in the Tower of London, no doubt fearing the worst.

The events of 1387 were both bizarre and frightening. Richard had raised a private army and attempted to wage war on his own subjects, seemingly with a view to condemning as traitors members of the nobility who had had the temerity to criticise him. This was unprecedented, and ultimately it signalled that Richard may even have been thinking about executions. To the political community, like many crises, all this had begun quite simply with concerns about the lack of direction in foreign policy, despite the payment of large amounts of taxation. Confronted with requests for more money and with growing rumours of the king's extravagance and lack of application, they had raised the alarm in Parliament. There is no doubt the crisis had been more serious than most. Hopes that Richard would provide leadership and a return to the glory days of his grandfather had been bitterly dashed as he advanced into adulthood. But Richard's reaction must have stunned his subjects. Failing entirely to see their defensive concerns and even threatening an alliance against them with the king of France himself, he must have seemed to inhabit an entirely different universe. Members of the nobility were fighting for their lives in 1387 – not against the French amassed with an army in the Channel, but against their own king.

Richard Humbled, 1387–8

Having despatched de Vere, the appellant lords were certain of victory. But they decided not to march on London immediately, remaining near Oxford until the New Year, only entering London briefly in late December to meet with the king in the Tower. It was a meeting for which they took no chances, arriving with five hundred armed men. There, they accused Richard of breaching his coronation oath and plotting against them, and they made a thinly veiled threat of deposition. They may even have briefly decided to depose him, but there are reports of disagreements between Gloucester and Henry Bolingbroke over who should succeed him, leading them away from the precipice. Gloucester would subsequently deny that he had any designs on the Crown in Parliament in February 1388, which lends credence to the story of the deposition: it was an odd thing to deny, if there was no substance to the rumours. Either way, the deposition did not go ahead. This left as many problems as it solved. Given the king's obvious attempt to destroy the appellant lords and in all probability his plan to have them tried for treason and executed, there was no reason to believe that he would suddenly relent and reform. This meant that for as long as Richard remained on the throne, the appellant lords were in significant personal danger; a combination of this ominous reality, the temperaments of Gloucester and Arundel, and the mood of the Commons in Parliament was to make 1388 even more lethal and dangerous than the year that preceded it.

Once the festivities of Christmas and the New Year were over, there was a swift takeover of government by the appellant lords – they could not risk the king regaining control and using it to destroy them. They compelled Richard to issue new writs summoning Parliament to convene at Westminster in February, with the clause about 'indifference to recent disputes' removed, and reform of the royal household began, paring down Richard's large and extravagant staff and followers to the essentials – in the buttery alone the commissioners were said to have found a hundred unnecessary servants. Clearly the appellant lords were bent not only on self-preservation but on carrying out the reforms they and so many others had demanded. Several of Richard's favourites in the household were also detained at this point, including Simon Burley, whose rise in status under Richard had been prodigious, and a number of soldiers with long records of service to the Crown. It was in effect a thorough purge – the work of strong-willed, frightened and desperate men. But in between the appellants and the king, there remained a group of moderate lords who were anxious to restore domestic peace, and the appellants had to ensure that these men were not alienated or Richard would surely use divisions among them to resume control. They therefore appointed a group of councillors 'for the continuous government of the king', its composition designed to secure the approval of the moderates.

Parliament began on 3 February 1388 with an elaborate ceremony: Richard opened the session with the core group of appellants, Gloucester, Arundel, Warwick, Bolingbroke and Mowbray, standing behind him in golden surcoats. Gloucester then knelt before the king and sought to excuse himself of conspiring to remove Richard from the throne. The king replied that the duke was blameless of any wrongdoing. Next, the appeal against de Vere, Pole, Neville, Tresilian and Brembre was read out and the appellants argued that the trial should take place in Parliament, with judgement by their peers with the king's assent, and not in the common-law courts. Their reasoning was that crimes as serious as those the five were alleged to have committed, which touched the person of the king himself and included noblemen among the accused, had to be a matter for Parliament. The logic being deployed here was in many ways a practical nicety: it was the only way the appellants could both get their appeal heard and ensure its success, as both common and civil lawyers had ruled categorically that the hearing of their appeal in Parliament was illegal. In many ways, they were as guilty as Richard himself in the extremity and political unacceptability of their actions. They achieved their desired outcome with the support of the Commons and their own overwhelming strength of force, the king having been effectively emasculated at Radcot Bridge. Only Brembre was present in Parliament, the other four accused having fled. Summons were issued three times in February for them to appear before the Lords. In their absence twelve secular lords were tasked with assessing the charges and deciding on due punishment. In all, thirty-nine charges were made against the five, including that they had enriched themselves, suborned the judges, plotted to kill the appellant lords, and persuaded Richard to make pacts with the French king while neglecting the defence of England. They were also said to have incited him to raise a retinue equipped with badges in a way that had never been done by a king before.

In the middle of February, the four who had absconded were pronounced guilty of treason and condemned to death, with the exception of Neville who, as a member of the clergy, was spared. Brembre was then brought into Westminster Hall for trial and pleaded not guilty, in the face of angry responses from the Commons that, had the appellants not got there first, they would have accused Brembre themselves. Brembre had made many enemies in London and those factions were out in force. Richard intervened to try to defend him, prompting outrage from the appellants. They were further angered when the investigating lords stated that Brembre had not done anything to warrant execution. Among the charges, the appellants had accused him of overseeing unlawful executions in London, and they now attempted to rouse the London factions in the Commons against the judgement, calling on the mayor and other officers for their view. The latter replied that they thought Brembre more likely to be guilty than not, which was enough to induce the Lords to reverse their judgement and sentence Brembre to death. Soon after this, Chief Justice Tresilian was discovered hiding in Westminster Abbey and executed; Brembre suffered the same fate a day after.

Lesser figures, including four of the king's chamber knights, Simon Burley, John Beauchamp of Holt, Sir John Salisbury and Ralph Berners, and the judges who had advised Richard in 1387, were impeached before the Commons. A sentence of death and forfeiture was issued for the judges, which was only commuted to exile in Ireland when both Archbishop Courtenay and the queen intervened, pleading for leniency. Simon Burley's fate was heavily debated, with Gloucester and Arundel unmovable on the sentence of death (even the other appellants felt that he should be spared). The queen apparently spent three hours on her knees in front of Arundel pleading for Burley's life. The only concession in the end was that he, Beauchamp and Berners were allowed the dubious mercy of being beheaded instead of hanged.

The brutality of the actions of the Commons and the appellants in these months understandably caused great concern among a number of the Lords. It is clear that some thought they had gone too far, and that Parliament had been used as a political weapon; and they were correct. The idea of judges being sentenced to death was particularly worrying. When Parliament resumed in June, provision was made at the behest of the Commons to establish that the trials in Parliament should not set a precedent, and in future it was declared that such trials should take place in the common-law courts. However, the appellants were also careful to enshrine in statute that any who tried in future to reverse the judgements of 1388 would be counted as traitors – they naturally feared reprisals. With Richard for the moment forced into quiescence, they went through the motions of a ceremony in Westminster Abbey in which both Lords and Commons renewed their oaths of allegiance to the king on the one hand, and Richard for his part gave them a promise that he would be 'a good king and lord' from thereon. This was a charade, but it was a necessary one to bring temporary closure to the episode.

On 4 June, what became known as the 'Merciless Parliament' was dismissed and the bloodletting was formally over. It had been the most violent and brutal Parliament since the institution began: even during the worst crises of Edward II's reign, it would have been unthinkable for so many close confidants of the king to be tried and executed in Parliament or anywhere else – Thomas of Lancaster's murder of Piers Gaveston had placed him firmly outside the bounds of acceptable behaviour and made him something of a political pariah. In 1388, Gloucester and Arundel, unlike Lancaster, were far from alone in their actions; they were accompanied by several other lords and supported by the Commons in Parliament, a mark of the increasing role of Parliament when compared with Edward II's reign. And while some of the motivation may have been faction or jealousy, for so many people to be moved to such extreme action demonstrates just how dangerous the king's friends, and by logical extension the king himself, were believed to be.

Richard's state after the execution and banishment of so many of his friends and allies can only be imagined. He had wanted the appellants defeated and condemned, destroyed even, but he had lacked the forces to enable him to inflict punishment on them in battle. He had lost everyone close to him, and his rule was now subject to close supervision by a Council. It was far from what he had envisaged in 1387.

New Beginnings? Royal Rule from 1389

In the months after the Merciless Parliament, Richard remained pliant. During the period after Parliament dispersed, he was even, perhaps surprisingly, angry when he heard about further Scottish incursions into the north of England following the end of the truce that summer. When soon afterwards, on 5 August, Henry Hotspur, son of the earl of Northumberland, was defeated and captured by the Scots at Otterburn, Richard even voiced a strong desire to lead an expedition. While the magnates on the royal Council felt that it would be wiser to wait until the New Year, and instead appointed military commanders to supervise and defend the Marches, these were positive, if unexpected, signs from the king.

In September 1388 Parliament swiftly reconvened in Cambridge and subsidies were raised for the defence of the border, though the Commons expressed considerable reluctance about paying more money, reflecting that there was already some dissatisfaction with the appellant regime. They also indicated that they would not support any further French expeditions while the danger from across the Channel remained low in the aftermath of Arundel's actions of 1387. The result was that peace negotiations restarted, and duly concluded in a series of truces. The Commons additionally demanded thoroughgoing reform of the Statute of Labourers and raised concerns about domestic law and order at the same time. Too many lords, they said, were giving out liveries to men who were creating disturbances locally; it was a matter the Commons had previously discussed, though studies of the localities do not suggest that it was in fact a source of significant problems. Whatever the case, the appellants and some of the other lords reacted testily to the Commons' complaints and Richard intervened to broker a compromise.

At this stage Richard appeared calm and acted with diplomacy. While some traits and patterns continued – he celebrated Christmas 1388 in his usual way with magnificent festivities at Eltham Castle in Kent – he remained co-operative under the tutelage of the Council. Then, on 3 May 1389, aged twenty-two, he suddenly took the initiative and declared himself of age to rule:

> For the twelve years since I became king, I and the entire kingdom
> have been under the control of others and my people burdened year on
> year with taxes. Now it is fitting that I should assume the conduct of
> affairs since I have reached the age of maturity. I shall work tirelessly so
> that my subjects shall live in peace and the realm prosper.

Reaching out to his subjects, and particularly the Commons, with what might even be called a 'manifesto' of low taxes, peace and good government, he was presenting himself as their ally, in complete contrast to earlier. The declaration was followed, to emphasise the king's good faith, by the postponement of the collection of some of the last subsidy and the appointment of peace commissions in all counties in July. Reforms were also made in respect of livery and maintenance, and new procedures were introduced to swear in all new sheriffs before both the king and the Council, to impress upon them the responsibilities of their office and their accountability for their actions; this was followed by a significant reduction in complaints of corruption. At the same time, Richard made changes to the composition of the Council, but although the appellants were removed, he was careful to appoint in their place long-established and respected Crown servants, including as treasurer Bishop Waltham of Salisbury, a man who was later to become very highly valued by the king. Edmund Stafford, the son of one of the Black Prince's retainers, who was trained in the civil law, was appointed keeper of the privy seal. He was an uncontroversial choice.

A further positive step was the planned return of John of Gaunt, who was then in Aquitaine. His campaign in Spain is often seen as a failure, but not only did he return a much richer man than he had been when he left England, he had achieved a settlement with Castile in which both parties agreed to work towards peace with France, and his daughters were now queens of both Portugal and Castile. When Gaunt returned in November

1389, the earlier rancour, even hatred, that Richard had expressed towards him seemed to have completely dissipated. Richard rode out to greet him a few miles from Reading, immediately giving him the kiss of peace. Gaunt was then granted an extension of his palatine powers in Lancashire for his heirs, a mark of the king's renewed favour, and in March 1390 he was additionally made duke of Aquitaine. Under Gaunt's influence, Gloucester returned to serve on the royal Council in January 1390 and Arundel in March. This was followed in August 1390 by an extravagant hunting party hosted by Gaunt on his estates in Leicester. Although Arundel did not attend, many others did, and a new spirit of co-operation and comradeship seemed to prevail. Under Gaunt's influence, Gloucester even received the grant of Holderness in Yorkshire in reversion from Queen Anne, and finally the promise of lands in place of his annuities.

Relations with France and Scotland began to improve at this time, too. Following the failure of an Arundel-led campaign to south-western France in June 1388 (the appellants had persuaded the Commons to grant a subsidy of £20,000 in recognition of their having dealt with the traitors and acted to save the realm from disaster), Gloucester and the Council had responded positively to new peace overtures from Philip of Burgundy. As the French were facing their own difficulties with internal rebellion, the idea of a settlement with England was as appealing across the Channel as it was to Richard II's exhausted English subjects. Peace with France also promised to bring with it at least a temporary truce with Scotland, as it would encompass the Scots as allies of the French. That would be a mercy in the aftermath of the heavy defeat inflicted on Hotspur's northern forces at Otterburn in 1388. Following the negotiations, a temporary truce was agreed on 18 July 1389, just weeks after Richard resumed control of government. Talks in pursuit of a permanent or long-term peace would follow for the next few years, resulting in a series of short-term truces, which became ever more important to the French in particular as Charles VI began to suffer from a series of bouts of psychosis from 1392 onwards. In negotiations for these, both Gaunt and Gloucester played a key role.

Yet while negotiations were positive, it proved impossible to agree a permanent treaty because of the vexed question of the sovereignty of Aquitaine. On the English side, armed risings even took place in both Cheshire and

Yorkshire in 1393, apparently in response to rumours that Gaunt and Gloucester might be about to surrender the king's position in the duchy, while in January 1394 Parliament was categorical that the English king should not pay homage to his French counterpart. Nonetheless, such was the desire for a longer peace on both sides that when these issues could not be permanently settled, a twenty-eight-year truce, the longest of the Hundred Years' War, was agreed instead in 1395 as part of wider arrangements for the marriage of Richard to Charles's daughter Isabella, following the death of Anne of Bohemia in June 1394. This, and the series of shorter truces that had preceded it, dramatically reduced the financial strain on England, and removed the prospect of an invasion. Politics seemed to be returning to a peaceful and collaborative modus operandi in the 1390s. Richard was not spending profligately, and he appeared to be working constructively with Gaunt and Gloucester.

But while political relationships seemed to be more settled and positive, Richard suffered a devastating blow personally in these years, when his beloved wife, Anne, died in June 1394, during a further outbreak of plague. She was only in her twenties. Richard was so distraught that he vowed not to enter any chamber she had been in for a year afterwards, and in 1395 he even had the royal manor of Sheen destroyed, his reaction to her death being reminiscent of Edward I when he lost his wife, Eleanor, in 1290, and a reminder of the devotion that could exist even in arranged royal marriages. Like Henry III and Eleanor, and Edward I and his own Eleanor, Richard and Anne had travelled almost everywhere together, and it was undoubtedly one of the major blows of his life to lose her. It may even have been the principal reason why, a week after Anne's funeral, he embarked on his first campaign to Ireland. It cannot have been a coincidence that he announced his intention to travel there just nine days after the queen's death.

The campaign was long overdue, the English position in Ireland having been significantly eroded since the 1360s. In fact, by the early 1390s it was so compromised that it was difficult to persuade anyone to take on the office of justiciar in the territory because of the real financial burden on the officeholder, who would have to subsidise their own costs. The English Exchequer and English lords with lands in the colony were in effect having to bankroll government there. It was not sustainable. Repeated calls had been made for Richard to travel to Ireland himself to restore lands to the English Crown that had been seized by rebels and to place the colony on a more secure long-term footing, but only now, in what was probably more of a reaction to Anne's death than an indication of commitment to kingly duty, did he seriously consider it. Taking an army of around eight thousand men, he spent autumn and winter 1394–5 bringing about the submission of rebels: it was to be his only real military achievement as king.

By early 1395, the Crown's position in Ireland was restored and Richard had been recognised by all the native leaders under his lordship. His next move was more controversial, and arguably foolish – he stated that all those who recognised his authority were to come under the protection of the English Crown. This meant that native Irish lords had almost as many rights as their English counterparts and could bring claims against them, which made the settlement of Ireland very difficult to manage. When Richard left the island in summer 1395, it fell to the young and inexperienced earl of March, who had taken over as lieutenant, to settle the plethora of pleas and disputes that had followed the king's declaration. This was much easier said than done, and problems in Ireland rumbled on for the next few years without resolution as the earl struggled to establish his authority. Richard had hardly shown an aptitude for the finer points of royal governance of his territories, but at least he had for once done what was broadly expected of him as king.

The internal and external peace of the early 1390s represented a welcome respite for the king's subjects. What had been a constant barrage of financial pressure on Parliament since the 1370s ceased, and with their pockets no longer empty from the demands of warfare, arguments and criticism of the government in the Commons became a thing of the past. A situation that had seemed hopeless on so many fronts seemed to have been transformed.

Plotting Revenge, 1389–97: Richard and the Appellants

The truth, though, was quite the opposite. Richard himself, despite outward appearances, remained largely unchanged. His 'manifesto' when he assumed control of government in 1389 marked the beginning of a clever and calculated campaign to detach the Commons from the Lords, and break up the alliance that had made possible the Merciless Parliament of 1388. He also worked swiftly to undermine the appellants' control of government: while he ensured that the appointments he made to the Council shortly after his announcement were uncontroversial in themselves, the dismissal of the appellant lords from it sent a clear signal. When they made overtures to him, he simply ignored them. There was a limit at this stage to how far he could exclude them in the medium term, and when worries were raised about their absence, he was forced to reappoint them, but a warning of the king's intentions had been issued.

In the same period Richard began to undermine Arundel, Warwick and Gaunt in other ways as well. First, when Arundel was removed from the Council in spring 1389, Richard saw to it that he lost his military commands too. Meanwhile, at a local level, Richard seems to have taken action that repeatedly served to undercut Arundel's position in Wales and the March. This seems to have been opportunistic rather than systematic, with Richard mostly just taking advantage of situations as they arose, but the effect was the same. As in the 1380s, each time the king was presented with the chance to augment his own position in the region, usually through lands passing to him when lords died leaving only minors or no heirs, Richard appointed household men and royal retainers to be their custodians. In February 1390, for example, after the death of the earl of Pembroke, John Hastings the Younger, Richard took the lands out of the hands of the appointed custodian, Sir William Beauchamp, who was not in his favoured circle, and began to insert members of his household into offices in them. It is likely that Arundel felt threatened by this as he proceeded swiftly to marry Philippa Mortimer, the widow of the earl, without the king's licence.

Later, following the deaths of local lords Nicholas, Lord Audley and Fulk, Lord Fitzwarin in July and August 1391, Richard managed to keep some of Audley's lands in royal hands by manipulating the evidence about rights of succession to it. Fitzwarin's heir, on the other hand, was a minor, which made it easy for Richard to place the wardship directly in the hands of household men. The lands of both men were in Arundel's own sphere of influence: Fitzwarin's castle of Whittington was in the middle of Arundel's Oswestry lordship, while Audley's lands were in the north Shropshire plain, where Arundel was dominant. There could be no mistaking what was happening: Richard was building up his own men on Arundel's doorstep. The following year Richard proposed that the nineteen-year-old earl of March, Roger Mortimer, whose lands were back in the custody of Arundel and others during his minority, should succeed his father as lieutenant of Ireland. Mortimer's father-in-law was Richard's favourite Thomas Holland, who quickly wrote in support to Richard, suggesting that Mortimer would need full custody of his lands if he were to have the resources to take up the position. This prompted Arundel and the other custodians to write arguing that the lands should not be granted prematurely. It seems Mortimer may have been content with the custodians' approach as he was later to be an appellant ally against the king, but again Arundel must have at least wondered about the motivations for Holland's actions. Like Warwick earlier, the earl also suffered the loss of key retainers to the king, some of whom were then given custody of lands in Arundel's sphere of influence.

Conclusively, Arundel was being deliberately undermined by a king who undeniably despised him. Relations between the two men worsened as the 1390s progressed: in August 1394 Arundel arrived late to the funeral of Queen Anne and then asked to leave early, prompting the grief-stricken king to seize a wand from one of the vergers and hit him so hard that he was knocked to the ground bleeding – it was said that had others not intervened, Richard would have killed the earl. The funeral service had to be delayed while the church was cleansed, and Arundel was then imprisoned in the Tower for a week. Bail cost him the huge sum of £40,000. This followed on from a scathing attack Arundel had launched on Gaunt in Parliament in January 1394, accusing him of being too close to the king, while Gaunt in turn accused Arundel of providing assistance to those who had revolted against the peace negotiations with France in Cheshire in 1393 (there is no evidence of this, though Arundel certainly did not provide any help putting down the rebellion). When Richard took his forces to Ireland in 1395 Arundel was notably not with them, and while he returned to court during Richard's absence, he played no part in government in these years.

A similar pattern arose in Richard's behaviour towards the earl of Warwick. In Warwick's lands in Warwickshire and Worcestershire, Richard both abused the law to achieve his ends and promoted his own men's causes in local disputes. Between 1391 and 1395, Warwick was excluded from all commissions to investigate trespasses and felonies committed against the king's tenants in Feckenham and Newbury in Worcestershire. Those appointed were associates of the king, often household men, who in some cases had no landed connection at all with the county. Richard himself retained several men whose pursuit of their own interests was to cause disorder in Warwickshire and Worcestershire. John Russell, Warwick's former retainer who had been recruited into the king's household in 1387, was one of these men. He fostered a circle of associates around him in Worcestershire in the early 1390s that was entirely separate from Warwick's affinity. Disputes arose and disorder followed, with the king notably supporting Russell and his associates against Beauchamp's people: at one point, with the king's support, Russell even brought about the impeachment of Warwick's steward in Parliament. This was a highly unusual legal procedure for someone not of magnate status and where matters of state were not involved; it had to have taken place with at least the king's tacit support. In Warwickshire, Richard's promotion of William Bagot, a notable member of the local gentry – who effectively became the key link between the king and the west Midlands – led to a similar upset in the balance of power. Richard even began to use the royal Council to enable him to intervene in his associates' favour in local disputes. He was to deploy the court of King's Bench in the same way in Lancashire against Gaunt later in the 1390s.

The final insult to Warwick came in 1397, when the king managed to wrest Gower in south-west Wales from him. The Beauchamp claim to Gower had a questionable history, and so when Thomas Mowbray, earl of Nottingham, brought a plea at Richard's prompting against the earl of Warwick in the court of King's Bench saying that Gower had originally been awarded to the Beauchamps in error, the result was inevitable. Richard used Warwick's earlier entry into Bishopston in Gower when the bishopric of Llandaff was vacant to argue that Warwick had acted in contempt of the king and derogation of the Crown. Warwick defended himself by saying that he was only emulating what his ancestors had always done during vacancies, an argument that left him exposed. Richard ordered him to repay all the money he had taken from the manor and fined him for contempt. Gower was then given to Mowbray by judgement of the court of King's Bench. Warwick was told to pay back all the profits he had drawn from the lordship over the last ten years, and as security he had to give seventeen manors to Mowbray. If he defaulted, he would lose the manors permanently. He also had to waive his right to any future attempt to recover Gower. The settlement was designed to bring Warwick to his knees after what by then amounted to a decade of consistent undermining of his position by the king in both Warwickshire and Worcestershire.

It is probably unsurprising, given the events of 1386-8, that Richard felt the way he did towards Arundel and Warwick, but the same cannot be said in relation to John of Gaunt, whom he had received back into England in 1389 with such fulsome ceremony. On the surface their relationship had been entirely repaired and Gaunt's influence restored. Yet in the localities, Richard was assiduously undermining the duke in exactly the same way as he was attacking Arundel and Warwick. Although armed uprisings that took place in Cheshire and Yorkshire in 1393, for example, were ostensibly protests about the peace negotiations being led by Gaunt and Gloucester, they were led by Richard's retainers Sir Thomas Talbot and Sir John Mascy. While Richard claimed that he had nothing to do with their declared bid 'to destroy the magnates of the realm', it is hard to imagine he played no part at all. In the same period, Richard was actively recruiting members of the Gaunt affinity into his own private affinity, and in the Midlands and Yorkshire Richard's associates were busy stirring up opposition to the Lancastrian affinity.

Richard worked on building up alliances within the nobility during this time too, attempting in particular to detach Thomas Mowbray and Gaunt's son Henry Bolingbroke from their appellant allies, making Mowbray captain of Calais in February 1391 and then justice of Chester and North Wales, and giving Bolingbroke a number of gifts, including an expensive breastplate, though tellingly Bolingbroke was not entrusted with any significant commands. Others were also carefully cultivated: the king's half-brother, John Holland, earl of Huntingdon, the man who had murdered Ralph Stafford on the way to campaign in Scotland, was made admiral and captain of Brest in place of Arundel in June 1389, and in February 1390 he became chamberlain of England. Both Holland half-brothers were given custody of several castles. Richard's cousin Edward, earl of Rutland, the son of Edmund of Langley, succeeded Huntingdon as admiral in 1391; and in Ireland in 1395, Huntingdon, Mowbray and Rutland, as well as the young earl of March, were given several titles. Proof of how closely trusted some of these men had become is found in the fact that Mowbray and Rutland were both part of the small embassy tasked with negotiating the king's second marriage, to Isabella of France, in 1395.

Richard's promotion of these favoured figures was serving to undermine local power structures and create resentment more widely than among the appellant lords. In the north, the Percy family found themselves systematically excluded from local government, while men like Thomas Mowbray, John, Lord Beaumont (a courtier friend of Richard) and John Holland, who had no landed connection in the borderlands, were promoted to lands and offices. Others were retained into the king's service, further isolating the Percies. One such retainer was Ralph Neville, John Neville's eldest son, who had succeeded his father in 1388. In May 1395, Richard retained Ralph as a king's knight with a fee of £130 a year. In the same year, as a mark of royal favour, he was granted the reversion of the lease of Richmond, and in November 1396, Richard also granted him the manor of Penrith and Sowerby in Cumberland. At the other end of the country, in Devon, the Courtenay earls similarly found themselves threatened by Richard's promotion of John Holland there. Even in Gaunt's stronghold of Lancashire Richard was retaining gentry in his service, directly cutting across Gaunt's affinity. He was also transferring cases from the palatinate justices, who should have been the superior source of legal authority, to the court of King's Bench, while local office was simultaneously used to promote men like Sir Ralph Radcliffe, a king's knight, who had been dismissed as sheriff of Lancashire in 1387 and arrested during the crisis of 1388. He became MP for Lancashire in 1397 and subsequently sheriff.

Despite attempting to create a picture of harmony and quiescence, it is obvious, then, that Richard was entirely unchanged in the 1390s. He spent the early and middle part of the decade systematically building up and promoting his own group of followers, and working to undermine the older nobles by whom he felt most threatened, notably Gaunt, Arundel and Warwick. Given his defeat in 1387 by the appellants and their retinues, it seems clear that underlying this must have been a determination never to be threatened again. And to achieve that end, he had adopted a two-pronged approach: to launch an outright challenge to his enemies' influence in the local areas that provided them with their military strength, and to build up his own allies and affinity. By the mid-1390s, the magnates had been successfully divided along exactly the lines Richard had intended, meaning that the older nobles had largely absented themselves from the royal court and retired to the relative safety of their lands and castles, while Richard's friends and followers were firmly present and in the ascendancy.

A New Interpretation of Kingship

Richard's pursuit of his own royal affinity in the 1390s was unlike anything seen before in post-Conquest England. All kings had their own household force, which waxed and waned depending on military commitments, dwindling in peacetime. By contrast, Richard's force was growing at a time of peace, and doing so dramatically: by 1395-6 there were 150 more men in the household than there had been in 1389; and by 1399 Richard had taken on 125 king's esquires for life and more on short-term contracts, and had retained more than 80 knights. The annual expenditure of Richard's wardrobe had risen hugely in the same period; by the mid-1390s alone, it was on a scale not seen since the 1360s, when Edward III had had many wartime ransoms at his disposal that Richard certainly did not possess. From late 1390 he also began distributing his livery and badges (the white hart and the sunburst) to his affinity, and all over England, especially in the north and the west, and in Wales, men were recruited specifically to represent Richard's direct personal interests: his own private army. They were then promoted and rewarded, often at the expense of his other subjects. The king had become partisan, another great lord, not the supreme adjudicator at the head of the body politic that he was supposed to be. It was pathological and dysfunctional, and it was surely destined to end in disaster.

Simultaneously, there was growing insistence on Richard's part on new forms of royal address and description. Around 1390, his subjects seem to have been instructed to refer to the king as 'prince', rather than as 'lord', the traditional title, and to address Richard as 'your majesty' and 'your highness' or 'very excellent and redoubtable and powerful prince'. Like Henry III, he began to venerate the cult of Edward the Confessor, England's only canonised king, giving gifts to his shrine at Westminster Abbey and restarting the renovation of the abbey, which had been abandoned after Henry's death. In 1392 he ordered a new portal at London Bridge containing stone images of himself and Queen Anne alongside shields that included the arms of the Confessor. To emphasise the blessedness of his own reign, in the late 1390s Richard commissioned what has become known as the Wilton Diptych, a painting depicting Richard offering England to the Virgin Mary as her dowry and receiving it back from her as guardian, to rule under her protection. Complementing all this was lavish spending on clothes and furs, and even a robe lined with precious stones which is said to have cost £20,000.

It was not odd for a king to want to emphasise his divine appointment, and in doing all these things Richard was in one sense only giving outward expression to his status. Increasing formality of address and an emphasis on hierarchy were also not unique to England in this period. The problem with Richard's actions was not the actions themselves so much as the extent to which, as in the 1380s, they reflected an obsessive focus on the due recognition of his status as king, in a way that had never been seen before: his subjects were even forbidden from looking him in the eye during the thrice-yearly crown-wearing ceremonies. That a pathological interpretation of kingly power underlay this is emphasised by the fact that in the same period Richard had a compilation of statutes relating to royal power specially made, and began to collect evidence of the miracles of Edward II. He also began a campaign at the papal curia for Edward II to be canonised, and made special arrangements with the abbot and convent of Gloucester for lights and ornaments to be maintained around Edward's shrine. Richard venerated, and thought others should venerate, a king who had tyrannised his subjects and murdered members of the nobility. It was an ominous sign, and doubly so when placed alongside a petition Richard managed to obtain from Parliament in late 1391 that he should henceforth be:

as free in his regality, liberty and royal dignity . . . as any of his noble progenitors . . . notwithstanding any former statute or ordinance to the contrary, notably in the time of King Edward the Second . . . and that if any statute was made in the time of the said Edward, in derogation of the liberty and freedom of the Crown, that it shall be annulled and of no force.

Yet more worrying was a clause Richard had included in the draft peace treaty with France in 1394 which had the king of France promise support for Richard 'against all manner of people who owe him any obedience and also to aid and sustain him with all their power against any of his subjects'. Not only had Richard not changed in any fundamental way since the 1380s, he was in fact contemplating a scenario in which he would again find himself at war with his own subjects. But this time, through the recruitment and deployment of a royal affinity, and with the support of the king of France, he did not intend to lose. There would be no repeat of the ignominious defeat that had occurred at Radcot Bridge.

Richard's resumption of governmental control caused a rise in very serious concerns about the king's behaviour. Worries about the failure to make peace with the appellants and their dismissal from the Council that were raised as early as autumn 1389 led to their reappointment and formal outward reconciliation in 1390 under the influence of Gaunt. Then, in 1391, there is evidence, through the reappointment of Bishop Arundel as chancellor in September and his subsequent actions, that attempts were being made to restrain the king. In particular, a royal order was given in December 1391 that Richard:

for certain reasons, with the assent of the Council . . . thought fit to revoke all letters patent heretofore granted by him of offices within his lordship of North and South Wales, except constableships of castles, being desirous that his justices there should dispose of those offices as was wont to be done in the time of the late prince, the king's father.

It is hard to believe that an order of this nature really came from Richard; given the appointments he had been making throughout 1390 and 1391, it seems more likely that the Council had intervened. In the early 1390s, the poet John Gower, who was closely connected with the Ricardian court, began to register his own disapproval of the king. In reworkings of his *Confessio Amantis* in the early 1390s, he removed his prayer for Richard and inserted instead a prayer for the state of England; perhaps even more tellingly, he made amendments to his *Vox Clamantis* in the same period, attributing the problems of the English realm to Richard rather than to the ubiquitous 'evil counsellors'. Such direct criticism of the king himself was rare, particularly so in not being made posthumously but while the king was still on the throne.

By the mid-1390s, Richard's policies were unsurprisingly placing a significant financial burden on his revenues, which were never supposed to bear such weight: in total the combined annual cost of his household departments had risen from around £21,000 in 1377–89 to more like £34,000 in 1392–5. They were to increase further in the final few years of the reign. Yet despite this, and the fact that the Commons were still being asked to pay taxation in this peacetime period for the maintenance of garrisons in places like Calais, they remained broadly quiet. Some of this may be because of the number of royal household men who were serving MPs; they were not inclined to bite the hand that fed them. But for the most part the Commons' lack of complaint was probably about the fact that, unlike in the 1380s, the threat of invasion was not imminent and the sums of money being requested in taxation were nothing like the previous decade. It was war and kingly failure in tandem that had generated acute political crisis, and the same perfect storm simply did not exist in the 1390s. What the 1390s show is that in normal circumstances the Commons, however much Parliament had developed in the last century, still had little inclination or incentive to get involved in everyday politics.

At the same time, Richard was being mostly careful not to be too overtly provocative; his actions were in some respects more subtle than in the 1380s. When the Council refused to accede to Mowbray's request for higher pay as warden of the March in the north of England in 1389, Richard initially left in pique for Kennington, but he soon saw fit to offer a compromise, something he would never have done previously. In the same year he received Gaunt with warmth and the kiss of peace on his return from Aquitaine, he agreed to a formal reconciliation with the appellants. In

1392, when the Council refused his request for the return of de Vere and Alexander Neville from the Continent, he did not demur, and he agreed to its subsequent request to promise never to recall the two infamous royal favourites. In return he achieved a promise of support against internal and external enemies from the Council – an ominous sign. Even when Richard took London into royal hands in 1392 (probably most immediately because he needed money), on the basis that there were 'errors in the government of the city' which Richard left unspecified, the liberties of the city were swiftly restored (during the king's pleasure) in return for a fine of £10,000. The seizure itself and the language in which London subsequently submitted to the king were in themselves alarming, but it was hard to argue with him even though he did not state explicitly what the supposed 'errors' were.

By the mid-1390s, Richard had succeeded in isolating the appellants and asserting his own power largely untrammelled. The removal of external threats had at the same time effectively neutralised Parliament. With all this accomplished, the obvious question in the appellants' minds must surely have been what he would do next. He had hinted repeatedly at revenge; their fear must have been that he would make good on his threats at the earliest opportunity.

Richard's Revenge, 1397

The year 1397 began without any immediate or obvious hint that Richard would follow his campaign to isolate the appellants by having Gloucester and Arundel killed and Warwick banished from the country for life – but that is what he did. Parliament convened in January to discuss a request from the king for funds for an expedition in support of the French in Italy to which he planned to send Thomas Mowbray and Edmund of Rutland. The reply of the Commons was to indicate their concern about the commitment, and then to prevaricate: some of the Lords were not there, they said, and so they could not make a decision. This in turn prompted disquiet on Richard's part about whether opposition was stirring in the Commons and he sent the chancellor to find out more. In response, the Commons indicated agreement that Richard must honour his commitment to the French, but they respectfully declined any responsibility for funding it themselves. They then seem to have presented the king with four petitions. One related to sheriffs and escheators, the Commons complaining that they were remaining in office beyond the allotted year, and that the social status of those appointed was not what it should be. Furthermore, they voiced continuing concern about the vulnerability of the Scottish Marches to attack, and about livery badges being given to esquires who were not resident in noble households, contrary to the previous order on this. Finally, they returned to the cost of the royal household, which they referred to as 'great and excessive'.

Richard's response to the petition was on one level restrained and measured: he promised to re-enact the legislation on the distribution of livery badges and protested that a sheriff could not learn his job in only a year. He returned the question of the defence of the Scottish Marches straight back to the Commons, saying he would be happy to follow suggestions by the Lords if they provided the money to make it possible. But in response to the petition relating to the royal household, he said he was deeply grieved; subjects seeking to govern the royal household undermined his regality and 'offended his majesty and the liberty which he had inherited against his ancestors'. He demanded to be told who had initiated the petition; when the Commons gave the king the name of a minor clerk, Thomas Haxey, the following day, they also admitted that the petition had been against the king's 'regality, royal estate and liberty'. Haxey himself only subsequently escaped death by virtue of being a cleric. The French plans for military action in Italy having collapsed, Richard then retracted his request for tax, but the atmosphere was ominous. The king had linked any questioning of his actions with treason, and that carried the ultimate penalty – the way was now effectively open to political murder. Richard's message was clear: the Lords and Commons in Parliament would raise complaints about the king's actions or behaviour in future at their peril. The healthy atmosphere of debate and challenge that had grown up in the century since the emergence of Parliament had been first stymied and then silenced.

From there, the situation deteriorated rapidly. Following the dissolution of Parliament, a Council was held in February, but Gloucester and Arundel ignored their summons to attend; Gloucester later complained about concessions by the king to the French. They clearly remained disaffected. In

July, Richard suddenly invited them both, as well as Warwick, to a banquet. Warwick was the only one of the three to attend. Gloucester excused himself on grounds of ill health, which seems to have been genuine. Arundel on the other hand, possibly fearing the worst, simply refused to come, and stayed sequestered in his castle at Reigate. The events of the banquet were bizarre: Richard had dinner with Warwick, apparently talking amiably to him throughout, and then, when it was over, had him arrested and taken to the Tower of London. The king then rode to Pleshey in the middle of the night with his cousin Edward, earl of Rutland, the Hollands, Thomas Mowbray and a number of household soldiers, and took Gloucester prisoner. When he pleaded for mercy, Richard allegedly said that he would show him as much mercy as Gloucester had himself to Simon Burley when the queen had spent three hours on her knees pleading for his life. Mowbray was then instructed to take Gloucester out of the country to Calais, where he was murdered. Forces were also sent to arrest Arundel, who was ultimately taken by treachery, having been prepared, characteristically, for a fight to the death. While all this was happening, the king was securing his own defences: on 13 July orders were sent to the sheriff in Cheshire to raise two thousand archers with all speed. Two days later a royal proclamation announced that the arrests were for 'the great number of extortions, oppressions, grievances etc. committed against the king and people, and for other offences against the king's majesty which shall be declared in the next Parliament, and not for the assemblies or risings occasioned by the uprising of 1387 and 1388'. It was important to stress that the action had been taken on the basis of new, not old offences, because disquiet was already being expressed publicly about what had happened, and Richard must have feared opposition. This way, he could maintain the moral high ground and buy himself time.

At a royal Council in Nottingham in August eight new appellant lords emerged under the king's aegis, and the tables were turned: this time it was not the king but Gloucester, Arundel and Warwick who were the accused. When the Council had ended, it was announced that the lords had been arrested for treason and would be tried in Parliament at Kingston-upon-Thames in September. The atmosphere in the lead-up to Parliament was tense, and the king, worried about opposition and a possible attempt to rescue the captives, gave orders to the sheriffs for all men in his pay to come armed. When Parliament opened, the resulting armed presence was disconcertingly large; all the lords who were trusted by Richard had also been asked to bring their retinues for protection, while the king's yeomen and retainers flanked the king himself. The layout of Parliament was itself different: a new, much higher throne had been made, with space next to it for the eight new appellant lords, and in front for the representative Lords and Commons. The even more exalted emphasis on the royal majesty which this signified was a sign of things to come. The composition of Parliament had been altered, too: the king's friend and former retainer of John of Gaunt, Sir John Bussy, was now speaker, while in the Commons 86 out of the 203 county representatives had never served as an MP before, possibly because experienced men were reticent about serving; the MPs also included a sizeable number of royal courtiers.

The chancellor, Edmund Stafford, bishop of Exeter, began by explaining that Parliament had been summoned to establish whether the rights of the Crown had been withdrawn or diminished. Shortly afterwards, the acts of the so-called Wonderful Parliament of 1386 were revoked and pardons given to all the commissioners of that year except Gloucester, Arundel and Warwick, and Arundel's brother, Thomas, who had since become archbishop of Canterbury. He was then impeached with no right of reply for his actions in 1386–8, and immediately banished. The eight new appellant lords, clothed in vibrant robes of red silk with a white border and gold embroidery, then presented their appeal against the three earls. When Gaunt, acting in his capacity as high steward of the realm, stated the charge to Arundel, he told Arundel that he deserved 'according to your idea of law to be condemned without answer' – given the actions of the Merciless Parliament, Gaunt took an understandable position. He ordered Ralph Neville, who was by now in receipt of a fee from Gaunt as well as the king, and had married the duke's daughter, to take away the earl's belt and scarlet hood. Arundel put up a spirited defence, citing the two pardons he had already received from the king, but he was summarily judged a traitor and sentenced to death. He was beheaded without ceremony shortly afterwards at Tower Hill. It was then announced that Gloucester was already dead, though unsurprisingly there was no admission that he had been murdered on Richard's personal instruction. He too was adjudged a traitor. Warwick made no attempt to defend himself, but instead pleaded for the king's mercy, confessing, according to one chronicler, 'like a wretched old woman . . . wailing and weeping and whining that he had done all'. This seems to have excited some compassion in Richard, who was later alleged to have said that Warwick's confession meant more to him than all the defaulted lands of Gloucester and Arundel. 'Moved by pity', Richard agreed to commute the sentence of execution to perpetual banishment to the Isle of Man.

The estates of all three men were sequestered and mostly redistributed immediately to Richard's close associates and relatives, five of whom were made dukes – Bolingbroke became duke of Hereford, Mowbray became duke of Norfolk, Richard's half-brother John and his nephew Thomas, son of Thomas Holland, became dukes of Exeter and Surrey respectively, and Richard's cousin Edward, earl of Rutland became duke of Aumerle. Walsingham, already critical of the king, referred to them mockingly as the 'duketti'. Earldoms were also granted to four of the king's favoured new courtiers, one of whom was Ralph Neville, who, on being elevated to Westmorland, achieved his father's unrealised aim of promotion to an earldom. At the same time, the county of Chester was made into a principality by parliamentary statute, an unprecedented elevation in status, and Arundel's estates in North Wales and Shropshire were 'annexed, united and incorporated' into it. One of Richard's final actions in this Parliament was to issue a general pardon, but it was announced that fifty unnamed persons were excluded from it; when pressed, the king still refused to name them, prompting a clamour of payments for individual pardons over the course of the following months, as large numbers of people, terrified of being among those marked as traitors, rushed to secure mercy. Parliament finished with the celebration of mass in Westminster Abbey and the swearing of oaths by the lords and clergy to uphold the acts of the 1397 Parliament.

According to the *Chronicle of the Treason and Death of Richard II* (*Chronique de la Traison et Mort de Richard II*), Richard's acts of revenge in 1397 were prompted by news that Gloucester, Arundel and Warwick were plotting against him, but there is little evidence of this, and none was presented at the trial in Parliament. It would surely have been used had it existed, because it would have been entirely convenient for the king to be able to cite something concrete. As it was, despite the proclamation that the earls had been arrested for new, not old offences, the reality was that nothing was presented at their trial. That the king had no intention of even producing a thin veil of new charges is indicated by the revocation of the acts of 1386 and the issue of a pardon excluding the earls and Archbishop Arundel before the trial had actually begun.

The timing of Richard's actions is probably best explained by reference to the French peace, which, with its in-built promise of support for the English king by his counterpart against all enemies, had been concluded in March 1396. Indeed, serious preparations for the final humbling of the lords seem to have begun shortly afterwards, in the autumn of 1396. Around that time Richard made a number of appointments to local offices that suggest that he intended to remove the appellants once and for all: members of the royal affinity were inserted into the sheriffdom of Herefordshire as well as the shared escheatorship with Gloucestershire, and a royal sergeant-at-arms was appointed to the escheatorship in Shropshire. Escheators were the people who would confiscate lands if an order or court judgement was given to do so, and that same royal bodyguard was the man subsequently tasked with the confiscation of Arundel property in Shropshire following the earl's arrest. In light of this, the restitution of the lordship of Gower to Mowbray, followed by the transfer to him of seventeen of the earl of Warwick's manors as security for the money Beauchamp had been ordered to pay to Mowbray, may have been similarly deliberate. This suggests that Richard made his move when he felt he could do so successfully.

Viewed empirically, the actions of John of Gaunt seem surprising, and we can only conclude that the duke's overriding loyalty to the Crown and to its prerogative must surely have influenced his actions in the late 1390s just as it had earlier. Unsurprisingly, he allegedly admonished Arundel for his attitude to the law when condemning him as a traitor in 1397. Regardless of Richard's provocation, Arundel's behaviour had at times been scandalous, not least at the funeral of Queen Anne. He had scarcely behaved with either nobility or dignity. Similarly, Gloucester was not beyond reproach – hot-headed and lacking in judgement, he had more than once been rehabilitated with the king by Gaunt.

But nonetheless Gloucester's murder must have frightened Gaunt, and it may well be that fear played a predominant part in Gaunt's actions as the decade wore on for other reasons, too. Although Richard had already begun retaining more people in Gaunt's sphere of influence in the north in the early 1390s, which had in turn prompted Gaunt to do the same, he had not at that stage been openly hostile. That began to change in around 1395, when Gaunt had been received back from Aquitaine by Richard in 1395 'without love', according to Walsingham. Thereafter the duke found himself much less frequently at the king's side or relied on for close counsel. Meanwhile, Richard increasingly used his prerogative judicial powers in Lancashire to undermine Gaunt's independence and authority there. In 1396–7, things went a step further: there were new rumours that plots were being hatched against Gaunt by allies of the king. As Richard launched his attack on Arundel, Gloucester and Warwick in 1397, Gaunt must have been seriously concerned that he might be next. In this context, he was probably very anxious to do nothing further to provoke the king: if he did, his estates and the inheritance of his son, Henry Bolingbroke, might well be at stake, as had been the case with the appellant lords. In other words, Gaunt simply could not afford to antagonise Richard.

That Gaunt was very concerned to keep in Richard's favour is amplified by advice he gave to Bolingbroke in early 1398 to reveal directly to the king a conversation with Mowbray, by then duke of Norfolk, in which Bolingbroke alleged that his friend had raised fears that Richard was planning the same fate for the two of them as had befallen Arundel, Gloucester and Warwick because of their involvement in the opposition of 1387–8. Bolingbroke did this in January 1398, and was ordered by Richard to repeat the story in Parliament at Shrewsbury later in the month. Unsurprisingly, an argument broke out between Bolingbroke and Mowbray in which the latter sought to defend himself. He knew only too well how dangerous a position he was in, as was Bolingbroke, if Richard were to suspect that he and Norfolk were plotting. The whole thing was a product of the terrifying atmosphere that prevailed following the destruction of the appellants.

It was in the end this argument and the way Richard responded to it that was to threaten the very inheritance Gaunt was seeking to protect and bring about Richard's own removal from the throne in 1399. For the moment, the king closed Parliament, took away Norfolk's offices of earl marshal and admiral of England and ordered him to appear before him in February. When Norfolk came forward, he denied all Bolingbroke's accusations, and without definitive proof on either side, the parliamentary committee appointed by the king to hear appeals decided that the only solution was trial by battle. In the meantime, Bolingbroke brought more accusations against Norfolk, saying that he was 'at the bottom of all the treasons' in England across the preceding two decades. The battle never took place: Richard stopped it just as the two men were preparing, banishing Norfolk from England for life and Bolingbroke from the realm for ten years.

As with Edward II, this episode and other aspects of Richard's behaviour – such as the fifty unnamed exclusions from the general pardon – demonstrate that the king, having apparently attained a position of unquestioned supremacy, was in fact at his least secure. His actions amounted to tyranny, and plots against him were almost bound to emerge as people sought to protect themselves when they became unsure whether they had fallen out of favour. Like his great-grandfather before him, Richard responded by attempting to shore up his position, packing offices across the country with men he thought would be loyal to him: in November 1397, eleven out of the twenty-seven sheriffs appointed were associated with the royal household or affinity. Similar action was taken with the peace commission. And, to enforce their loyalty, local communities were made to seal blank charters submitting themselves and their property to Richard's pleasure, a threat he could hold over them.

Meanwhile, through the royal Council, Richard was monitoring correspondence coming into and going out of the country, and the court of chivalry was tasked with dealing with traitors in the realm. In January 1398, Richard closed Parliament with another general pardon that enabled him to secure large peacetime grants of direct and indirect taxes. Parliament was now essentially under the king's personal control, as Richard also used the short session to vindicate the judges of 1387 and annul the judgements of the Merciless Parliament of 1388. There was an explicit threat here: the king would brook no opposition and would destroy as traitors anyone who questioned him. He similarly secured new powers for the committee that had been appointed in the 1397 Parliament to hear petitions, amending the Parliament roll to grant them power to investigate 'all other matters moved in the presence of the king and all things arising therefrom'. This was a major transfer of power away from Parliament and into the hands of the king's favourites. It is a moot point whether Richard intended ever to call Parliament again; after all, he had secured agreement to the wool and leather customs for life. In the remaining months of his reign, he certainly made no further attempts to convene it.

This period also witnessed further major recruitment to the royal affinity as the king sought to bolster his increasingly partisan and tyrannical authority; by autumn 1398 he had a permanently retained peacetime force of 750 men. More than three hundred archers divided into seven squadrons were at the heart of the retinue. They constituted Richard's personal bodyguard and went everywhere with him. There were then two further reserve forces each comprising well over a hundred men. Richard had in addition forced everyone who had been with the appellants in 1387-8 to buy an individual pardon from him, and seventeen counties that had supported the appellants were made to pay a high financial price to recover the king's favour. Any critics were rooted out and brought before the courts of the marshal and the constable. These were the beginnings of a reign of terror. As the king's megalomania grew, his status came to occupy more and more of his thoughts. He would sit on the throne from dinner until vespers, and anyone who caught his eye was made to bow before him.

In early 1399, no one could have told how exactly this would end, but as in 1326, the status quo was unsustainable. The king's tyranny – his refusal to play the role of protector of his subjects' property and his own very active threats to that property – had lost him all legitimacy. There were too many people who no longer had a stake in his kingship, and for whom coping with the potential chaos of Richard's removal would be preferable to his continued rule. If the last two centuries had established anything beyond doubt, it was that government had to act in the interests of the realm as a whole; it could not be partisan. And the king, like everyone else, was expected to abide by the law.

Over the years since 1215, structures and fora for dialogue and the giving of consent had developed which were now being overridden roughshod. It could not endure. What was needed, though, as in 1326, was a catalyst to set events in train. That was provided by the death of John of Gaunt, which Richard used to disinherit Bolingbroke, making his banishment for life. Richard followed this by enforcing direct loyalty to himself on the duke's Lancastrian retainers. Like his father before him, Ralph Neville found himself enveloped in high political machinations, forced to choose between the king and the duke: Richard told him he was willing to confirm the annuity of five hundred marks a year given to him by Gaunt, but only on the understanding that the now earl of Westmorland was 'retained to stay with the king only', a caveat Richard also put on other confirmations of Lancastrian annuities after Gaunt's death. For the moment, Neville and the others had no choice but to acquiesce.

The king's actions meant that like Roger Mortimer in 1326, Bolingbroke had nothing to lose by challenging the king. Soon Richard made the fatal mistake that opened the door to him: hearing of another rebellion in Ireland, he took the decision to cross the Irish Sea to bring his Irish opponents to heel. Richard's overconfidence at this point is somewhat staggering; although he took the heirs of Gloucester and Bolingbroke with him, he was accompanied by the leading earls and barons, leaving only his uncle Edmund of Langley, now duke of York, and the Council to guard the realm in his absence. Panic ensued in England on the king's departure, and rumours abounded that he was going to settle in Ireland, and that more nobles were to be murdered. The system broke down so badly that even the shire courts stopped convening. Government had almost immediately and completely collapsed.

Bolingbroke Becomes King

Bolingbroke did not waste his opportunity. Based at the French court in Paris, he was well placed to hear quickly of the king's departure for Ireland, and soon moved to mount an invasion. He wisely began from his landed base in the north of England, having sailed up the North Sea coast in early July 1399. There, many of his father's former retainers met him, prominent among whom was Ralph Neville, who took no time in declaring his loyalty to Bolingbroke and would thereafter be an important ally. Knowing that he would be best placed if he could create a physical division between Richard's councillors in London and the returning king, Bolingbroke did not attempt to take London, but instead headed south-west to Bristol. Delays to the king's departure from Ireland as Richard desperately sought to raise ships for his forces gave Bolingbroke the chance to bring about the duke of York's surrender. This happened relatively swiftly, probably because York was struggling in the face of mass desertion by the royal forces. Elsewhere Richard had sent John Montagu, earl of Salisbury – who had inherited his title in 1397 and quickly established himself as the king's favourite – to North Wales from Ireland with a small force. But Salisbury, hearing rumours that Richard had been killed, also struggled to hold his forces together, and Bolingbroke, marching to Conwy, easily took control of what had been the heart of Richard's realm, the 'inner citadel'. By the time Richard reached Conwy the war was lost. He was easily taken prisoner by the earl of Northumberland and quickly despatched to the Tower of London.

At this stage, it was not clear that Bolingbroke planned to claim the throne himself. On 19 August he issued summonses in Richard's name for Parliament to convene at Westminster at the end of September, and there is no indication that he intended to use it to make himself king. By the end of August, that had changed. A committee was appointed to consider 'the matter of setting aside King Richard, and of choosing the duke of Lancaster in his stead, and how it was to be done'. It was far from straightforward. Richard was Bolingbroke's prisoner, but he had made it abundantly clear that he had no intention of abdicating (despite what later Lancastrian propaganda was to claim). Both the earl of Northumberland and Ralph Neville were among those sent to the Tower to try to persuade Richard to resign his crown, but to no avail. Without an abdication there was no obvious precedent within England for removing the king. The only solution was to compile a list of Richard's crimes to demonstrate his tyranny, and present those to Parliament for adjudication, giving Parliament power and importance that it had never possessed before. When Parliament was confronted with the Articles of Accusation, there was no opposition: in fact, the assembled Lords and Commons agreed unanimously that the accusations made in the articles were true – notorious, even – and that

Richard should be deprived of his crown. For the first time ever, Parliament had been central to the removal of an anointed king of England.

In the end, the removal of Richard was achieved relatively easily, but it did not give Henry Bolingbroke an automatic claim to the throne. There were significant questions about his place in the line of succession. In dynastic terms, Edmund Mortimer, the eight-year-old heir to the earldom of March, was arguably the person best qualified to succeed Richard, as he was descended from Edward III's second son, whereas Bolingbroke was descended from his third son. On the other hand, Mortimer's claim was through the female line and Bolingbroke's through the male line. Initially, it seems that Bolingbroke thought this line of argument was not strong enough, and instead considered making his claim on the basis that Edmund Crouchback, of whom he was a direct descendant, was Henry III's first son and Edward I not the rightful king. But he quickly abandoned this approach. It was so fantastical that it was never likely to gain any traction, and why he considered it in the first place is an interesting question. He then seems to have thought about simply claiming the throne by right of conquest, but it was pointed out to him that a conqueror had no obligation to observe the laws and respect property. This would have raised fears about what he might do next; with Magna Carta and the rule of law so enshrined in English political dialogue, and Richard II's tyranny so alive in recent memory, it was far too provocative. In the end, Bolingbroke simply said that he claimed the throne by virtue of his descent from Henry III, leaving the details vague. It was the unprecedented and straightforward acceptance of the claim by the Lords and Commons in Parliament that enabled him to proceed. In other words, not only had Parliament, for the first time in history, sanctioned the removal of a monarch, it had also conferred legitimacy on a usurper. It was a measure of how far the role of the institution had developed over the course of its 150 years of existence.

On 29 September 1399, with this done, Parliament was dissolved and the following day a new Parliament was summoned in the name of Henry IV, king of England. But the situation remained far from straightforward: Henry had taken his throne by force, and he might be removed by the same means, especially with Richard alive and imprisoned at Pontefract in Yorkshire. He was never going to surrender quietly. That threat quickly materialised: in December a plot was hatched by Richard's 'duketti' to take Henry and his sons captive at New Year and replace him with Richard. Luckily the treachery of one of the earls meant that Henry became aware of the plan and was able to take defensive action that saw them defeated by the middle of January. By then, though, it was clear that Henry was far from safe on the throne, and that Richard remaining alive would continue to provide his enemies with a rallying point for action. The only solution was a brutal one: the death of Richard. With the former king still young and healthy, that could only mean his murder. Henry spent little time making the decision to dispense with his deposed rival, though he was later allegedly to have many nights disturbed by his conscience over the command. In February 1400, it came to pass that Richard died in unclear circumstances in his prison in Pontefract, and in a final but necessary indignity in order to quash future rumours of his survival, his body was transported to London and displayed for thousands to see at several points along the way. He was first buried at King's Langley in 1400, before being moved to his final resting place, Westminster Abbey, by Henry V in 1413.

The End of the Reign

Richard II's reign had begun in the most inauspicious circumstances: political division, military failure and economic collapse all bedevilled his minority. Whatever his personality, Richard would have faced great challenges once he assumed full control of his realm, but it was quickly clear that he would become part of the problem, not the solution. From the arrogant, lazy and somewhat feckless young man of the early reign, he developed into a paranoid, vindictive and vengeful tyrant. As with Edward II before him, Richard's tyranny would inevitably at some point elicit a challenge from someone with nothing left to lose, and after Richard had confiscated his inheritance, Henry Bolingbroke was an obvious candidate for an assault on Richard's position. Had he been in England rather than Ireland when the challenge came, it is a moot point whether Richard might have been able to deploy his hugely enhanced affinity to fight off the military challenge from the duke and his allies. No king before him had raised a personal military following on this scale in peacetime. On the

other hand, the allegiance of that following to the king was brittle – unsurprisingly, given Richard's behaviour. By 1399 he was effectively ruling from
a bunker, with government collapsing around him. Royal authority, by
definition, involved a compact between ruler and ruled. Richard wanted
no such compact, only personal status and power.

With Richard's failure and Bolingbroke's triumph, a new dynasty – the
Lancastrians – acceded to the throne. By this means, the greatest private
magnate in England and Wales became the embodiment of public authority. It is deeply ironic that Richard, who had acceded to the throne as the
embodiment of public authority, had fatally alienated the realm and forced
his own deposition by trying – through outrageous confiscation – to make
himself the most powerful private lord. In so doing, he effectively suborned
his public role as king to his personal, private interests, and surrendered his
kingly legitimacy. The challenge for Bolingbroke was how to effect a transformation in the opposite direction: from private lord to king. Gaining the
blessing of Parliament was only the start.

CONCLUSION: ENGLAND, ARISEN

Personalities and Politics

The story of politics in England between 1199 and 1399 is full of drama before the question of the development of the state is even mentioned. These two centuries witnessed savage internal conflict – including civil war, deposition, the murder of kings and the ruthless execution of rebel lords – as well as a devastating national pandemic in which somewhere between 30 and 50 per cent of the population perished, economic crisis and the first major peasant uprising in English history. The period also saw all-out war, as the English conquered Wales, attempted to subjugate Scotland and engaged in the prolonged diplomatic and military struggle to retain the English Crown's ancient lands in France that escalated into the Hundred Years' War. There were celebrated victories on land and at sea as well as ignominious defeats. And it was war that framed the foundation of England's pre-eminent chivalric companionship, the Order of the Garter. The great set-piece confrontations of the period – Bouvines, Evesham, Falkirk, Bannockburn, Halidon Hill, Sluys, Crécy, Neville's Cross, Poitiers – remain prominent, even epoch-making, in historical consciousness today, just as they resonated with contemporaries seven or eight hundred years ago.

Kings

Personalities illuminated the historical stage in thirteenth- and fourteenth-century England with their political nous, energy, sense of duty, bravery and charisma, as well as their incompetence, irresponsibility, narcissism, indolence and cruelty. Foremost among these characters were the six kings who ruled between 1199 and 1399. The best leaders are characterised by cognitive ability, emotional intelligence, courage and capacity for hard work, qualities that the kings of our period naturally possessed in varying measure.

King John's immense commitment and acumen in respect of royal administration, the energy with which he toured his realm and his attention to detail were worthy of his Angevin predecessors. But despite his undoubted ability, John lacked judgement, and his paranoia about threats to his position rendered him unable to keep allies and earn trust – and allegedly even to sleep. His cruelty meant that those who found themselves on the wrong side of him were often subjected to grievous torture and punishment. John's personality won him few, if any, lasting supporters, but above all it was his failure to retain the Angevin empire, particularly Normandy, together with his hugely expensive and ineffective attempt at its reconquest, the burdens of which fell disproportionately on his barons, that sparked the chain of events that led to Magna Carta. His death in the midst of a civil war meant that he left his infant son and heir the worst of legacies.

As the young Henry III grew into adulthood, he revealed himself to be a very different person from his father. Henry was a man of piety and intellectual simplicity, who was also notably humorous, forgiving and loving of his family, fiery but not cruel. He had a penchant for comfort and luxury. While he did not exhibit his father's brutality, he was also without his administrative competence and work ethic, and simply could not see what was required of him in light of Magna Carta. He provoked political opposition by promoting and rewarding unsuitable advisers, by failing to control government spending and by pursuing unrealistic foreign ambitions, in which his nobles had no confidence. The civil unrest in the 1250s and 1260s represented the nadir of Henry's reign. It was caused entirely by his poor governance, and might even have culminated in the ousting of the Plantagenet dynasty, had Simon de Montfort been successful in his aims. Ultimately, military victory over the rebels enforced peace, but if the reign did not end with civil war, Henry's failures meant that his son Edward received an inauspicious political inheritance.

Despite this handicap, Edward I's reign was one of great success. In his thirty-five years on the throne he broadly provided the exemplar of kingship that his father and grandfather could never supply. When he emerged into the political community as a teenager during the 1250s, his energy, determination, ability and strength of character were already abundantly clear, though initially his political behaviour exhibited dimensions of immaturity and misjudgement. While he remained an uncompromising character, given to periodic fits of uncontrollable rage, maturity brought Edward greater political steadiness. He was, in his own way, just as pious as his father and equally loving of his consort, but the interests of the realm and the duties of kingship soundly underpinned his political approach. With his grandfather's work ethic and more ambition than even John possessed, he was also responsibly minded. At his best he delivered a synchronicity with his subjects that was matched only by his grandson, Edward III.

In the intervening period, though, Edward II's reign showed how much damage a negligent king could do. Irresponsible, lazy, easily distracted and spiteful, he demonstrated no obvious commitment to anything other than his own pleasure and personal interests. His slothful attitude to government business and disregard for the realm's welfare degenerated over time into tyranny, as he sought revenge against his perceived enemies, abandoned all pretence at national defence and plundered the lands and goods of his own subjects. In Edward's youth his father had despaired of him and in middle age his subjects did the same – deposing him as 'incorrigible and without hope of amendment'.

Edward II's severe limitations and political travails in his early years have sometimes been attributed to an allegedly dysfunctional upbringing and a difficult inheritance. But the futility of such analyses is shown by the example of his eldest son. It is hard to think of a childhood more dysfunctional than that of Edward III – in which a teenager took his deposed father's throne, only to find himself kept under house arrest by his mother's lover, a tyrant who subsequently murdered his father and had his uncle executed. Nor is it easy to imagine a political inheritance more challenging than one in which a boy of seventeen had to seize control of his own kingdom in a bloody *coup d'état*, with royal coffers empty, lands lost and an aggressive enemy looking on from beyond the seas. But Edward III's kingship was highly successful: contemporaries said upon his death that he was 'the flower of kings past and [the] pattern for kings to come'. He revered his grandfather, Edward I, and sought to follow his example, taking his political innovations to their logical conclusion and even surpassing them – without provoking significant political conflict – because he was a valiant and committed leader, who cared about his people's welfare as well as his royal rights. Doubtless he was assisted by his personal charisma, reinforced by the awe in which a commander never defeated on the field of battle – and therefore repeatedly judged righteous by God – was naturally held.

Yet his legacy was not to be preserved. Despite the political division prevalent in the royal court as Edward III's final illness gave way to his grandson's compromised minority, it is hard to comprehend the mistrust and hostility that characterised Richard II's attitude towards his great lords from the very beginning of his personal rule. Like his great-grandfather, Edward II, whom he sought to absolve and even canonise later in life, his interests seem to have been wholly personally derived and focused. He was a dangerous combination of entitled, capricious, violent-tempered, paranoid, indolent and determinedly deaf to criticism. Political confrontation came almost as early in his reign as it had in that of Edward II, and like Edward, Richard responded only with fury to being held to account. Once he sought to rule fully unfettered, as he saw it, from 1397, his deposition as a tyrant had about it an air of depressing inevitability, reminiscent of the 1320s.

Nobles

While kings were the most important political actors in the period, the supporting cast of characters is equally colourful and integral. The more self-interested and ambitious they were, the greater the disruption they tended to cause. Ranulf of Chester always believed in his superior abilities and was a source of instability for those seeking to govern during Henry III's minority, while Peter des Roches and his nephew Peter des Riveaux were even more brazen. Des Roches may have believed in the right of the king to more freedom of action than the legacy of Magna Carta permitted, but his self-interest was never far from the surface. More complicated was Simon de Montfort. There is no doubt of his genuine commitment to aspects of political reform, but this sat uncomfortably alongside, and at times was subordinate to, his very powerful and dominating personal ambition. That ambition may even have stretched to the Crown itself, and it made him an especially dangerous opponent to the king.

Under Edward II and Richard II, many highly ambitious individuals established a frictional platform for themselves in the body politic.

Edward's favourite Piers Gaveston was perhaps more foolish and parading than nakedly ambitious (though he did promote his friends and relations in Gascony), but Hugh Despenser the Elder, Roger Mortimer, John Charlton, Roger Damory and – ultimately – Queen Isabella stand out for their self-promotion and willingness to clear almost any obstacle to their goals. Under Richard II, Robert de Vere, earl of Oxford and Simon Burley were prominent among the king's friends in attracting hostility for their ambition, lack of ability and perceived exploitation of the young king. Richard, earl of Arundel (d. 1397) was an irritant not only in opposition but also in government. Even more impossible to like was Thomas of Lancaster, whose stupidity, cynicism, narcissism and self-focus were as responsible for paralysing politics in the period 1312–20 as was the deleteriousness of Edward II. It was Hugh Despenser the Younger, however, who surpassed all other political actors in the thirteenth and fourteenth centuries in his greed, rapaciousness, cruelty, violence and paranoia. No other individual, not even a malign or incompetent king, produced such political tumult.

What is striking about these patterns of magnate-driven political friction or disruption is their location in the reigns of kings whose rule was weak, negligent or tyrannical. Kings who ruled well saw little political opposition. The only points in the reigns of Edward I and Edward III when great lords stood at the centre of political disagreement were when concerns about foreign and military policy combined with financial crisis, in 1297–1301, 1339–41 and the 1370s. This is not to suggest that troublesome individuals did not feature among the nobles when the throne was occupied by outstanding kings. Surely they must have done. But they did not create high political problems, probably because effective kingship left them no space in which they might do so.

Individuals of real talent, industriousness and responsibility, on the other hand, tended to stand out politically irrespective of kingly effectiveness. They shone in sometimes transformative ways for the realm or state. Under King John, Hubert Walter, the great administrator, and under Henry III, Peter de Raleigh, were responsible for governmental and legal reform. Among the nobility, William Marshal led the minority government of Henry III with dignity and gravitas until his death, while under Edward II, the earls of Warwick, Hereford and Pembroke were all identified and valued by contemporaries for their political leadership and wisdom; the latter in particular played a key role in delivering government in the 1310s. Undoubtedly, though, the best royal servants were empowered to have the most positive impact under competent and engaged kings.

If the behaviour of many of the protagonists of this period seems familiar in the modern period, it should not be surprising, because, while the context is in many ways different, human nature has not greatly changed. The motivations, and the best and worst qualities of political players, have endured. Almost all great lords – lay and ecclesiastic – were a source of stability rather than conflict. The medieval robber baron of popular consciousness is more a product of a generalised suspicion of elites than of historical fact. Perhaps only a minority of magnates were continuously engaged in the business of government in the interests of stability and the common good. But if the mass of lords broadly acquiesced in politics rather than seeking to steer them, they did so benignly rather than irresponsibly. What this period shows is that political leaders were usually working to keep the state functioning in the national interest as they saw it.

The Common Good

This was in part because of the power of the prevailing language of politics, which was focused on the common profit and the good of the realm. It was hard, if not impossible, to present political motivations and actions in any other light if they were to have legitimacy. Even during the crisis of 1258–67, when personal interests were perilously mixed with a desire for governmental reform, de Montfort and the rebel barons realised they had to speak of the common good. The same was true with the Articles of Accusation against Edward II, with the statements of the noble opposition in the 1380s and with the deposition articles of Richard II. Yet this was also about more than prevailing or convenient political rhetoric. The security of the social fabric, which combined social position with landed property, was vested in the continuation and stability of government and its structures. None of this is to deny the reality of self-interest. But in times of serious national crisis, consciously or subconsciously, people mostly understood that their individual and familial prospects were best served by the security that resulted from the pursuit of common interest.

This was displayed not just in the statements and actions of individuals but also in institutional behaviour – in the legal system and especially in Parliament, the most important representative institution to emerge in the period. It is only natural that the common law should have had at its heart the common good, and the language of the common law reflects this. Statutes, commissions and legal interventions from government frequently referenced the well-being or needs of the realm and the people. Legal process, particularly indictment and trial by jury, enrolled and invested the community in the business of the law. At its best, the law's intrusiveness, as the king pursued objectives or interests that did not always align completely with local assumptions or expectations, was tempered by the co-option of local perspectives through the commissioning of locally based justices, connected to and representative of the most important local networks and groupings. Its decision making on cases was usually characterised by alertness to local circumstances and the worthiness (in the moral at least as much as the social sense) of individuals. Those at work in the law – justices, jurors and administrators alike – were seeking to provide appropriate redress and to repair a torn social fabric. Plaintiffs and defendants might 'labour' a justice or juror, but we should remember that attempting such persuasion was at the time regarded as legitimate, within sensible bounds. Clear judicial venality and corruption, on the other hand, were strongly condemned, and the space for these to prosper in an emerging and professionalising legal system was progressively shut down during the reign of Edward III. Both Edward and his grandfather pursued what can only be described as personal crusades against perceived judicial corruption.

In Parliament both the Lords and the Commons represented the realm and its people's interests in formalising consent for government action. Again, the concept of the common profit predominated, whether applied to requests for taxation for war (as in 1297), demands for the hearing of petitions (under Edward II) or debates on the nature of royal justice (under Edward III). The overarching priority of Parliament was to protect the realm and its collective interests – broadly defined – while supporting the monarch. Parliamentary faction could develop, not least because Lords and Commons both represented a wide range of interests, from great landholders in the north to strongly entrepreneurial merchants in the south.

As Parliament grew, the scope for faction to emerge increased. Just as, at certain times, problematic individuals among the nobles disrupted politics, so could parliamentary faction, and the outcomes of parliamentary deliberations were sometimes far from satisfactory. The Parliament that backed the bishop of Norwich's ill-conceived and disastrous military campaign in Flanders in 1384 was dysfunctional. But when operating in tandem with a fair, grateful and attentive monarch, or efficient and enterprising officials (as in the 1270s and 1280s, or the 1340s and 1350s), it was characterised by unity of purpose and action. It supported the objectives and business of the king and government, while, where necessary, checking the burgeoning state in the interests of the people, though generally in a constructive manner.

The Emerging State

Governmental infrastructure and reach were transformed in England between 1199 and 1399, even allowing for the unusual strength of kingship and the extensive centralisation that had already occurred before the start of the period. A broader and more engaged group of figures contributed actively to decisions on foreign and military policy as well as to war finance. They did so in a Parliament that included lay and ecclesiastical magnates plus representatives of the gentry and urban communities. The royal legal system of the common law, established under Henry II and accessible to all the king's free subjects, had experienced vast growth in scale, scope and personnel. Even the king was accountable to it. Through the common law, royal government adjudicated disputes, provided redress for grievance and sought to tackle a wide range of crimes, down to village level and beyond, even in the furthest corners of the realm. A highly sophisticated and extensive governmental bureaucracy at Westminster and in the localities was staffed by an increasingly professional cadre of administrators and lawyers. On the field of battle, feudal conscripts had been replaced by expert, well-equipped and formidably organised professional soldiers, regionally recruited by specially contracted royal commanders from among the nobility and gentry, and transported overseas in some of Europe's most extensive and effective naval operations. The leading commanders were contracted to negotiate as well as fight on the king's behalf, and in times of truce characteristically featured prominently among the ranks of his diplomats.

People and Circumstances

The agency of individual kings and in particular the leadership skills they demonstrated or lacked had a dramatic effect on their realms. State growth ebbed and flowed between 1199 and 1399 in part because of kingly action or inaction. Under King John, Edward I and Edward III, significant expansion took place because they actively fostered or even demanded it, though John's actions were largely about the use of the law for his own ends, whereas both Edward I and Edward III saw the provision of justice as a matter of kingly duty. For the latter two, their commitment to offering their subjects more effective access to justice and maintaining order across the realm led to the dramatic expansion of legal mechanisms and structures, including numbers of legal personnel.

Henry III also significantly broadened the scope of the common law and access to it, particularly in the late 1240s and 1250s. But other aspects of state development in his reign resulted mainly from political tension (some of it inherited) rather than from direct and positive action by the king himself. Under Edward II and Richard II, state growth slowed. Edward's hand barely touched the tiller of royal government because he was so focused upon his personal affairs. His only engagement with the workings of government was devoted, from 1322, to maximising his personal wealth. Richard was similarly indolent and self-focused.

The monarchs' subjects also had agency. The common law proved remarkably popular with free men and women, and demand for it grew hugely between 1199 and 1399. This resulted in a proliferation of new writs and a vast expansion in the business of the royal courts, which in turn fostered innovations such as the regular commissions of assize and gaol delivery that went into the localities between the visitations of the general eyre. Even when kings made attempts to stem the flow of demand, as Edward I had to do in the 1280s, their success was limited because of the relentless pressure for access to the king's justice from below. That litigants were determined to use the common law is shown by numerous instances in which they creatively manipulated writs that did not really apply to their own circumstances or grievances to initiate a hearing – hence the cases of nominal conspiracy where no conspiracy was actually alleged, or the charges of supposed assault by force and arms that were actually about horses damaged by incompetent farriers or wine that had gone sour.

The growth of the state over these two centuries derived from the assertiveness of the king's subjects in other ways as well. The demand for the king to act within the law and to consult them before attempting to take money became entrenched during Henry III's minority, and it would have been hard for any king to jettison the embryonic structures that had emerged to facilitate those things. By the late fourteenth century, such change had morphed into both a bold Commons in Parliament, and further calls for representation and consultation among the peasantry. The demands by the peasant rebels of 1381 for equal treatment under the law owed a strong debt to those of their gentry and baronial forebears in 1215 and 1258. With Magna Carta having been regularly read out from the pulpit and in marketplaces across the land in the intervening 150 years, it is unsurprising that its principles were eventually espoused by a much wider social constituency.

Above all, though, it was war that built the state between 1199 and 1399. By generating actual or feared disorder, through invasion or (more commonly) the internal movement of troops, war prompted novel judicial interventions and solutions – such as the trailbaston commissions of 1305–7 or Edward III's use of the charges of conspiracy and treason in the mid-1340s and 1350s. War made military reorganisation and professionalisation necessary, and these were themselves dimensions of governmental expansion under Edward I and Edward III: if wars were to be won, armies had to be reformed to be more effective and disciplined, and the state had to lead in these areas. But most importantly, war produced taxation and Parliament. From the financial and logistical demands arose the series of military, financial and political crises out of which calls for representation and a formal process of consent and consultation emerged. It was war that gave rise to King John's greatest impositions, especially on the magnates, which led directly to the crisis of 1215 and Magna Carta, when they demanded the protection of the law from arbitrary exactions by the king. The subjection of the king to the law, and taxation as the solution to funding war, became established fixtures during Henry III's minority, because civil disharmony had to cease and because Henry again desperately needed money to respond to the French threat to his lands overseas. During Henry's adult reign, the growing political community began to define the parameters within which taxation would be given, repeatedly rejecting Henry's pleas for support for his military endeavours. It was these unsuccessful demands for taxation and Henry's arbitrary impositions on the knights of the shires that opened up the political space for further successful calls for representation and accountability. Henceforth, no sensible king could have thought that war would be funded by any means other than taxation, nor could he have believed that he could obtain those funds without the consent of the Commons in Parliament.

Under Edward I, Parliament and the taxation system became fully established (with the wider representation Parliament had first seen in the 1250s) and their status recognised, as the king sought to deal militarily with both perceived threats to English royal rights and authority in Wales and Scotland, and undoubted threats in France. Further development came in the 1290s, when, faced by multiple military threats and a shortage of money, Edward tried to specify the duty of his subjects to fund war in cases of urgent necessity, regardless of the impact on them. In this attempt to extend the power of the state, he was successfully resisted on the grounds that no king, no matter how serious his situation, had the right to damage the common good by impoverishing his people. In rebutting the king in this way, Parliament established an important principle and placed limits on the king's freedom of action and his government's ability to lay claim to his subjects' property, even during wartime. During the rule of Edward III, Parliament's effective centrality to a state expanding in response to martial pressure was cemented. Huge financial demands being made by war on the country prompted Parliament again to place certain limitations on the king's scope for fiscal action. Edward responded by actively embracing Parliament – both Lords and Commons – as necessary partners to a successful war effort. His success in creating, in this way, a new and shared state enterprise is shown by Parliament urging him, in the late 1350s, to continue his war with the French rather than make peace under terms that they considered insufficient.

It was harder for war to generate state development in the face of kingly neglect of defensive threats. There was anxiety in Parliament under Edward II, but ultimately the king's subjects struggled to force him to act. Yet some development still took place, in the hands of Edward's regional commanders in the north after Bannockburn, who learned early lessons from Robert Bruce that were duly translated into a transformed military under Edward III. During Richard II's minority, when those representing the king were very actively attempting to govern, Parliament's role in military policy grew because money on the scale needed could never have been found elsewhere, and royal government was repeatedly verging upon bankruptcy. The increased size of parliamentary representation at that time also created many more voices that expected to be heard in deliberations over taxation, added to which the economic collapse of the late 1370s meant that many who would normally contribute to taxation were seeking ways to retrench in the face of falling incomes – at exactly the time when the royal government needed more money to deal with the military threats from France and Castile. Consequently, during the early 1380s, Parliament came to flex its muscles more vigorously than at any time since its creation, and the peasantry was drawn into the payment of taxation and the wider political community as never before. But the Commons stopped short of demanding a say in determining strategy, still expressing a clear preference to be advised by the king and his Council. In the 1390s, once a truce and later peace with France had been concluded and taxation was no longer needed, Parliament played little role in politics until it was suddenly and unprecedentedly called upon to sanction the usurpation and accession of Henry Bolingbroke as king, signalling just how far Parliament had travelled in its first 150 years of existence.

There was one other, completely unanticipated event that had a major impact on the emerging state between 1199 and 1399: the sudden and cataclysmic arrival of the Black Death in 1348. Seen by contemporaries – including King Edward III – as God's judgement, plague critically changed England's demography, and therefore its social, economic and legal landscape. The governmental response under Edward III, of legislating for the first time to regulate the labour market, was itself an act of symbolic and significant state expansion. It is perhaps unsurprising that a king of Edward's ability should have thought along such sophisticated lines, especially in a period when rulers were in any case conceiving of state authority in such expansive terms. At the same time, the rising wealth of peasants, which arose from their decline in numbers during the first and subsequent outbreaks of plague, drew more of them than ever before into the political community as taxpayers and officials, and thereby into the embrace of the state. This of course was a development that was to have dramatic repercussions in the early years of Richard II's reign in the form of the Peasants' Revolt.

Structures, Ideas and Ideology

England's particular political structure and situation in 1199 gave rise to many of the subsequent developments in the state. By that year, the country had long recognised one king, and by contemporary European standards, government was already notably subject to direct royal control. The size and navigability of the country, as well the protection provided by the English Channel and the North and Irish seas against external threats, particularly from the Vikings, had made this much easier to achieve than in many countries. A clear contrast was France. Nearly five times the size of England and featuring a good deal of sparsely populated, upland and heavily wooded territory, it was never going to be as straightforwardly governable. Furthermore, English kings before and after 1199 were never confronted with the large, wealthy and semi-autonomous lordships within their nominal territory with which their counterparts across the Channel had to contend. The greatest lordships of the Welsh March were as nothing compared with Aquitaine, Brittany or Burgundy. Even in the most distant regions of England, where noble landholding was at its most cohesive and governmental lines of communication most stretched, many lords struggled to assert their jurisdictional independence. This was because the balance between lordly landed cohesion and royal reach still favoured the king. The early growth of London, as both a trading city and an administrative centre, additionally provided a focal point for royal government whose apparatus was already becoming too large and cumbersome to travel with the king. The emergence of Westminster as the seat of government did not, in that context, require a major leap.

Henry II's common law had itself been conceivable because the English king had long played an active role in the dispensation of justice, and the personnel of government, including royal justices, already existed to make its birth possible. The expansion of the common law and its personnel was equally natural, especially given its great popularity with the king's subjects, who flocked to its relative impartiality, recordability and enforceability. The rapidly growing demand for the common law among the king's subjects between 1166 and 1199 necessitated the law's further expansion to encompass a greater range of the problems they encountered in their everyday lives. It was a cycle of increase driving not just the provision of greater access to royal judges, but also the growth of legal education and the legal profession, as well as the range and scope of legal cases.

The emergence of Parliament and a system of national taxation, as well as the professionalisation of military service, were likewise made possible by existing structures. The tradition of magnates coming together to provide counsel to the king stretched back to before the Norman Conquest. The concept of such public counsel, even if that was not how it was termed, including nobles from throughout the realm, was firmly established by 1199. If a formal forum were going to emerge to discuss foreign and military policy, and the taxation it demanded, it was almost inevitable that it would take broadly representative, parliamentary form. Levies on the king's subjects were at the same time nothing new. They might previously have been predicated upon feudal obligations rather than on the idea of a joint enterprise for the defence of the rights of the English Crown, but the concept of national financial levies and the structures that already existed for collecting their proceeds in the localities formed an important basis for the formation of a system of national taxation in the thirteenth century. The same can be said of military service and the mechanisms that existed to raise troops across the realm. It was only a few short steps from feudal service to the nationally ordained array of troops to the professionalisation of the king's armies and the use of contracts to recruit them. All it required was a recognition of the efficiency and operational gains that might be made by more targeted and discriminating regional recruitment.

If the structural backdrop made many of the developments that took place both conceivable and likely, ideas and ideology (always permeated by religion) underpinned politics and change throughout Europe in the Middle Ages. In many ways these generated the forces that led to the governmental expansion and connected international conflict that the thirteenth and fourteenth centuries witnessed. From the twelfth century onwards, new ideas about royal authority and its sovereignty over other forms of authority were fostered as the study of Roman and canon law (the so-called 'learned laws') proliferated. This coalesced with innovations such as cursive script, and the consequent possibility of writing at much greater speed, to make the practical expression of this authority more realisable than ever before. It is little wonder that sovereignty and overlordship were matters for such serious consideration and debate across European polities in the thirteenth and fourteenth centuries, and lay at the heart of many conflicts.

The use of the terminology of sovereignty and overlordship by rulers, magnates and others was not simply a convenient excuse for seizing, or attempting to seize, power – in a mix of asserting authority and taking political control. These notions formed part of the ideological world in which popes, kings and their subjects operated, and could be powerful drivers of action in their own right. In the 1290s and 1330s alike, political expectations in England and France – where they were characteristically expounded by lords and lawyers in the royal court – led directly to conflict over sovereignty in Aquitaine and Scotland. This was precisely why Edward I sought to apply to John Balliol in Scotland the same burdensome feudal obligations to which he was being subjected by Philip IV in Aquitaine, and why earlier he had felt so strongly about English overlordship in Wales (though evidently a sense of racial superiority played its role, too). It was impossible not to think in such terms, given the language dominating political discourse and diplomacy. In the thirteenth century, again inspired by Roman law, notions of the public authority of the king or prince came to play a greater role in policymaking, and particularly in law-making across Europe. On this rested claims by kings – starting with John – to exercise their authority in the national or public interest (citing the 'common necessity'), to have access to their subjects' property by reference to the royal duty to maintain the common good, and to enhance their jurisdictional authority and the mechanisms by which they expressed it. It is no accident that Edward I promulgated as much legislation as he did, given the emphasis on the prince as lawgiver that predominated. As rulers interacted with their counterparts and other political actors across Europe and the British Isles, they were accessing the same authoritative texts and imbibing the same political ideas.

Just as rulers were inspired to claim ever more authority within their realms, and came to possess more ability to make real those claims, so their subjects across Europe responded by seeking to hold monarchs who were claiming ever greater public authority to account. Political crises, high and low, in England and beyond in the thirteenth and fourteenth centuries, were steeped with ideas about subjects' rights, across the social spectrum. The concerns of the earls of Hereford and Norfolk during the high political row over military policy and war finance in 1297 were naturally very different from those of Wat Tyler before and during the Peasants' Revolt of 1381, but their roots were similar. This was not about resisting or taking advantage of overbearing or incompetent kings; it was about the ideological, political, financial and legal structures subjects believed should underpin the relationship they had with their rulers. Arguments on consultation and consent, and representative institutions and the relationship between the king's subjects and the emerging state, also drew directly on pan-European ideas.

In this immensely fertile time for the generation of ideas, influences were not confined to the 'learned laws'. Another major lever on political actors was Aristotle, whose works were translated from Greek to Latin and thereby rediscovered in the mid-thirteenth century. The result was that writers like St Thomas Aquinas and, later in the century, Giles of Rome increasingly emphasised the divinely appointed and positive role of kings and governments, and the duty of the king to protect the 'common good' of his subjects. In this way, religious ideas and political ideas were brought together by theologians advising rulers – Aquinas was a notable figure at the French royal court in Paris, and Edward I may even have met him there.

By the late thirteenth century, thought had also developed under the influence of Aristotle's ideas to mean that a tyrant was considered not only to be a king who failed to adhere to the law but also one who acted against the common good of his realm. This idea was known and discussed in England. There are clear indications that Edward I himself was aware of the work of Aquinas and others – as were his counterparts in France, Spain, Hungary, Poland and elsewhere across the Continent. In fact, Giles of Rome was translated into every major European language. The so-called *Mirrors for Princes* written by Aquinas, Giles of Rome and others had a clear bearing on the behaviour of kings and their subjects, and their responses to each other across the Continent, and were even sometimes cited in political debate. The notion of the common good became a regular feature of English political discourse from the thirteenth century, either among opponents of the king or by rulers themselves. This was partly because they were using it to justify their actions, and partly because it had developed real meaning: it informed the definition of the power, duties and responsibilities of royal government that was emerging. It became embedded in the thinking not only of the most responsible and reflective political actors, but in wider society too. When Edward III talked – as he habitually did – about offences committed against the king and his people, it is evident that he regarded the two as indivisible. In 1199 King John had not thought in this way, and the difference between the attitudes of the two monarchs was not merely a reflection of their respective personalities.

Structures and ideas therefore provided the platform and reference points for political actors. It is difficult at times to disentangle the role of each in the developments that took place, and at many points they were inextricably connected. They could also generate their own, at times unstoppable, momentum. Philip VI in the mid-fourteenth century found himself harnessed to the idea that France would assert itself over the great lords who constituted its neighbours, essentially irrespective of his personal view (though it seems likely that he accepted it). But in reality he struggled to implement that political assertiveness in Aquitaine, in the deep south-west of his country, where his authority was weaker and subjects were less deferential, and to which his lines of communication and supply were vastly extended. By contrast, King John and his Angevin predecessors were able to assert their authority vigorously and effectively because of England's size and the distribution of landholding. Correspondingly, it is unlikely that kings could have implemented a desire to expand English royal government if London, Westminster and royal government in the shires had not already been so well developed. And while the legislative efforts of Edward

I and Edward III depended on the structures that were already in place, it is a moot point whether they would have been inspired to legislate on such a prolific scale had the public and legislative authority of the prince not been such a prominent part of political discourse at the time.

This unprecedented period saw, for an array of reasons, the origins of some of the most important constitutional features of the modern English, and British, landscape. Kings of England and their subjects in the thirteenth and fourteenth centuries were powerful agents in bringing about this critical change, but they were also shaped by the climate and circumstances they faced, and were swept along by near-irresistible political currents – with which they mostly swam. For all the strength and power of their personalities, it was therefore not one or even a series of individuals who determined the course of developments between 1199 and 1399, but a unique combination of people, circumstances, ideas and structures. The English state – precocious and distinct, and yet at the same time knitted inextricably into a political discourse that transcended national borders – had arisen.

NOTE ON SOURCES
and FURTHER READING

No history of late medieval England could be written without access to the extraordinary wealth of government records, many of them legal records, which survive in the UK in the National Archives at Kew, London. Key government instructions and responses have long been accessible in translation via the *Calendars of Patent, Close* and *Fine Rolls*, and digital copies of these are now freely available online. An excellent portal and guide to these and many other primary source materials is http://www.medievalgenealogy.org.uk and especially http://www.medievalgenealogy.org.uk/sources/rolls.

Historians of this period have benefited greatly from digitisation: many sources are now easily accessible from anywhere in the world. One major project has been the *Anglo-American Legal Tradition* (http://aalt.law.uh.edu/AALT.html) which has put many legal documents online, free of charge. The *Gascon Rolls Project* (http://www.gasconrolls.org) has made many of the records of the government of Aquitaine freely available. The digital library of sources created by the Institute of Historical Research, *British History Online*, is another superb resource with some documents free to view and others available on payment of a subscription (http://www.british-history.ac.uk). The *Oxford Dictionary of National Biography* (http://www.oxforddnb.com) can be accessed either via an individual subscription or through academic and public libraries, and there are detailed and penetrating profiles in it of many of the individuals featured in the book. Accessing them enabled us to build a strong chronology, and our narrative and analysis were also influenced by a number of the entries. Also vital to our research were the online records of Parliament, *The Parliament Rolls of Medieval England* (http://www.sd-editions.com/PROME/home.html). Finally, many documents from the period, including statutes and documentation from the various political crises, are available in the *English Historical Documents* series, which can be accessed in print and online via subscription (http://www.englishhistoricaldocuments.com). The best guide to chronicle sources is Antonia Gransden's work *Historical Writing in Medieval England*, which informed our writing. A number of chronicles are available either online or in print, some in translation and with helpful editorial input from academic historians. All the above have been crucial to us as authors and are excellent resources both for academic scholars and for the generally interested, though some require palaeographic and linguistic skills.

We are also indebted to the work of many modern historians. Below we have indicated specific areas in which others' work and ideas influenced the narrative in the preceding pages. What follows is also a guide to further reading. Starting points for a general overview of the period include David Carpenter's *The Struggle for Mastery*, a history of Britain that runs to 1284, Michael Prestwich's *Plantagenet England, 1225–1360*, and Gerald Harriss's *Shaping the Nation*, which begins in 1360. An older but still very useful work is May McKisack's *The Fourteenth Century*. The chronologies set out in all of these have been of great use to us in compiling this book. A recent, hugely important monograph is John Watts's *The Making of Polities*, a survey of political life in Europe that starts in 1300 but includes very useful background, discussing earlier developments as well as political ideas. This was a major stimulus for our discussions of the development of political ideas. A further monograph that influenced our thinking was Andrea Ruddick's ground-breaking *English Identity and Political Culture in the Fourteenth Century*. We were not able to explore the question of identity as much as we would have liked in the book, but what we have been able to say was greatly enriched by reading Andrea's work. Finally, although her work has focused primarily upon the fifteenth century, Christine Carpenter's thought has influenced us immensely. Her conception of medieval English politics and society is perhaps best summarised in her wonderful *The Wars of the Roses*.

On more specific themes, Antony Black's *Political Thought in Europe 1250–1450* is a very clear introduction to theory, as is the *Cambridge History of Medieval Political Thought c.350–1450*. The latter contains chapters on a wide variety of subjects. For the creation and development of the common law, see Paul Brand's *The Making of the Common Law* and John Hudson's *The Formation of the English Common Law*. Brand has also produced a very useful book on the law in the thirteenth century entitled *Kings, Barons and Justices*. On Parliament, see J. R. Maddicott's outstanding narrative *The Origins of the English Parliament 924–1327*; this has underpinned our writing and ideas about Parliament throughout a significant portion of the book. On armies and war, see Michael Prestwich's *Armies and Warfare in the Middle Ages: The English Experience*, and on the Hundred Years' War, Anne Curry's *The Hundred Years' War* is an excellent, thematic introduction. Also useful is her edited volume *The Hundred Years War Revisited*. Clifford Rogers's two books *War, Cruel and Sharp* and *The Wars of Edward III: Sources and Interpretations*, the former an analysis of Edwardian strategy as well as tactics, and the latter a highly valuable compendium of contemporary accounts of the war, are essential in different ways. Andrew Ayton and Philip Preston's *The Battle of Crécy, 1346* is an immensely stimulating volume of essays. Richard Barber's *Edward III and the Triumph of England* transports the reader to the world of warfare and chivalry, and provides excellent comment on chronicle sources. Other windows into the minds of protagonists are provided by *The Book of Chivalry of Geoffrey de Charny*, edited and translated by Richard Kaeuper, and Henry of Grosmont's *The Book of Holy Medicines*, edited and translated by Catherine Batt. The classic statement on chivalry remains Maurice Keen's *Chivalry*, and Juliet Barker's *The Tournament in England, 1100–1400* permits further insight into chivalric culture. Jonathan Sumption's multi-volume history of the Hundred Years' War provides the best diplomatic analysis and the most detailed account of the conflict. On Aquitaine, the best account of the duchy and the route to war in 1337 is Malcolm Vale's *The Origins of the Hundred Years War*. There are also a number of excellent books on both Scotland and Wales in this period. The epoch-making work of Rees Davies has been very important in our thinking and that of many other historians. We have been greatly indebted to his *The First English Empire*, his earlier *Lordship and Society in the March of Wales, 1282–1400* and his *The Age of Conquest: Wales 1063–1415*. A. D. M. Barrell's *Medieval Scotland*, Michael Brown's *The Wars of Scotland, 1214–1371* and Robin Frame's *The Political Development of the British Isles, 1100–1400* are all very interesting and particularly useful. Alice Taylor's ground-breaking *The Shape of the State in Medieval Scotland, 1124–1290* is recommended.

A controversial monograph – with whose central thesis we disagree, but which is highly stimulating – on the relationship between war and justice is Richard Kaeuper's *War, Justice and Public Order: England and France in the Later Middle Ages*. There is an important article that responds to the Kaeuper thesis by G. L. Harriss in the journal *Past and Present*: 'Political Society and the Growth of Government in Late Medieval England'. Tony Musson and Mark Ormrod's *The Evolution of English Justice: Law, Politics and Society in the Fourteenth Century* is an important summary of the development of the common law in the fourteenth century, which brings together an extensive, older historiography on law and justice. Critical to understanding how powerful judicial commissions worked in the localities is Edward Powell's *Kingship, Law and Society: Criminal Justice in the Reign of Henry V*. An older, but still very useful discussion of the interaction between law and the state is Gaines Post's *Studies in Medieval Legal Thought: Public Law and the State 1100–1322*. On the development of a system of public finance, the seminal text remains G. L. Harriss's *King, Parliament and Public Finance in England to 1369*. Harriss's arguments in *King, Parliament and Public Finance* greatly influenced our narrative of war-related crisis in Edward I's reign in particular, and of the development of Parliament under Edward III.

On King John, J. C. Holt is a towering presence. His monograph *Magna Carta* (now in its third edition) is the major historiographical work explaining how Magna Carta came about and what it meant. Holt's *The Northerners: A Study in the Reign of King John* also explains the particular role of the northern barons in the rebellion. It is to both these books that we owe our biggest debt for understanding the backdrop to Magna Carta, and the chapter on King John is heavily indebted to Holt's work.

Stephen Church's recent edited volume of essays, *King John: New Interpretations*, contains a number of interesting and useful pieces, especially those by Power, Barratt, Turner and Bradbury. There are biographies of King John by Ralph Turner, W. L. Warren and Sidney Painter which explore the reign and John himself in more detail. All three provided chronologies on which we depended in order to produce our chapter on King John.

On Henry III, David Carpenter is the most expert scholar and has inspired much of our writing. His *The Minority of Henry III* and more recently *Henry III: The Rise to Power and Personal Rule*, which runs to 1258 and will be followed by a second volume on 1258–72 in due course, are both outstanding books by someone who knows more about Henry III than any other historian, and were crucial to the construction of our narrative. Carpenter has also written a number of important articles on the reign, which have been collected together in his *The Reign of Henry III*. His work and ideas on the crisis of 1258 as well as on what was happening in the 1230s and 1240s, on the sheriffs and on Henry and Edward the Confessor underpinned our comments in those sections. We are especially indebted to him for our understanding of the genesis of the 1258 crisis. On Simon de Montfort, J. R. Maddicott's excellent biography both illuminates the man and provides a comprehensive and compelling account of events, particularly during the crisis period of the 1250s and 1260s. We relied heavily on it in constructing our account of the period from 1258 to 1265. Nicholas Vincent's book on Peter des Roches, *An Alien in British Politics, 1205–1238*, similarly paints a very helpful portrait of another controversial figure in the reign. Robert Stacey's study *Politics, Policy and Finance under Henry III*, which runs from 1216 to 1245, is an insightful and very detailed analysis of the interplay of the three areas in its title. This book was key to our discussion of what was happening in the 1230s and 1240s. Stacey and Carpenter differ in some of their interpretations, particularly in relation to how isolated Henry was from his magnates in the early 1240s, which makes for thought-provoking reading; in our discussion, we largely agreed with Carpenter's analysis. For the impact of Magna Carta in local society, J. R. Maddicott's article 'Magna Carta and the Local Community', which can be found in the journal *Past and Present*, is important. Tony Moore has done excellent research on local order under Henry III and we relied on it in our discussion of elements of Henry's approach to legal reform, especially in the late 1240s and early 1250s. Much of the relevant material is in his unpublished PhD thesis, *Government and Locality in Essex in the Reign of Henry III*, but his article '"If I Do You Wrong, Who Will Do You Right?": Justice and Politics during the Personal Rule of Henry III', in *Political Society in Later Medieval England*, edited by Benjamin Thompson and John Watts, is an excellent introduction to his work and ideas. Sophie Ambler has done outstanding research on the bishops under Henry III and her book *Bishops in the Political Community of England, 1213–1272* helped significantly with our understanding of the ecclesiastical side of politics and rebellion. On Henry's foreign policy, alongside Carpenter and Robert Stacey's book, we found Bjorn Weiler's *Henry III of England and the Staufen Empire 1216–1272* hugely informative and helpful.

On Edward I, there have been some important recent studies. Two works that build on entirely new research are Caroline Burt's *Edward I and the Governance of England* and Andrew Spencer's *Nobility and Kingship in Medieval England: The Earls and Edward I*. Spencer's work re-evaluates the relationship between Edward and his nobles in a much more positive and nuanced light than ever before and we were indebted to it in this chapter. Michael Prestwich remains the foremost expert on the reign as a whole, and his *Edward I* is a very useful and interesting political biography. His work on royal finances, *War, Politics and Finance under Edward I*, is helpful for anyone wanting to know more about the interrelationship between war and policy. We relied on all Prestwich's works for our interpretation of Edward I's reign, for chronologies and other details, and for arguments, especially in relation to war finance. There is also a recent collection of essays edited by Andrew Spencer and Andy King, *Edward I: New Interpretations*, with excellent contributions by a number of new and established scholars.

Our account and analysis of the reign of Edward II was based extensively upon the calendared governmental rolls, the rolls of Parliament, articles in the *Oxford Dictionary of National Biography*, the best chronicle of late medieval England, the *Vita Edwardi Secundi*, edited by Wendy Childs, and Seymour Phillips's excellent monograph biography, *Edward II*. Many years before the latter, which is somewhat more sympathetic towards Edward II than our own reading of the history, Phillips wrote an important biography of Aymer de Valence, earl of Pembroke, the political analysis of which is perhaps closer to our perspective. It was matched in the early 1970s by J. R. Maddicott's *Thomas of Lancaster* – with some of whose account of the rebel earl's motivations we differ. May McKisack's evergreen *The Fourteenth Century* also provides some very helpful analysis, as does, from the perspective of Queen Isabella, Helen Castor's terrific *She-Wolves: The Women Who Ruled England before Elizabeth*. We recommend Christopher Given-Wilson's *Edward II: The Terrors of Kingship*.

Original research in article form on the reign has been quite limited. Exceptions are recent articles on local order and justice by Caroline Burt: 'A "Bastard Feudal" Affinity in the Making? The Followings of William and Guy Beauchamp Earls of Warwick, 1268–1315' in the journal *Midland History*, and 'Local Government in Warwickshire and Worcestershire under Edward II' in *Political Society in Later Medieval England*, edited by Thompson and Watts. Nigel Saul's 'The Despensers and the Fall of Edward II' in *English Historical Review* explores the backdrop to the deposition, while Natalie Fryde's *The Tyranny and Fall of Edward II, 1321–1326* provides useful discussion. But our analysis of the tyranny, which significantly departs from most accounts, is based largely upon a re-examination of the published government records.

The study of Edward III's reign benefited enormously from the completion, before his untimely death, of Mark Ormrod's magisterial biography, *Edward III.* This provides a consistently excellent summary of recent research on Edward III, a good deal of which was written by Ormrod himself. James Bothwell's excellent *Edward III and the English Peerage: Royal Patronage, Social Mobility and Political Control in Fourteenth-Century England* has framed and enabled important analysis of the king's central relationship with his nobles, and G. L. Harriss's *King, Parliament and Public Finance to 1369* is, as we mentioned earlier, fundamental to any assessment of Edward III's statecraft, development of taxation and positive relationship with Parliament. The central issue of justice, once so controversial for the kingship of Edward III, is well summarised by Musson and Ormrod's *The Evolution of English Justice.* Robert C. Palmer's *English Law in the Age of the Black Death, 1348–1381* informed our sense of the legal and economic response to the great pestilence, but we also returned, after many years, to the pivotal work of Bertha H. Putnam on justice, especially *The Place in Legal History of Sir William Shareshull, Chief Justice of the King's Bench, 1350–1361.* The outstanding work of Clifford Rogers and Andrew Ayton on warfare and the Edwardian military revolution has already been cited, as has that of Malcolm Vale and Anne Curry, which explains causation and supplies wider context. Also influential to our narrative of military campaigns was Alfred H. Burne's *The Crécy War*, something of a period piece but one that captures the dynamism of the command exercised by Edward III and Henry of Grosmont particularly brilliantly. The most recent biography of the Black Prince, by Michael Jones, is a great read. While Ormrod's biography frames our account of politics in the 1360s and 1370s in particular, the bulk of our narrative and analysis is based on original research in the National Archives, especially in the legal records, and in the calendared governmental instructions and responses. Richard Partington's essays on the king's sergeants-at-arms (in *The Age of Edward III*, edited by James Bothwell), on Edward III and the nobility (in *Political Society in Medieval England*, edited by Thompson and Watts), and on law and justice (with Michelle Bubenicek, in *Government and Political Life in England and France, c.1300–1500*, edited by Christopher Fletcher, Jean-Philippe Genet and John Watts) underpin the argument.

There are several important works for Richard II's reign, including Nigel Saul's biography, which takes a particular line on Richard's approach to kingship, with which not everyone agrees. There is also Michael Bennett's excellent *Richard II and the Revolution of 1399.* Our chronological narrative was helped greatly by these works, alongside McKisack's *The Fourteenth Century* and Harriss's *Shaping the Nation.* Anthony Goodman's biography of John of Gaunt is a thought-provoking study of a controversial character, and significantly influenced our interpretation of

Gaunt's personality and motivations. Although Helen Castor's *The King, the Crown and the Duchy of Lancaster* is largely focused on the period after 1399, its introductory chapters are very valuable for understanding Richard II's reign and the contrast with Henry IV, particularly on the question of public and private power. Castor's work was central to our concluding points about the interrelationship between private lordship and public kingly authority under both Richard II and Henry IV; her forthcoming work on Richard II was too late to influence this book, but will undoubtedly be a compelling read. A. K. Gundy's book *Richard II and the Rebel Earl*, on Richard and the earl of Warwick, is an important monograph based on a wealth of new research in the archives that offers real insights into what Richard was doing in the localities, especially in the 1390s. This underpinned our narrative in that section of the book. Mark King has also recently done excellent work on the localities under Richard II. His article 'Richard II, the Mortimer Inheritance and the March of Wales, 1381–1384' in *Fourteenth Century England* is the source for our discussion of the inheritance, while his as yet unpublished outstanding PhD thesis *Richard II, Shropshire and the Northern March* was crucial for our discussion of the earl of Arundel in the localities and other observations on the March of Wales. Like Gundy, King sees Richard laying the groundwork for his coup of 1397 earlier in the 1390s. F. R. H. Du Boulay and Caroline M. Barron's edited volume *The Reign of Richard II*, although an older work, still contains a number of useful articles. Finally, Chris Fletcher's recent *Richard II: Manhood, Youth and Politics 1377–1399* is an interesting but controversial exploration of Richard, his outlook and the influences on him.

PICTURE CREDITS

INDEX